The Foundations of Behavioral Economic Analysis:
Volume 2

The Foundations of Behavioral Economic Analysis is also available in seven newly revised volumes published by Oxford University Press

The Foundations of Behavioral Economic Analysis: Volume 1
Behavioral Economics of Risk, Uncertainty, and Ambiguity

The Foundations of Behavioral Economic Analysis: Volume 2
Other-Regarding Preferences

The Foundations of Behavioral Economic Analysis: Volume 3
Behavioral Time Discounting

Forthcoming

The Foundations of Behavioral Economic Analysis: Volume 4
Behavioral Game Theory

The Foundations of Behavioral Economic Analysis: Volume 5
Bounded Rationality

The Foundations of Behavioral Economic Analysis: Volume 6
Behavioral Models of Learning

The Foundations of Behavioral Economic Analysis: Volume 7
Further Topics in Behavioral Economics

PRAISE FOR *"THE FOUNDATIONS OF BEHAVIORAL ECONOMIC ANALYSIS"*

"*The Foundations of Behavioral Economic Analysis* is a masterpiece. It covers the whole field of behavioral economics. And it is also an easy read, as beautiful examples throughout lead readers to appreciate behavioral decisions from the perspective of their own lifetime experience."
    George A. Akerlof, *University Professor, Georgetown University, and 2001 Nobel laureate in economics.*

"The publication of this book is a landmark occasion for the field of behavioral economics. Until now there has been no comprehensive survey of the field suitable for graduate students. Professor Dhami has thoroughly and rigorously filled that gap. The book will be placed in a handy place in my office since I plan to consult it regularly."
    Richard H. Thaler, *Charles R Walgreen Distinguished Service Professor of Economics and Behavioral Science, University of Chicago, and 2017 Nobel laureate in economics.*

"The seven volumes of *The Foundations of Behavioral Economic Analysis* offer a fascinating mix of theory and evidence and represent the most comprehensive synthesis of behavioral economics at an advanced level. They will be very useful for advanced researchers as well as for graduate students in behavioral economics and beyond."
    Ernst Fehr, *Professor of Economics, University of Zurich.*

"This series of seven volumes is a tour de force, a literal encyclopedia of behavioral economics. Its extraordinary breadth and depth, spanning all aspects from psychological foundations to the most recent advances and seamlessly integrating theory with experiments, will make it the must-have reference for anyone interested in this field, and more generally in where economics is headed. It will quickly become the standard textbook for all graduate courses in behavioral economics, and a much-thumbed companion for all researchers working at the frontier."
    Roland Benabou, *Theodore A. Wells' 29 Professor of Economics and Public Affairs, Princeton University.*

"In *The Foundations of Behavioral Economic Analysis*, Sanjit Dhami offers the first summary and exposition of research in this rapidly growing and increasingly influential subfield. The coverage is comprehensive, extending even to the recent subtopics of behavioral welfare economics and neuroeconomics. The book is distinguished by its detailed yet readable coverage of theory and evidence and its balanced discussion of the philosophical and methodological differences and similarities between 'behavioral' and neoclassical approaches to microeconomics. Select undergraduates, graduate students, and interested scholars will all gain from this masterful book."
    Vincent P. Crawford, *Drummond Professor of Political Economy, University of Oxford, and Research Professor, University of California, San Diego.*

"Economic theory in the twentieth century developed an extremely powerful repertoire of analytical techniques for studying human behavior, but labored under the rather bizarre misconception that the postulates of rational choice were sufficient to characterize economic behavior. Behavioral economics from the late twentieth century to the present demonstrated the explanatory power of hitching these analytical techniques to empirical data gleaned from laboratory and field experiments. The result has radically transformed economics as a scientific discipline, and the best is surely yet to come. Sanjit Dhami has performed a monumental task in consolidating this research and explaining the results in a rigorous yet accessible manner, while highlighting major controversies and sketching the central research questions facing us today."

Herbert Gintis, Santa Fe Institute.

"Displaying wit and wisdom, in *The Foundations of Behavioral Economic Analysis* Professor Dhami conveys both the substance and the excitement of the burgeoning field of behavioral economics. These remarkable volumes will serve as a reference for practitioners and a compelling entry-point for the curious."

George Loewenstein, Herbert A. Simon Professor of Economics and Psychology, Carnegie Mellon University.

"In the development of any field there comes a moment where the results already established must be synthesized, explained and consolidated both for those in the field and those outside. In these amazing volumes Sanjit Dhami has done just that and far more. This book will serve as an encyclopedic must-have reference for anyone seeking to do work in this field or just curious about it. The coverage is exhaustive and the exposition extremely clear and at a level suitable for advanced undergraduates, graduates students, and professionals. This is truly an achievement."

Andrew Schotter, Professor of Economics, New York University and Director, Center for Experimental Social Science.

"For someone, like myself, who started by being ignorant of the richness of the conversation within behavioral economics on a variety of issues, this magisterial volume is the ideal introduction, at once lucid and sophisticated."

Abhijit V. Banerjee, Ford Foundation International Professor of Economics, M.I.T.

"These seven volumes cover all relevant theoretical aspects of behavioral economics in great depth. A great strength is their comprehensiveness: they cover the whole field in a unified manner. They thus are unique in bringing to the fore the unity and diversity of the behavioral approach. The material is well-organized and accessible to a wide audience. It is invaluable to anyone teaching or studying any topic in behavioral economics, showing how the topic fits into the whole."

Peter Wakker, Professor of Economics, Erasmus University Rotterdam.

"Sanjit Dhami's *The Foundations of Behavioral Economic Analysis* is a major and most impressive achievement. It provides an exhaustive account and a masterful synthesis of the state of the art after more than three decades of behavioral economics. It has proven to be an indispensable reference for researchers in economics and psychology. The second, updated edition comes in seven volumes, and it is bound to become the standard text in graduate and advanced undergraduate courses on behavioral and experimental economics for many years to come."

Klaus M. Schmidt, Professor of Economics, University of Munich.

"This is the most complete and stimulating series of books on behavioral economics. With elegance and unprecedented elaborateness, it ties together a wealth of experimental findings, rigorous theoretical insights and exciting applications across all relevant fields of behavioral research. Sanjit Dhami's work has been shaped by numerous comments of the leaders in the field. Now, in the years to come, it will be the standard that shapes how the next generation of students and researchers think about behavior and its science."

Axel Ockenfels, University of Cologne, Speaker of the Cologne Excellence Center of Social and Economic Behavior.

"The expansion of behavioral economics during the past quarter century has been remarkable, much of it concerning strategic interaction and using tools from game theory. Sanjit Dhami's amazing book, now available in a convenient multi-volume format, summarizes—and even defines—the field, broadly as well as in depth. His coverage of theory as well as of experiments is superb. *The Foundations of Behavioral Economic Analysis* will be an indispensable resource for students and scholars who wish to understand where the action is."

Martin Dufwenberg, Karl & Stevie Eller Professor and Director of the Institute for Behavioral Economics at the University of Arizona.

"*The Foundations of Behavioral Economic Analysis* will be a central textbook for behavioral economics. One key feature is its appealing focus on the interplay between theory and evidence. For researchers, it will be a great source of information, puzzles, and challenges for the many years to come. It is a major achievement."

Xavier Gabaix, Pershing Square Professor of Economics and Finance, Harvard University.

"This is a unique and truly remarkable achievement. It is a magnificent overview of behavioral economics, by far the best there is, and it should define the field for at least a generation. But it is much more than that. It is also a brilliant set of original discussions, with pathbreaking thinking on every important topic. An invaluable resource for policymakers, students, and professors—and if they want to try something really special, for everyone else."

Cass Sunstein, coauthor of Nudge and Founder and Director of the Program on Behavioral Economics and Public Policy, Harvard Law School.

"This is truly an amazing work. It is unique in both comprehensiveness and depth. The author is to be applauded for producing what will surely be the standard reference for both researchers and students. And breaking it into seven volumes will greatly enhance its usability. I highly recommend these volumes to any serious reader in behavioral economics."

Gary Charness, Professor of Economics, University of California, Santa Barbara.

The Foundations of Behavioral Economic Analysis: Volume 2

Other-Regarding Preferences

SANJIT DHAMI

UNIVERSITY PRESS

UNIVERSITY PRESS

Great Clarendon Street, Oxford, OX2 6DP,
United Kingdom

Oxford University Press is a department of the University of Oxford.
It furthers the University's objective of excellence in research, scholarship,
and education by publishing worldwide. Oxford is a registered trade mark of
Oxford University Press in the UK and in certain other countries

© Sanjit Dhami 2019

The moral rights of the author have been asserted

First Edition published in 2019

Impression: 1

All rights reserved. No part of this publication may be reproduced, stored in
a retrieval system, or transmitted, in any form or by any means, without the
prior permission in writing of Oxford University Press, or as expressly permitted
by law, by licence or under terms agreed with the appropriate reprographics
rights organization. Enquiries concerning reproduction outside the scope of the
above should be sent to the Rights Department, Oxford University Press, at the
address above

You must not circulate this work in any other form
and you must impose this same condition on any acquirer

Published in the United States of America by Oxford University Press
198 Madison Avenue, New York, NY 10016, United States of America

British Library Cataloguing in Publication Data

Data available

Library of Congress Control Number: 2018959373

ISBN 978-0-19-883743-5

Printed and bound by
CPI Group (UK) Ltd, Croydon, CR0 4YY

Links to third party websites are provided by Oxford in good faith and
for information only. Oxford disclaims any responsibility for the materials
contained in any third party website referenced in this work.

To my Parents, wife Shammi, and son Sahaj

PREFACE TO VOLUME 2: BEHAVIORAL ECONOMICS OF RISK, UNCERTAINTY, AND AMBIGUITY

The Foundations of Behavioral Economic Analysis (henceforth, FBEA) was published by Oxford University Press in November 2016. It was the culmination of more than a decade of dedicated work. The book was quite well received and it was heartening to receive messages of support, encouragement, and appreciation from many quarters. Several reviews of FBEA have been published and they have praised the comprehensiveness, formal analysis, and the attention to empirical detail in the book. The book is increasingly taught around the world in behavioral and experimental economics courses in the leading economics departments. Encouragingly, it is also being used in more enlightened courses in economic theory, which was always an important objective of writing this book. The practice of ignoring the empirical evidence and the theoretical models in behavioral economics, in many courses in microeconomics, game theory, and contract theory, is one of the most retrogressive practices in the profession and a form of self-handicapping that is difficult to understand.

At 1796 pages (including unnumbered pages), FBEA is probably one of the longest economics books ever to have been published in a single volume. Binding the book was a major challenge, which Oxford University Press accomplished with great competence. Some friends have written on a lighter note about the physical size and the weight of the book. Samuel Bowles wrote to say that Herbert Gintis had presented him with a copy of the book on Christmas and that he had to hire a truck to take it home. In one of his reviews, Daniel Read congratulated me on writing the "War and Peace" of behavioral economics. Andrew Schotter wrote to say that he keeps one copy at home and another in his office in NYU to avoid carrying it on the New York subway. A friend who had purchased the paperback version took the drastic step of physically separating Part 4 on behavioral game theory (a good 320 pages long) to carry around with him. Xavier Gabaix is one of many readers who prefers the electronic version that makes issues of the size of the book irrelevant. However, at least some readers, and I am part of this group, tend to be old fashioned and prefer the printed version.

We did explore the idea of splitting FBEA into two volumes before it was published and this was put to an informal vote among 30 of the leading behavioral economists. They were almost equally split. OUP took the casting vote to decide on a single volume, understandably because there are not too many multiple volume mainstream texts in economics. As more feedback from the users of the book emerged, Adam Swallow, the commissioning editor at OUP, began exploring with me the possibility of splitting the book into multiple volumes. Just as publishing such a long book and making it available for teaching to several instructors prior to its publication was a novel and bold experiment in publishing, so too is the proposal to split it into multiple volumes. After extensive discussions at OUP, I was given the go ahead to pursue this exciting and unprecedented opportunity.

What we present to you here, after considerable thought, is a seven-volume book on behavioral economics that splits the nine parts of FBEA into the following topics: Behavioral economics of risk uncertainty and ambiguity (Volume 1); Other-regarding preferences (Volume 2); Behavioral economics of time discounting (Volume 3); Behavioral game theory (Volume 4); Bounded rationality (Volume 5); Behavioral models of learning (Volume 6); Further topics in behavioral economics that include emotions, behavioral welfare economics, and neuroeconomics (Volume 7). Other possible splits of FBEA were possible (e.g., combining Volumes 1 and 3; and Volumes 2 and 4), but none of these proposals offers the clean separation into the main topics in behavioral economics that the current split offers.

We believe that these seven volumes improve on FBEA for several reasons aside from just better portability of the print edition. First, it is a welcome opportunity to correct several typos and errors, as well as to improve the clarity of the text in many places. Second, it allows the updating of some of the material to reflect important recent scholarship in the form of a 'guide to further reading' at the end of each volume. This allows me to introduce several new concepts and tie them back to the discussion in the main text. Third, it gives readers the option to buy individual volumes, depending on their current research and teaching interests. However, those with a serious interest in economics, certainly all university academics, ought to consider reading all of the seven volumes. Fourth, given how daunting the prospect of revising the 1,800-page FBEA would have been, the split volumes increase the likelihood of a second edition to some, or all, of the volumes in due course.

For the benefit of readers who buy the separate volumes, or just a few of the volumes, we have taken several steps. Each of the volumes will have a new preface, a new introduction, and carry a reprint of the original preface in FBEA. This will give readers an opportunity to get acquainted with how and why this book came to be. The introductory chapter in FBEA covered important ground. In particular, the first 25 pages outlined the antecedents of behavioral economics, the role of scientific methodology, and the rationale for the experimental method. A lack of proper understanding and appreciation of these critical prerequisites may seriously hamper an understanding of the subject matter. For this reason, in each volume, we shall also print an edited version of the first 25 pages in FBEA. In these pages, I have also added a brief new subsection on replication of experiments. The remaining part of the introductory chapter in FBEA (pages 25–64) is printed only in Volume 1. I have taken care to remove as many typos and errors from the introduction of FBEA as I could find, and improved the clarity of the material in many places.

Readers will find that we have done many of the same things that we might have done in bringing out a second edition of FBEA in these seven volumes. We hope that our efforts in this direction will lead to a better understanding and appreciation of the subject matter of behavioral economics.

PREFACE TO THE FOUNDATIONS OF BEHAVIORAL ECONOMIC ANALYSIS

We print below the original preface to *The Foundations of Behavioral Economic Analysis* in Dhami (2016).

Neoclassical economics is a logically consistent and parsimonious framework of analysis that is based on a relatively small set of core assumptions, and it offers clear, testable, predictions. However, extensive and growing empirical evidence reveals human behavior that is difficult to reconcile within the typical neoclassical models. There has been a parallel development in rigorous theoretical models that explains better the emerging stylized facts on human behavior. These models have borrowed insights from psychology, sociology, anthropology, neuroscience, and evolutionary biology. Yet, these models maintain a distinct economic identity in terms of their approach, rigor, and parsimony. Collectively, these models form the subject matter of behavioral economics, which is possibly the fastest growing and most promising area in economics.

This book is an account of behavioral economics that starts with the basics and takes the reader to the research frontiers in the subject. Depending on how one chooses to use it, the book is suitable for courses at the advanced undergraduate, postgraduate, and research level in economics, and the related social sciences, including, but not restricted to, psychology, management, finance, political science, and sociology. The book should also serve as an essential reference book for anyone generally interested in behavioral economics at any level, and also serve to stimulate the interests of non-specialist academics, specialist academics who are looking for a bird's-eye view of the entire field, and policymakers looking for policy applications of behavioral economics. It would be desirable to assign this book as background reading to courses in economic theory. The book is also, in my view, the minimum subject matter that anyone who writes behavioral economics as their research interest, should be deeply familiar with.

In November 2003, two months after I joined the department of economics at the University of Leicester, I chanced upon an invitation to attend a talk by a colleague, Ali al-Nowaihi, on the subject of *prospect theory*. Ali, a mathematician by training, an economist by profession, and a keen student of the philosophy of science, put forward a Popperian view to evaluate economic theories. He argued that *expected utility theory* was decisively rejected by the evidence, and prospect theory was the most satisfactory decision theory currently available. As a purely neoclassically trained economist, I was troubled by the claims, but also extremely skeptical. For a start, prospect theory sounded like a strange name for a theory, and the evidence was largely "experimental," a data source, that I knew little about. As my defensive instincts started to kick in, I wondered if prospect theory really was so important, then surely my graduate courses, many taught by leading decision theorists, would have found some reason to mention it. Nor was there any mention of such a theory in conversations with colleagues at the two British universities where I had taught so far, or at seminars or conferences that I had attended.

However, rather than just dismiss Ali, a very likeable and respected figure in the department, I decided to put his seemingly extreme views to the test. One of my majors was in public economics, so I decided to conduct a prospect theory analysis of tax evasion in the hope of explaining the *tax evasion puzzles*, which had been outstanding for three decades (details in Part 1). There was already some preliminary work in this area that Ali had mentioned in passing, but none of the papers explained all the puzzles in one fell swoop, using all components of prospect theory. It took me just a few weeks to work out the results. To my utter amazement, prospect theory explained the qualitative and quantitative tax evasion puzzles. By contrast, the predictions based on an expected utility analysis were wrong by a factor of up to 100. This led to my first joint publication with Ali, with whom I have spent many years of fruitful collaboration since then.

This initial, and successful, encounter with prospect theory convinced me that I needed to explore behavioral economics in greater depth. Yet, around 2004, there was no definitive graduate text on behavioral economics. To be sure, there were many excellent sets of collected readings, and several insightful surveys and commentaries on selected aspects of behavioral economics that I eagerly read. In particular, while there were many excellent discussions of the experimental evidence, a full treatment of behavioral economic theory and its applications was missing. One could always pursue the journal articles, but the literature was already enormous, rapidly expanding, and scattered, which made it difficult to spot the links between the various models or to clearly visualize how the various pieces of the jigsaw fitted together. This book was motivated initially by the lack of a serious graduate book on the entire subject matter of behavioral economics, my desire to master behavioral economics, and to support my growing research agenda with Ali. In due course, and as the full range of the subject matter gradually dawned upon me, the scope of the book naturally became more ambitious and daring.

I strive to strike a balance between behavioral economic theory, the experimental evidence, and applications of behavioral economics. The choice of theoretical models in this book is dictated, first and foremost, by their ability to explain the empirical evidence. In some cases, where no decisive empirical evidence is available, I make a judgment on which models are more promising than others, although I give a wide berth to most models.

The main prerequisite for the book is training in the first two to three years of a reasonably good British or North American undergraduate degree in economics, or its equivalent. Any further concepts and techniques are introduced in the book, where needed. A prior course in behavioral economics is not a prerequisite for the book.

The book is divided into nine parts that cover decision making under risk, uncertainty, and ambiguity; other-regarding preferences; behavioral time discounting; models of behavioral game theory and learning; role of emotions in decision making; models of bounded rationality; judgment heuristics and mental accounting; behavioral welfare economics; and neuroeconomics. The book also considers a range of applications of the theory to most areas in economics that include microeconomics, contract theory, macroeconomics, industrial organization, labor economics, development economics, public economics, political economy, and finance. A set of exercises at the end of each part, except the part on neuroeconomics, serves to enhance the reader's understanding of the subject.

Behavioral economics is now a mainstream area in economics. One just has to look at the growing and large number of journal publications and Ph.D. theses every year; the Nobel Prizes to Herbert Simon, Daniel Kahneman, Robert Shiller, Alvin Roth, Vernon Smith, and George Akerlof; the John Bates Clarke medal to Matthew Rabin; the growing importance of behavioral economics among policymakers, as witnessed by the 2015 World Bank Development Report, and the formation of the behavioral insights team in the UK; and the choice of Richard Thaler as the incoming President of the American Economic Association.

It is fair to say that no self-respecting economics department can now afford to omit a course in behavioral economics from its undergraduate or graduate curriculum; indeed, doing so would be grossly unjust to its students and a retrogressive step. Nor can any academic economist, who wishes to retain professional honesty and a balanced opinion on the subject, afford to be unfamiliar with the subject matter of behavioral economics; I am often amused by the ignorance and arrogance of many who pass judgment on behavioral economics with supreme confidence, yet appear to have little understanding of it.

This book has taken more than ten years to write, and my debts are deep and profound. My first and foremost debt and gratitude is to my loving family without which this book could not have been written. To my parents, Manohar and Baljeet, for their unconditional lifelong love and support, and instilling in me the core values of honesty, commitment, and hard work. To my wife, Shammi, and my son, Sahaj, for their patience, sacrifice, unflinching support, and constant encouragement. When I started writing this book, Sahaj was in primary school, and in the month of its first publication, he could be packing his bags to join a university. I do not recommend this as the best template to encourage your son to write any books in the future. However, there are close parallels between Sahaj's educational journey from primary school to university, with my own journey in behavioral economics.

I owe a deep intellectual debt to my long-time coauthor and friend, Ali al-Nowaihi. I first learnt about prospect theory from him. I also owe my appreciation of methodology and the philosophy of science entirely to him. He has undertaken a larger burden of our joint research in the last few years, allowing me to be immersed in the book. For all these reasons, he is very much a coauthor of the book in spirit.

I am extremely grateful to many academics and Ph.D. students who unselfishly and generously contributed their time and efforts to reading drafts of various parts of the book. The participation of so many leading behavioral economists in the making of this book is unprecedented and has really made it into a public project for which I shall always be very grateful. Herbert Gintis, Martin Dufwenberg, and Vincent Crawford deserve special mention for being so very gracious with their inputs into most parts of the book, and very quickly responding to my queries.

Many others also played a critical role in the writing of this book and commented on material closer to their areas of interest, and/or offered valuable encouragement and advice. In particular, I wish to thank Mohammed Abdellaoui, Ali al-Nowaihi, Dan Ariely, Douglas Barrett, Björn Bartling, Karna Basu, Kaushik Basu, Pierpaolo Battigalli, Roland Bénabou, Florian Biermann, Gary Bolton, Subir Bose, David Colander, Andrew Colman, Patricio Dalton, Alexandra Dias, Florian Englmaier, Armin Falk, Ernst Fehr, Urs Fischbacher, Xavier Gabaix, Sayantan Ghosal, Uri Gneezy, Werner Güth, Shaun Hargreaves Heap, Fabian Herweg, Karla Hoff, Philippe Jehiel, David Laibson, George Loewenstein, Michel Marechal, Friederike Mengel, Joshua Miller, Axel Ockenfels, Amnon Rapoport, Ludovic Renou, Alvin Roth, Klaus Schmidt, Andrei Shleifer, Dennis Snower, Joe Stiglitz, Cass Sunstein, Richard Thaler, Jean-Robert Tyran, Klaus Waelde, Peter Wakker, Eyal Winter, and Peyton Young. I owe a profound intellectual debt to many others who did not read the book manuscript but whose work has greatly inspired me. These include Daniel Kahneman, Amos Tversky, Colin Camerer, Matthew Rabin, Herbert Simon, Robert Shiller, and George Akerlof. I am also very grateful to two successive Heads of the economics department at Leicester, Steve Hall and Chris Wallace, who tried to free up as much of my time as possible for writing the book.

I would like to specially acknowledge the enormous amount of work put in by two extremely conscientious and able Ph.D. students, Teimuraz Gogsadze and Junaid Arshad. They closely read and commented on successive drafts of the manuscript at all stages, offered very useful advice, and served as excellent sounding boards for new ideas. Jingyi Mao came up with a very nice cover for the book in a burst of creativity, for which I am very grateful. Other Ph.D. students who carefully read and commented on selected parts of the manuscript include: Ala Avoyan, Nino Dognohadze, Sneha Gaddam, Narges Hajimoladarvish, Emma Manifold, Jingyi Mao, Alexandros Rigos, David Tsirekidze, Yongli Wang, Mengxing Wei, and Mariam Zaldastanishvili.

I would be remiss not to thank the large number of other researchers whose work has made this book possible. I must also sincerely apologize to authors who feel that their work has been inadequately cited or not given the importance they feel that it deserves. To such authors, I say, omission of your papers does not mean that I necessarily viewed your papers as unimportant. In mitigation, I do not intend my book to be a survey of all the experimental results on all topics in behavioral economics; there are already excellent sources with this objective. And, quite possibly, I was simply unaware of your important work, which is in keeping with the evidence on limited attention and bounded rationality that plays an important role in this book.

I am very grateful to the team at Oxford University Press who have done an excellent job at all stages of this book. In particular, I would like to thank Adam Swallow, the commissioning editor for economics and finance at OUP for his patience, good cheer, organizational skills, and sound advice. Scott Parris, the economics editor at the US office of OUP, who retired just as this book was about to come out, was the first to spot the importance of this project. He offered very valuable advice and encouragement throughout the writing stage and played a key role in my decision to go with OUP. I must also thank Niko Pfund, the President of Oxford University Press USA, for his continued interest in the manuscript over several years, despite his many other responsibilities. The production and marketing teams at OUP were a pleasure to work with. Jon Billam took on the challenge of copy-editing an unusually large book with great enthusiasm. I am also very grateful to Emma Slaughter, the production editor for the book; Kim Stringer, the indexer; Kim Allen, the proofreader; Carla Hodge-Degler who took over as production editor from Emma; and to Leigh-Ann Bard, the marketing manager for the book.

CONTENTS

List of Figures	xxi
List of Tables	xxiii
Introduction to Volume 2	1
Introduction to Behavioral Economics and the Book Volumes	7
1 Some antecedents of behavioral economics	9
2 On methodology in economics	10
3 The experimental method in economics	16
3.1 Experiments and internal validity	17
3.2 Subject pools used in lab experiments	19
3.3 Stake sizes in experiments	20
3.4 The issue of the external validity of lab findings	20
3.5 The role of incentives in economics	22
3.6 Is survey data of any use?	25
3.7 Replications in experimental economics	27
4 Approach and organization of the book	28
5 Appendix A: The random lottery incentive mechanism	33
6 Appendix B: In lieu of a problem set	33
References for Introduction	38
1 The Evidence on Human Sociality	**42**
1.1 Introduction	42
1.2 Ultimatum and dictator games	47
1.2.1 The ultimatum game	47
1.2.2 The dictator game	50
1.2.3 Rationality of other-regarding preferences in dictator games	53
1.3 Gift exchange and trust games	55
1.3.1 The gift exchange game	55
1.3.2 The trust game, trust, and trustworthiness	64
1.4 Public goods games	68
1.4.1 Public goods game without punishments	68
1.4.2 Public goods game with punishments	69
1.4.3 Empirical evidence on public goods games	70
1.4.4 Heterogenous preferences and the pattern of contributions	74
1.4.5 Unproductive expenditures on public goods	77
1.4.6 Antisocial punishments	80
1.4.7 Evolution and reciprocity	83
1.5 How representative is the lab evidence?	84
1.5.1 The student subject pool and experimental scrutiny	84
1.5.2 The external validity of experiments on other-regarding preferences	86
1.6 Indirect reciprocity	93

2 Models of Other-Regarding Preferences — 96

- 2.1 Introduction — 96
- 2.2 The Fehr–Schmidt model — 100
  - 2.2.1 Fairness and market competition — 101
  - 2.2.2 Fairness and cooperation — 105
- 2.3 The ERC model — 108
- 2.4 Fairness and stochastic dominance — 110
- 2.5 Behavioral political economy — 115
  - 2.5.1 Existence of a Condorcet winner when voters have social preferences — 116
  - 2.5.2 Heterogeneity in voter preferences and redistribution — 121
- 2.6 Fairness, general equilibrium, and welfare — 125
- 2.7 Evidence on models of social preferences and reciprocity — 129
  - 2.7.1 The evidence on models of social preferences — 130
  - 2.7.2 The evidence on intentions and reciprocity — 132
- 2.8 A discussion of other promising models — 143
  - 2.8.1 The Charness and Rabin (2002) hybrid model — 143
  - 2.8.2 Models of interdependent preferences — 146
  - 2.8.3 The model of Cox, Friedman, and Gjerstad (2007) — 148
  - 2.8.4 A brief note on axiomatic foundations — 148

3 Human Morality and Social Identity — 152

- 3.1 Introduction — 152
- 3.2 Human virtues — 154
  - 3.2.1 Evidence on human virtues — 154
  - 3.2.2 A theoretical model of promises and threats — 160
- 3.3 Social identity — 165
  - 3.3.1 Evidence on social identity and other-regarding preferences — 166
  - 3.3.2 Identity and economic incentives — 173

4 Incentives and Other-Regarding Preferences — 177

- 4.1 Introduction — 177
- 4.2 Moral hazard and other-regarding preferences — 182
  - 4.2.1 Inequity aversion and moral hazard — 182
  - 4.2.2 Reciprocity and moral hazard — 189
- 4.3 Incomplete contracts under other-regarding preferences — 194
  - 4.3.1 Optimal contracts under self-regarding preferences — 197
  - 4.3.2 Optimal contracts in the presence of other-regarding preferences — 197
  - 4.3.3 Evidence on contract choice under contractual incompleteness — 205
- 4.4 Reciprocity and long-term contracts — 209
  - 4.4.1 The outcome with self-regarding preferences — 210
  - 4.4.2 The outcome with other-regarding preferences — 211
  - 4.4.3 Experimental results — 217
  - 4.4.4 The nature of the firm and other-regarding preferences — 221
- 4.5 Extrinsic and intrinsic motivation: theoretical framework — 226
  - 4.5.1 Self-signaling and social signaling — 227
  - 4.5.2 Intentions, altruism, and esteem — 233

4.6	Extrinsic and intrinsic motivation: empirical evidence	239
	4.6.1 Incentives may signal a hostile intent	239
	4.6.2 Control aversion and choking under high incentives	241
	4.6.3 Moral disengagement	248
	4.6.4 Morality may be difficult to signal in the presence of incentives	252
	4.6.5 Economic environment, learning, and incentives	255
	4.6.6 Crowding-in effect of incentives	258
5	**A Guide to Further Reading**	**262**
	5.1 More evidence from gift exchange experiments	262
	5.2 Social preferences and political choices	263
	5.3 Other-regarding preferences and children	263
	5.4 Other-regarding preferences around the globe	264
	5.5 Types of other-regarding preferences	264
	5.6 Recent evidence on human virtues	267
	5.6.1 Lab studies on lying behavior	267
	5.6.2 Artifactual and field studies of lying	268
	5.6.3 Markets and morality	270
	5.6.4 Public and private personas	272
	5.6.5 A microfoundation for gender differences in lying	273
	5.7 Norms and social preferences	274
	5.8 Exercises for Volume 2	280

References for Volume 2   285
Author Index   303
Subject Index   308

LIST OF FIGURES

1.1	The relation between effort and rent in the gift exchange game.	56
1.2	The effect of the equity norm on effort levels.	59
1.3	Behavior of workers' effort levels in the library task.	60
1.4	The relation between reciprocity and tenure.	61
1.5	Productivity of workers in different wage conditions.	62
1.6	Average responses for the positive reciprocity questions (left panel) and negative reciprocity questions (right panel).	63
1.7	Measures of trust and trustworthiness in a meta study.	65
1.8	The trust game in Huck et al. (2012).	67
1.9	Evolution of average contributions in three different treatments in the presence and in the absence of punishments.	71
1.10	Explaining the pattern of contributions when there is heterogeneity in social preferences.	76
1.11	Choice of institutions and contributions.	77
1.12	Contest expenditures in the treatments without punishment.	79
1.13	Actual and equilibrium rent dissipation.	81
1.14	Prosocial and antisocial punishment in the public goods game (left panel) and the relation between antisocial punishment and contributions (right panel).	82
1.15	Mean contributions in the P treatment (left panel) and the N treatment (right panel).	83
1.16	Results for the single- and double-anonymous treatments.	86
1.17	Workers' performance response to the wage increase (vertical axis), conditional on their fairness perceptions.	87
1.18	Checking the external validity of lab data on social preferences.	89
1.19	Average time spent on monitoring by different behavioral types. The bars represent standard errors of means.	91
1.20	Third party punishments in the dictator game.	95
2.1	The SSS and SFS economies.	123
2.2	The SSS, SSF, and FSF economies.	124
2.3	Modified ultimatum game.	134
2.4	Effect on b as a changes.	136
2.5	Normal form representation of a two-player, sequential, social dilemma game.	139
2.6	Cumulative distribution of the second player's cooperative decision (c1 to c6).	140
2.7	Two variations of the ultimatum game, indexed by the parameters x and y. The UG*x game is in the left panel and the UG*+y game is in the right panel.	141
2.8	Average rejection rates in the UG*x game.	141
2.9	Average rejection rates in the UG*+y game.	142
3.1	Results for the baseline treatment.	157

3.2	Messages sent by player A in each state.	159
3.3	The battle of sexes (BOS) game and the prisoner's dilemma game (PD).	169
3.4	Cooperation rates and beliefs in the modified trust game. Bars represent standard errors of means.	171
3.5	Group membership and punishment. Bars represent standard errors of means.	172
4.1	Share of bonus contracts and incentive contracts over successive rounds.	205
4.2	Relation between the actual bonus paid by the principal and effort level of the agent.	206
4.3	A comparision of the length of the worker–firm relationship under the two treatments.	217
4.4	Average temporal wage in each treatment.	218
4.5	Average temporal effort in each treatment.	219
4.6	Average earnings per trade of the workers and firms in each treatment.	219
4.7	Comparison of mean effort levels under various treatments.	220
4.8	Payoffs of the principal and agent in treatment RANDOM (left panel) and treatment FIXED (right panel).	225
4.9	Share of employment contracts in different treatments (left panel). Frequency of power abuse and share of employment contracts in each treatment (right panel).	225
4.10	Diagrammatic representation of the condition in (4.77).	229
4.11	Loci of combinations of (u_I, u_E) on which (4.86) binds.	232
4.12	A trust game that differentiates between voluntary and involuntary trust.	235
4.13	Effort and rents in three cases.	240
4.14	Effect of intentions in the trust game.	241
4.15	Median choice of action by the agent when the principal does, and does not, control.	242
4.16	Mean earnings as a percentage of maximum earnings in different games.	244
4.17	Mean earnings as a percentage of maximum earnings in different games.	245
4.18	Average profits and average effort levels conditonal on the employees' reputations.	246
4.19	Share of contract-F in each treatment.	247
4.20	Buyer/seller profits as a function of buyer/seller choices.	248
4.21	Average number of parents who arrive late.	250
4.22	Percentage of blood donors under varying levels of incentives.	253
4.23	The effect of incentives on prosocial behavior in different treatments. Vertical bars are standard errors of means.	254
4.24	Total public goods contributions over successive rounds when the incentives are varied.	257
4.25	Number of weekly visits to the gym. Error bars reflect one standard error.	260

LIST OF TABLES

2.1	Parameter estimates of the Fehr and Schmidt (1999) model of inequality aversion.	101
2.2	Payoffs of three players in three different allocations.	131
2.3	Summary of predictions for player B.	136
3.1	Payoffs of the players in each treatment in Gneezy (2005).	155
4.1	The cost of effort function.	210
4.2	The relevant economic information in each state of the world.	222

Introduction to Volume 2

Neoclassical economic theory typically relies on the assumption of self-regarding behavior, i.e., that individuals derive utility solely from their own pecuniary or non-pecuniary payoffs. We may term such preferences as *self-regarding preferences* and an individual with these preferences as a *self-regarding individual*.[1] This view of human behavior is often at odds with the evidence, particularly when interaction in small groups is considered but also, often in large-group interactions.

The evidence indicates that humans often exhibit direct or indirect concern about others for several reasons. As Gintis (2009, p. 49) puts it, "We conclude from behavioral game theory that one must treat individuals' objectives as a matter of fact, not logic." Individuals may care for others on moral grounds, or they may directly care about the pecuniary and non-pecuniary payoffs of others, or they may derive a warm glow from helping those who are less fortunate, or they may wish to punish others in the group whose treatment of them or of others in the group does not conform to expectations, or they may wish to signal desirable human qualities such as altruism or kindness to themselves and to others. In all these cases, humans exhibit *other-regarding preferences* (sometimes referred to as *social preferences*).

Volume 2 of the book studies the behavior of individuals with other-regarding preferences. The model with purely self-regarding preferences is unable to explain a range of phenomena from many diverse areas such as social dilemma situations, collective action, contract theory, the structure of incentives, political economy, and the results of several experimental games. By contrast, many of these phenomena can be explained by a model which recognizes that individuals have other-regarding preferences. On the other hand, many phenomena such as the behavior of competitive experimental market subjects seem to be in conformity with the model of self-regarding preferences (Roth et al., 1991).[2] However, in richer competitive environments, one still recovers a role for other-regarding preferences (Fehr et al., 1998). One challenge for theoretical research is to describe why the same individual exhibits other-regarding preferences

---

[1] The literature sometimes uses the term *selfish preferences* for *self-regarding preferences*. For most of the models that we consider, individuals try to maximize their objective functions, whether they have self-regarding or other-regarding preferences. For this reason, we find the term self-regarding to be more appropriate.

[2] Interestingly, in the Roth et al. (1991) experiments, bilateral behavior of subjects is consistent with models of social preferences. This dichotomy of behavior in multilateral and bilateral settings is not simply a figment of experimental data. Bolton and Ockenfels (2014) confirm these experimental findings from a field study based on eBay transactions. This also adds to a growing number of field studies that increasingly establish the external validity of lab experiments, a theme that we consider in more detail in Chapter 1.

in small groups, or in bilateral interactions, but self-regarding preferences in anonymous, large-group, market situations; see Fehr and Schmidt (1999) for a successful example of such a behavioral model.

Most experiments reveal a mixture of self-regarding and other-regarding preferences, but the relative fractions of players who exhibit the two types of preferences vary. For instance, for public goods experiments Fischbacher et al. (2001) show that 30–40% may have self-regarding preferences while the remaining may have other-regarding preferences. By contrast, the structural model estimates of Bruhin et al. (2018) for dictator games and trust games show that there are no self-regarding players; all players are other-regarding. An important and interesting issue for theoretical and empirical research is to examine the implications of such heterogeneity in preferences. We shall show that the introduction of even a small fraction of individuals with other-regarding preferences in a model with self-regarding preferences can substantially alter the results and vice-versa in applications ranging from public goods experiments, political economy, and contract theory.

Evidence for other-regarding preferences comes from many sources. Consider the following examples; the reader is invited to ponder if the model with purely self-regarding preferences could account for these results.[3]

1. Wages are usually not lowered in a recession as firms fear that this action may be construed by the workers to be *unfair* and have a negative effect on worker's *morale* (Bewley, 1999, 2005). The experimental findings of Fehr et al. (1993) and Fehr and Falk (1999) demonstrate that downward wage rigidity is caused by the belief on the part of employers that workers will reciprocate lower wages with lower levels of effort. For instance, in a double auction experiment, Fehr and Falk (1999) showed that employers accepted high wage offers in excess of the competitive level when the effort was endogenous. However, when the workers' effort was exogenously fixed, firms accepted the lowest wage offers. Thus, firms did not accept high wage offers purely for fairness considerations but also because they expected effort reciprocity on the part of workers. In actual practice, firms may prefer to hire workers who have other-regarding preferences because they may be expected to reciprocate positive actions by the firms and other co-workers in the team.
2. Consider a two-stage public goods game, where individuals make voluntary contributions to a public good, followed by the possibility of non-contributors being punished by the contributors. The model with purely self-regarding preferences predicts *free-riding*, i.e., zero contributions and no punishment of non-contributors by the contributors because bygones are bygones. In contrast, the experimental results show that individuals contribute more when others contribute more in previous rounds (Fischbacher et al., 2001). In experiments in many Western societies, we also observe the punishment of non-cooperators by cooperators and close to the first best level of contributions in the presence of punishments (Fehr and Gächter, 2000).
3. In one-shot interactions, in a range of experimental games considered below, such as the ultimatum game, the dictator game, and the trust game, people pass on far higher monetary amounts to others than are predicted by models of self-regarding preferences.
4. Kahneman et al. (1986) asked people if they would view a hardware store's action to increase the price of shovels following a snowstorm as fair? Most people thought that such

---

[3] It is possible that self-regarding preferences in conjunction with other auxiliary assumptions may explain these examples. However, if these assumptions are empirically rejected, then such explanations are ad hoc.

a price increase was unfair. However, they did not perceive an increase in price following an increase in the cost of inputs as unfair. In actual practice, many firms go to great lengths to establish their credentials for fair behavior.
5. Bargaining often stalls (*bargaining impasse*) in a range of situations, such as civil litigation, labor unrest, domestic strife, and clashes among religious and ethnic groups. An important psychological cause of bargaining impasse is that typically, individuals confuse what serves their self-interest and what is fair (Babcock and Loewenstein, 1997).[4]
6. Individuals make donations to charity, donate blood at Red Cross blood drives, and often volunteer time and money for prosocial actions. Such prosocial actions are often carried out for the benefit of non-kin members at a personal cost. The provision of monetary incentives for prosocial behavior may even be counterproductive (Titmuss, 1971; Bénabou and Tirole, 2003, 2006).
7. In one-shot interactions, such as in the trust game, pre-game *promises* and *threats* are predicted to be ineffective in altering behavior. Yet, such promises and threats are effective in generating more prosocial behavior (Ellingsen and Johannesson, 2004). Indeed, humans seem to value virtuous behavior such as honesty, fairness, and justice for its own sake; in neoclassical economics such behavior is *instrumental* but not *intrinsic*.
8. In one-shot interactions, when firms have a choice between a bonus contract and an incentive contract, the model with self-regarding preferences predicts the choice of an incentive contract. Bonus contracts should be ineffective in eliciting any effort from workers. Yet, we observe the predominant choice of bonus contracts in such a situation and much higher effort levels as well as profitability relative to incentive contracts (Fehr et al. 2007).
9. Military training programs typically focus on creating a separate identity—the identity of a soldier, in contrast to a civilian identity. A soldier's identity is associated with norms of behavior in particular situations that can be different from civilian norms of behavior in similar situations. These include the norms of *service before self*, courage, sacrifice, and fortitude under adversity. Similarly, firms try very hard to alter the identity of workers from *outsiders* into *insiders*. Insiders typically buy into the culture of the firm and subscribe to its objectives.

There has been a traditional aversion in economics to altering preferences/tastes in order to explain economic phenomena. This aversion may have been historically well-placed because the alternative could have been a proliferation of ad hoc models with preferences tailored to explain every possible situation. However, research in behavioral economics has provided a solid foundation, based on extensive experimental evidence, to propose models of other-regarding preferences. This is not ad hoc, and has enormously increased the ability of economic models to explain economic phenomena. Conversely, one may argue that in the face of overwhelming evidence that many humans exhibit some form of other-regarding preferences, it is ad hoc to focus exclusive attention on self-regarding preferences. As Gintis (2009, p. 49) puts it: "Self-regarding agents are in common parlance called sociopaths."

---

[4] We consider bargaining issues in Volume 4. Some of the reasons for bargaining impasse are as follows. First, confusion between self-interest and what is fair reduces the set of feasible agreements. Second, if each party believes that its (misplaced) notion of fairness is shared by the other party, then even potentially kind intentions by the other party could be perceived as being unkind. Third, psychological evidence indicates that parties in a bargaining situation are unwilling to settle below what they (mistakenly) perceive to be a fair entitlement. The reader might also wish to read a nice discussion of bargaining issues related to the issue of norms and social preferences in Crawford (1997, Section 5.3).

The argument that neoclassical economics does not rule out the role of other-regarding preferences is correct. Indeed, an older generation of economic models considered ideas such as *keeping up with the Joneses*, and *snob consumption* (Veblen, 1899; Duesenberry, 1949). However, while plausible, these models were not empirically well-founded and would not be able to explain the results from modern experimental games on fairness and reciprocity. In contrast, the current approach in behavioral economics offers empirically well-founded and parsimonious models of other-regarding preferences.

Let us consider some terminology that is used in models of other-regarding preferences. This terminology is by no means standard, partly because its origin straddles several disciplines such as economics, biology, anthropology, and sociology. Hence, we simply clarify the sense in which various terms are used in this book, without claiming that such usage is unique or the best possible.

Preferences are *altruistic* (respectively, *spiteful*) if one's utility is increasing (respectively, decreasing) in the consumption or well-being of others. Altruism is *unconditional kindness*, while spite is *unconditional unkindness*, irrespective of the behavior of other players. In practice, however, pure altruism is unable to explain a wide range of behaviors. For instance, it does not explain why many individuals are *conditional cooperators*, i.e., they cooperate only when others cooperate (as in successive rounds of a public goods game).[5] An *inequity averse* individual not only derives utility from own material consumption but also derives disutility from differences in own material consumption relative to the consumption of others. Such an individual dislikes relatively greater consumption (altruism) and/or relatively lower consumption (envy).

Reciprocal behavior can also be shown to arise in traditional economic analysis with self-regarding preferences. In classical game theory, in infinitely repeated games (or finitely repeated games with some uncertainty), cooperative behavior can be sustained in equilibrium. Such behavior is said to be *instrumentally reciprocal* because it is motivated purely by the prospect of a trade-off between short-run and long-run material gains.[6] By contrast, in a finitely repeated game, say, in a principal–agent relation, under self-regarding preferences, the outcome is that the worker shirks and output is low. However, under other-regarding preferences, theory and empirical evidence support superior cooperative outcomes (Brown et al., 2004, 2012). Thus, the evidence violates instrumental reciprocity here, and in many other classes of games.

Reciprocity that takes the form of responding to kindness and unkindness of others with like behavior, even in the absence of long-term considerations of costs and under complete certainty, may be termed as *intrinsic reciprocity*. People who exhibit such behavior are often described as *conditional cooperators*. The explanation of much human economic and social behavior relies on *intrinsic reciprocity*.

Altruism among kin members in humans is well documented. However, among humans, one also observes cooperation among non-kin group members and impressive division of labor at a level that is unprecedented in the animal kingdom (Wilson, 2012). Cooperation is much

---

[5] Axelrod and Hamilton (1981) conducted the classic experiments in reciprocity in the context of a sequence of repeated prisoner's dilemma games where there is some probability of the continuation of the game to the next period; see also Axelrod (1984). They found evidence for the superiority of the tit-for-tat strategy when subjects are randomly matched in each round of the game. In this strategy, subjects initially start by cooperating and then reciprocate in subsequent rounds, i.e., based on their experience in previous rounds, play defect in response to defect and play cooperate in response to cooperate. Such a strategy did best among the ones that were considered.

[6] A related concept from biology is that of *reciprocal altruism*. This involves a tendency to reward others in response to their kind behavior, when such net rewards may be expected to be reiprocated in the long term by others. See, for instance, Axelrod and Hamilton (1981) and Trivers (1971).

lower in primate societies with whom we share a common ancestor. Cooperation is well documented among ants, bees, and wild dogs, but this seems limited to genetic relations. Furthermore, humans are possibly unique among all animals to consider the fairness implications of their actions for kin and non-kin members.

An important component of human sociality is that group members often engage in costly punishment (respectively, costly rewards) of actions by third parties that are inimical (respectively, favorable) to some social goal or group norm. The punishers may not be directly affected by the actions of the third parties, yet they choose to punish/reward. Such costly punishment also takes place in finitely repeated games with no uncertainty, and no kin relation among group members. This form of reciprocity may be termed as *indirect reciprocity* and plays an important role in upholding group norms and social goals.

Strong reciprocity is a more encompassing concept that includes conditional cooperation and indirect reciprocity. Bowles and Gintis (2003) provide a working definition of strong reciprocity:

A strong reciprocator comes to a new social situation with a predisposition to cooperate, is predisposed to respond to cooperative behavior on the part of others by maintaining or increasing his level of cooperation, and responds to free-riding behavior on the part of others by retaliating against the offenders, even at a cost to himself, and even when he cannot reasonably expect future personal gains from such retaliation. The strong reciprocator is thus both a conditionally altruistic cooperator and a conditionally altruistic punisher whose actions benefit other group members at a personal cost.

In what follows, when there is no confusion, we shall mostly use the generic term reciprocity to denote various forms of reciprocity. How can we distinguish among various reciprocity concepts such as instrumental reciprocity, intrinsic reciprocity, and strong reciprocity? The solution is provided by carefully constructed experiments that are able to conduct sharp tests of the competing hypotheses and disentangle the various confounding factors. We shall review a range of such experimental studies below.

There are four chapters in Volume 2. We give a very brief introduction here; a more detailed introduction follows in each chapter.

Chapter 1 considers the empirical evidence on other-regarding preferences using a range of experimental games. These games include the *ultimatum* and *dictator games*, the *trust* and *gift exchange games*, and the *public goods game with and without punishments*. In this chapter, we also consider the external validity of lab experiments and objections to the student subject pool. We show that lab evidence is representative of real-world human behavior, and relative to other subject pools, the student subject pool delivers results in favor of the self–regarding model.

Chapter 2 considers models of *social preferences, type-based reciprocity, intentions-based reciprocity*, and other *hybrid models*.[7] We not only consider the leading theoretical models but also use empirical evidence to evaluate the relative success of these models. We show how these models can be used to explain the empirical evidence in Chapter 1. We give applications to behavioral political economy, and develop appropriate stochastic dominance concepts in the presence of other-regarding preferences. We also consider the implications of other-regarding preferences for a Walrasian competitive equilibrium as well as for the fundamental welfare theorems.

---

[7] The formal development of intentions-based reciprocity requires the use of psychological game theory, so it is postponed to Volume 4 of the book.

Chapter 3 considers two new topics, *human morality* and *social identity*, both of which are not traditionally considered in courses in neoclassical economics, in which agents are *amoral*. We first give the evidence on human morality, such as the aversion to lying, aversion to breaking promises, and wishing to uphold one's integrity. This is followed by an application to the hold-up problem in industrial organization. We then consider the evidence on social identity and explore applications on incentives in organizations.

Chapter 4 is the longest chapter in Volume 2. It considers issues of moral hazard and asymmetric information in the presence of other-regarding preferences, and the literature on complete and incomplete short-term and long-term contracts. Unlike many treatments of contract theory, we also closely consider the evidence on alternative contractual forms as well as the theoretical models and the relevant empirical evidence on *extrinsic* and *intrinsic motivation*.

Finally, the guide to further reading at the end of Volume 2 covers several interesting topics and it is an essential part of this volume. Among other topics, it presents new evidence on human morality and gives a self-contained discussion of *social norms*. The exercises for Volume 2 are situated at the end of the guide for further reading.

Introduction to Behavioral Economics and the Book Volumes

The *neoclassical framework* in economics provides a coherent and internally consistent body of theory that offers rigorous, parsimonious, and falsifiable models of human behavior.[1] Augmented with auxiliary assumptions, it is flexible enough to analyze a wide range of phenomena. In actual practice, the neoclassical framework includes, but is not restricted exclusively to, consistent preferences, subjective expected utility, Bayes' rule to update probabilities, self-regarding preferences, emotionless deliberation, exponential discounting, unlimited cognitive abilities, unlimited attention, unlimited willpower, and frame and context independence of preferences.[2] Neoclassical economics is also typically underpinned by optimization-based solution methods and an equilibrium approach.

In principle, the neoclassical framework is capable of relaxing many of its standard assumptions. For instance, it can allow for reference dependence preferences, social preferences, frame dependent preferences, and non-exponential models of discounting. However, these extensions are rare in actual practice, and when they are made, the neoclassical framework typically does not have fundamental new insights to offer. For instance, adding reference dependent preferences generates few, if any, insights in the absence of a theory about how human behavior differs in the domains of gains and losses relative to a reference point. Similarly, adding other-regarding preferences without attempting to fit such a model to the behavior of humans, particularly to the evidence from experimental games, offers little progress. For these reasons, my use of the term *neoclassical economics* is shorthand for *the typical practice in neoclassical economics*.

The intellectual developments in neoclassical economics are impressive. However, its empirical success in predicting and explaining human behavior is modest. Indeed, an impressive, thorough and detailed body of experimental, neuroeconomic, and field evidence, based on several decades of work, raises serious concerns about the core assumptions and predictions of neoclassical models. This has been matched by impressive theoretical developments, drawing on insights from psychology, biology, anthropology, sociology, and other social sciences, that has come to be

---

[1] I avoid the loaded term *standard economics* to refer to *neoclassical economics* because this might give the latter a certain empirical sanctity.

[2] I have deliberately avoided the word 'rationality' in this description of the neoclassical framework because it would have to be precisely defined. See Dhami and al-Nowaihi (2018) for the various senses in which rationality is used in neoclassical economics.

known as *behavioral economics*. These models have had much greater empirical success relative to neoclassical models.[3]

There is a danger that one may propose definitions of behavioral economics that are either too broad and have ambiguous scope, or are too narrow with limited scope; each of these outcomes would be unfair for a newly emerging field. Any falsifiable theory that replaces/modifies any of the core features of neoclassical economics, by alternatives that have a better empirical foundation in human behavior is a potential member of the class of behavioral economic theories, if it can pass stringent empirical tests.

The aim of this book is to offer an account of formal behavioral economic theory, its applications, and a discussion of the underlying experimental and field evidence.[4] The standard toolkit in neoclassical economics is adequate for the study of behavioral economics. Most behavioral models adopt an optimization framework, are typically underpinned by axiomatic foundations, are parsimonious, rigorous, falsifiable, and internally consistent.[5]

We do not attempt to pit behavioral economics against neoclassical economics in a paradigmatic battle. As in every science, we progress by taking account of evidence that suggests a refinement and improvement of existing models. In this case, the relevant improvement appears to have the steepest gradient in the direction of constructively incorporating insights from other behavioral sciences. The book outlines a new research program that offers a constructive way forward for economics by highlighting developments in behavioral economic theory, which also uses core insights from neoclassical economics. It is likely that in due course, behavioral economics will cease to exist as a separate field within economics, and this will become the normal way in which we do economics.

A distinction is sometimes drawn between experimental economics and behavioral economics.[6] However, the activity of behavioral economists and experimental economists has turned out to be complementary and collaborative, as in the natural sciences. It is often difficult to spot the dividing line between their work. For instance, experimental economists not only test the predictions of economic models, but their results have often been critical in suggesting further developments in behavioral models. Behavioral theorists on the other hand, often suggest experiments that could test their proposed theories.

The introduction to these volumes is a condensed version of the longer introduction in Volume 1 of *The Foundations of Behavioral Economic Analysis*. Section 1 briefly traces some of the historical developments that have led to modern behavioral economics. Section 2 considers important methodological issues that lie at the heart of how economists 'do' and 'should'

---

[3] Increasing the explanatory power of neoclassical economics is very worthwhile but Thaler (2015) adds another reason for studying behavioral economics in his inimitable style: "Behavioral economics is more interesting and more fun than regular economics. It is the un-dismal science."

[4] For a non-technical treatment of behavioral economics, the reader can consult the extremely readable and witty account by Thaler (2015) that offers a much more detailed historical account of developments in behavioral economics from the 1970s onwards from a personal perspective.

[5] I use the word "rigorous" purely for its practical appeal to most neoclassical economists but I agree with the sentiments expressed by Gintis (2009, p. xviii): "The economic theorist's overvaluation of rigor is a symptom of their undervaluation of explanatory power. The truth is its own justification and needs no help from rigor."

[6] Loewenstein (1999) gives a nice discussion of the methods in each of these areas and offers the following definition (p. F25): "BEs [behavioral economists] are methodological eclectics. They define themselves, not on the basis of the research methods that they employ, but rather their application of psychological insights to economics. In recent published research, BEs are as likely to use field research as experimentation... EEs [experimental economists] on the other hand, define themselves on the basis of their endorsement and use of experimentation as a research tool."

practice their craft. Section 3 considers the importance of the experimental method in behavioral economics. Section 4 briefly explains the organization of the book. There are two appendices. Appendix A outlines the random lottery incentive mechanism that lies at the heart of the modern experimental method in economics. Appendix B asks you to think of 50 questions as a problem set, but I deliberately give you very little structure at this stage in order to enable a free-spirited approach to the answers. Rigorous answers to these questions can be found in the book.

1 Some antecedents of behavioral economics

While Adam Smith's justly celebrated book, *The Wealth of Nations*, is widely cited, his other book, *The Theory of Moral Sentiments*, has received less attention. *The Theory of Moral Sentiments* reads like an agenda for modern behavioral economics; it recognizes many behavioral phenomena such as loss aversion, altruism, emotions, willpower, and the planner–doer framework (Ashraf et al., 2005). Classical economists such as Jeremy Bentham wrote about the psychological underpinnings of utility and Francis Edgeworth wrote about social preferences (Camerer and Loewenstein, 2004). Bardsley et al. (2010) trace the beginnings of experimental economics to the classical economists such as David Hume, Stanley Jevons, and Francis Edgeworth; Jevon's marginal utility analysis derived its motivation from experimental observations about the relation between stimuli and sensations.

Two factors contributed to the gradual elimination of psychology from economics. First, around the turn of the twentieth century, there was "a distaste for the psychology of their period, as well as the hedonistic assumptions of Benthamite utility" (Camerer and Loewenstein, 2004). The second was the revealed preference approach popularized by Paul Samuelson that emphasized the observation of *choice behavior* rather than the psychological foundations for choice behavior (Bruni and Sugden, 2007). Glimcher and Fehr (2014, p. xviii) write: "It cannot be emphasized enough how much the revealed-preference view suppressed interest in the psychological nature of preferences, because clever axiomatic systems could be used to infer properties of unobservable preference from choice."

Important, and path-breaking, developments in behavioral economics took place in the 1950s and 1960s that included: violations of the independence axiom of expected utility theory (Allais, 1953); violations of subjective expected utility (Ellsberg, 1961; Markowitz, 1952); demonstration of the importance of bounded rationality (Simon, 1978; Selten, 1998);[7] and early work on quasi hyperbolic discounting (Phelps and Pollak, 1968). However, at that time, this work struggled to get the attention that it deserved.

An important catalyst for the development of behavioral economics was the decline of the behavioralist school in psychology, and the emergence of cognitive psychology. Cognitive psychology emphasized the role of mental processes in the understanding of tasks involving decision making, perception, attention, memory, and problem solving. Some cognitive psychologists naturally turned their attention to testing their models against the neoclassical framework. The two most important cognitive psychologists in this category were Daniel Kahneman and Amos Tversky, whose work in the 1970s helped kick-start modern behavioral economics. Along with Richard Thaler, who was an economist by training, and was struggling to make sense of several

---

[7] Simon (1978) refers to Herbert Simon's Nobel lecture that traces the historical development of bounded rationality through the 1950s and 1960s. Selten (1998) is an English language version of a paper that appeared initially in German in 1962.

anomalies in neoclassical economics from the mid 1970s onwards, they are some of the earliest and most significant modern behavioral economists.

The second topic is the *role of experimental evidence in economics* that I consider in Section 3. The justification for this section is the continued skepticism of many economists about experimental economics, which constitutes an important part of the evidence base for behavioral economics. The following quote attributed to the Nobel Prize winner Gary Becker from a magazine interview (Camerer, 2015, p. 250) is probably not unrepresentative: "One can get excellent suggestions from experiments, but economic theory is not about how people act in experiments, but how they act in markets. And those are very different things. That may be useful to get suggestions, but it is not a test of the theory. The theory is not about how people answer questions. It is a theory about how people actually choose in market situations."

What follows is a somewhat long introduction, but this is a somewhat long book too. In mitigation, the first one third of the introduction largely deals with background material that reflects the somewhat unsettled nature of economics. My hope is that if a second edition of this book is ever written, then there would be enough convergence of views on this material, so that I can safely omit it.

2 On methodology in economics

University degrees in Economics and the natural sciences typically do not require formal courses in methodology. Yet, while all the natural sciences subscribe to the scientific method and students of natural sciences instinctively know that this means, economics has taken a very different, and pernicious, direction that has little basis in the scientific method. Consider, for instance, the following quote from Gintis (2009, p. xvi) that nicely captures the essence of the problem:

Economic theory has been particularly compromised by its neglect of the facts concerning human behavior... I happened to be reading a popular introductory graduate text on quantum mechanics, as well as a leading graduate text in microeconomics. The physics text began with the anomaly of blackbody radiation, ... The text continued, page after page, with new anomalies ... and new, partially successful models explaining the anomalies. In about 1925, this culminated with Heisenberg's wave mechanics and Schrödinger's equation, which fully unified the field. By contrast, the microeconomics text, despite its beauty, did not contain a single fact in the whole thousand-page volume. Rather the authors built economic theory in axiomatic fashion, making assumptions on the basis of their intuitive plausibility, their incorporation of the "stylized facts" of everyday life, or their appeal to the principles of rational thought.... We will see that empirical evidence challenges some of the core assumptions in classical game theory and neoclassical economics.

The actual practice of behavioral economics is influenced, directly or indirectly, by Popperian views on methodology (Popper, 1934, 1963). Popper begins by distinguishing between science and non-science. A scientific hypothesis must be falsifiable in the sense that it must specify the conditions under which the hypothesis can be rejected. Further, one can only refute theories but never prove that they are true. For instance, the observation of a million white swans is consistent with the hypothesis that "all swans are white" but does not prove that the hypothesis is true; for the very next observation could be a non-white swan.

The best recipe for the advancement of science, in the Popperian view, is to subject scientific hypotheses to stringent testing, i.e., expose the hypotheses to tests that are most likely to reject them. In the strict Popperian view, one observation that is contrary to a hypothesis rejects it. For instance, a single observation of a black swan rejects the hypothesis that all swans are white. Science progresses by advancing a new hypothesis that explains everything that a rejected hypothesis explained, but, in addition, it explains some new phenomenon that the rejected hypothesis could not. For an application of the Popperian position to economic contexts, see Blaug (1992), Hausman (1992), and Hands (2001).

One concern with the Popperian approach is that a test of a hypothesis is a joint test of the hypothesis and several auxiliary assumptions. Thus, a rejection may arise because the hypothesis is incorrect, or the auxiliary assumptions might have been rejected, or both; this is known as the *Duhem–Quine thesis* (DQT). For instance, in an experimental test that rejects mixed strategy Nash equilibrium, one might wonder if the rejection was caused by (1) one of several confounding factors, such as an inappropriate subject pool, unclear experimental instructions, and inadequate incentives, or (2) because subjects do not follow a mixed strategy Nash equilibrium. For this reason, a single refutation of a theory is not sufficient unless well replicated to account for all the main confounding factors that might be at play.

While the Popperian position is *prescriptive* (how should we best do science?), a *descriptive* view (how is science actually done?) was offered by Kuhn (1962). Kuhn noted that knowledge in science does not accumulate in a linear manner. He highlighted, instead, the role of periodic revolutions in science, or an abrupt transformation in the existing worldview, a *paradigm shift*. He distinguishes between three phases in the development of any science. In pre-science, there is no central paradigm, but there is an attempt to focus on a set of problems. In normal science, the longest of the three phases, there is the establishment of a central paradigm, great progress is made in answering many of the questions posed during pre-science, and much success is achieved in answering new questions. In a departure from the Popperian prescriptive position, in this phase, rejections of the paradigm are robustly challenged or ignored, and belief in the paradigm is unshakable. However, as anomalies gradually begin to accumulate, and reach a tipping point, a crises takes place in the paradigm. There is a sudden paradigm shift and a new paradigm that subsumes the old paradigm takes its place.

One prescriptive response to the DQT and to Kuhn's descriptive ideas, while retaining a Popperian approach, was proposed by Lakatos (1970) under the name: *The methodology of scientific research programs* (MSRP). Lakatos distinguished between a set of non-expendable statements or assumptions, which is the *hard core of a research program*, and a set of expendable auxiliary assumptions. In a distinctly non-Popperian recommendation, but reminiscent of the normal science phase of Kuhn, the hard core is insulated from refutation; this also addresses the DQT. For instance, Newtonian physics has a hard core that comprises the three laws of dynamics and a law of gravitation. Any refutation of the research program, in this phase, is then ascribed to a failure of the auxiliary assumptions, which are modified to explain the refutation.

One potential defense of this approach is that it allows for a period of time for the development of a new research program that can take account of the emerging refutations. However, a practical downside could be that proponents of a research program might engage in defensive methodology for far too long, and resist the development of a new research program that has a different hard core. To take account of this possibility, Lakatos termed a research program as *theoretically progressive* if refinements that take place by altering auxiliary assumptions but not the hard core, lead to the explanation of existing anomalies and to novel predictions. A research program is *empirically progressive* if the novel predictions are not refuted. Adherence to a hard core is only admissible if research programs are theoretically and empirically progressive.

Eventually anomalies play the most important part in giving rise to new research programs; Lakatos noted that all theories are born into and die in a sea of anomalies.[8] The reader may find below that the actual practice in behavioral and experimental economics appears to be closer to the Lakatosian view than the Popperian view.[9] For instance, in decision theory, the hard core may be thought to comprise completeness, transitivity, and first order stochastic dominance (Bardsley et al., 2010, p. 129). Indeed, neither expected utility theory nor the main behavioral alternatives such as rank dependent utility, theory of disappointment aversion, or prospect theory, are willing to relax the assumption of well-behaved preferences. This makes it difficult for most decision theories to explain framing effects, although prospect theory is potentially able to capture framing effects through changes in the reference point.

With this minimum background, consider "normal" practice in physics; I encourage the reader not to judge natural sciences by a few well-publicized outliers. In a letter to the *London Times*, dated November 28, 1919, Albert Einstein described his *theory of relativity* in comparison to *Newtonian physics*, to a lay audience. Einstein mentioned two predictions of his theory that had been confirmed (both in domains where his theory was most likely to fail, hence, these are "stringent tests"): (1) Revolution of the ellipses of the planetary orbits round the sun, which was confirmed for the orbit of Mercury. (2) The curving of light rays by the action of gravitational fields. He then mentioned one prediction that had not yet been confirmed (displacement of the spectral lines toward the red end of the spectrum in the case of light transmitted to us from stars of considerable magnitude); indeed, at the time Einstein published the theory of relativity, it was not even clear how to test this prediction. Einstein then wrote (p. 4): "The chief attraction of the theory lies in its logical completeness. If a single one of the conclusions drawn from it proves wrong, it must be given up."

I invite the reader to pause for a moment to compare Einstein's approach with the "mainstream" views in economics that I have outlined above. Indeed, as Bardsley et al. (2010, p. 8) note: "But it is surprisingly common for economists to claim that the core theories of their subject are useful despite being disconfirmed by the evidence."

In light of this brief discussion on methodology and an illustration of best practice in the natural sciences, let us return to the "neglect of the facts concerning human behavior in economics" that Herbert Gintis highlights above. Why should such a situation have arisen? In order to understand this state of affairs, consider the following three representative views, written by some of the leaders in neoclassical economics.

Dekel and Lipman (2010, p. 264) write: "Hence the choice of a model will depend on the purpose for which the model is used, the modeler's intuition, and the modeler's subjective judgment of plausibility.... One economist may reject another's intuition, and, ultimately, the marketplace of ideas will make some judgments."

Gilboa et al. (2014, p. F. 516) write: "In particular, we agree that: economic models are often viewed differently than models in the other sciences; economic theory seems to value generality and simplicity at the cost of accuracy; models are expected to convey a message much more than to describe a well-defined reality; these models are often akin to observations, or

---

[8] Closer to home, economists would remember the influential *anomalies feature* that Richard Thaler wrote for the *Journal of Economic Perspectives* from 1987 to 2006. Indeed, in the very first piece, Thaler, keenly aware of methodological issues, quoted from Thomas Kuhn.

[9] For a critique of the Lakatosian approach as applied to economics, see Hands (1991) and De Marchi and Blaug (1991).

to gedankenexperiments; and the economic theorist is typically not required to clearly specify where his model might be applicable and how."

Rubinstein (2006, p. 882) writes: "As in the case of fables, models in economic theory are derived from observations of the real world, but are not meant to be testable. As in the case of fables, models have limited scope. As in the case of a good fable, a good model can have an enormous influence on the real world, not by providing advice or by predicting the future, but rather by influencing culture. Yes, I do think we are simply the tellers of fables, but is that not wonderful?"

None of these representative quotes stresses the centrality of the empirical evidence in rejecting economic models or the need to design stringent tests to refute them; in fact economic models are not even meant to be tested. They also take a relativist position (one economist may reject another's intuition, and, ultimately, the marketplace of ideas will make some judgments) and take the role of models in economics as conveying "messages" or telling "fables".

Modern economics has been heavily influenced by the *instrumental position* taken by Friedman (1953), which is partly reflected in the three quotes above. Friedman argued that we should not judge economic theories by the realism of their assumptions but rather, by the accuracy of their predictions. He writes (p. 14): "Truly important and significant hypotheses will be found to have 'assumptions' that are wildly inaccurate descriptive representations of reality, and, in general, the more significant the theory, the more unrealistic the assumptions.... To be important, therefore, a hypothesis must be descriptively false in its assumptions." And shortly thereafter (p. 15) he writes: "To put this point less paradoxically, the relevant question to ask about the 'assumptions' of a theory is not whether they are descriptively 'realistic,' for they never are, but whether they are sufficiently good approximations for the purpose in hand."

A natural progression of Friedman's position can be found in Gilboa et al. (2014, F. 514): "Why does economic theory engage in relatively heavy technical analysis, when its basic premises are so inaccurate? Given the various violations of fundamental economic assumptions in psychological experiments, what is the point in deriving elaborate and carefully proved deductions from these assumptions? Why do economists believe that they learn something useful from analyzing models that are based on wrong assumptions?" Their answer to these questions is based on an identification of economic models with *case-based reasoning* rather than *rule-based reasoning*. Rule-based reasoning requires the formulation of general rules or theories. In contrast, case-based reasoning requires one to draw inferences based on similar past cases. The purpose of economic models, in this view, is to add to the bucket list of cases and analogies that can be used to draw inferences now, or at some point in the future.

These views give a fair bit of insight into contemporary thinking in economics about how we should go about practicing our craft. I also believe that acceptance of these views is widespread in the economics profession and many economists challenged on these views are surprised and outrightly dismissive. Initial intuition about economic models, whether motivated by existing empirical evidence, or a desire to make novel predictions, must begin from somewhere. Here, the role of initial conjectures as parables, useful stories, or fables to inform one's intuition about better and more complete models is surely important. But this cannot be the justification for continued reliance on a set of models that have faced persistent refutation, or to wish to shield them from refutation by seeking a special status for them.

Indeed, and it has to be said with great regret, many of the contemporary methodological views in economics are retrogressive and a license to engage in defensive methodology to protect the status quo. Friedman's approach has been much misused in economics. Consider the following entirely reasonable description of Friedman's approach to *model building* (as distinct from evaluating theories) in Gintis (2015, p. 223) that this book concurs with: "The goal of model-building [is] to create a tractable analytical structure, analyze the behavior of this structure, and test the fruitfulness of the results by comparing them with empirical data."[10]

The tendency to ignore or to discount experimental evidence in economics, despite its growing importance and prominence, when it contradicts neoclassical models is an indictment of the methodological approach taken in economics. Another important factor is that Friedman's instrumental position has been used as a license by some to make ad hoc auxiliary assumptions, and others to genuinely believe that their assumptions are literally true in an "as if" sense. Any empirical rejection of the "as if" assumptions is often rejected on the grounds that the evidence is flawed, untrustworthy, based on dubious experimental methods, or lacks external validity. This is a form of defensive methodology that is inimical to the progress of economics, and I urge the reader to resist it.

Behavioral economics offers an easier resolution of the "as if" approach. There is now compelling evidence, which shows that some of the central tenets of neoclassical economics are neither true in an "as if" sense, nor are their predictions always satisfactory when subject to stringent tests. So even on the grounds that Friedman favoured, *predictions of the relevant theory*, some of the central elements in neoclassical economics, such as self-regarding preferences, expected utility theory, exponential discounting, Bayes' Law, Nash equilibrium and its refinements, must either be significantly modified or abandoned. This book is replete with evidence that supports such a view. In particular, it is untenable to continue teaching the entire corpus of the existing status quo in economics on any scientific or logical grounds.

Schotter (2015) offers the following critique of Friedman's position. Suppose that assumptions x, y, and z lead to some theory T. Suppose also that one or more assumptions are violated by the empirical evidence, yet T makes a successful prediction. Then there are three possibilities. (1) The violated assumptions are superfluous for the theory, at least in the context where the theory was tested. (2) The violated assumptions counteract each other perfectly, so they do not affect the prediction. (3) The successful prediction is a fluke. Conversely, if the assumptions are correct and the model is complete then we expect T to make successful predictions anyway. Thus, it is difficult to justify a theory based on patently false assumptions. Schotter (2015, p. 63) observes, correctly: "after all, the assumptions are the theory."

My colleague, Ali al-Nowaihi, likes to give the following example that applies to birds who cannot swim (e.g., gannets can swim, so they are excluded). Birds fly, so one may theorize that they behave "as if" they understand the laws of aerodynamics. This is an admissible hypothesis, but then one must test the "as if" assumption. Given that air is basically a fluid, so birds might also be assumed to know the laws of hydrodynamics. If the "as if" presumption were true in this case, then birds released under water should try to swim, but they actually try to fly, and drown. Thus, the original "as if" supposition is false. If the "as if" assumptions are not tested properly, then we can never have any degree of confidence in the models based on these assumptions.

A common view in economics (shared unfortunately by some behavioral and experimental economists, I must add) appears to be that there is something rather difficult and unique about testing economic theories, relative to the natural sciences. So, at least implicitly, the argument goes, one needs to accord a "special status" to economic theories. Consider the following representative quote from Richard Lipsey's wonderful introduction to economics (Lipsey, 1979, p. 8)

---

[10] Readers interested in pursuing this approach further can consult Godfrey-Smith (2006, 2009) and Wimsatt (2007).

cited in Bardsley et al. (2010, pp. 6–7) that, I suspect, many economists would agree with: "Experimental sciences, such as chemistry and some branches of psychology, have an advantage because it is possible to produce relevant evidence through controlled laboratory experiments. Other sciences, such as astronomy and economics, cannot do this." A similar view is expressed in another celebrated text in economics (Samuelson and Nordhaus, 1985, p. 8): "Economists (unfortunately)... cannot perform the controlled experiments of chemists or biologists because they cannot easily control other important factors. Like astronomers or meteorologists, they generally must be content largely to observe." This mainstream view is contestable, and must be contested. There appears to be a misunderstanding about the relative difficulty of testing theories in the natural sciences and in economics.

The view that testing of theories is somehow easy or easier in the natural sciences, as compared to economics, must surely be deeply offensive and insulting to experimenters in the natural sciences. The Higgs boson or Higgs particle was proposed by British physicist Peter Higgs in the early 1960s, and it took 50 years of incredibly hard efforts to confirm the particle in 2013. Particle physicists did not seek a *special status* for this theory that could insulate it from rejection. The enormously high energies required to test for the Higgs particle required the construction of a very expensive and complex experimental facility, CERN's Large Hadron Collider, that eventually confirmed the theory. Note also that Peter Higgs was made to wait 50 odd years and given the Nobel Prize in physics only after his theory was confirmed. He was not given the Nobel on any of the following criteria: elegant and beautiful theory, useful model that helped the intuition of particle physicists, or a fable or useful story that aids in the understanding of how the universe began.

Astronomers who dealt with the question of the distance of earth from distant objects, or the chemical composition of stars that are millions of light years away, did not also seek a special status for their subject. They got on with the difficult job of seeking the relevant measurements, often using indirect evidence and clever implications of theory. They were eventually successful after several decades of work. Are economists seriously arguing that their measurement problems are more difficult than the problems in the natural sciences? Cosmic microwave background radiation was first proposed in 1948, but experimentally confirmed due to an accidental discovery in 1964. DNA was first isolated in 1869, but it took the most part of a century to find the double-helix structure of DNA, and confirm it by experimental evidence in 1953. The germ theory of disease was proposed in the mid sixteenth century, yet confirmation of the theory occurred in the seventeenth century. The pool of such examples is very large. The process of discovery, measurement, and of testing the theory, can be a long and arduous one; seeking a special status for the subject is defeatist and put bluntly, lazy.

Economists opposed to lab/field data are likely to argue that the behavior of humans is too noisy, heterogeneous, and fickle, which is not a problem in the natural sciences (e.g., atoms are, after all, not subject to mood swings). This overstates the degree of difficulty in testing economic theories, relative to those in the natural sciences on at least two grounds.

1. Experimental economics has discovered systematic human behavior in many of the most important domains in economics. A small sample includes reference dependence, loss aversion, non-linear probability weighting, conditional cooperation, intention-based reciprocity, present-biased preferences, and the importance of emotions such as regret, guilt, and disappointment. These behaviors are also underpinned by neuroeconomic evidence. Replication of standard experimental results is routine, and if similar subject pools and protocols are used, experiments produce replicable data. Examples are results from double

auction experiments, and a range of games that demonstrate human prosociality, such as the ultimatum game, the gift exchange game, the trust game, and the public goods game; these examples can be multiplied manyfold, as the results in this book attest.

2. If indeed human behavior is inherently too noisy and heterogeneous, then economic theory needs to focus more efforts in this direction. When Brownian motion was discovered in 1827 by Robert Brown, in the behavior of pollen grains, physicists did not throw up their arms in despair. Important work in the late part of the nineteenth century, and by Einstein in the early twentieth century, paved the way for describing not only the mathematics of Brownian motion, but also predicting the probability distribution of particles in Brownian motion. Perhaps, in an analogous manner, economic theories need to predict the probability distribution of economic behavior, which can then be tested in experiments.

Experimental economics in the lab, and in the field, has made enormous progress in developing new econometric techniques for small samples, and in novel experimental methods. It has also deeply enhanced our understanding of human behavior and allowed for stringent testing of economic theory. This progress is inconsistent with the view that we should grant a special status to economic theories that exempts them from careful and stringent testing. The differences in experiments in economics and the natural sciences are much smaller relative to the differences in attitudes and institutions in the two fields of study. Progress in economics will be substantially enhanced if we learn from best practice elsewhere, and give up our implicit demand for special status.

3 The experimental method in economics

Work on experiments in behavioral economics gained momentum following the seminal work of Daniel Kahneman and Amos Tversky in the 1970s. However, a number of important experiments in economics were also conducted in the late 1940s, the 1950s, and the 1960s. These include Edward H. Chamberlin's testing of general competitive equilibrium (Chamberlin, 1948); Maurice Allais's work on demonstrating violations of the independence axiom in expected utility theory (Allais, 1953); Vernon Smith's work on induced value elicitation and double auction experiments in competitive settings (Smith, 1962); and Sidney Siegel's experiments on bargaining (Siegel and Fouraker, 1960). Other prominent figures who were either involved in experimental economics, or expressed an interest in it during the 1950s and 1960s included Ward Edwards, Reinhard Selten, Martin Schubik, Herbert Simon, Charles Plott, Donald Davidson, and Pat Suppes; for a brief historical sketch, see Guala (2008) and Bardsley et al. (2010).

Experimental economics is now mainstream by most yardsticks, particularly in terms of its presence in peer-reviewed journals in economics. In his early surveys on experimental economics, Roth (1987, 1988) hoped that experimental economics would perform three kinds of functions: Speaking to theorists (testing economic theory), searching for facts (generating novel empirical regularities that could be modeled by subsequent theory), and whispering in the ears of princes (offering reliable policy advice). Roth (2015) takes stock of experimental economics on these criteria and finds that it is thriving. One of his case studies, on bargaining behavior, is outlined in detail in Volume 4 of the book.

At one level, there has been a complete denial of the usefulness of experiments in economics. Friedman (1953, p. 10) views the domain of empirical testing in economics to be naturally occurring field data: "Unfortunately, we can seldom test particular predictions in the social sciences by experiments explicitly designed to eliminate what are judged to be the most important disturbing influences. Generally, we must rely on evidence cast up by the 'experiments' that happen to occur." A modern critique of the experimental method in economics is offered by Levitt and List (2007). They list several objections to experimental results that I address in subsequent sections.

(1) Participants in experiments are subjected to unprecedented experimental scrutiny. Since subjects may perceive that they are being watched over by the experimenter, they may give responses that the experimenter really desires (*experimenter demand effects*; see Zizzo, 2010) or they may not reveal their true underlying preferences. For instance, they worry that participants may engage in more prosocial behavior than they really intend to.

Whilst I reserve my detailed responses to later sections, I find it somewhat curious that if subjects are accused of being influenced by experimenter demand effects, say out of reciprocity, guilt, or shame, then they appear to exhibit social preferences (or emotions reflected in beliefs may directly enter their utility functions, as in psychological game theory), which is precisely what is being disputed by the critics.

(2) In actual practice, human decisions are context-dependent and influenced by cues, social norms, and past experiences. It is not clear that experiments can capture these factors. For instance, participants in experiments may import an inappropriate "outside context" into their responses in experiments.

(3) Actual human behavior is strongly affected by stake sizes in experiments. Experiments are typically conducted with small stakes, so they might not capture the richness of human behavior that arises from varying stakes.

(4) There could be self-selection biases caused by student volunteers who might be particularly prosocial, younger, more educated, and have a higher need for approval, as compared to the average human population. In contrast, people who self-select themselves into real market situations, might be particularly suitable to do well in real markets.

(5) Choice sets in experiments might be particularly restrictive relative to the real world. For instance, there could be more prosocial options in experiments relative to the real world.

(6) The results of lab experiments may generalize poorly to real-world behavior for all of the reasons mentioned in (1) through (5), above. This issue of *external validity* of lab experiments is the main concern raised by the authors who write (p. 170): "Perhaps the most fundamental question in experimental economics is whether findings from the lab are likely to provide reliable inferences outside of the laboratory."

This discussion briefly encapsulates the modern case against experimental economics. Let us now briefly examine these claims.

3.1 Experiments and internal validity

Experiments allow for unprecedented control over the economic environment, hence, they have high *internal validity*, which is critical for stringent tests of economic theories. Internal validity is reduced when there are, for instance, selection issues, confounds in treatments, and unclear experimental instructions, all of which are carefully addressed in modern experimental work. Thus, in well-conducted experiments, the complicated identification strategies of field studies can be replaced by clever and much simpler experimental design.

For instance, suppose that a researcher is interested in testing if higher wages elicit higher effort in a firm; this is known as a *gift exchange game*. A field experiment is likely to be influenced by strategic behavior and reputational concerns of the workers and firms; field experiments in general, are likely to have lower internal validity. However, in a lab experiment, these factors are easily controlled, allowing one to cleanly separate the relation between a fair-wage and effort. The high degree of experimental control in lab experiments allows for replication of lab results. For the converse reason, the results of field experiments are more difficult, and sometimes impossible to replicate when one is given access to a unique field environment.

Experiments can also test the predictions of theory in a parameter space that might be difficult to observe in the field. This is similar to extreme stress tests of aircraft frames under conditions that are not normally encountered in the actual operation of the aircraft, or the exposure of bridge designs to extreme environmental conditions. In a nutshell, all this allows for more stringent tests of economic theory. Experiments are sometimes criticized on the grounds that the sample sizes are small. Falk and Heckman (2009) term this issue as a "red herring" on the grounds that there have been important developments in small sample econometrics, and many experiments do use large subject pools.

Camerer (2015) argues that there is no evidence of experimenter demand effects, despite the suspicion that there might be such effects; see also his discussion of the alternative interpretations of experimenter demand effects in Hoffman et al. (1998). There are several reasons why experimenter demand effects may be weak or non-existent. Such demand effects require two conditions. First, subjects must know the experimenter's preferred hypothesis. Second, they should be willing to sacrifice their own experimental earnings in order to favor the experimenter's preferred hypothesis.

On a-priori grounds, arguably, it is often quite hard for subjects to know the experimenter's preferred hypothesis. This arises particularly when (i) experimental instructions are carefully worded to prevent any such inference, and (ii) the experimenter might not be sure which of the competing hypotheses actually hold. However, if subjects can somehow guess the preferred hypothesis, then stakes can be raised to levels where they are too difficult to sacrifice for the sake of pleasing the experimenter. However, in most cases, the results with high stakes are not dramatically different from those with modest stakes (Camerer and Hogarth, 1999).[11] In three preference reversal experiments, Lambdin and Shaffer (2009) find that the percentage of subjects who were successfully able to guess the preferred hypothesis of the experimenter was 7%, 32%, and 3%.

The degree of anonymity in lab experiments can be varied, so it is an ideal environment to test for the effects of variation in the degree of anonymity (Bolton et al., 1998). One's actions are often observed by others in real-world situations, and in many field situations, where controlling for such scrutiny, and varying its level, is arguably even more difficult. The criticism of lab experiments on grounds of scrutiny (by the experimenter and other participants), also applies to field experiments, insofar as field subjects realize that they are in an experiment. Such experimenter demand effects may arguably, in many cases, be even stronger in field experiments, which are typically run in collaboration with governmental and semi-governmental bodies, and NGOs.

It is indeed the case that when subjects are observed in dictator game experiments in the lab, they give higher amounts (Dana et al., 2007; Haley and Fessler, 2005). In many real-world giving situations, actions are also observed by others; for instance, church collections that take the form

---

[11] Andersen et al. (2011) consider extremely high stakes ultimatum game experiments; the stakes vary from the equivalent of 1.6 hours of work to 1600 hours of work. The median offer by the proposer is to give 20% of the share to the respondent, but the rejection rate falls with the increase in the stake. In real life, we rarely make decisions involving 1600 hours of work, yet social preferences were not eliminated in the experiment.

of passing along a collection plate/basket, or having to declare one's charitable contributions for tax purposes. However, the effect of being observed disappears if one introduces a minimal element of strategic interaction as, say, in an ultimatum game (Barmettler et al., 2012). A more important determinant of giving in dictator games is whether income is earned or not. Giving in dictator game experiments falls to about 4.3% of an endowment of $10, when income is earned, relative to about 15% of the endowment in the case of unearned income (Cherry et al., 2002); the figure of 4.3% is closer to the corresponding field benchmark of charitable giving in the US, which stands at about 1% of income (Camerer, 2015).

A commonly heard critique of behavioral models of social preferences is that if experimentally observed social preferences are so important, then, putting it rather starkly, why do we not observe people giving envelopes stuffed with money to others (Bardsley et al., 2010, p. 53)? When dictators in experiments give out of earned income, then the extent of giving is not too far off from the rate of charitable giving (4.3% versus 1% for the case of US; see above). In the real world, subjects give money for charitable and other good causes out of after-tax income, which is not the case in the lab. So imagine that in dictator games in the lab with earned income, the dictator was told: "Here is your endowment of $10, which you have earned. We are taking 30% off as taxes, which we will partly use for redistributive purposes to the recipient in the experiment. How much of the rest will you offer to the recipient?" It would be surprising if the 4.3% giving in lab dictator games does not get closer to the 1% figure for charitable giving in the field. Similar observations apply to proposer offers and responder rejections in lab experiments that do not include a tax redistributive component. If this is the case, then giving in experiments may also be tapping into the innate human desire to redistribute to others, that is, at least partly, codified institutionally in the social welfare state.

3.2 Subject pools used in lab experiments

It is not unusual in many quarters to dismiss experiments conducted on students, the typical lab subject pool, as having limited or no relevance to testing economic theories. There are several objections to this claim that we now outline.

Economic theory does not specify the subject pool on which its predictions are to be tested. Gilboa et al. (2014, p. F516) write "the economic theorist is typically not required to clearly specify where his model might be applicable and how." Clearly, one cannot have it both ways by not specifying a subject pool and then objecting to a particular subject pool. This view has been popularized in Vernon Smith's *blame the theory argument*. Writing in the context of incentives in experiments, Smith (2001) writes in his abstract: "The rhetoric of hypothesis testing implies that game theory is not testable if a negative result is blamed on any auxiliary hypothesis such as 'rewards are inadequate.' This is because either the theory is not falsifiable (since a larger payoff can be imagined, one can always conclude that payoffs were inadequate) or it has no predictive content (the appropriate payoff cannot be prespecified)."

One concern with the student subject population is that students might not have the necessary and relevant experience to conform to the predictions of the theory. However, one can allow lab subjects to gain experience in the lab by repeatedly making decisions; indeed, many lab experiments examine such learning effects and the effects of experience. We postpone a fuller discussion of these issues to Section 3.4, where we consider the external validity of lab experiments.

Students possess higher than average education and intelligence, which should be rather favorable to tests of neoclassical economic theory that requires economic agents to possess high levels of cognitive ability. It often comes as a surprise to the critics, but student subjects are much less prosocial relative to non-student subject pools (Falk et al., 2013; Carpenter and Seki, 2011; Anderson et al., 2013).[12] In a review of 13 studies that satisfy stringent tests of comparability, Fréchette (2015) finds that either there was very little difference between the behavior of students and professionals, or students were actually closer to the predictions of neoclassical theory. CEOs are often more trusting as compared to the student population (Fehr and List, 2004). More prosocial students do not self-select themselves as subjects in experiment (Cleave et al., 2012). Students who self-select themselves into experiments are motivated by monetary rewards (Abeler and Nosenzo, 2015), or interest in experimental lab tasks (Slonim et al., 2013). This evidence stands in contrast to the characterization of students in Levitt and List (2007) (based on two studies conducted in the 1960s) as scientific do-gooders who cooperate with experimenters to seek social approval.

3.3 Stake sizes in experiments

Economic theory does not specify the size of the stakes for which its predictions hold. Experimental economics is typically criticized for its low stakes. The evidence on stake size effects is mixed. However, many experimental results continue to hold, at least qualitatively, even with higher stakes (Slonim and Roth, 1998; Cameron, 1999). The most prominent effect of stakes arises when one moves from hypothetical payoffs to some strictly positive incentives. However, there is much less difference between moderate and high stakes; in particular, the main effect is a reduction in the variance of responses (Camerer and Hogarth, 1999).

There are two issues with high stakes, which are understated in many critiques of experimental economics. First, the vast majority of decisions that we make in real life are low stake decisions. How many times do we buy a car, a house, or a consumer durable such as a TV/laptop? Second, the main evidence for stake effects comes from experiments themselves. Third, as Thaler (2015) notes, the insistence on high stakes arises presumably because we are supposed to pay greater attention to economic decisions involving high stakes. But our success and expertise in making economic decisions is as much a matter of practice and learning. Since high stakes decisions are rare, we get limited opportunities to learn and make optimal decisions; the converse is true of low stakes decisions. Hence, there is no supposition that high stakes decisions should be closer to the predicted outcomes in neoclassical economics. So, he argues, correctly, that economists need to make up their minds whether they wish to insist on high stakes or low stakes as the appropriate test of their theories. Either way, experiments still offer the most natural environment to test the effect of stakes, which is an argument for more, not fewer, experiments.

3.4 The issue of the external validity of lab findings

Camerer (2015) distinguishes between the *policy view* and the *scientific view*. In the policy view, generalizability of lab findings to the field, or *external validity*, is essential. In the scientific view, all properly gathered evidence, including lab and field evidence, serves to enhance our understanding of human behavior. In this view, there is no hierarchical relation between lab and field evidence, and it is a mistake to pose the issue as if one had to make a choice between the two kinds of evidence. Camerer (2015, p. 251) explains cogently: "In this view, since the goal is to understand general principles, whether the 'lab generalizes to the field' (sometimes

---

[12] However, student subjects might be more prosocial when it comes to volunteering time (Slonim et al., 2013).

called 'external validity' of an experiment) is distracting, difficult to know (since there is no single 'external' target setting), and is no more useful than asking whether 'the field generalizes to the lab.'"

To understand Camerer's argument more fully, consider the following simple formalization in Falk and Heckman (2009). Suppose that we are interested in some variable Y that can be explained fully by the variables $X_1, X_2, \ldots, X_n$ and the "true" functional relation between them is given by $Y = g(X_1, X_2, \ldots, X_n)$, which is sometimes known as an *all causes model*. A researcher may be interested in examining the causal effect of X_1 on Y, holding fixed all other variables $\widehat{X} = (X_2, X_3, \ldots, X_n)$. For instance, in gift exchange experiments, Y is the level of effort of a worker and X_1 is the level of wage paid by the firm. The all causes model will typically include many factors in the vector $\widehat{X}$, such as the number of firms and workers, choice sets, payoff functions, incentives, demographic characteristics, regulatory environment, and moral and social characteristics of the parties involved.

When the relevant hypothesis is tested in the lab, the researcher estimates a model of the form $Y = f(X_1, X^L)$, rather than the all causes model $Y = f(X_1, \widehat{X})$, where $X^L \neq \widehat{X}$; X^L includes variables such as incentives given in the experiment, the endowments of subjects, the subject pool, context, and the structure of payoffs. One may also conduct field experiments in which one estimates a model of the form $Y = f(X_1, X^{F_1})$, where $X^{F_1} \neq \widehat{X}$, and typically $X^{F_1} \neq X^L$. Field experiments are conducted with a particular subject pool, such as sports card traders in List (2006).

The typical claim by critics of the experimental method is that $f(X_1, X^L)$ does not satisfy external validity, but $f(X_1, X^{F_1})$ does satisfy it. Now suppose that we are interested in examining the gift exchange relation in yet another population of subjects in the field, say, part time employees at General Motors. This gives rise to yet another estimated relation $Y = f(X_1, X^{F_2})$, where X^{F_2} reflects the set of variables and their characteristics in this field experiment. Is there any particular reason why the results based on the model $Y = f(X_1, X^{F_1})$ are more relevant, as compared to $Y = f(X_1, X^L)$, for predicting the causal effects of X_1 in the relation $Y = f(X_1, X^{F_2})$? Camerer (2015, p. 256) offers his assessment (expressed in our notation): "If the litmus test of 'external validity' is accurate extrapolation to X^{F_2}, is the lab X^L necessarily less externally valid than the field setting X^{F_1}? How should this even be judged?" Falk and Heckman (2009, p. 536) go slightly further: "The general quest for running experiments in the field to obtain more realistic data is therefore misguided. In fact, the key issue is what is the best way to isolate the effect of X_1 while holding constant $\widehat{X}$."

Since the criterion for external validity is unclear, it is best to treat lab and field evidence as complementary. Lab evidence allows for much tighter control of the variables in $\widehat{X}$. Field experiments allow for a larger variation in some aspects of $\widehat{X}$ (e.g., different subject pools with different demographic and social characteristics) while lab experiments allow for larger variation in other aspects of $\widehat{X}$ (e.g., exploration of the parameter space for values that can be hard or rare to find in the field). Lab experiments allow for greater replication because they are less costly and the economic environment in the lab can be more tightly controlled, while any specific field environment could be fairly unique.

We review the evidence for the generalizability of lab evidence to the field in many parts of this book. We end this section with the following bold claim from Camerer (2015, p. 277) made from studies where the lab and field evidence can be well matched: "There is no replicated evidence that experimental economics lab data fail to generalize to central empirical features of field data (when the lab features are deliberately closely matched to field features)." Readers interested in these issues can further consult Camerer (2015, pp. 281–5) for a list of studies that show a good association of lab behavior with field behavior in studies where it is more difficult to match the lab and the field evidence due to differences in the design or subject population.

Not everyone within the experimental economics community is willing to dismiss the importance of external validity. For instance, Kessler and Vesterlund (2015) believe that aiming for external validity is important, that qualitative experimental results have high degree of external validity, and that the concerns about external validity pertain only to quantitative experimental results. However, using a relatively large number of studies, Herbst and Mas (2015) show that peer effects on worker output in lab experiments and field studies from naturally occurring environments are quantitatively very similar. Hence, experiments appear to have external validity, even for quantitative estimates.

In light of the discussion above, the reader may perhaps appreciate better the view taken in this book that all sources of evidence, lab experiments, field experiments, and field data are equally valid and complementary in nature.

3.5 *The role of incentives in economics*

The norm in experimental economics is that all decisions made by subjects, or any elicitations of their underlying preferences in experiments, should be incentive compatible. It would currently be near impossible to get an experimental paper published in an economics journal if it did not respect incentive compatibility, preferably by using monetary rewards. In contrast, psychology does not require similar adherence to incentives. Camerer and Hogarth (1999) perform a meta-study of 74 studies, over the period 1990–8, in the leading economics journals: *American Economic Review*, *Econometrica*, *Journal of Political Economy*, and *Quarterly Journal of Economics*. Not a single experimental study in this sample was published without the use of incentives. In a meta-study over the period 1988–97, Hertwig and Ortmann (2001) found that only 26% of the articles published in a leading journal in psychology, the *Journal of Behavioral Decision Making*, used monetary task related incentives.

Economists have traditionally viewed effort as aversive and requiring scarce cognitive resources. Hence, they believe that people will exert effort only if the marginal disutility of effort is exceeded by the marginal utility of monetary incentives (*extrinsic motivation*). By contrast, psychologists have stressed the *intrinsic motivation* of subjects in experiments that does not require task related monetary incentives. Psychologists do pay subjects a show-up fee and/or course credit because it may be unethical to pay less than a minimum wage for a student's time and also because the fixed fee may elicit a reciprocal response by priming intrinsic motivation. Another difference between experiments in economics and psychology is that in the former, experimental practice is much more standardized and regulated (Hertwig and Ortmann, 2001). For instance, deception is taboo in economics experiments, but its practice is variable in psychology experiments.

Smith (1976) made an early recommendation for the use of incentives, based on his experience in double auction experiments. Employing monetary incentives in experiments is also a common recommendation by some of the pioneers in the field (Davis and Holt, 1993; Roth, 1995; Smith, 1991; Smith and Walker, 1993). The effectiveness of incentives, particularly in settings outside double auction experiments, is an empirical question. Several meta studies of the effect of incentives are now available, which show that the effect of monetary incentives on effort and performance in experiments is quite subtle. Neither of the following two extreme positions is supported by the evidence: Incentives make no difference and incentives remove all behavioral anomalies.

However, there is a caveat to these meta studies. Since the underlying preferences are unobserved, in experiments, task performance and incentive compatibility are measured by compliance with the predictions of the underlying theory. However, the underlying theory might itself be refuted by the evidence. One might then fall back on measuring the effect of incentives on the effort undertaken by the subjects (an input), rather than the performance in the task (the output); for a brief survey of these studies, see Bardsley et al. (2010, Chapter 6). However, in many tasks, effort might not improve performance. For instance, consider subjects in experiments engaged in non-trivial strategic interaction. In most games, it would be hard for the players to hit upon the Nash equilibrium purely by deduction, even if incentives were high.

The results reported in the careful meta-study by Camerer and Hogarth (1999) are particularly instructive. In many economic environments, such as choosing among risky gambles, market trading, and bargaining, the weight of the evidence (and the modal result) shows that increasing incentives does not change the average behavior. However, incentives often reduce the variance of outcomes. Incentives may sometimes harm the performance of subjects in experiments, for instance, subjects may choke under pressure (Ariely et al., 2009); their intrinsic motivation may be crowded out, and they may engage in too much payoff-reducing experimentation to avoid negative incentives such as punishments (Hogarth et al., 1991);[13] they may place too great a reliance on personal judgment, when relying on public information would have improved payoffs (Arkes et al., 1986); they may experience motivational crowding-out, e.g., in the presence of incentives, individuals do not feel responsible for their own behavior (Gneezy and Rustichini, 2000b); individuals might be insulted by the low level of incentives (Gneezy and Rustichini, 2000a). However, for another set of problems, mostly in judgment tasks, financial incentives affect average performance. Typically, the nature of these tasks is such that increased effort improves performance. Examples include memory retrieval tasks, tasks where recalling the play in previous rounds improves predictions, or mundane tasks such as piece-rate clerical work where one might be easily bored, e.g., counting the number of occurrences of a particular alphabet on a page of English text.

The meta-study by Bonner et al. (2000) supports the results of the Camerer–Hogarth study. They find that incentives have little effect in problem solving tasks, highest positive effects in tasks where effort improves performance (e.g., clerical tasks, pain endurance, or detecting typos on a page), and weak positive effects in judgment tasks. Hertwig and Ortmann (2001) find moderately positive effect of incentives. However, their sample size is small. Only 48 out of 186 studies (26%) that they considered used financial incentives. Of these, only ten explored the effect of monetary payments. One of their suggestions is to use different treatments that do use and do not use monetary incentives to build a better picture of the effect of incentives.

Clearly, a reduction in the variance of responses in the presence of incentives, in some experiments, is desirable on the grounds that it improves the statistical power of tests. However, economics advocates a cost–benefit approach, and research funding for experiments is a scarce resource. Hence, one has to trade off the reduced variance against performing more experiments with bigger subject pools in the absence of monetary incentives. Greater variance of responses produces more outliers, but as Camerer and Hogarth (1999, p. 31) point out, there are alternative solutions: "Of course, other methods might work the same magic more cheaply. Trimmed means and robust statistical methods also reduce the influence of outliers."

---

[13] For a formal model that shows the trade-off between intrinsic and extrinsic motivation, see Bénabou and Tirole (2003).

So what explains the absolute adherence of experimental economists to incentives as a matter of norm? Bardsley et al. (2010, pp. 249–50) conjecture a cynical explanation: "A reason often given to psychologist's opposition to them is that incentives present an obstacle to less-experienced researchers who find it harder to secure research funding. It may be that economists are less concerned by the presence of such obstacles, or even that some actively promote the use of incentives as a barrier to entry." Many psychologists remain unconvinced of the arguments that experimenters in economics propose in favor of using incentives. For instance, Read (2005, p. 265) concludes his paper as follows: "... there is no basis for requiring the use of real incentives to do experimental economics."

The decision to employ incentives is a part of the experimental design. But as a practical matter, experimenters interested in publishing their work in economics journals have little choice in this matter. A second issue in the design of experiments is the level of incentives and the context. Gneezy and Rustichini (2000b) use four different levels of incentives, zero, low, medium, and high, to check for the level effect and conduct two different experiments to check for context effects. In one experiment, the IQ experiment, they find that incentives improve performance when one compares the levels low and high; but there was no difference between medium and high incentives. In the second experiment, the donations experiment, donations were highest when no incentives were given; in this case, intrinsic motivation is superior to extrinsic motivation. Using the same dataset, Rydval and Ortmann (2004) find that ability levels of individuals explained greater variation in performance relative to incentives. The assessment offered by Bardsley et al. (2010, p. 253) on the level of incentives is this: "The message seems to be that in terms of the impact on cognitive effort allocation the presence of task related incentives matters more than their level."

How can an experimental economist who has decided to run experiments using incentives ensure that the responses by the subjects are incentive compatible? Typically, incentive compatibility in experiments has been defined with respect to expected utility theory; however, the behavior of the majority of people is not consistent with expected utility theory. Hence, judging incentive compatibility is a vexed task. For instance, the leading method of ensuring incentive compatible choices, the *random lottery incentive scheme* (RLI), that we outline in Appendix A, depends crucially on the *independence axiom* of expected utility theory. However, if the decision maker does not follow expected utility but follows, say, rank dependent utility or prospect theory, then the independence axiom does not hold. Thus, choices are not guaranteed to be incentive compatible.

The evidence against expected utility is now overwhelming, as we do indeed explore in this book, and the independence axiom has been rejected in many empirical tests (e.g., *Allais paradox*). Bardsley et al. (2010) argue, however, that despite the rejection of the independence axiom, empirical evidence shows that the random lottery mechanism does not bias results. They write (p. 270): "it may simply be a happy coincidence that the RLI works, by engaging a particular mental heuristic that promotes unbiased task responses." Some readers might find this argument to be weak, and will wish to seek further clarification of the underlying mechanism that makes RLI an empirically attractive option.

Another popular incentive compatible mechanism in experiments that relies on an expected utility formulation is the *Becker–DeGroot–Marshak mechanism* (BDM) (Becker et al., 1964). This is typically employed in eliciting the willingness to pay and the willingness to accept for an object. Subjects in their roles as sellers are asked to state their valuation, v, for an object. A random price, p, is then drawn. If $p \leq v$, then a seller is not allowed to sell but if $p > v$, then the seller must sell. Subjects who follow expected utility should report their true valuations. To see this, suppose that the seller's valuation for an object is believed to be distributed randomly over the interval $[\underline{v},\overline{v}]$, the true valuation is v, and the price is drawn randomly from the interval $[\underline{v},\overline{v}]$, using the distribution F. Suppose that the seller chooses to declare a low valuation, $v_L < v$. In this case, the seller chooses to forgo a profitable opportunity to sell if the price turns out to be in the interval $(v_L, v]$ and the expected forgone profits are $\int_{v_L}^{v} (v-p) dF(p) > 0$. Thus, the seller never declares a low valuation. Now suppose that the seller declares a high valuation, $v_H > v$. In this case, the seller risks the potential expected loss $\int_{v}^{v_H} (v-p) dF(p) < 0$, so he never overstates his valuation. In short, the BDM is incentive compatible under expected utility. A direct implementation of the BDM has been found not to be incentive compatible (Bohm et al., 1997). However, suppose decision makers are presented with ascending or descending prices and must choose to trade or not at these prices. In the end, one of the trades is picked at random and paid off. There is some evidence that this version of the BDM may be incentive compatible (Braga and Starmer, 2005).

Similar calculations as employed in the BDM show that the *second price auction* (bidders bid simultaneously, and the winner pays the second highest bid) is also incentive compatible under expected utility. Bardsley et al. (2010, Chapter 6) review evidence which shows that the responses in BDM and the second price auction are sensitive to experience and, in later rounds, valuations are likely to converge to the true values. But the evidence on the incentive compatibility of variants of the *Vickery auctions* (which is a more general form of second price auctions) is mixed. They write (p. 274): "the efficacy of particular elicitation mechanisms can vary across different types of tasks. Indeed, whether an elicitation mechanism works may depend on the kind of research question that motivates its use."

To summarize, the discussion on incentive compatible elicitation mechanisms in experiments raises uncomfortable questions for the practice of experimental economics. First, predicted incentive compatibility relies on theories such as expected utility theory that have inadequate empirical support. Second, there are no universally agreed on mechanisms that will guarantee incentive compatibility in experiments and it very much comes down to a matter of judgment of the experimenter. Third, despite the firm insistence of experimental economists to use task related incentives, the theoretical response to these problems (e.g., the development of incentive compatibility under behavioral decision theories) appears to be inadequate.

3.6 Is survey data of any use?

Section 3.5 shows that there is often merit in the use of incentives, e.g., usefulness in double auction experiments, judgment tasks, effort related responses as in clerical tasks, and reduction in variation of responses. However, it is fair to say that the empirical case for the use of incentives in experiments is not as strong as is typically made out within the experimental economics community. Hence, one needs to consider other sources of data too in order to build a composite picture of human behavior. Most economists mistrust *survey data* and data based on *hypothetical questions* on the grounds that subjects are not incentivized to reveal their true preferences. This is due to the traditional belief in economics that people mainly have *extrinsic* rather than *intrinsic* motivation.

In the history of behavioral economics, the reliance on hypothetical questions and survey data often gave rise to deep insights that allowed for major advances. Two prominent examples include the work of Daniel Kahneman and Amos Tversky on prospect theory (Kahneman and Tversky, 1979) based on hypothetical questions in lab experiments, and the work of Daniel Kahneman, Richard Thaler, and Jack Knetsch on fairness motivations in humans (Kahneman et al., 1986) based on hypothetical questions posed in telephone surveys. Kahneman and Tversky (1979) is the second most cited paper in all of economics, the catalyst for the Nobel prize to Kahneman, and the source of prospect theory, which is currently the most satisfactory decision theory under risk, uncertainty, and ambiguity.[14] Yet the paper is based on hypothetical, non-incentivized, lab experiments. Any guesses if it would have been published in an economics journal today?

Another merit of studies based on hypothetical, non-incentivized, questions is that they can complement lab experiments in certain areas. Here, we consider two examples from the work of Daniel Kahneman and Amos Tversky.

> **Example 1** Consider the identification of loss aversion (losses bite more than equivalent gains) in Kahneman and Tversky (1979). In lab experiments, it is not always easy to induce loss aversion over "large losses" because it is considered unethical in experimental economics to leave subjects out-of-pocket. The main alternative in lab experiments is to give subjects money upfront to ensure they are never out-of-pocket. However, this may contaminate their responses by the "house money effect" (gamblers who win money in a casino are more likely to gamble with it; as they say, easy come easy go). Hence, if the intrinsic motivation of subjects to answer lab questions can be trusted, then there is no harm in presenting them with hypothetical loss scenarios.
>
> **Example 2** Consider the following hypothetical, non-incentivized, lab questions from experiments conducted in a seminal paper by Kahneman and Tversky (1984). The percentage of subjects choosing each response is given in brackets.
> Imagine that the US is preparing for the outbreak of an unusual Asian disease, which is expected to kill 600 people. Two alternative programs to combat the disease have been proposed. Assume that the exact scientific estimates of the consequences of the programs are as follows:
> Positive Framing: If program A is adopted, 200 people will be saved. If program B is adopted, there is a one-third probability that 600 people will be saved and a two-thirds probability that no people will be saved. Which of the two programs would you favor? (72% chose A, 28% chose B).
> Negative Framing: If program C is adopted, 400 people will die. If program D is adopted, there is a one-third probability that nobody will die and a two-thirds probability that 600 people will die. Which of the two programs would you favor? (22% chose C, 78% chose D).
> Relative to the status quo, positive framing presents data in terms of "lives saved," while negative framing presents the same data in terms of "lives lost." Options A and C are identical, and options B and D are also identical. Under frame-invariance, the typical assumption in neoclassical economics, if A is chosen over B then C must be chosen over D (and vice versa). However, in the domain of gains (lives saved relative to the status quo), the majority (72%) chose the safe option (A) over the risky option (B). In the domain of losses (lives lost relative to the status quo) the majority (78%) chose the risky option (D) over the safe option (C). This establishes several results. First, behavior is not frame-invariant. Second, the results are not consistent with expected utility. Third, subjects are risk averse in gains and risk seeking in losses; this is one of the important insights of prospect theory.[15]

---

[14] The source for the "second most cited paper" claim is Table 2 in Kim et al. (2006).
[15] To be more precise, there is a *fourfold classification of risk attitudes* under prospect theory that depends jointly on the shapes of the probability weighting function and the utility function. The details are given below in Chapter 2.

These results have survived several challenges (e.g., choices over incentivized lotteries) and even professional physicians and World Bank staff behave in the same manner as lab subjects. Clearly this experiment cannot be run in the lab because it would be unethical to take a life.

Thaler (2015, p. 47) writes on the aversion to survey data: "This disdain [for survey data] is simply unscientific. Polling data, which just comes from asking people whether they are planning to vote and for whom, when carefully used by skilled statisticians ... yield remarkably accurate predictions of elections. The most amusing aspect of this anti-survey attitude is that many important macroeconomic variables are produced by surveys! ... 'jobs' data ... come from surveys conducted by the Census Bureau. The unemployment rate, ... is also determined from a survey that asks people whether they are looking for work. Yet using published survey data is not considered a faux pas in macroeconomics. Apparently economists don't mind survey data as long as someone other than the researcher collected it."

Happiness economics, which we consider in Volume 7 is based almost entirely on survey data. Policymakers appear to take serious interest in this area and survey measures of well-being and happiness are highly correlated, which is consistent with the standard that one might expect from incentivized responses. Furthermore, firms often use information gleaned from market surveys to introduce new products about which consumers have no prior experience, and alter the characteristics of existing products; the consequences of these decisions run into billions of pounds every year.

Consider an example where incentives make the problem even worse. Using hypothetical, non-incentivized questions, Lichtenstein and Slovic (1973) asked people to chose between a less risky *P*-bet (high probability of winning a low prize) and a more risky $-bet (a low probability of winning a high prize). When asked to choose directly between the two bets, most people chose the low risk option, the *P*-bet. Yet, most people assigned a higher certainty equivalent to the $-bet as compared to the *P*-bet. Thus, we have a case of *preference reversals* that cannot be explained by any model of consistent preferences. Grether and Plott (1979) suspected that the problem was caused by hypothetical choices. However, when they re-ran the experiments using incentivized subjects, the incidence of preference reversals worsened.

In sum, there are no grounds to outrightly reject survey data. Survey data has pitfalls, for instance, poll data sometimes gives misleading results, however the benefits of survey data outstrip the potential pitfalls. But other data sources also have limitations; hence, it is important to use all sources of data, surveys, experiments, and field evidence, to build a more complete picture of human behavior.

3.7 Replications in experimental economics

Replications of existing research in economics is not a hugely active area, and certainly less active relative to psychology, which has led to a replication crises in that subject because the majority of studies could not be replicated.[16] Camerer et al. (2016) replicate 18 between-subjects lab experiments published in the two leading journals, *American Economic Review* and the *Quarterly Journal of Economics*, between 2011 and 2014. They find that for 11 out of the 18 studies (61.1%) there is a significant effect in the same direction ($P < 0.05$) as reported in the main finding of

---

[16] For replications in psychology, see, for instance: Open Science Collaboration (2015). Estimating the reproducibility of psychological science: *Science* 349(6251). For a discussion of replications in several areas of economics, see the May 2017 issue (Volume 107, No. 5) of the *American Economic Review*.

each study; three more studies are also close to being successful. The remaining studies fail the replication test on this criterion. Using another method of assessment, they constructed 95% confidence intervals of the main effect size for each paper; 12 of the 18 replications (66.7%) fall within this confidence level. How high are these successful replication rates? This is a relative question, and we simply do not have enough studies in economics and in psychology to make a comparison. When compared with this small number of studies, the authors report that the stated replication rates in economics experiments are relatively higher, but could be improved further.

Replications are critical, but they are not the only yardstick on which we should judge research. After all, if the original research questions were uninteresting and the research design was flawed, the replication can, at best, do no better. There have been suggestions to raise the significance levels for new results (Benjamin et al., 2018). Furthermore, the dependence of preferences on context, frame, and culture is widely evidenced in behavioral economics. These findings suggest that research in behavioral economics may not always be easy to replicate unless a range of contextual, cultural, and frame-dependent factors are controlled for.

4 Approach and organization of the book

This seven-volume book is an attempt to take stock of behavioral economics and aims to serve several purposes: A course text for advanced students in economics and other social sciences, a research handbook for behavioral economists, and an invitation to economists and other social scientists of all persuasions to explore this exciting new field. In its teaching role, the book would ideally be taught in a yearlong course in behavioral economics, supplemented by readings that reflect the interests of the instructor. A good example is a typical two-semester North American-style course that has 13 weeks of teaching in each semester; students meet each week for a two-hour lecture and a one-hour problem-solving class. This book tries to standardize the material in behavioral economics so that students can see behavioral economics as a coherent and widely applicable body of theory, much as they might see any other established area in economics. It is also intended to 'nudge' many idiosyncratic course outlines, that pass for behavioral and/or experimental economics at the moment, to adopt a more balanced approach.

Given the scope of the book, one can also construct a large number of coherent and interesting single-semester courses not just in behavioral economics but also in behavioral decision theory, behavioral macroeconomics, behavioral industrial organization, behavioral contract theory, topics in behavioral economics, and the like. I believe that the book should also be essential background reading for any advanced course in microeconomics in order to address Herbert Gintis' (2009, p. xvi) concern raised in Section 2, till the time that microeconomics books respond in a satisfactory manner to his suggestion.

Despite the size of the book, it is, I believe, the "minimum" amount of material that any academic who declares behavioral economics or experimental economics as their research interest, must have deep, rather than passing, familiarity with.

As the reader may have guessed from Sections 2 and 3, my main criterion for including models in this book is their consistency with the evidence, unless there is significant merit in using a model for pedagogical or other reasons. Most of the models that I use can typically explain at least as much as neoclassical models, but can also better explain data from other domains of human behavior. It is entirely possible, of course, to append auxiliary assumptions to standard neoclassical models to explain almost any set of stylized facts. However, I try to stay away from models in which these auxiliary assumptions are ad hoc fixes.

I encourage the reader to keep an open mind about behavioral economics models and judge models by the relevant empirical evidence. Models in behavioral economics are as theoretically rigorous as models in neoclassical economics, if rigor is an important criteria for the reader. Gilboa (2009, Section 7.1) may well be right that all models are ultimately wrong. Even if this statement were true, we must consistently strive to improve our models in the light of rejections, in order to make better predictions and improve our understanding of human behavior. The sequence of these improved models may or may not ever converge to the "true model." Yet, each time we reject a model and put in its place a new one that makes better predictions, we make progress.

The level of honesty that we need as a profession is captured in the words of the Nobel Prize-winning physicist Richard Feynman (1965, p. 158) that economists would do well to embrace: "But experimenters search most diligently, and with the greatest effort, in exactly those places where it seems most likely that we can prove our theories wrong. In other words, we are trying to prove ourselves wrong as quickly as possible, because only in that way can we find progress." The "all models is wrong critique" is unhelpful at best and, if used inappropriately, it is likely to hinder progress in the subject.

For many of the topics, the book is organized in the following general style. A neoclassical theory is outlined, followed by a review of the evidence for it. If the weight of the evidence is inconsistent with the theory, then the behavioral alternatives and the evidence for or against them is described. There is a range of applications in the book for many of the behavioral theories that the reader/instructor can choose from. In order to help readers who might not be familiar with the full range of topics in behavioral economics, I err on the side of longer introductions to most of the chapters. As a first pass, readers may wish to skim through the introductions to the various volumes and chapters, in order to get a bird's-eye view of the material. This should enable readers to draw up a priority list of topics that they would wish to read or teach in their courses. I deliberately shy away from offering such a list of topics to the reader, and like a good restaurant, prefer to fall back on offering a wide menu of tempting choices, hoping that you, the reader, will keep coming back, and spread the word.

Some readers may feel that it is presumptuous to include the word "foundations" in the title of this book. However, in justification, I believe that there is now a sufficiently rich body of lab and field evidence that is well described by models of behavioral economic theory. The richness of human behavior that we can account for with these models is unprecedented in modern economics. A few of the areas in behavioral economics, notably *neuroeconomics*, are very young and I have some hesitation in bringing this material under the rubric of a book that claims to describe the foundations of a subject. Yet, omitting this material is not an attractive option, and I have erred on the side of inclusion.

I also try to flag up material that is speculative, yet promising, or where the evidence base is not sufficiently established at this point in time. Behavioral economics continues to be work in progress and despite the huge increase in understanding attained over the last several decades, a lot needs to be done. Writing this introduction upon completion of the book, and reflecting on the material, I must confess that I have never personally felt so enriched, yet so ignorant, in my life. I hope that the serious, and just the plain curious, among you, come away with a similar sentiment after reading this book.

The book is organized into seven volumes structured into multiple chapters; there are exercises at the end of each volume. The order of the volumes reflects, at least partially, the historical development of the subject, and also bears some similarity with the organization of a typical course in microeconomics. Each volume begins with an introduction to the material in that volume, and each chapter has a separate, but more detailed, introduction.

The table of contents give a bird's-eye view of what is inside the book and I will not bore you with a semi-verbatim description. I should make a few broad comments though, about my organization of the material. I focus mainly on topics that readers may find to be in an unexpected location within the book.

The book opens with Volume 1 on *behavioral decision theory* because playing a game against nature under risk, uncertainty, and ambiguity, in a static setting, is one of the simplest economic problems; this abstracts from temporal and strategic concerns. However, there is an important overlap between risk preferences and time preferences, which is split between Volume 1 and Volume 3 on time preferences. Many readers might have wished to see a more thorough treatment of ambiguity. However, most of the modern developments in ambiguity are within the confines of the neoclassical models. An important behavioral literature on source-dependent preferences is now beginning to develop that highlights the role of prospect theory. The literature on behavioral models of ambiguity aversion has been gaining momentum in the last few years, as evidenced from our discussion in the guide to further reading at the end of Volume 1.

Microeconomics texts typically begin with a discussion of the properties of human preferences, which are regarded as the primitives of the model. Most evidence now indicates that there is a mixture of individuals with purely *self-regarding preferences*, as in neoclassical economics, and those with *other-regarding preferences*. Volume 2 considers the evidence on *human sociality* and behavioral models that take account of this evidence. There is also a discussion of the implications of social preferences for competitive general equilibrium, which typically comes much later in a microeconomics course. Two important topics that lie at the heart of human motivation in economics, *social identity* and *human virtues*, appear in a stand-alone chapter in Volume 2. The inclusion of these major topics should be less surprising than the fact that most microeconomics texts have somehow contrived to exclude them.

An explicit time dimension is not fundamental to the material in Volumes 1 and 2. In Volume 3, we consider the evidence on time preferences and *behavioral models of time discounting*. The treatment of time preferences is excessively narrow in neoclassical microeconomics texts. This is because the entire psychology of time preferences is captured by a single parameter, the discount rate, in the exponential discounted utility model—the main model of time preferences in neoclassical economics. This is not just unsatisfactory in light of the richness in observed time preferences, but exponential discounting is strongly rejected by the evidence, perhaps even more so than expected utility theory.

Volume 3 is the slimmest of the seven volumes but there is likely to be much that is new and unfamiliar to many readers. This will require investment in learning new machinery such as *subadditivity*, *attribute-based models* of time preferences, and *models of reference time preferences*. I advise the serious reader to persevere with Volume 3. It is worth telling an anecdote that the reader may wish to keep in mind when an unfamiliar topic is encountered in Volume 3. When George Loewenstein, one of the leaders in time discounting, first saw the material in Volume 3, he particularly commended me for including *subadditivity* (i.e., discounting depends on how one partitions a given interval of time). However, when another group of non-specialists read the same material as part of a group reading seminar in a leading university, they were put off by the "unusual and new" concept of subadditivity. The reason subadditivity is there in the book is because it is currently supported by the evidence; its current popularity/aesthetic appeal (or lack of it) are criteria that, for this book, are not relevant.

Volume 4, perhaps the longest of the seven volumes, is on *behavioral game theory*. Classical game theory revolutionized economics by forcing it to specify explicitly the economic environment, set of players, sequence of moves, and the mapping of histories to payoffs. Anyone comparing industrial organization theory before the advent of game theory with modern industrial organization theory will immediately notice the much greater clarity achieved by modern game theoretic models (think, e.g., of models of entry deterrence). Gintis (2009) advocates keeping game theory as the common toolkit for all social sciences despite pointing out serious shortcomings in classical game theory, for instance, the assumption of common priors and the justification for a Nash equilibrium. The approach in this book concurs with this sentiment. Despite widespread belief to the contrary, the evidence has not been too kind to classical models of game theory. This is particularly the case for observed behavior in the early rounds of a game, and for equilibrium refinements that require high cognitive requirements. In particular, it stretches the imagination to believe that players could arrive at a Nash equilibrium purely by a deductive process. For instance, the cooperation rate in many static prisoner's dilemma game experiments is about 60%; cooperation here is a dominated strategy, which in classical game theory, ought never to have been played.[17]

We consider at length the evidence for classical models of game theory and the leading behavioral alternatives. Many of the main behavioral alternatives, such as *level-k models*, the *cognitive hierarchy model*, and the *quantal response equilibrium*, relax the "equilibrium in beliefs" assumption, or the assumption that players play a best response. There are several other behavioral models of strategic interaction that are in the fray. While the empirical evidence is not always consistent with these models, the most heartening aspect of the discourse in behavioral game theory is that we are actually using empirical evidence to choose among the models. You cannot convince the leaders in this field, say, Vincent Crawford or Colin Camerer, about your proposal for a new solution concept in game theory by simply appealing to the aesthetic appeal of your proposed model, or its ability to tell a useful story, or a fable, if it is not supported by the evidence. I have decided to include the topic of *psychological game theory* in Volume 4. I anticipate that some instructors may have wished to place this topic in Volume 7 on emotions, because it also deals with *anger* and *guilt*, while other instructors may have wished to see it in Volume 2, because it also deals with intentions-based reciprocity. My relatively detailed treatment of this material reflects my preference to see this material given more prominence in modern behavioral economics.

Volume 5 considers *models of bounded rationality*, and I personally believe that it is of enormous significance for the future direction of behavioral economics. It is split into three chapters. The chapter on *judgment heuristics*, a topic that owes its origin and importance to Tversky and Kahneman (1973, 1974), brings into sharp focus the debate about the relative suitability of the *optimization approach*, and the *heuristic-based approach* to economic models.[18] This chapter is a must-read for anyone who believes that the standard neoclassical framework is satisfactory on the grounds that its predictions match the data in an 'as if' sense. The chapter on *mental accounting* considers work that Richard Thaler almost single-handedly pioneered. It deserves to see much more development and interest among theorists working in behavioral economics. The reader may not have expected a chapter on *behavioral finance* in Volume 5 but there is no better place to illustrate bounded rationality and the inefficiency of markets in the very market that is typically held up as a model of efficiency in neoclassical economics.

---

[17] Social preferences alone cannot explain behavior of the players in the prisoner's dilemma game; see al-Nowaihi and Dhami (2015).

[18] For a discussion of alternative views on the optimization versus heuristics debate, the reader may consult the June 2013 issue of the *Journal of Economic Literature*, Volume 51, No. 2.

Volume 6 outlines the evidence on human learning and introduces traditional as well as the newer *behavioral models of learning*. I also give chapter-length treatments of *evolutionary game theory* and *stochastic social dynamics*. An appendix briefly introduces the reader to the necessary technical machinery on deterministic and stochastic dynamical systems. Some instructors would have wished to see the chapter on evolutionary game theory in Volume 4. One aim of this chapter is to provide evolutionary foundations for human sociality that we covered in Volume 2, and also introduce some newer and interesting topics, such as *gene-culture coevolution* that justify the location of this chapter in a volume on learning. Volume 6 is particularly instructive in evaluating the common claim that a Nash equilibrium arises if sufficient learning opportunities are provided to the subjects. A separate chapter-length treatment on stochastic social dynamics in Volume 6 might be unexpected, even for many behavioral economists who do not typically include this topic in their courses. However, I believe that this material needs to be taken more seriously, and all students of behavioral economics should have at least a basic familiarity with it.

The final volume, Volume 7, considers three different topics: emotions, behavioral welfare economics, and neuroeconomics.

Neoclassical economics typically focuses on cold and emotionless deliberation. Part 1 in Volume 7 considers the role of emotions in explaining economic phenomena. Instructors interested in teaching a course that focuses on emotions will need to combine the material here with that from other parts of the book, such as psychological game theory (Volume 4), models of regret and disappointment aversion (Volume 1), and issues of self-control and present-biased preferences (Volume 3). We also consider the Gul–Pesendorfer model of temptation that some readers might have preferred to situate in Volume 3, where issues of present-biased preferences are discussed. I have also placed the important policy relevant topic of *happiness economics* here, insofar as happiness may be considered as a type of emotion. The evidence base in happiness economics is typically constructed using survey data that not all economists are comfortable with (see Section 3.6 above), which has hampered its acceptability within academic economists. I urge economists to take this material more seriously, particularly given the correlations between various measures of well-being and happiness. Some readers may find *models of dual selves* to be somewhat out of place in this part; I partly share this concern but it was not immediately clear where better to situate this important topic.

Part 2 in Volume 7 considers issues in *behavioral welfare economics*, which is an area that is likely to experience more development in the future. If people have behavioral biases relative to the neoclassical model, then should we respect those biases or not? The debate is not just about *libertarianism* and *paternalism*, but also about exactly what these terms mean in the presence of behavioral biases.

Part 3 in Volume 7 gives a very brief tour of *neuroeconomics* that highlights the neuroeconomic foundations of just a few selected aspects of human behavior from the first four volumes of the book. In particular, I make no attempt at completeness in the treatment of neuroeconomics; several excellent and more authoritative sources are available (e.g., Glimcher et al., 2009; Glimcher and Fehr, 2014).

There are some notable omissions from the book that are partly dictated by technological considerations such as the physical size of the book, the current importance of these topics in behavioral economics, and last but not least, by my own lack of competence in these areas. *Complexity theory* and its implications for public policy do not figure in this book; readers can pursue Mitchell (2009) for an introduction, followed by Colander and Kupers (2014) for policy issues. I have also omitted a discussion of *agent-based computational models*; readers can begin with Tesfatsion and Judd (2006) and Farmer and Foley (2009). I also give insufficient attention to the *epistemic foundations of equilibrium concepts* in classical and behavioral game theory; see Dekel and Siniscalchi (2015) for a recent review and Gintis (2009) for a critique of the epistemic foundations of classical game theory.

5 Appendix A: The random lottery incentive mechanism

Consider the *random lottery incentive mechanism* (RLI) that is widely employed to pay subjects in experiments. Suppose that expected utility maximizing subjects in an experiment perform n tasks from a set of tasks $T = \{t_1, \ldots, t_n\}$. Let task t_i involve choosing from a set of lotteries, $\mathcal{L}_i$ and define $\mathcal{L} = \cup_i \mathcal{L}_i$ as the set of all lotteries considered in the n tasks. Consider a subject in the experiment whose preferences over pairs of elements in $\mathcal{L}$ are represented by $\succeq$. At the beginning of the experiment, subjects are told that one of the tasks will be picked at random once all tasks are completed, and their choice in that task will be paid to them for real. Let us abstract from issues of a possible show-up fee for the experiment that we have already commented on above.

Suppose that in any task, t_i, the most preferred lottery of the subject is L_i^*. Conditional on the incentive structure described above, should the subject choose L_i^*? An elicitation method is incentive compatible if the answer is yes. The probability that task i is chosen to be rewarded at the end of the experiment is $\frac{1}{n}$. With the complementary probability $1 - \frac{1}{n}$, any of the other $n-1$ tasks might be chosen to be rewarded. Let the choice made by the subject on any task $t_j, j \neq i$ be L_j. Let us denote by $(L_1, p_1; \ldots; L_i^*, p_i; \ldots; L_n, p_n)$ the compound lottery in which lottery L_j is played with probability p_j. From the *independence axiom* of expected utility theory that should be familiar to most undergraduates in economics (see Volume 1 for details), we know that since $L_i^* \succeq \widehat{L}_i$ for all $\widehat{L}_i \in \mathcal{L}_i$, it follows that

$$\left(L_1, \frac{1}{n}; \ldots; L_i^*, \frac{1}{n}; \ldots; L_n, \frac{1}{n}\right) \succeq \left(L_1, \frac{1}{n}; \ldots; \widehat{L}_i, \frac{1}{n}; \ldots; L_n, \frac{1}{n}\right) \text{ for all } \widehat{L}_i \in \mathcal{L}_i. \tag{1}$$

In words, the independence axiom says that if $L_i^* \succeq \widehat{L}_i$ then the decision maker prefers any mixture of lotteries that gives L_i^* over an identical mixture that contains $\widehat{L}_i$ in its place. Thus, the subject will choose L_i^* in task t_i. We can show this to be true for all tasks $t_j \in T$. Thus, RLI is incentive compatible.

6 Appendix B: In lieu of a problem set

This section poses 50 problems that you will encounter in this book and tailored to the material presented in the introduction. If you are already familiar with a particular problem, just move on to the next one. The problems range from straightforward applications of the material in the introduction to slightly more challenging ones. I deliberately avoid giving too much structure to the problems, so that you can try to solve them by writing your own models in a free-spirited manner. If you wish to use the neoclassical model to solve a problem, then think carefully about the auxiliary assumptions that you invoke. In particular, do ask yourself if the auxiliary assumptions that you use are ad hoc or not. You will encounter the solutions to these problems, and many others, as you progress through the book; this will also give you an opportunity to check your initial responses.

1. Many taxi divers quit too early on rainy days in New York when the effective wage rate is actually very high. In other words, why is it so hard to find a taxi on a rainy day in New York?
2. Why do owners of objects, humans, or chimps, value them more than non-owners (under neoclassical economics, everyone should value objects at their opportunity cost)?
3. If people play Russian roulette, why are they likely to pay more to reduce the number of bullets from 1 to 0, as compared to from 4 to 3 (check that under expected utility these two choices should be equally valuable)?
4. From 1926 to about the mid 1980s, the annual real return on stocks has been about 7% with a standard deviation of 20%, while the annual real return on treasury bills has been less than 1%. In neoclassical economics, a coefficient of relative risk aversion of about 30 can explain these findings, but the actual coefficient is around 1. This is the *equity-premium puzzle*. How can you explain the equity-premium puzzle?
5. A decision maker has initial wealth, w. Suppose that at all levels of wealth, he prefers to keep his wealth rather than play the lottery L_1 : win $11 or lose $10 with equal chance, for any w. Then, under expected utility theory, the decision maker will prefer the lottery L_1 to the lottery L_2 : lose $100 and win an infinite amount with equal probability (*Rabin's paradox*). Thus risk aversion over small stakes, under expected utility theory, implies implausible risk aversion over large stakes. Does expected utility correctly encapsulate the risk attitudes of an individual? Can you think of modifications to expected utility that will explain Rabin's paradox?
6. For an amateur tax evader, the actual probability of audit is 1–3% and the penalty for being caught is (i) return of evaded taxes, plus (ii) fine at the rate of 1–2 times evaded tax. A quick back of the envelope calculation will show that this implies a return on tax evasion of about 96–98%. If you are an expected utility maximizer and have a coefficient of relative risk aversion of about 70 or above, you will pay your taxes; but, empirically, the coefficient is about 1. Since there are very few assets with this return, why do people pay any taxes?
7. Why do people not buy insurance against very low probability events such as natural hazards, even when insurance is better than actuarially fair and the losses of insurance firms are underwritten by the government?
8. In everyday conversations about risky decisions, people speak of *optimism, pessimism, disappointment*, and *regret* (think only of pure risk in a simple game against nature). Can neoclassical decision theory under risk account for these emotions?
9. In recessions, why do firms typically prefer to lay-off workers rather than cut wages?
10. Why do most people find a cut in the nominal wage of 5% under zero inflation to be more unfair relative to a nominal wage increase of 2% under 7% inflation? What are the implications for macroeconomics?
11. In experiments on redistributive taxes, why do people often choose a smaller, more equally distributed, cake as compared to one in which they get a larger share of a very unequally distributed cake?
12. Should we generally expect any difference in outcomes relative to the neoclassical case if a minority of players have other-regarding preferences (i.e., also care about payoffs of others in addition to their own)? You may think of optimal contracts (static and finitely repeated) between a principal and two agents in a production task where both agents are essential. One of the agents has self-regarding preferences, but the other has other-regarding preferences; the principal does not know who's who.

13. Why are individuals often willing to punish third-parties for observed norm violations between other players even when their own payoffs have not been affected?
14. Why do workers often respond to higher wage offers of firms by working harder, even in 'static games', where they could take the money and run? Why, in these static problems, may firms choose to offer high wages that exceed the opportunity cost of hiring workers? How might you distinguish the predictions of this model from the model of efficiency wages?
15. Why may firms sometimes choose to offer non-enforceable bonus contracts to workers in preference to enforceable incentive contracts, even in static problems? And why might the choice of effort by workers under bonus contracts be relatively higher as compared to that under incentive contracts?
16. Why do moral suasion, trust, and giving workers a goal/sense of purpose or a particular company identity, often outperform monetary incentives?
17. Why do people not lie maximally even when their behavior is guaranteed to remain completely anonymous? And why do we teach children not to lie, act morally rather than opportunistically, and help those who are less fortunate, rather than the neoclassical prescriptions about human behavior (maximize your payoffs/utility subject to technological constraints, but ignore any moral or ethical considerations relative to payoff maximization)?
18. Consider Akerlof and Kranton's (2005, p.9) description of the following initiation process at the US West Point military academy. "On plebes' first day…they strip down to their underwear. Their hair is cut off. They are put in uniform. They then must address an older cadet, with the proper salute…must stand and salute and repeat, and stand and salute and repeat, until they get it exactly right, all the while being reprimanded for every tiny mistake." How would an economist brought up on the theory of incentives and organizations make sense of this initiation ceremony?
19. Why does the law make a distinction between murder and manslaughter, assigning much lower punishments for manslaughter for the same harm to the victim?
20. Most people would prefer one apple today to two apples tomorrow, but they prefer two apples in 51 days to one apple in 50 days. How can you explain this preference reversal?
21. Discounting over an entire time interval $[t,,\bar{t}]$ in one go, turns out to be smaller, relative to discounting over n successive sub-intervals $[t,,t_1],[t_1,,t_2],\ldots,[t_{n-1},\bar{t}]$; this is known as *subadditive discounting*. Under exponential discounting, the two answers should be identical. What modifications do you think are needed to the exponential discounting model to explain this empirical finding?
22. Why does the data (e.g., for the US) show a sharp drop in consumption at retirement?
23. Why do people simultaneously hold illiquid assets and credit card debt?
24. Why do people procrastinate so much?
25. Why do people often pay more for an annual gym membership when they could save money on a pay-as-you-go basis?
26. In normal form games in which a Nash equilibrium can be found with more than 2–3 steps of iterated elimination of dominated strategies, the experimental evidence often shows that the outcome is not a Nash equilibrium. Does this evidence cause you to have any reservations about equilibrium concepts in classical game theory or a desire to modify them? If so, how?
27. Why do we observe far more cooperation in a one-shot prisoner dilemma game (about 60% of the time) relative to the prediction of classical game theory that predicts no cooperation under the assumption that people have self-regarding preferences? Bear in

mind that the prisoners' dilemma game is possibly the most widely used game in the social sciences as a metaphor for human cooperation (or the lack of it), so this is not an unimportant result that can be ignored.

28. Empirical evidence shows that in centipede games, the backward induction outcome (play down at the first node) is played less than 10% of the time. In six-node centipede games, in a majority of the cases, players move across to at least the fourth node. How can you explain these findings? Does your explanation have testable implications?

29. If you are unconvinced by the experimental method, can you come up with a few "stringent" non-experimental tests of classical game theory using real-world data?

30. Why do bargaining negotiations often stall with adverse consequences for both parties (union strikes, wars, family gridlocks over issues) even when issues of asymmetric information are not salient? This is particularly the case in conditions where the classical alternating offers bargaining game predicts an immediate bargaining solution without delay.

31. You live in Italy and as most folks who live there, you typically don't tip cab drivers. However, one week you go abroad, and take a taxi to a friend's house who lives in the countryside in a country where there is a norm for tipping taxi drivers. A 70-year-old meek-looking and frail taxi driver delivers you safely to your destination. Would you honor the norm of tipping him or just walk away? Suppose you answered that you would pay the tip. Is your behavior consistent with classical game theory? If not, then which feature of classical game theory could be altered to explain your tipping behavior?

32. Why are winners of common value auctions often 'cursed' in the sense that they make far less money than they anticipated?

33. Eyetracking data from a three-round, two-player bargaining game whose structure is hidden from view, but searchable by using mouse clicks, reveals the following. Most subjects search for payoffs and the size of the cake to be divided in each round, forward from the first round rather than backward from the third round. Furthermore, subjects trained in backward induction do search backwards more often. Does this in any way make you uneasy about equilibrium concepts in classical game theory, or would you simply discount this evidence?

34. Why do interrogators often conduct around-the-clock interrogation of suspects?

35. Why might many people end up marrying or proposing marriage/seeking divorce without sufficient deliberation, or buy consumer durables in haste? Can you think of any legal interventions that take such human behavior into account? Would such legal interventions be necessary for the typical individual in the neoclassical framework?

36. Why are we typically happy to buy consumer durables on installments, yet prefer to prepay for a holiday?

37. Why do smokers and alcoholics often pay money at rehab clinics to get rid of their addictions? Recall that the typical model of addiction in neoclassical economics assumes that people choose to get rationally addicted, taking account of the relevant costs and benefits now, and in the future.

38. Why do many cigarette smokers report an increase in happiness following an increase in excise duty on cigarettes (based on US and Canadian data)?

39. A town is served by two hospitals. In the larger hospital, about 45 babies are born each day, and in the smaller hospital, about 15 babies are born each day. As you know, about 50% of all babies are boys. However, the exact percentage varies from day to day. For a period of one year, each hospital recorded the days on which more than 60% of the babies born were boys. Which hospital do you think recorded more such days? 53 students in the sample

said that both hospitals are equally likely to have recorded such days and 21 students each chose the larger and the smaller hospital, respectively. Are the students behaving like the agents in neoclassical economics (sometimes known as *Econs*)? If not, what does their behavior reveal?

40. Why do sales at lotto stores that have sold a winning ticket soar in the immediate weeks following the lotto win (this positive effect on sales persists for up to 40 weeks following the lotto win)? How can you test the hypothesis that "the winning store just produced more interest among the local population to buy more lotto tickets, so that this finding is perfectly consistent with neoclassical economics"?
41. Why do so many mergers fail, yet we often observe waves of mergers from time to time?
42. Why do people find it more difficult to make a choice when the set of choices expands (people choose easily among three types of jams, but often struggle to choose among 27 types of jams)?
43. There is much cross-country variation in organ donation rates in European countries (98% in Austria, but 12% in Germany; 99.9% in France, but 17.7% in the UK; 85.9% in Sweden, but 4.25% in Denmark). It turns out that in countries with high organ donation rates, people are automatically enrolled in the organ donation program, but can opt-out if they wish. The situation is exactly the reverse in countries with low organ donation rates, where people can opt-in if they wish. Can this empirical fact be explained under neoclassical economics? If you answer yes, then be careful in stating your auxiliary assumptions and think of the evidence for these assumptions.
44. There are only two cab companies in the city, Green and Blue; 85% of the cabs are Green. There was an accident last night. A witness comes forward to testify that the cab involved in the accident was Blue. In similar conditions, the reliability of the witness is 80%, i.e., the probability that he gets it wrong is 20%. What is the probability that the actual cab involved in the accident was Blue? The median and modal response was 80%. Are the students behaving like the agents in neoclassical economics? If not, what does their behavior reveal?
45. Why do buyers of a new car often find that the particular model they drive suddenly appears more common on the roads?
46. Why do marketing people play on alternative ways of framing information that has identical information-content? Why for instance, may swimsuit models be placed next to sports cars in advertisements, when the main role of advertisement in the neoclassical framework is to convey information to potential buyers?
47. Why do sales drop if publicly known sales taxes are displayed on price stickers rather than being added at the check-out counter?
48. Why might the financial market price skewness in asset returns?
49. Why are so many financial crises accompanied by no-news (i.e., no information related to fundamental values)?
50. Consider the probability of success that entrepreneurs assign to their startups. In one empirical study, only 5% of startup entrepreneurs believe that their odds are any worse than comparable enterprises and a third believe that their success is assured. Based on French data, 56% expect 'development' and only 6% of startup entrepreneurs expect 'difficulty'; three years on, the respective figures are 38% and 17%. Empirically, only half of all startups survive beyond three years and the high failure rate among startups is widely reported in the popular press. How can we square these figures with the supposed rationality of participants in corporate finance? How should we react to this sort of evidence?

REFERENCES FOR INTRODUCTION

Abeler, J. and Nosenzo, D. (2015). Self-selection into laboratory experiments: pro-social motives versus monetary incentives. *Experimental Economics* 18(2): 195–214.

Allais, M. (1953). La psychologie de l'homme rationnel devant le risque: critique des postulats et axiomes de l'école Américaine. *Econometrica* 21: 503–46.

al-Nowaihi, A. and Dhami, S. (2015). Evidential equilibria: heuristics and biases in static games of complete information. *Games* 6(4): 637–77.

Andersen, S., Ertaç, S., Gneezy, U., Hoffman, M., and List, J. A. (2011). Stakes matter in ultimatum games. *American Economic Review* 101(7): 3427–39.

Anderson, J., Burks, S. V., Carpenter, J. et al. (2013). Self-selection and variations in the laboratory measurement of other-regarding preferences across subject pools: evidence from one college student and two adult samples. *Experimental Economics* 16: 170–89.

Ariely, D., Bracha, A., and Meier, S. (2009). Doing good or going well? Image motivation and monetary incentives in behaving prosocially. *American Economic Review* 99(1): 544–55.

Arkes, H. R., Dawes, R. M., and Christensen, C. (1986). Factors influencing the use of a decision rule in a probabilistic task. *Organizational Behavior and Human Decision Processes* 37: 93–110.

Ashraf, N., Camerer, C. F., and Loewenstein, G. (2005). Adam Smith, behavioral economist. *Journal of Economic Perspectives* 19(3): 131–45.

Bardsley, N., Cubitt, R., Loomes, G., Moffatt, P., Starmer, C., and Sugden, R. (2010). *Experimental Economics: Rethinking the Rules*. Princeton, NJ: Princeton University Press.

Barmettler, F., Fehr, E., and Zehnder, C. (2012). Big experimenter is watching you! Anonymity and prosocial behavior in the laboratory. *Games and Economic Behavior* 75(1): 17–34.

Becker, G. M., Degroot, M. H., and Marschak, J. (1964). Measuring utility by a single-response sequential method. *Systems Research* 9: 226–32.

Bénabou, R. and Tirole, J. (2003). Intrinsic and extrinsic motivation. *Review of Economic Studies* 70(3): 489–520.

Benjamin, D. J., Berger, J. O., Johannesson, M., Nosek, B. A., Wagenmakers, E. J., Berk, R., and Morgan, S. L. (2018). Redefine statistical significance. *Nature Human Behaviour* 2(1): 6–10.

Blaug, M. (1992). *The Methodology of Economics, Or, How Economists Explain*. Cambridge and New York: Cambridge University Press.

Bohm, P., Lindén, J., and Sonnegård, J. (1997). Eliciting reservation prices: Becker-DeGroot-Marschak mechanisms vs. markets. *Economic Journal* 107: 1079–89.

Bolton, G. E., Zwick, R., and Katok, E. (1998). Dictator game giving: rules of fairness versus acts of kindness. *International Journal of Game Theory* 27(2): 269–99.

Bonner, S. E., Hastie, R., Sprinkle, G. B., and Young, S. M. (2000). A review of the effects of financial incentives on performance in laboratory tasks: implications for management accounting. *Journal of Management Accounting Research* 13: 19–64.

Braga, J. and Starmer, C. (2005). Preference anomalies, preference elicitation and the Discovered Preference Hypothesis. *Environmental and Resource Economics* 32: 55–89.

Bruni, L. and Sugden, R. (2007). The road not taken: how psychology was removed from economics, and how it might be brought back. *Economic Journal* 117: 146–73.

Camerer, C. F. (2015). The promise and success of lab-field generalizability in experimental economics: a critical reply to Levitt and List. In G. R. Fréchette and A. Schotter (eds.), *Handbook of Experimental Economic Methodology*. Oxford: Oxford University Press. pp. 249–95.

Camerer, C. F., Dreber, A., Forsell, E., Ho, T.-H., Huber, J., Johannesson, M., Kirchler, M., Almenberg, J., Altmejd, A., Chan, T., et al. (2016). Evaluating replicability of laboratory experiments in economics. *Science* 351(6280): 1433–6.

Camerer, C. F. and Hogarth, R. M. (1999). The effects of financial incentives in experiments: a review and capital-labor-production framework. *Journal of Risk and Uncertainty* 19(1–3): 7–42.

Camerer, C. F. and Loewenstein, G. (2004). Behavioral economics: past, present, future. In C. F. Camerer, G. Loewenstein, and M. Rabin, (eds.), *Advances in Behavioral Economics*. New York: Russell Sage, pp. 3–51.

Cameron, L. A. (1999). Raising the stakes in the ultimatum game: experimental evidence from Indonesia. *Economic Inquiry* 37(1): 47–59.

Carpenter, J. P. and Seki, E. (2011). Do social preferences increase productivity? Field experimental evidence from fishermen in Toyama Bay. *Economic Inquiry* 49(2): 612–30.

Chamberlin, E. H. (1948). An experimental imperfect market. *Journal of Political Economy* 56(2): 95–108.

Cherry, T., Frykblom, P., and Shogren, J. (2002). Hardnose the dictator. *American Economic Review* 92(4) 1218–21.

Cleave, B. L., Nikiforakis, N., and Slonim, R. (2012). Is there selection bias in laboratory experiments? The case of social and risk preferences. *Experimental Economics* 16(3): 372–82.

Colander, D. and Kupers, R. (2014). *Complexity and the Art of Public Policy: Solving Society's Problems from the Bottom Up*. Princeton, NJ: Princeton University Press.

Dana, J., Weber, R. A., and Kuang, J. X. (2007). Exploiting moral wriggle room: experiments demonstrating an illusory preference for fairness. *Economic Theory* 33: 67–80.

Davis, D. D. and Holt, C. A. (1993). *Experimental Economics*. Princeton, NJ: Princeton University Press.

De Marchi, N. and Blaug, M. (eds.) (1991). *Appraising Economic Theories: Studies in the Methodology of Research Programmes*. Cheltenham: Edward Elgar.

Dekel, E. and Lipman, B. L. (2010). How (not) to do decision theory. *Annual Review of Economics* 2: 257–82.

Dekel, E. and Siniscalchi, M. (2015). Epistemic game theory. In H. P. Young and S. Zamir (eds.), *Handbook of Game Theory with Economic Applications*, Volume 4. Amsterdam: Elsevier, pp. 619–702.

Dhami, S. and al-Nowaihi, A. (2018). Rationality in *Economics: Theory and Evidence*. CESifo Working Paper No. 6872. Forthcoming in *Handbook of Rationality*. Cambridge, MA: MIT Press.

Ellsberg, D. (1961). Risk, ambiguity, and the Savage axioms. *Quarterly Journal of Economics* 75(4): 643–69.

Falk, A. and Heckman, J. J. (2009). Lab experiments are a major source of knowledge in the social sciences. *Science* 326: 535–38.

Falk, A., Meier, S., and Zehnder, C. (2013). Do lab experiments misrepresent social preferences? The case of self-selected student samples. *Journal of the European Economic Association* 11(4): 839–52.

Farmer, J. D. and Foley, D. (2009). The economy needs agent-based modelling. *Nature* 460: 685–6.

Fehr, E. and List, J. A. (2004). The hidden costs and returns of incentives: trust and trustworthiness among CEOs. *Journal of the European Economic Association* 2(5): 743–71.

Feynman, R. (1965). *The Character of Physical Law*. Cambridge, MA: MIT Press.

Fréchette, G. R. (2015). Laboratory experiments: professionals versus students. In G. R. Fréchette and A. Schotter (eds.), *Handbook of Experimental Economic Methodology*. Oxford: Oxford University Press, pp. 360–90.

Friedman, M. (1953). *The Methodology of Positive Economics*. Chicago: University of Chicago Press.

Gilboa, I. (2009). *Theory of Decision Under Uncertainty*. Cambridge: Cambridge University Press.

Gilboa, I., Postlewaite, A., Samuelson, L., and Schmeidler, D. (2014). Economic models as analogies. *Economic Journal* 124: F513–F533.

Gintis, H. (2009). *The Bounds of Reason: Game Theory and the Unification of the Behavioral Sciences*. Princeton, NJ: Princeton University Press.

Gintis, H. (2015). Modeling homo-socialis: a reply to critics. *Review of Behavior Economics* 2: 211–37.

Glimcher, P. W., Camerer, C. F., Fehr, E., and Poldrack, R. A. (2009). *Neuroeconomics*. Amsterdam: Academic Press, Elsevier Inc.

Glimcher, P. W. and Fehr, E. (eds.) (2014). *Neuroeconomics*. Amsterdam: Elsevier Inc.

Gneezy, U. and Rustichini, A. (2000a). A fine is a price. *Journal of Legal Studies* 29(1): 1–17.

Gneezy, U. and Rustichini, A. (2000b). Pay enough or don't pay at all. *Quarterly Journal of Economics* 115(3): 791–810.

Godfrey-Smith, P. (2006). The strategy of model-based science. *Biology and Philosophy* 21: 725–40.

Godfrey-Smith, P. (2009). Models and fictions in science. *Philosophical Studies* 143: 101–16.

Grether, D. M. and Plott, C. (1979). Economic theory of choice and the preference reversal phenomenon. *American Economic Review*. 69(4): 623–38.

Guala, F. (2008). Experimental economics, history of. In S. N. Durlauf and L. E. Blume (eds.), *The New Palgrave Dictionary of Economics*. 2nd edition. Basingstoke: Palgrave Macmillan.

Haley, K. J. and Fessler, D. M. T. (2005). Nobody's watching? Subtle cues affect generosity in an anonymous economic game. *Evolution and Human Behavior* 26(3): 245–56.

Hands, D. W. (1991). The problem of excess content: economics, novelty, and a long Popperian tale. In M. Blaug and N. DeMarchi (eds.), *Appraising Economic Theories*. Cheltenham: Edward Elgar, pp. 58–75.

Hands, D. W. (2001). *Reflections Without Rules: Economic Methodology and Contemporary Science Theory*. Cambridge: Cambridge University Press.

Hausman, D. (1992). *The Inexact and Separate Science of Economics*. Cambridge: Cambridge University Press.

Herbst, D. and Mas, A. (2015). Peer effects on worker output in the lab generalize to the field. *Science* 350: 545–9.

Hertwig, R. and Ortmann, A. (2001). Experimental practices in economics: a methodological challenge for psychologists? *Behavioral and Brain Sciences* 24(3): 383–403.

Hoffman, E., McCabe, K. A., and Smith, V. L. (1998). Behavioral foundations of reciprocity: experimental economics and evolutionary psychology. *Economic Inquiry* 36: 335–52.

Hogarth, R. M., Gibbs, B. J., McKenzie, C. R. M., and Marquis, M. A. (1991). Learning from feedback: exactingness and incentives. *Journal of Experimental Psychology: Learning, Memory and Cognition* 17: 734–52.

Kahneman, D., Knetsch, J. L., and Thaler, R. H. (1986). Fairness as a constraint on profit seeking: entitlements in the market. *American Economic Review* 76(4): 728–41.

Kahneman, D. and Tversky, A. (1979). Prospect theory: an analysis of decision under risk. *Econometrica* 47(2): 263–91.

Kahneman, D. and Tversky, A. (1984). Choices, values, and frames. *The American Psychologist* 39: 341–50.

Kessler, J. B. and Vesterlund, L. (2015). The external validity of laboratory experiments: the misleading emphasis on quantitative effects. In G. R. Fréchette and A. Schotter (eds.), *Handbook of Experimental Economic Methodology*. Oxford: Oxford University Press, pp. 391–406.

Kim, E. H., Morse, A., and Zingales, L. (2006). What has mattered to economics since 1970. *Journal of Economic Perspectives* 20, 189–202.

Kuhn, T. S. (1962). *The Structure of Scientific Revolutions*. Chicago, IL: University of Chicago Press.

Lakatos, I. (1970). Falsification and the methodology of scientific research programmes. In I. Lakatos and A. Musgrave (eds.), *Criticism and the Growth of Knowledge*. Cambridge: Cambridge University Press.

Lambdin, C. G. and Shaffer, V. A. (2009). Are within-subjects designs transparent? *Judgement and Decision Making* 4(7): 554–66.

Levitt, S. D. and List, J. A. (2007). What do laboratory experiments measuring social preferences reveal about the real world? *Journal of Economic Perspectives* 21(2): 153–74.

Lichtenstein, S. and Slovic, P. (1973). Response-induced reversals of preference in gambling: an extended replication in Las Vegas. *Journal of Experimental Psychology* 101(1): 16–20.

Lipsey, R. G. (1979). *An Introduction to Positive Economics*. 5th edition. London: Weidenfield and Nicholson.

List, J. A. (2006). The behavioralist meets the market: measuring social preferences and reputation effects in actual transactions. *Journal of Political Economy* 114(1): 1–37.

Loewenstein, G. F. (1999). Experimental economics from the vantage-point of behavioural economics. *Economic Journal* 109(453): 25–34.

Markowitz, H. (1952). The utility of wealth. *Journal of Political Economy* 60(2): 151–58.

Mas-Collel, A., Whinston, M. D., and Green, J. R. (1995). *Microeconomic Theory*. New York: Oxford University Press.

Mitchell, M. (2009). *Complexity: A Guided Tour*. Oxford: Oxford University Press.

Phelps, E. and Pollak, R. A. (1968). On second best national savings and game equilibrium growth. *Review of Economic Studies* 35(2): 185–99.

Popper, K. (1934). *Logik der Forschung* (Hutchinson & Company published the translation by Karl Popper titled *The Logic of Scientific Discovery* in 1959).

Popper, K. (1963). *Conjectures and Refutations: The Growth of Scientific Knowledge*. London: Routledge and Kegan Paul.

Read, D. (2005). Monetary incentives, what are they good for? *Journal of Economic Methodology* 12(2): 265–76.

Roth, A. E. (1987). Laboratory experimentation in economics. In T. Bewley (ed.), *Advances in Economic Theory, Fifth World Congress*. Cambridge: Cambridge University Press, pp. 269–99.

Roth, A. E. (1988). Laboratory experimentation in economics: a methodological overview. *Economic Journal* 98: 974–1031.

Roth, A. E. (1995). Introduction to experimental economics. In J. H. Kagel and A. E. Roth (eds.), *The Handbook of Experimental Economics*. Princeton, NJ: Princeton University Press, pp. 3–109.

Roth, A. E. (2015). Is experimental economics living up to its promise? In G. R. Fréchette and A. Schotter, (eds.), *Handbook of Experimental Economic Methodology*. Oxford: Oxford University Press, pp. 13–40.

Rubinstein, A. (2006). Dilemmas of an economic theorist. *Econometrica* 74(4): 865–83.

Rydval, O. and Ortmann, A. (2004). How financial incentives and cognitive abilities affect task performance in laboratory settings: an illustration. *Economics Letters* 85: 315–20.

Samuelson, P. A. and Nordhaus, W. (1985). *Economics*. New York: McGraw Hill.

Schotter, A. (2015). On the relationship between economic theory and experiments. In G. R. Fréchette and A. Schotter (eds.), *Handbook of Experimental Economic Methodology*. Oxford: Oxford University Press, pp. 58–85.

Selten, R. (1998). Features of experimentally observed bounded rationality. *European Economic Review* 42(3–5): 413–36.

Siegel, S. and Fouraker, L. E. (1960). *Bargaining and Group Decision Making*. New York: McGraw-Hill.

Simon, H. A. (1978). Rational decision-making in business organizations. Nobel Memorial Lecture, December 8, 1978.

Slonim, R. and Roth, A. E. (1998). Learning in high stakes ultimatum games: an experiment in the Slovak Republic. *Econometrica* 66(3): 569–96.

Slonim, R., Wang, C., Garbarino, E., and Merret, D. (2013). Opting-in: participation bias in economic experiments. *Journal of Economic Behavior and Organization* 90: 43–70.

Smith, V. L. (1962). An experimental study of competitive market behavior. *Journal of Political Economy* 70: 111–37.

Smith, V. L. (1976). Experimental economics: induced value theory. *American Economic Review* 66: 274–9.

Smith, V. L. (1991). Rational choice: the contrast between economics and psychology. *Journal of Political Economy* 99: 877–97.

Smith, V. L. (2001). From old issues to new directions in experimental psychology and economics. *Behavioral and Brain Sciences* 24(3): 428–9.

Smith, V. L. and Walker, J. M. (1993). Monetary rewards and decision cost in experimental economics. *Economic Inquiry* 31: 245–61.

Tesfatsion, L. and Judd, K. L. (eds.) (2006). *Handbook of Computational Economics, Volume 2: Agent-Based Computational Economics*. Amsterdam: North-Holland.

Thaler, R. H. (2015). *Misbehaving: The Making of Behavioral Economics*. New York: W. W. Norton.

Tversky, A. and Kahneman, D. (1973). Availability: a heuristic for judging frequency and probability. *Cognitive Psychology* 5(2): 207–32.

Tversky, A. and Kahneman, D. (1974). Judgment under uncertainty: heuristics and biases. *Science* 185: 1124–30.

Wimsatt, C. W. (2007). *Re-Engineering Philosophy for Limited Beings*. Cambridge, MA: Harvard University Press.

Zizzo, D. J. (2010). Experimenter demand effects in economic experiments. *Experimental* 13(1): 75–98.

CHAPTER 1
The Evidence on Human Sociality

1.1 Introduction

In this chapter, we review the evidence from several kinds of experimental games. These include the *ultimatum game*, the *dictator game*, the *gift exchange game*, and *public goods games* with and without punishments. In small group interaction, particularly in bilateral interaction, these experiments reject the notion that humans have purely self-regarding preferences. The behavior of a majority of people is consistent with other-regarding preferences and conditional reciprocity, although a significant minority exhibits purely self-regarding preferences. An important finding, from these experiments, is that the introduction of a small fraction of individuals with other-regarding preferences in a population of self-regarding individuals can result in a large change in the outcomes (Fischbacher et al., 2001; Fehr and Fischbacher, 2005; Fischbacher and Gächter, 2010).

Section 1.2.1 considers the ultimatum game, one of the most widely replicated experimental games in economics. In this two-player game, originally introduced by Güth et al. (1982), a *proposer* proposes to share a part of his endowment with a *responder*. The only action of the responder is to accept or reject. If accepted, the split proposed by the proposer is implemented, but if rejected, both get nothing. The prediction under self-regarding preferences is that the responder will be offered the smallest indivisible part of the endowment by the proposer. By contrast, the results are consistent with other-regarding preferences. Mean offers are 30–40% of the endowment and the median offers are 40–50% of the endowment.

These results continue to hold when the stakes are raised, say, up to an equivalent of about 62 hours of work (Slonim and Roth, 1998). But, for extremely large stakes, equivalent to 1600 hours of work, the responders' rejection rates fall but the median offer by the proposer is still about 20% of the endowment (Andersen et al., 2011). However, these stakes are too large relative to those that are commonly observed in real life among individuals. The evidence also indicates that there is some interaction between experience and the choices made in the ultimatum game but the self-regarding outcome is still not achieved. It would seem, therefore, that for most people other-regarding preferences are very hard to switch off and most of us may be intrinsically disposed to exhibit at least some altruism and reciprocity, even when the stakes are reasonably high. We postpone a formal definition of *reciprocity* to Volume 4, where we introduce the machinery of psychological game theory. Humans exhibit conditional reciprocity if they respond to the kind actions of others with kindness, and unkind actions with unkindness.

It has been alleged by some critics that subjects play prosocially in ultimatum games because they mistakenly apply repeated game heuristics to an essentially static but multi-stage game

(Binmore, 1998). However, the evidence from ultimatum games does not support this view (Fehr and Fischbacher, 2002). There is wide variation in the offers made by proposers and in the rejection rates of responders in different societies (Henrich et al., 2001). This cautions us against generalizing results too much from one culture to another. Interestingly, contrary to what students of economics may have been led to believe, offers and rejection rates are higher in societies where market exchange is more prevalent, although the direction of causality is difficult to establish with the available evidence. Indeed, market exchange requires a high degree of interpersonal trust especially because contracts may often be verbal and informal.

In Section 1.2.2, we consider the dictator game, which is a variant of the ultimatum game in which the responder has no actions, so the proposer's proposed split is always implemented. Nevertheless, proposers still make a mean offer of about 15–20% of the endowment in this case (Forsythe et al., 1994). This establishes two results. (i) Since the mean offer is lower relative to the ultimatum game, high offers in the ultimatum game arise partly for strategic reasons, i.e., to ensure acceptance of the offer by conditionally cooperative responders. (ii) Since the mean offers are strictly positive in the dictator game, proposers exhibit altruism.

Recent scholarship gives a more nuanced view of the results from dictator games but it also suggests that these results may not be portable to other games. A distinction has been drawn between *genuine altruists* and *reluctant altruists* (Dana et al., 2006). A reluctant altruist is someone who, for instance, may give money to a beggar should he unexpectedly run into one, but prefers to be on the other side of the road if he spots the beggar from a distance. There are many reasons why people may behave more altruistically in dictator games when they perceive they are being watched (Haley and Fessler, 2005). For instance, people may dislike falling short of the expectations of others about their actions (*guilt*). Emotions such as guilt may directly enter one's utility function. Formal modeling of these issues requires the machinery of *psychological game theory* that is considered in Volume 4 (Geanakoplos et al., 1989; Battigalli and Dufwenberg, 2009). Another potential explanation is that *identity* and *self-esteem* may be important determinants of the desire to appear fair to oneself and to others (Bénabou and Tirole, 2011).

In Section 1.2.3, we consider dictator game experiments that allow us to draw inferences about the rationality of subjects (Andreoni and Miller, 2002). Subjects in these experiments reveal that they have other-regarding preferences because they make strictly positive offers in the dictator game, yet the same subjects satisfy the *generalized axiom of revealed preference* (GARP). Hence, there is nothing irrational about other-regarding preferences.

Section 1.3 considers two related games, the *gift exchange game* and the *trust game*. We first consider the gift exchange game (Akerlof, 1982; Fehr et al., 1993; Fehr et al., 1997) in Section 1.3.1. A firm (player 1) makes a contract offer (w_b, e_n) to a worker (player 2) that specifies a binding wage level, w_b, and a non-binding effort level, e_n. The contract may offer *positive rents* to the worker, i.e., a wage (net of effort costs) that is greater than the outside option. If the contract is accepted, the worker chooses an actual effort level, e_a. Since the wage is binding, if workers have self-regarding preferences, they should shirk, i.e., $e_a = 0$. Anticipating this, firms should offer $w_b = 0$, so the rents of workers should be zero. By contrast, the experimental findings are that (i) workers are offered positive rents, and (ii) the rents and actual effort levels of workers are positively correlated. These results provide important confirmatory evidence for other-regarding preferences. In experiments that allow firms to punish shirking workers when $e_a < e_n$, results show that shirking is significantly reduced. If the firm were self-regarding, punishments should be ineffective because bygones are bygones in classical game theory.

The results of experiments in the gift exchange game have been extended in several directions. The effects of a wage decrease may have a more pronounced effect on effort as compared to a wage increase (Kube et al., 2006). This result is consistent with the findings of Bewley (1999) that firms are reluctant to cut wages in a recession in order to preserve the morale of its workers. As in the ultimatum game, there are cultural differences in the degree of sociality in the gift exchange game (Charness et al., 2004). Fehr et al. (1998) embed a gift exchange game within competitive markets where quality is endogenous. They find substantial departures from the competitive equilibrium outcome. Thus, current competitive equilibrium experiments (see Volume 4 of the book) that justify the equilibrium outcome may not be rich enough to deal with all the relevant aspects. The idea that sociality may survive and affect outcomes in competitive markets is one of the most important results in this volume.

When the gift exchange game is played with a firm and two or more workers, then additional insights emerge, depending on the relative pay and effort levels of the workers. It turns out that the degree of sociality in gift exchange games is influenced by the degree of *social comparisons* in the workplace (Gächter et al., 2012; Abeler et al., 2010; Cohn et al., 2011). The degree of sociality also depends on whether the workers' rent is monetary or non-monetary (Kube et al., 2012). Recent work explores the *duration effects* of the gift exchange relation. Gneezy and List (2006) conclude that the effects are short-lived. However, Bellemare and Shearer (2007) find that the short-lived effects only apply to workers who are hired on the spot market. By contrast, workers with longer tenure exhibit stronger reciprocity and long-lived effects of gift exchange. The predictions of the gift exchange game are confirmed by survey evidence (Dohmen et al., 2009).

In the gift exchange game, the total surplus is controlled by player 2, the worker, who exerts mutually beneficial effort. In Section 1.3.2, we consider the *trust game* in which player 1 determines the surplus in the relation (Berg et al., 1995). Both players are given an identical initial endowment, $e > 0$, by the experimenter. Player 1, the *trustor*, chooses an investment, $i : 0 \leq i \leq e$. The experimenter then multiplies this investment by a number $m \geq 1$ and passes it on to player 2, the *trustee*. The trustee voluntarily returns an amount of money $r : 0 \leq r \leq mi + e$ to the trustor. The numbers i (investment) and r (return) are, respectively, taken as measures of *trust* and *trustworthiness*. If players are self-regarding, then the subgame perfect outcome of the trust game is $i = r = 0$. By contrast, the meta-study of Johnson and Mislin (2011) shows that, pooling across all regions, trustors invest 50.2% of their endowment and trustees return 37.2% of the feasible amount. But there is significant regional heterogeneity (e.g., North Americans send back significantly more than Africans), older people are more trusting, students are less trusting, stakes do not appreciably affect the results, and the results depend on the value m. Overall, these results confirm the presence of other-regarding preferences and intrinsic reciprocity.

When subjects have an opportunity to examine the history of the other player in trust games, most players choose to do so. Interestingly, subjects may use the past levels of "trust" exhibited by other players to also infer their "trustworthiness," suggesting that these two human virtues may be correlated (Charness et al., 2011). In an interesting experiment, Eckel and Petrie (2011) offer subjects a chance to view a photograph of their opponent at a price. They find that there is a stable demand curve for these photographs. Conditional on having observed the opponent's picture, players behave more prosocially. White trustors discriminate between white and black trustees, investing more if the trustee is white. Black trustors do not discriminate. There are hardly any gender differences in prosocial behavior. On the whole, there appears to be an information value in a face.

Section 1.4 considers *public goods games*. Section 1.4.1 considers the basic model *without punishment* and Section 1.4.2 *with punishments*. In these games, a group of individuals simultaneously choose their level of contributions to a public good that is non-rival in consumption and non-excludable. For each extra unit of contributions to the public good, each individual receives an identical per unit benefit from the public good that is less than the private marginal cost of the contribution. If all contributors have self-regarding preferences, then the unique prediction of the model is that all players will *free-ride*, i.e., each player will contribute zero. In the model with punishments, there is a second stage in which, once the contributions are revealed, players can engage in costly punishments of other players. However, under self-regarding preferences, in the second stage, bygones are bygones, so players should not punish others. Without the threat of punishments, the predicted results with and without punishments are identical, i.e., everyone free-rides.

The evidence from public goods games, in Section 1.4.3, rejects the predictions of the self-regarding model, irrespective of whether punishments are available or not (Fehr and Gächter, 2000). In the absence of punishments, contributions typically start off from a high level and then gradually decay over successive rounds of the experiment. Self-regarding preferences cannot explain the pattern of decay, nor the reason why contributions start off from a high level, once the game is restarted. When punishments are allowed, then the outcome is close to the first best. Contributors punish non-contributors when the game is played in most Western countries where the *rule of law* and the *norm of civic cooperation* are high (Herrmann et al., 2008).

The evidence on various aspects of the public goods game is rich and extensive. The negative net effects of costly punishments that are sometimes found when the experiment is repeated over a few rounds, typically ten, are reversed when the experiment is repeated a large number of times, say, 50 rounds (Gächter et al., 2008). This informs our view of why punishments may have evolved; they are efficiency enhancing in enforcing social norms, provided the game is played over sufficiently many rounds. A combination of rewards and punishments elicits even greater cooperation as compared to the use of these instruments on their own (Sefton et al., 2007). Non-monetary punishments such as ostracization may also be effective in securing cooperation (Masclet et al., 2003; Cinyabuguma et al., 2005). Endogenous group formation in which players or the experimenter choose group members based on their past contributions influences contributions (Chaudhuri and Paichayontvijit, 2006; Gächter and Thöni, 2005; Page et al., 2005). Face to face communication enhances cooperation, but it is predicted to be ineffective under self-regarding preferences (Bochet et al., 2006). Publicly given, intergenerational, advice achieves nearly 90% of the socially optimal contributions (Chaudhuri et al., 2006).

In Section 1.4.4, we consider an explanation of the pattern of contributions in public goods games based on heterogeneous other-regarding preferences (Fischbacher et al., 2001; Fehr and Fischbacher, 2005; Fischbacher and Gächter, 2010). This model highlights two fundamental features of many social dilemma situations. (i) There is a mix of people with self-regarding and other-regarding preferences. (ii) There are profound implications of having even a small fraction of subjects with one type of preferences in the presence of the other type. Suppose that in a public goods game, a majority of the subjects have other-regarding preferences and we begin with initially high levels of cooperation. Then the presence of a minority of subjects with self-regarding preferences may drive contributions to low levels. The reason is that over successive rounds of the game, as contributors discover that some of the other players are free-riders, negative reciprocity kicks in, and they respond with successively lower contributions. Thus, we cannot conclude, by observing a lack of cooperation, that most players have self-regarding preferences.

In Section 1.4.5, we consider games in which two rival groups expend costly resources to win a contest and the prize is shared equally among the members of the winning group (Abbink et al., 2010). Thus, the prize has the nature of a public good. Examples include countries going to war, trade union strikes, and firms lobbying for a government contract. The winning probability, for any group, depends on the relative resources expended. If both groups increase their expenditures in the same proportion, their payoffs fall, but winning probabilities are unaltered. Thus, if the groups can coordinate, they can simultaneously, and proportionally, reduce their expenditures without altering winning probabilities, but increasing their payoffs; this is the sense in which the expenditures are unproductive. Each group, by incurring such expenditures, reduces the winning probability of the other group, a negative externality that it does not take into account. Empirical evidence shows that the unproductive expenditures are much higher than the Nash predictions.

Section 1.4.6 considers cultural differences in the nature of punishments in public goods games (Herrmann et al., 2008). In societies where the *rule of law* and the *norm of civic cooperation* is strong, one observes *prosocial punishments*, i.e., cooperators punish non-cooperators and this enhances prosociality. However, in other societies where one observes a weaker rule of law and a weaker norm of civic cooperation, one observes *antisocial punishments*, i.e., non-cooperators may punish the cooperators in revenge for having been punished in the past. This has adverse effects on the level of contributions in public goods games. One reason for the net negative effect on payoffs in the presence of antisocial punishments is that experiments may overstate the extent of punishment opportunities that we observe in society. For instance, societies typically engage in collective punishments through a legal code. It is quite likely that private punishments may be harsher relative to those prescribed by the legal code, however, experiments typically do not distinguish between the two. When one allows for credible punishments over a reasonably high number of rounds, then the net effect of punishments is positive (Gächter et al., 2008).

Section 1.4.7 gives some observations on the evolutionary sources of reciprocity. Volume 6 of the book considers this material in greater detail.

Section 1.5 considers the issue of the *external validity* of lab experiments as well as other possible *biases* in such experiments. The introduction to the book also gives a detailed consideration of these issues, so the treatment here minimizes the degree of overlap between the two. Several concerns have been raised about the validity of lab experiments (Levitt and List, 2007). Section 1.5.1 considers the criticism that the typical experiment is conducted with students, and more prosocial students may have been self-selected into the experiments. Being watched by the experimenter may bias the behavior of subjects in experiments (*experimental scrutiny effects*). Furthermore, students may deliberately appear more prosocial, anticipating that this is what the experimenter desires (*experimenter demand effects*). An increasingly robust finding in the emerging experimental literature is that the student population is less prosocial as compared to the general population (Falk et al., 2013; Carpenter and Seki, 2011; Fréchette, 2015). If anything, this biases the results in favor of the textbook self-regarding model. More prosocial students do not self-select themselves into experiments (Cleave et al., 2012). Experimental scrutiny does not necessarily lead to more prosocial behavior (Barmettler et al., 2012).

In any case, even if experimental scrutiny were important, as is suggested in several experimental papers, then it too makes a powerful case for the importance of other-regarding preferences. If the presence of a stranger (the experimenter) in the room switches on other-regarding preferences, then it is quite plausible that most human activity, which is carried out in the direct presence or indirect presence[1] of others is similarly affected. It would appear that the negative implications of experimental scrutiny may have been exaggerated, even if such scrutiny were important.

---

[1] For instance, a party that is unfairly treated in a bilateral exchange can disseminate such information to others, including legal institutions if the behavior is illegal.

A rapidly expanding body of empirical literature, that we consider in Section 1.5.2, supports the external validity of lab experiments (Camerer, 2015). Japanese fishermen who operate in a collective manner in the field (sharing of costs and the fish catch) are also more prosocial when they play the public goods game in the lab (Carpenter and Seki, 2011). The conditional reciprocity of fishermen estimated in the lab is a significant predictor of their field productivity. Subjects who reveal more self-regarding preferences in the lab are also less likely to increase their effort in the real world, following a wage increase (Cohn et al., 2012).

Shrimpers and fishermen in northeastern Brazil who behave more selfishly in public goods games also behave more opportunistically in the field (Fehr and Leibbrandt, 2011). More prosocial behavior in the lab is correlated with better market performance (Leibbrandt, 2012). In Ethiopia, subjects who cooperate more in the public goods game also behave in a less opportunistic manner in their real-world activity that involves forest management (Rustagi et al., 2010). A greater degree of trustworthiness in trust games predicts a greater likelihood of repaying loans in a microcredit program in Peru (Karlan, 2005). Chicago MBA students who exhibit more trustworthiness in the lab are also more likely to make charitable donations (Baran et al., 2010). Similar results are true for Swiss students (Benz and Meier, 2008).

In a game played between two players, if a third party who has no material stakes in the game, is willing to engage in costly punishments and rewards, then it exhibits *indirect reciprocity* (Gintis, 2009). In the final part of the chapter, in Section 1.6, we consider the extensive evidence in favor of indirect reciprocity (Seinen and Schram, 2001; Engelmann and Fischbacher, 2009; Fehr and Fischbacher, 2004).

1.2 Ultimatum and dictator games

1.2.1 *The ultimatum game*

The *ultimatum game,* introduced by Güth et al. (1982), is played between two players, a *proposer* and a *responder*. The *proposer* is given an integer monetary amount x by the experimenter. Suppose that the smallest indivisible amount of money is one cent. The proposer offers a share $s \in \{0, 0.01, 0.02, \ldots, x.00\}$ to the *responder*. If the responder accepts the offer, then the proposer's initial offer is implemented and the dollar payoffs of the proposer and the responder are, respectively, $y_P = x - s$, and $y_R = s$. If the responder rejects the offer, the respective dollar payoffs are $y_P = 0$, and $y_R = 0$.

If both players have self-regarding preferences, then in the subgame perfect outcome, the respective dollar payoffs are $y_P^* = x - 0.01$, $y_R^* = 0.01$. If the amount $x is infinitely divisible, then the subgame perfect outcome is $y_P^* = x$, $y_R^* = 0$.[2] The experimental results do not support this prediction. The results have been summarized in several places.[3] The gist of the experimental results is as follows. (1) The mean offer is $s = 0.3x$ to $0.4x$. (2) The median offer is $s = 0.4x$ to $0.5x$. (3) There are rarely any unfair offers ($s = 0$ or $0.1x$) or over-fair offers ($s > 0.5x$). (4) Low offers are often rejected.

---

[2] If the amount $x were infinitely divisible with α being the smallest equal part, then the subgame perfect outcome is $y_P^* = \lim_{\alpha \to 0}(x - \alpha) = x$, $y_R^* = \lim_{\alpha \to 0}\alpha = 0$.
[3] See, for instance, Camerer (2003), Camerer and Thaler (1995), Thaler (1988), Güth and Tietz (1990), Roth et al. (1991).

These results continue to hold in several studies conducted in high stakes games. For instance, Cameron (1999) conducted high stakes experiments in Indonesia in which x ranged from 5,000 to 200,000 rupiahs (about three months' wages). The mean offer was $s = 0.4x$ to $0.45x$. Respondents were more likely to accept offers when stakes were high while the behavior of the proposers hardly changed.[4]

Slonim and Roth (1998) consider experiments with varying stakes in the Slovak Republic in which x equals 2.5, 12.5, and 62.5 hours of wages respectively. The rejection rates in the low and the high stakes conditions are similar in the first round and fall slightly in the high stakes condition by round ten, the last round of the experiment. This indicates that there is some interaction of experience and stakes in the rejection rates of offers. However, the mean and median offers are very similar in the low and the high stakes conditions. Exit interviews show that the main motive for the rejection of low but positive offers is that responders find them to be *unfair*.

Carpenter et al. (2005) find that for moderately high stakes, a given proportional increase in stakes leads to a much less proportionate fall in the offers made by the proposer.[5] For instance, a ten-fold increase in stakes from $10 to $100 leads to a halving of the median offer from 40% to 20%, and to an even lower proportionate fall in the average offer from 33% to 25%. Andersen et al. (2011) raise the stakes beyond the levels of most previous studies. Their study, carried out in a northeastern Indian village, allowed stakes to vary between 20 rupees to 20,000 rupees (1.6 hours of work to 1,600 hours of work).[6] They find that although the median offer by the proposer is to give 20% of the share to the respondent, the rejection rate falls with an increase in the stake.[7] As the authors correctly point out, these results do not invalidate the practical applicability of earlier results because one does not typically encounter real-life situations with such high stakes and the bulk of market transactions are low stakes transactions.

The ultimatum game has been mostly played with university students. In an interesting study, Henrich et al. (2001) explore cross-cultural variations in the ultimatum game. In this study, evidence was gathered from 15 small-scale societies across 4 continents and 12 countries. The predictions of the ultimatum game with self-regarding preferences are not borne out in any of these societies. The mean offers were quite variable (26–58%) relative to experiments done previously with university students where the mean offers are 43–48%. In some societies, even low offers were rarely rejected, while in others, even extremely generous offers were rejected because in such societies, the rejection of a gift is considered tantamount to the rejection of subordination.

The two main factors that enhanced sociality in the results of Henrich et al. were the following. (1) *Market integration* in the community, i.e., the predominance of buying/selling and working for a wage. (2) *Cooperation in production*, i.e., whether production is carried out on an individual basis or it is cooperative, e.g., in a team environment. These two factors enhanced sociality in the sense of higher offers by proposers and accounted for 66% of the variation in the outcomes in the ultimatum game. On average, people from the least market-integrated communities offered about one-quarter of the stake. By contrast, those from the most integrated communities, such as rural Missouri, offered roughly half. Thus, *markets may foster sociality*, an idea that might seem surprising to some students of mainstream economics because this is hardly ever highlighted.

---

[4] Similar findings are reported in Fehr et al. (2014) and Hoffman et al. (1996).
[5] See also List and Cherry (2008).
[6] By way of comparison, in the study by Slonim and Roth (1998), the highest stake level is 62.5 hours of wages.
[7] In one condition, they find that at the highest level of the stake the rejection rate falls to 0%.

The results of the ultimatum game are sensitive to how much proposers feel that they are entitled to their endowments—a sort of *entitlement norm*. A feeling of entitlement may be created by simply announcing an entitlement (Hoffman and Spitzer, 1982; Cherry et al., 2002), or by having a contest to choose proposers to play a high stakes ultimatum game (List and Cherry, 2000), or by having the proposer earn the endowment (Parrett, 2006). The greater is the entitlement offered to the proposers, the lower is their offer to the responder. Harrison and McCabe (1996) find that the outcomes in an ultimatum game depend on the history of offers and rejections in previous rounds of the game, which might serve to establish a *fairness norm*.

Binmore et al. (1995) and Roth and Erev (1995) have used learning models to explain the results of the ultimatum game in terms of purely self-regarding preferences. The basic argument is that there is an asymmetry between the learning propensities of proposers and responders when the proposers make low offers. The payoff loss to a responder from rejecting a low offer is very low but for a proposer it is very high. Hence, proposers quickly learn not to make very low offers and responders learn very slowly not to reject very low offers. Over time, which can involve thousands of iterations, the behavior with self-regarding preferences can be shown to converge close to the subgame perfect outcome ($y_P^* = x$, $y_R^* = 0$). There are two problems with this approach. First, there is no guarantee that convergence takes place in any sensible amount of time. Second, the structure of the ultimatum game is incredibly simple and it seems unlikely that subjects are making systematic mistakes of this sort.

Binmore (1998) explains the results of the ultimatum game in terms of social norms. The idea is that in the real world, subjects in experiments may be used to playing repeated games. Hence, in the laboratory, they may mistakenly apply repeated game heuristics to the static ultimatum game and cooperate even when the subgame perfect outcome requires them not to cooperate. It is likely that individuals, in their role as subjects in experiments, bring with them real-world norms into the lab (see, for instance, the variation in offers in different cultures in the study by Henrich et al., 2001). However, whether subjects mistake a static context (the ultimatum game) for a repeated game is an empirical question. And the empirical evidence rejects this view. The same subjects in experiments behave very differently in the lab when they play static games and when they play repeated games where reputation building is important.[8] Furthermore, neuroeconomic evidence does not support the view that subjects make mistakes in these simple games.[9]

Fehr and Fischbacher (2003) conducted experiments with the ultimatum game in which ten proposers and ten responders met each other over successive rounds. No players are paired more than once. In the *reputation condition*, the past behavior of the responders is made public, while in the *no-reputation condition* it is private information to the responder. In the reputation condition, responders have an opportunity to develop a reputation for being tough by rejecting low offers, which is costly in the short run. The gain from such an action is the possibility that future proposers may make high offers to them. The average acceptance thresholds were significantly higher in the reputation condition relative to the no-reputation condition.

Some related issues in ultimatum games are also considered in the section on bargaining games in Volume 4.

---

[8] See, for instance, Andreoni and Miller (1993), Engelmann and Fischbacher (2009), Fehr and Fischbacher (2003), and Gächter and Falk (2002).

[9] A region of the brain, the dorsal striatum, associated with the reward circuits of the brain is activated when subjects punish behavior that is perceived to be unfair; see, for instance, de Quervain et al. (2004). Knoch et al. (2006) show that an impairment of the prefrontal cortex that is associated with rational thinking reduces the ability of subjects to reject unfair offers.

1.2.2 The dictator game

It is useful to compare the predictions of the ultimatum game with the *dictator game* for additional insights. The dictator game is similar to the ultimatum game except that the responder (sometimes referred to as the *receiver*) is passive and has no actions. Thus, the dictator's offer is always implemented. If all individuals had purely self-regarding preferences, then the prediction is that the dictator will keep all the money and offer none to the receiver. On the other hand, a strictly positive, but relatively lower, offer in the dictator game would indicate the following. (1) Proposers are inequity averse, or altruistic.[10] (2) Higher offers in the ultimatum game are made partly for strategic concerns such as fear of rejection, say, because receivers may have inequity averse preferences.

Forsythe et al. (1994) find that proposers' offers are higher in ultimatum games relative to dictator games. They find that the average offers made by the proposers in dictator games are between 10% and 25%. While these offers are lower, on average, relative to those found in ultimatum games, the offers are still significantly higher than zero. The results of this study have been replicated many times. The interested reader can consult Camerer (2003, p. 57) for a useful table of results. The mean transfer, across studies, made by the proposer in dictator games is roughly 15–20% of the endowment.

List (2007) broadens the action set of the proposer in dictator games to allow for both positive and negative transfers. This is achieved by first giving an endowment to the proposer and the respondent. Negative transfers mean that the proposer is allowed to take money from the respondent's endowment. The main finding is that this reduces the average and median offers made by the proposer, yet the equilibrium outcome under self-regarding preferences (i.e., the proposer makes a offer of zero) does not arise. Levitt and List (2007) explain these findings in terms of the attempts by subjects in experiments to find *contextual clues* in the game in order to apply appropriate norms. For instance, the expansion of the action set of the proposer in dictator games to negative transfers, reduces the scope of what might be construed as a self-regarding offer.

Haley and Fessler (2005) find that when dictators make their proposal where they perceive that they are being watched, say, merely by having pictures of eyes in the room, then they tended to make more generous offers. Similar results are found in a related context, where a picture of eyes elicited greater voluntary contributions, relative to a picture of flowers (Bateson et al., 2006). However, in games with minimal strategic elements, such as in the trust game, these results do not survive. No effect of the eyes cue was found for either prosocial individuals or self-regarding individuals in the trust game experiments of Fehr and Schneider (2010).

In general, there is wide variation in the offers made in dictator games that are quite sensitive to simple framing effects. These results point to the high degree of sensitivity of the results under dictator games to framing effects and experimental protocol relative to those of, say, the ultimatum games. Despite its popularity, the dictator game might not be a particularly good game to test alternative theories that require even a modicum of strategic interaction (Fehr and Schmidt, 2006).

Dana et al. (2006) consider a variant of the dictator game in which dictators were given an initial amount of $10. In the first experiment, once the dictators had made their choices, but

---

[10] Selten and Ockenfels (1998) consider a modified dictator game, called the *solidarity game*. In this game, players had an ex-ante chance to be dictators and receivers and outcomes were risky. They find it difficult to explain the behavior of a set of their subjects (36% of the total) using altruism alone.

before these choices were communicated to receivers, dictators were given the option of exiting the game with $9. If dictators wished to exit the game in this manner, receivers were not informed of the dictator's offer, or the game they were playing. Despite the fact that dictators could get a higher payoff by playing the dictator game than exiting in this manner, a significant percentage, 28%, choose the exit option.

In a second experiment, in the private condition, receivers did not know if the money offered to them came from the dictator or the experimenter, thus, the dictator's intentions are not revealed. In this case, 1 out of 24 dictators exited. However, when the first experiment was replicated, 9 out of 24 dictators exited. These results show that at least for a significant minority of the dictator subjects, the offers may reflect their desire not to appear overly self-regarding to the receivers.

Dana et al. (2007) introduce a degree of opacity in a variant of the usual dictator game. In the *baseline treatment* with the usual and fully transparent dictator game, the dictator can choose one of two actions, A or B with respective payoffs (6,1) and (5,5) (the first payoff is the dictator's and the second is the receiver's). Thus, by accepting a small reduction in his own payoff by a unit, the dictator can enhance the payoff of the receiver by four units. In the *hidden payoff treatment*, the payoff of the receiver is uncertain, so the respective payoffs from the actions A and B are shown to be (6,?) and (5,?). All subjects were told that the payoffs from A and B are equally likely to be either (i) (6,1) and (5,5), or (ii) (6,5) and (5,1). In each case, the proposer can, costlessly and voluntarily, choose to reveal the payoffs by clicking a button on a computer screen but this information could not be seen by the receiver. Altruistic motives, for instance inequity aversion, suggest that the dictator would choose B in case (i) and A in case (ii).[11]

If inequity aversion is the dominant motive, then the proportion of dictators who choose B in the baseline treatment should be the same as the proportion of dictators who click to reveal the payoffs in the hidden payoff treatment. A high proportion, 74% (14 out of 19), of the dictators in the baseline treatment chose B. This could be either because they are inequity averse or that they did not wish to appear non-altruistic. However, in the hidden payoff treatment, 56% of the proposers did not choose to click the button to reveal the payoffs. The difference in the proportion of dictators who choose to ensure a generous offer in the two treatments is statistically different. Thus, the authors conclude that the desire to appear fair to others and possibly to oneself is an important determinant in dictator games, which cannot be accommodated by current models of inequity aversion. These results resonate with the observation of why one might cross to the other side of the street to avoid a beggar. In conjunction, these findings suggest that in dictator games, many dictators may be *reluctant altruists*. One way in which these findings and those on antisocial punishments in public goods games (see below) can be explained is by a more explicit theoretical model of the microfoundations of human identity and morality. For progress in this direction, see Bénabou and Tirole (2011).

However, it has proved hard to replicate results on moral wiggle room in games where some strategic interaction is involved. For instance, van der Weele et al. (2014) show that moral wiggle room in the trust and the moonlighting games does not reduce reciprocity. This is another instance of why results in the dictator game are quite special and non-robust with respect to other domains.

Ockenfels and Werner (2012) conduct Internet experiments with a large, diverse, subject pool, using the dictator game. The size of the cake that the dictator shares can be small or large. In the

---

[11] Some may argue that this substantially alters the dictator game, the essence of which is that the respondent's payoff equals the proposer's endowment minus the amount the proposer wishes to keep for himself.

Noinfo treatment, the receiver never discovers the size of the cake; he only observes the dictator's offer. In the Info treatment, after the dictator has made his offer, the receiver is informed about the size of the cake. In the Noinfo condition, when the cake is *large*, the dictator typically offers a share to the receiver that is less than one half of the *small cake*. Hence, the dictator hides behind the "small cake effect." By contrast, when the cake is small there is very little difference between the results in the two treatments. These results suggest that giving in dictator games is influenced by second order beliefs, i.e., what the dictator believes the receiver believes he will get. It may be the case that the dictator is overcome by guilt if the dictator believes that the receiver believes that he will get more than the dictator actually gives (Battigalli and Dufwenberg, 2007). In other contexts, several papers have demonstrated an *audience effect* on giving.[12] These are all cases in which second order beliefs influence one's action. The appropriate framework to rigorously analyze these concerns is psychological game theory (see Volume 4).

Andreoni and Bernheim (2009) consider the norm of sharing 50–50 in dictator games. About 20–30% of the dictators offer a 50–50 split to the receiver. This can be explained by the dictator's desire to appear fair to the receiver, particularly if there are shared social norms about equitable splits. It is important to consider the influence of social norms of sharing in many of the experimental games on other-regarding preferences, an area that is likely to gather more steam in the future.

Lotz et al. (2013) ask if there is a fraction of *genuine altruists* as distinct from *reluctant altruists*, and if we can predict the nature of altruism? They invoke an underlying measure of altruism known as justice sensitivity (JS) that has been used by several psychologists to explain individual-level differences in behavior (Schmitt et al., 1995; Schmitt et al., 2010). Subjects are asked 40 questions and asked to rate each on a scale of 0 (strongly disagree) to 5 (strongly agree). Examples of questions include the following: I cannot easily bear it when people profit unilaterally from me; It bothers me when someone gets something they don't deserve; I have a bad conscience when I receive a reward that someone else has earned. These responses are used to derive measures of sensitivity to becoming a victim of injustice (JS_{victim}), sensitivity of a neutral observer ($JS_{observer}$), sensitivity of an actual perpetrator ($JS_{perpetrator}$), and sensitivity of a passive beneficiary ($JS_{beneficiary}$). The last three measures are combined into a single measure—JS_{others}. The main findings are as follows. At the aggregate level, the authors replicate the result that dictators wish to avoid appearing unfair. However, at the individual level, those with a high JS_{others} score are genuine altruists with stable other-regarding preferences and those with a low JS_{others} score are reluctant altruists. This appears to be an important advance in the literature; it not only suggests a more nuanced view of the dictator game but could also help reconcile conflicting results in this game.

In Volume 7 of the book, in the chapter on emotions, we make the distinction between *deliberative choices* and *automatic choices*. Deliberative choices involve the cognitive part of the brain, the prefrontal cortex (system II), that takes account of the long-run consequences, the costs and benefits, and the morality of one's action. By contrast, automatic choices are associated with the more primitive part of the brain, the limbic system (system I); these are quick, instinctive, reactive, pre-programmed choices that may respond to a range of emotions such a fear, anger, and anxiety. Are the choices of players in ultimatum and dictator games deliberative or automatic? One branch of the literature argues that preferences for fairness are deliberative choices. In

---

[12] See, for instance, Soetevent (2005) in the context of charitable giving in churches and Rege and Telle (2004) in the context of public goods games.

support, this literature cites evidence that kindergarten children make more self-regarding choices (an automatic response), while adults are more likely to make other-regarding choices. Hence, fairness preferences may be acquired. A second literature, that is neurobiological and behavioral, suggests that fairness preferences are an automatic response in adulthood.

Neither of the two systems, system I or system II, has primacy over the other. However, system II can use a scarce, but easily depleted, resource, *willpower*, in order to control system I. Hence, willpower-depleted choices are more likely to be in greater conformity with system I. In Halali et al. (2013), subjects first participate in 20 incongruent trials of a *Stroop task*. For instance, they may be shown a red colored ink that is named blue. Subjects then have to suppress their automatic response of saying "red" by saying "blue" instead. This is presumed to deplete their willpower (particularly if the questions are posed rapidly). The evidence suggests that their automatic responses can then be elicited.

In the ultimatum game, following depletion of willpower, proposers make relatively fairer offers. Furthermore, the difference in the choices made under systems I and II (corresponding to relative depletion of willpower) is statistically significant. There are two possibilities. (P1) The automatic response is fear of rejection by the receiver, so the offers are higher. (P2) The automatic response is more fair as compared to a deliberative response that is more self-regarding. But if P2 is the correct explanation, then we should also observe more fair offers in the dictator game. By contrast, the automatic response in dictator games is to make more self-regarding offers. This implies that P1 is the more likely explanation, i.e., the automatic response is strategic—fear of rejection. The authors also confirm similar findings for receivers in other work.

1.2.3 Rationality of other-regarding preferences in dictator games

The rationality of other-regarding preferences hinges on whether they are complete and transitive. An obvious test is to observe the relevant restrictions on actual demand curves, such as the Slutsky restrictions on the cross partial derivatives of Hicksian demands. If this test is satisfied, then the demand curves are the outcome of a utility maximization exercise. But in actual practice, it is hard to observe demand curves.

An alternative approach, using *revealed preference*, is to directly observe the market prices $(p_1, p_2, \ldots, p_n)$ and the associated levels of demands $(x_1^*, x_2^*, \ldots, x_n^*)$.[13] Thus, our observations are a sequence of price–quantity pairs $(p_i, x_i^*)_{i=1}^n$. A utility function, u, *rationalizes* these observations if for any $i = 1, \ldots, n$ we have $u(x_i^*) \geq u(x_i)$ for all x_i such that $p_i x_i^* \geq p_i x_i$. Thus, x_i^* is revealed to be preferred to all other consumption bundles, x_i, that the consumer is able to afford at the price p_i. In this case, we can infer that the data was generated by a utility maximization process. Hence, the underlying preferences are rational, i.e., complete and transitive.

A sufficient condition to guarantee rationality and, hence, the existence of a utility function that rationalizes the data is the *generalized axiom of revealed preference* (GARP). Suppose that choices are generated by utility maximization. Suppose also that we observe that at price p_i, consumption bundle x_i^* was chosen when another bundle $\bar{x}$ was available and affordable, i.e., $p_i x_i^* \geq p_i \bar{x}$. In this case, x_i^* is *directly revealed preferred* to $\bar{x}$; we write this as $x_i^* D \bar{x}$. If choices were generated by utility maximization, then we must have $u(x_i^*) \geq u(\bar{x})$.

We may also, in our data, observe a series of binary choices of the following form: $x_i^* D x_j$, $x_j D x_k, \ldots, x_n D \bar{x}$. In this case, we say that x_i^* is *revealed preferred* to $\bar{x}$; we write this as $x_i^* R \bar{x}$.

---

[13] Each x_i^* may be a vector, in which case the corresponding price, p_i, is also a vector.

If choices were indeed generated by utility maximization, then we may again conclude that $u(x_i^*) \geq u(\bar{x})$.

Suppose that we impose the restriction of local non-satiation on the utility function, i.e., $u(x) < u(x+\varepsilon), \varepsilon > 0$. In this case, if data are generated by utility maximization, the observation $p_i x_i^* > p_i \bar{x}$ would imply that $u(x_i^*) > u(\bar{x})$. In particular, it cannot be that $u(x_i^*) = u(\bar{x})$. For if it were, then, given $p_i x_i^* > p_i \bar{x}$, we can find some x in the neighborhood of $\bar{x}$ that is affordable, $p_i x_i^* \geq p_i x$, yet, it gives higher utility, $u(x_i^*) = u(\bar{x}) < u(x)$, on account of non-satiation. But this contradicts that x_i^* was chosen at a price p_i.

Now suppose that we observe that at price p_i, consumption bundle x_i^* was chosen when another bundle $\bar{x}$ was strictly cheaper, i.e., $p_i x_i^* > p_i \bar{x}$. In this case, we say that x_i^* is *strictly directly revealed preferred* to $\bar{x}$; we write this as $x_i^* SD \bar{x}$.

> **Definition 1.1** *(Generalized axiom of revealed preference, GARP): Suppose that x_i^* is chosen at a price p_i when $\bar{x}$ is available and affordable. If $x_i^* R \bar{x}$, then it cannot be the case that $\bar{x} SD x_i^*$.*

Andreoni and Miller (2002) test for GARP in the dictator game, using the following method. Suppose that a dictator is given an income y and he wishes to propose the split (y_P, y_R). For every unit of income that the dictator wishes to give to the responder, he needs to give $p y_R$ units to the experimenter, where $p > 0$. The experimenter then credibly gives y_R units to the responder. The variable p may be thought of as the price of giving. If the dictator has other-regarding preferences, then he solves a standard utility maximization problem in which he maximizes $u(y_P, y_R)$, subject to the budget constraint $y_P + p y_R = y$. The levels of income used were $y = 40, 60, 75, 80, 100$, and the prices used were $p = 0.25, 0.33, 0.5, 1, 2, 3, 4$.

Andreoni and Miller (2002) use Afriat's *critical cost-efficiency index* (CCEI) to measure whether a violation of GARP is severe or not. The CCEI gives an indication of how much of the budget must be shrunk in order to rationalize the data. The closer the index is to 1, the less severe are the violations. Out of 176 subjects, there were 18 violations of GARP, i.e., the choices of 18 subjects cannot be rationalized by utility maximization. Based on the CCEI index, there were only four violations. Random choice, on the other hand, would have led more than three-quarters of the subjects to violate GARP. With the exception of three subjects, the observed data can be rationalized by a quasiconcave utility function. This evidence suggests that the subjects are rational and one can find a utility function that rationalizes the choices that they have made.

At a price of $p = 1$, the dictator gave away, on average, about 23% of the endowment, which is similar to the results in Forsythe et al. (1994). There is heterogeneity among the subjects and only a small minority are unconditional altruists. A little less than a quarter of the subjects behaved as if they had self-regarding preferences, 14.2% of the subjects tried to equalize their payoffs with the other player (Leontief preferences), and 6.2% of the subjects had preferences of the perfect substitutes form.

Results along similar lines, i.e., consistency with GARP and heterogeneity at the individual level, when CES utility functions are fitted to individual-level data in dictator games, are also reported by Fisman et al. (2007). In a more recent study, Iriberri and Rey-Biel (2013) also implement a similar framework to that in Andreoni and Miller (2002) and Fisman et al. (2007) in dictator games. They find that self-regarding preferences are the most common (47%), followed by inequity averse preferences (21%), social welfare maximizers (19%), and competitive preferences (13%).

Volk et al. (2012) elicit contribution rates of subjects in public goods games (see Section 1.4) at three different dates: in the base period, and 2.5 months and 5 months from the base period. They classify subjects into three categories: conditional cooperators, free-riders, and others. At the aggregate level, the distribution of the level of cooperation is unchanged at the three dates. This is important because most inferences in public goods games are drawn at the aggregate level (see Section 1.4 below). There is variation in intertemporal stability of preferences at the individual level. While two-thirds of the subjects stay in their category at all three dates, a third switch categories.[14] Personality traits, in particular the trait of being *agreeable*, is a significant predictor of temporal stability of preferences at the level of the individual.

In conclusion, there is nothing irrational about other-regarding preferences.

1.3 Gift exchange and trust games

1.3.1 *The gift exchange game*

The *gift exchange game* was introduced by Fehr et al. (1993). Its objective was to test for the presence of *intrinsic reciprocity*, using a labor market setting. It drew on the insights of Akerlof (1982) and Akerlof and Yellen (1990), who had already explored departures from competitive market outcomes in macroeconomic models by using notions of fairness and reciprocity in labor markets. In exploring the effects of wage rates greater than the market clearing wage rates, as in models of efficiency wages, Akerlof (1982, p. 544) writes: "On the worker's side, the 'gift' given is work in excess of the minimum work standard; and on the firm's side the 'gift' given is wages in excess of what these women could receive if they left their current jobs." These critical insights pervade the literature that followed.

Consider the gift exchange game used in the experiments conducted by Fehr et al. (1997). Subjects in experiments were assigned to one of two roles: a principal or an agent. The identities of trading partners were not revealed to any experimental subject, ruling out repeated game effects and any attempts to build a reputation for cooperative behavior. Principals offer a contract (w_b, e_n) to agents that specifies a *binding* wage level, w_b, and a *non-binding* effort level, e_n. Since a binding effort level cannot be specified, there is contractual incompleteness in the model. The wage level can be chosen from the set $\{0, 1, 2, \ldots, 100\}$, while the effort level can be chosen from the set $\{0.1, 0.2, \ldots, 1\}$. Let e_a be the *actual* effort level chosen by the agent. The payoff of the principal is $100 e_a - w_b$. The payoff of the agent is $w_b - c(e_a)$, where $c(e_a)$ is an increasing and convex function of effort with the endpoints given by $c(0.1) = 0$ and $c(1) = 18$. The outside option of the agent is zero.

If all agents possess self-regarding preferences, then the outcome is very simple. Because the effort level is non-contractible, each self-regarding agent chooses the lowest effort level, $e_a = 0.1$. The rational, forward-looking, principal correctly anticipates this, so he offers a wage $w_b = 0$, which ensures that the individual rationality constraint of the agent binds, i.e., $w_b = c(0.1) = 0$.

Suppose that the agent has *other-regarding preferences* or *intrinsic reciprocity*, and that this is known to the principal. In this case, the principal anticipates that the intrinsic reciprocity of the agent would induce him to reciprocate higher wage offers with higher actual effort levels. If the cost of eliciting higher effort is not too high, then it may be optimal to offer $w_b > 0$ and, on account of gift exchange, one would expect to observe $e_a > 0.1$.

---

[14] These estimates on stability are higher than some of the other estimates; see, for instance, Muller et al. (2008).

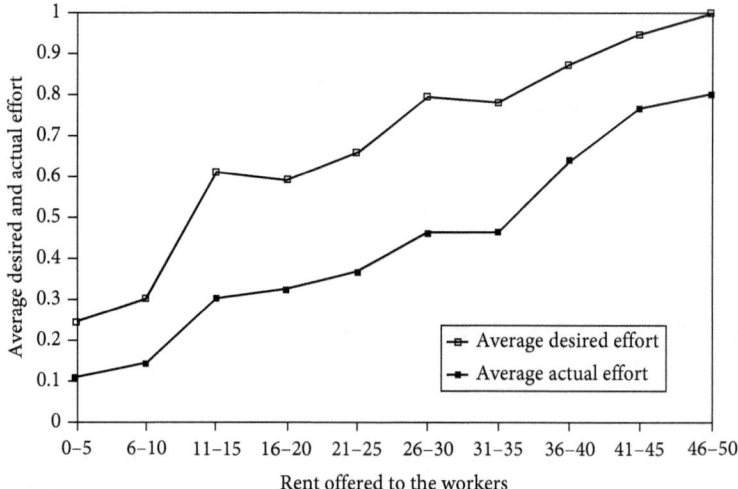

Figure 1.1 The relation between effort and rent in the gift exchange game.
Source: Reprinted from European Economic Review, 46: 687–724. Fehr, E. and Falk, A. "Psychological foundations of incentives." © 2002, with permission from Elsevier.

The experimental results are depicted in Figure 1.1, where the vertical axis measures the actual effort, e_a, and the non-binding contractual effort level, e_n. The horizontal axis measures the level of rents, $w_b - c(e_n)$, embodied in a contract. The following conclusions arise.

1. There is a direct relation between e_a and $w_b - c(e_n)$. Hence, workers respond to higher rents by actually working harder. These results are consistent with at least some fraction of the workers having a preference for intrinsic reciprocity but are consistent with principals having either self-regarding or other-regarding preferences. (a) Even principals with self-regarding preferences who are aware that the agents have intrinsic reciprocity will wish to tap into such reciprocity by offering higher wages that elicit higher effort, provided that eliciting effort is not too costly. (b) So long as a high enough fraction of workers has intrinsic reciprocity, the principal will have an incentive to offer rents, i.e., wages greater than the market clearing level even if other workers have purely self-regarding preferences.
2. Conditional on any given level of rents, there is some shirking, i.e., $e_a < e_n$.
3. There is a significant fraction of self-regarding agents who put in the minimum effort level, $e_a = 0.1$. Fehr and Falk (2002) summarize the weight of the evidence from several studies and suggest an indicative figure for the fraction of self-regarding subjects that lies between 40% and 60% percent. The remaining fraction is accounted for by subjects who have other-regarding preferences.[15]

Suppose now that, ex-post, the principals can punish workers who work less than the contracted level, $e_a < e_n$, and reward those who work more than the contracted level, $e_a \geq e_n$. If all principals had purely self-regarding preferences, then introducing such an option should

---

[15] For an estimation of the relative proportions of self-regarding and other-regarding economic agents, see also Berg et al. (1995), Fehr and Falk (1999), McCabe et al. (1998), Abbink et al. (2000).

have no effect. This is because at the end of the game, bygones are bygones and punishments do not directly increase the material utility of individuals. However, if principals are believed to have other-regarding preferences or intrinsic reciprocity, then agents rationally believe that they could be punished for underperforming.[16] Hence, we may expect an increase in actual effort, e_a. The main results in Fehr et al. (1997) are as follows.

1. If $e_a < e_n$, then principals punish in 68% of the cases.
2. If $e_a \geq e_n$, then principals reward in 41% of the cases.
3. Workers seem to anticipate the principal's reciprocity. When $e_a < e_n$, workers anticipate being punished in 54% of the cases. When $e_a > e_n$, workers expect to be rewarded in 98% of the cases.
4. The presence of rewards and punishments decreases shirking from 83% of the cases to only 26% and increases the average level of effort from 0.37 to 0.65.

The gift exchange game has been replicated a large number of times. The general finding of a positive relation between mean effort level and the rent offered by the principal is quite robust.[17] Many studies, some reviewed below, indicate that the positive relation between effort and wages is less strong than originally thought but that there is a much stronger reduction in effort following a wage decrease. Thus, wage decreases appear to be much more costly relative to the gains to firms from equivalent increases in wages. For instance, the elasticity of effort with respect to a wage increase is 0.15 in Gneezy and List (2006) and 0.30 in Kube et al. (2006). However, the elasticity is 0.82 for a wage decrease in Kube et al. (2006).

Fehr et al. (2009) conjecture two reasons for the finding of a weak positive effect of rents on effort in the empirical literature. First, the sample sizes are quite small. Second, the base wage over which rents are offered is already too high. Evidence indicates that workers are more likely to make a greater increase in effort if the base wage is perceived as unfair.

Falk (2007) ran the following field experiment with a non-student population. A Swiss charity made two different kinds of gifts in solicitation letters sent out to 10,000 potential donors. In the baseline case of the *no gift condition*, no gift was included. In the *small gift condition*, the request for donations was accompanied by a single card from a child in Bangladesh. In the *large gift condition*, four such cards were included. The relative frequency of donations in the no gift condition, small gift condition, and the large gift condition was respectively 12%, 14%, and 21%. These differences were statistically significant, which confirms the insights of the gift exchange game. Further, there was insignificant intertemporal substitution in the sense that larger donations in the current period did not crowd out future donations.

Indirect evidence of gift exchange is also found in situations where strikes or other labour relation disruptions in companies lead to a perception of unfairness on the workers' part. If workers perceive that they are unfairly treated, they then tend to reduce effort. Such indirect evidence has been found by Mas (2006) at the New Jersey police department, Mas (2008) at Caterpillar, Krueger and Mas (2004) at Bridgestone/Firestone tires, and Lee and Rupp (2007) for airline wage settlements.

---

[16] Principals may well have such preferences. Fehr and List (2004) use the trust game in Fehr and Rockenbach (2003), which was performed on students, to examine the behavior of CEOs in Costa Rica. They find that CEOs are actually more trusting and trustworthy relative to students.

[17] See, for instance, Charness (2000), Fehr et al. (1993, 1998), Fehr et al. (2007), Fehr and Falk (1999), Gachter and Falk (2002), and Hannan et al. (2002).

Do the results of the gift exchange experiments survive with an increase in stakes? Fehr et al. (2002) conducted experiments in Russia where subjects earned, on average, the monetary equivalent of one week's worth of wages in one condition, and 10 week's worth of wages in another condition. No significant differences were found in the results between the two conditions. These stakes are high enough to cover many real-world economic transactions.

The gift exchange experiments of Charness et al. (2004) show that there are possibly cultural differences between European and US subjects in experiments. The US subjects engage in lower levels of gift exchange. They also find negative effects on the magnitude of gift exchange when payoff tables are provided. However, it is not clear why the provision of these tables should matter, e.g., does it clarify the structure of the problem or does it induce particular framing effects?

GIFT EXCHANGE AND COMPETITIVE EQUILIBRIUM

The results of Fehr et al. (1998) speak to the class of results that find support for the predictions of competitive market equilibria in experimental markets (Smith, 1962; Davis and Holt, 1993).[18] Fehr et al. (1998) embed a gift exchange game within competitive markets by allowing sellers to choose a variable quality for a good (see the introductory chapter in Volume 1 for more details). If buyers pay a higher price, then sellers can choose to supply them with a higher quality. Under self-regarding preferences, the sellers should supply the lowest quality, and anticipating this, buyers should offer low prices. By contrast, the experimental evidence shows that buyers offer a higher price in anticipation of reciprocal behavior on the part of sellers, who reciprocate by supplying higher quality. The outcome of the experiments departs significantly from the competitive market equilibrium predictions, due to fairness and reciprocity considerations. Furthermore, such reciprocal behavior has a positive effect on the profits of buyers. In conjunction with the results from ultimatum games that reveal more prosocial behavior in the presence of greater market integration, these results challenge the conventional view that markets necessarily produce self-regarding outcomes.

GIFT EXCHANGE AND SOCIAL COMPARISONS

The standard gift exchange experiments assume a bilateral employment relation, i.e., there is one principal and one agent. This feature is relaxed in several experiments. Maximiano et al. (2007) extend the standard framework to allow for four workers working for the same principal and find that the effort levels of the workers in the bilateral and multilateral conditions are very similar.

Social comparisons seem to be an important determinant of reciprocity. Gächter et al. (2012) modify the gift exchange game by considering one employer and two employees. The employer announces a publicly observed wage. The employees then choose their effort levels sequentially. Employee 1 chooses his effort level first, which is observed by employee 2, who then chooses his effort level. When the wage level is high enough, then a higher effort level by employee 1 is followed by a higher effort level by employee 2. This effect is over and above the normal effort levels in the gift exchange game. Cohn et al. (2011) consider randomized field experiments in which teams of two agents are paired with a principal. They consider two separate treatments. In the first, the wages of both agents are cut by 25%, while in the second, the wage of only one of the two agents is cut by 25%. The effort level of the agent whose wage is cut in the second treatment decreases twice as much (by 34%) relative to that in the first treatment (by 15%). This demonstrates that social comparisons play an important role in gift exchange experiments.

---

[18] The results of experimental competitive markets are discussed in more detail in Volume 4 of the book.

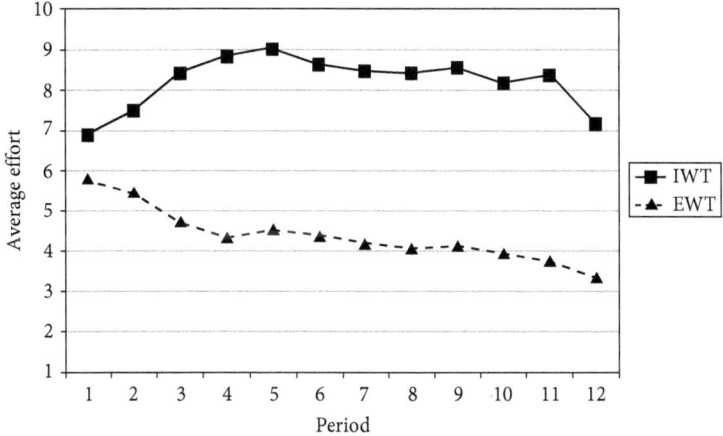

Figure 1.2 The effect of the equity norm on effort levels.
Source: "Gift exchange and workers' fairness concerns: When equality is unfair," Abeler, J., Altmann, S., Kube, S., and Wibral, M., Journal of the European Economic Association, 8(6): 1229–1324. © 2010 European Economic Association.

In an interesting set of experiments, Abeler et al. (2010) consider repeated interaction between a principal and two agents. Neither effort nor wages are contractible. In one treatment, the equal wage treatment (EWT), both workers are paid equal wages, so there is no horizontal inequity. In a second treatment, the individual wage treatment (IWT), unequal wages are allowed. EWT may be viewed as fair if both workers put in identical levels of effort. However, in the case of unequal efforts, an EWT may be perceived as unfair and, hence, may prove detrimental to effort. The experimental results support these findings; see Figure 1.2 for the average effort level across 12 rounds. In the EWT treatment, the worker who initially puts in a higher level of effort responds to equal wages by putting in a lower effort level in the next round. Effort, in this treatment, moves downwards over successive rounds. By contrast, in the IWT, the worker who puts in a lower effort level in one round, receives a lower wage from the principal and responds by putting in a higher effort level in the next round. In this case, effort increases over successive rounds. Average wage is positively correlated with the effort levels as in gift exchange games.

Kube et al. (2012) find that gift exchange is more effective when the firm offers a non-monetary reward to the worker as compared to a monetary reward. Students are hired for a data entry task and earnings of 36 euros for a three-hour task are announced. In the *monetary gift treatment*, subjects discover that their wage has been unexpectedly raised to 43 euros. In the *material gift treatment*, workers unexpectedly receive a material gift worth 7 euros. Workers respond by entering 6% more data in the first treatment but 30% more data in the second treatment. Interestingly, in a binary choice comparison, workers preferred to receive 7 euros in preference to the gift. This suggests that the gift is not perceived to be more valuable, however, the gift seems to have a signaling value, which elicits greater effort.

GIFT EXCHANGE AND DURATION EFFECTS

Gneezy and List (2006) make two extensions to the standard gift exchange game. First, they look at field experiments rather than lab experiments. Second, they focus on studying the effort provision of workers over an extended period of time. In one of their tasks, the library task, workers were recruited with an offer of an hourly wage of $12 for six hours of work. They were not told that they were participating in an experiment. In the no-gift treatment, workers were paid a flat wage of $12/hour as promised. In the gift treatment, they were unexpectedly paid an increased, but flat, wage of $20/hour. Effort was initially higher in the second treatment, possibly on account of the gift exchange motive. However, gradually, over six hours, the effort levels in the two treatments converged, as shown in Figure 1.3.

These results beg two questions. First, what are the reasons for the downward movement in effort in the gift treatment? The authors' preferred explanation is that workers in the second treatment have not had a chance to figure out the game with a cool head (the so-called *hot state, cold state* comparison). However, an alternative explanation, based on the adjustment of the reference points, also appears plausible. The reference point of workers whose wage has gone up, may adjust upwards, so that the unexpected increase in wage no longer seems like a gift after the adjustment has been made. Second, if real-world firms are rational, then firms should eventually learn that the effects of gift exchange do not last long. So instead of offering a flat unexpected increase in wage to $20/hour, it might well be optimal to offer a gradual increase in the wage rate in small increments to elicit a positive incremental effort level over time. In this sense, the Gneezy and List (2006) results enrich the insights from the gift exchange game by offering insights about duration effects.

Bellemare and Shearer (2007) point out that the Gneezy and List (2006) results rely on observations taken from spot markets but do not speak to the issue of the long-term relations between workers and firms. They examine the effect of a one-off surprise bonus of $80 in a tree planting firm in British Columbia where the average daily earnings were $200. There are workers of varying tenure length within the firm. The results are shown in Figure 1.4 for two typical profiles of workers who begin their employment at the age of 20 and 28, respectively. The effort levels of workers, measured in terms of the number of trees planted daily, are observed over six weeks. Significant long-term effects on the effort levels are found in workers with longer tenure, after controlling for planter-fixed effect, weather, and day-of-week effect (to control for fatigue). Such effects are insignificant for workers with very short tenures (as in the spot markets of Gneezy and List, 2006). In general, there is a positive relation between reciprocity and tenure. This complements nicely the Gneezy–List results suggesting that the gift exchange relationship survives over the long term, provided there are long-term relations between the firm and the workers. Indeed this might even provide a new rationale for long-term relations in firms.

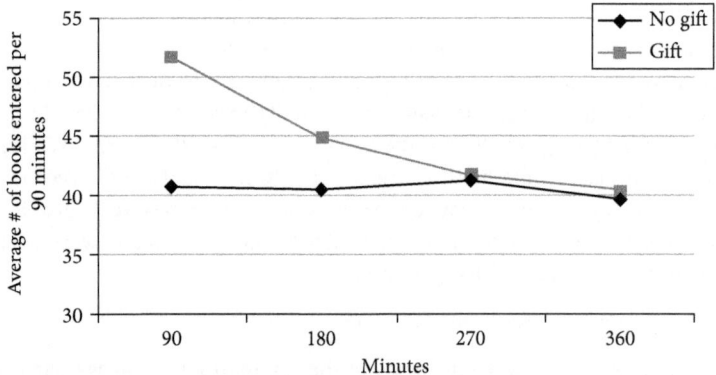

Figure 1.3 Behavior of workers' effort levels in the library task.
Source: Gneezy and List (2006) with permission of the Econometric Society.

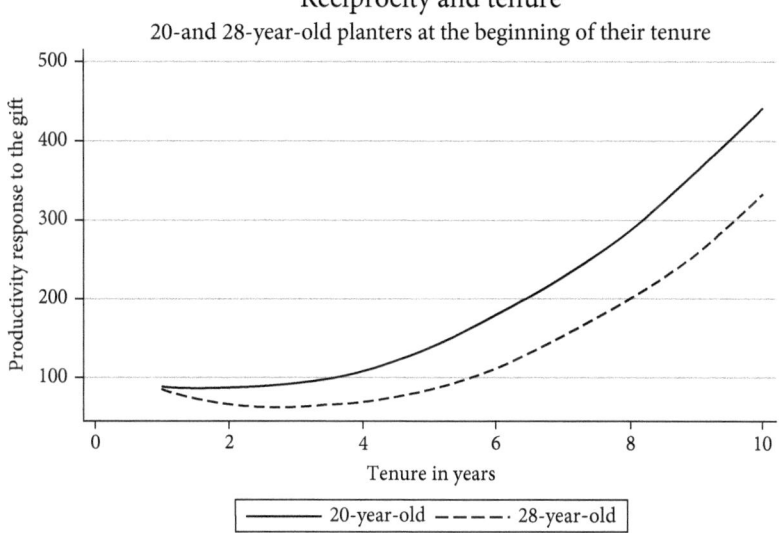

Figure 1.4 The relation between reciprocity and tenure.
Source: Reprinted from Games and Economic Behavior, 67(1): 233–44. Bellamere, C. and Shearer, B., "Gift giving and worker productivity: evidence from a firm level experiment." © 2009, with permission from Elsevier.

REFERENCE DEPENDENCE AND GIFT EXCHANGE

The evidence shows that other-regarding preferences can be reference dependent (Fehr et al., 2009). This may interact with gift exchange issues that future research can examine. Thus, labor market policy interventions such as minimum wage laws could alter the worker's perception of a fair wage, leading them to alter their effort decisions. Hence, after the introduction of minimum wage laws, firms may find that they must pay higher wages or be perceived as unfair. The experiments of Brandts and Charness (2004) show that market competition and minimum wage laws do not have a significant effect on the results of gift exchange experiments, although effort is somewhat lower in the presence of minimum wages. In contrast to these results, Owens and Kagel (2010) find that in gift exchange experiments, the effect of a minimum wage is to increase effort levels. Falk et al. (2006) explore the relation between minimum wages and fairness and find that the minimum wage raises the reservation wage of workers. It is interesting that if minimum wage laws are repealed, then workers do not reduce their notion of a fair wage by as much as the drop in the minimum wage, giving rise to a sort of *ratchet effect*. Hence, firms may find it difficult to reduce wages, giving rise to downward rigidity in wages.

Kube et al. (2013) use a field study to examine the contention by Bewley (1999) that firms are reluctant to cut wages for fear of reducing morale and effort. The authors allow for an exogenous variation in the wage in a one-shot interaction between a firm and its workers. Student-workers are hired to undertake a data entry task and informed that the projected wage is EUR 15/hour for six hours. This was intended to serve as a reference point for the wage that workers could expect. In the baseline treatment, students were actually paid EUR 15/hour. In the PayCut treatment, they were paid EUR 10/hour, and in the PayRise treatment they were paid EUR 20/hour. These variations in the wage levels were not related to the past level of wages, a problem that often arises in actual firm-level data.

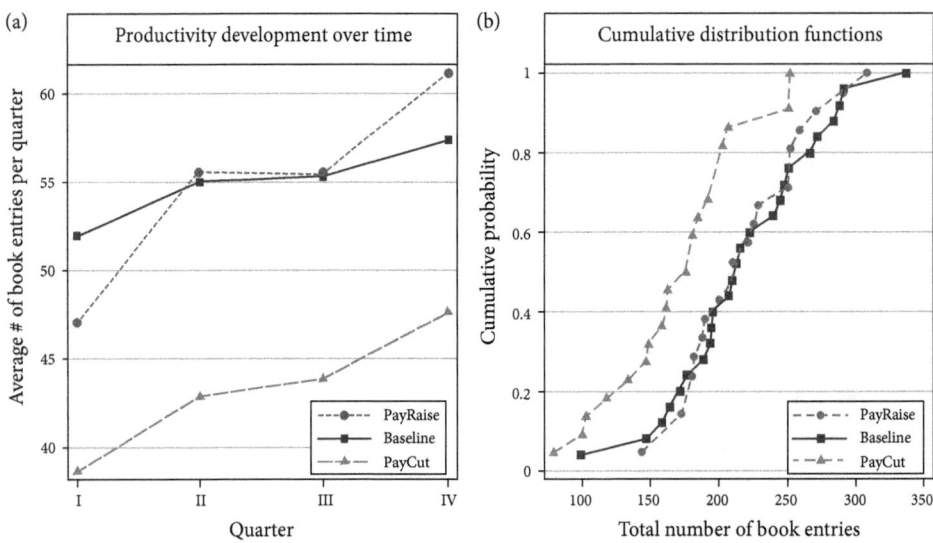

Figure 1.5 Productivity of workers in different wage conditions.
Source: "Do wage cuts damage work Morale? Evidence from a natural field experiment," Kube, S., Maréchal, M. A., and Puppe, C., Journal of the European Economic Association, 11(4): 853–70. © 2013 by the European Economic Association.

The results are shown in Figure 1.5. In the left panel, each quarter on the horizontal axis represents a 90-minute period. The average number of books marked was significantly lower in the PayCut treatment as compared to the Baseline treatment, and this difference is stable over time. On average, the number of books marked was 21% lower in the PayCut treatment, relative to the Baseline treatment. By contrast, the difference between the PayRise and the Baseline treatments was not statistically different. Thus, the evidence is not consistent with positively reciprocal behavior but it is consistent with negatively reciprocal behavior and with Bewley's findings. In the right panel of Figure 1.5, we plot the cumulative distribution functions of the number of book entries. The PayCut distribution is first order stochastically dominated by the distributions in the other two treatments.

These results can be explained by models of inequity aversion if one assumes that all players consider only the incomes earned during the field experiment and ignore outside incomes (narrow bracketing). The results can also be explained by models of reciprocity. The authors show that the model by Cox et al. (2007) can explain their findings.

SURVEY EVIDENCE FOR GIFT EXCHANGE

Most of the results on the gift exchange game have been based on experimental findings. In a novel study, Dohmen et al. (2009) use panel survey data from the German Socio-Economic Panel Study (SOEP) from the 2005 wave. Many economists have aversion to survey evidence on a-priori grounds,[19] but a-priori grounds can also be used to defend survey evidence, particularly if people respond to survey questions, using their intrinsic motivation, and have some aversion to lying (see Chapters 3 and 4). Indeed, survey evidence is routinely used by government agencies

---

[19] The standard arguments are that survey evidence is typically not as tightly controlled as lab experiments, there is no guarantee that the responses are incentive compatible, and face-to-face interaction while collecting the evidence may bias choices.

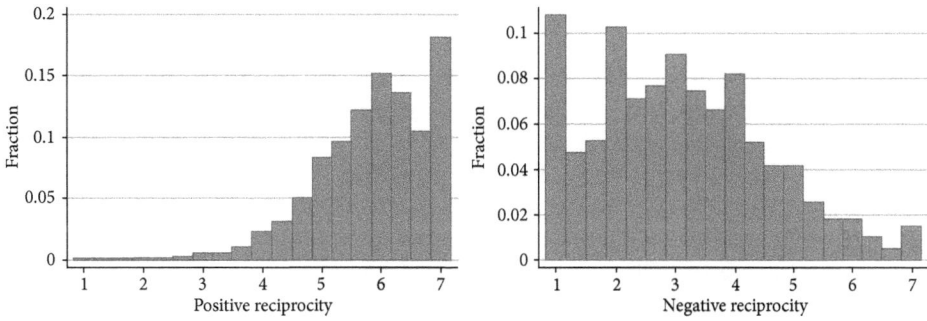

Figure 1.6 Average responses for the positive reciprocity questions (left panel) and negative reciprocity questions (right panel).

Source: "Homo reciprocans: Survey evidence on behavioral outcomes," Dohmen, T., Falk, A., Huffman, D., and Sunde, U., The Economic Journal, 119(536): 592–612. © The Authors. Journal compilation © Royal Economic Society 2009.

and firms as the basis of important decisions. Six interesting questions on reciprocity were asked in the 2005 wave of the SOEP. These were as follows.

(1) If someone does me a favor, I am prepared to return it.
(2) If I suffer a serious wrong, I will take revenge as soon as possible, no matter what the cost.
(3) If somebody puts me in a difficult position, I will do the same to him/her.
(4) I go out of my way to help somebody who has been kind to me before.
(5) If somebody offends me, I will offend him/her back.
(6) I am ready to undergo personal costs to help somebody who helped me before.

Questions 1, 4, and 6 elicit positive reciprocity and 2, 3, and 5, negative reciprocity of the responders. Responders had to rank their response on a scale of 1 (does not apply) to 7 (applies perfectly).

The results are shown in Figure 1.6, averaged across the positive reciprocity questions (1,4,6) and the negative reciprocity questions (2,3,5); the vertical scales in the left and the right panels are different. For the three positive reciprocity questions, less than 5% of the responders answer 1 (does not apply) and the modal response is 6 or 7. For the three negative reciprocity questions, the modal response is a 1 or 2 and 10% choose a 6 or 7. There is heterogeneity in responses in both cases but there is significantly greater heterogeneity in the negative reciprocity questions. Positive reciprocity weakens as the costs of reciprocal behavior increases. The response 7 (fully agree) is chosen by 60% when there is no cost (Q1), by 35% when responders need to go out of their way (Q4), and by 22% when there is a personal cost (Q6). While modal responses are low for negative reciprocity, these responses do not appear to be sensitive to the costs of reciprocity. An important finding in this study is that the correlation between positive and negative reciprocity is quite low, 0.021. Hence, the extent of negative reciprocity in a responder may not allow one to predict very well the extent of positive reciprocity.

Suppose that we interpret overtime work as a measure of reciprocity and assign to it a binary variable (1 if overtime, 0 if no overtime).[20] A probit regression shows that individuals who score high on the positive reciprocity questions are also more likely to do overtime work and

---

[20] Obviously, overtime work could be entirely supply-side driven, and reflect responder circumstances unrelated to reciprocity.

individuals who score highly on the negative reciprocity questions less likely to do so. Not only does the effect of reciprocity, measured in 2005, show up in overtime work in the current year 2005 but also in future years, 2006, 2007. Positive reciprocity has an even stronger effect on the probability of overtime work, when responders perceive that they are paid a fair wage. A similar effect of reciprocity on absenteeism is found.

Mincer-type equations are traditionally used in economics to explain earnings as a function of several explanatory variables such as individual characteristics and educational attainment. The authors get all the classical effects[21] but, in addition, positive reciprocity enhances earnings in current and future years. However, there is no significant effect of negative reciprocity. Furthermore, individuals who are positively reciprocal are less likely to be unemployed, more likely to have a larger number of close friends, and more likely to report greater satisfaction with life.

1.3.2 The trust game, trust, and trustworthiness

The trust game was introduced by Berg et al. (1995), which in turn is a simplified version of a game in Camerer and Weigelt (1988). Consider a static game, played between an *investor* and a *respondent*, sometimes known, respectively, as the *trustor* and the *trustee*. Each player is endowed with some fixed level of endowment, say, 10 MUs (an MU is a unit of money in the experiments). The investor must decide to send, or invest, an amount $i \in \{0, 1, 2, \ldots, 10\}$ to the responder, via the experimenter. The experimenter multiplies the amount by a number $m > 1$, known as the *multiplier*, which captures the market return and passes it on to the responder; $m = 3$ in many experiments. The responder then returns an amount $r \in \{0, 1, 2, \ldots, 10 + mi\}$ back to the investor. The respective payoffs of the investor and the responder at the end of the game are $10 - i + r$ and $10 + mi - r$.

Definition 1.2 *(Trust and trustworthiness)*: *The numbers i and r are, respectively, measures of trust and trustworthiness.*

RELATION BETWEEN THE GIFT EXCHANGE GAME AND THE TRUST GAME

The reader may have noted the similarity in the structure of the trust game with the gift exchange game. The surplus in the trust game, found by adding the payoffs of the two players is $20 + (m - 1)i$, which is increasing in the investment made by the investor. By contrast, the surplus in the gift exchange game is $\theta e_a - c(e_a)$, where $\theta > 0$ is the marginal product of effort; for instance, $\theta = 100$ in the Fehr et al. (1997) experiments described above. If θ exceeds the marginal cost of effort (which is typically the case in experiments), then the surplus is increasing in the effort level. From these observations, the main difference between the two games is that in the trust game, the first mover (investor) can increase the surplus through his actions (investment). By contrast, in the gift exchange game, it is the second mover (the worker) who can increase the surplus through his action (effort level).

If subjects in experiments have self-regarding preferences and are rational, then the responder will never send any money back to the investor ($r = 0$). The rational investor correctly anticipates the responder's behavior, and sends an amount, $i = 0$. Thus, the unique subgame perfect outcome is $i = r = 0$.

---

[21] For instance, men are paid more than women, experience has an increasing and concave effect on earnings, and education has a positive effect on earnings.

By contrast, if subjects in experiments have other-regarding preferences (or intrinsic reciprocity), then responders are likely to reciprocate higher levels of i with higher levels of r. One would then expect $i > 0$ and $r > 0$. This prediction is borne out by the evidence. Responders typically return back the investment that they have received from the investor. The investor finds that his investment is, at least mildly, profitable, so he sends a strictly positive amount. However, small upward jumps in i are typically ineffective in eliciting greater r, relative to larger jumps in i.

A large number of replications of the trust game have been conducted. The interested reader may consult the meta-study by Johnson and Mislin (2011) that draws on 161 replications of the trust game with a total of 23,000 respondents. They measure trust by a variable pSent, and trustworthiness by a variable pReturn, defined respectively as $i/10$ and $r/(10 + mi)$, i.e., the fraction of total amounts available that are sent by each of the players. These measures are shown in Figure 1.7.

Across all studies, the mean amount sent by the investor, pSent, is .502 (so investors send about half their wealth), while the mean amount sent by the responder, pReceive, is .372 (so responders send about 37.2% of their wealth). For instance, if initial endowments are 10 each, $m = 3$, and $i = 5$, then $r = 9.3$. The meta-study reveals many other interesting features. The amounts sent are larger when interacting with a human, as compared to a non-human, subject such as a computer; older people send larger amounts; significantly lesser amounts are sent in Africa as compared to North America; students send a significantly lower amount as compared to the non-student population; reducing the multiplier from 3 to 2 reduces the amount returned by the respondent. An important finding from the meta-study is that stakes do not have any affect on the results.

The experimental results in Charness et al. (2011) show that providing a history of the behavior of respondents alters the amounts transferred by the investors. When given a choice of exploring past data on the history of the responders, 70% of the investors choose to check the relevant history. Past behavior that is more trusting and trustworthy gives rise to greater trust. However, subjects also use past data on trust to infer greater trustworthiness, suggesting that these two measures may be correlated. Does it pay to trust based on past data? The answer is yes, in both treatments, although in only one treatment is it statistically significant.

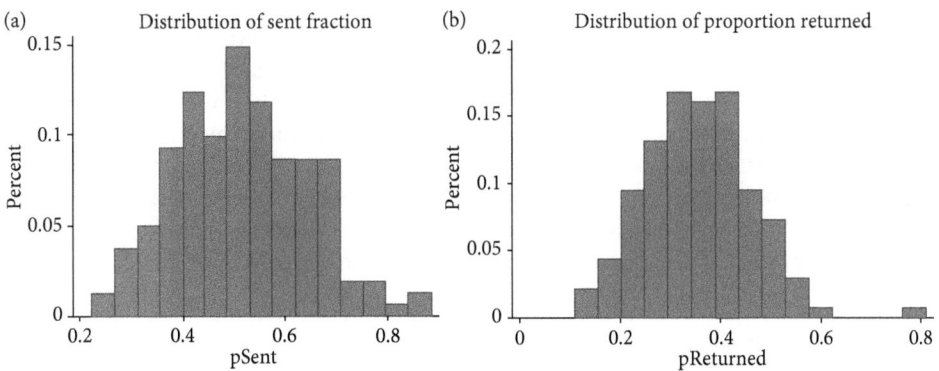

Figure 1.7 Measures of trust and trustworthiness in a meta study.

Source: Reprinted from Journal of Economic Psychology, 32(5): 865–89. Johnson, M. D. and Mislin, A., "Trust games: a metaanalysis." © 2011, with permission of Elsevier.

Eckel and Petrie (2011) consider a trust game in which investors and responders can, by paying a price, look up a photograph of the other player.[22] They explore if the amount of trust and trustworthiness changes as a result of looking at a photograph of the other player. The motivation for this paper is earlier work that discovered a link between economic decisions and human characteristics such as beauty, ethnicity, and gender.[23] In their trust game experiments, both parties are endowed with ten tokens each (each token is equivalent to $1.5). In various sessions, the subjects face different prices for buying photographs of the other player. Not all subjects decide to purchase the photographs. At the lowest price of $0.20, 50% of the subjects buy the photographs, and they respond to an increase in price by reducing their demand for photographs. Hence, there appears to be a downward sloping demand curve for photographs.

The difference between the demands for photographs of investors and responders is not statistically significant. However, investors are willing to pay more for the photographs, relative to responders, because their decision in a trust game is relatively more strategic. There is no gender difference in the demand for photographs, but there is an ethnic difference. White investors are 40% more likely to wish to buy photographs as compared to subjects of any other ethnicity. Conditional on buying a photograph, white investors discriminate in their investment, i, based on the ethnicity of the responder. On average, they send 3.6 tokens to a black responder and 5.5 to a white responder; the difference is statistically significant. Black investors send significantly fewer tokens than whites, but they do not discriminate in their investment choices based on ethnicity.[24] There is no difference in the number of tokens sent based on the relative genders of the investor and the responder.

For responders, the response, r, to the amount sent by the investor, i, is upward sloping. The highest slope of the response function is for white responders. In general, conditional on observing a photograph, responders send more tokens to the investor, relative to the case where they do not see a photograph. In their roles as responders, both blacks and whites send more tokens back to an investor of the same ethnicity. The authors conclude that the "informational value of a face is non-zero." However, the informational value differs for different ethnic groups.

The terms *trust* and *trustworthiness* have a precise meaning in the trust game. Outside the context of this game, trust might need a more formal definition. In applied economic work, various proxies for trust are used. This literature indicates that measures of trust are correlated with GDP, growth, inflation, volume of trade, and the propensity to invest in the stock market. What sort of trust does the trust game capture? There have been attempts to answer this question in terms of altruism and *betrayal aversion*. For a fuller discussion of these very interesting issues and the formal definitions of the relevant terms, see the excellent survey by Fehr (2009).

The trust game is not the only context in which *trust* and *trustworthiness* have been measured. Bolton et al. (2004) consider these concepts in the context of feedback systems in online electronic purchases such as those on Amazon and eBay.[25] In these experiments, a buyer first chooses to buy or not. If the buyer chooses to buy, he needs to pay the money upfront. The seller

---

[22] In related research, dictators give only a third as much to an anonymous responder relative to the case where they are told that the responder is the Red Cross; see, for instance, Eckel and Grossman (1996).

[23] See Croson and Gneezy (2009) for a survey of the link between decisions and gender. For the link between beauty and decisions, see, for instance, Hamermesh and Biddle (1994), Mobius and Rosenblat (2006), and Andreoni and Petrie (2008).

[24] The authors conjecture that whites are in a majority, so they are more likely to be "teachers in school or bosses in workplace" hence, they are less likely to be discriminated against.

[25] See also the follow-up paper by Bolton et al. (2013) that speaks to the limitations of field studies in online auctions in engineering changes that might promote more trust through various feeback systems.

then chooses to dispatch the good or not. The seller's action is subject to moral hazard because he might choose not to dispatch the promised good. This setting characterizes many forms of online purchases. Three markets are considered. In the *strangers market*, buyers and sellers meet only once and do not have access to each other's transactions history. In the *feedback market*, an online system tracks the previous shipping decisions of the seller and reveals them to the buyer at the time of the buying decision. However, buyers and sellers are randomly paired in each round. Finally, in the *partners market*, feedback is as in the feedback market, but the buyer and seller pairings are unaltered over the experiment.

In this online experimental market, we may define *efficiency* by the percentage of potential transactions completed. *Trust* is measured by the percentage of buyer orders and *trustworthiness* by the percentage of seller dispatches, once the buyer has decided to buy. On all these indicators, the partners market does the best, followed by the feedback market, while the strangers market performs the worst. The reason for the difference is that each of these markets has different incentives for building reputations, and there are differences in the quality and interpretation of feedback. For instance, we may use information on the last item shipped, or not shipped, by the seller as a predictor of trust in each market. Such information has no effect on trust in the strangers market (because such information is not available). However, conditional on the last item being shipped, in the feedback market, the probability of trust doubles from 33% to 65%. The effect on trust in the partners market is even stronger. The quality of feedback in the partners market is superior because current feedback improves one's own future buying decisions. By contrast, in the feedback market, the benefit accrues to others. Thus, the partners market form is superior, relative to the others, in the internalization of information externalities arising on account of the feedback.

The experimental results of the ultimatum game show that market integration and cooperation in production are associated with greater sociality. Huck et al. (2012) consider whether increased competition can enhance sociality and efficiency in trust games.[26] They consider the game in Figure 1.8, originally due to Bohnet et al. (2005). The trustor (player 1) has two strategies: Trust (T) or not trust (N). The trustee (player 2) also has two strategies: Honor trust (h) or exploit trust (e). The game has a unique subgame perfect Nash equilibrium (N,e). The *trust rate* is defined as the percentage of times the trustor plays T and the *honor rate* is the percentage of times the trustee plays h. The efficiency rate is defined as the percentage of times one observes the outcome (T, h).

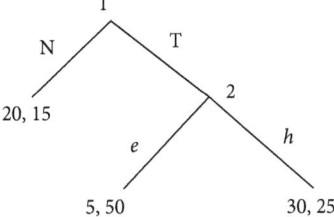

Figure 1.8 The trust game in Huck et al. (2012).
Source: Reprinted from Games and Economic Behavior, 76(1): 195–209. Huck, Steffen, Lünses, Gabriele, and Tyran, Jean-Robert, "Competition fosters trust." © 2012, with permission from Elsevier.

---

[26] Trust can also be influenced negatively by the degree of inequality in outcomes in a game; see, for instance, Hargreaves Heap et al. (2013).

In the *control treatment*, the stage game is played repeatedly over 30 rounds with randomly matched players. In the original experiments by Bohnet et al. (2005), in the control treatment, the efficient outcome (T, h) is played only 5% of the time and, as expected, the trust and honor rates are very low. Huck et al. (2012) introduce additional treatments to isolate the effect of competition. Over the 30 rounds, subjects are assigned either to the role of trustors or trustees over the entire duration of the experiment. A "market" has four trustors and four trustees. In the private information treatment (pi), each subject is informed of only their own past interactions (their actions and the actions of the other player) in the game. In the full information treatment (fi), all trustors have access to the histories of all the trustees. There is a second dimension to these treatments. In the random matching treatment each trustor is randomly assigned to a trustee in each round. In the endogenous matching treatment, the trustors choose which trustee they would like to be matched with. Since trustors compete for trustees, this is known as the *treatment with competition*.[27]

The results are as follows. In the control treatment, the results are similar to those in Bohnet et al. (2005). The efficiency rate is only 8% and the trust rate and the honor rates are identical at 28%. In the case of random matching, private information (pi) and full information (fi) give similar results but with vastly improved rates of sociality relative to the control treatment—the trust rate almost doubles to 50%, the honor rate doubles to 69%, and the efficiency rate quadruples to 36%.[28] However, the most dramatic effect arises in the treatment with competition, irrespective of whether information was private or full. For instance, in the full information treatment with competition, the trust rate, honor rate, and the efficiency rates are respectively 0.90, 0.94, and 0.85, roughly triple those in the control treatment.[29]

Burnham et al. (2000) postulate that humans have a friend or foe (FOF) mental mechanism. Depending on whether humans perceive their opponent to be a friend or a foe, they make different choices. The authors test for such a mechanism by priming subjects in two-player trust games. For instance, if the other player is termed as a "partner" he might be perceived as a friend and if he is termed as an "opponent" he might be perceived as a foe. They find that partners trust more than opponents. They also find twice the level of trustworthiness among partners relative to opponents.

1.4 Public goods games

In this section, we separately consider the public goods game with and without punishments, followed by an examination of the evidence on such games.

1.4.1 *Public goods game without punishments*

There are $i \in N = \{1, 2, \ldots, n\}$, $n \geq 2$, risk-neutral individuals and each has an initial endowment $y > 0$, expressed in some monetary units. They simultaneously decide on their respective

---

[27] If a trustee is matched with more than one trustor in any round, the trustee can choose only one action. His total payoff for that round is the sum of his payoff across all matchings.

[28] These findings are in line with those in Bolton et al. (2004) who also find that giving feedback to players about past play improves sociality.

[29] In other contexts, with similar endogenous matching of participants, Page et al. (2005) show that contributions in public goods games improve and Bohnet and Kübler (2005) show that cooperation improves in social dilemma games.

contributions, $g_i \geq 0$, to a public good. The total monetary contribution towards the public good is given by $G = \sum_{i=1}^{n} g_i$. The monetary payoff, m_i, of individual $i \in N$ is given by

$$m_i = y - g_i + rG; \quad \frac{1}{n} < r < 1, \tag{1.1}$$

where r is the monetary equivalent of the return, or benefit, to an individual, arising from one unit of the public good, G.

Definition 1.3 *The variable r in (1.1) is called the marginal per capita return (MPCR).*

The Nash equilibrium outcome of this game when individuals have self-regarding preferences is characterized by complete *free-riding*; it is derived in the next proposition.

Proposition 1.1 *(i) In the unique Nash equilibrium, all self-regarding individuals make zero contributions, i.e., $g_i^* = 0$ for any $i \in N$. (ii) By contrast, the social optimum is characterized by $g_i^* = y$ for all $i \in N$.*

Proof: (i) Recall that all individuals are risk-neutral. To check that in a Nash equilibrium $g_i^* = 0$ for any $i \in N$, let the vector of contributions of others $\mathbf{g}_{-i}^* = \mathbf{0}$. Using (1.1),

$$\frac{dm_i}{dg_i} = r - 1 < 0; \because r < 1,$$

hence, $g_i^* = 0$, which proves the result.

(ii) The social objective function is $W = \sum_i m_i = ny - G + rnG$. To find the social optimum, note that

$$\frac{dW}{dg_i} = rn - 1 > 0; \because \frac{1}{n} < r,$$

hence, in the social optimum, $g_i^* = y$ for all $i \in N$. ∎

1.4.2 Public goods game with punishments

In the public goods game with punishments, there are two stages. In the first stage, one plays the public goods game without punishments. In the second stage, once the individual contributions, $g_1, g_2, \ldots, g_n$, are public information, each player simultaneously chooses a punishment vector $\mathbf{p}_i = (p_{i1}, \ldots, p_{in})$ where p_{ij} is the punishment inflicted by player i on player j at a cost of c per unit and $0 < c < 1$. In this game, the utility function of a risk-neutral individual i with self-regarding preferences is given by

$$m_i = y - g_i + rG - c\sum_{j \neq i} p_{ij} - \sum_{j \neq i} p_{ji}. \tag{1.2}$$

The first three terms in (1.1), (1.2) are identical. The fourth and fifth terms, respectively, in (1.2) capture the cost of punishing others and the cost of being punished by others.

Definition 1.4 *(Efficiency of punishment): Equation (1.2) assumes a linear punishment technology. For any player i, it costs c units (in some appropriate units, such as experimental* tokens) to punish player j, $j \neq i$, by 1 unit. The efficiency of punishment is defined by $1/c$. A lower cost of punishment/unit corresponds to a higher efficiency of punishment.

Proposition 1.2 *When all players have self-regarding preferences, the Nash equilibrium of the public goods game with punishments and without punishments is identical, i.e., in equilibrium the contribution of any player is $g_i^* = 0$ for all $i \in N$.*

Proof: Conditional on any vector of first stage contributions $(g_1, g_2, \ldots, g_n)$ consider the subgame that begins with the decision by players to engage in punishment. Conditional on the punishment vectors of others, $\mathbf{p}_{-i}$, the choice of $\mathbf{p}_i = \mathbf{0}$, maximizes m_i. Hence, it is a dominant strategy, for each player, to not engage in any punishment in the subgame. Given that the second stage outcome is $\mathbf{p}_i = \mathbf{0}$ for all $i \in N$, the first stage payoffs in (1.1), (1.2) are identical. Hence, using Proposition 1.1, $g_i^* = 0$ for all i. ∎

Proposition 1.2 shows that in this multi-stage game, punishments are never optimal for players with self-regarding preferences because bygones are bygones. Hence, any threats to engage in punishment are not credible, thus, punishments carry no bite.

1.4.3 Empirical evidence on public goods games

How do the results in Propositions 1.1, 1.2 compare with the empirical evidence? Experiments on public goods games without punishments typically proceed as follows. There are a fixed number of rounds, say, ten, and a certain number of subjects in experiments, say, $n = 6$. At the start of the experiment, subjects are given some endowment (tokens or points), say, $y = 20$, that can be redeemed at the end of the experiment for money. In each period, subjects are asked to contribute to a common pool or a public account, which captures the idea of a public good. After the contributions have been made, the experimenter places some percentage, say 30% (so $r = 0.3$), of the total amount in the public account into the private account of each individual. This captures some level of uniform benefits from the provision of the public good.

At the end of each period, all subjects are able to observe the total amount in the common pool as well as the individual contributions of others. In public goods games with punishments, a second stage is added to the first in which contributors can punish non-contributors at some personal cost. Typically, for each token surrendered by a punisher to the experimenter, the recipient of the punishment has to surrender more than one token depending on the efficiency of punishment (see Definition 1.4). The same sequence of play then takes place in the subsequent rounds.

The socially efficient outcome is for each individual to put all the endowment into the common pool (Proposition 1.1(ii)). In the socially efficient outcome, each subject parts with the 20 units of endowment but receives $0.3(20 \times 6) = 36$ from the experimenter, for a net gain of 16. However, the essence of the privately optimal solution is that conditional on others contributing, any individual can do better by not contributing, i.e., free-riding. For instance, if the first five players contribute, then by not contributing, the sixth player's payoff is $20 + 0.3(20 \times 5) = 50 > 36$. Thus, in a Nash equilibrium, nobody contributes (see Proposition 1.1(i)).

Experimental evidence on public goods games without punishments typically shows that subjects begin by contributing about half of their endowments to the common pool. The contributions then begin to drop in subsequent rounds and towards the last round, the contributions for most subjects are nearly zero, as predicted by the model with self-regarding preferences.[30] This evidence from the later rounds is sometimes taken as supportive of the predictions of the

---

[30] See, for instance, Andreoni (1988), Isaac et al. (1985). The results from a wide range of studies on this issue are surveyed in Dawes and Thaler (1988) and Ledyard (1995).

model with self-regarding preferences (Proposition 1.1). However, on the whole, this pattern of contributions is not consistent with self-regarding preferences because it does not explain (i) why contributions are initially high, and (ii) why if the game is restarted, the contributions typically jump up to a higher level (Fehr and Fischbacher, 2003).

The results of the public goods game with punishments under self-regarding preferences (see Proposition 1.2) are rejected by the evidence. For instance, Fehr and Schmidt (1999) report that, on average, across various studies considered by them, 73% of the subjects choose $g_i = 0$ in the public goods game without punishments. By contrast, on average, 80% cooperated fully in the public goods game with punishments.

The experimental results of Fehr and Gächter (2000) reject the predictions in Proposition 1.2. First, cooperators in public goods games are willing to engage in costly punishment of the free-riders, although such punishments do not give them any material benefits. Second, the extent of punishment inflicted on the free-riders depends on the magnitude of free-riding. Third, in the presence of punishment, there is less free-riding. Thus, potential free-riders seem to realize that they are likely to be punished if they free-ride.

More fully, Fehr and Gächter (2000) used ten rounds and four subjects in each group. They consider the following three treatments. In the *partner treatment*, the same four subjects remained in the group for the ten periods. In the *stranger treatment*, subjects were randomly reassigned at the end of each period, not ruling out the possibility that some subjects may be matched with each other in more than one period. Finally, the *perfect stranger treatment* is similar to the stranger treatment except that it was ensured that no two subjects get matched in the same group in more than one period. The public goods game with punishments was played in the first ten rounds followed by the public goods game without punishments in the next ten rounds. The results are shown in Figure 1.9.[31]

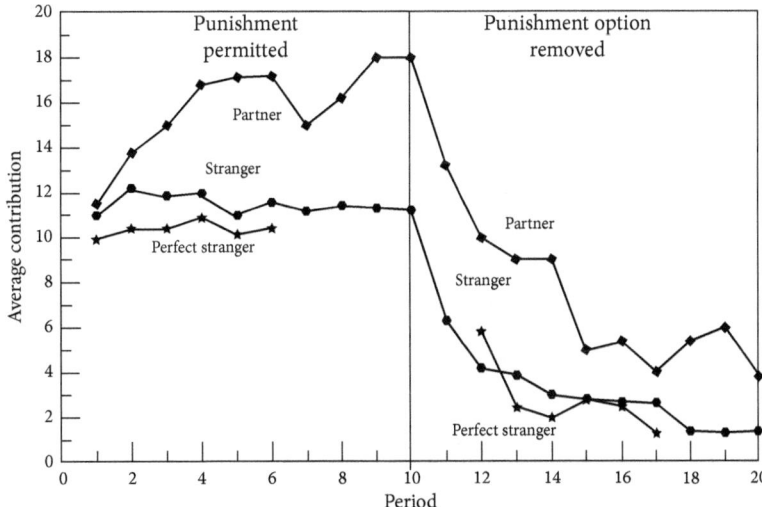

Figure 1.9 Evolution of average contributions in three different treatments in the presence and in the absence of punishments.
Source: Fehr and Gächter (1999).

---

[31] The gaps in the curve representing the perfect stranger treatment arose because of the finiteness of the number of participants in the experiment.

In the first ten rounds, when costly punishment is allowed, cooperation as measured by average contributions is mostly increasing in all treatments. In the last ten rounds, when the punishment option is removed, we get the standard result that cooperation deteriorates over time. In the partner treatment, when punishment is permitted, one achieves close to full cooperation (i.e., the socially efficient outcome) by round ten. Furthermore, the cooperation level in the partner treatment is greater than any of the other two treatments. Once a group member is punished, it is likely that all subjects in a group believe that inadequate contributions will almost certainly invite credible punishment. The cooperation levels in the other treatments, while lower than the partner treatment, are still impressive and much higher than the prediction of zero cooperation under self-regarding preferences (see Proposition 1.2).

The punishment levels remain at high levels in the final rounds when there is little or no future to worry about. Thus, these punishments are not carried out for instrumental reasons, such as preventing future levels of shirking. Rather, these punishments appear to reflect the innate desire to discipline violators of the norm of cooperation, and/or to derive hedonic utility from punishing non-cooperators. In Volume 7 we show that the neuroeconomic evidence supports this view (de Quervain et al., 2004).

We now give a brief and selective overview of some further results on public goods games. By varying the MPCR (see Definition 1.3), Brandts and Schram (2001) find that conditional cooperation is not caused by errors on the part of subjects in experiments. Kurzban and Houser (2004) find that the fraction of subjects who exhibit a preference for conditional cooperation is stable across various public goods games; about 65% of subjects appear to be conditional cooperators. Thus, the results of the public goods game are not simply errors, they indicate a preference for reciprocity.

As in many other experimental games on human sociality, there are cultural variations in prosocial behavior for the public goods game. Kocher et al. (2008) find variation in the fraction of subjects who are conditional cooperators in a sample from the US, Austria, and Japan. The highest percentage of conditional cooperators are in the US, at 80.6%; the respective figures for Austria and Japan are 44.4% and 41.7%. Brandts et al. (2004), however, find little variation in the fraction of conditional cooperators in the US, Spain, Japan, and the Netherlands. Herrmann and Thöni (2009) find fairly stable fractions of conditional cooperators (about 56%) that do not depend on rural/urban regions, or on several socioeconomic variables.

Gächter et al. (2008) consider the effects on the degree of cooperation by varying the number of replications of the public goods game (10 and 50 rounds respectively) with two treatments, punishment, P, and no punishment, N. This gives four sets of experiments: 10P, 50P and 10N, 50N. They wish to test if the consequences of costly punishments on payoffs in 10P experiments, relative to the benefits of increased cooperation, are eliminated or reversed in 50P experiments. They find that the highest levels of cooperation and the maximum payoffs among the four cases arise in the 50P game; in particular, these exceed the observed levels for the 10P case. Towards the final rounds of the 50P game, the contribution levels stabilize and one observes very little punishment. Thus, an observation of little punishment does not mean that punishments are ineffective. Rather very little punishment may be required if individuals make high contributions to the public good; see also Gintis and Fehr (2012).

Sefton et al. (2007) consider the possibility of both positive punishment (sanctions) and negative punishment (rewards) in public goods games. They find that a combination of rewards and punishments elicits greater cooperation relative to punishments or rewards alone. However, in their setup, the efficiency of punishment (see Definition 1.4) is only 1. Nikiforakis and Normann (2008) vary the efficiency of punishment and consider the effect on the extent of cooperation. They consider four levels of efficiency, $1/c$, namely, 1, 2, 3, and 4. They find that the contributions to the public good are increasing in the efficiency of punishment. For very efficient punishments ($\frac{1}{c} = 3, 4$) they achieve contributions that are close to the socially optimal solution. Using data on Dutch subjects in their experiments, Egas and Riedl (2008) also find that the level of contributions are at the socially optimal level for $\frac{1}{c} = 3$, and older subjects are more likely to punish non-contributors.

There are two opposing effects on cooperation as the group size increases under the assumption that the cooperation of group members can only be elicited through costly monitoring. In a larger group, there could be a greater incentive to free-ride because the probability one may be monitored by any single player is smaller. However, a countervailing force in a larger group is that there are more monitors. The net effect on the probability of detection of non-cooperation, and, hence, the incentive to free-ride, is not clear. Carpenter (2007) considers simulated automata and finds that larger groups are more efficacious in making higher contributions, and they exhibit a lower level of free-riding.

In the typical public goods experiments, punishments are monetary. In traditional societies, however, punishments often take a non-monetary form, such as ostracization and other social sanctions. Masclet et al. (2003) consider a public goods game in which, in addition to monetary punishments, subjects can assign between 1 and 10 "disapproval points" to non-contributors that do not affect their monetary payoffs. They find that both monetary and non-monetary punishments produce greater cooperation as compared to the case of no punishments. However, while in the initial rounds of the experiment, non-monetary punishment is quite effective, subsequently, monetary punishment is more effective.

Cinyabuguma et al. (2005) consider another form of non-monetary punishment, namely, expulsion of free-riders by a majority vote. Expelled members can play subsequent rounds of the public goods game but their endowments are halved. Individuals who are expelled, or if a vote is taken on their expulsion, respond by contributing more in subsequent periods. Not many expulsions take place to ensure high contributions, possibly because the threat of expulsion is a sufficient deterrent. The expelled members are typically those who contribute the least, so punishments are not antisocial. There is a fairly rich and varied literature on the differential responses of individuals to democratically and non-democratically chosen policies. For instance, Dal Bó et al. (2010) show that players cooperate more in prisoner's dilemma games when a policy, say, punish if others do not cooperate, is chosen democratically rather than randomly by a computer.

In a public goods game, Chaudhuri and Paichayontvijit (2006) find that 62% of the subjects are conditional cooperators. If information is given to subjects about the conditional cooperation of other subjects, then conditionally cooperative subjects are found to increase their contributions. Page et al. (2005) allow for the endogenous formation of groups in the sense that subjects can express a preference for who they would like to be paired with after being provided with information about the contributions of others. This also facilitates high levels of contributions to public goods, even in the absence of punishment.

Several other papers study the implications of matching *like-minded players*, in the sense of similarity in contributions in a public goods game, into separate groups. It is found that the contributions in the initial rounds of the public goods game are a useful measure of cooperative disposition (Gunnthorsdottir et al., 2007). Gächter and Thöni (2005) conduct an initial round of a public goods experiment and based on the contributions, they group the top three contributors in the first group, the next three in the second group and so on. Each group then plays a public goods experiment over ten rounds with an MPCR (Definition 1.3) chosen to be 0.6.

Even in the absence of any punishment, the average contributions in the first group are nearly socially optimal.[32]

Monetary and non-monetary punishments are not the only mechanisms used to elicit greater contributions. Bochet et al. (2006) allow for several kinds of communication devices such as *face-to-face* (direct communication for five minutes prior to the game), *chat-room* (communication via a computer monitor), and *numerical cheap talk* (each person types in a number indicating his/her intended contribution to the public good that is seen by others but no further communication is allowed). Face-to-face communication is the most effective form and achieves total contributions that are about 96% of the socially optimal solution.

Chaudhuri et al. (2006) explore the implications of several forms of intergenerational advice given by one generation of players playing the public goods game to the next generation. They allow for several treatments that are differentiated on the basis of whether the advice is given to one member of the next generation, or to all members, and if this advice is publicly announced or not. Publicly announced advice is most effective in eliciting the greatest level of contributions, that is 90% of the socially optimal level.

Iturbe-Ormaetxe et al. (2011) consider *threshold public goods games* in which the public good materializes only when total contributions exceed a certain threshold level. In one treatment, the public goods provision game (PGP), subjects simultaneously contribute towards a public good and if the total contributions exceed a threshold, the public good is provided to all participants. In a second treatment, the public goods deterioration (PGD) treatment, subjects are initially endowed with a public good. But they are told that the good will completely deteriorate in the future, unless a threshold amount of voluntary contributions are raised to prevent the deterioration. In standard theory, one should not expect any difference in the results in the PGP and PGD treatments. By contrast, the authors find that the contributions are significantly higher in the PGD treatment. They explain their results using prospect theory. The presence of an initial entitlement to the public good in the PGD treatment creates a higher reference point. Since losses bite more than equivalent gains in prospect theory (loss aversion), subjects are willing to pay relatively more to avoid degradation of the public good. This result is analogous to the explanation of the endowment effect (see Volume 1 of the book).

1.4.4 Heterogenous preferences and the pattern of contributions

In public goods games, the *expectations of the contributions of others* is a critical factor in determining one's own contributions. Subjects in experiments initially contribute about 40–60% of their endowments.[33] In the absence of punishments, why does the level of cooperation drop off in successive rounds of the public goods game? One possible explanation is that subjects gain experience and, hence, learn how to maximize their self-regarding payoffs. But this does not explain why these subjects start with high cooperation rates if they are asked to play a repeated public goods contribution game once again (Andreoni, 1988).

---

[32] The level of contributions in the other groups are quite high as well. While the contributions in the second group are also high, the average contributions among the lowest group from round four onwards are about half the social optimum. The authors conjecture that the results for the lowest group arise on account of strategic considerations while those among the higher groups arise on account of conditional reciprocity.

[33] See, for instance, Dawes (1980) and Fischbacher et al. (2001). For an extensive survey of the results till about 1995, see Ledyard (1995).

The leading candidate for the explanation of these stylized facts is a theory that recognizes the role of reciprocity and the heterogeneity of players. The evidence is consistent with the view that a fraction of the subjects are conditional cooperators, while the remaining have self-regarding preferences. In repeated public goods games, the evidence in Fischbacher et al. (2001) indicates that 10% of the subjects always match the expected average contribution of others, 14% fully match the expected contributions of others until they spend half their endowments, 40% match the expected contributions of others to a lesser extent, 30% are free-riders, and the remaining 6% have no well-defined behavioral pattern.[34]

For the moment, let us ignore the last group which has no well-defined pattern, and find the rational expectations equilibrium of the model. Denote the expected average contribution of others by $\bar{y}^e$. Suppose that subjects have spent less than half their endowments. Then the behavior of the first two groups, constituting 24% of the population, is given by $y_1 = a_1 + \bar{y}^e$ and that of the third group, constituting 40% of the population, is given by $y_2 = a_2 + b_2 \bar{y}^e$, where $0 < b_2 < 1$ and $a_1, a_2 \geq 0$ are constants that are independent of $\bar{y}^e$. For the 30% who are free-riders, the contributions are $y_3 = 0$. Hence, conditional on $\bar{y}^e$, total contributions $y = 0.24 y_1 + 0.40 y_2 + 0.30 y_3$ can be written as

$$y = f(\bar{y}^e) = a + b\bar{y}^e, \tag{1.3}$$

where $a = 0.24 a_1 + 0.4 a_2 \geq 0$ and $b = 0.24 + 0.4 b_2 < 1$.

A rational expectations equilibrium requires us to find the fixed point of $y = f(\bar{y}^e)$. For one parameterization of the model, $y = f(\bar{y}^e)$ is depicted in Figure 1.10 by the line labeled "average conditional contribution." Crucially, this line is flatter than the 45° line, which is also shown. Suppose that we begin at an initial level of cooperation of 80% and subjects best respond to the observed contributions in the previous period. There is then a gradual temporal decay in cooperation until an equilibrium is achieved with an aggregate contribution of about 10%. The following important lessons emerge from this analysis.

1. Despite the fact that the self-regarding individuals are in a minority (30%), they drive down the level of cooperation of the conditionally cooperative players, who in this case are in a majority (64%), from a high level (80%) to a very low level (10%).
2. One cannot infer the incidence of reciprocity/altruism in a population, just by observing the final outcome. In this case, the aggregate equilibrium contribution of 10% hides the fact that more than half the players are conditional cooperators.
3. Upholding the belief that others will cooperate is very important for a cooperation norm to develop. If the possibility of punishment of non-cooperators is introduced, and the punishment technology is effective enough, then cooperation can be sustained.[35] The credibility of punishment, which arises from intrinsic reciprocity, prevents the non-cooperators from free-riding, hence, strengthening the belief that others will cooperate.

---

[34] For an early use of the term "conditional cooperation" in the context of public good experiments, see Sonnemans et al. (1999). Keser and van Winden (2000) find that as many as 80% of the experimental subjects behave in a conditional manner. Fischbacher and Gächter (2010) find that 55% of their subjects are conditional cooperators and 23% are free-riders.

[35] See Fehr and Schmidt (1999), Fehr and Gächter (2002), Ostrom et al. (1992), and Yamagishi (1986).

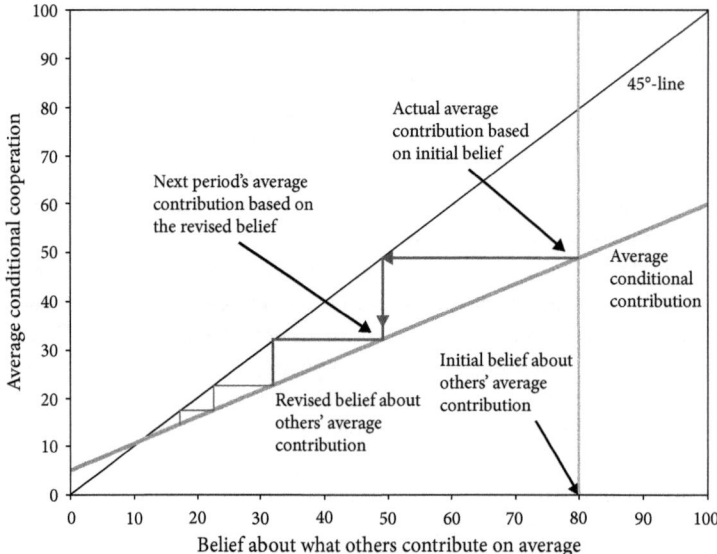

Figure 1.10 Explaining the pattern of contributions when there is heterogeneity in social preferences.
Source: Fehr and Fischbacher (2005).

Gürerk et al. (2006) conduct public goods experiments in which individuals self-select themselves into two possible "institutions" over 30 rounds. In any round, there are three stages. In stage 1, subjects choose among two institutions, a *sanctioning institution* (SI) and a *sanction-free institution* (SFI). Only in the SI can subjects engage in ex-post rewards and punishments. In stage 2, subjects are grouped by their chosen institution, given an endowment of 20 MUs, and play a simultaneous move public goods game. In stage 3, subjects may positively or negatively sanction other players in their group, if their institutional choice allows it. At the end of each round, subjects learn the payoffs of other players in each institution before playing the next round, where they get an opportunity to once again choose one of the two institutions.

The results are shown in Figure 1.11. In the first round, the results are as follows. The majority institutional choice is to shun sanctions; 36.9% choose SI to SFI. Of those who chose SI, almost half contribute at least 15 MUs (high contributors) and nearly three-quarters engage in punishment of low contributors. The neoclassical prediction with self-regarding preferences is that players should not engage in any ex-post punishments in this finitely repeated, full information game. High contributors in the SI comprise 13.1% of the total population of 84 subjects, and may be termed as strong reciprocators. This is in contrast to the outcome in the SFI, where 43.4% are free-riders and only 11.3% are high contributors. Only 2.4% of the subjects in SFI may be classified as strong reciprocators. Across both institutions, 15.5% are strong reciprocators in the first round.

Over time, subjects endogenously choose the SI, so that it becomes the predominant institution. Furthermore, average contributions in the SI reach almost first best levels of 20 MUs, while those in the SFI converge to near 0 MUs. In round 30, for instance, the average contribution in the SI is 19.4 MUs, while that in the SFI is 0 MUs.

What causes the switch in institutions to a more cooperative form? Suppose that individuals mimic the high payoff players. After round five, the payoff of high contributors in the SI is

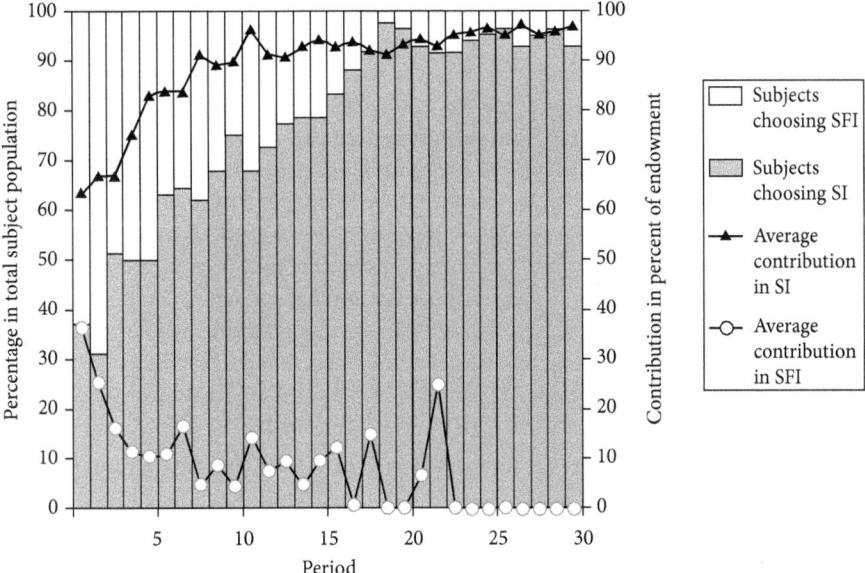

Figure 1.11 Choice of institutions and contributions.

Source: From Gürerk, Ö., Irlenbusch, B., and Rockenbach, B. "The competitive advantage of sanctioning institutions," Science (2006), 312(5770). Reprinted with permission from AAAS. Readers may view, browse, and/or download material for temporary copying purposes only, provided these uses are for non commercial personal purposes. Except as provided by law, this material may not be further reproduced, distributed, transmitted, modified, adapted, performed, displayed, published, or sold in whole or in part, without prior written permission from the publisher.

higher than the payoff of high/low contributors in the SFI and also higher than the payoff of low contributors in the SI. This provides a powerful incentive for free-riders in the SI to switch to high contributions in subsequent rounds. Furthermore, 80.3% of subjects who switch institutions from the SFI to the SI, immediately increase their contributions as they gain membership of the SI. In a significant finding, 27.1% of subjects who make this institutional switch, convert from being free-riders (0 MUs) to full cooperators (20 MUs). Thus, subjects quickly internalize the norm of contributions and punishments when they switch to a cooperating group; this is reminiscent of conformist behavior in models of cultural selection. Conversely, those who switch in the opposite direction, SI to SFI, immediately reduce contributions in a similar manner.

1.4.5 Unproductive expenditures on public goods

In the standard public goods experiments, punishments enhance efficiency and improve individual payoffs. However, in another class of public goods games, punishments may deter efficiency. Consider wasteful expenditures that might be incurred by groups of players in rent-seeking games to obtain a prize. The prize has the nature of a public good; it is non-rival and non-excludable for members of the winning group. For instance, two countries fighting a war over rights to a territory, a trade union striking for better wages, ethnic conflicts in countries, R&D competition among firms, several firms lobbying for a government contract, and two political parties fighting an election. These disputes could be between groups of people, or between individuals, or between individuals and groups. Abbink et al. (2010) consider this class of problems using Gordon Tullock's rent-seeking model.

Let there be two competing groups, $j = A, B$. The number of group members are $n_j = 1, 2, 3$, or 4 players depending on the treatment; when $n_j = 1$, the group comprises a single individual. The composition of the groups stays the same over successive rounds of the experiment. Each player is given an initial endowment of $E = 1000$ points, which can either be used to buy contest tokens (one point can be exchanged for one token), or be added to one's points balance, which can be redeemed for money at the end of the experiment. The objective is to win a prize of 1000 tokens, which is given to each player in the winning group. The total prize received by a winning group of size $N \in \{n_A, n_B\}$ is $1000N$. Thus, the prize has the characteristic of a public good among members of the winning group (non-rival in consumption and non-excludable).

Each team member, in each group, simultaneously chooses to buy a contest token. Denote the number of tokens purchased by player i in group $j = A, B$ by t_{ij}. Suppose that the total number of contest tokens purchased by groups A and B is $T_A = \sum_{i=1}^{n_A} t_{iA}$ and $T_B = \sum_{i=1}^{n_B} t_{iB}$. As in Tullock's model, the probability that any of the two groups, $j = A, B$, wins the prize equals $\frac{T_j}{T_A + T_B}$. The payoff of any risk-neutral player i in any of the groups $j = A, B$ in any round of the experiment is given by

$$\pi\left(t_{ij}, T_A, T_B\right) = E + \frac{T_j}{T_A + T_B} 1000 - t_{ij}. \tag{1.4}$$

There are 20 rounds of the experiment. In each round, each player from each group selects the number of contest tokens to buy. Using (1.4), the first order conditions with respect to t_{ij}, $j = A, B$, for an interior solution, give rise to two equations: $(T_A + T_B)^2 = 100 T_B$ and $(T_A + T_B)^2 = 100 T_A$. It follows that, in a Nash equilibrium, $T_A = T_B$. Setting $T_A = T_B$ in any of the first order conditions, one gets the Nash prediction $T_A^* = T_B^* = 250$.[36] The Nash equilibrium does not impose any restrictions on the contest tokens purchased by individuals, so long as $\sum_{i=1}^{n_j} t_{ij} = 250$, $j = A, B$.

In a Nash equilibrium, both groups buy identical number of tokens, so the winning probability for each group is $\frac{1}{2}$. Since $\frac{T_j}{T_A + T_B}$ is not defined for $T_A = T_B = 0$, if both groups coordinated by mutually reducing their respective total expenditures to any smallest possible amount $\epsilon > 0$, then their winning probability is also $\frac{1}{2}$. However, since expenditure on tokens reduces utility, at least for large groups (see (1.4)), the total expenditure on tokens across both groups $\sum_{j=1}^{n_j} \sum_{i=1}^{n_i} t_{ij}$ may be viewed as the extent of wasteful or unproductive expenditures.

We denote a generic treatment by $x : y$, where $x = n_A$ and $y = n_B$. The first three treatments are: 1:1, 1:4, and 4:4. In the fourth treatment, denoted by 4:4P, a punishment option is allowed and each group has four members. In treatment 4:4P, at the end of each round, after observing the contributions of other group members, costly punishment of one's group members is allowed. Sacrificing a token reduces the number of tokens of the punished player by three tokens. As in public goods games with self-regarding preferences and punishments, bygones are bygones, so we should not observe any punishments in equilibrium. Thus, the Nash equilibrium of the games 4:4 and 4:4P is predicted to be identical when individuals have self-regarding preferences.

---

[36] If one incorporates risk aversion in the payoff functions of individuals, then it can be shown that the equilibrium purchase of contest tokens is smaller.

We next define a measure of the total unproductive expenditures (tokens plus punishment expenditures) across both groups as a percentage of the total amount won, 1000N.

Definition 1.5 *(Rent dissipation):* The "rent dissipation not accounting for punishment costs" is given by $\sum_j \sum_i t_{ij}/1000N$, where N is the number of members in the group that wins the prize. Suppose that player i in group j inflicts a total punishment of p_{ij} tokens on other group members. Then "rent dissipation accounting for punishment costs" is given by $\sum_j \sum_i (t_{ij} + p_{ij})/1000N$.

In the fifth, and last, treatment denoted by 4:4/40, the treatment in which $n_A = n_B = 4$ is conducted over 40 rounds, instead of 20 rounds.

The results are as follows. Figure 1.12 considers treatments 1:1, 1:4, and 4:4 in which there is no punishment. It shows the average contest expenditures over the 20 rounds as well as the benchmark Nash equilibrium prediction of a contest expenditure of 250 tokens. When a single individual plays against a team of players (as in the treatment 1:4), then in the curve labeled (Teams), the sum of the expenditures of all team members is shown, while in the curve labeled (Individuals) only the individual expenditure of the singleton member is shown.[37]

In each of the treatments, the difference between the Nash prediction and the actual expenditures is statistically significant.[38] On average, individuals spend about twice the Nash prediction and teams spend about four times the Nash prediction. The average contributions reduce in

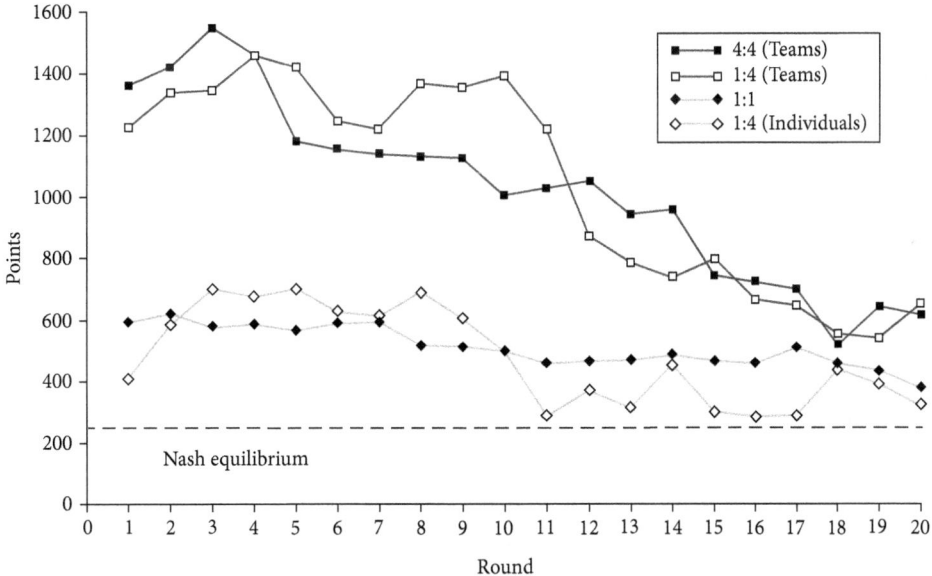

Figure 1.12 Contest expenditures in the treatments without punishment.
Source: Abbink et al. (2010) with permission from the American Economic Association.

---

[37] Thus, the curve labeled 1:4 (Individuals) shows the expenditure by the single team member of group A, while the curve labeled 1:4 (Teams) shows the expenditure by the combined team members of group B. The curve labeled 4:4 (Teams) shows the average across each of the two teams.
[38] This is not a new result; see Abbink et al. (2010) for the relevant references.

successive rounds in the direction of the Nash prediction. Yet in the last five rounds, when contributions are lowest, in treatments 1:4 and 4:4, they are still significantly higher relative to the Nash prediction in a statistical sense. Teams contribute significantly more towards conflict expenditures relative to individuals.

The downward trend in contributions over successive rounds makes one wonder if with sufficiently many rounds, the contributions would converge to the Nash prediction. However, when the 4:4/40 treatment is run, the contributions stabilize by round 30, so that there is no significant difference in contributions between rounds 31–35 and 36–40. The average contributions still remain significantly above the Nash prediction.

The effect of punishments is seen by comparing the two treatments, 4:4P, and 4:4. The punishment option significantly increases the level of conflict expenditures. Expenditures in treatment 4:4P are everywhere above the levels of the 4:4 treatment and higher in a statistically significant sense, even in the last five rounds. Indeed, if one adds the conflict expenditures across both teams of four players, they are nearly equal to the prize that the winner gets (4×1000). This dissipates almost the entire gains from the costly contest.

The punishment option is frequently used by the subjects in experiments in experimental games when it is available, as in public goods games. In classic public goods games experiments, due to free-riding, the actual contributions are lower than the socially optimum level, which is typically full contribution of the endowments (Fehr and Gächter, 2000). In this case, punishments nudge the contributions towards the social optimum and increase the payoffs of players. However, in the case of conflict expenditures, even though the prize has the features of a public good, the players contribute higher than the target (Nash equilibrium) and punishments drive the contributions further away from equilibrium and reduce the payoffs of players.

Figure 1.13 shows the extent of rent dissipation in the presence and in the absence of punishment for each of the four treatments, for each quarter of the 20 rounds. For the 4:4P treatment we show, separately, rent dissipation, while accounting for and not accounting for punishment (Definition 1.5). Rent dissipation is very high for the 1:1 treatment.[39] Interestingly, rent dissipation in the 4:4P treatment is higher than the 4:4 treatment and even higher than the 1:1 treatment. Thus, unlike the public goods game, punishments lead to huge, non-productive, expenditures in this case.

1.4.6 Antisocial punishments

The efficiency enhancing role of punishments in public goods experiments has mainly been documented in experiments conducted in the US and in Western Europe. In these societies, the indices for the *norms of civic cooperation* and *rule of law* are high.[40] Norms of civic cooperation encompass attitudes to tax evasion and abuse of the welfare state, while rule of law reflects peoples' trust in law enforcement institutions. Herrmann et al. (2008) consider the role of punishments in public goods games in 16 diverse societies (see Figure 1.14 for a list) with varying norms of civil cooperation and the rule of law.

The subject pool is undergraduate students who were similar in age and socio-demographic characteristics. The main finding is the presence of *antisocial punishments*, i.e., punishment of cooperators by non-cooperators, in public goods games that can reduce the level of cooperation.

---

[39] Recall that in the definition of rent dissipation, the denominator is 1000N, where N is the number of members in the group that wins the prize. *Ceteris paribus*, rent dissipation is highest when $N = 1$.

[40] These indices can be found, for instance, in the World Values Survey (see http://www.worldvaluessurvey.org/).

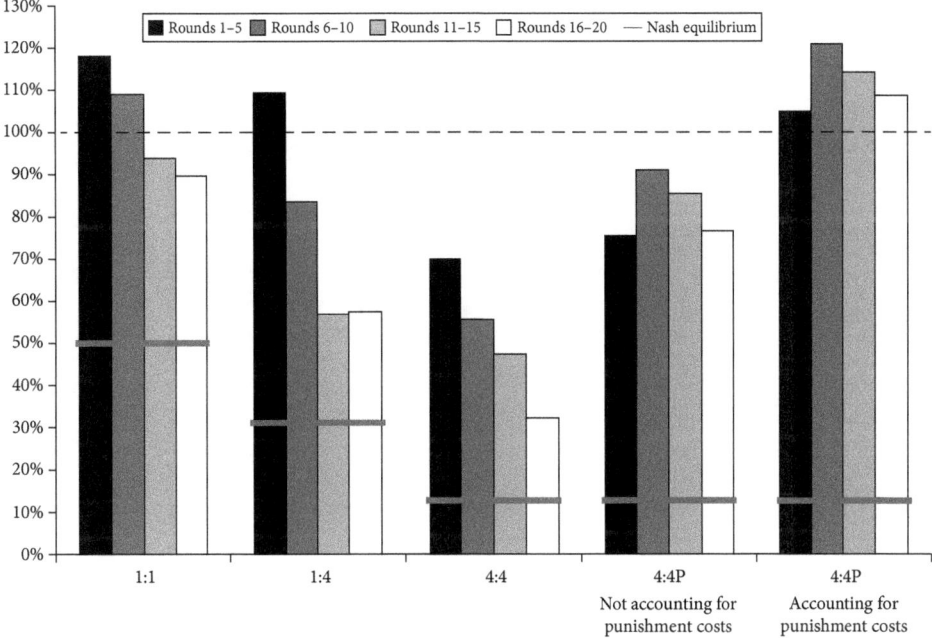

Figure 1.13 Actual and equilibrium rent dissipation.

Source: Abbink et al. (2010) with permission from the American Economic Association.

Groups of four players played the public goods game over ten rounds in the no punishment (N) and the punishment (P) treatments. Each subject had an initial endowment of 20 tokens, and for each token contributed to the public good, each player received a return of 0.4 tokens (in the terminology of Section 1.4.1, $r = 0.4$).

Figure 1.14 (left panel) shows the mean level of *prosocial punishments*, i.e., punished players contribute lower amounts, and *antisocial punishments*, i.e., punished players contribute higher amounts. Five categories of punishment are shown. The category labeled $[x,y]$, $x < y < 0$ shows the punishment of someone who contributed between x to y tokens less than the punisher (prosocial punishment). When $0 < x < y$, the category $[x,y]$ shows the punishment of players who contributed between x to y tokens more than the punisher (antisocial punishment). Prosocial punishment is widespread and the degree of variability is low. However, there is high variability in the level of antisocial punishment and differences in such punishments across groups are statistically significant.[41] The right panel of Figure 1.14 shows a negative relation between the mean levels of antisocial punishment and contributions to the public good (Spearman's correlation coefficient is −0.87). Thus antisocial punishments are associated with detrimental social outcomes.

One possible determinant of antisocial punishment is the human desire for revenge. Indeed, controlling for the level of contributions, the amount of punishment in period $t − 1$ is a significant determinant of the level of antisocial punishment in period t. This effect is highly significant

---

[41] In a follow-up study, Gächter and Herrmann (2009) find large cross-cultural differences in the antisocial punishment of prosocial cooperators in four cities in Russia and Switzerland.

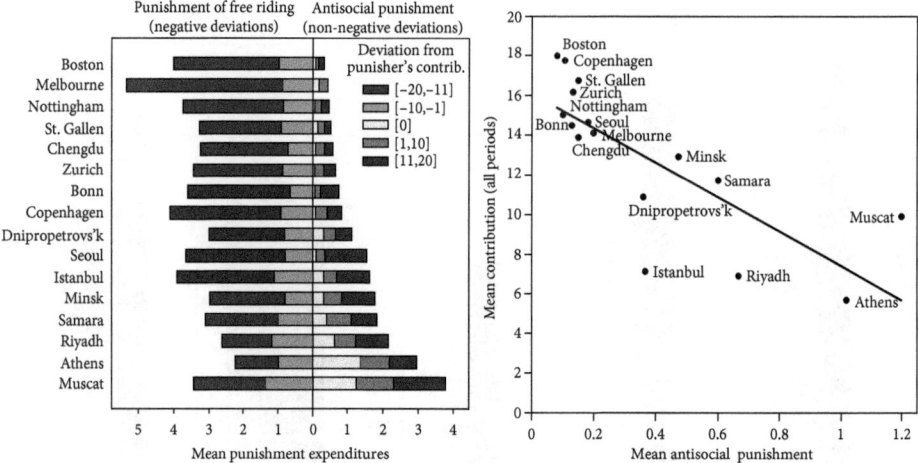

Figure 1.14 Prosocial and antisocial punishment in the public goods game (left panel) and the relation between antisocial punishment and contributions (right panel).

Source: From Herrmann, B., Thöni, C., and Gächter, S., "Antisocial punishment across societies," Science (2008), 319(5868). Reprinted with permission from AAAS. Readers may view, browse, and/or download material for temporary copying purposes only, provided these uses are for noncommercial personal purposes. Except as provided by law, this material may not be further reproduced, distributed, transmitted, modified, adapted, performed, displayed, published, or sold in whole or in part, without prior written permission from the publisher.

in seven groups, weakly significant in two groups and insignificant in the remaining groups. In all the groups, the level of cooperation stabilized over successive rounds in the P condition (LHS panel of Figure 1.15). However, unlike the earlier experimental results, punishments did not necessarily lead to high levels of contributions. By contrast, in the N condition (RHS panel of Figure 1.15), the level of contributions converged towards low levels in most groups, although there is still significant variability by round ten. In both treatments, history plays a powerful role. Groups that start off at higher levels of contributions continue at a higher level throughout the ten rounds of the experiment. On the whole, the cooperation level was relatively higher in the P treatment, in a weakly significant sense, in eleven groups, while there was no significant difference in the other five groups.

Thus, a central message here is that when one allows for cultural variations and departures from Western subject pools, the efficacious effect of social sanctions cannot be taken for granted. A regression analysis shows that antisocial punishments are more likely to be carried out in groups where the norm of civic cooperation and the rule of law is weak. Both variables are statistically significant when antisocial punishments take place. However, with prosocial punishments, the rule of law is no longer significant in explaining the differences in contribution rates. In interpreting these results, Gintis (2009, p. 81) writes: "The success of democratic market societies may depend critically upon moral virtues as well as material interests, so the depiction of economic actors as 'homo economicus' is as incorrect in real life as it is in the laboratory."

Falk et al. (2005) explore the motivation for private sanctions in a three-player prisoner's dilemma game. After the strategy choices have been made, by giving up a unit of their payoffs, players who sanction can reduce the payoff of another player by an amount $\gamma \geq 1$. In the high sanctions treatment (high γ), they find that 68.5% of the cooperators punish defectors.

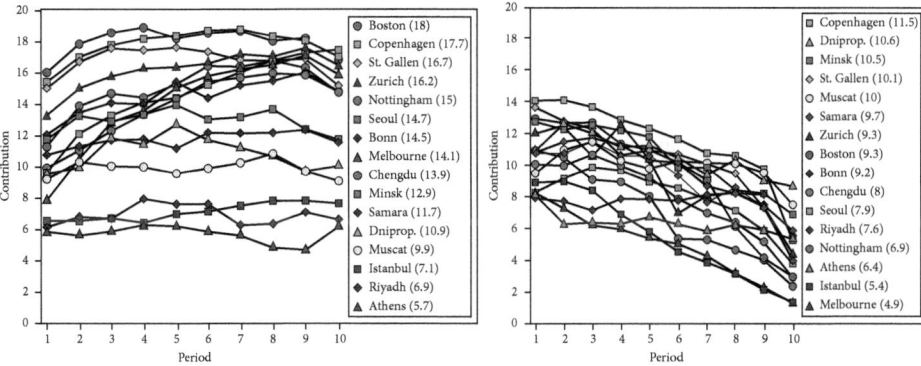

Figure 1.15 Mean contributions in the P treatment (left panel) and the N treatment (right panel).

Source: From Herrmann, B., Thöni, C., and Gächter, S., "Antisocial punishment across societies," Science (2008), 319(5868). Reprinted with permission from AAAS. Readers may view, browse, and/or download material for temporary copying purposes only, provided these uses are for noncommercial personal purposes. Except as provided by law, this material may not be further reproduced, distributed, transmitted, modified, adapted, performed, displayed, published, or sold in whole or in part, without prior written permission from the publisher.

Indeed, cooperators almost exclusively punish defectors. About 40% of defectors imposed sanctions on other defectors. However, 34% of defectors punished other cooperators—a form of antisocial punishment. At the individual level, cooperators punish more than defectors. In the low sanctions condition ($\gamma = 1$), sanctions cannot reduce payoff differences. Only 2.2% of the defectors punished others but nearly 60% of the cooperators punished other defectors; intentions based-theories may provide one possible explanation.

1.4.7 Evolution and reciprocity

Why does reciprocity arise? The literature arising from theories of evolution, based on the framework of a *selfish gene*, argues that altruism is fitness reducing (Dawkins, 1989). Reciprocity in this framework is a *maladaptation* (Ghiselin, 1974; Hamilton, 1964; Trivers, 1971; Williams, 1966). However, the propensity of individuals to cooperate with others and act in a prosocial manner, reviewed above, especially those who are not related by kin, suggests that self-interest is not the only motive. In other words, there is support for conditional reciprocity, which includes intrinsic reciprocity. Gintis (2000) shows that starting from a population of purely self-regarding individuals, mutants who have regard for others can successfully invade the population, i.e., purely self-regarding preferences is not an evolutionary stable strategy. In equilibrium, there is a polymorphic population that consists of both self-regarding and reciprocal types. The intuition is that during times of hardship, e.g., wars and famine, and in cooperative activities, such as hunting, the ability to cooperate is essential for survival. Purely self-regarding phenotypes will find it difficult to survive such periods. Hence, a certain critical number of prosocial types may become essential to tide over such times. Furthermore, in group conflict, altruism may result in an increase in the fitness of the group, which is a controversial idea in biology. These issues are sufficiently vexed, and important at the same time, that they require a fuller treatment and the development of the relevant analytical machinery (Bowles and Gintis, 2013; Gintis et al., 2001; Gintis et al., 2003). These issues are considered in Volume 6.

1.5 How representative is the lab evidence?

Can lab experiments provide a useful guide to the choices of individuals in the field? This is the issue of *external validity* of lab experiments that is already considered in detail in the introductory chapter in Volume 1; the interested reader is advised to read both treatments in conjunction because they often consider non-overlapping issues. Consider some possible objections to the external validity of the lab experimental evidence in the context of other-regarding preferences (Levitt and List, 2007). First, there may be adverse selection among students who volunteer for experiments. For instance, those with preferences for reciprocity may self-select themselves to participate in these experiments leading to an overestimation of reciprocity among humans. Second, subjects in experiments may simply be acting in a reciprocal manner because they believe that this is what the experimenter wishes to demonstrate (*experimenter demand effect*).[42] Third, subjects in experiments interact anonymously with others in the experiment whereas most real-world data is generated by personal interaction among people. These are legitimate concerns. The aim of this section is to examine the empirical evidence for such concerns. Recent scholarship allays fears over many of these concerns.

1.5.1 *The student subject pool and experimental scrutiny*

Falk et al. (2013) examine the criticism that the experimental results derived from the student population may have biased the findings. From 2004 to 2009, 89% of the studies considered by them used the student population as subjects in experiments. This is a particularly valuable study because it elicits fairness concerns of the student and the non-student populations, using the same experimental protocol. A variant of the trust games is used to elicit fairness preferences.

The main findings are as follows. First, students with reciprocal preferences are not more likely to be self-selected into experiments. Second, the non-student subject pool exhibits more reciprocity in the sense that responders return significantly more money to the proposer in the trust game. So if anything, the student population may lead to downwardly biased inferences about the degree of reciprocity. A range of other evidence supports the assertion that the non-student population is relatively more prosocial; see, Fehr and List (2004), List (2004), Bellemare et al. (2008), Carpenter et al. (2008), Burks et al. (2009), and Baran et al. (2010). In a gift exchange game, Hannan et al. (2002) also find lower reciprocity among undergraduate students relative to MBAs under identical experimental conditions. Their explanation is that MBAs have greater experience in job environments where gift exchange is important.

Cleave et al. (2012) conduct experiments with 1,173 students that play a trust game and a lottery choice task in a classroom experiment. The resulting data are assumed to be the preferences of the general student population. These 1,173 students are then invited to participate in a lab experiment. Those who turn up for the lab experiment exhibit preferences similar to those of the general student population. Thus, the authors conclude, it is not necessarily the case that more prosocial students select themselves into lab experiments.

Could students simply be making more prosocial choices in the lab because they perceive that this is what the experimenter desires (experimenter demand-effects and experimental scrutiny)? Or, perhaps, they may feel that self-regarding or greedy choices are likely to be frowned upon by

---

[42] For a thought-provoking discussion of the issues involved in such *experimental demand effects*, and how they might be minimized, see Zizzo (2010).

other observers (*audience effect*), hence, they may, falsely, exhibit other-regarding preferences in the lab? These concerns are articulated in Levitt and List (2007). Bandiera et al. (2005) find that the monitoring of workers, relative to non-monitoring, induces more prosocial behavior. Recall also the discussion on Haley and Fessler (2005), above, in which simply showing subjects a pair of eyes in dictator games may induce them to give more, yet these results do not carry over to games with strategic concerns (Fehr and Schneider, 2010).

Barmettler et al. (2012) directly address the question of experimental scrutiny in a carefully controlled experiment using three experimental games, a dictator game, an ultimatum game, and a trust game. In the dictator and the ultimatum games, the first mover, respectively, the dictator and the proposer, was given CHF 20 to allocate between himself and the second mover (the receiver/responder). In the trust game, the trustor and the trustee were given an endowment of CHF 10 each. Each subject played each game only once in a between-subjects design.

The typical method of conducting these experimental games is through a computer interface. However, this requires the presence of an experimenter who may scrutinize the choices that students make. For this reason, the authors conduct their experiments with paper and pen in a classroom, and the students were seated sufficiently far apart to ensure anonymity of choices. The students were provided packages with colored envelopes and pens and a personal ID number that only they knew. They made their choices on paper and stuffed the choices back into the envelopes. The envelopes were collected by the experimenters, and the relevant payments based on the choices were put back into the envelopes.

In the single-anonymous treatment (S), at the end of the experiment, the subjects reported their id numbers to the experimenter who matched it to the envelopes and handed the envelopes to the subjects. In this case, the experimenter could have observed the choices of the students. In the double-anonymous treatment (D), the subjects collected their payments directly, and privately, from a table on which the envelopes with ID numbers were placed. In this case, the experimenter could not identify the choices made by the participants.

The results are shown in Figure 1.16. In none of the three games and for any player in any role (proposer or responder, trustor or trustee), is there any statistically significant difference in the choices of the players across treatments S and D. In the dictator game, in treatment S, the median amount transferred by dictators is CHF 3.9, while in treatment D it is 3.6; the difference is statistically insignificant. These results are consistent with the results in Hoffman et al. (1994) for dictator games who varied the degree of experimental anonymity but the results were not statistically different.

For the ultimatum game, the mean offer of the proposer is CHF 8.6 in treatment S and CHF 8.3 in treatment D. The difference is statistically insignificant and the median offers are identical. The behavior of responders in treatments S and D is not statistically different.[43] In the trust game, the median transfer by the trustor in treatment D is CHF 8, while in treatment S it is CHF 7. In this case as well, the differences are statistically insignificant and the average transfers are identical.

Critics of the effect of experimental scrutiny on other-regarding preferences have perhaps been too harsh. If experimental scrutiny turns out to be important, it would serve to illustrate the powerful role of other-regarding preferences. Some critics argue that simply by having an observer (an experimenter) in the room or having a picture of a pair of eyes of an anonymous

---

[43] Bolton and Zwick (1995) find significant effects of anonymity on the results for ultimatum games in some of the trials. But anonymity only explains a small percentage of the departures from equilibrium play in their experiments. Barmettler et al. (2012) also note procedural differences across the single- and double-anonymous treatments in Bolton and Zwick (1995).

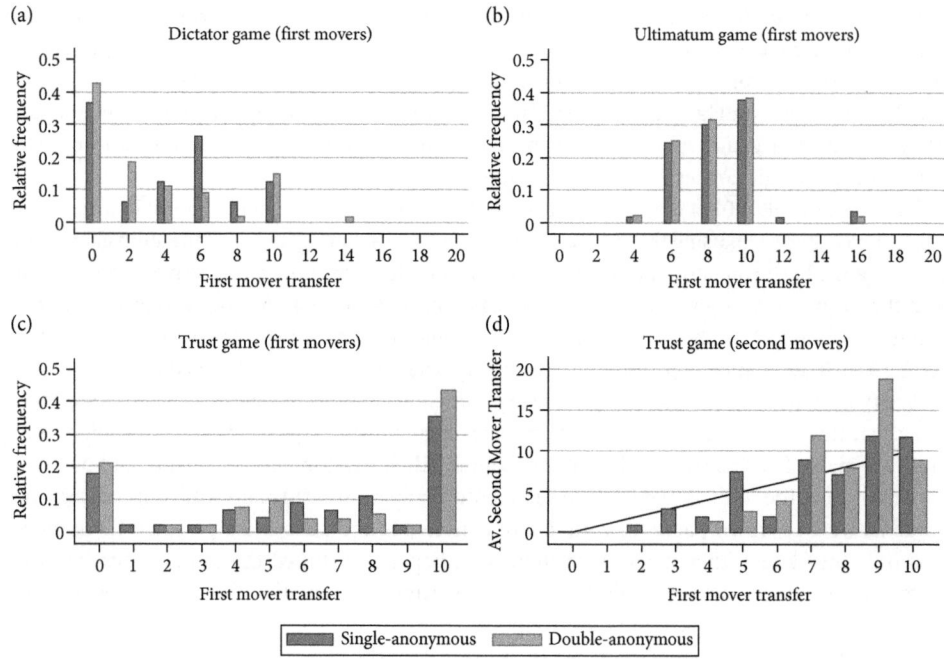

Figure 1.16 Results for the single- and double-anonymous treatments.

Source: Reprinted from Games and Economic Behavior, 75(1): 17–34. Barmettler, F., Fehr, E., and Zehnder, C., "Big experimenter is watching you! Anonymity and prosocial behavior in the laboratory." © 2012, with permission from Elsevier.

individual in the room seems to switch on other-regarding preferences. Many real-world interactions are either directly observed by third parties or allow for credible information transmission to third parties. Using the critics' argument, institutions that wish to promote human sociality then appear to have an extremely low-cost method of switching on other-regarding preferences in most cases. This is in line with anthropological findings of cooperation in small groups of individuals; see Gintis (2009).

1.5.2 The external validity of experiments on other-regarding preferences

Cohn et al. (2012) address issues of the external validity of lab experiments in the gift exchange game. Using a Swiss subject pool, where subjects distributed newspapers at train stations and other public places, working on a regular hourly pay of CHF 22, they implemented an increase in salary of CHF 5 to CHF 27. They found that only workers who felt that the original salary was unfair responded by putting in more effort. Those who felt that the original salary was fair, did not increase their effort in a statistically significant manner; Figure 1.17 shows the workers' average performance and the standard errors. In a lab experiment, conducted on the same subjects, they were able to elicit the other-regarding preferences of the subjects. Those subjects who behaved selfishly in the lab did not increase their effort in the field, following a wage increase, regardless of whether they considered the original salary (CHF 22) to be fair or unfair. Thus, the effect shown in Figure 1.17 is driven by workers who were prosocial in the lab. In this case, behavior in the lab appears to have a high degree of external validity.

Carpenter and Seki, (2011) study the behavior of two types of fishermen in Toyama Bay, Japan, who mainly fish for shiroebi (Japanese glass shrimp). The *poolers* who have been operating as

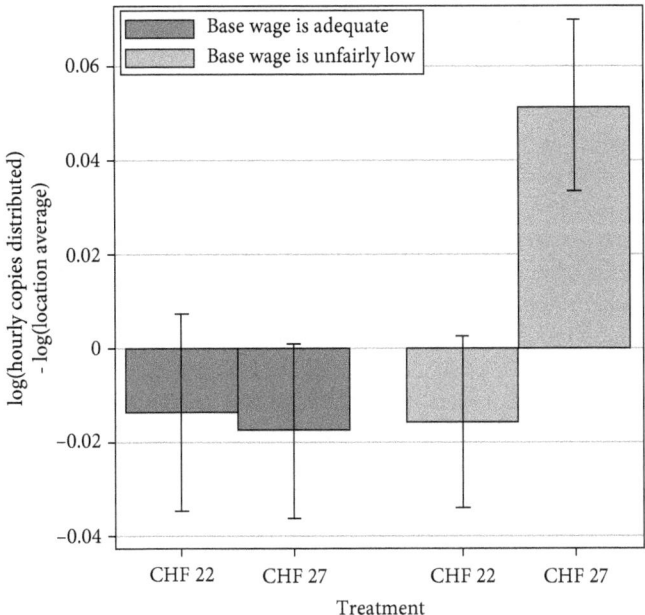

Figure 1.17 Workers' performance response to the wage increase (vertical axis), conditional on their fairness perceptions.
Source: Cohn et al. (2012). Reproduced with permission. © INFORMS, http://www.informs.org.

such since the early 1960s, pool their incomes, expenditures, and the fish catch. This activity requires substantial coordination, cooperation, and concern among the individuals. The second group of fishermen, the *non-poolers*, who have been operating since 1992, work on an individual basis; they do not pool their resources, or the fish catch. The aim of the study is to see if there is a link between the other-regarding preferences of the two groups, as elicited by a *modified public goods game* (MPG game) and the choice of their real-life activity, poolers or non-poolers. Thus, the study directly addresses the issue of the external validity of lab experiments on other-regarding preferences.

In the MPG game, conducted in 2003, groups of four individuals are formed, and the experimenter gives each individual an initial endowment that is equivalent to about USD 4.30. The experiment lasted less than an hour and each participant earned USD 73.19, on average. The experiment is conducted separately with poolers, non-poolers, and students recruited from nearby universities.

In the first five rounds of the experiment, the participants play a standard public goods game without punishments. The experimenter doubles the total contributions of the group and then redistributes the resulting total among the four members. Since the return on a unit of contribution is 0.5 for each group member, it is optimal to free-ride if one has purely self-regarding preferences. The efficient outcome is for each individual to contribute their full endowment. In the remaining five rounds of the experiment, a *social disapproval protocol* is unexpectedly introduced at the end of each round. According to this protocol, the contributions of all group members are randomized and shown to the others. Conditional on having observed the contribution of others, group members can then buy, at a cost of 10 yen each, either a smiley face (to indicate approval) or a sad face (to indicate disapproval). These faces are then shown to the group at the beginning of the next round, so that group members can gauge the approval levels of others.

The MPG game allows the experimenter to identify several aspects of the other-regarding preferences of poolers, non-poolers, and students. For instance, when individual contributions in round t are regressed on total contributions in round $t-1$, the intercept term recovers the degree of *unconditional cooperation*, while the slope term recovers the degree of *conditional cooperation*. Similarly, the propensity to send sad faces recovers *disapproval*, and the reaction in round t to the number of sad faces based on contributions in round $t-1$, recovers *response to disapproval*.

One can now directly examine the productivity of fishing boats belonging to poolers and non-poolers and examine if productivity is affected by (1) conditional cooperation, (2) unconditional cooperation, (3) propensity to show disapproval, and (4) response to disapproval. A range of other control variables, e.g., the experience of the fishermen, is carefully introduced. Conditional cooperation, recovered from the lab evidence, is significantly positively correlated with actual productivity of the fishermen. This tendency is stronger for poolers as compared to the non-poolers. Conditional cooperation in the lab is the single most important variable in explaining the higher productivity of poolers relative to non-poolers.

The propensity to show disapproval is also a statistically significant factor in explaining higher productivity, although the response to disapproval is not positively related to productivity. Finally, poolers are found to exhibit greater unconditional cooperation in the lab, relative to non-poolers. It is eminently possible that many decades of being involved in team production has shaped the other-regarding preferences of poolers. As in Falk et al. (2013), the finding here is that the student population is less cooperative. The authors remark in their conclusion that: "This sort of result—students being less pro-social than field participants—has become a 'stylized fact' of the field experimental literature."

Fehr and Leibbrandt (2011) study the behavior of fishermen in rural fishing villages in northeastern Brazil. There are two kinds of individuals. Those who catch shrimp (shrimpers) and those who catch fish (fishermen). The shrimpers and the fishermen operate on a lake that has common property rights with no legal limits on the amount of the catch and the costs of fishing are relatively small. The main focus is on the fishing instruments used. Shrimp traps with small holes or fishing nets with smaller holes increase the catch but create an immediate and future negative externality for others. Shrimpers and fisherman are aware of this channel of causality.

The size of the holes is taken as a measure of the cooperation of the shrimpers and the fishermen. The smaller the holes, the less cooperative is the observed behavior. Shrimpers and fishermen first play a public goods game (PG). Each participant is also asked to state, prior to making their contributions, the contributions that they expect of others. It is found that the expected contributions of others are the best predictor of one's contributions in the PG game, which suggests the presence of conditional cooperation. In a separate experiment, the time preference parameters of the shrimpers and fishermen are also elicited because the negative externalities accrue now and in the future.

Figure 1.18 illustrates the main insights of the paper. The horizontal axis classifies the contributions in the PG game into three categories—low, medium, and high. The vertical axis measures the actual hole size used by shrimpers and fishermen. More cooperative behavior in the PG game is also associated with a larger hole size, which corresponds to greater cooperation in the field data. Fehr and Leibbrandt (2011, p. 1146) write: "We show that there is no insurmountable gap between the laboratory and the field, even though the context in our laboratory environment differs from the field context in important ways." Impatience, as measured in the time preference

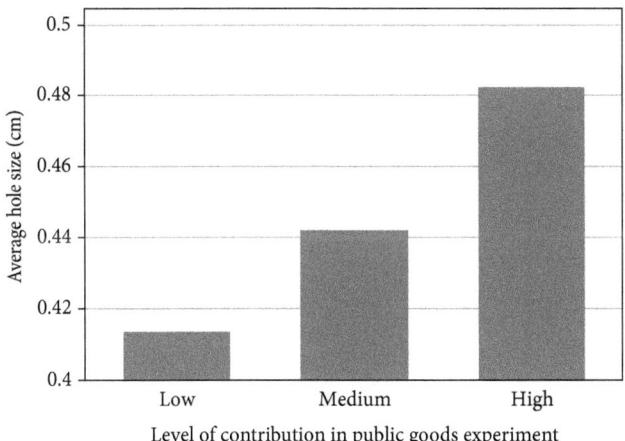

Figure 1.18 Checking the external validity of lab data on social preferences.
Source: Reprinted from Journal of Public Economics, 95(9–10): 114–55. Fehr, E. and Leibbrandt, A., "A field study on cooperativeness and impatience in the Tragedy of the Commons." © 2011, with permission from Elsevier.

experiments, is not related to contributions in the public goods game. Hence, while both cooperation and impatience are important in the degree of exploitation of common resource problems, they operate through separate channels.

The subject pool in Leibbrandt (2012) is shrimp fisherman in Brazil who sell their shrimp, individually, in open air markets. The fishermen participate in a public goods experiment (PGE) and a risk aversion experiment in which the identity of the opponents is kept anonymous. In the PGE, each player is given 10 MUs (monetary units). In the unique Nash equilibrium, each player should free-ride and in the socially optimal equilibrium, each player should contribute all 10 MUs. The number of MUs that are contributed is used to measure the *degree of prosociality*. This allows the segregation of all subjects into two pools.

Those that contribute less than 4 MUs (54.6%) are classified as *less prosocial* and those who contribute 4 MUs or more (45.4%) are classified as more prosocial. Following the collection of lab data, two kinds of real-life data are collected from the shrimp sellers. First, survey data on various aspects of their sociality. Second, actual data on prices and quantities sold. The results are as follows.

1. Less prosocial sellers are more likely to sell their shrimp catch at a relatively lower price. Except for a minimal range of prices, the distribution function of the price of shrimps sold by more prosocial sellers first order stochastically dominates the distribution function of less prosocial sellers. Sellers who completely free-ride in the PGE, achieve the least shrimp price per unit. Controlling for several other factors (shrimp size, risk aversion, experience, gender, and color of shrimp) sociality, as observed in the lab, has a significantly positive effect on the prices of the individual shrimp sellers.
2. More prosocial sellers are less likely to lose important buyers and more likely to have trade relations of greater duration. For instance, 59.3% of the less prosocial sellers had trade relations less than or equal to three years, while the corresponding figure for more prosocial sellers is 37.7%. The average duration of the trade relationship for more prosocial sellers is six years, and the corresponding figure for less prosocial sellers is 4.5 years.

3. In the self-reported surveys, more prosocial sellers also report greater confidence in the extent to which they can signal their trustworthiness.

These results are intriguing. Future research can check for the robustness of these findings in other contexts and clarify the transmission mechanism between other-regarding preferences and the relevant economic variables. However, this research rules out two of the channels that were considered to be important. (1) Prosocial players self-select themselves into jobs with higher earnings and productivity. (2) Prosocial individuals earn more because they interact better with colleagues. Explanation 1 does not work because both types of sellers are found in the same profession and the second explanation does not work because this is a market in which the sellers are individual players. The authors conjecture an explanation along the lines of Bowles et al. (2001). Since prosocial sellers are less likely to engage in opportunistic behavior with buyers, they reap the reputational benefits in terms of the volume and the terms of trade.

Rustagi et al. (2010) consider issues of forest conservation, a common property resource, in Ethiopia. The Bale Oromo people in the Bale region were given property rights over the forest in return for managing the forest cover through conservation efforts, sustainable tree felling, and monitoring misuse by others. In the first stage of the experiment, a public goods game was played with the subjects. Groups of two players were formed. Each of the players had to give a response to how much they would contribute, conditional on the seven possible levels of contributions of the other players; this is the *strategy method* of eliciting choices. One of the players was then picked at random and asked to make an offer, following which the other player's offer, revealed from the strategy method, is implemented.

A player is defined to be a conditional cooperator if his contribution is increasing in the perceived contribution of the other player. Based on the experimental results, players are categorized into four types. The most interesting types in the current context are the *free-riders*, or type 0 players (11.49%), *weak conditional cooperators*, or type 2 players (11.63%), and *strong conditional cooperators* or type 3 players (34.02%); the remaining players, type 1 players, have mixed preferences and it is difficult to classify them cleanly into any of these three categories. The main difference between weak and strong conditional cooperators is the difference in statistical significance of the correlation between their contributions and the contributions of others.

In terms of forest management, the main indicator of cooperation is the extent of costly personal monitoring of the forest, say, through forest patrols, to prevent misuse of the common resource. The main hypothesis is that cooperation in the public goods game and the degree of cooperation in managing the common forest resource are correlated. This is borne out by the evidence, as shown in Figure 1.19. There is a statistically significant relation between cooperation in the lab and in the field. The authors conclude on p. 964: "In sum, better forest management outcomes are not only a result of conditional cooperators being more likely to abide by the local rules of the group but also being more willing to enforce these rules at a personal cost."

Karlan (2005) considers participants in a microcredit program in Peru. The participants are members of a non-profit group lending organization in Ayacucho, Peru that allows poor women to borrow and save. Loans are given for a period of four months and the organization actively encourages members to develop a savings habit. In the first step, these participants play a standard trust game. The amount given by the first mover (investor or trustor) is an indication of the degree of *trust*, while the amount sent back by the second mover (the responder or trustee) is often termed as the degree of *trustworthiness*.

The aim of this study is to see if actions taken in the trust game can predict the outcomes of the financial decisions a year later. In relation to the outcomes in the trust game, the two main

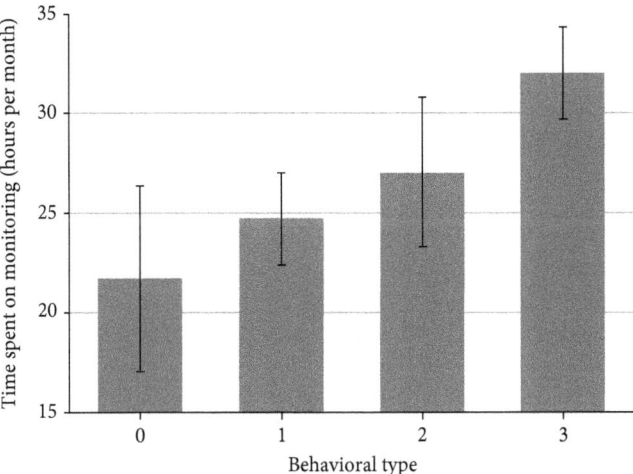

Figure 1.19 Average time spent on monitoring by different behavioral types. The bars represent standard errors of means.

Source: From Rustagi, D., Engel, S., and Kosferd, M. "Conditional cooperation and costly monitoring explain success in forest commons management," Science (2010), 330(6006). Reprinted with permission from AAAS. Readers may view, browse, and/or download material for temporary copying purposes only, provided these uses are for noncommercial personal purposes. Except as provided by law, this material may not be further reproduced, distributed, transmitted, modified, adapted performed, displayed, published, or sold in whole or in part, without prior written permission from the publishers.

hypotheses are the following.[44] (1) A greater degree of trustworthiness should be associated with a greater likelihood of repaying loans. (2) A higher degree of trust should be associated with a greater gambling instinct. Such players should save less. Both hypotheses are confirmed by the evidence.

Hargreaves Heap et al. (2012) test the external validity of lab experiments on prosociality on the Gisu people in eastern Uganda. The Gisu are known for individualistic behavior and relatively low levels of prosociality, even with insiders in the same village or people sharing a common lineage. The authors played the trust game with the Gisu and tested two hypotheses. The first is that the Gisu are expected to exhibit relatively less prosocial behavior compared to the typical lab findings. The second is that even when one observes prosocial behavior, insiders will be favored less relative to the typical experimental findings. The authors are unable to reject any of these hypotheses.

Baran et al. (2010) consider the entire 2008 cohort of Chicago MBA students. These students play the trust game in one of their courses. As a measure of trustworthiness, 83.8% of the students in their role as the trustee, return at least 30% of the amount sent to them by the trustor. Eighteen months later, the same students are followed up to observe the amount of donations they make back to the school. Trustworthiness in the trust game is a significant predictor of the actual donations made by the students. Thus, lab experiments have high external validity and subjects do not just exhibit more trustworthiness in experiments to appear nice to the experimenter. The

---

[44] The author also considers a public goods game and results of a General Social Survey that we do not report here.

authors feel that their results are strong enough to conclude that: "In sum, our paper provides evidence that lab measures are a reasonably accurate way of predicting individual behavior in the field, bolstering support for using laboratory experiments to measure other-regarding preferences. It also supports the claim that reciprocity is an important—even characteristic—preference of many, but not all, individuals."

Benz and Meier (2008) consider University of Zurich students who are asked each semester, at the time of renewal of their registration, if they would like to, anonymously and voluntarily, contribute to one of two funds. Fund A helps students in financial difficulties and one can contribute CHF 7 (about USD 5) and Fund B supports foreign students at the University of Zurich and one can contribute CHF 5 (about USD 4). The students can also choose not to contribute to any fund. The decisions of the students are taken as the relevant field data.

These students subsequently participate in one of two experiments where they allocate an endowment of CHF 12 given to them by the experimenter. In the first experiment, the social funds experiment, 99 students are asked to contribute to the same fund (or not contribute at all) that they did in the field experiment in the university. In the second experiment, 83 students are asked to choose to contribute between two randomly chosen charities outside the university. The students were not aware that they were participating in a scientific study that was comparing their field and experimental actions. The field and the experimental data are in close agreement. For instance, the average contribution of the students in the social funds experiment was CHF 9.46, while in the field study they had contributed CHF 9.07 in the previous semester and CHF 9.55 in the four semesters after the experiment took place. This indicates external validity of lab evidence; similarity in prosocial behavior from earned/unearned income; and stable preferences.

List (2006) reports on lab and field experiments conducted with sports card traders.[45] The lab experiments are carefully conducted in a location very near the field experiments and are closely matched in protocol. The study examines whether sellers reciprocate higher price offers of buyers by offering sports cards of higher quality, and whether this response differs in the lab relative to the field. Overall, quality for each price is lower in the field relative to that in the lab. For instance, the average quality offered by sellers for price offers of $20 by buyers in the lab and the field are respectively 3.1 and 2.3; the corresponding figures for a price offer of $65 are 4.1 and 3.1. However, the response of price to quality is comparable in the lab and in the field.

Levitt and List (2008) interpret the results in List (2006) as greater reciprocity in the lab relative to that in the field. However, Camerer (2015) re-examines this data in a within-subjects analysis in which the same individuals participated in the lab and the field experiments. He shows that the data reported in Levitt and List (2008) is for a smaller sample of non-local dealers only who account for just 30% of the sample. It turns out that the non-locals are indeed relatively more reciprocal in the lab. However, this result reverses for the local dealers (70% of the sample) who are relatively more reciprocal in the field. Pooling across the two kinds of dealers, and using three different statistical tests of significance, no firm conclusions can be drawn for the difference between lab and field data. Camerer concludes (p. 271): "To be crystal clear, I am not sure whether dealers behave differently in the lab and the field, in the most closely matched comparison of lab-market and field (cards)." Camerer (2015) reviews a set of papers where the lab features are deliberately matched with field features to ensure comparability between the two. He finds only one paper, by Stoop et al. (2012), based on data collected from fishermen in Holland, where

---

[45] See also the introduction of this book for a more detailed account of this research.

prosociality in the lab is weaker relative to the field experiments. Even in this case, he believes that (p. 275): "it is not strong evidence because there are many differences between field and lab."

1.6 Indirect reciprocity

A variety of games studied above, e.g., the ultimatum game, gift exchange game, trust game, public goods game, illustrate the powerful role of reciprocity. *Indirect reciprocity*, refers to the actions taken by a third party (e.g. social approval or disapproval) on observing kind or unkind behavior between at least two other parties; the payoffs of the third party are not necessarily directly influenced. The term indirect reciprocity was used by Alexander (1987) who invoked it to provide an evolutionary basis for cooperation and punishment in human societies.

Seinen and Schram (2001) use the *helping game* to illustrate the importance of indirect reciprocity. Subjects in the experiment were paired randomly in repeated bilateral interactions. In each interaction, one of the subjects was given the role of a donor and the other, the role of a recipient. The only decision for the donor is to decide to *give* an amount of money, $m > 0$, at a cost $c > 0$ such that $c < m$, or to *pass* the opportunity to give, in which case, the game ends. The recipient is passive in each interaction. The act of giving (or helping) is what gives this game its name.

All individuals are given "scores" that reflect their social status. A score at any point in time, indicates the number of times that an individual chose to give (helpful choice) as a donor, in the past six decisions. Hence, the social status of an individual belongs to seven possible categories: $0, 1, \ldots, 6$. For instance, a social status of 4 means that the individual chose to give four times in the past six rounds, but declined the opportunity to give twice. Cost, c, can be either high (*HC* treatment) or low (*LC* treatment), and information on social status can either be public (*I* treatment), or private (*N* treatment). The interactions between these four categories are then considered. For instance, *LCI* is the treatment in which costs are low and information about social status is public. The results are as follows.

1. The highest fraction of helpful choices is in the *LCI* treatment and the lowest in the *HCN* treatment.
2. The difference in the fraction of helpful choices between the following pairs of treatments is statistically significant at the 5% level: *LCI-HCN* and *HCI-HCN*.
3. Subjects with high social status are almost always reciprocated.[46] This provides evidence of indirect reciprocity. Thus, it seems entirely rational for subjects to build a reputation for helping using the channel of indirect reciprocity.
4. Subjects are often found to be using cutoff rules, e.g., help the recipient if her social status is greater than some cutoff level.
5. There are interesting dynamics, which suggest that the initial level of social status in a critical minimum level of the population is crucial in determining whether, over time, the subjects will evolve towards higher or lower cooperation.

---

[46] Hargreaves Heap and Varoufakis (2002) first consider the effect of endogenously generated social status in a hawk-dove game. Then, their subjects play a modified hawk-dove game that adds an extra pure strategy—cooperate. Subjects who were discriminated against in the first game were more likely to cooperate with each other in the second game.

Engelmann and Fischbacher (2009) argue that the study by Seinen and Schram (2001) confounds two factors—indirect reciprocity and strategic considerations. So, donors might wish to give for two possible reasons. (1) For strategic reasons, in order to build a reputation in terms of social status, so that in their future roles as recipients, they receive greater help from the donors. (2) On account of indirect reciprocity, to reward recipients whose social status is high. In their experimental design, the donor can give up 6 units of the experimental money to enable the recipient to receive 15 units. The game was repeated over 80 rounds. For some subjects, the *social status* based on scores (number of times they helped in five previous times in the role of donors) was made public in the first 40 rounds, and for the rest, in the last 40 rounds.

Thus, in any round, one could observe the interaction among subjects with different social status. When information was made public, the donor was told about the social status of the recipient before making the decision to give. Evidence was found for both confounding factors—indirect reciprocity and strategic considerations. For instance, 25% of the subjects did not help when the social status was not made public but did help when it was made public. This is evidence of strategic considerations. There is a positive relation between the giving actions of donors and the social status of recipients, irrespective of the social status. However, the amount of help given to those with high social status is twice as much as that given to those with low social status, which provides evidence of indirect reciprocity.

In an interesting variant of the dictator game, Fehr and Fischbacher (2004) introduce the possibility of third party punishment. If the third party is willing to incur a private loss, but achieves no personal gain to enforce a "norm of giving," then it furnishes evidence for indirect reciprocity. In this third party punishment game (TPG), there are three players. Player A (the proposer) has an endowment of 100 MU (unit of money in the experiments), player B (the respondent) has 0 MU, and player C (the third party) has 50 MU. A dictator game is played between players A and B. Player C observes the game, and in his role as the third party, decides whether to punish or reward player A for this actions. By spending 1 MU, C can reduce A's payoff by 3 MU, however, there is no direct personal benefit to C from punishing player A. All players know the extensive form of the game. The experimenters conjecture that there is some sort of *fairness norm* which applies to the TPG, so that player C is predicted to punish low offers by player A.

Figure 1.20 shows that the magnitude of punishment meted out by player C is higher if the dictator makes a lower transfer. The very fact that punishments are undertaken by player C indicates that preferences are not self-regarding. Since 50-50 is a potentially salient fairness norm, in 55% of the cases, player C punishes A when offers to B fall below 50%. It is interesting that 70–80% of player *B*s expect A to be punished when the offer falls below 50%. Many institutions in society, such as the police, law, third party intervention in bargaining, and regulation, ensure that powerful parties do not exploit their monopoly positions.

Charness et al. (2008) consider a trust game in which the material payoff of a third party is unaffected by the decisions of the other two parties who play a trust game. They consider three separate treatments. Treatment 1 is a baseline treatment, which is the standard trust game in the absence of a third party. Treatment 2 allows the third party to punish the trustee for not sending enough money back to the trustor. Treatment 3 allows the third party to reward the trustor for receiving an insufficient amount of money from the responder. In Treatments 2 and 3, the actions of the trustee and the trustor are found to be altered towards greater trust and trustworthiness, relative to the baseline treatment in which the third party is absent. For instance, the trustor sends 60% more to the trustee in Treatment 2. However, there is no appreciable difference in the amount sent when there is the possibility of third party reward. This is the main result

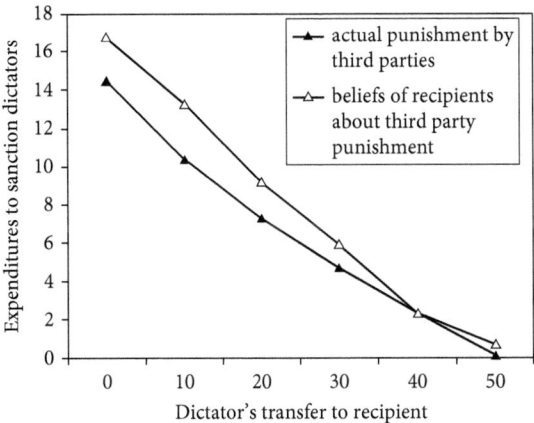

Figure 1.20 Third party punishments in the dictator game.

Source: Reprinted from Evolution and Human Behavior, 25(2): 63–87. Fehr, E. and Fischbacher, U., "Third-party punishment and social norms," © 2004, with permission from Elsevier

in the paper; recall that in the trust game, the trustor controls the surplus in the relationship, so he is the more important player. The interpretation of the results for the trustee are more complicated because he is influenced not just by the amounts sent by the trustor, but also by third party punishment. Yet, on the whole, trustees too return a higher amount to the trustor in the presence of third party punishment.

CHAPTER 2
Models of Other-Regarding Preferences

2.1 Introduction

An impressive range of theoretical models have been developed to address the empirical findings on other-regarding preferences. For pedagogical ease, we have found it useful to split other-regarding preferences in the following manner.

In *models of social preferences*, decision makers care not only about their own payoffs but also the payoffs of others in some reference group. In *models of interdependent preferences*, decision makers respond to the actions of others, conditional on the perceived type of others. For instance, altruistic individuals may respond in an altruistic manner if they perceive others to be altruistic, but not if others are perceived to be self-regarding. In *models of intention-based reciprocity*, the perceived *intentions* of others are the critical determinant of how one responds to the actions of others. The types of others (e.g., altruistic or self-regarding) are irrelevant in these models. Finally, there are *hybrid models* that combine two or more of the earlier models and/or use a richer array of social objectives that individuals might have, such as the *maximization of efficiency* or the *utility of the worst-off member* of society.[1]

We begin with some simple examples. Consider a set of individuals $i \in N = \{1, 2, \ldots, n\}$ whose respective monetary payoffs are denoted by $y_1, y_2, \ldots, y_n$. Suppose that the preferences of any individual $i \in N$ can be represented by a utility function.

Example 2.1 (Altruism): Individual $i \in N$ has purely self-regarding preferences if, his utility function is $u_i = u_i(y_i)$. Such preferences are unable to explain the results of the experimental games considered in Chapter 1 such as the ultimatum game, the trust game, the gift exchange game, and the public goods game.

Let $\mathbf{y}_{-i}$ be the vector of payoffs of all individuals other than individual i. Preferences of individual $i \in N$, are said to be altruistic if the utility function can be written as $U_i = U_i(y_i, \mathbf{y}_{-i})$, such that (1) there exists at least one element y_j in $\mathbf{y}_{-i}$ such that $\frac{\Delta U_i}{\Delta y_j} > 0$, and (2) there does not exist any y_k in $\mathbf{y}_{-i}$ such that $\frac{\Delta U_i}{\Delta y_k} < 0$. From the evidence reviewed

---

[1] This distinction is by no means unique, or universally agreed upon (see footnote 1 in Dufwenberg and Kirchsteiger 2004, p. 269). For instance, our suggested terminology does not readily admit emotions such as *guilt* and *anger*. However, psychological game theory is treated separately in Volume 4 of the book.

in Chapter 1 we know the following. Behavior in dictator games seems to accord with such preferences, and is, in some cases, enhanced when players feel that they are being watched. In a modified dictator game, Andreoni and Miller (2002) found that the behavior of subjects was consistent with the generalized axiom of revealed preference (GARP), so such preferences are not irrational. There was substantial heterogeneity in the actions of subjects. The behavior of 23% of the subjects was spiteful, i.e., they acted so as to reduce the payoffs of others. Purely altruistic preferences cannot also explain the behavior in trust games as well as in public goods games with punishments that relies on conditional reciprocity.

Example 2.2 (Envy): Suppose that we have only two players, $n = 2$. Consider the utility function due to Bolton (1991),

$$U_i = U_i\left(y_i, \frac{y_i}{y_j}\right); \; i,j = 1,2 \text{ and } i \neq j,$$

where $\frac{\partial U_i}{\partial y_i} > 0$, and $\frac{\partial U_i}{\partial \frac{y_i}{y_j}} > 0$ if $y_i < y_j$, which captures envy, but $\frac{\partial U_i}{\partial \frac{y_i}{y_j}} = 0$ if $y_i \geq y_j$. However, envy alone cannot explain why individuals give a positive amount in the dictator and the ultimatum games. It also does not explain behavior in the trust game or the gift exchange game.

Examples 2.1 and 2.2 suggest that neither altruism, nor envy, alone, can provide the foundations for a model of social preferences. A more complete description of human behavior requires an integration of selfishness, altruism, and envy. The model of Fehr and Schmidt (1999) (henceforth, FS) that we consider in Section 2.2, incorporates these diverse concerns. Furthermore, any model that aspires to explain social preferences must, at a minimum, explain the findings of the basic experimental games in Chapter 1.

In the FS model, inequity is self-centered. Individuals compare their own payoff with the payoffs of those who are better off (envy) and those who are worse off than them (altruism). The FS model does not invoke the beliefs of players about others (first order beliefs) or the beliefs of players about the beliefs of others (second order beliefs), so, it does not model the role of *intentions*; a rigorous analysis of these concerns requires the machinery of psychological game theory (see Volume 4 for details).

The FS model can successfully explain many of the findings of the experimental games in Chapter 1; these include the ultimatum game (Section 2.2.1, below), the dictator game, the gift exchange game, and the public goods game with and without punishments (Section 2.2.2, below). The channel through which the FS model explains positive giving in ultimatum and dictator games is altruism. A similar channel facilitates *trust* and *trustworthiness* in the trust game. However, envy and altruism, jointly, need to be invoked to explain the results of the public goods games with punishments. One difficulty that the FS model faces is in the explanation of some of the results from the dictator games that we reviewed in Chapter 1. This includes, in particular, the empirical finding of reluctant altruism; yet, these results are far less important in games that include a modicum of strategic concerns such as the ultimatum game.

Another great merit of the FS model is that it can simultaneously explain other-regarding behavior in bilateral or small group interaction and self-regarding behavior in competitive market settings. We explore these issues in Section 2.2.1 through an example of the ultimatum game by successively allowing for *proposer competition* and *responder competition*. Once we allow for such competition, the outcome of the ultimatum game with social preferences, under certain restrictions on the magnitude of altruism and envy, is identical to the outcome with self-regarding preferences. For instance, in the presence of responder competition, each responder is reluctant to reject an unfair offer by the proposer because another responder might accept it. This allows the proposer to get away with offering the minimum possible amount. Will the proposer wish to offer the minimum amount? The answer is affirmative, if the altruism of the proposer is low enough.

A second model of inequity aversion that we consider, in Section 2.3, is the *equity, reciprocity, and competition* (ERC) model of Bolton and Ockenfels (2000). In this model, players care about the absolute magnitude of their payoff, and their payoff relative to the total payoff of others, but do not care about the distribution of payoffs of others. In two-player games, such as ultimatum and dictator games, the ERC model and the FS model often yield similar predictions.[2] In games with three or more players, however, the predictions of the two models may differ substantially. The reason is that in the ERC model, a player does not care about the payoffs received by each of his opponents individually as long as the average payoff remains constant. For example, in the public goods game with punishment, ERC predicts that a contributor is indifferent whether to punish a free-rider or another contributor, because punishing either of them affects the average payoff in the same way, while FS predicts that the free-rider will be punished.

The predictive ability of many theoretical models of self-regarding preferences hinges critically on answering the following question: Given two income distributions P and Q, which does the individual prefer? In a major advance, Rothschild and Stiglitz (1970, 1971) showed that the relevant concepts are *first and second order stochastic dominance*. However, these concepts are not sound for individuals who have social preferences, such as those of the Fehr–Schmidt form. In Section 2.4, we outline newer statistical concepts that are appropriate for individuals with Fehr–Schmidt preferences (Dhami and al-Nowaihi, 2013). We also clarify the relation of these newer dominance concepts with Lorenz dominance, which should facilitate applications of social preferences in the income distribution literature.

The FS model fits well the evidence on the behavior of subjects in experiments on societal redistribution. This evidence suggests that explanations for societal redistribution could be underpinned by social preferences and the innate desire of humans to be fair. By contrast, the existing theoretical literature on political economy assumes self-regarding preferences. Section 2.5 explores the implication of other-regarding preferences for understanding societal redistribution in a simple general equilibrium model with endogenous labor supply (Dhami and al-Nowaihi, 2010a,b). Two main results are established in this section. First, the conditions for the existence of a *Condorcet winner* under social preferences are natural and intuitive. Second, when there is a mixture of self-regarding and other-regarding voters, then the outcomes can be counter intuitive. Even if self-regarding voters are in a majority, the preferred policy of the other-regarding voters may prevail, i.e., be a Condorcet winner, and vice versa. An important determinant of the eventual redistributive outcome is the skill distribution and the inequality aversion of other-regarding voters.

Section 2.6 considers the Walrasian competitive equilibrium and the fundamental welfare theorems when consumers have other-regarding preferences (Dufwenberg et al., 2011). Using a separability condition on preferences, we establish a link between the Walrasian equilibria of an economy with other-regarding preferences and a related economy with self-regarding

---

[2] An interesting exception is a variant of the ultimatum game in which the proposer receives ϵ and the responder receives 0 if the proposer's offer is rejected. In this game, ERC predicts that any positive offer will be accepted because the relative payoff position of the responder is always worse than if he rejects the offer. In contrast, the FS model predicts that unfair offers are rejected.

preferences. In general, the fundamental welfare theorems need not hold. But with an appropriate *social monotonicity condition*, restrictions on preferences to *well-being externalities*, and lump-sum transfers, we establish the analogue of the second fundamental welfare theorem. Interestingly, there is a close link between some of these results and the simple general equilibrium model of redistribution that we consider in Section 2.5, below.

Section 2.7 considers the evidence on models of fairness and reciprocity. Formal models of reciprocity require the apparatus *of psychological game theory* that is postponed to Volume 4 of the book. In Section 2.7.1, we consider a range of evidence that incorporates a desire for efficiency and surplus maximization over inequity aversion (Charness and Rabin, 2002; Engelmann and Strobel, 2004). However, evidence has also accumulated for the opposite view, in favor of inequity aversion (Bolton and Ockenfels, 2006). On account of their training, economics students may bias results in favor of efficiency, while inequity aversion remains fairly salient for non-economics students (Fehr et al., 2006).[3] The evidence against inequity aversion has typically come from dictator games. However, in games where all players have an economically meaningful action, there is support for models of inequity aversion. For instance, in a gift exchange game, when workers have a chance to maximize the surplus in the relationship at a personal cost, they typically do not do so (Fehr et al., 1993, 1998). If surplus maximization were the overriding concern then, in gift exchange experiments, for any wage offered by the firm, we should always observe the worker putting in the maximum level of effort. But, as we saw in Chapter 1, what we observe is a positive relation between effort and wages (gift exchange).

In models of social preferences, such as Fehr and Schmidt (1999) and Bolton and Ockenfels (2000), intentions of other players do not matter. By contrast, intentions seem important to humans, e.g., the law makes a distinction between murder and manslaughter. Section 2.7.2 considers the experimental evidence for the role of intentions (Falk et al., 2008). This evidence rejects models of pure social preferences and models of pure reciprocity. It seems that the evidence is best described by models that combine the role of intentions, social preferences, and reciprocity such as the model by Falk and Fischbacher (2006).

Section 2.7.2 considers some caveats to the evidence on intentions. First, the early literature did find it hard to discover clinching evidence of intentions that could not be explained by other-regarding preferences (Blount, 1995; Charness, 2004; Bolton et al., 1998). Second, more recent evidence shows that in some cases, other-regarding preferences explain the evidence better than intentions. However, in other cases, both intentions and other-regarding motives are unable to explain the evidence (Bolton and Ockenfels, 2005). In this case, one may need to explore other avenues, possibly *procedural theories of fairness*, *fairness norms*, or bring into consideration reference points for fairness.

Section 2.8 considers several *hybrid models* that combine elements of social preferences and reciprocal intentions. Some models combine intentions with social preferences and other social objectives such as efficiency (Charness and Rabin, 2002). In models of *interdependent preferences*, people favor others who are perceived to be similarly fairness-minded (Levine, 1998; Cox et al., 2007). These models analyze intentions in a reduced form manner and do not employ the tools of psychological game theory. The section concludes with a note on the axiomatic foundations of social preference models (Segal and Sobel, 2007; Neilson, 2006).

---

[3] In Charness and Rabin (2002) and Engelmann and Strobel (2004), the predominant subject pool is economics students.

2.2 The Fehr–Schmidt model

Fehr–Schmidt (1999), henceforth FS, develop a model of social preferences that simultaneously explains both fairness-induced behavior in small group interaction and self-regarding behavior in market settings. Their work also indicates that the presence of a small fraction of self-regarding individuals within a group of individuals who have social preferences (and vice versa) may have important implications for the observed outcome.

Formally, consider a set of n individuals, $N = \{1,2,\ldots,n\}$. For any player $j \in N$ define the set $N_{-j} = N - \{j\}$. N_{-j} is called the reference set with respect to individual j. The respective monetary payoffs of the individuals are $y_1, y_2, \ldots, y_n$. The payoffs of all individuals other than i are denoted by the vector $\mathbf{y}_{-i}$. For any $i \in N$ the Fehr–Schmidt utility function of an individual (or FS utility function) is given by

$$U_i(y_i, \mathbf{y}_{-i}; \alpha_i, \beta_i) = y_i - \frac{\alpha_i}{n-1} \sum_{j \neq i} \max\{y_j - y_i, 0\} - \frac{\beta_i}{n-1} \sum_{j \neq i} \max\{y_i - y_j, 0\}, \quad (2.1)$$

where $\alpha_i \geq 0$ and $0 \leq \beta_i < 1$. Most experimental evidence indicates that $\beta_i \in [0,1)$ and $\beta_i < \alpha_i$. An individual is said to have *social preferences* or *other-regarding preferences*, if at least one of β_i and α_i is non-zero.

The FS utility function has several important features. First, inequity is modeled as *self-centered inequity aversion*, i.e., one's own income becomes the reference point with respect to which incomes of others are compared. Furthermore, inequity among other members of the reference group, i.e., among N_{-i}, is not taken into account by individual i. Second, the theory is silent on the composition and size of the reference group, N_{-i}. Third, the FS utility function reduces to that of a self-regarding individual when $\beta_i = \alpha_i = 0$. Fourth, although (2.1) restricts itself to the linear payoffs case, the theory allows U_i to be non-linear in the payoffs. Fifth, intentions, as in Rabin (1993), or average income, as in Bolton and Ockenfels (2000), do not play a role. Sixth, $\beta_i < 0$, on account of individuals who might derive pleasure from being better off than others (e.g., status-seeking individuals), is ruled out. However, in most cases this feature does not affect the results considered by FS. Seventh, while there is an upper bound on β_i there is none on α_i.[4] Eighth, $\beta_i < \alpha_i$ implies that the player suffers more from marginal changes in *disadvantageous inequity* (the second term in (2.1)) rather than marginal changes in *advantageous inequity* (the third term in (2.1)). Ninth, payoffs are normalized to take account of the number of players, hence, the second and third terms in (2.1) are divided by $n-1$.

Unlike models that incorporate only altruism or envy (see Examples 2.1, 2.2 above), the FS model incorporates both concerns. Individuals with such preferences, therefore, care about how unequal their incomes are, relative to those who are richer and those who are poorer. For this reason, the class of such models is also sometimes known as *models of inequity aversion*. Table 2.1 gives the reader an indication of the magnitudes of α, β from various studies reported in Eckel and Gintis (2010). The estimates suggest that $\beta < 1$ and typically $\beta < \alpha$. Most tests

---

[4] To see why β_i is restricted to be less than one for all i, consider the following simple example. Suppose that the incomes are arranged in increasing order, so $y_n = \max\{y_1, y_2, \ldots, y_n\}$ and $\beta_n \geq 1$. Then (2.1) implies that

$$U_n(y_n, \mathbf{y}_{-n}; \alpha_n, \beta_n) = (1 - \beta_i)y_n + \frac{\beta_i}{n-1}[y_1 + y_2 + \ldots + y_{n-1}].$$

If $\beta_i \geq 1$ then the RHS is non-increasing in y_n, so (provided this does not change the income rankings) throwing away a dollar increases the payoff of player n, which seems unreasonable.

Table 2.1 Parameter estimates of the Fehr and Schmidt (1999) model of inequality aversion.

Study and population	Mean parameter values	
	α	β
Fehr and Schmidt (1999)		
Calibration (calculated from reported distributions)	0.85	0.315
Standard deviation	(1.119)	(0.252)
Bellemare, Kroger, and van Soesta (2008)		
Population sample, Dutch adults	1.892	0.801
	(0.640)	(0.921)
High education and below 35	1.018	−0.271
	(0.325)	(0.503)
Goeree and Holt (2000)[b]		
Student proposers	0.84	0.66
	(0.160)	(0.080)
Student responders	0.84	0.12
	(0.160)	(0.020)
Ellingsen and Johannessen (2004)[c]		
Student subjects	0.31	0.36
95% Confidence Interval	(0–1.2)	(0.25)–0.5
Daruvala (2009)[d]		
Student subjects	0.952	0.344
Standard deviation	(1.039)	(0.294)

Standard errors in parentheses, unless otherwise indicated. (a) Specification included variables to measure intentions, and is embedded in a logit decision framework; (b) Specification included logit decision framework; a common parameter was estimated; (c) Estimated from graphs; (d) Mean and standard deviation value calculated by the author from individual data.
Source: Eckel and Gintis (2010).

of inequity averse preferences have been done on aggregate level data. Using a within-subjects design, Blanco et al. (2011) report differences in the estimated parameters of inequity aversion at the aggregate level and the individual level. Fisman et al. (2007) report substantial heterogeneity at the level of individuals in social preferences. For a debate on the calibration of the Fehr–Schmidt model, see the 2010 issue of the *Journal of Economic Behavior and Organization*, Volume 73.

The model described in (2.1) is the linear version of the FS model. The non-linear version has also been used to explain important phenomena such as societal redistribution. See, for instance, Dhami and al-Nowaihi (2010a,b), which is discussed in Section 2.5 below.

2.2.1 Fairness and market competition

We now demonstrate how the FS model can explain the anomalies generated by the ultimatum game. Denote the proposer and the responder in the ultimatum game as, respectively, players 1 and 2. The share received by the responder is denoted by s, assumed perfectly divisible, while the proposer's share is $1 - s$.

Lemma 2.1 *The responder accepts all offers $s \geq 0.5$. There is a critical share, $s_c < 0.5$, such that the responder (1) rejects all offers $s < s_c$, and (2) accepts all offers $s \geq s_c$.*

Proof of Lemma 2.1: Suppose that $s \geq 0.5$. From (2.1), the responder's utility is $U_2 = s - \beta_2[s - (1-s)] = \beta_2(1-s) + s(1-\beta_2)$, which is positive because $\beta_i \in [0,1)$. Hence, the responder will always accept $s \geq 0.5$. Now suppose that $s < 0.5$. From (2.1), the responder's utility is $U_2 = s - \alpha_2[(1-s) - s] = s(1 + 2\alpha_2) - \alpha_2$. For this to be positive we require that

$$s \geq s_c = \frac{\alpha_2}{1 + 2\alpha_2}; \ s_c < 0.5. \tag{2.2}$$

Hence, the responder will accept all offers $s \geq s_c$ and reject all offers $s < s_c$. ∎

The critical threshold, s_c, is increasing and strictly concave in α_2. In the limiting case $\alpha_2 \to \infty$, $s_c = 0.5$.

Proposition 2.1 *The equilibrium share offered by the proposer to the responder is given by*

$$s^* = \begin{cases} s_c & \text{if } \beta_1 < 0.5 \\ 0.5 & \text{if } \beta_1 > 0.5 \\ s \in [s_c, 0.5] & \text{if } \beta_1 = 0.5 \end{cases}$$

Proof of Proposition 2.1: It is simple to check that the proposer will not offer a share $s > 0.5$ to the responder. From Lemma 2.1 we know that the responder will accept any share $s : s_c \leq s \leq 0.5$. Let us consider such a share, s. From (2.1), the proposer's utility is $U_1 = (1-s) - \beta_1[(1-s) - s]$, so $\frac{\partial U_1}{\partial s} = 2\beta_1 - 1$. Thus, if $\beta_1 < 0.5$, then $\frac{\partial U_1}{\partial s} < 0$, so the proposer should offer the minimum share that will be accepted by the responder, i.e., $s^* = s_c$. If $\beta_1 = 0.5$, then $\frac{\partial U_1}{\partial s} = 0$, so any feasible share $s^* \in [s_c, 0.5]$ that will be accepted is offered. If $\beta_1 > 0.5$, then $\frac{\partial U_1}{\partial s} > 0$, so we have a corner solution, $s^* = 0.5$. ∎

The predictions of the theory seem to match the stylized facts reasonably well in Western societies. First, there are rarely any offers above 0.5. Second, offers of 0.5 are readily accepted and low offers (presumably below s_c) are rejected.

It is possible that one (or both) of the parties has asymmetric information about the preference parameters of the other party. For instance, suppose that the proposer has asymmetric information about the responder's disadvantageous inequity parameter, α_2. In particular, suppose that the proposer knows that α_2 has support $[\underline{\alpha}, \overline{\alpha}]$ and a distribution function $F(\alpha_2)$. From Lemma 2.1, we know that the offer will only be accepted by the responder if $s \geq s_c$. So, using (2.2), $\Pr(s \geq s_c) \Leftrightarrow \Pr\left(\alpha_2 \leq \frac{s}{1-2s}\right) = F\left(\frac{s}{1-2s}\right)$, which is increasing in s. Hence, the probability that an offer is accepted by the responder is increasing in the offer, s. This is also consistent with the empirical evidence.

The results derived above change dramatically when there is one-sided market competition either among proposers or among respondents. This is well known in experimental economics. For instance, Davis and Holt (1993) make six concluding remarks to their book. In the very first, they state that *competitive market predictions have been observed in a rich variety of circumstances and in literally hundreds of instances*. Furthermore, they remark that experimental behavior approximates the competitive outcome even in the absence of the limiting cases (i.e., a large number of traders or complete information). These insights also apply to the predictions of the FS model for the ultimatum game as we now see.

MARKET GAMES WITH PROPOSER COMPETITION

Consider $n > 2$ players, where the first $n-1$ players are proposers and the nth player is the single responder in an ultimatum game. The proposers simultaneously make an offer to the responder. Each proposer's offer takes the form of a share $s \in [0,1]$ that is offered to the responder. Denote the maximum offer among the proposers by $\bar{s} = \max\{s_i\}$, $i \in N/n$. If $\bar{s}$ is unique, then the corresponding proposer gets to make that offer, with probability 1, to the responder. If, however, $k > 1$ proposers make the same offer, $\bar{s}$, then each of these proposers makes an offer to the responder with probability $1/k$. If the responder rejects the offer, everybody gets zero. If the responder accepts an offer s from the jth proposer, then their respective payoffs are $s, 1-s$ and everybody else gets zero.

We first consider the benchmark result when all players have self-regarding preferences.

> **Lemma 2.2** *Suppose that all individuals are self-regarding. In any subgame perfect outcome, at least two proposers must offer $\bar{s} = 1$, which is accepted by the responder.*

Proof of Lemma 2.2: Suppose to the contrary that there is some $s : 0 < s < 1$ that is an equilibrium. Any of the proposers can now offer $s + \epsilon$, $\epsilon > 0$, which will be accepted by the responder and improves the payoff of the proposer. Furthermore, there cannot be a single proposer who offers $\bar{s} = 1$ in equilibrium. If this is the case, then let the next best offer by any proposer be $\tilde{s}$. The original proposer can now lower his offer to any number in $(\tilde{s}, 1)$. Such an offer is accepted by the responder and improves the payoff of the original proposer. Hence, the unique equilibrium offer is $\bar{s} = 1$, which is made by at least two proposers. ∎

In the face of proposer competition, the responder reaps all gains from trade. These results are consistent with the experimental evidence in Roth et al. (1991).

What is the equilibrium outcome when all n players have social preferences? It turns out that the outcome is identical to that obtained under self-regarding individuals. We first prove an intermediate result that extends Lemma 2.1 to $n - 1$ proposers.

> **Lemma 2.3** *The other-regarding responder will accept any offer $s \geq 0.5$.*

Proof of Lemma 2.3: For $s \geq 0.5$, the utility of the responder from accepting the offer is

$$U_n = s - \frac{\beta_n}{n-1}[s - (1-s)] - \frac{(n-2)\beta_n}{n-1}(s - 0). \tag{2.3}$$

Since $0 < \beta < 1$, so $U_n \geq 0$. Since, $U_n \geq 0$ if an offer $s \geq 0.5$ is accepted and $U_n = 0$ if the offer is rejected, hence, the offer is accepted. ∎

> **Proposition 2.2** *Suppose that all agents have other-regarding preferences given in (2.1). In the ultimatum game with proposer competition, the unique subgame perfect equilibrium outcome is for at least two proposers to offer $s = 1$, which is accepted by the responder. All gains from trade accrue to the responder.*

Proof of Proposition 2.2: Using Lemma 2.3, the responder will accept $s = 1$. We want to show that there cannot be an equilibrium in which $0.5 \leq s < 1$ is offered and accepted by the responder. Suppose that $\hat{n}$ proposers, such that $1 \leq \hat{n} < n-1$, offer $0.5 \leq \bar{s} < 1$ in equilibrium and their offer is accepted. Order, without loss of generality, the proposers as follows $1, 2, \ldots, \hat{n}, \hat{n}+1, \ldots, n-1$. The proposers $\hat{n}+1, \ldots, n-1$ offer less than $\bar{s}$, say, 0 (this does not alter the proof). Now choose any proposer i from among $\hat{n}+1, \ldots, n-1$. If he offers some $s_i < \bar{s}$, then proposer i does not win the contest and there are two other players who have a greater payoff: the proposer who wins and the responder, hence, using (2.1), his payoff is

$$U_i(s_i) = 0 - \frac{\alpha_i}{n-1}[(1-\bar{s}-0) + (\bar{s}-0)] = -\frac{\alpha_i}{n-1}. \tag{2.4}$$

If proposer i instead offers $\bar{s} + \epsilon, \epsilon > 0$, then he wins the contest for sure. In this case one player, the responder, has a greater payoff than him (on account of Lemma 2.3), while $n - 2$ players have a lower payoff. Using (2.1), his payoff is

$$U_i(\bar{s}+\epsilon) = [1-(\bar{s}+\epsilon)] - \frac{\alpha_i}{n-1}[(\bar{s}+\epsilon) - [1-(\bar{s}+\epsilon)]] - \frac{\beta_i(n-2)}{n-1}[1-(\bar{s}+\epsilon)]. \tag{2.5}$$

From (2.4), (2.5), it is straightforward to check that $U_i(\bar{s}+\epsilon) - U_i(s_i) > 0$. Hence, we derive a contradiction, so any $s < 1$ cannot be an equilibrium offer.

Now let $\hat{n} = n - 1$ and an offer $0.5 \leq \bar{s} < 1$ that is accepted (see Lemma 2.3). Each proposer then wins the contest with probability $\frac{1}{n-1}$. Any of the proposers can offer an amount $\bar{s} + \epsilon$, ϵ sufficiently small and be ensured to win with probability 1. This improves the payoff of the proposer and contradicts the original equilibrium.

Hence, any $s < 1$ cannot be an equilibrium offer. ∎

MARKET GAMES WITH RESPONDER COMPETITION

Now consider the possibility of responder competition. Suppose that the first player is the proposer, while players $2, 3, \ldots, n$ are responders. The proposer makes an offer, followed by the responders' decisions to accept or reject. Among the set of responders who accept the offer, one is randomly chosen with uniform probability. The payoffs of the proposer and the winning responder are $1 - s, s$, while all others get zero. If no responder accepts, then all players get zero.

Lemma 2.4 *Suppose that all players are self-regarding. In any subgame perfect outcome, the proposer offers $\bar{s} = 0$, which is accepted by at least one responder.*

Proof of Lemma 2.4: Analogous to the proof of Lemma 2.2, so it is omitted. ∎

There is less experimental evidence for market games with responder competition, relative to those with proposer competition. In ultimatum games with two responders, if any responder rejects an offer, the other responder might accept it. Hence, punishing the proposer for low offers is more difficult. One should expect that the same offers are less likely to be rejected in the presence of responder competition.

These predictions are borne out in Fischbacher et al. (2009) where subjects were randomly rematched every period to ensure that the game remained a one-shot interaction. When a single proposer is matched with a single responder, the responder gets, on average, about 40%. In the case of two responders, the share is about 14% lower, and in the final period, it dips below 20%. When there are five responders, the responder's share is about 10% in the last 10 rounds of a 20-round experiment.

An important implication of these results is that if individuals have self-regarding preferences, then adding another responder (competition) should have no impact on the outcome and the proposer receives the entire surplus. Thus, the introduction of competition is neutral in terms of the outcome. However, the introduction of competition when agents have social preferences alters the outcomes significantly. Hence, the self-interest model understates the role of competition. The experimental results of Güth et al. (1997) also bear out these results.

The next proposition shows that in the presence of social preferences, the outcome under responder competition is identical to that under self-regarding preferences. We leave the proof as an exercise for the reader.

Proposition 2.3 *Let the advantageous inequality parameter of the proposer, β_1, be bounded above by $(n-1)/n$. Suppose that we limit attention to $s < 0.5$. Then there exists a subgame perfect outcome in which each responder accepts any $0 \leq s < 0.5$ and the proposer offers $s = 0$.*

This is not the only equilibrium of the model; an exercise at the end asks for other equilibria.

Propositions 2.2, 2.3 show that in the presence of competition, the preferences of individuals, self-regarding or other-regarding, do not matter for the results. Why? The reason is that each individual is too small to influence the degree of inequality in society. Hence, this makes the pursuit of individual self-interest more beneficial (through the first term in (2.1)), while at the same time turning the inequality to his advantage, which is preferable because $\beta_i < \alpha_i$. When individuals have a greater opportunity to influence the degree of inequality, e.g., by altering the level of effort in a principal–agent relationship, then other-regarding preferences have an even greater influence on the outcome, as we shall see later.

An important implication is that if individuals are "small," then fairness issues are less important in the market for goods (as Propositions 2.2, 2.3 exemplify) but are of greater importance in labor markets where endogenous effort has a greater influence on outcomes.

2.2.2 Fairness and cooperation

We now apply the FS preferences to an explanation of the results from public goods games. The implications of these results go beyond the public goods game. In finite multi-stage games with self-regarding players, cooperation is difficult to achieve under full information, because the tendency for opportunistic behavior in the last stage unravels all the way back to the initial stage. However, if players have other-regarding preferences, then they might not engage in opportunistic behavior in the last stage because of inequity aversion. Furthermore, if some players have initially managed to increase their relative payoffs by behaving in an opportunistic manner, they might be punished by the other-regarding players, who desire greater equality of payoffs. This imparts credibility to the punishment of opportunistic behavior. Contrast this with the non-credibility of punishments in a finite multi-stage full information game with self-regarding players.

To examine the issues involved, we use the public goods game, described in Section 1.4. The monetary payoffs in the game without punishment and with punishment are given by (1.1), (1.2). The utility of an other-regarding individual i is of the FS form,

$$U_i = m_i - \frac{\alpha_i}{n-1} \sum_{j \neq i} \max\{m_j - m_i, 0\} - \frac{\beta_i}{n-1} \sum_{j \neq i} \max\{m_i - m_j, 0\}. \quad (2.6)$$

PUBLIC GOODS GAME WITHOUT PUNISHMENTS

Using (1.1), in the public goods game without punishments, $m_j - m_i = g_i - g_j$. Thus, using (2.6), the utility of player $i \in N = \{1, 2, \ldots, n\}$ is

$$U_i = y - g_i + rG - \frac{\alpha_i}{n-1} \sum_{j \neq i} \max\{g_i - g_j, 0\} - \frac{\beta_i}{n-1} \sum_{j \neq i} \max\{g_j - g_i, 0\}. \quad (2.7)$$

Lemma 2.5 *A sufficient condition for an other-regarding player with preferences given in (2.7) to choose $g_i^* = 0$ is that $r + \beta_i < 1$.*

Proof of Lemma 2.5: From (2.7), by contributing an extra unit to the public good, the monetary cost to an individual is $1 - r$. To see the maximum possible monetary benefit from this action, suppose that, among the set of contributors, this agent contributes the least. From (2.7), by contributing an extra unit, the benefit to this lowest contributor is a reduction in advantageous inequity by $\frac{\beta_i(n-1)}{n-1} = \beta_i$. Hence, the maximum possible benefit to player i is $\beta_i - (1 - r)$, which is negative if $r + \beta_i < 1$. ∎

Proposition 2.4 *Let $\tilde{n} \in \{0, 1, \ldots, n\}$ be the number of other-regarding players with $r + \beta_i < 1$. If $\tilde{n} \geq \frac{r}{2}(n-1)$, then there is a unique equilibrium in Nash contributions such that $g_i^* = 0$ for all i.*

The proof of Proposition 2.4 is left to the reader as an exercise. From Lemma 2.5, $r + \beta_i < 1$ guarantees free-riding. Proposition 2.4 shows that if a lower bound is put on the number of free-riders, then all other-regarding players do not contribute. If the number of free-riders is large enough, in the sense specified in Proposition 2.4, then contributors to the public good would suffer too much disadvantageous inequity from contributing. Hence, they do not contribute. In this case, the result in Proposition 2.4 matches with the empirical evidence that there is little voluntary contribution in public goods games without punishments. There are, however, other equilibria in which a fraction of the agents contribute a positive amount; an exercise asks you to show this.

PUBLIC GOODS GAME WITH PUNISHMENTS

The possibility of punishment alters the results of public goods games with other-regarding individuals quite dramatically. Suppose that there are some free-riders in the first stage. Then first stage contributors, who are other-regarding, have an incentive to punish the free-riders in the second stage. Contributors in the second stage face disadvantageous inequity relative to the free-riders, because the latter get exactly the same level of benefit from the public good but have not paid adequately. How much do the contributors care about this inequity? The answer depends on their inequity aversion parameter α_i. If this is large enough, then a contributor can make a credible threat to punish the free-riders. If the punishment has sufficient bite for the non-contributors, then it can reduce or eliminate free-riding, which is in line with the experimental evidence. These ideas are formalized below.

Definition 2.1 *A conditionally cooperative enforcer is characterized by two conditions: (1) $r + \beta_i > 1$, and (2) a willingness to cooperate if others cooperate.*

Proposition 2.5 *Suppose that there are $n_c \in \{0, 1, \ldots, n\}$ conditionally cooperative enforcers. Order the players such that the first n_c are conditional cooperators, $1, 2, \ldots, n_c$,*

$n_c + 1, \ldots, n$. The remaining players are self-regarding, i.e., $\alpha_j = \beta_j = 0$, $j = n_c + 1, \ldots, n$. Let

$$\frac{\alpha_i}{(n-1)(1+\alpha_i) - (n_c - 1)(\alpha_i + \beta_i)} > c, \tag{2.8}$$

where c is the cost per unit to punish another player; $\frac{1}{c}$ is also known as the *efficiency of punishment* (see Definition 1.4). The following constitutes a subgame perfect equilibrium. In the first stage, all individuals contribute an identical amount $g_i = \bar{g} \in [0, y]$. The second stage strategies are as follows. If all individuals contribute $\bar{g}$ in the first period, then there are no punishments. If player $j \in \{n_c + 1, \ldots, n\}$ contributes $g_j < \bar{g}$, then each player $i \in \{1, 2, \ldots, n_c\}$ inflicts a punishment $p_{ij} = (\bar{g} - g_j)/(n_c - c)$. There is no punishment inflicted by any players outside this set. If any of the conditionally cooperative enforcers $i \in \{1, 2, \ldots, n_c\}$ contributes $g_i < \bar{g}$ or any player chooses $g > \bar{g}$, then a Nash equilibrium of the punishment game is played.

Proof of Proposition 2.5: Suppose that some player $j \in \{n_c + 1, \ldots, n\}$ contributes $g_j < \bar{g}$ and all other players follow their equilibrium action. Then, given the punishment strategies outlined in the proposition, in conjunction with the monetary payoff given in (1.2), it can be checked that

$$m_j = y - g_j + r\left[(n-1)\bar{g} + g_j\right] - n_c\left(\frac{\bar{g} - g_j}{n_c - c}\right),$$

and for any player $i \in \{1, 2, \ldots, n_c\}$,

$$m_i = y - \bar{g} + r\left[(n-1)\bar{g} + g_j\right] - c\left(\frac{\bar{g} - g_j}{n_c - c}\right),$$

$$\Rightarrow m_i = y - \left(\frac{n_c - c}{n_c - c}\right)(\bar{g} - g_j + g_j) + r\left[(n-1)\bar{g} + g_j\right] - c\left(\frac{\bar{g} - g_j}{n_c - c}\right),$$

$$\Rightarrow m_i = y - g_j + r\left[(n-1)\bar{g} + g_j\right] - \left(\frac{\bar{g} - g_j}{n_c - c}\right)(n_c - c + c) = m_j.$$

Thus, the deviator gets the same payoff as the enforcer. Because the non-deviating, non-enforcers, do not punish they get the highest payoff. Hence, it is better for a deviating non-enforcer to be a non-deviating, non-enforcer.

We now need to check two conditions.

I. Each of the enforcers finds it worthwhile to carry out the stated punishment: Suppose that an enforcer $i \in \{1, 2, \ldots, n_c\}$ reduces punishment of some deviating player j by an amount $\epsilon > 0$ from the stated level $p_{ij} = (\bar{g} - g_j)/(n_c - c)$. This has three main effects.

1. Relative to the other non-deviating, non-enforcers, $n_c + 1, \ldots, n$, enforcer i increases their own payoff by $c\epsilon$ (the effective cost of the punishment) for a benefit in disadvantageous inequity of

$$\frac{\alpha_i}{n-1}\left[n - (n_c - 1)\right]c\epsilon. \tag{2.9}$$

2. Relative to the other $n_c - 1$ enforcers who stick to the stated level of punishment, the payoff of a deviating enforcer goes up. This results in an additional cost to enforcer i in terms of advantageous inequity of

$$\frac{\beta_i(n_c - 1)}{n-1}c\epsilon. \tag{2.10}$$

3. Relative to the defector, the payoff of player i has gone up by ϵ on account of the reduction in punishment. So player i finds that disadvantageous inequity has gone up by an amount

$$\frac{\alpha_i}{n-1}[\epsilon - c\epsilon]. \tag{2.11}$$

Subtracting (2.10), (2.11) from (2.9) and simplifying, we get the required condition (2.8).

II. *Each of the enforcers finds it worthwhile to contribute $\bar{g}$*: Suppose that one of the conditional enforcers $i \in \{1, 2, \ldots, n_c\}$ reduces his contribution of the public good from the stated level $\bar{g}$ to $\bar{g} - \eta$, $\eta > 0$. Ignore punishments in the second stage for the moment. This increases the monetary payoff by $(1-r)\eta$ but creates more advantageous inequality (a cost) with respect to all other players by an amount $\frac{\beta_i(n-1)}{n-1}\eta$. The net effect is $\eta(1 - r - \beta_i)$ which, using Definition 2.1, is negative for a conditionally cooperative enforcer. If we include second stage punishments, the net effect is even more negative. Hence, it does not pay to reduce contributions from the stated amount. ∎

2.3 The ERC model

Bolton and Ockenfels (2000) propose a model of *equity, reciprocity*, and *competition* (ERC), a model of social preferences that is closely related to a model in Bolton (1991).[5] ERC applies to both extensive form and normal form games. Suppose that there are n players, $i = 1, 2, \ldots n$. Payoffs to all players are non-negative monetary payoffs. Denote by $x_i \geq 0$, the payoff of player i. The sum of the total payoffs is $S = \sum_{i=1}^{n} x_i$. The relative payoff of player i, also called the *motivation factor*, is given by

$$r_i = r_i(x_i, S, n) = \begin{cases} x_i/S & \text{if } S > 0 \\ \frac{1}{n} & \text{if } S = 0 \end{cases}. \tag{2.12}$$

The utility function (the authors prefer the term, *motivation function*) of player i is $u^i = u^i(x_i, r_i)$. Using (2.12), it is given by

$$\begin{cases} u^i\left(x_i, \frac{x_i}{S}\right) & \text{if } S > 0 \\ u^i\left(x_i, \frac{1}{n}\right) & \text{if } S = 0 \end{cases}. \tag{2.13}$$

The assumptions on the utility function are as follows.

A1: u^i is twice continuously differentiable in x_i, r_i.
A2: u^i is increasing and concave in x_i ($u_1^i \geq 0$, $u_{11}^i \leq 0$).
A3: For any given monetary payoff, the utility function u^i is maximized at $r_i = 1/n$ and is strictly decreasing and strictly concave in r_i around this point.

Assumption A3 builds into the model the importance of an equal division of the social surplus (the authors term equal division as the *social reference point*). The crux of the model is the trade-off created by assumptions A2 and A3. From A2, the individual prefers to increase

---

[5] For an understanding of the evolution of this model, see the section on bargaining games in Volume 4. For an earlier published motivation behind the ERC model, see Bolton and Ockenfels (1998).

her monetary payoff. However, from A3, for any monetary payoff, the individual prefers equal division. Population heterogeneity is introduced by how different individuals view this trade-off.

ERC and FS preferences do not nest each other, and nor do their empirical predictions. ERC is able to explain several stylized facts from experimental results, among them, the following. Why do proposers give more in ultimatum, as compared to dictator games? Why is there a positive association between effort and rents in the gift exchange game? In dictator games, ERC predicts that the proposer will keep between half and all of the money. It also predicts that zero offers will be rejected in ultimatum games and the rejection rates will increase as the proposer's offer falls. The ERC model also explains the competitive outcomes under proposer competition in an ultimatum game. The ERC model allows for asymmetric information, and it can also explain the data in three-player ultimatum games where a passive third party appears to be treated unfairly, relative to the predictions of the Fehr–Schmidt model (Bolton and Ockenfels, 1998).

By contrast, there are other predictions of the ERC theory that are at variance with the evidence. In the ERC model, individuals compare their payoff with the aggregate payoff of others. In this sense, ERC has a less nuanced notion of inequality, relative to the FS model. In particular, individuals using ERC preferences do not care about interpersonal comparisons of their own payoff and the payoffs of others. The following experimental games show that this gives rise to different predictions relative to the FS model.

Suppose that a player has the mean payoff. Now consider a mean preserving spread of the payoff distribution. ERC predicts that the player's utility should be unaffected. However, the experimental results of Charness and Rabin (2002) do not support this prediction; utility falls with the mean preserving spread. By contrast, the FS utility of a player will be affected by such mean preserving changes.

The ERC model is not able to explain the outcomes in public goods games with punishments. In the second stage of this game, individuals with ERC preferences will not punish the non-contributors because they are not concerned with individual payoffs. Sensing this, potential non-contributors will not contribute. Hence, the prediction of the ERC model is that the outcome of the public goods games with and without punishments should be identical. This is strongly refuted (see Section 1.4.3). Antisocial punishments (see Section 1.4.6) are inconsistent not just with the ERC model but also with many other models of social preferences. However, observed punishments in most experiments conducted in Western societies are prosocial. When the institution of punishment is enshrined via an upfront referendum, then punishments are not antisocial, nor are punishments antisocial when there is a norm for punishing non-cooperative behavior, or punishments elicit feelings of guilt and shame (Tyran and Feld, 2006; Herrmann et al. 2008; Carpenter et al., 2009). These kinds of punishments have relatively greater external validity, and the FS model explains them well.

The ERC model also finds it difficult to explain the results of games that demonstrate indirect reciprocity (see Section 1.6). Consider, for instance, the following variant of the third party punishment game. There are three players A, B, and C with respective endowments S, 0, $S/2$. Players A and B play a dictator game with A being the first mover (so B has no meaningful actions to take). Player C can punish player A if the offer of player A to B is considered inadequate. For each unit of money that player C spends on the punishment, the monetary payoff of player A is reduced by three units. The total surplus in the game is $S + S/2 = 3S/2$. The relative share of player C, in the absence of punishment, is $1/3$, thus, given assumption A3, the Bolton–Ockenfels model predicts no punishment. In most experiments, the majority of C players undertake some form of punishment, which is at variance with the ERC model.

Charness and Rabin (2002) consider a variant of the third party punishment game. Suppose that three players A, B, and C have respective shares given by (x_1, x_2, x_3). Player C is now given a choice between the following two allocations: (575, 575, 575) and (900, 300, 600). Player C gets the fair share (a third) in both allocations. The Bolton–Ockenfels model predicts that player C will choose the second allocation because, among the two, it gives player C a higher material payoff (Assumption A2). The experimental evidence is that 54% of the subjects prefer the first allocation. Self-interest alone predicts that C will choose the second allocation, hence, we cannot conclude that the choice of the remaining 46% supports the Bolton–Ockenfels model.

Although the experimental evidence from the simple games considered above does not always support the Bolton–Ockenfels model, as no model of other-regarding preferences is supported in all possible experiments, it is nevertheless an important milestone in the development of models of social preferences. It formalizes an important intuitive insight about how people may behave in certain situations. The model may perhaps perform even better in more cognitively challenging games with a very large number of players, where one might only have a rough notion of one's position relative to the aggregate.

2.4 Fairness and stochastic dominance

Given two probability distributions over outcomes, it is critical to be able to answer the question of which distribution an individual prefers. Under self-regarding preferences, this question has been the cornerstone of many important advances in economic theory. The relevant machinery to deal with these issues is *first and second order stochastic dominance* and *generalized Lorenz dominance*.[6] What can we say when individuals have social preferences?

Dhami and al-Nowaihi (2013) show that the standard concepts of *first order and second order stochastic dominance* as well as *generalized Lorenz dominance* are no longer valid when one has social preferences of the FS form. They propose alternative dominance concepts that are suitable for such social preferences. In this section we consider their work.

Consider n possible income classes. Income, y, of any member belongs to the set of possible incomes $\mathbf{Y} = \{y_1 < y_2 < \ldots < y_n\}$. Under any distribution function, P, over this set of incomes, the proportion of individuals with income y_i is denoted by $p_i \geq 0$, $\sum_{i=1}^{i=n} p_i = 1$. The *cumulative probability distribution* is given by $P_0 = 0$, $P_j = \sum_{i=1}^{i=j} p_i$, $j = 1, 2, \ldots, n$. Denote by Π, the set of all such distributions over $\mathbf{Y}$.

The *cumulative of the cumulative distribution* is given by $\widetilde{P}_0 = 0$, $\widetilde{P}_j = \sum_{i=1}^{i=j} P_i$, $j = 1, 2, \ldots, n$. Let $\widetilde{\Pi}$ be the set of all such distributions. The average, or mean, of $y_1, y_2, \ldots, y_n$ under the distribution $P \in \Pi$ is

$$\mu_P = \sum_{i=1}^{i=n} p_i y_i.$$

Let $u(y_i)$ be the utility function of an individual who has self-regarding preferences and has the income y_i. Denote by $\mathbf{u}$ the class of all non-decreasing utility functions.

In this section we will work with the general form of Fehr–Schmidt preferences, sometimes known as the *non-linear form of Fehr–Schmidt preferences*. These preferences modify the linear form of FS preferences given in (2.1) as shown in the next definition. For axiomatic foundations of such preferences, see Section 2.8.4 below.

---

[6] See Rothschild and Stiglitz (1970, 1971).

Definition 2.2 *(General form of FS utility):* Consider the income distribution, P, and $u \in \mathbf{u}$. The general form of the Fehr–Schmidt utility function (FS) for an individual with income $y_j \in \mathbf{Y}$ is given by

$$U(y_j, P) = u(y_j) - \beta \sum_{i=1}^{j-1} p_i [u(y_j) - u(y_i)] - \alpha \sum_{k=j+1}^{n} p_k [u(y_k) - u(y_j)], \alpha \geq 0, 0 \leq \beta < 1.$$

For two income distributions, P and Q, (2.14) gives (2.14)

$$U(y_j, P) - U(y_j, Q) = \beta \sum_{i=1}^{j-1} (q_i - p_i) [u(y_j) - u(y_i)] + \alpha \sum_{k=j+1}^{n} (q_k - p_k) [u(y_k) - u(y_j)].$$

(2.15)

For an individual with self-regarding preferences, $\alpha = \beta = 0$, so

$$U(y, P) = u(y). \quad (2.16)$$

The approach in the literature is to begin with a purely statistical definition of a dominance concept and then to establish its economic relevance (or *soundness*) by relating it to the relevant decision theory. In the discrete case, first and second order dominance are defined as follows.

Definition 2.3 *(First order stochastic dominance):* Let $P, Q \in \Pi$. Then P first order stochastically dominates Q ($P \succsim_1 Q$) if $P_j \leq Q_j$ for $j = 1, 2, \ldots, n$. If, in addition, the inequality is strict for some j, then P strictly first order stochastically dominates Q ($P \succ_1 Q$).

Definition 2.4 We say that the income levels are equally spaced if for some positive real number, δ, $y_{i+1} - y_i = \delta$ for $i = 1, 2, \ldots, n-1$.[7]

Definition 2.5 *(Second order stochastic dominance):* Suppose that incomes are equally spaced (Definition 2.4).[8] Let $P, Q \in \Pi$. Then P second order stochastically dominates Q ($P \succsim_2 Q$) if $\widetilde{P}_j \leq \widetilde{Q}_j$ for $j = 1, 2, \ldots, n$ and if $\mu_P \geq \mu_Q$.[9] If, in addition, one of these inequalities is strict, then P strictly second order stochastically dominates Q ($P \succ_2 Q$).

Propositions 6.8 and 6.9 consider the classical case in which self-regarding individuals maximize their expected utility behind a veil of ignorance (Mas-Colell et al., 1995, Chapter 6). Recall $\mathbf{u}$ is the class of all non-decreasing utility functions.

Proposition 2.6 Let $P, Q \in \Pi$. Then $P \succsim_1 Q$ if, and only if, for any $u \in \mathbf{u}$,

$$\sum_{i=1}^{i=n} p_i u(y_i) \geq \sum_{i=1}^{i=n} q_i u(y_i), \quad (2.17)$$

---

[7] This is not restrictive because we can always introduce extra income levels, each with probability zero, to achieve equal spacing. For example, suppose $y_1 = 5, y_2 = 7, y_3 = 11$, which is not equally spaced, and $P_1 = \frac{1}{3}$, $P_2 = \frac{2}{3}$. Consider $y_1 = 5, y_2 = 7, y_3 = 9, y_4 = 11$, which are equally spaced, and $Q_1 = \frac{1}{3}, Q_2 = \frac{2}{3}, Q_3 = \frac{2}{3}$. Both P and Q describe the same reality.
[8] Often "equal spacing" is not stated as part of the definition of second order stochastic dominance. But then it has to be stated in the propositions. We find it more convenient to state this in the definition. This assumption is not needed in the continuous case.
[9] Often the condition $\mu_P \geq \mu_Q$ is not included as part of the definition of second order stochastic dominance. But then it needs to be included in the statement of the relevant propositions. It is slightly simpler to include $\mu_P \geq \mu_Q$ as part of the definition of second order stochastic dominance.

and $P \succ_1 Q$ if, and only if, the inequality in (2.17) is strict for all strictly increasing $u \in \mathbf{u}$.

Choosing $u(y) = y$ as a candidate function in Proposition 2.6 we get that if $P \succsim_1 Q$ ($P \succ_1 Q$), then the restrictions on the means under P and Q is $\mu_P \geq \mu_Q$ ($\mu_P > \mu_Q$).

Proposition 2.7 *Let $P, Q \in \Pi$. Then $P \succsim_2 Q$ if, and only if, for any concave $u \in \mathbf{u}$,*

$$\sum_{i=1}^{i=n} p_i u(y_i) \geq \sum_{i=1}^{i=n} q_i u(y_i), \tag{2.18}$$

and $P \succ_2 Q$ if, and only if, the inequality in (2.18) is strict for all strictly increasing strictly concave $u \in \mathbf{u}$.

Propositions 2.6 and 2.7 assume self-regarding individuals who follow expected utility behind a veil of ignorance. This falls within the domain of normative economics. However, we are interested in the more realistic ex-post situation where individuals with FS preferences know their income level and the income levels of others in their reference group (there is no uncertainty). The question that we address is: Which distribution will such individuals choose?

Example 2.3 *Consider three income levels, $0, 25, 50$ and two distributions, P, Q defined in the Table below, where $\frac{1}{6} \leq \varepsilon \leq \frac{5}{6}$.*

y	$y_1 = 0$	$y_2 = 25$	$y_3 = 50$
$p(y)$	0	1/3	2/3
$q(y)$	1/6	ε	$(5/6) - \varepsilon$
$P(y)$	0	1/3	1
$Q(y)$	1/6	$(1/6) + \varepsilon$	1
$\tilde{P}(y)$	0	1/3	4/3
$\tilde{Q}(y)$	1/6	$(1/3) + \varepsilon$	$(4/3) + \varepsilon$

From the above table it can be easily seen that $P \succ_1 Q$. Also from the above table it is clear that $P \succ_2 Q$ ($\mu_P = \frac{125}{3} > \frac{125}{3} - 25\varepsilon = \mu_Q$). For the individual with income $y_2 = 25$, we can find from (2.15)

$$U(25, Q) - U(25, P) = \alpha \left(\varepsilon - \frac{1}{6} \right) [u(50) - u(25)] + \frac{\beta}{6} [u(0) - u(25)] \tag{2.19}$$

It is easy to construct examples where an individual with Fehr–Schmidt preferences strictly prefers the dominated distribution Q to P. For example, let $\varepsilon = \frac{1}{3}$ and take u to be any strictly increasing own utility function. Take $\alpha = 1$ and $\beta = 0$. Consider an individual with income 25. Then, from (2.19) we get $U(25, Q) - U(25, P) = \frac{u(50) - u(25)}{6} > 0$.

Example 2.4 *In FS preferences, see (2.14), $\beta > 0$ captures altruism or compassion towards individuals who are poorer. Hopkins (2008) differentiates between the sign of β in two different literatures. In behavioral economics, where models of social preferences have gained* increasing acceptance, $\beta > 0$. But in happiness economics, $\beta < 0$ is allowed for. Hopkins (2008) refers to $\beta < 0$ as "pride," "competitiveness," or "downward envy." Consider now some implications of pride ($\beta < 0$) rather than altruism ($\beta > 0$) in the data given in Example 2.3. Let u be any strictly increasing own utility function. Take $\alpha = 1$ and $\varepsilon = \frac{1}{6}$. Then, from (2.19) we get that $U(25, Q) - U(25, P) = -\frac{\beta}{6}(u(50) - u(25))$. Clearly the choice between P, Q now hinges solely on the sign of β. An individual with altruism prefers P to Q but an individual with pride prefers Q to P. Dhami and al-Nowaihi (2013) show formally that an individual with pride will always prefer the dominated distribution.

These examples beg the question: what are the appropriate dominance concepts for FS preferences? The next remark provides a clue to the answer.

Remark 2.1 *Begin with an income distribution $P \in \Pi$, under which an individual has the Fehr–Schmidt preferences given in (2.14) and has income y_j. Consider two income levels, y_s, y_t, such that $y_s < y_t < y_j$, $p_s < 1$ and $p_t > 0$. Suppose that we obtain the distribution Q from P by transferring a fraction Δ of individuals from the income class y_t to y_s, where $0 < \Delta < \min\{1 - p_s, p_t\}$, then from (2.15) $U(y_j, P) - U(y_j, Q) = \beta \Delta [u(y_t) - u(y_s)] > 0$. Thus individuals with FS preferences dislike "rich to poor transfers" among people poorer than them. Now consider two income levels, y_l, y_m, such that $y_j < y_l < y_m$, $p_l < 1$ and $p_m > 0$. Obtain a new distribution Q by transferring a fraction Δ of individuals from the income class y_m to y_l, where $0 < \Delta < \min\{1 - p_l, p_m\}$, then from (2.15) $U(y_j, Q) - U(y_j, P) = \alpha \Delta (u(y_m) - u(y_l)) > 0$. Thus, individuals with FS preferences like "rich to poor transfers" among people richer than them.*

Consider the following example that illustrates some of the main ideas in Dhami and al-Nowaihi (2013). The relevant data is given in the table below, where $0 < \epsilon < \frac{1}{6}$. We are interested in the individual with income of $y_3 = 50$ who has FS preferences.

y	$y_1 = 0$	$y_2 = 25$	$y_3 = 50$	$y_4 = 75$	$y_5 = 100$
$p(y)$	0	$1/3$	$(1/3) + 2\epsilon$	$(1/3) - 2\epsilon$	0
$q(y)$	ϵ	$(1/3) - \epsilon$	$1/3$	$(1/3) - \epsilon$	ϵ
$P(y)$	0	$1/3$	$(2/3) + 2\epsilon$	1	1
$Q(y)$	ϵ	$1/3$	$2/3$	$1 - \epsilon$	1
$\widetilde{P}(y)$	0	$1/3$	$1 + 2\epsilon$	$2 + 2\epsilon$	$3 + 2\epsilon$
$\widetilde{Q}(y)$	ϵ	$(1/3) + \epsilon$	$1 + \epsilon$	2	3

Below income $y_3 = 50$, distribution Q moves some richer individuals to a poorer income level and a fraction 2ε of individuals with income $y_3 = 50$ are distributed equally between the higher income levels of 75 and 100. Using (2.15), a simple calculation shows that an individual with income $y_3 = 50$ prefers the distribution P to the distribution Q. What inferences can we draw from this unambiguous preference for P? An examination of the table reveals that the following restrictions apply:

$$P_i \leq Q_i,\ P_k \geq Q_k;\ i < 3,\ k \geq 3. \tag{2.20}$$

$$\widetilde{P}_i \leq \widetilde{Q}_i,\ \widetilde{P}_k \geq \widetilde{Q}_k;\ i < 3,\ k \geq 3. \tag{2.21}$$

From (2.20), neither distribution first order stochastically dominates the other, and, from (2.21), neither distribution second order stochastically dominates the other. Thus, a-priori, one cannot predict which distribution would be preferred by an individual with self-regarding preferences. But we shall see that these restrictions are ideal to determine which of the distributions is preferred by an individual with FS preferences whose income is $y_3 = 50$. One can make the following simple calculations using (2.15), for any $u \in \mathbf{u}$,

$$U(50, P) - U(50, Q) = \beta \varepsilon \left[u(25) - u(0) \right] + \varepsilon \alpha \left[u(75) - u(50) + u(100) - u(50) \right] > 0,$$

as claimed. We did not need to invoke the concavity of the utility function for this example because it satisfies (2.20), in which case it is sufficient that $u \in \mathbf{u}$.

In the case of first and second stochastic dominance (Definitions 2.3, 2.4) the dominant distribution, P, has a mean that is no lower than the dominated distribution, Q. This need not be the case under our proposal for FS dominance (see below). From the data given to us,

$$\mu_Q - \mu_P = 50\epsilon > 0.$$

Thus, the preferred distribution in this case, P, has a lower mean. The reason is that, for $\alpha > 0$, a reduction in the mean can be associated with a reduction in disadvantageous inequality for an individual with income y_j without affecting that individual's income. For instance, this could happen by destroying some of the wealth of individuals with income higher than y_j (but still leaving them with incomes no less than y_j). This is supported by the evidence where subjects in experiments prefer a smaller cake which is more equitably distributed.[10]

The conditions in (2.20), (2.21) are examples of the more general conditions that are developed in Dhami and al-Nowaihi (2013). They call these conditions, respectively, *first order FS dominance* and *second order FS dominance*. We state these conditions and some of the relevant results below that the reader is asked to prove in the exercises.

Definition 2.6 *(First order Fehr–Schmidt dominance)*: Consider an individual with income $y_j \in Y$. Let $P, Q \in \Pi$. Then P first order FS_{y_j} dominates Q ($P \succeq_{FS1_{y_j}} Q$) if

(a) $P_i \leq Q_i$ for each $i = 1, 2, \ldots, j-1$, and
(b) $P_k \geq Q_k$ for each $k = j, j+1, \ldots, n-1$.

If, in addition, one of these inequalities is strict, then we say that P strictly first order FS_{y_j} dominates Q ($P \succ_{FS1_{y_j}} Q$).

Thus, distribution P first order FS dominates Q for an individual of income level $y_j \in Y$ if it first order stochastically dominates below y_j and is first order stochastically dominated above y_j. Second order FS dominance that we now define relies on a similar interpretation.

Definition 2.7 *(Second order Fehr–Schmidt dominance)*: Let $P, Q \in \Pi$, $y_j \in Y$. Then P second order FS_{y_j} dominates Q ($P \succeq_{FS2_{y_j}} Q$) if

---

[10] See, for instance, Ackert et al. (2007), Bolton and Ockenfels (2006), and Tyran and Sausgruber (2006).

(a) Incomes are equally spaced (Definition 2.4),
(b) $\widetilde{P}_i \leq \widetilde{Q}_i$ for each $i = 1, 2, \ldots, j-1$, and
(c) $\widetilde{P}_k \geq \widetilde{Q}_k$ for each $k = j, j+1, \ldots, n-1$.

If, in addition, one of the inequalities in (b) or (c) is strict, then we say that P strictly second order FS_{y_j} dominates Q ($P \succ_{FS2_{y_j}} Q$).

Proposition 2.8 (Dhami and al-Nowaihi, 2013): Consider an individual with income $y_j \in Y$. Let $P, Q \in \Pi$. Then P first order FS_{y_j} dominates Q ($P \succeq_{FS1_{y_j}} Q$) if, and only if, $U(y_j, P) \geq U(y_j, Q)$ for all $u \in \mathbf{u}$, $\alpha \geq 0$ and $\beta \in [0, 1)$.

Proposition 2.9 (Dhami and al-Nowaihi, 2013): Let $P, Q \in \Pi$, $y_j \in Y$. Let P second order FS_{y_j} dominate Q ($P \succeq_{FS2_{y_j}} Q$). Then $U(y_j, P) \geq U(y_j, Q)$ for all $\alpha \geq 0$, $\beta \in [0, 1)$ and all concave $u \in \mathbf{u}$.

The next proposition establishes a partial converse of Proposition 2.9.

Proposition 2.10 (Dhami and al-Nowaihi, 2013): Let $P, Q \in \Pi$ and $y_j \in Y$. Suppose incomes are equally spaced (Definition 2.4). Suppose $\widetilde{P}_{j-1} = \widetilde{Q}_{j-1}$. If $U(y_j, P) \geq U(y_j, Q)$ for all $\alpha \geq 0$, all $\beta \in [0, 1)$ and all concave $u \in \mathbf{u}$, then P second order FS_{y_j} dominates Q ($P \succeq_{FS2_{y_j}} Q$).

In the model with self-regarding preferences, the relation between second order stochastic dominance and generalized Lorenz dominance is a crucial one.[11] Indeed, such a relation is often used in a justification of cross-country ranking of income distributions. Dhami and al-Nowaihi (2013) show that an analogous result holds for the case of FS preferences. It turns out that a slight modification of second order FS dominance is equivalent to a modified form of generalized Lorenz dominance. This makes available the full toolkit of dominance concepts for social preferences of the FS form.

2.5 Behavioral political economy

The explanation of societal redistribution is one of the central problems in political economy. Existing explanations rely on voters who have self-regarding preferences.[12] In the literature, the simplest political institution is *direct democracy* in which voters vote directly to choose between alternative policies. This is not only an important benchmark institution, its role in actual policy choice has been expanding.[13] For these reasons, we restrict ourselves to direct democracy in this section.

The recent empirical literature strongly supports the role of social preferences in voting models (Ackert et al., 2007; Bolton and Ockenfels, 2006; Tyran and Sausgruber, 2006). These papers establish that voters often choose policies that promote equity/fairness over purely self-regarding considerations. Bolton and Ockenfels (2006), for instance, examine the preference for equity versus efficiency in a voting game. Groups of three subjects are formed and are presented with two alternative policies. One policy promotes equity, while the other promotes efficiency. The final

---

[11] See Lambert (2001) for a statement and proofs of the relevant results and a good discussion of the issues.
[12] For a wide-ranging review, see Persson and Tabellini (2000).
[13] See, for instance, Matsusaka (2005).

outcome is chosen by a majority vote. About twice as many subjects in experiments preferred equity as compared to efficiency.[14]

Experimental results on voting under direct democracy lend support to the FS model. Tyran and Sausgruber (2006) explicitly test for the importance of the FS framework in explaining the experimental results on voting. They conclude that the FS model predicts much better than the standard model with self-regarding preferences. In addition, for the three income classes in their experiments, the FS model provides, in their words, "strikingly accurate predictions for individual voting in all three income classes."

The econometric results of Ackert et al. (2007), based on their experimental data, lend further support to the FS model in the context of redistributive taxation. The estimated coefficients of altruism and envy in the FS model are statistically significant and, as expected, negative in sign. In the context of voting experiments, Bolton and Ockenfels (2006) conclude that "while not everyone measures fairness the same way, the simple measures offered by [Bolton and Ockenfels (2000)] or FS provide a pretty good approximation to population behavior over a wide range of scenarios that economists care about."

Economy-wide voting under direct democracy is impersonal and anonymous, thereby making it unlikely that intentions play any important role. Hence, FS preferences are a particularly good vehicle through which to model social preferences in a voting context. In the discussion below we use the term *self-regarding voter model* when all voters have self-regarding preferences and the term *other-regarding voter model* when at least some voters have social preferences.

Dhami and al-Nowaihi (2010a, 2010b) provide the relevant theoretical results that are motivated by the experimental results and open the way for further applications of the other-regarding voter model. In particular, the neoclassical results on the existence of Condorcet winner derived for self-regarding voters no longer apply for other-regarding voters. Dhami and al-Nowaihi (2010a) derive conditions for the existence of a Condorcet winner when all voters have a social preference of the FS form. Dhami and al-Nowaihi (2010b) consider the implications for societal redistribution when there is a mixture of other-regarding and self-regarding voters. We consider these two contributions below.

2.5.1 Existence of a Condorcet winner when voters have social preferences

We consider a standard, general equilibrium model with endogenous labor supply that gives the simplest trade-off between equity and efficiency.[15] Let there be $n = 2m - 1$ voters who combine the roles of producer-consumers and voters. Let the skill level of voter j be $s_j, j = 1, 2, \ldots, n$, where $0 < s_i < s_j < 1$, for $i < j$. Denote the skill vector by $\mathbf{s} = (s_1, s_2, \ldots, s_n)$ and the median skill level by s_m. Each voter has a fixed time endowment of one unit, so supplies l_j units of labor and enjoys $1 - l_j$ units of leisure, where $0 \leq l_j \leq 1$. Labor markets are competitive and each firm has access to a linear production technology. Thus, firm j, represented by voter j, produces an amount y_j such $y_j = s_j l_j$. Hence, the wage rate offered to each voter coincides with the marginal product, i.e., the skill level, s_j. Thus, the before-tax income of voter j is given by $y_j = s_j l_j$. Denote the average before-tax income by $\bar{y} = \frac{1}{n} \sum_{j=1}^{n} y_j$.

---

[14] Furthermore, even those willing to change the status quo for efficiency are willing to pay, on average, less than half relative to those who wish to alter the status quo for equity.

[15] This is also known as the Roberts–Romer–Meltzer–Richards model (or RRMR model) based on the names of economists who formally articulated it in seminal contributions to political economy. For the relevant references, see, for instance, Persson and Tabellini (2000) and Dhami and al-Nowaihi (2010 a,b).

The government operates a linear progressive income tax system. This is characterized by a constant marginal tax rate, t, $t \in [0,1]$, and a uniform transfer or benefit, b, to each voter that equals the average tax proceeds, thus, $b = t\bar{y}$. The budget constraint of voter j is given by $0 \leq c_j \leq (1-t)y_j + b$, which can be written as

$$0 \leq c_j \leq (1-t)s_j l_j + b. \tag{2.22}$$

We define a voter's preferences in two stages. First, let voter j have a continuous *own-utility* function, $\tilde{u}_j(c_j, 1 - l_j)$, defined over own-consumption, $c_j > 0$, and own-leisure, $1 - l_j$, $0 \leq l_j \leq 1$. Each voter has a twice continuously differentiable, and identical, utility function

$$\tilde{u}_j = \tilde{u}(c_j, 1 - l_j). \tag{2.23}$$

Differences in c_j and l_j across voters arise only due to differences in skill levels but not due to differences in the utility functions. We assume that own-consumption is always desirable, so $\tilde{u}_j$ is a strictly increasing function of c_j. Second, voters have *other-regarding preferences* as in Fehr–Schmidt (1999). Let $\mathbf{c}_{-j}$ and $\mathbf{l}_{-j}$ be the vectors of consumption and labor supplies, respectively, of voters other than voter j. Then the *FS-utility* of voter j is[16]

$$\tilde{U}_j\left(c_j, l_j; \mathbf{c}_{-j}, \mathbf{l}_{-j}, t, b, \alpha, \beta, \mathbf{s}\right) = \tilde{u}_j - \frac{\alpha}{n-1} \sum_{k \neq j} \max\left\{0, \tilde{u}_k - \tilde{u}_j\right\} - \frac{\beta}{n-1} \sum_{i \neq j} \max\left\{0, \tilde{u}_j - \tilde{u}_i\right\},$$

where, for other-regarding voters, $0 < \beta < 1$ and $\alpha > 0$ with the typical experimental finding suggesting that $\alpha > \beta$. For *self-regarding* voters $\alpha = \beta = 0$, so $\tilde{U}_j = \tilde{u}_j$. Thus, $\tilde{u}$ is also the utility function of a self-regarding voter, as in the standard model. The other-regarding voter cares about own payoff (first term), payoff relative to those where inequality is disadvantageous (second term) and payoff relative to those where inequality is advantageous (third term).

Since $\tilde{u}_j$ is a strictly increasing function of c_j, and since $\alpha \geq 0$ and $0 \leq \beta < 1$, it follows that $\tilde{U}_j$ is also a strictly increasing function of c_j. Hence, the budget constraint (2.22) holds with equality. Substituting $c_j = (1-t)s_j l_j + b$, from (2.22), into the utility function of a self-regarding voter, $\tilde{u}_j(c_j, 1 - l_j)$, we get

$$u_j = u\left(l_j; t, b, s_j\right) = \tilde{u}((1-t)s_j l_j + b, 1 - l_j). \tag{2.24}$$

Correspondingly, eliminating own-consumption, the FS-utilities take the form

$$U_j\left(l_j; \mathbf{l}_{-j}, t, b, \alpha, \beta, \mathbf{s}\right) = u_j - \frac{\alpha}{n-1} \sum_{k \neq j} \max\left\{0, u_k - u_j\right\} - \frac{\beta}{n-1} \sum_{i \neq j} \max\left\{0, u_j - u_i\right\}. \tag{2.25}$$

We consider a two-stage game. In the first stage, all voters vote directly for their most preferred redistributive tax rate. If a median voter equilibrium exists, then the tax rate preferred by the median voter is implemented—the outcome in this case is known as a *Condorcet winner*. In the second stage, all voters make their labor supply decision, conditional on the tax rate chosen by the median voter in the first stage. On choosing their labor supplies in the second stage, the

---

[16] Here, we consider the non-linear version of FS preferences; see Fehr and Schmidt (1999) and Definition 2.2.

announced first period tax rate is implemented. In the second stage, the voters play a one-shot Nash game: each voter, j, chooses his/her labor supply, l_j, given the vector, $\mathbf{l}_{-j}$, of labor supplies of the other voters, so as to maximize his/her FS-utility (2.25).

The solution is by backward induction. So consider first, the second stage. Given the tax rate, t, and the transfer, b, both determined in the first stage, the voters play a one-shot Nash game to determine their labor supplies (in the subgame determined by t and b).

Proposition 2.11 *(Dhami and al-Nowaihi, 2010a): In the second stage of the game, voter j, whether other-regarding or self-regarding, chooses own labor supply, l_j, so as to maximize own-utility, u_j defined in (2.24), given t, b, and s_j.*

The proof of Proposition 2.11 is left as an exercise for the reader. From Proposition 2.11, an other-regarding voter, despite having social preferences, chooses labor supply exactly like a self-regarding voter. However, when making a decision on the redistributive tax rate in the first stage (see below), the two kinds of voters make different choices. In other words, in two separate domains, redistributive choice and labor supply, the other-regarding voter behaves *as if* he had social preferences in the first domain and self-regarding preferences in the second. In this respect, these results are similar to the contrast between the results in the ultimatum game with and without proposer (or responder) competition in Section 2.2.1.[17] Note that Proposition 2.11 would not hold if in the FS utility function of voter j in (2.25), the u_i, $i \neq j$, entered non-additively. However, the empirical evidence supports the adopted form for the FS-utility function in the voting domain.

For the generic utility function $\widetilde{u}(c, 1-l)$, defined in (2.23), we use the standard notation $\widetilde{u}_1 = \frac{\partial \widetilde{u}(c,1-l)}{\partial c}$ and $\widetilde{u}_2 = \frac{\partial \widetilde{u}(c,1-l)}{\partial (1-l)}$. The utility function has the following, plausible, properties:

(a) $\widetilde{u}_1 > 0$, (b) $l > 0 \Rightarrow \widetilde{u}_2(c, 1-l) > 0$, (c) $\widetilde{u}_2(c,1) = 0$, (d) $\widetilde{u}_1(c,0) \leq \widetilde{u}_2(c,0)$, (2.26)

(a) $\widetilde{u}_{11} \leq 0$, (b) $\widetilde{u}_{12} \geq 0$, (c) $l > 0 \Rightarrow \widetilde{u}_{22}(c, 1-l) < 0$, (d) $(\widetilde{u}_{12})^2 \leq \widetilde{u}_{11}\widetilde{u}_{22}$. (2.27)

From (2.26a), the marginal utility of consumption is positive, while (2.26b) implies that marginal utility of leisure is positive, unless $l = 0$ in which case (2.26c) says that the consumer is satiated with leisure. From (2.26d), when a consumer has no leisure, she always (weakly) prefers one extra unit of leisure to one extra unit of consumption. (2.27a) says that marginal utility of consumption is non-increasing. From (2.27b), consumption and leisure are complements, while (2.27c) implies that the marginal utility of leisure is strictly declining unless, possibly, the consumer is satiated with leisure (in which case $\widetilde{u}_{22}(c,1) = 0$). Conditions (2.26) and (2.27) guarantee that a maximum exists, that it is unique and that it is an interior point ($0 < l_i < 1$), unless $t = 1$ in which case the maximum will lie at $l_i = 0$. Conditions (2.27a,c,d) guarantee that $\widetilde{u}$ is concave.

We list, in Lemmas 2.6 and 2.7 below, some useful results; the proofs are left as an exercise for the reader. Lemma 2.6 shows that there is a unique solution to the labor supply of an individual and characterizes other useful properties of labor supply. For instance, the optimal labor supply is decreasing in the redistributive tax rate (conflict between efficiency and equity).

---

[17] In other contexts, individuals might, for instance, send their own children to private schools (self-interest) but could at the same time vote for more funding to government-run schools in local or national elections (public interest). Thus, individuals can put on different hats in different situations.

Lemma 2.6 *(Properties of labor supply; Dhami and al-Nowaihi, 2010a):*

(a) Given t, b, and s_j, there is a unique labor supply for voter j, $l_j = l(t, b, s_j)$, that maximizes self-regarding utility $u(l_j; t, b, s_j)$ defined in (2.24),

(b) $t \in [0, 1) \Rightarrow 0 < l_j < 1$,

(c) $l_j = 0$ at $t = 1$,

(d) $t \in [0, 1] \Rightarrow \left[\frac{\partial u}{\partial l_j}(l_j; t, b, s_j)\right]_{l_j = l(t, b, s_j)} = 0$,

(e) $l(t, b, s_j)$ is continuously differentiable,

(f) $\frac{\partial l(t, b, s)}{\partial b} \leq 0$,

(g) for each $t \in [0, 1]$, the equation $b = \frac{1}{n} t \sum_{i=1}^{n} s_i l(t, b, s_i)$ has a unique solution $b(t, \mathbf{s}) \geq 0$; and $b(t, \mathbf{s})$ is continuously differentiable.

Substituting optimal labor supply, given by Lemma 2.6(a), in $u(l_j; t, b, s_j)$ we get the indirect self-regarding utility function of voter j,

$$v_j = v(t, b, s_j) = u(l(t, b, s_j); t, b, s_j). \tag{2.28}$$

Lemma 2.7 lists some useful properties of the indirect utility function, v. In particular, v is increasing in the lump-sum transfer, b. If the tax rate is bounded away from 1, then v is increasing in the skill level of the individual, s, and decreasing in the redistributive tax rate, t (holding fixed, b). In Lemma 2.7, the distinction between the results at $t = 1$ and $t \in [0, 1)$ follow from Lemma 2.6(b), (c)

Lemma 2.7 *(Properties of the indirect own utility function; Dhami and al-Nowaihi, 2010a):*

(a) $\frac{\partial v}{\partial b} > 0$,

(bi) $\left[\frac{\partial v}{\partial s}\right]_{t=1} = 0$, (bii) $t \in [0, 1) \Rightarrow \frac{\partial v}{\partial s} > 0$,

(ci) $\left[\frac{\partial v}{\partial t}\right]_{t=1} = 0$, (cii) $t \in [0, 1) \Rightarrow \frac{\partial v}{\partial t} < 0$,

(di) $\frac{\partial^2 v}{\partial s \partial b} \leq 0$, (dii) $\left[\frac{\partial^2 v}{\partial s \partial b}\right]_{t=1} = 0$.

Substituting labor supply, $l(t, b, s_j)$, into $y_j = s_j l_j$ gives before-tax income $y_j(t, b, s_j) = s_j l(t, b, s_j)$.

We now solve the first stage problem of the choice of the optimal tax rate. Substituting labor supply, $l(t, b, s_j)$, into the utility function, $U_j(l_j; \mathbf{1}_{-j}, t, b, \alpha, \beta, \mathbf{s})$, and using (2.25) and (2.28), the indirect utility function, $V_j(t, b, \alpha, \beta, \mathbf{s})$, of voter j is given by

$$V_j(t, b, \alpha, \beta, \mathbf{s}) = v_j - \frac{\alpha}{n-1} \sum_{k \neq j} \max\{0, v_k - v_j\} - \frac{\beta}{n-1} \sum_{i \neq j} \max\{0, v_j - v_i\}, \tag{2.29}$$

where v_j is defined in (2.28). In the light of Lemmas 2.7(bi) and 2.7(bii), (2.29) becomes

$$V_j(t, b, \alpha, \beta, \mathbf{s}) = v_j - \frac{\alpha}{n-1} \sum_{k > j} [v_k - v_j] - \frac{\beta}{n-1} \sum_{i < j} [v_j - v_i]. \tag{2.30}$$

We now introduce two further assumptions, A1 and A2, followed by the main result.

A1: $t \in [0, 1) \Rightarrow \frac{\partial^2 v}{\partial s \partial t}(t, b, s) < 0$, where v is defined in (2.28).

Recall, from Lemma 2.7(cii), that $t \in [0,1) \Rightarrow \frac{\partial v}{\partial t} < 0$. Hence, $\frac{\partial}{\partial s}\left(t\frac{\partial v}{\partial t}\right) = t\frac{\partial^2 v}{\partial s \partial t} < 0$ can be interpreted as saying that an extra 1% on the redistributive tax rate hurts a poor person less than a rich person. Thus Assumption A1 roughly says that redistributive taxes hurt the poor less than the rich. This is the basic foundation of the modern welfare state.[18]

A2: $\frac{\partial V_j}{\partial t}(t, b, \alpha, \beta, \mathbf{s}) \leq 0$.

Since $\frac{\partial v}{\partial t} < 0$, for $t < 1$ (Lemma 2.7(cii)), an increase in tax (benefit, b, remaining fixed), is undesirable for a self-regarding-voter, which is entirely reasonable. Assumption A2 extends this to other-regarding voters as well. It implies that envy is not so great as to make an other-regarding voter prefer an increase in tax, even if it has no gain for anyone in terms of an increase in the benefits, b (b is held fixed in computing $\frac{\partial V_j}{\partial t}$ in A2).

Thus, conditions A1 and A2 bear an intuitive interpretation. Dhami and al-Nowaihi (2010a) show that the class of utility functions that satisfy assumptions A1 and A2 is very large. They also discuss the interpretation of assumptions A1, A2 in terms of a voter's own-utility $\widetilde{u}_j(c_j, 1 - l_j)$ but there are no obvious insights to be gained from this.

Proposition 2.12 *(Dhami and al-Nowaihi, 2010a): Under assumptions A1 and A2 a majority of the other-regarding voters prefer the tax rate that is optimal for the median-skill voter.*

The modern literature on political economy when voters are self-regarding depends critically on the conditions for the existence of a Condorcet winner. Proposition 2.12 gives the analogous conditions when voters have social preferences of the FS form. Future research can extend these results to other models of social preferences.

So far, we have assumed that all voters have social preferences. However, the evidence typically reveals a mixture of self-regarding and other-regarding individuals. The next section considers the implications of such a mixture for optimal redistribution. In order to prepare the ground for the next section we give some intermediate results.

Substituting labor supply, $l(t, b, s_j)$, into $y_j = s_j l_j$ gives before-tax income $y_j(t, b, s_j) = s_j l(t, b, s_j)$. Substituting $b(t, \mathbf{s})$, given by Lemma 2.6(g), into the indirect self-regarding utility function (2.28), gives

$$w_j(t, \mathbf{s}) = v\big(t, b(t, \mathbf{s}), s_j\big). \tag{2.31}$$

Let

$$W_j(t, \alpha, \beta, \mathbf{s}) = V_j(t, b(t, \mathbf{s}), \alpha, \beta, \mathbf{s}), \tag{2.32}$$

where $b(t, \mathbf{s})$ is given by Lemma 2.6(g). Then (2.30) can be written as

$$W_j(t, \alpha, \beta, \mathbf{s}) = w_j(t, \mathbf{s}) - \frac{\alpha}{n-1}\sum_{k>j}\big[w_k(t, \mathbf{s}) - w_j(t, \mathbf{s})\big] - \frac{\beta}{n-1}\sum_{i<j}\big[w_j(t, \mathbf{s}) - w_i(t, \mathbf{s})\big], \tag{2.33}$$

where w_j is defined in (2.31). This gives the Fehr–Schmidt utility of an individual with skill level s_j that depends only on the redistributive tax rate, t.

---

[18] Assumption A1 is satisfied, for instance, in the important case of quasi-linear preferences, which is widely used in this literature.

2.5.2 Heterogeneity in voter preferences and redistribution

We now examine some of the insights from Dhami and al-Nowaihi (2010b) who consider the implications for societal redistribution arising from a mixture of other-regarding and self-regarding voters. Consider the model in Section 2.5.1 but assume, for pedagogical ease, that voters belong to one of three categories: poor, middle class, and rich, whose skills are ordered as $s_1 < s_2 < s_3$. We also assume that voters have identical α, β parameters.[19] Each type of voter can have either self-regarding preferences ($\alpha = \beta = 0$) or other-regarding preferences ($\alpha, \beta \neq 0$). One can assume either that there is a large number of voters who are uniformly distributed over the three skill levels or just three voters, one of each type. We use the latter interpretation below.

We assume that the self-regarding utility function is quasi linear, with constant elasticity of labor supply, which is the most commonly used functional form in various applications of the median voter theorems.

$$\widetilde{u}(c, 1 - l) = c - \frac{\epsilon}{1 + \epsilon} l^{\frac{1+\epsilon}{\epsilon}}, \qquad (2.34)$$

where ϵ is the constant elasticity of labor supply, assumed positive.[20] One can check that the more general case considered in Lemmas 2.6 and 2.7 continues to hold. Using (2.33), (2.34), and Lemmas 2.6 and 2.7, we can prove the next proposition.

Proposition 2.13 *(Dhami and al-Nowaihi, 2010b) (Existence of optimal tax rates): Consider $W_j(t, \alpha, \beta, \mathbf{s})$ defined in (2.33).*

(a) *Given α, β and $\mathbf{s}$, $W_j(t, \alpha, \beta, \mathbf{s})$ attains a maximum at some $t_j \in [0, 1)$.*
(b) *Whenever there is an interior solution to the tax rate, the tax rate, t_j, preferred by voter j, is unique.*
(c) *$W_j(t, \alpha, \beta, \mathbf{s})$ is strictly increasing on $[0, t_j)$ and strictly decreasing on $(t_j, 1]$.*
(d) *t_j is non-decreasing in α, β.*

The final result in Proposition 2.13(d) deserves to be commented upon. The intuition is that an increase in α_j increases disutility arising from disadvantageous inequity. By increasing the redistributive tax rate, the voter reduces, relatively, the utility of anyone who is richer, hence, reducing disadvantageous inequity. On the other hand, an increase in β_j increases disutility arising from advantageous inequity. An increase in the redistributive tax benefits everyone poorer than the voter relatively more, thus, reducing advantageous inequity.

For the three-voter model, poor, middle class, and rich, there are $2^3 = 8$ possible combinations of the preferences of voters. Denoting by S and F, respectively, a self-regarding and a fair (or other-regarding) voter, the eight possible combinations of the voters, each combination arranged in order of increasing skill level from left to right, are: *SSS*, *SSF*, *SFS*, *SFF*, *FSS*, *FSF*, *FFS*, *FFF*. For instance, *SFF* denotes an economy in which the lowest skill voter is self-regarding and the middle and high skill voters are both fair. Since the experimental evidence is that 1/3 to 2/3 of the participants are self-regarding, the most important cases are *SSF*, *SFS*, *SFF*, *FSS*, *FSF*, *FFS*.

Proposition 2.13 tells us about the features of the most preferred tax rate by any voter. Does a Condorcet winner exist in this economy? We cannot directly apply the results of Proposition 2.12

---

[19] For the case where the fairness parameters of voters can differ, so that the fairness parameters of voter $j = 1, 2, 3$ are summarized α_j, β_j, see Dhami and al-Nowaihi (2010b).
[20] The case $\epsilon = 1$ has special significance in the literature. In this case, $\widetilde{u}(c, 1 - l) = c - \frac{1}{2}l^2$.

because we now have a mixture of self-regarding and other-regarding voters. The main result is summarized in Proposition 2.14.

Proposition 2.14 *(Dhami and al-Nowaihi, 2010b): Let*

$$\theta_1 = \frac{s_2^{1+\epsilon} - s_1^{1+\epsilon}}{s_3^{1+\epsilon} - s_2^{1+\epsilon}}; \; \theta_2 = \frac{2}{2+\theta_1},$$

then,[21] for the three-voter model:

(a) *The median-skill voter with skill s_2 is the Condorcet winner. Let t_j, $j = 1, 2, 3$ be the most preferred tax rate of voter j. Then the most preferred tax rates are ordered by magnitude as $t_3 < t_2 < t_1$, in the following cases:*
   (i) *SSS, FSS, FFS, and FFF,*
   (ii) *SFS and SFF, if $\frac{\alpha}{2-\beta} < \theta_1$,*
   (iii) *SSF and FSF, if $\beta < \theta_2$,*

(b) *The low-skill voter with skill s_1 is the Condorcet winner, and $t_3 < t_1 < t_2$, in cases SFS and SFF, if $\theta_1 < \frac{\alpha}{2-\beta}$,*

(c) *The high-skill voter with skill s_3 is the Condorcet winner, and $t_2 < t_3 < t_1$, in cases SSF and FSF, if $\theta_2 < \beta$.*

We now offer a discussion of Proposition 2.14.

In cases *SSS, FSS, FFS,* and *FFF*, the median-skill voter is decisive in the redistributive tax choice (Proposition 2.14a(i)). Note that in the cases *SSS, FSS,* the median-skill voter is self-regarding, while in cases *FFS* and *FFF* the median-skill voter is other-regarding. Hence, in these four cases, the redistributive outcome in the case of a mixture of voter types is identical to a hypothetical economy in which all voters are of the same type as the median-skill voter. So, for instance, the redistributive outcome in the *FSS* economy is the same as that in an *SSS* economy, while the outcome in the *FFS* economy is identical to the *FFF* economy.

The same result is also true for the other four cases *SFS, SFF, SSF,* and *FSF* provided that the relevant upper bounds on α and/or β are satisfied (Proposition 2.14a(ii) and a(iii)). In each of these eight cases, the tax rate implemented is the tax rate, t_2, preferred by the median-skill voter.

If the upper bounds in Proposition 2.14a(ii), a(iii) are not satisfied, then the median-skill voter is no more decisive. From Proposition 2.14b, in cases *SFS* and *SFF*, the low-skill (and self-regarding) voter becomes decisive, and the implemented tax rate is t_1. From Proposition 2.14c, in cases *SSF* and *FSF*, the high-skill (and other-regarding) voter becomes decisive, and the implemented tax rate is t_3.

Note that in all such cases, *the implemented tax rate is the median tax rate and not, necessarily, the tax rate preferred by the median-skill voter.*

Consider the four striking cases in the following corollary to Proposition 2.14.

Corollary 2.1

(a) *For SFS, the majority of voters are self-regarding yet, if $\frac{\alpha}{2-\beta} < \theta_1$, then a majority votes for the tax rate preferred by the median-skill other-regarding voter (Proposition 2.14a(ii)).*

---

[21] It can be proved that the constant θ_1 is, for the three-voter case, directly proportional to the ratio of advantageous to disadvantageous inequality for voter 2; see Dhami and al-Nowaihi (2010b). θ_2 depends inversely on θ_1.

(b) For SFF, the majority of voters are fair yet, if $\theta_1 < \frac{\alpha}{2-\beta}$, then a majority votes for the tax rate preferred by the low-skill self-regarding voter (Proposition 2.14b).

(c) For SSF, the majority of voters are self-regarding yet, if $\theta_2 < \beta$, then a majority votes for the tax rate preferred by the high-skill other-regarding voter (Proposition 2.14c).

(d) For FSF, the majority of voters are fair yet, if $\theta_2 < \beta$, then a majority votes for the tax rate preferred by the median-skill self-regarding voter (Proposition 2.14a(iii)).

Denote by t_j^S and t_j^F to be the most preferred tax rates of voter j if he is, respectively, self-regarding and fair (or other-regarding). From Proposition 2.14a(i), in an SSS economy, the median-skill voter is decisive, so $t_3^S < t_2^S < t_1^S$ because richer self-regarding voters prefer a lower redistributive tax. This is shown in Figure 2.1 by the curve labeled abc. Now suppose that we replace the *self-regarding* median-skill voter in an SSS economy by an other-regarding voter to generate the SFS economy. There are two cases:

(a) If the inequality $\theta_1 < \frac{\alpha}{2-\beta}$ holds, then from Proposition 2.14b, for the SFS economy, we get the ranking of most preferred tax rates to be $t_3^S < t_1^S < t_2^F$. This is shown in Figure 2.1 by the curve adc. The tax rate of the low-skill self-regarding voter, t_1^S, is now able to defeat any of the other two tax rates in a pairwise contest (either of the other two classes of voters find it optimal to align with the low-skill voter against the tax proposal of the third voter). The optimal tax rate of the lowest-skill voter becomes the decisive redistributive choice. Hence, in moving from the SSS to the SFS economy, there is a jump in the tax rate from point b to point a (or from t_2^S to t_1^S).

(b) If the restriction $\frac{\alpha}{2-\beta} < \theta_1$ holds, then we get the case in Proposition 2.14a(ii). In this case, the ranking of tax rates, for the SFS economy, is $t_3^S < t_2^F < t_1^S$, so the median skill voter is also the decisive median voter. In Figure 2.1, this ranking of tax rates is shown by the curve aec. In this case, as we transit from the economy SSS to the economy SFS, there is a smaller upward jump from point b to point e.

In Proposition 2.14b, the crucial inequality is $\theta_1 < \frac{\alpha}{2-\beta}$; for the SFS economy, the relevant curve is adc in Figure 2.1. To see why this inequality is important, suppose that there is pairwise voting between the two tax rates, t_1^S, t_2^F. For the high-skill voter (whose skill level is s_3) to prefer the tax rate of the low-skill voter, t_1^S, the optimal tax rate of the middle-skill voter, t_2^F, should be "too high" in the sense that $t_1^S < t_2^F$. In this case, a majority (the rich and the poor) will prefer the tax rate t_1^S to t_2^F. The following factors help to satisfy the inequality $\theta_1 < \frac{\alpha}{2-\beta}$, and, hence, are conducive to t_2^F being "too high."

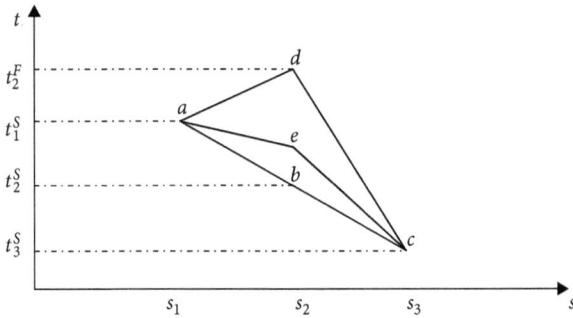

Figure 2.1 The SSS and SFS economies.

(a) High inequity aversion, as captured by the magnitudes of α, β: From Proposition 2.13d, higher magnitudes of the inequity aversion parameters, α, β, increase the optimal tax rate for other-regarding voters, so increase t_2^F.

(b) High skill inequality at the upper end of the skill distribution ($s_3 - s_2$) and low inequality at the lower end of the income distribution ($s_2 - s_1$) reduce θ_1 and increase t_2^F: To see this, suppose that $s_3 - s_2$ increases because of an increase in s_3. This leads to an increase in disadvantageous inequity faced by a voter of skill level s_2. Self-regarding voters would like to redistribute more when the rich get richer because average incomes increase, so the lump-sum available for redistribution is higher. Other-regarding voters have an additional motive to redistribute more, namely, that it reduces disadvantageous inequity. This facilitates an increase in t_2^F.

For self-regarding voters, a decrease in the low-skill level reduces the redistributive tax rate. The intuition is that reduction in low-skill income reduces average income available for redistribution, hence, reducing the marginal benefits of increasing the tax rate. For other-regarding voters, however, the results can go either way. The reason is that on the one hand, the other-regarding voter is influenced by very similar considerations to the self-regarding voter (because the other-regarding voter also cares about "own" payoff). However, on the other hand, the empathy/concern for poorer voters, on account of the disutility arising from advantageous inequity induces the other-regarding voter in the opposite direction, i.e., greater redistribution. The interplay between these two opposing factors determines if the other-regarding voter will respond, unlike the self-regarding voter, by redistributing more in response to poverty. The restriction $\theta_1 < \frac{\alpha}{2-\beta}$ ensures that overall, one gets the ranking $t_3^S < t_1^S < t_2^F$ for the optimal tax rates of the three voting classes.

In Figure 2.2, we illustrate the second generic case when $\theta_2 < \beta$ (see Proposition 2.14c). For the benchmark SSS economy, we know from Proposition 2.14a(i), that the median-skill voter, of skill s_2, is decisive, so $t_3^S < t_2^S < t_1^S$. Thus, the SSS economy is represented by the line abc. Now replace the highest-skill self-regarding voter by an other-regarding voter to generate the economy SSF. Under the restriction specified in Proposition 2.14c ($\theta_2 < \beta$), the economy SSF is shown in Figure 2.2 by the curve abe and one gets the ordering of tax rates to be $t_2^S < t_3^F < t_1^S$. In this case, the rich but other-regarding voter is decisive because the proposed tax rate, t_3^F, can defeat any of the other two proposed tax rates in a pairwise contest. Under the restriction $\theta_2 < \beta$, the FSF economy is also shown in Figure 2.2, by the curve dbe. The decisive median voter is again the rich other-regarding voter, who is not the median-skill voter.

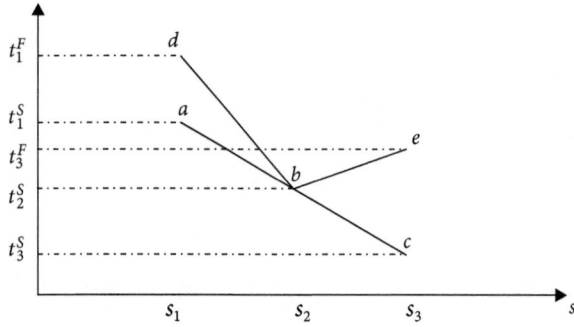

Figure 2.2 The SSS, SSF, and FSF economies.

Why does the restriction $\theta_2 < \beta$ not involve α? The reason is that for the cases in Figure 2.2 to arise, we need the most preferred tax rate of the rich other-regarding voter to be high enough, in the sense that $t_2^S < t_3^F$. The rich other-regarding voter faces no disadvantageous inequality, which explains the absence of the parameter α. However, if β is high enough, then the rich other-regarding voter suffers sufficiently highly from advantageous inequality with respect to the other two class of voters. In particular, if $\theta_2 < \beta$, then $t_2^S < t_3^F$, which leads to the surprising outcome in Proposition 2.14c.

2.6 Fairness, general equilibrium, and welfare

In the presence of other-regarding preferences, can we invoke the standard machinery of general equilibrium and welfare economics? For instance, we know from undergraduate microeconomics that in the presence of consumption externalities, the fundamental welfare theorems need not hold. Such consumption externalities are also reflected in social preferences; see, for instance, the Fehr–Schmidt preferences in (2.1). The relevant issues are addressed by Dufwenberg et al. (2011). In this section we give readers a flavor of their results.[22]

Consider a production economy with goods (inputs and outputs) indexed by $l \in \{1, 2, \ldots, L\}$, profit maximizing firms indexed by $j \in \{1, 2, \ldots, J\}$, and utility maximizing consumers indexed by $i \in \{1, 2, \ldots, I\}$. The price of good l is $p_l \geq 0$, and the price vector of all goods is given by p. The production set of firm j, $Y_j \subseteq \mathbb{R}^L$, is closed and bounded; negative and positive entries in the production set are, respectively, inputs and outputs. The profit function of firm j is given by $\pi_j(p)$; its existence for all p is guaranteed by the assumptions. The set of all possible production profiles is given by $Y = \Pi_{j=1}^J Y_j$, and the typical element is denoted by y. Consumer i has an initial endowment of $e_i \in \mathbb{R}_+^L$, and the consumption vector given by $x_i \in \mathbb{R}_+^L$. The consumption vector of all I consumers is $x \in \mathbb{R}_+^{LI}$. All firms are owned by consumers. The share of consumer i in firm j is θ_{ij}, hence, the income of the consumer is $w_i = pe_i + \sum_{j=1}^J \theta_{ij} \pi_j(p)$.

Denote by $B_i = \{x_i \in \mathbb{R}_+^L : px_i \leq w_i\} \subseteq \mathbb{R}_+^L$, the non-empty and compact budget set of consumer i. Let $B = (B_1, B_2, \ldots, B_I)$ be a profile of budget sets of all consumers and $\mathcal{B}$ be the set of all budget profiles. Other-regarding preferences are captured by defining, for any consumer i, a binary preference relation, $\succsim_i$, over objects in the set $\mathbb{R}_+^L \times \mathcal{B}$; each object (x, B) is a pair of the consumption profile of all consumers and of the budget sets of all consumers. It will sometimes be convenient to write (x, B) as (x_i, x_{-i}, B) where x_{-i} is the consumption profile of all consumers other than consumer i.

Definition 2.8 *The preferences of the individuals satisfy the following properties:*

(a) *Strictly monotone in own consumption: Fix x_{-i}, B and let $x_i \geq x_i'$ but $x_i \neq x_i'$. Then strict monotonicity requires $(x_i, x_{-i}, B) \succ_i (x_i', x_{-i}, B)$, where $\succ_i$ is the strict preference relation.*

(b) *Continuous: Fix any x', B. The set $P = \{(x, B) : (x, B) \succsim_i (x', B)\}$ is closed.*

(c) *Strictly convex over own consumption: Fix x_{-i}, B. Let $x_i \neq x_i'$ and $(x_i, x_{-i}, B) \succsim_i (x_i', x_{-i}, B)$. Then strict convexity requires that for $\alpha \in (0, 1)$, $(\alpha x_i + (1-\alpha)x_i', x_{-i}, B) \succ_i (x_i', x_{-i}, B)$.*

---

[22] We omit the proofs. However, the proofs use standard arguments used in graduate texts in microeconomics.

Under these assumptions, suppose that each preference relation, $\succsim_i$, can be represented by a continuous utility function $U_i(x,B) : \mathbb{R}_+^{LI} \times \mathcal{B} \to \mathbb{R}$. Clearly, this utility function is more general than the standard one because utility also depends on the budget sets. For instance, an individual may be envious of another who has the ability to buy a larger basket of goods.

> **Definition 2.9** *(Economy): An economy $\mathcal{E}$ is described by the vector $(I, e, \{U_i\}, J, Y, \theta)$, i.e., the set of players, their endowments, their utility functions, the set of firms, their production sets, and the shares of consumers in each firm.*

We have assumed that the budget set is compact, the utility function of each consumer is continuous, and preferences are strictly convex, so the demand function exists and for consumer i it is given by $d_i(x_{-i}, B) \in \arg\max_{x_i \in B_i} U_i(x_i, x_{-i}, B)$. Thus, the optimal demand of any consumer, d_i, depends directly on the consumption levels and the budget sets of others. This contrasts with the neoclassical case of self-regarding preferences in which the direct effects of the consumption and budget sets of others are absent. Can one impose conditions on $U_i(x_i, x_{-i}, B)$ such that these effects are also absent when we allow for other-regarding preferences? If so (see below), consumer i is said to behave as-if-classical.

> **Definition 2.10** *(As-if-classical consumers): Consumer i behaves as-if-classical if d_i does not depend on x_{-i}, B_{-i}, where B_{-i} gives the profile of budget sets of all consumers other than i.*

The actions of others do determine prices, p, hence, also w_i. These factors also determine d_i, hence, even as-if-classical consumers are "indirectly" influenced by the actions of others.

The demand functions of consumer i, $d_i(x_{-i}, B)$, for the L goods can be written as $d_i(x_{-i}, B_i, B_{-i})$. Substituting the optimal demands in the definition of the budget sets we can write $B_i = B_i(p, w_i)$. Hence, we may write the demand functions of consumer i as $d_i(p, w_i, x_{-i}, B_{-i})$.

The next definition is helpful to determine the conditions on preferences that ensure consumer i behaves as-if-classical.

> **Definition 2.11** *(Separable preferences): Given any two consumption profiles, x, x', and two budgets sets, B, B', the preferences of consumer i are said to be separable if*
> $$(x_i, x_{-i}, B) \succsim_i (x'_i, x_{-i}, B) \Leftrightarrow (x_i, x'_{-i}, B') \succsim_i (x'_i, x'_{-i}, B').$$

In Definition 2.11, preferences over own consumption bundles are independent of the consumption bundles and budget sets of others.

> **Proposition 2.15** *(Dufwenberg et al., 2011): Separable preferences have a utility representation given by $V_i(m(x_i), x_{-i}, B)$, where (i) V_i is increasing in m, and (ii) the function $m: \mathbb{R}_+^L \to \mathbb{R}$, known as the consumer's "internal utility function," is continuous, strictly monotone, and strictly quasi-concave.*

The importance of separable preferences is shown in the next proposition.

> **Proposition 2.16** *(Dufwenberg et al., 2011):*
>
> (i) *If the preferences of consumers can be written as $V_i(m(x_i), x_{-i}, B)$ (Proposition 2.15), then the consumer behaves as-if-classical (Definition 2.10).*
> (ii) *If $d_i(p, w_i, x_{-i}, B_{-i})$ is continuously differentiable in (p, w_i), then consumers behave as-if-classical if the utility function can be represented as $V_i(m(x_i), x_{-i}, B)$ (Proposition 2.15).*

The conditions in Proposition 2.16 hold for Fehr–Schmidt preferences, as we now show in the next example.

Example 2.5 *(Weighted utilitarian preferences; Dhami and al-Nowaihi, 2010a,b): Consider the Fehr–Schmidt preferences given in 2.1. Define the sets A_i and D_i as the set of consumers with respect to whom consumer i has respectively, advantageous and disadvantageous inequality. So*

$$A_i = \{j : i \neq j \text{ and } x_j \leq x_i\}, \tag{2.35}$$
$$D_i = \{k : k \neq i \text{ and } x_k > x_i\}. \tag{2.36}$$

Denote the respective cardinalities of these sets by $|A_i|$ and $|D_i|$. Then FS-utility can be written in a way that is reminiscent of the weighted utilitarian form:

$$U_i = \omega_{ii} x_i + \sum_{j \neq i}^{I} \omega_{ij} x_j, \tag{2.37}$$

where,

$$\begin{aligned} j \in A_i &\Rightarrow \omega_{ij} = \frac{\beta}{n-1} > 0, \\ i = j &\Rightarrow \omega_{ii} = 1 - \frac{|A_i|\beta}{n-1} + \frac{|D_i|\alpha}{n-1} > 0, \\ k \in D_j &\Rightarrow \omega_{ik} = -\frac{\alpha}{n-1} < 0. \end{aligned} \tag{2.38}$$

Furthermore, the weights sum up to one, i.e., $\sum_{j=1}^{I} \omega_{ij} = 1$. For self-regarding consumers, $\omega_{ii} = 1$ and $\omega_{ij} = 0$ $(i \neq j)$. Clearly (2.37) is of the same form as V_i (Proposition 2.15), hence, the consumer must behave as-if-classical.

We are now interested in exploring the link between the Walrasian equilibrium of an economy with other-regarding preferences, and the Walrasian equilibrium with self-regarding consumers.

Definition 2.12 *A Walrasian equilibrium is given by a triple of prices, consumption profiles, and production plans of firms, i.e., (p^*, x^*, y^*), such that: (i) Each x_i^* maximizes the utility of the consumer U_i, subject to the budget constraint B_i, (ii) Each y_j^* maximizes the profit function of the firm, π_j, subject to the production set Y_j. (iii) All markets for the L goods clear.*

Definition 2.13 *Consider any economy $\mathcal{E} = (I, e, \{U_i\}, J, Y, \theta)$ (Definition 2.9). The corresponding 'internal economy' is defined by $\mathcal{E}^{Int} = (I, e, \{m_i\}, J, Y, \theta)$, where m_i is defined in Proposition 2.15.*

In Definition 2.13, the only difference between an economy and its internal economy is that in the latter, all consumers are self-regarding. The next proposition gives the link between the Walrasian equilibria of the two economies.

Proposition 2.17 *(Dufwenberg et al., 2011): Suppose that the preferences of all consumers are separable (Definition 2.11) and strictly monotone in own-consumption. Then the set of Walrasian equilibria of the two economies, $\mathcal{E}$ and $\mathcal{E}^{Int}$ are identical.*

Example 2.6 *(Dhami and al-Nowaihi, 2010a,b): Section 2.5, above, gives a behavioral political economy application in a simple general equilibrium model of endogenous labor supply. Lemma 2.6 shows that there is a unique labor supply for voter j, $l_j = l(t, b, s_j)$, that maximizes own-utility $u(l_j; t, b, s_j)$ despite the fact that voter j has other-regarding preferences. In other words, the voter behaves as-if-classical. The same individual with Fehr–Schmidt preferences behaves as if he had self-regarding preferences when he chooses labor* supply but other-regarding preferences when he chooses the redistributive tax rate. This result was puzzling to the authors and they used it to argue that preferences may be context dependent.[23] The second stage general equilibrium outcome in this model is identical for voters who have self-regarding or other-regarding preferences. This result was given before the more general insights of Dufwenberg et al. (2011) were known, albeit in the specific context of voting.[24]

We now consider issues of welfare economics. Here, the analysis requires a more restricted version of $V_i(m(x_i), x_{-i}, B)$.

Definition 2.14 *(Well-being externalities): Well-being externalities arise if the utility function of any consumer i is given by $W_i(m_i, m_{-i})$, where m_i is given in Proposition 2.15. W_i is increasing in each argument and $m_k(x_k)$ is increasing for each k.*

Example 2.7 Consider two examples of well-being externalities. The first one is due to Edgeworth (see citation in Dufwenberg et al. 2011).

$$W_i(m_i, m_{-i}) = m_i + \frac{\eta_i}{I-1}\left(\sum_{k \neq i} m_k\right),$$

where $\eta_i > 0$ captures altruism, while $\eta_i < 0$ captures spite. The second example is a version of the Bolton–Ockenfels ERC model.

$$W_i(m_i, m_{-i}) = m_i - \eta_i \left| m_i - \frac{\sum_k m_k}{I} \right|; 0 \leq \eta_i < 1.$$

Definition 2.15 *(Feasibility and Pareto optimality): An allocation $x = (x_1, x_2, \ldots, x_I)$ is feasible if there exists some production plan $y = (y_1, y_2, \ldots, y_J) \in Y$ such that $\sum_{i=1}^{I} x_i \leq \sum_{i=1}^{I} e_i + \sum_{j=1}^{J} y_j$. A feasible allocation, x, is Pareto optimal if there does not exist another feasible allocation x' such that at least one consumer is better off and no consumer is worse off.*

We first show by an example that the second fundamental welfare theorem need not hold.

Example 2.8 *The object of this example is to show that Pareto efficient allocations need not be Walrasian equilibria in the presence of other-regarding preferences. Suppose that there are two consumers ($I = 2$), two goods ($L = 2$), and the (identical) utility functions of the consumers are given by*

$$W_i = m_i - 2m_k, i \neq k \text{ and } m_i(x_i) = h(x_{i1}) + h(x_{i2}), h' > 0, h'' < 0. \tag{2.39}$$

The aggregate endowment of each of the two goods is 1. The allocation $((0,0),(0,0))$ is not a Walrasian equilibrium of the internal economy $\mathcal{E}^{Int}$ (Definition 2.13) because preferences are strictly monotone, yet no consumer consumes anything. However, given (2.39), $((0,0),(0,0))$ is Pareto optimal.

---

[23] The authors argued that: "For example, individuals, when making a private consumption decision might act so as to maximize their selfish interest. But in a separate role as part of the government, as a school governor or as a voter, could act so as to maximize some notion of public well being. Individuals might, for instance, send their own children to private schools (self interest) but could at the same time vote for more funding to government run schools in local or national elections (public interest)."

[24] The orginal results were presented in the Public Economics Weekend, held at Leicester in 2006.

Example 2.8 indicates that additional restrictions on preferences are required for the standard welfare theorems to hold in the presence of other-regarding preferences. In particular, we would like to rule out the pathological case of Example 2.8.

Definition 2.16 *(Social monotonicity): Consider an allocation, x. Then there exists another allocation z such that $z \geq 0$ and*[25]

$$W_i(m_i(x_i+z_i), m_{-i}(x_{-i}+z_{-i})) > W_i(m_i(x_i), m_{-i}(x_{-i})),$$

where $\sum_{k=1}^{I} z_k = z$ and at least one element of the vector z is strictly positive.

Definition 2.13 requires that redistributing an extra amount of resources to all consumers increases everyone's utility. This rules out the extreme case of spite in Example 2.8.

Proposition 2.18 *(Dufwenberg et al., 2011): Suppose that the utility function exhibits well-being externalities (Definition 2.14) and the social monotonicity condition (Definition 2.16) holds.*

  (i) *The set of Pareto optimal allocations of the economy $\mathcal{E}$ is a subset of the Pareto optimal allocations of the economy $\mathcal{E}^{Int}$.*
  (ii) *Every Pareto optimal allocation of the economy $\mathcal{E}$ can be obtained as a Walrasian equilibrium if lump-sum transfers are allowed.*

Proposition 2.18(i) shows the relation between the Pareto optimal equilibria of economies with other-regarding and self-regarding preferences. Proposition 2.18(ii) is the analogue of the second welfare theorem but for other-regarding preferences. The social monotonicity condition by itself does not ensure that Pareto efficient equilibria can be implemented as a Walrasian equilibrium unless lump-sum transfers are allowed; the next example discusses this point.

Example 2.9 *Suppose that there are three consumers and one good. The endowment of consumer 1 and consumer 3 is one unit each of the good, while consumer 2 has zero units (so $e = (1, 0, 1)$). Consumer 2 has purely self-regarding preferences. The utility of consumer 1 is $W_1 = x_1 + \frac{2}{3}x_2$ and the utility of consumer 3 is $W_3 = x_3 + \frac{2}{3}x_2$. Suppose that we allow for voluntary lump-sum transfers of goods between the three consumers and the social monotonicity condition (Definition 2.16) holds. Consumers 1 and 3 do not want to transfer any of the good to consumer 2 because giving up a unit costs 1 but gives a marginal benefit $\frac{2}{3} < 1$. Hence, the economy is stuck with the initial allocation $e = (1, 0, 1)$, yet it is Pareto dominated by the allocation $(0, 2, 0)$. Thus, no Walrasian equilibrium can implement the Pareto optimal allocation $(0, 2, 0)$.*

2.7 Evidence on models of social preferences and reciprocity

In this section we consider first the evidence on models of social preferences (Section 2.7.1) followed by the evidence on the role intentions (Section 2.7.2).

---

[25] We use here the notation $\geq$, which applies the *greater than or equal to* operation to elements of vectors.

2.7.1 The evidence on models of social preferences

One criticism of the inequity aversion models is that they do not specify the reference group over which an individual compares his payoff (Sobel, 2005). However, the reference group can be elicited from subjects in experiments and alternative assumptions on the reference group can be experimentally tested. Given individual heterogeneity, it may be undesirable for the theory to specify a reference group. Some individuals may simply compare their consumption with those on the street that they live in, others with colleagues in the workplace, still others with the population of subjects in similar professions, and so on.

Some models introduce the possibility that individuals care for the total economic surplus (Charness and Rabin, 2002). A natural way to test the relative concerns for surplus maximization and inequity aversion is to construct experiments that set these two opposing concerns against each other.[26] The main result of these papers is that in dictator games, a non-negligible fraction of proposers are willing to take an action that increases the total surplus, even at a cost in terms of personal payoff, and even if this increases disadvantageous inequity for them.

Andreoni and Miller (2002), and Andreoni and Vesterlund (2001) vary the price at which the proposer can transfer a unit of money to the responder in dictator games. Normally, in dictator games, by giving up a unit of money, the dictator can transfer a unit of money to the receiver (the 1:1 case). In the 1:1 case, experimental evidence shows that the dictator never proposes to transfer more than half the amount. Now suppose that we reduce the price of giving by using other ratios such as 1:2 (i.e., for every unit given up by the dictator, 2 units are transferred to the responder), and 1:3. In these cases, Andreoni and Miller (2002) and Andreoni and Vesterlund (2001) find that in a non-negligible fraction of cases, the dictators end up with less money relative to the receiver, but the total surplus between the two parties is higher. Such results are not consistent with models of inequity aversion models such as the ERC model, the Fehr–Schmidt model, and the composite model of Falk and Fischbacher (2006). There is substantial heterogeneity at the level of the individual. Andreoni and Vesterlund find that 44% of the subjects are completely self-regarding, 35% seem to have egalitarian preferences (they try to equalize payoffs), and only 21% are surplus maximizers.

Charness and Rabin (2002) consider the following two payoff-pairs in a dictator game: (400, 400) and (400, 750), where the first figure represents the dictator's payoff, while the second figure is the responder's payoff. Of the subjects 31% are found to be egalitarian, which is similar to the finding in Andreoni and Vesterlund (2001). To check for the presence of individuals who might not be willing to make the surplus maximizing choice at a cost to their own payoff, consider another choice condition: (400, 400) versus (375, 750). In this case, only 49% make the surplus maximizing choice, because it reduces own-payoff by 25. When income disparities are increased further, e.g., in the choices (400, 400) and (400, 2000), then 62% make the egalitarian choice in preference to the surplus maximizing choice.

Iriberri and Rey-Biel (2013) find that in dictator games, there is heterogeneity in preference types (self-regarding, social welfare maximizing, inequity averse, and competitive); almost half the subjects are self-regarding. We have noted above, reservations about the use of the dictator game results to draw robust conclusions about social preferences (Fehr and Schmidt, 2006). However, an interesting element of the results in this paper is that people alter their preference

---

[26] See, for instance, Andreoni and Miller (2002), Andreoni and Vesterlund (2001), Bolle and Kritikos (1998), Charness and Rabin (2002), Cox (2000).

Table 2.2 Payoffs of three players in three different allocations.

Allocation	A	B	C
Person 1	9	8	11
Person 2	8	8	10
Person 3	4	8	9
Total	21	24	30

Source: Engleman and Strobel (2004).

types depending on the available social information (e.g., about the actions of others); this is suggestive of interdependent preferences. There is also substantial heterogeneity in beliefs about others that is dependent on one's preference type.

Engelmann and Strobel (2004) present the following example that illustrates concerns for efficiency and inequity aversion. There are three individuals and three possible allocations, A, B, and C; Table 2.2 shows the payoffs of the three players in the three different allocations. Suppose that individual 2 is asked to choose between allocations A and B, which give the individual an identical payoff of 8. Inequity aversion theories predict that individual 2 will choose allocation B over A because it has a more equitable payoff. However, there is another potential explanation. Allocation B is more efficient as compared to A (joint surplus being 24 rather than 21). So it might well be the case that what seems to be a choice based on inequity aversion is really a concern for efficiency. Thus, based on this choice alone we cannot distinguish between theories of choice that are based on inequity aversion and surplus maximization.

Now suppose that individual 2 has a choice between all three allocations, A, B, and C. Suppose that allocation C is chosen. This will provide support for selfishness (2's payoff is highest in allocation C), efficiency (joint surplus is highest in allocation C), inequity aversion,[27] and maximin preferences (the poorest individual is best off in allocation C). Engelmann and Strobel (2004) perform experiments to disentangle these three effects, namely, efficiency, inequity aversion, and maximin preferences. They conclude that a concern for efficiency and Rawlsian preferences, jointly, is more important, relative to a concern for inequity aversion. This result supports the Charness and Rabin (2002) model (see Section 2.8), over models of inequity aversion.

Preferences for efficiency and Rawlsian maximin, relative to inequity aversion were discussed in a series of papers in the December 2006 issue of the *American Economic Review*. Bolton and Ockenfels (2006) run fresh experiments to show that there is a greater willingness to pay by individuals to achieve an equitable outcome rather than an efficient one. Engelmann and Strobel (2006) argue that a potential confounding factor in these experiments is that the gains from efficiency are lower than the gains from equity.

Fehr et al. (2006), however, show that the results of Engelmann and Strobel (2004) are driven by the presence of economics students who learn about the importance of economic efficiency in their first year. After replicating several experiments in Engelmann and Strobel, they find that the dominance of the efficiency motive holds true only for economics and business administration students. Non-economist subjects find inequity aversion more attractive relative to efficiency.

---

[27] The reader can easily check that, for person 2, the Fehr–Schmidt utility is higher for distribution C as compared to distribution A.

The evidence on the surplus maximizing motive comes largely from dictator games in which only one player has a non-trivial action. There are several issues with using the dictator game for detecting the presence of a surplus maximization motive (Fehr and Schmidt, 2006). First, it is not clear if the dictator game is a good analogy for real-world economic situations (even charities may be pro-active, not passive). Second, as we have seen above, the results of the dictator games, unlike those of the ultimatum games, are not very robust, hence, this may not be a particularly suitable game to test surplus maximization. Third, there are end game effects (as in Andreoni and Miller, 2002), where the predictions of a surplus maximization preference are not borne out in the final periods of the experiment. These final period effects can be accounted for by models of inequity aversion and intention-based reciprocity. Fourth, what if we introduced the possibility of an element of strategic consideration in which more than one player has a non-trivial choice? Is there a reduction in the surplus maximizing choice in this case? The experiments of Fehr et al. (1993, 1998) that we consider next are important in this regard.

Fehr et al. (1993, 1998) embed a gift exchange game in a strategic environment. A proposer (firm) makes a wage offer that is observed by the responder (worker) who then chooses a non-binding effort level. Since the effort level is non-binding, the responder has a non-trivial choice that can affect the total surplus in the relation. An increase in the effort level by the responder increases the total surplus by five units on average. If surplus maximization is the overriding objective, certainly more important than outcome inequality and reciprocity, then we should observe the responder putting in the maximum possible effort level. Furthermore, we should not observe any correlation between wages and effort levels. Both these implications are rejected by the evidence. In no more than 2% of the cases does the responder undertake an effort level such that the proposer's payoff is relatively greater. There is also a clear correlation between the wage offered and the effort level undertaken. The actual effort level undertaken by the responder is significantly below the maximum feasible effort level.

When subjects punish others in public goods games in the lab, there are two possible motives. First, subjects may wish to act in a *reciprocal manner*. For instance, contributors may punish non-contributors. A second motive may be to equalize payoffs. In a nice experimental design, Dawes et al. (2007) offer a way of separating the two motives. They replace the first (cooperation) stage in a Fehr–Gächter type cooperation and punishment game with a random allocation of incomes to the players that mimics the income distribution in Fehr and Gächter (2002) after the first stage. Then they give the players in stage 2, a possibility to reward or punish others in the group by assigning reward or punishment tokens to them. Interestingly, players with below-average incomes are often rewarded while players with above-average incomes often get punished. In this set up, reciprocity can play no role at all but FS or ERC-type inequity aversion can. However, ERC cannot explain this pattern of targeting rewards and punishments. This result suggests that inequity aversion (apart from reciprocity) as in the Fehr and Schmidt (2007) model is a powerful force in sanctioning behavior in public goods games.

2.7.2 The evidence on intentions and reciprocity

The *state of mind* of the accused and his/her *intentions* are of crucial importance in most legal systems when dealing with murder. The law, in most countries, defines *murder* as the *intentional* killing of another human being with full premeditation. On the other hand, the killing of a human carried out under some form of *diminished responsibility* that reflects *less than full intentionality* is treated differently.[28] In particular, the killing of a human where there is a clear lack of *intent* to kill is termed as *manslaughter* and it carries a lower penalty than premeditated murder.

Murder and manslaughter are two extreme categories with several others in between. For instance, in the Canadian legal system, murder is further classified into first and second degrees based on *intent* of the perpetrator. First degree murder is the intentional killing of a human being with premeditation, while second degree murder does not involve premeditation, e.g., killing in the heat of the moment, but nevertheless, with intent to kill, which distinguishes it from manslaughter.[29]

The *inequity aversion* models of Fehr and Schmidt (1999) and Bolton and Ockenfels (2000) are purely outcome oriented, and ignore the role played by intentions. In many contexts, one's behavior is determined by beliefs about the intentions of others. For instance, charitable giving in which one does not know the identity of the receiver of a gift might well be motivated by issues of inequity aversion. On the other hand, a firm contemplating a wage cut might be concerned that workers may form negative inferences about its intentions and may respond with negative reciprocity in the form of low effort.

An early experiment that considered the role of intentions in the ultimatum game was conducted by Blount (1995). In ultimatum games, if the initial offer is made by a computer generated random number (random offer condition) or a third party (third party condition), then the offer does not reveal any information about the intentions of the proposer. Hence, if intentions-based motives are the only explanation behind the results of the ultimatum game, we should observe no rejections in these two cases. Relative to the benchmark case, where a human proposer makes an offer, Blount (1995) finds that the rejection rates of responders decline significantly in the random offer condition. However, there is no significant change in the third party condition. The first result provides support for intentions-based models. But the second result (no significant change in the third party condition) contradicts intentions-based explanations and is consistent with models of inequity aversion.[30] Using the ultimatum game, Offerman (2002) finds that intentional low offers are 67% more likely to be followed by actions of opponents that are payoff reducing. Kagel et al. (1996) also find that the rejection rates in ultimatum games are higher when intentionally unequal proposals are made.

Falk et al. (2003) consider the modified ultimatum game in Figure 2.3 to isolate the role of intentions. The proposer, labeled by P, has two choices, 1 and 2, in offering a split of 10 dollars. The responder, labeled by R, has a choice to either accept (action a) or reject (action r). The payoffs are shown at each end node. Two variations of the game are considered. In the first variant, game A, the payoffs from the strategy pair (2, a) are (5, 5), while in the second variant, game B,

---

[28] Several factors may indicate diminished responsibility. These include, insanity, depression, side effects of certain medications, and even post-natal depression (in the case of murder of a child by the mother).

[29] Intentions can also be transferrable, within the law, in the following sense. In English law, transferred malice occurs when an individual, say A, is attacked with an intention to kill but in fact another individual, say B, is killed. The perpetrator, say individual C, can be charged with the murder of individual B.

[30] There were some pecularities in these experiments that may or may not account for these conflicting results. For instance, in two out of the three treatments, subjects made decisions in the roles of proposers and responders but the payment they received was for one of these two roles, which was only subsequently revealed to them. Furthermore, in one treatment, deception was involved—subjects thought they were making the decisions as proposers but, in fact, the experimenter made the proposals.

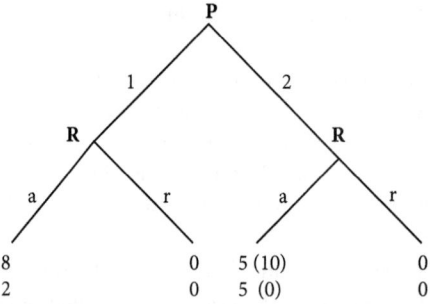

Figure 2.3 Modified ultimatum game.

Source: "On the nature of fair behavior," Falk, A., Fehr, E., and Fischbacher, U., Economic Inquiry, 41(1): 20-6. © 2007, John Wiley and Sons.

the payoffs from the strategy pair (2, a) are (10, 0). In all other respects, the payoffs from the two games are identical.

Consider game A and let the proposer choose strategy 1. In the absence of reciprocity, and based purely on self-interest, the best response of player 2 is to accept, resulting in the payoff pair (8, 2). However, in the presence of reciprocity and intentions, while deciding to accept or reject the offer, the responder brings into consideration the fact that the proposer has not chosen strategy 2, a relatively fairer strategy, which would have ensured payoffs of (5, 5). This reveals to the responder that the proposer's intentions *could have been fairer*.

Now consider game B. If the proposer chooses strategy 1 over strategy 2, the responder knows that the proposer gave up a likely payoff of 10 and chose a payoff of 8 instead. This reveals to the responder that the intentions of the proposer *could have been less fair*. Hence, if intentions are important, then the responders in game B should be more likely to accept the proposer's offer of an 8–2 split, despite the fact that the outcome (8, 2) is identical in both games. The essential feature of reciprocity is not necessarily to alter the distribution of payoffs but to respond to kindness and unkindness with like behavior.

Falk et al. (2003) find that the 8–2 split is rejected in 44.4% of the cases in game A but it is rejected in only 8.9% of the cases in game B. This runs counter to the predictions of the inequity aversion theories, which would predict that the rejection rates should not be different in the two games because the outcome (8, 2) is identical in both. However, the fact that there should be any rejection rate at all for game B suggests that the reciprocity approach based on intentions does not provide a full explanation either. Clearly more empirical work in this area will provide a fuller picture.

One possible implication of intentions driven behavior for public goods games is the following. The extent of punishment meted out by cooperators to non-cooperators should depend on the difference in their contributions, which reveals the extent of unkindness of non-cooperators. Fehr and Gächter (2002) found this to be the case in their public goods experiments. They found that the single most important predictor of the punishment meted by contributors to non-contributors was the difference in contributions between the two players. Furthermore, 75% of all punishments were carried out by contributors whose contributions were above average.

In order to isolate the role of intentions, Falk et al. (2008) use the moonlighting game, which is due to Abbink et al. (2000). There were 112 subjects in the experiment. The moonlighting game allows one player, say *A*, to be kind or unkind in the first stage and then, in the second stage, allows another player, say B, to reciprocate with rewards or punishments. Each player starts with an initial endowment of 12 monetary units of experimental money (MU). Player A chooses some action $a \in \{-6, -5, \ldots 0 \ldots, 5, 6\}$ in the first stage. If $a > 0$, then player A sacrifices a tokens but player B receives a tokens (kind intentions), while if $a < 0$, then player B must surrender a tokens to A (unkind intentions). In the second stage, conditional on A's action, player B takes some action $b \in \{-6, -5, \ldots, 17, 18\}$. If B chooses $b > 0$, then B gives an amount b to A (reward) and if $b < 0$, then B loses b, while A loses $3b$ (punishment).

The experiment allows for two treatments. In the *intentions treatment* (I-treatment), players choose their actions freely, so intentions can be inferred from actions. In the *no-intentions treatment* (NI-treatment), a random device is used to choose A's action, so intentions cannot be inferred. The ex-ante predictions are as follows.

1. If both A and B have self-regarding preferences, then the solution, using backward induction, is simple. In the second stage, when it is B's turn to move, bygones are bygones. B maximizes her payoff by choosing $b = 0$. Anticipating B's actions, A takes maximum advantage by choosing $a = -6$.
2. Suppose individuals care only about outcomes and ignore intentions, as in the inequity aversion models of Fehr and Schmidt (1999) and Bolton and Ockenfels (2000). Then, a higher action by player A, reduces A's payoff. Since player B dislikes inequality, she should respond by contributing more. Thus b should be increasing in a. In particular, when $a = 0$, then $b = 0$. However, since there is no role for intentions, we do not expect any difference among the I-treatment and the NI-treatment.
3. Suppose now that only intentions (but not outcomes) matter.[31] One can construct plausible equilibria such that a larger contribution, a, by player A, signals better intentions. In this case, in the I-treatment, we expect player B to reciprocate A's action, so b is predicted to be increasing in a. In the NI-treatment, however, intentions cannot be inferred, so the model predicts $b = 0$ for all actions taken by player A. Finally, in models that take account of both intentions and outcomes, e.g., Falk and Fischbacher (2006), one expects b to be increasing in a. However, when intentions are revealed, as in the I-treatment, then we expect b to respond even more strongly to a on account of reciprocity. The predictions are summarized in Table 2.3.

The experimental results are shown in Figure 2.4. The horizontal axis is player A's action, a, while the vertical axis is player B's action, b, in response to A's action. In the I-treatment, average and median action of player B is increasing in the action of player A. This contradicts the prediction of self-regarding preferences, $b = 0$ for all a. The median response in the NI-treatment is consistent with the prediction of the self-regarding preferences ($a = b = 0$). The difference in the intentions and the no-intentions treatment is statistically significant and intentions matter in the domain of both positive and negative reciprocity (recall that a can be negative or positive). Thus, the results also reject the "outcomes only" models (see second row of Table 2.3).

Regression results also show that reciprocity is not completely wiped out in the NI-treatment. This is seen by running a regression of b on a constant term, α_0, the action a of player A, a dummy variable d that equals 1 for the I-treatment and zero otherwise, and, finally, the interaction term,

---

[31] Dufwenberg and Kirchsteiger (2004) and Falk and Fischbacher (2006) consider the role of intentions and outcomes; see the material on psychological game theory in Volume 4 of the book.

136 | CHAPTER 2 *Models of Other-Regarding Preferences*

Table 2.3 Summary of predictions for player B.

Model	I-treatment	NI-treatment
Standard prediction	$b=0, \forall a$	$b=0, \forall a$
Only payoff consequences matter (Fehr–Schmidt and Bolton–Ockenfels)	b increases in a	exactly the same behavior as in I-treatment
Only fairness intentions matter (Dufwenberg–Kirchsteiger)	b increases in a^0	$b=0, \forall a$
Payoff consequences and fairness intentions matter (Falk–Fischbacher)	b increases in a	b increases in a but *less* than in the I-treatment

Source: Falk et al. (2008).

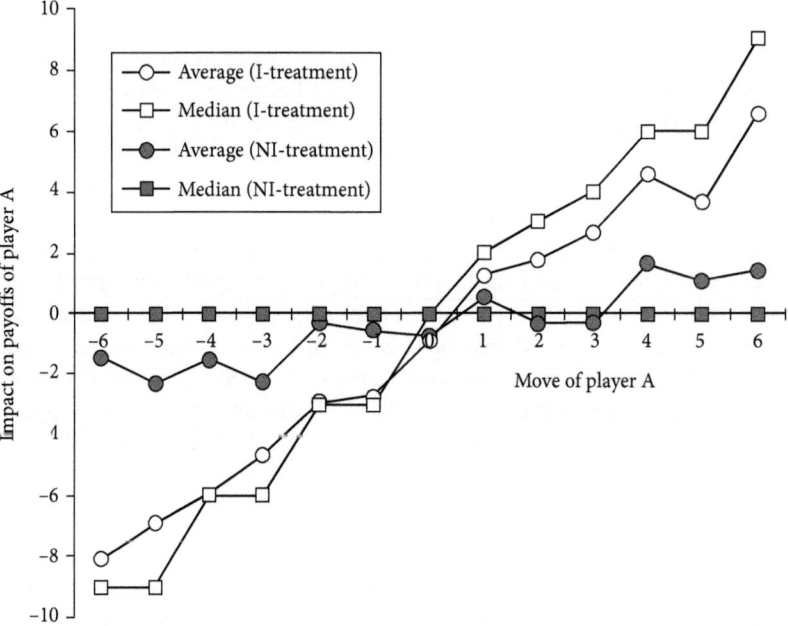

Figure 2.4 Effect on b as a changes.
Source: Reprinted from Games and Economic Behavior, 62(1): 287–303. Falk, A., Fehr, E., and Fischbacher,U., "Testing theories of fairness-intention matter." © 2008, with permission from Elsevier.

$a \times d$. The sum of the coefficients on the constant term and on the action "a," give the additional amount of b that is elicited in the NI-treatment. This is positive and statistically significant, which is not consistent with the prediction in Dufwenberg and Kirchsteiger (2004). In conclusion, the aggregate evidence is that outcomes and intentions are both important, hence, more general models such as the one by Falk and Fischbacher (2006) have a better chance of succeeding.

The experiment also generated data at the disaggregated level, i.e., on individual choices. The percentage of subjects in the role of player B whose behavior corresponds to self-regarding preferences ($b = 0$ for all a), increases from 0 to 30 as one goes from the I to the NI treatments. Hence, a substantial part of the behavior is explained by fairness intentions. The percentage of subjects who exhibit positive or negatively reciprocal behavior, reduces from 76 to 30 as one moves from the I to the NI treatment. But importantly, reciprocity is not completely wiped out even in the NI treatment. About 40% of the subjects continue to exhibit reciprocal behavior. This supports the assertion that intentions alone do not drive human behavior; the concern for fair outcomes also plays an important role.

One set of experiments finds little evidence that fairness intentions play an important role in the domain of positively reciprocal behavior (Bolton et al., 1998; Cox, 2000; Charness, 2004), while another set of results suggests that intentions are important in the domain of negatively reciprocal behavior (Blount, 1995; Offerman, 2002). By contrast, the experimental results of Falk et al. (2008), described above, find clear evidence that reciprocal intentions are important in the domain of positively and negatively reciprocal behavior. What accounts for the differences in results?

Falk et al. (2008) raise four main concerns about earlier experimental work in explaining the differences from their results. First, in some of the experiments, a significant number of the subjects had an efficiency motive in the sense that they were willing to tolerate a reduction in their own payoffs to increase the total size of the cake. This may have confounded the reciprocity motive. Second, in some experiments, the repeated trials could have introduced noise and spillovers across the periods, making it difficult to isolate intentions. Third, in some experiments, the fairness or unfairness of actions is not salient enough to signal intentions of subjects. Fourth, the intentions and the no-intentions treatments in some of the experiments might not have been well differentiated.

Cox (2004) considers variants of the trust game. In treatment 1, which is similar to the moonlighting game above, Player A is given $10 to pass on to player B, via the experimenter. The experimenter triples the amount that A has offered, before passing it on to B. Player B can then return any amount to player A. In treatment 2, Player B does not have the opportunity to return any money to player A. Finally in treatment 3, player A does not move, but the experimenter makes a move on behalf of player A, passing on the same amount as in treatment 1. The main difference between treatments 1 and 3 is that player A's intentions can be inferred in treatment 1 but not from treatment 3. So, if players were purely inequity averse, then one should not observe any difference between the results of the two treatments. The experimental results show that player B returns more money in treatment 1 and, in particular, returns more when player A offers more money, hence, demonstrating the role of intentions and reciprocity.

Bartling and Fischbacher (2012) consider a four-player dictator game. There are two possible dictators, players A and B, and two possible receivers, players C and D. There are only two possible allocations. The *fair allocation* in which each player gets a payoff of 5, and the *unfair allocation* in which players A and B get a payoff of 9 each and players C and D get a payoff of 1 each. In the no-delegation treatment, player A has to directly choose among the fair and the unfair allocations. In the delegation treatment, player A delegates player B to make the allocation decision (player B cannot refuse). In the *punishment option*, player C observes the chosen allocation and can then engage in punishing players A and B. In the *no-punishment option*, player C cannot punish.

Under pure inequity aversion, the choice of delegation by A should not matter to the punishment decision of player C. However, the choice of allocation and the choice of delegation both convey important information about the intentions of each of the players A and B. While such intentions can be difficult to pin down, the paper makes progress in this direction. For instance, in one treatment, called *asymmetric*, A can either choose the fair allocation (but not the unfair allocation), or delegate the choice to B, who can then choose among the fair and the unfair allocations. In this case, delegation by A clearly reveals unkind intentions because there is some likelihood that B may choose the unfair allocation, so player A gets 9 instead of 5, while players C and D get the low payoff of 1 each.

The main findings are as follows. When the fair option is chosen by either A or B there is no punishment. The dictator (A or B) who chooses an unfair allocation is punished more and there is very little punishment of the other player. Thus, one observes more delegation by player A to player B when the punishment option by player C is available. Thus, by delegating to B, player A also shifts most of the punishment to B if an unfair allocation is chosen.

When player A delegates to player B who then chooses an unfair offer then player A is punished relatively more as compared to the case when he directly chooses the unfair allocation. In this case, C may believe that A could have chosen the fair allocation but chose instead to delegate to B who chose an unfair allocation, hence, revealing possibly unkind intentions on the part of A. As compared to the symmetric case (where A can choose among the fair and unfair allocations), punishment of player A by player C is significantly higher in the asymmetric treatment if B chooses the unfair allocation. The reason is that this clearly reveals, to player C, the unkind intentions of player A.

INTENTIONS, INEQUITY AVERSION, AND FAIRNESS REFERENCE POINTS

Most people would concede the importance of the *intentions motive* in influencing the actions of players. However, the relative importance of the *intentions motive* (the *attribution hypothesis*) and other-regarding preferences (the *distribution hypothesis*) has been an area of some conflicting views; see Bolton et al. (2008). See also the comments by Falk et al. (2008) on the possible reasons for the differences in results between the early and the later work.

The early literature found it difficult to produce evidence on the sole importance of the attribution hypothesis. The evidence is probably better described by a combination of the attribution hypothesis and the distribution hypothesis. However, in this section, we shall see that some of the evidence begs for the introduction of even newer theoretical considerations such as a *procedural approach to fairness* and/or a better understanding of a *fairness reference point*.

We have considered issues of a fairness reference point in relation to the work of Gneezy and List (2006) and Fehr et al. (2009), elsewhere in this chapter. Bolton et al. (2005) consider experimental evidence based on the ultimatum game that may form the basis of theoretical work on a procedural approach to fairness. The main idea of these experiments is that individuals are willing to accept an unfair outcome, provided it is the outcome of a procedure that is agreed to be fair. The authors give two insightful examples of the importance of their approach.

> **Example 2.10**   *In a court case in 1842 (US v. Holmes), crew members of a ship were found guilty of throwing 14 non-crewmen overboard from a leaky and crowded lifeboat. However, the guilty verdict centered not on throwing the 14 non-crewmen overboard (perhaps this was unavoidable) but rather on the unfairness of the "procedure" that excluded everyone from the crew to be thrown overboard. The judge ruled that the victims should have been chosen by a fair lottery that included both crew and non-crew members.*

> **Example 2.11**   *A consortium of eight US states (the Southeast Compact) chose North Carolina as a destination for a radioactive waste management facility, using a lottery method. The North Carolina legislature accepted the decision on the grounds that they were chosen based on a fair procedure.*

Existing theories of social preferences and intentions are neutral towards the perceived fairness of procedures that govern outcomes. Rather, their interest centers around the fairness of outcomes and the kindness of intentions. Clearly, if the outcomes are sensitive to the perceived fairness of the procedure, then we need a broader model; the experimental evidence in Bolton et al. (2005) makes such a case.

Recall that Blount (1995) produced mixed evidence for the role of intentions—rejection rates in ultimatum games were very similar in the baseline and the third party treatments, which actually contradict the intentions motive. Another set of experiments, conducted around the mid 1990s and reported in Charness (2004), applied Blount's idea to a gift exchange game.[32] Consistent with the attribution hypothesis, he found a positive correlation between the actions of two players (gift exchange). However, when the first mover's action are allocated to a third party or chosen randomly, so intentions are impossible to infer, the contributions by the second player are even higher. This contradicts the attribution hypothesis. Normal form representation of a two-player, sequential, social dilemma game.

Similar difficulties in finding support for the intentions hypothesis were encountered by Bolton et al. (1998), which is an early, published, experimental contribution. They consider a two-player sequential game; players observe a 3 × 6 normal form game (see Figure 2.5). However, as explained below, they actually play a 2 × 6 normal form game in three different treatments. The row player always has the choice of the middle row (m), in each treatment. But in three different treatments, he can choose one additional row from among the top (t) or bottom (b) rows. The choice of the additional row reveals important information about the intentions of the row player. The column player chooses between columns, c1 to c6, and has a dominant action, c1, irrespective of the choice of the row player. However, by successively choosing actions c2, c3, . . . , c6 he can, at some personal cost to his payoffs, increase the payoff of the row player, such that the total surplus increases (social dilemma game). Once each player chooses his actions, payoffs are determined as in Figure 2.5.

In the baseline treatment, treatment II, the row player picks his second row to be m, thus, the choice by the row player is irrelevant. This is the *no free choice treatment* because the intentions of the row player cannot be inferred.

In treatment I, the row player picks his second row to be b. This is the *positively reciprocal treatment* because by choosing m over b, the row player can improve the payoff of the column player, for any action chosen by the column player. The column player can now, if he wishes, reward the kind intentions of the row player by a choice that is different from the dominant action, c1. The higher the chosen column number, the greater is the reward for kind intentions;

	c1	c2	c3	c4	c5	c6
t	800, 2050	1000, 2000	1200, 1950	1400, 1900	1600, 1850	1800, 1800
m	900, 1650	1100, 1600	1300, 1550	1500, 1500	1700, 1450	1900, 1400
b	1000, 1250	1200, 1200	1400, 1150	1600, 1100	1800, 1050	2000, 1000

Figure 2.5 Normal form representation of a two-player, sequential, social dilemma game.
Source: Experimental Economics, "Measuring motivations for the reciprocal responses observed in a simple dilemma game," 1(3), 1998, 207-19, Gary Bolton, Jordi Brandts, and Axel Ockenfels. © Economic Science Association. With permission of Springer.

[32] Earlier versions of these results circulated in a working paper, circa 1996.

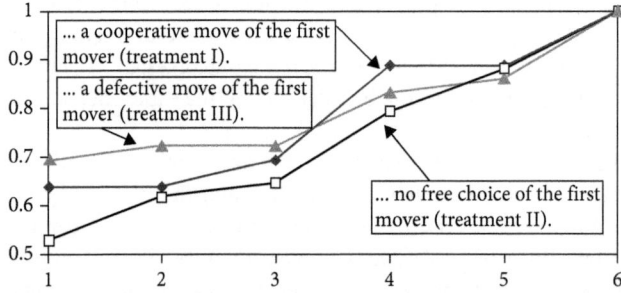

Figure 2.6 Cumulative distribution of the second player's cooperative decision (c1 to c6).
Source: Reprinted from Bolton, G. E., Brandts, J., Katok, E., Ockenfels, A., and Zwick, R., "Testing theories of other-regarding behavior: A sequence of four laboratory studies," in C.R. Plott and V. L. Smith, eds., Handbook of Experimental Economics Results. Copyright © 2008, with permission from Elsevier.

we shall refer to this as the degree of *cooperative behavior* of the column player; this is the horizontal axis in Figure 2.6. One can then compare the results in treatments I and II, say, when player 1 chooses m, to determine the extra contribution of intentions to the outcome. Finally, in the *negatively reciprocal treatment*, treatment III, the row player chooses row t as his second row (so the choice is between the two rows t and m). In this case, by choosing m, the row player signals to the column player that he has unkind intentions. Again, one may compare the choices with treatment II to infer the marginal effect of intentions.

The results are shown in Figure 2.6 in terms of the cumulative frequencies of the cooperative choices of the column player in each treatment. Thus, a higher graph indicates a less cooperative choice (this just follows from first order stochastic dominance). The choices by the column player, particularly departures from action c1, can be used to infer reciprocal behavior in both reciprocity treatments, I and III. Notice, from Figure 2.6, that in the no free choice treatment (treatment II), about half the column players choose an action higher than c1. Thus, there is a significant element of other-regarding preferences that can be noiselessly isolated from any reciprocity considerations. However, when the three distributions in Figure 2.6 are compared using the relevant statistical tests, one cannot reject the null hypothesis that the contributions of the column player belong to the same underlying distributions. Nor can we reject similar null hypotheses when the contributions under any two treatments are compared in a pairwise manner. The authors conclude (p. 213): "Hence our statistical tests imply that all of the observed reciprocal action is attributable to the distribution hypothesis."

Bolton and Ockenfels (2005) observe variations in the results from ultimatum games, say, the probability of responder rejections, as one alters the parameters in the game; they refer to this as *stress testing* the results. The two variations are shown in their multiplicative and additive forms, respectively, in the left and right panels of Figure 2.7. A proposer has a cake of size $4 that he can split with the responder. The proposer has two actions; action l is the more equitable choice, while action r is less equitable. The responder observes the action chosen by the proposer, then chooses to accept, a, or reject, r.

Consider first the multiplicative game in the left panel of Figure 2.7. In this game, stress testing involves varying the values of $x = 0.2, 0.6, 1$ and 1.2; each of these games is known as UG*x. The payoffs of both players are not required to sum up to $4. When $x = 1$ this is a standard ultimatum game. Notice, in particular, that the parameter x does not influence the payoff of the responder.

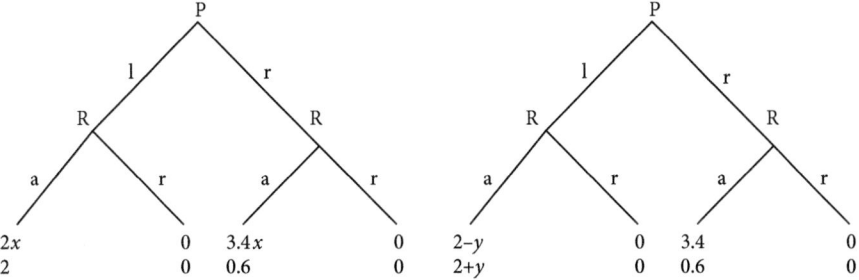

Figure 2.7 Two variations of the ultimatum game, indexed by the parameters x and y. The UG*x game is in the left panel and the UG*+y game is in the right panel.

Source: Economic Theory, 25(4): 957–82. "A stress test of fairness measures in models of social utility," Bolton, G. and Ockenfels, A. © Springer-Verlag 2005. With kind permission from Springer Science and Business Media.

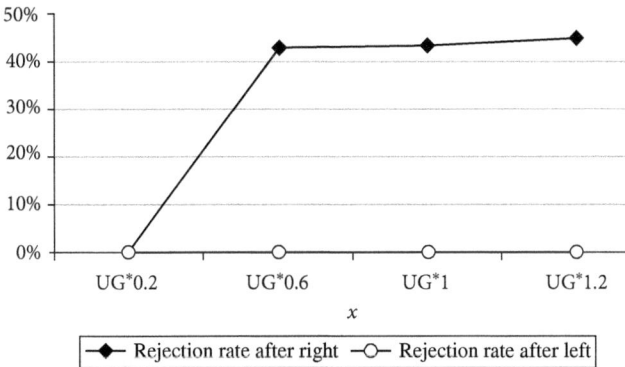

Figure 2.8 Average rejection rates in the UG*x game.

Source: Economic Theory, 25(4): 957–82. "A stress test of fairness measures in models of social utility," Bolton, G. and Ockenfels, A. © Springer-Verlag 2005. With kind permission from Springer Science and Business Media.

Under self-regarding preferences, the subgame perfect outcome of any UG*x game is (r,a). Given the *kindness functions* used by the authors,[33] purely intentions-driven models predict that the size of x should not influence the rejection rates of the responder. However, the magnitude of x does influence the relative payoffs of the two players, hence, models of other-regarding preferences predict variability of rejection rates with respect to x.

The results on the rejection rates of responders in the UG*x game are shown in Figure 2.8. There are no rejections when the proposer plays the strategy l. However, when the proposer plays the strategy r, rejection rates rise sharply from zero in the UG*0.2 game to 43% in the UG*0.6 game but, thereafter, these rates stabilize. This is inconsistent with the attribution hypothesis.

What explains the sharp rise in rejections between the UG*0.2 game and the UG*0.6 game? Consider the following explanation. When $x = 0.2$, both players get an equal payoff of 0.6 when the proposer chooses r. However, when $x > 0.2$, we get highly unequal payoffs from the action

---

[33] For a fuller discussion, see the discussion on psychological game theory in Volume 4.

profile (r,a) in any UG*x game. The responder gets 23% of the cake in UG*0.6 and 13% in UG*1.2. One may conjecture that starting from a 50% share of the cake in UG*0.2, a 23% share of the cake appears highly unattractive, hence, rejections increase dramatically between UG*0.2 and UG*0.6. However, the difference between a 23% and 13% share of the cake is less dramatic, hence, it elicits a smaller difference in rejection rates between UG*0.6 and UG*1.2.

In the UG*x game we varied *distributive measure of fairness* and held the *kindness measure* fixed. We now flip these roles in the UG* $+y$ game in the right panel of Figure 2.7, where $y \in \{-1.6, 0, 0.8, 1.6\}$. The subgame perfect outcome is (r,a). Since the payoffs following the choice of r by the proposer are independent of y, the distribution hypothesis predicts that the rejection rates must be identical in any UG* $+y$ game. The rejection rates following a choice of l by the proposer are predicted to fall between the games UG* -1.6 and UG* $+0$. However, the distribution hypothesis cannot predict the rejection rates following a choice of l by the proposer as y increases beyond zero. The reason is that the absolute payoff increases but the relative payoff falls (think, e.g., of the Fehr–Schmidt model).

By contrast, the intentions-based hypothesis (attribution hypothesis) predicts that as y increases, the rejection rates following a choice of r by the proposer should increase. The reason is that the proposer leaves only 0.6 for the responder by playing r when he could have left a lot more by playing l. This is the sense in which the *kindness measure* is varied in the UG* $+y$ game.

The average rejection rates are shown in Figure 2.9. As predicted by the distribution hypothesis, the rejection rates following a choice of l by the proposer fall sharply between the games UG* -1.6 and UG* $+0$. However, the rejection rates following the choice of r by the proposer are different in the various UG* $+y$ games. Hence, there is mixed support for the distributional hypothesis. Following a choice of r by the proposer, as y increases from -1.6 to 0, the rejection rates increase; this supports the attribution hypothesis. However, as y increases beyond 0, the rejection rates fall, contradicting the attribution hypothesis. In a strict sense, these results reject both distribution-only and attribution-only hypotheses.

What accounts for the rejection rates in the UG* $+y$ game? One plausible conjecture is that the responder's notion of what is *fair* depends on y. When $y = 0$, the payoffs from the strategy pair (l, a) are (2, 2), which may possibly serve as a *reference point for fairness*. In this case, the rejections

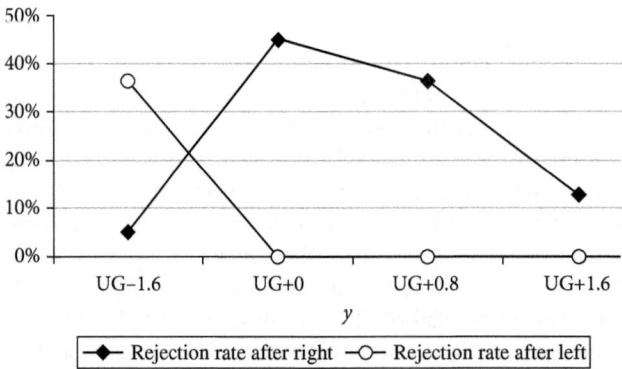

Figure 2.9 Average rejection rates in the UG*+y game.

Source: Economic Theory, 25(4): 957-82. "A stress test of fairness measures in models of social utility," Bolton, G. and Ockenfels, A. © Springer-Verlag 2005. With kind permission from Springer Science and Business Media.

following a choice of r by the proposer that give rise to unequal payoffs are maximal (Figure 2.9). As y increases, the payoffs from the strategy pair (l, a), given by $(2-y, 2+y)$, become increasingly unequal. Thus, the new reference point for fairness may have become more unequal, prompting a greater acceptance rate following the choice of r by the proposer. Indeed, when $y=-1.6$, the rejection rate following a choice of r by the proposer is the lowest. This suggests an alternative approach to the distributional and the attribution hypotheses in which there is an explicit consideration of the reference point for fairness.

2.8 A discussion of other promising models

In this section, we consider other models of fairness and reciprocity such as the hybrid model of Charness and Rabin (2002), and models of interdependent preferences. We describe the relevant theory and also pit the models against the evidence.

2.8.1 The Charness and Rabin (2002) hybrid model

Charness and Rabin (2002) argue that experiments that test for social preferences have been unduly restrictive in the sense of giving too few options to the subjects in experiments. For instance, in the context of experiments in the ultimatum game, they argue that (1) a responder only has the option to accept or reject, which rules out other interesting choices such as "social objectives," and (2) the structure of the game ensures that the only retaliatory instrument (rejection of the responder's offer) reduces inequality between the two players. They design experiments that allow for a larger range of choices for subjects in experiments. One of their main findings is that very few subjects are willing to sacrifice their own money in order to reduce inequality by lowering the payoffs of others. Half of the subjects are willing to reduce their own payoffs in order to make inequality-increasing sacrifices.

This does, however, run counter to the experimental results from public goods games with punishments as well as those from experiments conducted in a voting context (see Section 2.5 above). Charness and Rabin (2002) write (p. 5): "Indeed, while our analysis stresses that our data contradict difference-aversion models, we do not think we have conclusively disproved these models. Fehr and Schmidt [1999], for instance, have argued that only 40 percent of subjects need be difference-averse to explain the phenomena they explain. This is arguably consistent with our data."

Charness and Rabin (2002) present two versions of a theoretical model. The models combine inequity aversion and the role of intentions, hence, they may be termed as *hybrid models*. The first version is a model of social preferences. Suppose that the set of individuals is $N=\{1,2,\ldots n\}$, and individuals are given respective allocations or consumption levels, $x_1, x_2, \ldots, x_n$. The social welfare function is defined as

$$W = \delta \min\{x_1, x_2, \ldots, x_n\} + (1-\delta)(x_1 + x_2 + \ldots + x_n); \delta \in (0,1). \tag{2.40}$$

Social welfare is a convex combination of a Rawlsian maximin criterion reflecting Rawlsian inequity aversion (first term), and the sum of individual payoffs reflecting altruism and/or efficiency (second term). The utility of any individual $i \in N$ is defined as follows,

$$U_i = \lambda x_i + (1-\lambda)W,$$

where $\lambda \in (0,1)$ and W is defined in (2.40). When $n=2$, denoting the two players by A, B, and $A \neq B$, the utility function for player A is given by:

$$U_A = \begin{cases} x_A + (1-\lambda)(1-\delta)x_B & \text{if } x_A < x_B \\ (1-\delta+\lambda\delta)x_A + (1-\lambda)x_B & \text{if } x_A \geq x_B \end{cases}. \tag{2.41}$$

For the preferences given in (2.41), the indifference curves in (x_A, x_B) space are kinked and downward sloping. To see this, we can use (2.41) to calculate the marginal rates of substitution (MRS) in each of the two outcome domains:

$$\frac{dx_B}{dx_A} = \begin{cases} MRS_{AB}^- = \frac{-1}{(1-\lambda)(1-\delta)} & \text{if } x_A < x_B \\ MRS_{AB}^+ = \frac{-(1-\delta+\lambda\delta)}{(1-\lambda)} & \text{if } x_A \geq x_B \end{cases}.$$

The absolute value of the slope is greater when $x_A < x_B$ because $\left|MRS_{AB}^-\right| > \left|MRS_{AB}^+\right|$. Hence, when $x_A < x_B$, the opportunity cost of a unit of x_A for player A, expressed in terms of x_B is relatively higher. Thus, individuals are more reluctant to accept a reduction in their payoffs when they are behind others as compared to the case where they are ahead of others.

This model is able to explain why proposers in dictator games give a strictly positive amount to receivers and why trustees in trust games return a strictly positive amount to the investor. However, it is not able to explain why subjects in experiments retaliate and reduce the material payoffs of others at a cost to themselves as, for instance, in public goods games with punishments.

For this reason, Charness and Rabin propose a second version of their model, in which players are affected by outcome differences as well as the intentions of other players. Like models of interdependent preferences that we consider below, this model ignores the more rigorous framework of psychological game theory in which beliefs are modeled endogenously; see Volume 4 of the book. By contrast, the Charness and Rabin (2002) and Levine (1998) models opt for a reduced-form framework that may be more tractable.

Suppose that there are two individuals, A and B, with respective material payoffs, x_A and x_B. Then, the preferences of player B are represented by the following utility function (the utility function of player A is analogously written by swapping the indices A and B).

$$U_B(x_A, x_B) = \begin{cases} (1-\rho-\theta q)x_B + (\rho+\theta q)x_A & \text{if } x_A \leq x_B \\ (1-\sigma-\theta q)x_B + (\sigma+\theta q)x_A & \text{if } x_A > x_B \end{cases}. \tag{2.42}$$

The payoff of any player is a weighted average of one's own payoff and the payoff of the other player. The weights depend on one's relative payoff with respect to the other player and also the intentions of the other player. In (2.42), $q = -1$ if player A has revealed negative intentions and $q = 0$ otherwise. The parameters of social preference are ρ, σ, θ. The first two, ρ, σ, relate to inequity aversion, while θ captures the role of intentions.

Suppose first that $\theta = 0$, so ignore the role of intentions for the time being.

1. An individual is said to have *competitive preferences* if $\sigma \leq \rho \leq 0$. In this case

$$U_B(x_A, x_B) = \begin{cases} x_B + |\rho|(x_B - x_A) & \text{if } x_A \leq x_B \\ x_B - |\sigma|(x_A - x_B) & \text{if } x_A > x_B \end{cases}.$$

Hence, player B derives utility from a higher material payoff and disutility from a lower payoff. Furthermore, since $|\sigma| > |\rho|$, player B exhibits a form of loss aversion; it is more painful to fall behind in material payoffs. Similar comments apply to player A.

2. The *difference aversion* (or *inequity aversion*) models of Bolton and Ockenfels (2000), Fehr and Schmidt (1999), and Loewenstein et al. (1989) can be represented by $\sigma < 0 < \rho < 1$. In this case, using (2.42) and continuing to assume that $\theta = 0$, we get

$$U_B(x_A, x_B) = \begin{cases} x_B - \rho(x_B - x_A) & \text{if } x_A \leq x_B & \text{(Altruism)} \\ x_B - |\sigma|(x_A - x_B) & \text{if } x_A > x_B & \text{(Envy)} \end{cases}.$$

Difference aversion and reciprocity can be combined, as in Falk and Fischbacher (2006), but without the apparatus of psychological games, by allowing $\theta \neq 0$. Suppose now that $\theta > 0$. Let $q = -1$, i.e., player B believes that player A has revealed negative intentions. Then, from (2.42), player B reduces the weight that she places on the payoff of player A, relative to her own payoff. This is quantitatively similar to a reduction in σ or ρ.

Charness and Rabin then define a *reciprocal fairness equilibrium* (RFE). The RFE is defined in the context of a richer model in which there are n players and there is a *demerit profile* $\rho = (\rho_1, \rho_2, \ldots, \rho_n)$. The ith element of the demerit profile, $\rho_i \in [0,1]$, indicates how much player i "deserves" in the view of the other players. The weight placed on player i's payoff in the utility function of other players is decreasing in ρ_i. The demerit of any player is unanimously agreed upon by all other players by comparing the strategy of player i to some selfless standard of behavior. One can extend (2.40) to write the preferences of player i in this case as

$$U_i = (1-\lambda)x_i + \lambda \left(\delta \min \left\{ x_i, \min_{j \neq i}(x_j + d\rho_j) \right\} \right) \qquad (2.43)$$
$$+ \lambda(1-\delta)\left(x_i + \sum_{j \neq i} \max\{1 - k\rho_j, 0\} x_j - f \sum_{j \neq i} \rho_j x_j \right).$$

where $d, k, f \geq 0$ are the model parameters. When $d = k = f = 0$, then (2.40), (2.43) are identical. Player i places less weight on the payoff of player j when d, k are large. When f is large, and ρ_j is large, then player i might derive utility from a reduction in the payoff of player j.

An RFE is a profile of strategies and a demerit profile such that (1) each player maximizes his payoff given in (2.43), and (2) the demerit profile is consistent with the profile of strategies. It is difficult to use the RFE concept except for simple games and the large number of parameters creates difficulties in testing the model. The demerit profile is defined only in equilibrium, which makes it a difficult concept to use in the presence of multiple equilibria—a problem that is not uncommon in many models in economics.

Does the experimental data reveal that subjects have maximin preferences? The results of Engelmann and Strobel (2004), reviewed above in Section 2.7.1, reveal some support for such preferences but also persuasive evidence to the contrary. In the three player ultimatum game, the experimental evidence is that the passive receiver typically gets nothing (Riedl and Vyrastekova, 2002). This is clearly evidence against maximin preferences. Fréchette et al. (2003) also find evidence against maximin preferences. In a group of five players, they ask one player to make a proposal to allocate a fixed sum of money among the five players. The support of at least three players (majority rule) is needed to implement the proposal. In 65% of the cases, the winning proposal made no allocation to two of the five players. Hence, all gains are mopped up by the winning coalition.

Okada and Riedl (2005) perform another experiment with a strategic element. There is one proposer and two responders. The proposer allocates a given amount to himself and the other two players; denote this allocation by (x_1, x_2, x_3). If the proposer decides to form a three-person coalition, the total amount to be allocated is 3000. If he decides to form a two-person coalition, the total amount available is an element of the set $\{1200, 2100, 2500, 2800\}$. For the proposer's offer to be successful, both responders must accept the offer in the three-person coalition and the single responder must accept the offer in the two-person coalition. The prediction of maximin preferences is that the proposer chooses a three-player coalition and $x_1 = x_2 = x_3$. When the amounts available for the two-player coalition are high enough (2500, 2800), then 90% of the players choose the two-player coalition. The three-player coalition is chosen by most proposers only when the amount available to the two-player coalition shrinks sufficiently, i.e., to 1200.

These results suggest that in strategic situations, the maximin motive does not seem to be always salient. On the other hand, in dictator games, there is a strictly positive level of giving to the responder that is consistent with the presence of such a motive. It is conceivable that the maximin motive is probably more important in non-strategic settings such as charity, or in the context of anonymous voting for national referenda. The reader may also wonder if these results negate models of inequity aversion, such as the Fehr–Schmidt model. The answer depends on what is the appropriate reference group. From models of social identity (see Chapter 3), we know that individuals treat *ingroup* and *outgroup* members differently, and passive outsiders, in the experiments reported above, may be perceived as outgroup members. In this case, there is no violation of models of inequity aversion. Indeed, using these ideas one might better endogenize the issue of reference groups in models of inequity aversion.

2.8.2 Models of interdependent preferences

In models of *interdependent preferences*, actions taken by a player depend on the perceived type of the other player. For instance, altruistic players may wish to be kind to other altruistic players but not to other non-altruistic players. Let us consider the model of interdependent preferences in Levine (1998).[34]

Suppose that there are n players and the game has an extensive form representation. At any end node, player $i = 1, 2, \ldots, n$ has *direct utility* u_i. Each player has a type that is characterized by some altruism coefficient, $a_i \in (-1, 1)$. We say that the individual is spiteful if $a_i < 0$, self-regarding if $a_i = 0$, and altruistic if $a_i > 0$. A higher value of $a_i > 0$ denotes a more altruistic player. The altruism-adjusted or composite utility of player i is

$$v_i = u_i + \sum_{j \neq i} \beta_j u_j; \; \beta_j = \frac{a_i + \lambda a_j}{1 + \lambda}; \lambda \in [0, 1]. \tag{2.44}$$

---

[34] For the Ellingsen and Johannesson (2008) model of type-based reciprocity, see Volume 4.

In the special case $\lambda = 0$, we have $v_i = u_i + \sum_{j \neq i} a_i u_j$. So, depending on the sign of a_i, we have a model of *pure altruism* or *pure spite*, as in Ledyard (1995). When $a_i = 0$ and $\lambda = 0$ for all i, then we get the self-regarding case, $v_i = u_i$.

Players' concern for fairness is captured in the following manner.

1. If $\lambda > 0$ and $a_i > 0$, $a_j > 0$, then $\beta_j > 0$, so the payoff of altruistic players is increasing in the payoff of other altruistic players. If $\lambda > 0$, then β_j is increasing in a_j, i.e., the weight put on player j's payoff is increasing in the altruism of player j.
2. When $\lambda > 0$ and $a_i > 0$, $a_j < 0$ such that $\frac{a_i}{\lambda} < |a_j|$ we have $\beta_j < 0$. In this case, the utility of an altruistic player i is decreasing in the spiteful player j's payoff. So essentially, individuals want to be nice with altruistic individuals and spiteful with spiteful ones.

Population heterogeneity is introduced by assuming that a_i is drawn from some cumulative distribution function, $F(a)$, that is common knowledge to the players. However, a_i is privately known to player i only. Hence, the underlying game is one of private information about the types of others, where a type is the degree of altruism of a player. Players, through their actions, can reveal their private information about their altruistic coefficient, a_i. As in the Fehr–Schmidt model, the payoffs of other players are taken into account, but in addition, the types of the other players are also taken into account. An objective of the model is to explain the results of small-stake experiments, so, typically $u_i(x_i) = x_i$.

The data from the ultimatum game is used to estimate the value of λ and to calibrate the distribution $F(a)$. Using these parameters, the model is able to explain why some individuals contribute in public goods games or why strictly positive offers are rejected in ultimatum games. However, it cannot explain why there is positive giving in the dictator game. Another potential issue, common with other signaling games, is that there might be a multiplicity of equilibria.

Rotemberg (2008) proposes another model of interdependent preferences to account for the results of the ultimatum and dictator games. One of the motivations of this paper is that the model by Levine (1998) is unable to explain the results of the modified dictator game of Charness and Rabin (2002); it predicts far too much spite relative to what is observed. In an ultimatum game, the responder's utility in Rotemberg's model is given by

$$U_R = x_R + \left(a_R - f\left(a_P^e, a_{\min}\right)\right) x_P,$$

where x_R and x_P are the respective payoffs of the responder and the proposer, a_R is the responder's altruism, a_P^e is an estimate made by the responder of the proposer's altruism, $a_{\min}$ is some minimum level of altruism, and f is a function such that

$$f = \begin{cases} 0 & \text{if } a_P^e > a_{\min} \\ 1 + a_R & \text{if } a_P^e \leq a_{\min} \end{cases}.$$

Thus, if the perceived altruism of the proposer falls below a certain level ($a_P^e \leq a_{\min}$), then U_R is decreasing in the proposer's payoff. As a_P^e changes and $a_P^e - a_{\min}$ alters signs, we are likely to observe discontinuous jumps in the actions of the responder from acceptance to rejection; this is consistent with the experimental findings. The responder's decision to accept or reject makes the proposer's payoff risky. This is incorporated by specifying the proposer's utility function to be

$$U_P = E\left[x_P + a_R x_R\right]^\gamma,$$

where $\gamma > 0$ captures the degree of risk aversion of the proposer. In order to explain the data, it is assumed that the proposer is risk loving, i.e., $\gamma > 1$. Under the assumptions made above, the model explains well the data from the ultimatum game. However, it is not clear how well the model explains results from other experimental games on human sociality.

2.8.3 The model of Cox, Friedman, and Gjerstad (2007)

Cox, Friedman, and Gjerstad (2007) propose a flexible utility function with interdependent preferences that applies to sequential two-person games of perfect information. The utility function of player i is

$$U_i = \begin{cases} \frac{1}{\alpha}\left(x_i^\alpha + \beta x_j^\alpha\right) & \text{if } \alpha \neq 0 \\ \left(x_i x_j\right)^\beta & \text{if } \alpha = 0 \end{cases}, \quad (2.45)$$

where $\alpha \in (-\infty, 1]$ captures the ease of substituting x_j for x_i, and $\beta \neq 0$ is the *emotional state* of the player. In (x_i, x_j) space, the slope of an indifference curve for the preferences given in (2.45) is

$$MRS_{i,j} = \beta^{-1} \left(\frac{x_j}{x_i}\right)^{1-\alpha}, \quad (2.46)$$

where $\frac{x_j}{x_i}$ gives the relative payoffs of the two players. When $\alpha = 1$, $MRS_{i,j} = \beta^{-1}$, i.e., the allocations of the two individuals are substitutes. For $\alpha < 1$, one recovers the standard case of convex indifference curves. When $\alpha = 0$, MRS_{x_i, x_j} is constant along any ray from the origin, so we get homothetic preferences. Leontief preferences correspond to $\alpha \to -\infty$.

Let $\pi_i^{\max}(s_j)$ be the maximum payoff that player i can get, conditional on the strategy, s_j, of player j and let $\overline{\pi}_i$ be some reference payoff of player i. The *reciprocity motive* of player j, denoted by ρ_j, is defined as $\rho_j = \pi_i^{\max}(s_j) - \overline{\pi}_i$.

The parameter β depends positively on the reciprocity motive, i.e., $\beta = \beta(\rho_j)$, which is an increasing function.[35] If $\rho_j < 0$, then player j is believed to have unkind intentions towards player i. In this case, $\beta(\rho_j) < 0$, so U_i is decreasing in x_j. Hence, player i would want to be unkind to player j.

The authors estimate the parameters of their model using data from ultimatum games and the Stackelberg duopoly game in Huck et al. (2001). The model fits well the data from these games. It remains to see if it also fits the data from other experimental games on human sociality.

2.8.4 A brief note on axiomatic foundations

We have considered three main kinds of theoretical models. Models of social preferences (e.g., Fehr and Schmidt, 1999), models of interdependent preferences (e.g., Levine, 1998), and models of intentions-based reciprocity (e.g., Charness and Rabin, 2002).[36] The aim of these models is to propose psychologically plausible utility functions that can explain a range of experimental

---

[35] In the more general model $\beta = \beta(\rho_j, \phi)$, where ϕ is a variable that measures status. β is assumed to be increasing in both arguments.

[36] For a formal consideration of models of intentions-based reciprocity, based on the more satisfactory framework of psychological game theory, see Volume 4 of the book.

results. It is not always clear, however, what restrictions on preferences are required for these utility functions.

Segal and Sobel (2007) make progress on this issue. We give a purely heuristic outline of the relevant conditions. They ask: what axioms need to be imposed in order to generate preferences for fairness and reciprocity? Segal and Sobel specify preferences directly over the profile of mixed strategies. Suppose that the generic mixed strategies of two players i,j in a two-player game are denoted by σ_i and σ_j, respectively. They define a preference relation for the ith player as $\succeq_{i\sigma_j}$ that is defined directly over the mixed strategies of player i, but conditional on the mixed strategy followed by player j, σ_j. More generally, the preference relation can depend on the entire mixed strategy profile of the players, which the authors call the *context* of the game.

Suppose that the following conditions hold: (1) Preferences over outcomes satisfy the axioms of expected utility. (2) Preferences over mixed strategies, $\succeq_{i\sigma_j}$, satisfy the continuity and the independence axioms. These two axioms are as stated under expected utility (see Volume 1), but the objects over which they are stated are mixed strategies. (3) The self-interest axiom holds in the sense that if all other players are indifferent between two mixed strategies, then one chooses the mixed strategy that gives a higher own-payoff. Under these conditions, Segal and Sobel show that the preferences $\succeq_{i\sigma_j}$ can be represented by a utility function of the following form.

$$U_i = v_i(\sigma_i,\sigma_j) + \alpha_{i,\sigma_j} v_j(\sigma_i,\sigma_j), \qquad (2.47)$$

where $v_i(\sigma_i,\sigma_j)$ is the utility of the ith player from material payoffs that arise from the strategy profile (σ_i,σ_j). The parameter α_{i,σ_j}, which can be either positive or negative, depends on the strategy of the opponent. Although the authors do not use these terms, the sign of the parameter α_{i,σ_j} captures strategy-dependent altruism ($\alpha_{i,\sigma_j} > 0$), or strategy-dependent spite ($\alpha_{i,\sigma_j} < 0$). Several models that are discussed in Volume 2, on altruism, spite, and inequity aversion, are special cases of (2.47), although in these models, altruism/spite are not dependent on the strategy of the opponent.

The following example demonstrates the implications of the preferences in (2.47).

	AM	PM
AM	$10(1+i\alpha), 10$	$0,0$
PM	$0,0$	$10(1+i\alpha), 10$
ALL	$7+10i\alpha, 10$	$7+10i\alpha, 10$

The column player is a plumber and the row player is a homeowner who has a leaky faucet. The plumber can either come in the morning (AM), or in the evening (PM). The homeowner needs to take time off from work to facilitate the plumber's access to the faucet. If the homeowner takes time off in one session (either AM or PM), then it is not as damaging to his material payoff as taking the whole day off (the strategy, ALL). The plumber has purely self-regarding preferences, while the homeowner has social preferences. The homeowner places a weight $\alpha > 0$ on the payoff of the plumber. In this sense the homeowner is altruistic.

The joint payoffs are maximized if the plumber and the homeowner can coordinate on the time (AM or PM); the parameter i, in the payoff matrix, captures feelings of reciprocity of the homeowner towards the plumber. Suppose that the plumber plays the two strategies, AM and PM, with respective probabilities $p, 1-p$. If the plumber plays a pure strategy, i.e., $p=0$ or $p=1$, the homeowner assigns "kind" intentions as the plumber is viewed as willing to coordinate (assuming the mixed strategy is observed). In this case, $i = 1$, which implies positive reciprocity from the homeowner. However, if the plumber plays a purely mixed strategy, i.e., $p > 0$, then the plumber does not seem interested in coordinating and may cause the homeowner to take a full day off. The homeowner then assigns unkind intentions, $i = -1$, i.e., the homeowner places a negative weight on the payoffs of the plumber (negative reciprocity).

1. Suppose first that the plumber plays a pure strategy (so $p = 0$ or $p = 1$). If $p = 1$, then AM is strictly dominant for the homeowner, and if $p = 0$, then PM is strictly dominant for the homeowner. Hence, the two pure strategy Nash equilibria are (AM, AM) and (PM, PM).
2. Suppose that the homeowner has purely inequity averse preferences and does not care about intentions, so that $i = 1$ for all values of x. In this case, it is easy to check that (AM, AM) and (PM, PM) are still the Nash equilibria of the game.
3. Now suppose that intentions too matter, so $i = -1$ if the plumber plays a strictly mixed strategy, and $i = 1$ if he plays a pure strategy. We want to show that, in this case, the strategy ALL might be a part of the Nash equilibrium strategy profile. Define $g(\alpha) = \frac{0.7-\alpha}{1-\alpha}$. For ALL to dominate AM we require that $g(\alpha) > p$ and for ALL to dominate PM we require that $p > 1 - g(\alpha)$. Hence, the following is a mixed strategy Nash equilibrium. The homeowner plays ALL and the plumber plays AM with a probability p such that $g(\alpha) > p > 1 - g(\alpha)$. For instance, if $\alpha = 0.1$, then $g(0.1) = 2/3$. Hence, any p such that $\frac{2}{3} > p > 1/3$ is sufficient is induce the homeowner to play ALL in the Nash equilibrium.

Neilson (2006) provides axiomatic foundations for the Fehr and Schmidt (1999) preferences. The key axiom is *self-referent separability* that we consider heuristically. Suppose that we have three players. Consider ordered tuples of the allocations of the three players (x_1, x_2, x_3), where x_i is the allocation of player $i = 1, 2, 3$. Suppose that the first player reveals the preference

$$(60, 60, 60) \succeq (60, 80, 40). \tag{2.48}$$

The payoff of the first player is common to both choices. The standard separability axiom requires that for any x_1, it must be the case that $(x_1, 60, 60) \succeq (x_1, 80, 40)$. In particular, it must be the case that $(50, 60, 60) \succeq (50, 80, 40)$. But this has the implication that player 1 prefers an allocation in which he is ranked third in the income distribution rather than second. In other words, the separability axiom is not sensitive to one's rank in the income distribution.

The main thrust of a modified separability axiom, *the self-referent separability axiom*, is to take account of the rank of players making choices. Suppose that the set of feasible allocations of players belong to some set X. The following two conditions are required for this axiom to be satisfied in the context of this three person game.

1. Starting from any symmetric allocation, if a player prefers to add $y \in X$ to his allocation rather than $y' \in X$, then he should do so for any other symmetric allocation also. Formally, for any $x, y, z, y' \in X$,

$$\text{if } (x+y, x, x) \succeq (x+y', x, x), \text{ then } (z+y, z, z) \succeq (z+y', z, z).$$

2. Starting from any two symmetric allocations, if a player prefers adding some amount $y \in X$ to the outcomes of the other players for one allocation, he should also prefer to do so for any other amount $y' \in X$. Formally, for any $x, y, z, y' \in X$,

$$\text{if } (x, x+y, x+y) \succeq (z, z+y, z+y), \text{ then } (x, x+y', x+y') \succeq (z, z+y', z+y').$$

Proposition 2.19 *(Neilson, 2006): Suppose that there are $n \geq 2$ players. Consider any allocation $x = (x_1, x_2, \ldots, x_n)$ of payoffs to the n players. The preference ordering satisfies self-referent separability if and only if there exist functions $u_1, \ldots, u_n$ such that preferences can be represented by a function U of the form*

$$U(x) = u_1(x_1) + \sum_{i=2}^{n} u_i(x_i - x_1). \tag{2.49}$$

Several inequity averse utility functions, for instance, the Fehr–Schmidt (1999) utility function, are of the same form as (2.49). In (2.49), one's own consumption bundle is the reference point against which the consumption bundles of others are compared. As the reader may have guessed, one can also get a representation for prospect theory type preferences using similar axioms; see Neilson (2006).

CHAPTER 3
Human Morality and Social Identity

3.1 Introduction

In neoclassical economics, there is no explicit role for *character virtues*, such as the desire to be honest, to keep promises, to avoid deception and lies, and to be fair to one's fellow human beings. Neoclassical economics assumes that people are disposed to tell *selfish black lies* (Erat and Gneezy, 2012), i.e., lies that benefit the individual but also typically harm others. By contrast, we do observe individuals whose behavior accords well with "good" character virtues. The explanation for such behavior in neoclassical economics is *instrumental* because individuals are *consequentialists*. In this view, individuals strategically exhibit the relevant character virtues, based on a cost–benefit analysis. Neoclassical economics, thus, takes a fairly dim view of human nature, relative to many of the other social sciences in which humans *intrinsically* display character virtues.

The purpose of the first part of this chapter (Section 3.2) is to give experimental evidence on the source of human character virtues—instrumental, or intrinsic. Furthermore, we wish to apply these concepts to a theoretical model of promises and threats. We begin, in Section 3.2.1, with some of the relevant evidence. The evidence shows that character virtues may directly provide utility to humans, say, on account of enhanced self-esteem. Such character virtues are likely to determine behavior, particularly when the gains from non-virtuous behavior are small. Humans are not likely to lie for small gains, but as the gains become large, the morality of a fraction of the subjects is loosened (Gneezy, 2005; Gneezy et al., 2013; Gibson et al., 2013). Character virtues may also depend on the prevalence of such character virtues in the population. For instance, bribing a traffic policeman, or evading taxes may be considered less non-virtuous in societies where such activity is more widely prevalent.

In an interesting experiment, Fischbacher and Föllmi-Heusi (2013) asked subjects to privately roll a six-sided dice, and then self-report the outcome. The distribution of self-reported outcomes can now be compared with the predicted statistical distribution where each of the six outcomes, 1 to 6, occur with probability 1/6. Roughly 40% of the subjects are *completely honest*, even when lying could have improved their payoffs. A significant fraction of the subjects tell *partial lies*, even when lying maximally would have improved material payoffs (see also Gneezy et al., 2013). About 22% behave in a manner that is consistent with the selfish black liars assumed in neoclassical economics. We also report the results of a similar elicitation by Pruckner and Sausgruber (2013), who report non-conclusive evidence on gender differences in lying, as well as the importance of many non-economic factors in the lying decision.

In neoclassical economic theory, *promises* and *threats* are simply cheap talk. By contrast, a significant fraction of subjects in experiments honor their promises (Ellingsen and Johannesson, 2004; Charness and Dufwenberg, 2006; and Vanberg, 2008). We consider some of the relevant evidence in Section 3.2.2. We also consider here, a theoretical model of promises and threats in a buyer–seller problem in which there is the possibility of the hold up of the seller's investment (Ellingsen and Johannesson, 2004). When the buyer and the seller have other-regarding preferences, and there is a cost of breaking a promise, or of not carrying out a threat, two things happen. First, promises and threats become effective, and alter the eventual outcome; this is confirmed by the experimental results. Second, the effect of other-regarding preferences can magnify the cost of breaking a promise and the cost of not carrying out a threat.

One may also carry out promises and threats for reasons other than the costs of lying. For instance, promises may induce others to form trusting beliefs. If one cares for the beliefs of others then one may suffer from *guilt* by breaking the original promise (Charness and Dufwenberg, 2006). Issues of guilt and the relevant empirical evidence is considered in Volume 4 of the book. However, the results of Vanberg (2008) support the *cost of lying* explanation of breaking promises.

Section 3.3 considers the topic of *social identity*, which traditionally is a part of the subject matter of social psychology. Our focus, however, is on exploring the recent advances from the rapidly expanding literature in economics. In *social identity theory*, one's *social identity* refers to the *social category* one belongs to, such as black or white, blue collar worker or white collar worker, and soldier or civilian. Different identities may be triggered by different social contexts. For instance, a national identity may apply to a football supporter when his country plays against another, and a club identity when his preferred club plays against another. Once the social identity of a group is taken on, group members prefer to conform to the group norm.

In most classic experiments on social identity, individuals are *primed* for a group identity. There is evidence that even a *minimal group identity*, based on trivial characterizations, say, blue and red groups, may alter the behavior of group members. The typical finding is that one favors one's own group members, or the *ingroup*, relative to non-group members, or the *outgroup* (Billig and Tajfel, 1973; Tajfel and Turner, 1986).

In Section 3.3.1, we consider the evidence from recent experiments in economics on social identity. The Asian American identity is associated with the norms of hard work and patience. When Asian Americans are primed for their identity, they make more patient choices than whites. By contrast, in the unprimed condition, their choices are more impatient than whites (Benjamin et al., 2010). Altruism and envy are found to be stronger towards ingroup members and players are more likely to forgive unfavorable behavior by an ingroup member relative to an outgroup member (Chen and Li, 2009).

Charness et al. (2007) play a two-player battle of sexes (BOS) game and a two-player prisoner's dilemma (PD) game. They find that subjects make more aggressive choices (e.g., defect in the PD game) when group membership is highly salient (e.g., choices are made in front of other group members who observe the outcomes immediately). When a player observes that the opponent is making choices under highly salient group membership, he/she responds by making more accommodating choices (e.g., cooperate in the PD game). When group membership is less salient, the percentage of aggressive choices drops significantly.

Goette et al. (2012) argue that real-life social groups (SG) exhibit far more social ties and friendships between group members relative to the minimal groups (MG) in experiments. Based on field studies on Swiss army trainees, they find that there are qualitative and quantitative differences between the behavior of SG and MG group members that can be used to reconcile existing results. There is significantly greater cooperation between SG members and they punish defecting ingroup members as much as defecting outgroup members. However, while MG members punish defecting outgroup members as much as SG members do, they punish ingroup members far less.

Since ingroup members engage in unfavorable behavior towards outgroup members, one might wonder if the existence of groups reduces overall welfare. Hargreaves Heap and Zizzo (2009) argue and empirically show that group membership confers private hedonic benefits. Taking account of these hedonic benefits produces an overall positive effect of group formation.

Section 3.3.2 considers a simple principal–agent model of the interaction between identity and incentives (Akerlof and Kranton, 2000, 2005, 2008). The principal has the choice of appointing a supervisor to monitor the non-contractible effort level of the agent. However, the very act of appointing the supervisor alters the identity of the agent, who now considers himself an outsider. When the principal has the option of appointing a supervisor, yet does not appoint one, then the agent feels trusted, and dons the identity of an insider.

If the agent considers himself as an insider he internalizes a *higher effort norm*. Thus, choosing not to appoint a supervisor has a cost and a benefit for the principal. The cost is the inability to engage in ex-post punishments, such as fines, if the agent shirks; this reduces deterrence. The benefit is that since the agent internalizes a higher effort norm, the individual rationality constraint of the agent can be satisfied at a lower expected wage cost. These sorts of trade-offs then determine the optimal organizational design.

3.2 Human virtues

We separate the discussion in this section into two parts. In the first part, we discuss the empirical evidence on *lying behavior*. In the second part, we consider formal models of *promises* and *threats*.

3.2.1 Evidence on human virtues

While the interest in human attitudes to lying in economics is a relatively recent and growing phenomenon, psychologists have been interested in these issues for much longer (Vrij, 2000, 2008). In neoclassical economics, one takes a fairly dim view of human nature. Using the terminology of Erat and Gneezy (2012), neoclassical economics assumes that humans feel no remorse in telling *selfish black lies*. Typically, such lies benefit the person telling the lie but harm the other party. In particular, an individual telling selfish black lies suffers no decrease in utility on account of the lies. Neoclassical economics then proceeds to determine incentive compatible mechanisms that induce truth-telling, purely in response to the underlying economic incentives. The dismal nature of this view of human nature is not a reason to reject it. Our interest, below, is in empirically pitting this view against alternative views of human nature.

In contrast to selfish black lies, *white lies* do not harm the other party, and may indeed contribute to increasing the utility of others. Erat and Gneezy (2012) give two insightful examples. Consider a supervisor giving feedback to a failing employee. If the feedback is entirely truthful, it may seriously undermine the employee's confidence in undertaking future tasks. Shading the truth may be efficacious in meeting longer-term objectives. In other contexts, doctors may sometimes give placebos to patients when they fully know that the placebo has no pharmacological effect.

Two further categories of white lies have also been used in empirical work. A player who tells *altruistic white lies* may be harmed by the lies, but the intention is to increase the payoff of the other party. A player tells *Pareto white lies* when such lies improve the payoffs of both players.

It is also useful to consider the following terminology in Gneezy (2005). Suppose that action A involves a lie but action B does not, yet both actions lead to the same monetary payoff for a player. If the player is indifferent between the actions A and B, we say that the player takes a *consequentialistic approach*. Players in neoclassical economics are consequentialists. Otherwise, if there is a preference for one action over the other, the player takes a *non-consequentialistic approach*. The bulk of the empirical evidence indicates that the actions of players are non-consequentialistic.

In cheap talk games, unlike signaling games, the messages sent by players do not affect the payoffs of players. Rather, the messages influence the beliefs of the other player about the state of the world, hence, they indirectly influence payoffs through their effect on actions. Gneezy (2005) considers cheap talk games between two players; the three treatments in his experiments are shown in Table 3.1. In each treatment, player 1 (the sender) has two possible choices: A and B. Player 2 (the receiver) does not see the payoffs; however, player 1 can see the payoffs.

Player 1 sends one of two possible messages to player 2. Message A says: "Option A will earn you more money than option B." Message B says: "Option B will earn you more money than option A." Message B is a *lie* because for all three treatments, player 2 gets a lower payoff from option B. By contrast, the sender always gets a higher payoff from option B. Player 2 observes the message and then chooses either option A or B. Player 2's chosen option is then implemented. The structure of the game is not rich enough for a signaling equilibrium to be sustained; player 2 does not even know if the incentives of the two players are aligned or not.

Out of the 50 participants who were assigned the role of a sender, in an incentive compatible elicitation, 82% expected the receiver to follow their message. This was close to the actual percentage of receivers who did follow the messages, 78%. Thus, conditional on their messages being largely followed, if senders are assumed to tell selfish black lies, then they should always choose the option that maximizes their payoff (message B in all treatments).

Table 3.1 Payoffs of the players in each treatment in Gneezy (2005).

Treatment	Option	Payoff of	
		Player 1	Player 2
1	A	5	6
	B	6	5
2	A	5	15
	B	6	5
3	A	5	15
	B	15	5

Notice that the incentive to lie for player 1 (choosing message B) is different in each of the three treatments on two different counts. First, the gain in own-payoff is 1 for treatments 1 and 2 but it is 10 for treatment 3. Second, the loss to player 2 from being lied to is 1 in treatment 1 but 10 in treatments 2 and 3. The percentage of player 1s who lied in treatments 1, 2, and 3, respectively, is 36, 17, and 52 and these percentages are statistically different. In treatments 1 and 2, the personal gain from lying is 1, however, the loss to player 2 increases from 1 to 10. This reduces the fraction of player 1s who lie by more than half. However, in treatments 2 and 3, the loss to player 2 is 10 in each case but the personal gain to player 1 increases from 1 to 10. This significantly increases the percentage of player 1s who lie to 52. This experiment shows that the extent of lying responds to the gain from lying and the cost to the other player. However, it cannot cleanly separate the *role of other-regarding preferences* from *aversion to lying*.

In a separate questionnaire, Gneezy (2005) asks a different set of players to judge the fairness of lies with different consequences. University of Chicago students are asked which of the following two lies is more unfair. In one case, the seller sells a car to a buyer without revealing that it will cost $250 to fix a pump in the car. In another, the seller does not reveal that the brakes are faulty, which will also cost $250 for the gullible buyer to fix. A significantly higher percentage of the respondents judged the second scenario (faulty brakes) to be the more unfair of the two lies, despite identical monetary costs of repair. Subjects are not merely consequentialists but they apparently care about the higher potential risk to the buyer in the second case. If the responses of these subjects are more generally representative of the population, then we can trust a car salesman to more accurately report the condition of the brakes as compared to the air-conditioner.

Hurkens and Kartik (2009) reconsider the results of Gneezy (2005) and show that they are unable to reject the hypothesis that the data comes from a population of players of two types. Type I never lies whatever the cost (ethical types) and Type II always lies (unethical type).[1] However, if the types are fixed, this evidence begs the question of why the extent of lying responds to the incentives to lie in so many diverse contexts.

Gibson et al. (2013) conduct a decision theoretic lab experiment in which the confounds of strategic considerations and other-regarding preferences are eliminated. In the truth-telling task, subjects, in their role as the CEO of a company, had to decide on two possible earnings announcements that affected their own payoffs. A higher announcement is a lie but also increases their payoff. In several different treatments, the payoff differences between truth-telling and lying are different. For instance, in one treatment, the choice was between announcing 31 cents/share and 35 cents/share and the higher announcement led to 5 times higher earnings for the CEO. The subjects are told that the lie is within the bounds of what could be defended on accounting grounds.

If the subjects were of only two types, ethical and unethical, then we should not get any variation in the levels of truthfulness as the incentive to lie varies. The ethical types should never lie and the unethical types should always lie. In contrast, the extent of lying was sensitive to the incentive to lie. The authors find that the most significant factor in the decision to lie is the intrinsic cost of lying, which ties in with the results of Gneezy (2005). Hence, people seem to have underlying preferences over how much they are willing to lie as incentives for lying vary.

Fischbacher and Föllmi-Heusi (2013) introduce a novel method of measuring the extent to which people lie, even when the individual responses cannot be checked for lying. Subjects in

---

[1] For an early theoretical attempt at modeling two-type models of this sort, see Koford and Penno (1992).

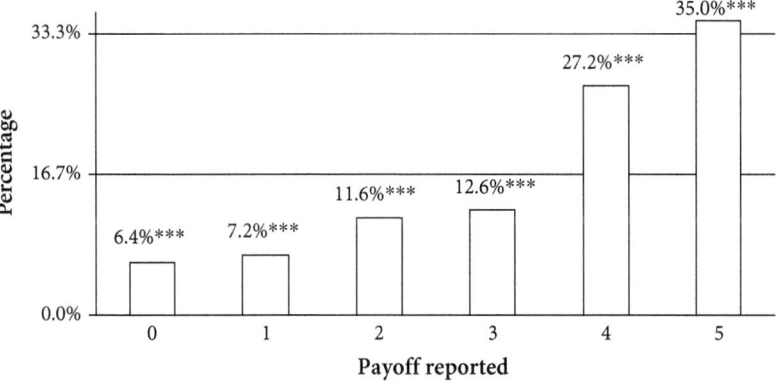

Figure 3.1 Results for the baseline treatment.

Source: "Lies in disguise: an experimental study on cheating," Fischbacher, U. and Föllmi-Heusi, F. Journal of the European Economic Association, 11(3): 525–47. © 2013 by the European Economic Association.

the experiment are asked to roll a dice and privately observe the outcome of the dice. To ensure anonymity, the experimenter is not present in the room when each participant privately rolls the die. For the numbers 1, 2, 3, 4, and 5, the payoff equals the self-reported outcome from the roll of the dice. If the claimed number is 6, then the payoff is zero. The experimental design ensures that subjects can never be found out if they cheat. The distribution based on the claimed numbers is then compared to the predicted statistical distribution of outcomes in which each number comes up with a probability 1/6 or 16.7%. Several control treatments were used that varied the level of stakes, created a negative externality on another player from lying, and created even higher levels of anonymity.[2]

The results of the baseline treatment for 389 participants are shown in Figure 3.1. On the horizontal axis are the payoffs of the player that simply correspond to the self-reported number on the dice (recall that for a report of 6 on the dice, the payoff is zero). The vertical axis measures the percentage of subjects who report being in each category; the theoretical prediction of 16.7% is also shown. The stars denote the significance levels for a two-sided binomial test of the differences in the observed percentage of players who self-report in each category from the theoretical prediction of 16.7%. The results are as follows.

1. A Kolgomorov–Smirnov test rejects the hypothesis that the observed distribution is identical to the predicted uniform distribution where each number occurs with a chance of 16.7%.
2. Numbers below 4 and the number 6 are underreported as they lie below the 16.7% line, while the numbers 4 and 5 are overreported. Since only 16.7% of the subjects are predicted to get a 6 and anybody who does not get a 6 is unlikely to report a 6, it is significant that 6.4% nevertheless report 6. This is contrary to the assumption of selfish black liars in neoclassical economics. Assuming that the proportion of intrinsically honest players is independent of

---

[2] In this treatment, participants shredded any pieces of paper they had written on and directly took prize money from an envelope without the intervention of the experimenter.

the number arising on the throw of the dice, then, since $\frac{6.4}{16.7} = 0.38323$, the proportion of intrinsically honest subjects is 38.3%.
3. The number 5 is payoff maximizing, yet 16.7% of the subjects would have got a 5 anyway, hence, the percentage of people who are unethical income maximizers is $\frac{6}{5}(35 - 16.7) = 21.96\%$.
4. More than 16.7% of the subjects report the number 4. Hence, there is a set of subjects who lie but do not lie maximally. These may be termed as partial liars. Such behavior could arise, for instance, if subjects wish to maintain a positive self-image.

A similar elicitation method is used by Prucker and Sausgruber (2013) using field data. They conducted their field experiments in two towns in Austria. Several tabloids operate under an *honor system* in which newspapers are sold on the street using a booth filled with newspapers. Customers pay into a padlocked cashbox. The payments are not monitored, so customers can pay an amount below the price of the newspaper or not pay at all. There is very little gain from not paying and a very small probability of non-payments being discovered. The authors run two different treatments by posting a note on the booth.

In the treatment LEGAL, a note is posted on the booth, reminding customers of the legal norm of paying for the newspaper. In treatment MORAL, the posted note appeals to the honesty of the customers, so it primes them to follow a social norm. The newspaper costs 0.60 euros and only a third of the customers pay a strictly positive amount. Average payment in the LEGAL treatment is 0.061 euros and average payment in the MORAL treatment is 0.14 euros. Thus, the MORAL treatment is more effective. The authors conjecture that there is, in fact, a moral norm of payment and when subjects are primed to consider it, self-interest is reduced somewhat in favor of a social norm of honesty.

Abeler et al. (2014) conducted a field study in Germany. Participants were contacted by phone, asked to toss a coin that only they privately observe, and report the result on the phone. Subjects received a payoff of 15 euros if they report tails. Under self-regarding preferences and amoral preferences, all subjects should report tails. Using the method introduced by Fischbacher and Föllmi-Heusi, the reported distribution of tails is compared to the predicted theoretical distribution. Almost all subjects told the truth; indeed the percentage reporting tails is lower than 50%. The authors conclude that the results are consistent with a cost of lying and that lab experiments understate the costs of lying and overstate the extent of amoral preferences.

Mazar et al. (2008) used two different treatments. In the first treatment, the experimenter checked answers to 20 maths questions and students were paid according to the number of correct answers. This establishes a benchmark distribution of marks. In the second treatment, subjects could mark the questions themselves (based on an answer key provided by the experimenter), then shred their answers and self-report the number of correct answers to claim the payment. Students in treatment 2 reported solving 10% more questions as compared to treatment 1. If students did not feel any unease at telling selfish black lies, then all of them should have reported 100% correct answers, given that this would have maximized their payoffs, particularly when the probability of being caught was zero.

Gneezy et al. (2013) introduce a third method of measuring lying aversion. Two individuals A and B are paired to play a simple sequential sender–receiver game. Only player A observes a randomly determined state of the world $s \in S = \{1, 2, \ldots, 6\}$; each of the states is equally likely. Player A then sends a message $r \in S$ to player B. The message is truthful if $r = s$, otherwise it is a lie. Player B observes the message and then chooses an action $a \in S$. The payoff of player A, π_A, is linearly increasing in r but it does not depend on the state, s, or the action, $a \in S$, of player B.

The payoff of player B, π_B, depends on his action a and the truthfulness of A. The exact payoffs are as follows.

$$\pi_A = 10 + 2r \text{ and } \pi_B = \begin{cases} 10 & \text{if } r = a \text{ and } r = s \\ 0 & \text{if } r = a \text{ and } r \neq s. \\ 3 & \text{if } r \neq a \end{cases}$$

Thus, player B gets the highest payoff when A sends a truthful message that is believed by player B. If player B chooses not to believe the message of player A (truthful or not), then he gets a fixed payoff of 3. If untruthful messages are believed, then B's payoff is zero. A player who is disposed to tell selfish black lies, as in neoclassical economics, would choose the message $r = 6$ in every state, s. The incremental payoff to player A from lying increases as s decreases.

The results with 72 subjects, who were rematched randomly over 24 rounds are as follows. The messages sent by player A in each state are shown in Figure 3.2. Each column corresponds to the percentage distribution of messages, $r \in S$, sent by player A for each state, $s \in S$. The sizes of the circles reflect the fraction of choices in each category. Along the diagonal, we get the percentage of truthful messages sent by A. Since the incentive to lie increases as s falls, it is not surprising that as s increases, messages are increasingly truthful.

Another indicator of this is the top row in Figure 3.2, which shows a message of $r = 6$ for each $s \in S$. As s increases from 1 to 5, the percentage of player As who lie maximally ($r = 6$) falls; these differences are statistically significant. These results are consistent with those of Gneezy (2005) reviewed above. As in Fischbacher and Föllmi-Heusi (2013), many players are partial liars but the percentages here are smaller; for instance, for states $s = 1, 2,$ and 3, there are 10% partial liars. There is also an element of other-regarding preferences in the results that is revealed

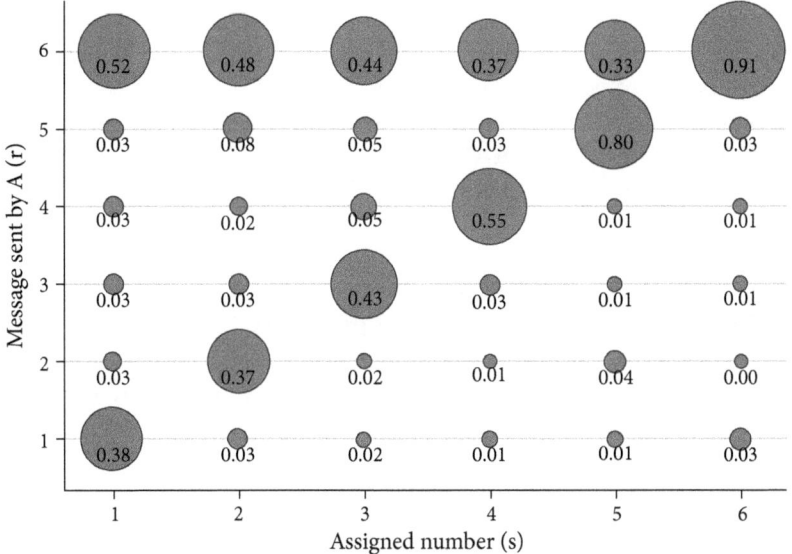

Figure 3.2 Messages sent by player A in each state.

Source: Reprinted from Journal of Economic Behavior of Organization, 93: 293–300. Gneezy, U., Rockenbach, B., and Serra-Garcia, A., "Measuring lying aversion." © 2013, with permission from Elsevier.

over successive rounds of the experiment. Player As are less likely to lie in period t if their lie in period $t-1$ reduced B's payoff.

As in many of the other results reported in this section, a very large fraction of player Bs choose to follow player A's message (i.e., $a = r$). For $r = 1, 2, \ldots, 5$, in 85–89% of the cases we have $a = r$ but when $r = 6$ we have $a = r$ for only 46% of player Bs. There is evidence of learning over successive rounds; player Bs reduced their dependence on messages by A if they were lied to in the previous period. On the whole, excluding $r = 6$, player Bs significantly improved their payoffs from following the message of player A.

A developing theoretical literature introduces a cost of lying in the players' utility functions.[3] Serra-Garcia et al. (2013) consider the efficacy of cheap talk in asymmetric information, sender–receiver, games. They consider two kinds of messages that can be sent by the sender—a message about the private information of the sender or a message about the action of the sender. In these kinds of games, there are two equilibria. In the *babbling equilibrium*, the receiver ignores the message sent by the sender. However, in the *influential equilibrium*, there is a separating equilibrium in which different types of senders send different messages and the receiver conditions his actions on the message of the sender. Under the *cost of lying assumption*, the only equilibrium that survives is the influential equilibrium.

There is a growing literature that examines the differential propensities of men and women to lie. For instance, Dreber and Johannesson (2008) find that men are more likely than women to tell a selfish black lie. Childs (2012) finds no gender differences in lying. However, when the stakes are reduced, in a similar game to Dreber and Johannesson, no gender differences are found by Gylfason et al. (2013). Erat and Gneezy (2012) show that men are more likely to tell a selfish black lie and a Pareto white lie. However, women are more likely to tell an altruistic white lie. This contributes to a developing literature that requires further replication and testing; for a survey on gender differences in preferences, see Croson and Gneezy (2009).

Conrads et al. (2013) find that individuals are more prone to lying under team incentives relative to piece rates. The reason is that under team incentives, players may be able to spread the consequences of lying among other team members. Cappelen et al. (2013) consider the non-economic correlates of lying. They find that the non-economic factors are as important as the economic ones. Participants who gave larger amounts in dictator games are also less likely to lie in sender–receiver games. They do not find a gender effect of lying, although females are slightly more prone to lie than males, a finding that is in contrast to earlier work. Other variables that correlated with lying were age, a measure of other-regarding preferences, and the nature of the lie, e.g., the incidence of lying falls when the message of the sender involves personal content.

3.2.2 A theoretical model of promises and threats

In neoclassical economics, promises or threats are not credible unless instrumentally rational self-regarding players respond to reputational concerns, or to third party enforcement. In the absence of these conditions, verbal commitments, in the form of *promises* or *threats*, are predicted to be ineffective. This is in contrast with the view taken in psychology and sociology, where such verbal communication can be efficacious; Volume 4 of the book considers experimental evidence that supports this view. Ellingsen and Johannesson (2004), henceforth EJ, examine the predictions from these conflicting approaches in a variant of the hold-up problem.

---

[3] See, for instance, Ellingsen and Johanneson (2004), Kartik et al. (2007), and Kartik (2009).

Consider a multi-stage, two-player, game between a seller (S) and a buyer (B). In stage I, the seller can, at a fixed cost, $F > 0$, make an investment decision $I \in \{0,1\}$. $I = 0$ denotes foregoing the investment opportunity, and $I = 1$ denotes making the investment. The gains from trade in stage II are $g \in \{0, G\}$. If $I = 1$, then $g = G > F$, otherwise if $I = 0$, then $g = 0$.

If $I = 1$, then, in stage II, let x_S, x_B be, respectively, the seller's and buyer's shares of the gains from trade, G. Following, $I = 1$, the buyer proposes a split of G by making a proposal $x = \{x_S, x_B\}$ such that $x_S + x_B = G$. The seller makes the binary accept/reject decision $a(x) \in \{0,1\}$. If the decision is to accept ($a = 1$), the proposal x is implemented, and if it is to reject ($a = 0$), both get zero. The outside option of the seller is zero. In the experiments, the unit of currency is Swedish Kroner (SEK), $F = 60$ and $G = 100$.

Let us first consider the theoretical predictions under the benchmark case of self-regarding preferences.

Proposition 3.1 *Suppose that the seller and the buyer have self-regarding preferences. Then, in the unique subgame perfect equilibrium of the game: $I = 0$, $x_B = G$, $x_S = 0$, and $a = 1$. Furthermore, any promises made by the buyer or the seller at any stage do not influence the outcome.*

Proof: In stage II, the seller will accept any non-negative offer because the outside option is zero, so $a = 1$. Knowing this, the buyer offers $x_S = 0$, so $x_B = G$. In stage I, the ex-ante utility of the seller from $I = 1$ is $-F < 0$ and from $I = 0$ it is 0. Thus, $I = 0$ is optimal. The reason that promises have no effect in the game is that players have self-regarding preferences and there is no cost of breaking a promise. ∎

Let us now examine the experimental results to see if the predictions of the self-regarding model in Proposition 3.1 hold. EJ consider three treatments. In the first treatment, no communication is allowed. In the second treatment, the buyer sends a message to the seller before the seller makes the investment decision. In the third treatment, the seller sends a message to the buyer along with his investment decision $I \in \{0,1\}$. Clearly, messages in the second treatment are of the nature of promises. For instance, the buyer might *promise* in his message to the seller that "I shall share the net gains from trade, $G - F$, equally with you." Messages in the third treatment are of the nature of *threats*. For instance, in his message to the buyer, the seller might issue the threat that "If you make me a low offer, I will reject your offer and each of us will get zero."

The experimental results reject the predictions of Proposition 3.1, and are as follows. In treatment 1, a third of the sellers choose $I = 1$ and the modal offer by buyers is to split the net gains from trade $G - F = 40$ equally, thus, the modal proposal is $x_S = 80, x_B = 20$. However, the mean offer in treatment 1 is $x_S = 48.57$ and mean profit of the seller, $x_S - F = -12.86 < 0$.

The presence of communication in treatments 2 and 3 increases the mean offer. The mean offer in treatment 2 (buyer communication) is the highest and it is significantly higher than in treatment 1; the mean profit of the seller in treatment 2 is 8.75. The two most frequent proposals made by the buyer in treatment 2 were $x_S = 60$ (so seller's net profit, $x_S - F$, is zero), and $x_S = 80$ in which case the seller's net profit is 20. Out of the 30 pairs of subjects, in three cases, sellers accepted an offer that made them a loss.

The mean offer in treatment 3 is lower but not statistically different from that under treatment 2. Nine out of the 21 messages in treatment 3 contained threats; however, these threats were not very credible and often ignored by the buyers. The vast majority of the seller messages (16 out of 21) suggested splitting the net gains from trade equally but in the majority of cases (9 out of 16), the buyers made lower offers to the seller. This is in keeping with the nature of the hold-up problem; once the seller sinks the investment, the buyer can hold-up the seller, ex-post.

The failure of the predictions of the model with self-regarding preferences is problematic because the hold-up problem is of fundamental importance in industrial organization and in contract theory. EJ suggest that the explanation lies in other-regarding preferences, modified to take account of a cost of breaking the promise.

Suppose that the seller and the buyer in the EJ model have Fehr–Schmidt preferences as in (7.1), so that the Fehr–Schmidt utility of the seller is denoted by $U_S(x,I,a;\alpha_S,\beta_S)$, where α_S, β_S are the preference parameters of the seller. The buyer's Fehr–Schmidt utility is denoted by $U_B(x;\alpha_B,\beta_B)$, where α_B, β_B are the preference parameters of the buyer and $x = \{x_S, x_B\}$. Suppose that there is mutual knowledge of the utility functions, U_S and U_B.

Proposition 3.2

(a) If $\beta_B > \frac{1}{2}$, then in the unique subgame perfect equilibrium of the model: $I = 1$, $x_B = \frac{G-F}{2}$, $x_S = \frac{G+F}{2}$ and $a = 1$.

(b) If $\beta_B < \frac{1}{2}$, then in the unique subgame perfect equilibrium of the model, $I = 0$.

Proof: Consider a seller who, in stage II, is making his acceptance decision, having observed the buyer's proposal $x = \{x_S, x_B\}$, and conditional on having chosen $I = 1$ in stage I. The stage II payoffs of the seller and the buyer are, respectively, $x_S - F$ and x_B, where $x_S + x_B = G$. Suppose that the buyer does not make any overfair offers, so the buyer's payoff is relatively greater (we appeal to the ultimatum game for this sort of evidence[4]). Denote the utility of the seller from accepting ($a = 1$) and rejecting ($a = 0$) the proposal, respectively, by $U_S(x,1,1;\alpha_S,\beta_S)$ and $U_S(x,1,0;\alpha_S,\beta_S)$. Thus,

$$U_S(x,1,1;\alpha_S,\beta_S) = x_S - F - \alpha_S[x_B - (x_S - F)] \text{ and } U_S(x,1,0;\alpha_S,\beta_S) = -F - \alpha_S F. \quad (3.1)$$

Substituting $x_B = G - x_S$ in (3.1), the smallest offer x_S that the seller accepts such that $U_S(x,1,1;\alpha_S,\beta_S) \succ U_S(x,1,0;\alpha_S,\beta_S)$ is

$$\underline{x}_S = \frac{\alpha_S G}{1 + 2\alpha_S} > 0. \quad (3.2)$$

A rational buyer with mutual knowledge of Fehr–Schmidt preferences knows that any offer to the seller below $\underline{x}_S$ will be rejected (recall that under self-regarding preferences, buyers offered $x_S = 0$). Thus, the maximum monetary payoff of the buyer is $G - \underline{x}_S$.

In making his proposal, $x = \{x_S, x_B\}$, the buyer takes the subsequent behavior of the seller, in (3.2), as given. Suppose that we are interested in the case where the buyer demands more than half the net surplus, i.e., $x_B \geq \frac{G-F}{2}$, so that the buyer's payoff is relatively greater. Since $x_S = G - x_B$, the condition $x_B \geq \frac{G-F}{2} \Leftrightarrow x_S \leq \frac{G+F}{2}$. Also notice that $\frac{G+F}{2} > \underline{x}_S$. Thus, the buyer chooses x_B in order to maximize $U_B(x;\alpha_B,\beta_B) = x_B - \beta_B[x_B - (x_S - F)]$ subject to the constraints $x_S + x_B = G$ and $0 < \underline{x}_S \leq x_S \leq \frac{G+F}{2}$. This is equivalent to the problem of choosing x_B in order to maximize

---

[4] This assumption comes with the caveat that in some cultures overfair offers are not unheard of; see Henrich et al. (2001).

$$U_B(x;\alpha_B,\beta_B) = x_B - \beta_B[x_B - (G - x_B - F)], \quad (3.3)$$

subject to $\frac{G-F}{2} \leq x_B \leq G - \underline{x}_S$. From (3.3) we have

$$\frac{dU_B}{dx_B} = 1 - 2\beta_B.$$

Suppose that $1 - 2\beta_B < 0 \Leftrightarrow \beta_B > \frac{1}{2}$, then the buyer chooses the lower limit $x_B = \frac{G-F}{2}$, so $x_S = G - x_B = \frac{G+F}{2}$. In this case, it is optimal in the first stage for the seller to choose $I = 1$.

When, $\beta_B < \frac{1}{2}$, $\frac{dU_B}{dx_B} > 0$, so the buyer chooses the upper limit $x_B = G - \underline{x}_S = G\left(\frac{1+\alpha_S}{1+2\alpha_S}\right)$. The ex-ante utility of the seller from investing in this case is $U_S(\underline{x}_S, 1, 1; \alpha_S, \beta_S) = \underline{x}_S - F - \alpha_S[G - \underline{x}_S - (\underline{x}_S - F)] = -F - \alpha_S F < 0$, which is lower than the outside option of zero. Hence, $I = 0$. ∎

The inequity aversion parameters of both players, α_S and β_B, determine the size of the offer and the investment decision. If the advantageous inequity parameter of the buyer, β_B, is high enough ($\beta_B > 1/2$), then the buyer offers to share equally in the gains from trade, inducing the seller to make the investment in stage I. If $\beta_B < 1/2$, then the ex-post hold-up problem is serious enough for the seller to prevent any investment in stage I. From (3.2), we have that the seller's minimum acceptable share is increasing in the gains from trade, G, as well as the disadvantageous inequity parameter of the seller, α_S. The higher is α_S, the more likely the seller is to reject an offer by the buyer, eliciting higher offers for the seller in equilibrium.

Social preferences of the Fehr–Schmidt form are consistent with the experimental findings in EJ of strictly positive offers made by buyers and the investment choice, $I = 1$, of the sellers. However, these preferences still do not explain the role of communication in enhancing investment by sellers. In order to incorporate the role of communication, EJ introduce a cost of breaking a promise. This cost, l, is incurred only if a promise is broken.

Suppose that $\beta_B < \frac{1}{2}$, so that $1 - 2\beta_B > 0$. We know that, in this case, from Proposition 3.2, the seller is offered $\underline{x}_S$ but the seller does not find it worthwhile to invest ($I = 0$). Can the buyer *promise* to offer more to the seller, say, x_S^*, in order to induce first stage investment ($I = 1$)? Let us assume that the buyer does not make overfair offers, so he does not offer to share more than half the net gains from trade. Thus, the buyer promises to give a share, x_S^*, to the seller that satisfies

$$\underline{x}_S < x_S^* \leq \frac{G+F}{2}.$$

If the buyer keeps his promise, then the utility of the buyer is

$$U_B(x_S^*,.) = G - x_S^* - \beta_B[G - x_S^* - (x_S^* - F)].$$

If the buyer does not keep his promise and reverts back to his ex-post optimal level of offer $\underline{x}_S$ then his utility is

$$U_B(\underline{x}_S,.) = G - \underline{x}_S - l - \beta_B[G - \underline{x}_S - (\underline{x}_S - F)],$$

where l is the cost of breaking the promise. It is optimal for the buyer to keep his promise if $U_B(x_S^*,.) \geq U_B(\underline{x}_S,.)$, so the lowest promise of the seller's share is

$$x_S^* = \min\left\{\frac{G+F}{2}, \underline{x}_S + \frac{l}{1-2\beta_B}\right\}.$$

Since we are considering the case $0 < 1 - 2\beta_B < 1$, we have $\frac{l}{1-2\beta_B} > l$. Thus, the presence of inequity aversion on the part of the players magnifies the effect of the costs of breaking the promise. If players had entirely self-regarding preferences, so $\beta_B = 0$, then the effect of promises does not get magnified.

Consider now the case of seller communication when there is a cost of not carrying out a threat. Suppose that the seller threatens to reject any unfair offers $x_S < F + \frac{G-F}{2} = \frac{G+F}{2}$. We are interested in the maximum offer $\widehat{x}_S < \frac{G+F}{2}$ that the seller can credibly threaten to reject.

Using (3.1), we can find $\widehat{x}_S$ from the following condition

$$\widehat{x}_S - \alpha_S[G - \widehat{x}_S - (\widehat{x}_S - F)] - l = -\alpha_S F, \qquad (3.4)$$

where l is the cost of not carrying out the threat by accepting any infinitesimal amount less than $\widehat{x}_S$. Solving out for $\widehat{x}_S$ from (3.4), and using the upper bound $\frac{G+F}{2}$ on $\widehat{x}_S$ we get

$$\widehat{x}_S = \min\left\{\frac{l + \alpha_S G}{1 + 2\alpha_S}, \frac{G+F}{2}\right\}.$$

The seller will always get an ex-post offer of $\underline{x}_S = \frac{\alpha_S G}{1+2\alpha_S}$ in (3.2). However, the cost of breaking threats, l, can give the seller an extra minimum payoff of $\frac{l}{1+2\alpha_S}$, which is decreasing in α_S. Thus, as the degree of disadvantageous inequity suffered by the seller, α_S, increases, the set of offers that he can credibly threaten to refuse, shrinks. This reduces the commitment value of threats. A simple application of L'Hôpital's rule shows that $\lim_{\alpha_S \to \infty} \widehat{x}_S = \frac{G}{2}$, thus, as $\alpha_S \to \infty$, the seller cannot threaten to reject even $\frac{G}{2}$, which splits the gross gains equally (i.e., not taking account of F). In this case, the ex-post monetary payoff of the seller is $\frac{G}{2} - F$, which for the EJ experiments ($F = 60$ and $G = 100$) is a negative number.

The experimental data in EJ does show that seller threats are not very potent, while buyer promises are far more effective; this qualitative feature is consistent with the proposed theoretical model. However, in order to explain the quantitative features of the data, one has to allow for a distribution of values for α and β (and possibly also of l) across the population.[5]

In contrast to EJ, Charness and Dufwenberg (2006) locate the explanation for the efficacy of promises in *guilt-aversion*. Subjects who break a promise experience *guilt* when they let down the payoff expectations of others. An understanding of this mechanism requires the machinery of *psychological game theory* that is considered in Volume 4 of the book. A-priori, one possible objection to the explanation offered by EJ may be that they assume the very result they wish to prove, by including a cost of breaking a promise in their objective function. There are two responses. First, EJ make very precise predictions that differ between buyers and sellers, which can be tested. Second, one chooses among different explanations of the same phenomenon not by a-priori plausibility but by putting them to a stringent empirical test.

Vanberg (2008) pits the two competing explanations by EJ and Charness and Dufwenberg (2006) empirically against each other. He argues that the experiments by Charness and Dufwenberg are not able to distinguish between the two competing explanations. Thus, he

---

[5] Indeed, Fehr and Schmidt (1997) use such a distribution from experimental data to explain their own findings. For instance, α takes the values 0, 0.5, 1, and 4 for, respectively, 30, 30, 30, and 10 % of the players. The parameter β takes the values 0, 0.25, and 0.6 for, respectively, 30, 30, and 40 % of the players.

designs experiments in which the predictions of the two explanations can be neatly distinguished. The main finding is that the results are consistent with a model in which people have a preference for keeping their promises, as in EJ.

3.3 Social identity

Individuals may "identify" themselves with certain *social categories*. *Social identity* refers to one's social category. For instance, an individual's identity could be manager or worker, blue collar or white collar worker, black or white, member of a club or a non-member, and soldier or civilian. Each social category is governed by a *norm* of behavior that specifies the *ideal behavior* of a member in each situation.[6] Different social contexts may trigger different identities—a family identity, a regional identity, or a national identity (Turner et al., 1987).

Let us begin with an example. Akerlof and Kranton (2005, p. 9) describe the following initiation at the US West Point military academy. "On plebes' first day ... they strip down to their underwear. Their hair is cut off. They are put in uniform. They then must address an older cadet, with the proper salute ... must stand and salute and repeat, and stand and salute and repeat, until they get it exactly right, all the while being reprimanded for every tiny mistake." How should an economist brought up on the theory of incentives and organizations make sense of this?

Akerlof and Kranton (2005, p. 9) offer an answer: "Economists' current picture of organizations and work incentives has no place for the West Point program ... The Army's aim at West Point is to change cadets' preferences. They wish to inculcate non-economic motives in the cadets, so that they have the same goals as the U.S. Army. Alternatively stated, the goal of West Point is to change the identity of the cadets, so they will think of themselves, above all else, as officers in the U.S. army. They will feel bad about themselves—they will lose utility—if they fall short of the ideals of such an officer."

The effect of social identity has also been documented for some of the experimental games considered in Chapter 1. For instance, Ockenfels and Werner (2014) show that dictators transfer a higher amount to responders who are perceived to share a common group identity. Second order beliefs of the dictator are important too. When the dictator believes that the responder is unsure of the common group identity, he transfers a lower amount.

There are three main components of social identity theory. In the first, *categorization*, the individual players are classified into the relevant categories, say, gender, race, nationality, and profession. In the second, *identification*, individuals identify with the characteristics of the category in which they are categorized; perhaps individual identity imparts greater self-esteem. Other members of the same group are often called insiders or *ingroup members* and members of other groups are called outsiders or *outgroup members*. Identification might involve adopting the stereotypical behaviors of one's group members. It also typically involves favoring the ingroup members over outgroups. In the third, *social comparison*, individuals compare their own group to other groups on some criteria, which is also possibly stereotypical.

Research in *social psychology* has typically employed the technique of inducing *artificial group identities* through a process of *priming* the individuals; see Tajfel et al. (1971) for the classic experiments. The typical experiment then observes the effect of such priming on the behavior of subjects towards ingroup and outgroup members. The experimental process involves

---

[6] For early developments in social identity theory, see Tajfel and Turner (1979).

finding the *minimal group* such that the weakest possible identification with the group produces discriminatory behavior towards ingroup and outgroup members.

An important finding of this research is that with most minimal groups, and even the most trivial categorization, say, into blue and red groups, there is relatively more favorable behavior towards ingroup members; for surveys, see Tajfel and Turner (1986) and McDermott (2009). Even when subjects know that the assignment to groups is random, they continue to discriminate in favor of insiders (Billig and Tajfel, 1973). These findings suggest that humans might be hardwired, perhaps for evolutionary reasons, to take on social identities that can create both socially harmful and socially helpful outcomes.[7] Examples of socially harmful outcomes might be intolerance, discrimination, and prejudice, whereas socially helpful outcomes might arise from internalizing desirable norms of hard work and honesty; for instance, when Asians in the US are primed for their Asian identity, they achieve greater educational and professional success.

3.3.1 Evidence on social identity and other-regarding preferences

Benjamin et al. (2010) explain how priming of subjects to induce group identities can be used in experiments to explain the choices of subjects. Suppose that an individual belongs to some category C, and chooses some action, $x \in X$, where X is some finite set of actions; more generally, x could be a vector of actions. If the individual did not belong to any category, then his most preferred action would have been x_P. However, the target action (possibly a norm) for a member of category C is x_C. The individual must choose x in order to maximize his utility, given by

$$U = -w(s)(x - x_C)^2 - [1 - w(s)](x - x_P)^2, \qquad (3.5)$$

where $w(s)$ is the weight that the individual puts on conforming with his category norm, x_C. In (3.5), the individual derives disutility from a weighted combination of departures of his action, x, from the category norm, x_C, and his privately optimal choice, x_P. The variable s may be thought of as the strength of affiliation with one's category, and could reflect the extent of priming in the experiment. The restrictions on $w(s)$ are that $w(0) = 0$ and $w' > 0$, so greater priming induces a greater weight on conforming with group norm. The first order condition is sufficient and solving it we get the optimal choice

$$x^* = w(s)x_C + [1 - w(s)]x_P, \qquad (3.6)$$

which is just a weighted average of the group norm and the privately optimal choice. Several conclusions can be drawn from (3.6). First, because $w' > 0$, as the strength of affiliation with one's category, s, increases, the optimal choice x^* becomes closer to the category norm, x_C. Suppose that starting from some level of strength, s, priming of subjects induces an extra affiliation, ε, to one's category, so that the final level of strength is $s + \varepsilon$. Then, expanding $x^*(s + \varepsilon)$ around $x^*(s)$ using a first order Taylor series approximation, and using (3.6),

$$x^*(s+\varepsilon) - x^*(s) \approx \varepsilon \frac{dx^*(s)}{ds} = \varepsilon w'(s)(x_C - x_P).$$

---

[7] Henri Tajfel, one of the poineers of social identity theory was a Polish Jew who suffered extreme hardships in Nazi concentration camps and lost his family. His interest in social identity theory was possibly fueled by the prejudice and discrimination that he personally experienced.

Since $w' > 0$, the effect of priming on optimal choices depends on whether $x_C \gtreqless x_P$. Also, $\frac{d}{ds}\left(\frac{dx^*(s)}{ds}\right) = w''(s)(x_C - x_P)$, which depends on the sign of $w''(s)$ and whether $x_C \gtreqless x_P$. Thus, a-priori it is not necessarily the case that on the margin, priming is more effective for those individuals who identify more strongly with a category. These considerations could be important in understanding the behavior of individuals in social identity experiments.

Benjamin et al. (2010) consider the following stylized facts, using US data. First, Asian Americans accumulate more human capital and save more in tax-deferred savings accounts relative to white Americans. Controlling for observable demographic features, black Americans do relatively worse than white Americans on these counts. Second, women appear to take lower risks than men in financial investments, and also behave relatively more conservatively in the lab. Further, it has been advanced that the norms in each of these groups (by ethnicity and gender) may be responsible for these findings. For instance, it is believed that the Asian American identity is associated with the norm of patience, while the non-immigrant black identity with the opposite norm—impatience and risk taking. Similarly, the male identity may be associated with taking more risks than the female identity.[8] Clearly non-experimental data is fairly noisy in this respect because it includes many other confounds, such as peer pressure, income levels, and various socioeconomic aspects. Hence, the authors propose an experimental test.

After being primed for Asian, black, or gender identities, the risk preferences of the subjects and the time preferences are elicited. Priming took the form of background questionnaires in which the questions highlighted racial or gender identities. For instance, there were questions about languages spoken at home and how long the immigrant family had been in the US. In terms of the simple theoretical framework proposed above, x equals risk or time preferences and x_C are the relevant category norms. For instance, if $x_P = \theta_P$ is the discount rate of an unprimed Asian American, then $x_C = \theta_C < \theta_P$ is the discount rate of an Asian American who has been primed for his more patient Asian identity.

The results are as follows. Unprimed Asians are more risk-averse and more impatient than whites. However, when primed with their Asian identity, the impatient choices drop by 14%, which is significant at the 1% level. Primed Asians require much lower interest rates to defer payments from a current date to a future date.[9] For a current amount of $4 and payments deferred by a week, the elicited percentage interest rate falls by three-quarters when primed for the Asian identity.

The difference between the impatient choices of primed and unprimed whites and primed and unprimed immigrant blacks are not statistically significant. However, contrary to the received view, in terms of their time preference, primed native blacks respond in the same direction as primed Asians, i.e., become more patient. Individuals who are primed for gender do not make choices that are any different from the unprimed condition.[10] Shih et al. (1999) find that when subjects are primed separately for Asian and gender identities, and given a maths test, they do best when primed for the Asian identity and worse when they are primed for the female identity.

---

[8] We refer the reader to the large number of references on these claims in Benjamin et al. (2010).

[9] Denote current income as Y_0, next year's income as Y_1, annual interest rate as r and the annual discount rate as θ. Then the elicited interest rate r^e makes the decision maker indifferent between the two choices: Y_0 and Y_1. Thus, $Y_0 = \frac{Y_1(1+r^e)}{1+\theta}$, so a lower r^e reveals a lower θ, and a more patient individual.

[10] This is consistent with the results of Cadsby and Maynes (1998) who also find that gender has little effect on contributions in public good experiments when subjects are primed for gender identities in a pregame questionnaire.

Chen and Li (2009) consider the effect of social identity on other-regarding preferences. Each of their treatments has four stages. In the first stage, the subjects are categorized into groups. The groups are formed, based on the preferences of subjects for paintings by one artist over another artist.[11] In stages 2 and 3, the group identities are strengthened through two tasks. In the first task, subjects were quizzed about the names of artists for a set of paintings. Correct answers were rewarded with tokens that could be cashed for money from the experimenter. Subjects were allowed to consult their group members (but not the members of the other group) in searching for the correct answer. In the second task, subjects were given a set of tokens and had to decide, over five rounds, how to allocate them to other players. The identity of the other players was varied between ingroup and outgroup members. The players knew that one of the rounds would then be randomly picked and played for real money. Two further control groups were constructed in which the identity of the subjects towards their ingroup members was not primed in this manner.

Once group identity was induced and enhanced in this manner, in the final stage, stage 4 of the experiment, subjects played several two-person sequential move games from Charness and Rabin (2002). In these games, player 1 chooses between two actions, stay out or enter. If player 1 stays out, the game ends with exogenously given payoffs, and if player 1 enters, then player 2 chooses between two possible payoff allocations for the player. The strategy method is used to elicit the choices. Player 2 is asked to make a choice in each of the two cases, assuming that player 1 has stayed out and that player 1 has entered. The games are differentiated by the actions of both players. For instance, in making his choice, player 2 could choose an option where no sacrifice is involved in ensuring that player 1 gets a higher payoff, or where such a sacrifice is involved, or where the sacrifice actually reduces the payoff of player 1. The choices reveal the extent to which players appear to exhibit elements of other-regarding preferences towards others.

The results are as follows. For stage 2 of the treatment, players allocated significantly more tokens to ingroup members relative to outgroup members. This replicates the often found result that minimal groups favor ingroup members. From the choices made in stage 4 of the experiment, players exhibit altruism towards opponents if their payoff is greater and envy if it is lower. However, altruism and envy are relatively stronger towards ingroup members.

Other interesting results arise by observing the behavior of player 2 when the decision of player 1 (to enter or stay out) conveys information about intentions. In this case, results can be further sharpened by observing cases where player 2 sacrifices own-payoff to get player 1 a better payoff, and where the sacrifice in own-payoff leads to lower payoff for player 1. Here, the results, based on a logit specification, are as follows. Players are 18.6% likely to reward ingroup members more than outgroup members. Social preferences matter in the sense that player 2 is less likely to reward player 1 if player 2's payoff is relatively lower—so envy limits positive reciprocity.

For every 100 token disadvantageous gap, player 2 is less likely to reward player 1 by 7.8%. Since the strategy method is used to elicit the choices of player 2 for both possible choices of player 1 (stay or enter), we can determine if player 2 is likely to reward or punish unfavorable choices. It turns out that player 2 is more likely to reward favorable behavior by an ingroup player 1 and also more likely to forgive unfavorable behavior by an ingroup player 1. Finally both players are more likely to choose the joint payoff maximizing choice when they are ingroup members.

---

[11] The painters are two modern artists. Based on the names of the painters, the two groups are the "Klee" and "Kadinsky" groups. To control for possible salience effects of the names of the artists, two control groups—the Maize and Blue groups were also used.

Cohn et al. (2013) conduct a field study of prison inmates from Switzerland's largest adult penitentiary. Their aim is to see if imprisonment fosters a criminal identity. In the baseline treatment, criminals were asked to report the number of heads in ten tosses of a coin that they privately observed. The reported outcomes were then compared to the statistical average of 50% heads. Criminals misreported 20% of the times. When criminals were primed for their criminal identity (e.g., by asking what they were convicted for) they cheated even more—now they misreported 32% of the times. By contrast, in a placebo condition, subjects were recruited from the general population. In this case, when primed for a criminal identity (reading a short text profile describing a criminal or a non-criminal person), the percentage of misreported heads fell from 14% to 10%.

In Charness et al. (2007), subjects are assigned to one of two groups, row players (R) and column players (C), in the prisoner's dilemma game (PD) and the battle of sexes game (BOS). These games are shown in Figure 3.3.[12] The PD has a unique Nash equilibrium (B,B). The BOS game has two pure strategy Nash equilibria (A,A) and (B,B) and a mixed strategy Nash equilibrium in which each player plays his preferred strategy (A for row player and B for column player) with probability 0.75.

Players in the PD game are said to be *aggressive* if they play B and *accommodating* if they play A. In the BOS game, aggressive players play their preferred strategy, and accommodating players play the opponent's preferred strategy. Players are randomly assigned as row players (category label R) and column players (category label C). Once the category labels (R and C) are assigned to the players, they go to their respective rooms labeled R and C. If a game is played in room R, then the row player is termed as the host and the column player is termed as the guest. Similarly, in room C, the column player is the host and the row player is the guest.

The treatments exploit two dimensions. In the *audience treatment*, the other group members sit in a semi circle behind the player when he makes the decision, but do not otherwise interfere in actual choices made. This is intended to induce greater salience of group membership. In the *no-audience treatment*, other group members do not watch. In the second dimension, the *feedback treatment*, all people in the room immediately learn the outcome, while in the *no-feedback treatment*, the payoffs are revealed only at the end of the session. The payoffs of any player are made up of two components—their own-payoffs in games when they make active decisions and a one third stake in the payoffs of one's ingroup members when others in the ingroup play the games.

When group membership is more salient (audience treatment) subjects are more likely to choose the action that maximizes their own payoff. For the row player, these actions are B in the PD game, and A in the BOS game. However, when this salience is reduced (no-audience

Battle of sexes game			Prisoner's dilemma game		
	A	B		A	B
A	3, 1	0, 0	A	5, 5	1, 7
B	0, 0	1, 3	B	7, 1	2, 2

Figure 3.3 The battle of sexes (BOS) game and the prisoner's dilemma game (PD).
Source: Charness et al. (2007) with permission from the American Economic Association.

[12] Volume 4 of the book considers the experimental results on these two classes of games in detail.

treatment) these aggressive choices are reduced. In the audience treatment, in the BOS, hosts are aggressive in 84% of the cases and guests accommodate in 65% of the cases. By contrast, in the no-audience treatment, these numbers are significantly lower at 60% and 38% respectively. Thus, hosts are more aggressive when they play in front of an audience of their ingroup members. Guests seem to anticipate this behavior and are more accommodating. Similarly, the feedback treatment makes group membership more salient and creates effects similar to those in the audience treatment. When group membership is most salient, in the treatment with audience effects and feedback effects, almost all hosts are aggressive (95%) and this is again well anticipated by the guests who accommodate even more.

In the PD game, hosts accommodate in 62% of the cases when there is no audience and feedback. However, when group membership is most salient (audience plus feedback) hosts only accommodate in 28% of the cases. The effect of group membership is smaller but still significant for guests. In the case of no audience and feedback, guests accommodate in 45% of the cases but this reduces to 34% in the audience and feedback treatment.

Goette et al. (2012) consider the external validity of minimal groups (MG) created in the lab in which ingroup members may have limited interaction with each other. They argue that real-world groups are, instead, characterized by strong interactions among ingroup members. These members have social ties and friendships between each other, which may generate empathy and prosocial behavior within the group. Denote the treatment with real social groups by SG treatment. The main research objective is to examine the behavior of subjects in minimal and real social groups. In each of the MG and SG treatments, members of groups are randomly assigned, rather than endogenously assigned. Individuals only knew whether the player they interacted with is an ingroup or outgroup member but not the identity of the player; this rules out strategic, reputation building, motives.

The subjects in the experiment were Swiss army trainees who stayed in the same platoon once they joined the Joint Officer Training Program (JOTP). The subjects had performed a range of joint tasks together, possibly enhancing their group identity. The random assignment of the trainees to a platoon (each platoon has 21 members) comprises one *real social group* (SG). Assignment to a platoon enhances social identity among platoon members as they do a variety of joint tasks during a three-week period. In contrast, the minimal group, MG, is formed simply on the basis of random choice, using the social security numbers of the army trainees. This is a minimal group because all members are part of the JOTP, yet, unlike the SG, may belong to different platoons, so have not necessarily interacted over the three weeks of platoon training. In the experiments, subjects are simply told of the ID number of the platoon of the opponent as a method of identifying ingroup and outgroup members.

The subjects played a modified trust game, akin to a simultaneous move prisoner's dilemma. Two players, A1 and A2, were given 20 points. They simultaneously decide to send up to 20 points to the other player. The experimenter doubled the points that were passed to the other player. Sending 0 points may be considered to be the *defection decision* and sending all 20 points may be considered to be the *cooperative decision*. In the ingroup condition, the opponent was a member of the same platoon, while in the outgroup condition, he was a member of another platoon.

In experiment 1, players simply choose the number of points to send to the other player. In experiment 2, the possibility of third party punishment was allowed with the introduction of players B1 and B2, each of whom was allocated 70 points. Having observed the actions of player Aj, $j = 1, 2$, player Bj could punish player Aj. Punishment took the form of each player Bj being allowed to spend up to 10 deduction points aimed at player Aj. For each point surrendered by player Bj, player Aj lost 3 points. This allows one to test for altruistic norm enforcement. Players B1 and A1 form an ingroup and players B2 and A2 form another ingroup. The payoffs (one point equalled 0.25 CHF) were mailed to the home addresses of the trainees, ten days after the end of the course, on completion of the JOTP.

Panel A in Figure 3.4 shows the cooperation rates in the MG and the SG treatments. In Figures 3.4, 3.5 we use the convention that other A players are all referred to as A2 players and all players that a player B can punish are called A1 players. In both treatments, MG and SG, there is significant, positive, ingroup bias in cooperation rates. Averaged across both treatments, the cooperation rate with ingroup members is 65%, while that with outgroup members is 50%. The difference in cooperation rates towards ingroup and outgroup members in the MG treatment is 10%, but it is 20% in the SG treatment. Thus, there is a significant quantitative difference in the two treatments. The actual differences in cooperation rates are also evident in the beliefs of the players (Panel B); ingroup members are believed to be significantly more cooperative.

Figure 3.5 shows that the behavior in treatments MG and SG is qualitatively different. In the MG treatment (Panel b), when player A1 defects, the punishment is smaller for ingroup members relative to outgroup members. But when A1 cooperates, punishment of ingroup members and outgroup members is similar in both MG and the SG treatments; some punishment still takes place because players do not fully cooperate. In the SG treatment (Panel a), punishment of outgroup members for defection is nearly identical to ingroup members. Another interesting finding is that defection against ingroup members is punished relatively more highly in the SG treatment (see Figure 4 in Goette et al., 2012). By contrast, there is no such difference in the MG treatment. Thus, third party norm enforcement is stronger when the group identity is stronger (SG treatment).

These qualitative and quantitative differences between the SG and MG treatments can potentially reconcile the differences in existing results between minimal and real groups. For instance, for real groups (akin to the SG treatment) Bernhard et al. (2006) find that tribes in Papua New Guinea punish ingroup and outgroup members equally for defection. However, Chen and Li (2009) using minimal groups (akin to the MG treatment) find that ingroup members are punished less than outgroup members.

Yamagishi and Kiyonari (2000) find that the effects on cooperation rates are different in a simultaneous and sequential move prisoner's dilemma game. The argument is that in the

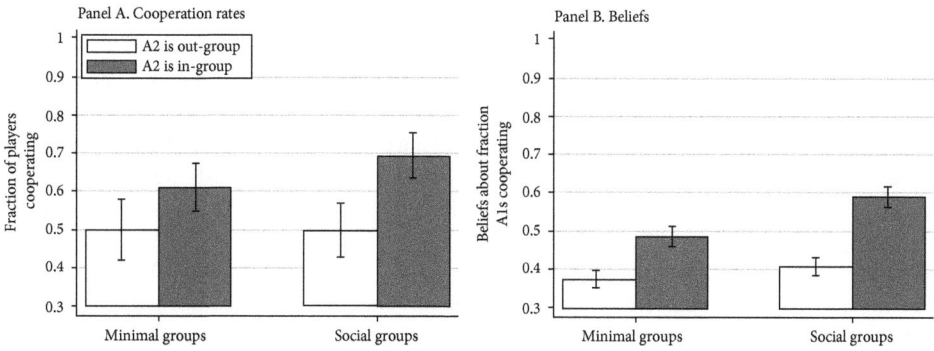

Figure 3.4 Cooperation rates and beliefs in the modified trust game. Bars represent standard errors of means.

Source: Goette et al. (2012) with permission from the American Economic Association.

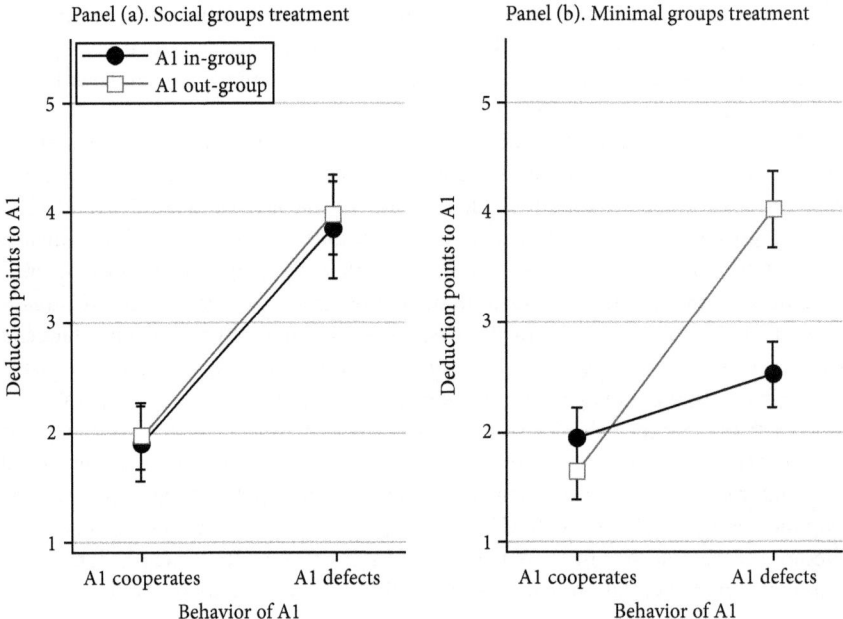

Figure 3.5 Group membership and punishment. Bars represent standard errors of means.
Source: Goette et al. (2012) with permission from the American Economic Association.

sequential game, non-cooperative behavior is punished anyway by the second mover, removing the need for group identity to sustain cooperative behavior. Guala et al. (2013) show that common knowledge of group affiliation enhances cooperation rates in a prisoner's dilemma game.

Chen and Chen (2011) consider *minimum effort games* that are considered, in detail, in Volume 4 of the book. In such games, the payoffs of players are decreasing in their own action, but increasing in the minimum action of the group. There are several possible symmetric Nash equilibria in which all players choose the same action. In the Pareto efficient Nash equilibrium, all group members choose the highest possible action. The authors show that when subjects are not primed for any identity, they choose an inefficient action. However, once individuals are primed for group identity (e.g., by undertaking group tasks), and learning is allowed, then individuals choose the efficient equilibrium.

Hargreaves Heap and Zizzo (2009) consider a trust game played by players from two groups of players. They verify the usual finding of more cooperative behavior towards ingroup members relative to outgroup members. They argue that while this clearly improves the welfare of ingroup members, it reduces the welfare of outgroup members. On net, the outcome may reduce aggregate welfare, which is a potentially negative outcome of group affiliation. What accounts for the psychological benefits from joining a group? In order to elicit the value that people place on belonging to a group, they run artificial markets in which participants can trade in their group membership for a price. The elicited prices suggest that people derive psychological benefits that exceed the material benefit of belonging to the group. When one adds these psychological benefits to the net welfare computed above, the overall social welfare of group formation is non-negative.

3.3.2 Identity and economic incentives

Identity economics is the study of identity, norms, and ideal behavior. It offers a radically different view of incentives, one that is not new to sociologists but would be to many economists. Several decades of experiments in social psychology show that it might be optimal for organizations to alter the identity of its members, so that they internalize the mission and objectives of the organization and think of themselves as *insiders* in the organization. Clearly, if this can be done successfully, then identity may substitute, perhaps partly, for the monetary costs of incentives to ensure that members work to fulfill the objectives of the organization that they work for. We draw on Akerlof and Kranton (2000, 2005, 2008) in our discussion of the relevant issues in this section.

Consider a prototype principal–agent model in which the agent can choose among two possible actions, high and low, H, L, which give rise, respectively, to the effort levels, $e_H > e_L$. The profits of the principal can either be high, π_H, or low, π_L, $\pi_H > \pi_L$. The actions of the agent induce a probability distribution over profits. Under action H, the profits π_H, π_L are equally likely, while under action L, the profit level π_L occurs with probability 1. The principal cannot observe the effort level but can condition wage payments to the agent, w, on the profit levels, π_L, π_H. For any wage–effort pair, (w,e), define

$$u(w,e) = \ln w - e. \tag{3.7}$$

We shall enrich this prototype model below.

Denote the identity of the agent by $I_c \in \mathbb{R}$, where c indexes the identity of the agent. We distinguish between two identities. In the first, the agent identifies himself as part of the group that he works with; we call this the *insider identity* or *group identity* ($c = G$). In the second, the agent considers himself to be an outsider; we call this the *outsider identity* ($c = O$). Identity $c \in \{O, G\}$ is associated with the norm of an ideal effort level, e_c. The norm of effort for insiders is likely to be higher than for outsiders, so $e_G > e_O$. Thus, it is cheaper to elicit higher effort from insiders. The utility of the agent when his identity is c, is given by

$$U(w,e;c) = u(w,e) + I_c - \mu_c |e_c - e|, \tag{3.8}$$

where u is defined in (3.7), and $\mu_c > 0$ is a scaling parameter. In standard textbook economics models, the utility of the agent is given by $u(w,e)$. By contrast, in models of identity, the agent additionally derives direct utility from his identity, I_c, and disutility from deviations of effort from the norm for the identity group (last term in (3.8)).

Since $e_G > e_O$, the principal needs to offer relatively lower wage differentials (across the two effort levels, high and low) to insiders, for eliciting high effort. In other words, when there are two effort levels, then, under an insider identity one would expect to observe flatter wage profiles. This result need not hold under more than two effort levels, because an insider identity may also induce the principal to elicit an even higher effort level. Thus, incentives and identity are complements when there are two effort levels but may become substitutes when there are more than two effort levels.

The firm may consider altering the worker's identity from an outsider to an insider if the cost of doing so is low enough. The benefits are twofold. First, the incentive cost of eliciting the same effort level is lower. Second, a lower variation in wage is preferred by the risk averse insider, reducing the incentive costs of the firm. We now consider some of these issues in a model of optimal hierarchical organizational design (Akerlof and Kranton, 2008).

Suppose that a risk-neutral principal hires an agent with the preferences given in (3.8). The principal can either hire a supervisor or not. The supervisor obtains hard evidence of action L with probability $p > 0$, but cannot obtain verifiable evidence of action H. In the event that the supervisor reports hard evidence of a low level of effort, e_L, the principal levies a fine $f > 0$ on the agent.

The presence or the absence of the supervisor alters the identity of the agent and this is borne out by evidence from social psychology experiments (Jex and Britt, 2008). In the presence of the supervisor, the agent feels as an outsider (identity $c = O$) and in the absence of the supervisor, the agent feels trusted, so he has an insider or group identity (identity $c = G$). The principal understands, correctly, the agent's identity under various regimes.

The assumptions on the ideal effort levels are as follows: (1) The ideal effort level of an outsider is $e_O = e_L$. (2) The ideal effort level of an insider is the effort level $e_G = e_M$, corresponding to some action M on the part of the agent such that $e_L < e_M < e_H$. Under action M, the probability of getting high profits, π_H, is $\frac{\theta}{2}$ and the probability of getting low profits π_L, is $1 - \frac{\theta}{2}$, where $0 \leq \theta \leq 1$. The outside option of the agent is given by $\bar{u}$.

The principal offers a profit-contingent wage to the agent, (w_H^c, w_L^c), where w_j^c is the contracted wage when the observed profit is π_j, $j = L, H$, and the identity of the agent is $c \in \{O, G\}$. Effort is non-contractible. The expected profit of the principal from inducing the high effort level, e_H, when the agent's identity is c is given by

$$\Pi(c) = \frac{1}{2}(\pi_H - w_H^c) + \frac{1}{2}(\pi_L - w_L^c).$$

The expected profit, if other effort levels are to be induced can be found analogously.

PRINCIPAL APPOINTS A SUPERVISOR (REGIME I)

When the principal appoints a supervisor (Regime I), the agent takes the identity of an outsider, so $e_O = e_L$. Suppose that the principal wishes to induce the effort e_H. The expected profit of the principal is

$$\Pi(O) = \frac{1}{2}(\pi_H - w_H^O) + \frac{1}{2}(\pi_L - w_L^O).$$

The individual rationality constraint (IR), ensures that the agent receives at least as much as the outside option.

$$\frac{1}{2}\ln w_H^O + \frac{1}{2}\ln w_L^O - e_H + I_O - \mu_O|e_L - e_H| \geq \bar{u}. \text{ (IR)}$$

The incentive compatibility constraint (IC) of the agent ensures that action H is preferred to action L. Note that the identity of the agent stays the same under both actions and depends only on the organizational structure (supervisor or no supervisor). If the agent chooses action L, the outcome π_L obtains with probability 1. An audit by the supervisor reveals, with probability p, that the agent chose L in which case the agent is fined an amount f. Hence, the IC is given by

$$\frac{1}{2}\ln w_H^O + \frac{1}{2}\ln w_L^O - e_H - \mu_O|e_L - e_H| \geq (1-p)\ln w_L^O + p\ln(w_L^O - f) - e_L. \text{ (IC)}$$

Finally, there is a limited liability constraint (LLC), which ensures that the agent's payoff after paying a fine cannot be driven below $l > 0$.

$$0 < l \leq w_L^O - f. \text{ (LLC)}$$

The IR binds in equilibrium. If not, then the principal can increase profits by reducing the incentive payments w_H^O and w_L^O. The IC also binds in equilibrium. If not then the principal can increase his profits by reducing w_H^O. The RHS of the IC is decreasing with respect to p, hence, the payoff of the agent from taking the action L is lower under better supervision. However, since the IC must bind, there are two ways of restoring the binding IC after an increase in p: Either w_H^O goes down or w_L^O goes up or a bit of both. We collect these results in the next lemma.

Lemma 3.1 *When the principal appoints a supervisor, then more effective supervision associated with a higher probability of detection, p, induces a flatter optimal wage profile (the gap between w_H^O and w_L^O is lower). This also reduces the expected cost of the incentive payment to the principal.*

THE PRINCIPAL DOES NOT APPOINT A SUPERVISOR (REGIME II)

When the principal does not appoint the supervisor (Regime II), he chooses not to monitor the agent, so the agent has an insider or group identity, $c = G$. The norm-driven ideal effort level of the agent is $e_G = e_M$. Suppose, initially, that the principal wishes to induce the high action, H. The expected profit of the principal is

$$\Pi(G) = \frac{1}{2}\left(\pi_H - w_H^G\right) + \frac{1}{2}\left(\pi_L - w_L^G\right).$$

The individual rationality constraint of the agent is

$$\frac{1}{2}\ln w_H^G + \frac{1}{2}\ln w_L^G - e_H + I_G - \mu_G |e_M - e_H| \geq \bar{u}. \text{ (IR)}$$

There are two incentive compatibility constraints, IC1 and IC2. The principal needs to ensure that the agent prefers the effort level e_H to e_M (IC1) and the effort level e_H to e_L (IC2). Recall that the probability of outcome π_H under the action e_M is $\frac{\theta}{2}$.

$$\frac{1}{2}\ln w_H^G + \frac{1}{2}\ln w_L^G - e_H - \mu_G |e_M - e_H| \geq \frac{\theta}{2}\ln w_H^G + \left(1 - \frac{\theta}{2}\right)\ln w_L^G - e_M. \text{ (IC1)}$$

$$\frac{1}{2}\ln w_H^G + \frac{1}{2}\ln w_L^G - e_H - \mu_G |e_M - e_H| \geq \ln w_L^G - e_L - \mu_G |e_M - e_L|. \text{ (IC2)}$$

As in Regime I, there is also a limited liability constraint in Regime II. Note in IC1 and IC2 that the identity of the agent stays the same under different effort levels in this regime. The lack of supervision has costs and benefits. The cost is that, ex-post, the agent is not punished for exerting a low effort level. The benefit is that with a group identity, the ideal effort level of the agent is higher, $e_M > e_L$. Since $e_L < e_M < e_H$, it follows that $|e_M - e_H| < |e_L - e_H|$, thus, the individual rationality constraint is easier to satisfy in Regime II relative to Regime I. So, the wage costs are also relatively lower in Regime II.

When might the principal not wish to induce the high effort level, e_H, in Regime II and settle for the intermediate effort, e_M? To answer this question, rewrite IC1 as follows

$$\frac{(1-\theta)}{2}\left(\ln w_H^G - \ln w_L^G\right) - (1+\mu_G)(e_H - e_M) \geq 0. \text{ (IC1)}$$

As $\theta \to 1$, it becomes prohibitively expensive to elicit the effort level, e_H; in this case one would need an extremely steep wage profile for IC1 to hold. The reason is that, as $\theta \to 1$, an agent with identity G finds that he gets only marginally higher wage payments by exerting the higher effort level, e_H, but substantially greater disutility from having to compromise on the ideal effort level, e_M. Under such identity concerns, the principal may find it optimal to induce the ideal effort level of the agent, e_M. In this case, the relevant incentive compatibility constraint, which ensures that the agent chooses the effort level e_M rather than e_L is given by IC3:

$$\frac{\theta}{2}\ln w_H^G + \left(1 - \frac{\theta}{2}\right)\ln w_L^G - e_M \geq \ln w_L^G - e_L - \mu_G |e_M - e_L|. \text{ (IC3)}$$

Or,

$$\frac{\theta}{2}\left(\ln w_H^G - \ln w_L^G\right) \geq (1 - \mu_G)(e_M - e_L). \text{ (IC3)}$$

The factors that make it easier for IC3 to hold and, hence, more likely that the principal will successfully induce e_M, are (1) $\theta \to 1$, $\mu_G \to 1$, and (2) the gap between e_M and e_L is small.[13]

---

[13] For a richer and more encompassing model of identity, see Bénabou and Tirole (2011). Benjamin et al. (2010) consider the effect of ethnic, racial, and gender identity norms on risk and time preference.

CHAPTER 4
Incentives and Other-Regarding Preferences

4.1 Introduction

Traditional economic theory extolls the virtues of incentives, typically high-powered, in models where individuals have self-regarding preferences. By contrast, real-world incentives are typically low-powered. Consider the quote from the empirical study by Lemieux et al. (2009): "in the United States only 37 percent of individuals have some kind of pay-for-performance component to their compensation and that among those who do the median magnitude of these incentives is only 3.5 percent of their base wage."

Models of *multitask agency* have already shown that high-powered incentives may be counterproductive. For instance, in the presence of high rewards on easily observed tasks, agents may put disproportionately less effort into tasks that are valuable for the principal, yet are hard to observe and reward formally. However, the experimental results show that even when agents have a single task, the optimal incentives may be low powered. This does not mean, of course, that incentives are unproductive. For instance, recall that the evidence in Chapter 1 shows that punishments (negative incentives) are efficacious in public goods games. However, the evidence from behavioral economics shows that the effect of incentives on human behavior is far more nuanced than can be accounted for by models of self-regarding preferences.

In Section 4.2, we consider the effects of other-regarding preferences on incentives in the presence of *moral hazard*. The agent's effort is either not observable or is observable but not verifiable, hence, wage contracts can be conditioned only on the observable and verifiable outcomes, such as output levels.

Section 4.2.1 considers the effect of inequity aversion on optimal wage schemes when a principal observes a noisy signal of the agent's effort level. Following Itoh (2004), consider two effort levels, two output levels, and a self-regarding principal. The agent is other-regarding (in the Fehr–Schmidt sense) and suffers inequity aversion with respect to the principal. The presence of moral hazard gives rise to rents for the worker, as in models of self-regarding preferences. However, the principal needs to offer even higher rents to an inequity averse agent to compensate for the agent's disadvantageous inequity, relative to the principal.

Suppose that there are several agents who suffer from inequity aversion with respect to each other but not with respect to the principal. Each agent works on an independent project, but inequity aversion creates interlinkages between the outcomes on the projects. In this case, the choice among alternative forms of compensation schemes such as *team incentives*, *relative performance evaluation*, and *independent contracts*, depends on the degree of advantageous and disadvantageous inequity suffered by the agents. For instance, if the advantageous inequity of the winning agent is too high, then relative performance evaluation creates higher disutility to the winning agent. Hence, to ensure satisfaction of the incentive compatibility constraint, the principal needs to offer a higher level of rents. By contrast, team incentives do not create inequality aversion, so they may be preferred to relative performance evaluation.

Inequity aversion reduces a player's utility when, relative to another player, his payoff is greater (altruism) or lower (envy). By contrast, *reciprocity* induces players to reciprocate kind actions of others by kindness and unkind actions by unkindness. Section 4.2.2 considers the implications of reciprocity for optimal contracts in a principal–agent problem with moral hazard. Ideally, one would wish to use the machinery of psychological game theory (see Volume 4 of the book) to model issues of reciprocity. This allows for the endogenous determination of beliefs about others. However, here we follow Englmaier and Leider (2012) in modeling reciprocity in a simpler, reduced-form, manner.

Suppose that the outside option of the agent is zero. If the principal leaves positive rents to the agent, the agent perceives this to be a kind action and may reciprocate by aiding the principal in increasing profits. The implications for optimal contracts under moral hazard are profound, even in this reduced-form model. For instance, it has been a puzzle why real-world contracts are so low-powered relative to the predictions of agency models of moral hazard with self-regarding preferences. In the presence of reciprocity, however, it can be shown that even a *flat wage schedule* can implement high levels of effort, provided that the principal leaves sufficiently high rents with the agent. The reason is that the reciprocity induced by these rents elicits high effort level from the agent, as in gift exchange games.

Section 4.3 considers a principal–agent problem with non-verifiable effort and other-regarding preferences of the Fehr–Schmidt form (Fehr et al., 2007). The principal is uncertain whether the preferences of the agent are self-regarding or other-regarding. In addition to the standard *incentive contract*, we consider here a *trust contract* and a *bonus contract*. In the incentive contract, the principal can invest in a costly monitoring technology that gathers hard evidence of the shirking of the agent with some probability. In the event that shirking is discovered, the principal can levy a fine. Clearly, if the detection technology is effective and the level of fines is high enough, the agent will never shirk under an incentive contract. In a trust contract and a bonus contract, by contrast, the principal foregoes investing in the monitoring technology, even when such a choice is available. This is interpreted by the agent as *kind intentions* on the part of the principal. By contrast, the offering of an incentive contract is interpreted as unkind intentions.[1] Thus, other-regarding agents behave as if they were self-regarding in the presence of incentive contracts but other-regarding in the presence of trust and bonus contracts.

In a trust contract, the principal offers a fixed, contractible, wage despite not having the ability to monitor the agent. Clearly, the success of such a contract relies on the reciprocity of agents, as in gift exchange experiments. In a bonus contract, by contrast, the principal promises a bonus at the end of the game, after having observed the outcome. If the agents believe in the principal's reciprocity, then they know that if they work hard, they will be rewarded ex-post; this is true both for self-regarding and other-regarding agents. The incentive contract is least incomplete (effort can always be enforced with high enough detection probability and fines), the trust contract is

---

[1] This is consistent with the empirical results that are reviewed below.

more incomplete (effort can never be enforced), and the bonus contract is the most incomplete (effort and the bonus level are unenforceable).

The benefit of the incentive contract is that it allows for the monitoring and punishment of shirking agents, while the cost is that such contracts cannot tap into the reciprocity of the other-regarding agents. On net, such contracts may elicit lower effort levels and output levels. The advantage of the trust and the bonus contracts is that they can tap into agents' reciprocity, but the disadvantage is that they cannot dissuade purely self-regarding agents from shirking. The eventual outcome depends on these competing trade-offs. The greater the probability that the agent is self-regarding, the more successful will an incentive contract be. The other-regarding principal suffers from disadvantageous inequity when he encounters a self-regarding agent. But if the disadvantageous inequity parameter of the principal is low, the costs of offering a trust and a bonus contract are low relative to the positive reciprocity obtained from the other-regarding agent.

The empirical evidence on contractual choice in the presence of such contractual incompleteness issues is considered in Section 4.3.3 (Fehr et al., 2007; Fehr and Schmidt, 2007). It turns out that the bonus contract is empirically the most widely chosen contractual form. The effort levels and the profits of the principal are also the highest under a bonus contract. By contrast, if the principal and the agent were purely self-regarding, the incentive contract always dominates the bonus contract.

We also examine the empirical choice of organizational forms in the presence of the classical hold-up problem between two parties (Fehr et al., 2008). The prediction of the model with self-regarding preferences is that residual control rights should be given to the party that makes the investment. Joint ownership, by contrast, is predicted to stifle investment because it creates the problem of ex-post hold-up. However, the empirical evidence shows that when given a choice, most players choose joint ownership because it is more conducive to reciprocal behavior.

In Section 4.4, we introduce the possibility of *two-sided asymmetric information* and *long-term contracts* in a principal–agent relationship (Brown et al., 2004, 2012). Our aim is to characterize the perfect Bayesian equilibrium in the model. The firm (principal) and the worker (agent) both have asymmetric information about each other's type; types can be either self-regarding or other-regarding. In a model with a finite number of periods, we allow firms to either hire workers in a spot market condition, or choose to endogenously maintain long-term relations with them.

When workers have other-regarding preferences, in the last period, they will not choose their effort opportunistically. Their inequity aversion induces an effort level higher than the minimum effort level that would be chosen by a purely self-regarding agent. Analogously, other-regarding principals will wish to offer rents in the last period. In the penultimate period, workers with self-regarding preferences may not wish to shirk because if they are revealed to be shirkers they will be fired from their job and forgo rents in the final period. One can work this logic backwards and ensure that workers get rents in equilibrium and, irrespective of their type, put in an effort level greater than the purely self-regarding one. The evidence supports the predictions of this model. One observes the endogenous formation of long-term relations. Effort levels, profits, and rents are higher in long-term relations, relative to spot-market or short-term relations. The formation of social ties in the relation induces even greater cooperation in long-term relations (Van Dijk et al. 2002).

Section 4.4.4 addresses the ambitious question of why firms exist. Or, under what conditions will an employer choose an *employment contract* over a *sales contract*? An employment contract gives greater ex-post flexibility to the employer, but also opens up the possibility that the employer may exercise his residual control rights in a manner that is disadvantageous to the employee. By contrast, a sales contract prevents the possibility of ex-post abuse of the contract by the employer but suffers from the absence of the ex-post flexibility of an employment contract. It turns out that the presence of other-regarding preferences and long-term endogenous contracts play a key role in identifying a new set of transaction costs that explain the existence of vertical integration (Bartling et al., 2013). We shall consider the relevant theoretical framework, but particularly the empirical evidence, in some detail.

In contract theories with self-regarding preferences, cleverly designed incentives typically have a positive impact on effort, output, and profits. However, it is well known that even with self-regarding preferences, incentives may not always have the desired effects. First, incentives can be conditioned only on a limited number of variables that may be observable and verifiable, such as revenues or output. Second, under *multi-task agency*, where the agent simultaneously chooses effort levels on several distinct tasks, which are observed with error, incentives for more easily observable and verifiable tasks may shift attention away from other, valuable, but less-well observed tasks (Holmstrom and Milgrom, 1991). Third, when tournaments among workers are organized, they might sabotage each other or not cooperate with each other. A large amount of experimental and field evidence now demonstrates the presence of other-regarding preferences in worker–firm relations.[2] This creates further issues with the use of incentives in principal–agent problems.

An emerging literature explores the effectiveness of incentives, not only by using other-regarding preferences, but also by invoking additional features such as identity, reputational concerns, asymmetric information, self-signaling, and social signaling motives for one's actions.[3] For instance, anonymous donations are rare, yet are considered to be very commendable, and boasting of one's charitable donations is looked down upon. Clearly, models that incorporate social signaling of one's intentions are a promising candidate to explain such phenomena. Models that explain monetary charitable giving as a signal of one's wealth cannot sometimes explain in-kind donations such as volunteering for social causes and donating blood. In taking such actions, the individual could be self-signaling respectable human qualities such as altruism or kindness.

In Section 4.5, we consider theoretical models of *intrinsic* and *extrinsic* motivation. Extrinsic motivation refers to human endeavor that arises purely as a response to external material incentives. Any remaining motivation that is independent of incentives offered by another party, is intrinsic. Section 4.5.1 considers first a principal–agent framework in which the agent has asymmetric information about the cost of the project (Bénabou and Tirole, 2003). The agent observes a private signal of the cost and the level of bonus offered by an informed principal. We show that in a perfect Bayesian equilibrium of the model, a higher bonus offered by the principal conveys bad news to the agent about the cost. Hence, incentives may deter the effort of the agent. These models can potentially explain actions in situations where one party to a formal or informal contract has private information (child rearing, education, monitoring of employees).

One needs a different theoretical framework to explain *prosocial decisions* such as blood donations, charitable giving, and voting (Bénabou and Tirole, 2006). In this case, incentives may signal to others that the individual's motivation is not intrinsic. Examples of such incentives include direct incentives for blood donations and tax-exempt charitable donations. Hence, there is likely to be a trade-off from the use of incentives. Incentives may activate extrinsic motivation but reduce the potential of individual actions to signal to themselves and others, their intrinsic

---

[2] See, for instance, Fehr et al. (1997), Fehr and Schmidt (1999), Fehr and Gächter (2000), Bandiera et al. (2005), Falk et al. (2005), Fehr et al. (2007), DellaVigna (2009), Sloof and Sonnemans (2011).
[3] See Bénabou and Tirole (2003, 2006, 2011) for an extensive discussion of these issues.

motivation. These theoretical models do not, however, address the question of whether they can explain the experimental evidence from the dictator, ultimatum, trust, and public goods games.[4]

Section 4.6 considers the empirical evidence on extrinsic and intrinsic motivation. Section 4.6.1 shows that incentives may signal a *hostile intent*. In gift exchange games, the effort level is higher when no incentives are used, relative to negative incentives (fines) and positive incentives (bonuses). Within the two incentive treatments, effort levels are higher under positive, as compared to negative incentives (Fehr and Gächter, 2001). In trust games, when a fine is available but not used, it produces the highest level of trustworthiness (Fehr and Rockenbach, 2003).

Section 4.6.2 shows that incentives may conflict with the desire of agents for *autonomy* and *independence* (Deci and Ryan, 1985; Deci et al., 1999). In trust games, when the trustor announces a target back-transfer from the trustee, the degree of trustworthiness falls (Falk and Kosfeld, 2006). Relatively high monetary incentives can arouse the agent excessively and the agent may be distracted by the high reward. It is possible that under these conditions, the agent *chokes* and produces a lower level of performance, as, for instance, in a penalty kick taken in a high pressure football game (Ariely et al., 2009a).

When employers are given an opportunity to screen the past history of the workers, relative to a base treatment where such screening is not allowed, one observes important implications for contract choice (Bartling et al., 2012). Employees who develop good reputations by putting in high effort levels in the past are rewarded with good jobs that have high wages and are subject to low levels of control. On the other hand, employees who do not develop such reputations are offered bad jobs (low wages, high control, and low surplus). The possibility of screening spurs workers to work harder in order to build a reputation. Even self-regarding workers mimic other-regarding workers to partake in this reputation building exercise in order to increase their payoffs.

Section 4.6.3 considers the possibility that economic agents may *switch off their ethicality* in the presence of incentives; a phenomenon that psychologists refer to as *moral disengagement*. The moral frame of the dictator game can be changed if it is framed as an exchange game, leading to lower transfers from the dictator (Hoffman et al., 2008). Similarly, when a *competitive environment* is introduced in ultimatum games, proposers make lower offers (Schotter et al., 1996). In field studies of common property resources, regulation produces less cooperative outcomes as compared to communal cooperative efforts (Cardenas et al., 2000).

Fines on parents for arriving late in day care centers in Haifa induced parents to arrive even later. In the absence of fines, a reciprocity relation between carers and parents ensured that they did not arrive as late (Gneezy and Rustichini, 2000a). When students were primed to collect money for a good cause, but not given incentives, they produced greater collections, relative to low incentives. Higher incentives increased collections relative to low incentives, but not relative to the case of no incentives and priming for a good cause (Gneezy and Rustichini, 2000b).

Section 4.6.4 shows that incentives may reduce the ability of people to signal their human virtues, hence reducing prosocial behavior. Titmuss (1971) argued that blood donations are likely to be higher on a voluntary basis as compared to incentivized blood donations. Swedish data on blood donations showed that while there is no crowding-out effect of incentives for men, there is a statistically significant crowding-out effect for women (Mellström and Johannesson, 2008). However, the emerging evidence points to an even more nuanced set of effects. Non-monetary

---

[4] But also see Benabou and Tirole (2011), whose motivation is to explain experimental evidence that may be anomalous for some of the models of social preferences, such as reluctant altruism in dictator games.

incentives may actually improve blood donations (Lacetera et al., 2012; Goette and Stutzer, 2008). In contrast, several studies find no effect of incentives on blood donations (Reich et al., 2006; Goette et al., 2010).

Monetary incentives given to high school students, preparing for their Bagrut certification in Israel, are ineffective for boys but effective for girls whose predicted grades are higher than the average (Angrist and Lavy, 2009). When charitable donations are publicly observed, then incentives reduce the signaling value of such donations, reducing the level of donations (Ariely et al., 2009b).

Section 4.6.5 considers the effect of the economic environment. For instance, the legal environment and the strength of law enforcement has an effect on the trustworthiness of agents in a principal–agent relation (Bohnet et al., 2001). *Moral suasion* may be effective in inducing contributions in public goods games, while regulation to contribute a certain minimum level may have a long-run detrimental effect (Reeson and Tisdell, 2008). Bicycle couriers who receive performance-related pay are likely to cooperate less in sequential prisoner's dilemma games. By contrast, those on a fixed hourly wage or members of cooperatives are more likely to cooperate (Burks et al., 2009). This also contributes towards establishing the external validity of lab experiments.

Section 4.6.6 considers situations in which there is synergy between incentives and prosocial behavior. Punishments in public goods games are less likely to be *antisocial punishments* (non-contributors punishing contributors) when punishments for non-cooperation elicit shame and guilt (Herrmann et al. 2008; Carpenter et al., 2009). When sanctions are imposed in public goods games to punish non-contributors, based on a referendum among players (rather than individual sanctions), they are likely to be more effective. Such sanctions are also more likely to elicit feelings of shame and guilt (Tyran and Feld, 2006).

No significant link is found between intrinsic motivation and incentives in a field study conducted in US schools. However, while incentives for output (final grades) are ineffective, incentives for inputs, e.g., attendance and good behavior, are more effective (Fryer, 2011). The effects of short-term educational incentives are likely to be gender specific and age specific. Further, when incentives are given with delay they are less effective (Levitt et al., 2012). Incentives to exercise over a long term are more effective than short-term incentives (Charness and Gneezy, 2009).

4.2 Moral hazard and other-regarding preferences

In this section, we consider a traditional principal–agent framework in which there is moral hazard and only the agent has other-regarding preferences. We will, in turn, consider the effects of *inequity aversion* (Section 4.2.1) and *reciprocity* (Section 4.2.2) on optimal contracts. Here we restrict attention only to state-contingent wage contracts. The subsequent sections will consider a richer range of contracts such as trust and bonus contracts, as well as issues of asymmetric information.

4.2.1 Inequity aversion and moral hazard

Consider the following simple model, due to Itoh (2004), using the standard moral-hazard framework, that should be familiar to undergraduate students in economics. A risk-neutral principal hires a risk-neutral agent to engage in a project that has two possible observable and verifiable outcomes (outputs), $0 \leq y_L < y_H$. The agent can choose one of two unobservable (or observable but non-verifiable) actions $a_0 < a_1$. The cost of the actions is given by $c(a_i)$, $i = 0, 1$. Action a_i results in the outcome y_H with probability p_i, and $p_1 > p_0$. Thus, the higher action induces a higher probability of the higher outcome. The reservation utility of the agent is normalized to zero.

A contract (w_L, w_H) specifies a wage $w_j \geq 0$, $j = L, H$, contingent on the only observable and verifiable outcome, i.e., y_j. The constraint $w_j \geq 0$ reflects *limited liability*. We rule out renegotiation of contracts.

The principal has self-regarding preferences and his profit is given by

$$\pi_j = y_j - w_j, j = L, H. \tag{4.1}$$

The agent has other-regarding preferences with respect to the payoffs of the principal. His utility function is of the Fehr–Schmidt form and is given by

$$u(w_j, \pi_j, a_i) = \begin{cases} w_j - c(a_i) - \alpha \gamma v(w_j - \pi_j) & \text{if } w_j \geq \pi_j \\ w_j - c(a_i) - \alpha v(\pi_j - w_j) & \text{if } w_j \leq \pi_j \end{cases}; j = L, H, i = 0, 1, \tag{4.2}$$

where $\alpha > 0$, $|\gamma| < 1$, and v is an increasing function. Typical, under Fehr–Schmidt preferences, $\beta = \alpha \gamma$ (see (2.1)). If $\gamma > 0$, then the agent suffers from advantageous inequity. But if $\gamma < 0$, then the agent derives satisfaction or pride in coming out ahead; see also the discussion on these issues in Section 2.4. When $w_j = \pi_j$, we have $u(w_j, \pi_j, a_i) = w_j - c(a_i)$, so there are no inequity concerns. Notice that in (4.2), the disutility of effort does not enter into the comparison of the agent's payoff with the principal's payoff; this assumption can be relaxed.

For pedagogical reasons, we make the following two simplifying assumptions.

A1. The principal always wishes to induce the higher action, a_1, from the agent (possibly because y_H is high enough).

A2. The second assumption involves the following relatively innocuous normalization

$$c(a_0) = 0, c(a_1) = c > 0, y_L = 0. \tag{4.3}$$

Let us first consider the textbook case of self-regarding preferences ($\alpha = 0$). The results are summarized in the next proposition.

Proposition 4.1 *Suppose that the agent has self-regarding preferences ($\alpha = 0$).*

(i) *Let the action of the agent be observable and verifiable. Any combination (w_L, w_H) such that $w_L + p_1 (w_H - w_L) = c$, is able to implement the first best contract.*

(ii) *Under moral hazard, the first best contract does not satisfy the incentive compatibility conditions of the agent.*

(iii) *Under moral hazard, the unique optimal second best contract specifies $w_L = 0$ and $w_H = \frac{c}{p_1 - p_0}$.*

(iv) *The outside option of the agent gives a payoff of zero, yet the agent earns positive rents in the second best contract.*

Proof: Define the following first differences.

$$\Delta w = w_H - w_L, \Delta p = p_1 - p_0. \tag{4.4}$$

The expected utility of the agent from the contract (w_L, w_H), when the agent puts in effort a_1 is $(1 − p_1)w_L + p_1 w_H − c$; this can be written as $w_L + p_1 \Delta w − c$. The incentive compatibility (IC) constraint and the individual rationality (IR) constraint are given by

$$\begin{cases} IC: & w_L + p_1 \Delta w − c \geq w_L + p_0 \Delta w \\ IR: & w_L + p_1 \Delta w − c \geq 0 \end{cases}.$$

Using the notation in (4.4) the IC and IR constraints can be written compactly as

$$\begin{cases} IC: & \Delta p \, \Delta w \geq c \\ IR: & w_L + p_1 \Delta w \geq c \end{cases}.$$

(i) If the action of the agent is observable and verifiable, then the only relevant constraint for the principal is the IR constraint. The principal can directly specify an action and implement it. Leaving any rents to the agent, beyond the agent's outside option of zero, reduces the principal's profits, hence, the IR constraint binds. Thus, any combination (w_L, w_H) such that $w_L + p_1 (w_H − w_L) = c$, is able to implement the first best contract.

(ii) From (4.3), $y_L = 0$, hence, we pick the first best contract $(w_L, w_H) = \left(0, \frac{c}{p_1}\right)$ such that the IR constraint binds. Substitute into the LHS of the IC constraint, we get $\Delta p \, \Delta w = \Delta p w_H = c \left(1 − \frac{p_0}{p_1}\right) < c$, which violates the IC constraint.

(iii) Under moral hazard, the principal maximizes expected profits $p_1 y_H − w_L − p_1 \Delta w$, or minimizes expected cost, $EC = w_L + p_1 \Delta w$, subject to the IC, IR, and the limited liability constraints. Both IC and IR constraints cannot bind at the same time. For instance, using $(w_L, w_H) = \left(0, \frac{c}{p_1}\right)$, if the IR constraint binds, we get the contradiction in part (ii). In particular, the agent must get some rents under moral hazard from taking the higher action a_1. Thus, the IR constraint does not bind. The IC constraint must bind in equilibrium. If not, then the principal can reduce w_L, w_H by a small amount $\varepsilon > 0$. This does not alter the IC and for a sufficiently small ε, the IR constraint continues to hold. However, the principal's expected costs are reduced. Thus, IC must bind, so, $\Delta p (w_H − w_L) = c$. Thus, the principal's expected cost is $EC = w_L + c \frac{p_1}{\Delta p}$, which is minimized by choosing $w_L = 0$ and choosing $w_H = \frac{c}{\Delta p}$. Thus, the optimal contract under moral hazard specifies $(w_L, w_H) = \left(0, \frac{c}{\Delta p}\right)$.

(iv) Substituting the optimal wage contract in (iii) into the LHS of the IR constraint, we get $c \frac{p_0}{\Delta p} > c$. Thus, the agent gets strictly positive rents under the optimal contract. ∎

Let us now consider the optimal contract when the agent has other-regarding preferences $(\alpha > 0)$. We restrict attention to optimal contracts where $w_L = 0$. This restricts the class of optimal contracts, but under certain conditions it is without loss of generality.[5]

Using (4.1), (4.2) the assumptions in (4.3) imply that when $j = L$ we have $w_L = \pi_L = 0$. So, in this case, there are no inequity aversion issues to consider. Thus, inequity aversion has bite only when $j = H$. Using (4.1),

---

[5] See Itoh (2004) for the conditions under which such a contract is optimal. For instance, if there is a limited liability condition on the principal, then there is no loss in generality in assuming $w_L = 0$ because no output is produced in this state of the world (from (4.3), $y_L = 0$).

$$w_H \geq \pi_H \Leftrightarrow w_H \geq \frac{y_H}{2} \text{ and } w_H \leq \pi_H \Leftrightarrow w_H \leq \frac{y_H}{2}. \quad (4.5)$$

The incentive compatibility (IC) condition of the agent requires that the agent prefers the high action, a_1, over the low action, a_0. Using (4.2) we know that there are two cases to consider: $w_H \geq \pi_H$ ($\Leftrightarrow w_H \geq \frac{y_H}{2}$) and $w_H \leq \pi_H$ ($\Leftrightarrow w_H \leq \frac{y_H}{2}$). Using (4.1), (4.2), (4.3), (4.5), when $w_H \geq \frac{y_H}{2}$, the IC condition of the agent requires that

$$p_1 \left(w_H - c - \alpha\gamma v(2w_H - y_H)\right) + (1-p_1)(0 - c - 0) \geq$$
$$p_0 \left(w_H - \alpha\gamma v(2w_H - y_H)\right) + (1-p_0) \times 0. \quad (4.6)$$

When $w_H \leq \frac{y_H}{2}$, the IC condition requires that

$$p_1 \left(w_H - c - \alpha v(y_H - 2w_H)\right) + (1-p_1)(0 - c - 0) \geq$$
$$p_0 \left(w_H - \alpha v(y_H - 2w_H)\right) + (1-p_0) \times 0. \quad (4.7)$$

Simplifying (4.6), (4.7) we can write the incentive compatibility condition as

$$\begin{cases} w_H - \alpha\gamma v(2w_H - y_H) \geq \frac{c}{p_1 - p_0} & \text{if } w_H \geq \frac{y_H}{2} \quad (IC^+) \\ w_H - \alpha v(y_H - 2w_H) \geq \frac{c}{p_1 - p_0} & \text{if } w_H \leq \frac{y_H}{2} \quad (IC^-) \end{cases}. \quad (4.8)$$

We have denoted the incentive compatibility conditions in the advantageous inequity and the disadvantageous inequity cases, respectively, by IC^+ and IC^-. Given the evidence on ultimatum games, where proposers typically do not offer more than half the share of the pie, we focus here on the case represented by IC^-. The optimal contract in this case, when the agent has other-regarding preferences, is described in the next proposition; readers interested in exploring the implications of the case IC^+, may do so as an exercise.

Proposition 4.2 Suppose that $\frac{y_H}{2} \geq \frac{c}{\Delta p}$, where Δp is defined in (4.4).
(i) In the optimal second best contract, $w_L = 0$ and w_H satisfies

$$w_H - \alpha v(y_H - 2w_H) = \frac{c}{\Delta p}.$$

(ii) The expected payment made by the principal in the optimal contract is increasing in α, and strictly increasing in α if $\frac{y_H}{2} > \frac{c}{\Delta p}$.
(iii) In the optimal second best contract, the agent earns positive rents.

Proof: (i) Since we are interested only in the case described by IC^-, let us find the set of values of w_H for which IC^- holds. For $w_H = \frac{y_H}{2}$, IC^- implies that $w_H = \frac{y_H}{2} \geq \frac{c}{\Delta p}$, which is also the assumed condition in the Proposition. The LHS of IC^- is increasing in w_H, so let us find the minimum value of $w_H = \widehat{w}_H$ for which IC^- holds; this value is given by the solution to

$$\widehat{w}_H - \alpha v(y_H - 2\widehat{w}_H) = \frac{c}{\Delta p}. \quad (4.9)$$

Thus, the set of contracts for which IC^- holds is given by the interval $w_H \in \left[\widehat{w}_H, \frac{y_H}{2}\right]$, where $\frac{y_H}{2} \geq \frac{c}{\Delta p}$; the higher the output in the good state of the world, the wider is the interval of incentive compatible contracts. It is now sufficient to show that $\widehat{w}_H$ satisfies the individual rationality constraint of the agent, IR, when the principal wishes to induce the high action, a_1. The relevant IR is given by

$$\widehat{w}_H - \alpha v(y_H - 2\widehat{w}_H) \geq \frac{c}{p_1}. \tag{4.10}$$

Using (4.9), we can rewrite (4.10) as $\frac{c}{\Delta p} > \frac{c}{p_1}$, which is true, hence, IR is satisfied (by assumption, the optimal $w_L = 0$).

(ii) The minimum expected payment of the principal is $p_1 \widehat{w}_H$. It suffices to show that $\widehat{w}_H$ is increasing in α. Differentiating the LHS of (4.9) with respect to α we get $\frac{\partial LHS}{\partial \alpha} = -v(y_H - 2\widehat{w}_H)$, which is strictly negative if $y_H > 2\widehat{w}_H$, thus, the optimal level of $\widehat{w}_H$ must increase to compensate for the fall in the LHS, in order to restore the equality in (4.9). If $\frac{y_H}{2} = \frac{c}{\Delta p}$, then we get the case $\widehat{w}_H = \frac{y_H}{2} = \frac{c}{\Delta p}$, but then $\widehat{w}_H$ is independent of α and $\frac{\partial LHS}{\partial \alpha} = 0$.

(iii) From the last sentence of the proof to (i), $\frac{c}{\Delta p} > \frac{c}{p_1}$, thus, the IR holds with a strict inequality and the agent earns positive rents. ∎

Comparing Propositions 4.1, 4.2, the agent earns rents in the optimal contract when effort is unobservable, irrespective of whether he has self-regarding or other-regarding preferences. From Proposition 4.2(ii), the other-regarding preferences of the agent reduces the material payoff of the principal. The reason is that when the realized output is y_L, there are no equity comparisons. However, when the realized output is y_H, the agent suffers from disadvantageous inequity if the wage in that state, w_H, is low. In order to ensure that the IC constraint of the agent binds in that state, the principal ends up offering a higher wage, and reducing his own profits.

In the presence of multiple agents, it may be that the reference group of the agent is not the principal, but rather the other agents. Consider two agents and to each of the agents, the principal offers an independent project (we rule out joint production). Each project has the same technology as in the case of the single agent. Thus, each agent exerts two possible levels of effort, $a_0 < a_1$, and there are two possible probabilistic outcomes for each agent, $0 \leq y_L < y_H$. The higher outcome is more likely for each agent under higher effort, i.e., $p_1 > p_0$. It is possible in this case that $\gamma < 0$, i.e., agents derive greater utility by coming out ahead of the other agent. Let w_{jk}^n be the wage offered to agent $n = 1,2$ if the outcome of that agent's project is y_j and the outcome of the other agent is y_k such that $j,k = L,H$. For pedagogical simplicity we make the following assumption.

A3. The agents are symmetric in the sense that they have identical α, γ. The function v is also identical for both agents and is given by $v(x) = x$. The reference group for each agent is the other agent. As in the case of a single agent, we restrict attention to the case in which if an agent gets a low outcome y_L, then his wage is zero, i.e., $w_{LL}^n = w_{LH}^n = 0$ for $n = 1,2$.[6] The optimal contract is symmetric, so $w_{jk}^1 = w_{jk}^2 = w_{jk}, j,k = L,H$.[7] The objective of the principal is to minimize the expected payment across both agents.

Remark 4.1 *An immediate implication of assumption A3 is that it suffices to find the optimal values of only w_{HH} and w_{HL}.*

---

[6] Itoh (2004) shows that this restriction is without loss in generality.
[7] To be sure, w_{jk}^1 is the wage paid to agent 1 when his output is y_j and the output of agent 2 is y_k. Analogously, w_{jk}^2 is the wage paid to agent 2 when his output is y_j and the output of agent 1 is y_k.

Assume now that assumptions A1, A2, and A3 hold. From assumption A1, the principal wishes to implement the high action from both agents.

The action a_1, by each of the agents can result in four possible pairs of outcomes (y_H, y_H), (y_H, y_L), (y_L, y_H), and (y_L, y_L). These outcomes correspond to the respective pairs of wages (w_{HH}^1, w_{HH}^2), (w_{HL}^1, w_{LH}^2), (w_{LH}^1, w_{HL}^2), (w_{LL}^1, w_{LL}^2) that occur with the respective probabilities p_1^2, $p_1(1-p_1)$, $(1-p_1)p_1$, and $(1-p_1)^2$; denote by W the set of all wage pairs.

Suppose that we get the outcome pair (y_j, y_k), so that the corresponding tuple of wages is (w_{jk}^1, w_{kj}^2). In this state, the utility of agent 1 from action a_1 is

$$u(w_{jk}^1, w_{kj}^2, a_1) = \begin{cases} w_{jk}^1 - c - \alpha\gamma(w_{jk}^1 - w_{kj}^2) & \text{if } w_{jk}^1 \geq w_{kj}^2 \\ w_{jk}^1 - c - \alpha(w_{kj}^2 - w_{jk}^1) & \text{if } w_{jk}^1 \leq w_{kj}^2 \end{cases}. \quad (4.11)$$

The utility of agent 2 can be written analogously. From assumption A3, the contracts are symmetric, hence, we can dispense with superscripts for players. Using (4.11), we can write the expected utility of any agent from the action, a_i, $i = 0, 1$,

$$Eu(W, a_i) = p_i^2(w_{HH} - c(a_i)) + p_i(1-p_i)[w_{HL} - c(a_i) - \alpha\gamma w_{HL}] \\ + (1-p_i)p_i[-c(a_i) - \alpha w_{HL}] - c(a_i)(1-p_i)^2. \quad (4.12)$$

From any agent's perspective, the first and the last terms correspond to the outcomes (w_{HH}, w_{HH}) and (w_{LL}, w_{LL}) that occur with respective probabilities p_i^2 and $(1-p_i)^2$. In each of these states, there are no equity concerns, and by assumption, $w_{LL} = 0$. The middle two terms correspond to the outcomes (w_{HL}, w_{LH}) and (w_{LH}, w_{HL}) that occur with respective probabilities $p_i(1-p_i)$ and $(1-p_i)p_i$. In each case, inequity concerns are important (see (4.11)) and we have assumed that $w_{LH} = 0$. Simplifying (4.12) we get

$$Eu(W, a_i) = p_i[p_i w_{HH} + (1-p_i) w_{HL} - (1-p_i)\alpha w_{HL}(1+\gamma)] - c(a_i). \quad (4.13)$$

Since we would like to implement the high action, a_1, thus, it follows that the individual rationality constraint of any agent is $Eu(W, a_1) \geq 0$, or

$$p_i[p_i w_{HH} + (1-p_i) w_{HL} - (1-p_i)\alpha w_{HL}(1+\gamma)] - c(a_i) \geq 0. \text{ (IR)} \quad (4.14)$$

Using (4.3) and (4.13), the incentive compatibility constraint is $Eu(W, a_1) \geq Eu(W, a_0)$, or

$$p_1 w_{HH} + (1-p_1) w_{HL} + \alpha w_{HL}[p_1 - 1 - (1-p_1)\gamma] \geq \frac{c}{p_1 - p_0}. \text{ (IC)} \quad (4.15)$$

From Remark 4.1, the objective of the principal is to choose w_{HH} and w_{HL} in order to minimize his expected cost

$$2p_1(w_{HL} + p_1(w_{HH} - w_{HL})),$$

subject to the IR and the IC of the agents in (4.14) and (4.15).

We introduce some useful terminology about the kinds of contracts that can be offered.

Definition 4.1 In a "team contract," both agents receive a higher wage if their projects simultaneously succeed relative to the case where at least one project fails, i.e., $w_{HH} > w_{HL}$. In a "relative performance contract," if one project fails and the other succeeds, the successful agent gets a higher wage relative to the case where both projects succeed, i.e., $w_{HH} < w_{HL}$. In an "independent contract," $w_{HH} = w_{HL}$, thus, the success or failure of the project of one agent is irrelevant for the wage of the other agent.

As one may expect, under self-regarding preferences, the independent contract is optimal because the problems of both agents are completely de-coupled; the proof is left for the reader.

Proposition 4.3 Under self-regarding preferences ($\alpha = 0$), the optimal contract offered by the principal is non-unique. Any pair (w_{HL}, w_{HH}) that satisfies $p_1 w_{HH} + (1-p_1) w_{HL} = \frac{c}{(p_1-p_0)}$ is optimal. In particular, the independent contract in which $w_{HH} = w_{HL} = \frac{c}{p_1-p_0}$ is also optimal.

The optimal contract under other-regarding preferences is described next; the proof is left for the reader. The intuition behind the result is provided below.

Proposition 4.4 Under other-regarding preferences ($\alpha > 0$), the optimal contract offered by the principal depends on the parameters of the model in the following manner.

(i) If $\gamma > \frac{p_1}{1-p_1}$, then the optimal contract is an extreme "team contract"

$$w_{HL} = 0 \text{ and } w_{HH} = \frac{c}{p_1(p_1-p_0)}.$$

The expected payment of the principal is independent of α and γ.

(ii) Let $\gamma < \frac{p_1}{1-p_1}$ and $\gamma \leq \frac{1}{\alpha} - \frac{L_H}{L_L}$, where $L_H = \frac{p_1}{p_0}$ and $L_L = \frac{1-p_1}{1-p_0}$ are the likelihood ratios of getting the high and the low outcomes under, respectively, the high and the low actions. Then, the optimal contract is an extreme "relative performance evaluation contract,"

$$w_{HH} = 0 \text{ and } w_{HL} = \frac{c}{(p_1-p_0)(1-p_1)} \frac{1}{+\alpha[p_1-\gamma(1-p_1)]}.$$

The expected payment of the principal is decreasing in α and increasing in γ.

(iii) If $\gamma < \frac{p_1}{1-p_1}$ and $\gamma > \frac{1}{\alpha} - \frac{L_H}{L_L}$, then

$$w_{HL} = \frac{c}{(p_1-p_0)} \frac{1}{\alpha L_H} \text{ and } w_{HH} = \frac{c}{(p_1-p_0)} \frac{1-p_1}{p_1 L_H}\left(\frac{L_H}{L_L} - \frac{1-\alpha\gamma}{\alpha}\right),$$

and the expected payment from the principal to the agents is increasing in γ, but is independent of α.

We now discuss the results in Proposition 4.4. Inequity averse agents are motivated by two considerations that do not influence agents with self-regarding preferences. Such agents dislike being behind, as reflected in the size of α, and dislike being ahead if $\gamma > 0$, as reflected in the size of $\alpha\gamma$ (which equals β in the Fehr–Schmidt model). Agents are behind when their action leads to the output y_L, while the other agent's action leads to the output y_H. Agents are ahead in the converse case. The outcome depends on which of these two influences dominate.

For instance, in Proposition 4.4(i), when γ is large (or $\frac{p_1}{1-p_1}$ is small), then agents derive an even larger disutility from being ahead. Thus, when an agent produces y_H and the other agent produces y_L, his wage is $w_{HL} = 0$. An extreme form of team incentives is preferred to relative performance incentives in this case by paying a positive wage only if both agents are successful in producing y_H. Since there is no inequity in equilibrium, the payments of the principal are independent of α and γ. Thus, extreme team incentives ensure that agents never get left behind each other (provided they both put in the high effort level, a_1).

In Proposition 4.4(ii), we have the opposite case when γ is small. An extreme example of this case arises when $\gamma < 0$, i.e., an agent derives pride from coming out ahead. In this case, the inequity cost to the agent from being ahead is small (or negative if $\gamma < 0$), so, the opposite of team incentives, relative performance evaluation, is efficient.[8] However, in this case, since positive wages are paid to one of the agents only when that agent produces a high output and the other a low output, issues of inequity aversion will be central to the satisfaction of the incentive compatibility conditions. Hence, the expected payment of the principal does depend on α and γ (and it is increasing in γ, as suggested by the intuition, above).

In general, the inequity aversion of the agents makes the individual rationality constraint of the agents most costly for the principal to satisfy if $\alpha(1 + \gamma) > 1$ (see (4.14)), resulting in larger wage payments relative to the self-regarding case. When $p_1 \to 1$, the signal (i.e., the realized output) is increasingly informative of the agent's effort. Both conditions, $\gamma < \frac{p_1}{1-p_1}$ and $\gamma \geq \frac{1}{\alpha} - \frac{L_H}{L_L}$, are likely to hold, so we have the case in Proposition 4.4(iii). In this case, a contract that is intermediate between an extreme team incentive contract and an extreme relative performance evaluation contract is offered. Each agent is offered a positive wage whenever his project does not fail. Comparing Propositions 4.3, 4.4, the optimal contract under self-regarding preference is non-unique but the introduction of even a small amount of other-regarding preferences ($\alpha > 0$) gives rise to a unique contract.[9]

Rey-Biel (2008) also considers inequity aversion in a situation where a principal hires two agents. The agents are inequity averse towards each other but not towards the principal. The main difference from the model in Itoh (2004) is that there is *joint production* of a single good between the two agents and there is no uncertainty. Hence, the outcome provides a noiseless signal of the effort levels of the agents. The principal who has self-regarding preferences exploits the inequity aversion of the two agents in designing the optimal wage contracts in the following manner.

The optimal wage levels are high and equal when both agents work hard (and a high output level is produced), thus, there is minimal inequity aversion. However, when the outcome signals with certainty that one of the agents has not worked hard but the other has, then the wage levels are used to deliberately create high inequality among the agents. Since the agents dislike inequality, it is easier for their incentive compatibility conditions to be satisfied in the presence of inequity aversion. Relative to purely self-regarding agents, the principal is able to induce a higher effort level at a lower wage cost when agents are inequity averse.

4.2.2 Reciprocity and moral hazard

Having considered the effects of *inequity aversion* in the presence of moral hazard, we now consider the influence of *reciprocity*. We follow the model of Englmaier and Leider (2012) but restrict attention to two actions, two outcomes, a risk-neutral principal and a risk averse

---

[8] Further issues of the optimality of relative performance evaluation under inequity averse agents are explored in Bartling (2011).
[9] For a consideration of issues similar to Itoh (2004) see Bartling and von Siemens (2010) and, in a continuous outcome framework, Englmaier and Wambach (2010).

agent. The rigorous modeling of these issues requires the use of psychological game theory; see Volume 4 of the book. By contrast, Englmaier and Leider (2012) take a simpler, direct, and reduced-form approach.

The model is similar to that in Section 4.2.1. The agent chooses among two unobservable actions $a_0 < a_1$. The cost of action $i = 0, 1$ is c_i. Each action probabilistically determines one of two observable output levels, $0 \leq y_L < y_H$. Action a_i results in the outcome y_H with probability p_i such that $p_1 > p_0$. The utility function of the agent, defined over material rewards, u, is increasing and concave (we did not invoke risk aversion in Section 4.2.1). The outside option of the agent is zero. The *monotone likelihood ratio property* (MLRP) holds, i.e., $\frac{p_1}{p_0} > \frac{1-p_1}{1-p_0}$, so the relative probability of getting a higher signal under a higher action is greater.

A contract specifies, for $j = L, H$, a triple (w_L, w_H, a), where $w_j \geq 0$ is the wage if the realization of output is y_j and $a \in \{a_0, a_1\}$ is the *non-contractible, desired level of effort*. The agent has limited liability ($w_j \geq 0$) and there is no renegotiation of contracts. We assume that the principal always wishes to induce the higher action, a_1. Thus, we wish to focus attention on contracts of the form (w_L, w_H, a_1) in which the principal optimally chooses w_L, w_H. Let $u_H = u(w_H)$ and $u_L = u(w_L)$ and define the following

$$\bar{u}(a_i) = p_i u_H + (1 - p_i) u_L - c_i, \quad \bar{\pi}(a_i) = p_i y_H + (1 - p_i) y_L, \qquad (4.16)$$

where $\bar{u}(a_i)$ and $\bar{\pi}(a_i)$ are, respectively, the expected utility of the agent (net of effort costs) and the expected output of the principal when the agent chooses the action a_i, $i = 0, 1$. Conditional on any level of expected wage, the expected output, $\bar{\pi}$, is directly proportional to the principal's expected profit. Thus, when considering the effort choice of the agent, it is pedagogically convenient to refer to $\bar{\pi}$ as the expected profit of the principal. Define the following first differences

$$\Delta c = c_1 - c_0, \quad \Delta \bar{\pi} = \bar{\pi}(a_1) - \bar{\pi}(a_0).$$

Consider the contract (w_L, w_H, a_i), in which the desired, but non-contractible, effort is a_i. The utility of the agent from this contract when he chooses the action $a_j \in \{a_0, a_1\}$ is denoted by $U(a_j, a_i)$ and is given by

$$U(a_j, a_i) = \bar{u}(a_j) + r \bar{u}(a_i) \bar{\pi}(a_j), \quad r > 0. \qquad (4.17)$$

Conditional on the contract (w_L, w_H, a_i), the first term on the RHS is the expected utility of the agent when he chooses the action a_j. The second term captures considerations of reciprocity. In judging the kindness of the principal, the agent takes the outside option, normalized to zero, as the fair level of utility. But if $\bar{u}(a_i) > 0$, the agent derives positive rents from the contract, so he reciprocates by engaging in gift exchange. This is reflected in the interaction of the agent's rents from the intended contract with the expected profit of the principal from the action chosen by the agent, a_j. The parameter $r > 0$ reflects the relative weight placed on reciprocity considerations. The greater is r and the higher the level of rents, the greater is the level of internalization of the principal's expected profit by the agent.

We assume that the principal always finds it optimal to implement the action a_1. For the principal, maximizing expected profits $p_1(y_H - w_H) + (1 - p_1)(y_L - w_L)$ is equivalent to minimizing expected wage costs. Thus, the principal's problem, P0, is

$$w_L^*, w_H^* \in \underset{w_j \in [0, y_j], \, j = H, L}{\arg\min} \bar{w}(a_1) = p_1 w_H + (1 - p_1) w_L \qquad (4.18)$$

subject to

$$U(a_1, a_1) \geq U(a_0, a_1) \quad \text{(IC)}$$
$$U(a_1, a_1) \geq 0. \quad \text{(IR)}$$

The optimal wage profile w_L^*, w_H^* must induce the choice of a high effort level, a_1 (incentive compatibility constraint, IC) and provide the agent with at least his reservation utility of zero (individual rationality constraint, IR).

The main difference from the standard moral hazard problem is that the principal can induce a high effort level through two channels. (1) By optimally offering a mix of w_L, w_H, as in models of self-regarding preferences. (2) By offering rents to the worker, which tap into the worker's reciprocity and internalize the objective of producing high expected output for the principal.

Consider the transformation introduced by Grossman and Hart (1983). Let

$$w_j = h(u(w_j)), h = u^{-1}, \text{ so } h' > 0 \text{ and } h'' > 0, j = H, L. \quad (4.19)$$

The implications in (4.19) are drawn from the standard properties of inverse functions and the fact that $u' > 0$ and $u'' < 0$.[10] Using (4.17), (4.19), and the notation $u_j = u(w_j), j = L, H$, we can rewrite the principal's problem, P0. The new, but equivalent, problem, P1, eliminates the wage levels and is expressed in terms of utilities of the agent in the two states $j = L, H$:

$$u_L^*, u_H^* \in \arg\min V = p_1 h(u_H) + (1 - p_1) h(u_L)$$

subject to

$$\bar{u}(a_1) - \bar{u}(a_0) + r\bar{u}(a_1)(\bar{\pi}(a_1) - \bar{\pi}(a_0)) \geq \Delta c \quad \text{(IC)}$$
$$\bar{u}(a_1) + r\bar{u}(a_1)\bar{\pi}(a_1) - c_1 \geq 0. \quad \text{(IR)}$$

The optimal choices $u_j^*, j = H, L$ are restricted to the compact interval $[u(0), u(y_j)]$. In problem P1, in order to induce the high effort, a_1, the principal minimizes a convex function (recall $h'' > 0$) subject to linear constraints. Thus, the satisfaction of the first order conditions with the relevant complementary slackness conditions is necessary and sufficient for an optimal solution.

We may now speak of the optimal contract as the triple (u_L^*, u_H^*, a_1), which allows us to recover the optimal wage contract (w_L^*, w_H^*, a_1) through the relation $w_j^* = h(u_j^*)$.

Let the Lagrangian of the constrained minimization problem, P1, be denoted by L and let λ_{IC} and λ_{IR} be the Lagrangian multipliers on the IC and IR constraints. The first order conditions with respect to u_L and u_H are

$$u_L : h'(u_L) = \lambda_{IC} \left[1 - \frac{1 - p_0}{1 - p_1} + r\Delta\bar{\pi} \right] + \lambda_{IR}(1 + r\bar{\pi}(a_1)). \quad (4.20)$$

$$u_H : h'(u_H) = \lambda_{IC} \left[1 - \frac{p_0}{p_1} + r\Delta\bar{\pi} \right] + \lambda_{IR}(1 + r\bar{\pi}(a_1)). \quad (4.21)$$

---

[10] For any feasible point, x, in the domain of h, $h'(x) = \frac{1}{u'(h(x))}$ and $h''(x) = -\frac{1}{(u'(h(x)))^2} u''(h(x)) h'(x)$. Thus, if u is increasing and concave, then the inverse, h, is increasing and convex.

In addition, we have the Kuhn–Tucker complementary slackness conditions, i.e.,

$$\lambda_{IC}\frac{\partial L}{\partial \lambda_{IC}} = 0, \lambda_{IR}\frac{\partial L}{\partial \lambda_{IR}} = 0. \tag{4.22}$$

Denote the minimum value of the objective function of the principal by

$$V(r, \Delta\overline{\pi}) = p_1 h(u_H^*) + (1-p_1) h(u_L^*). \tag{4.23}$$

We first state the benchmark textbook result in the absence of reciprocity ($r = 0$).

Proposition 4.5 (*Optimal contracts in the absence of reciprocity*): Suppose that reciprocity is absent ($r = 0$). Then, in the optimal contract, (u_L^*, u_H^*, a_1):

(i) The first order conditions are

$$h'(u_L) = \lambda_{IC}\left[1 - \frac{1-p_0}{1-p_1}\right] + \lambda_{IR}, \tag{4.24}$$

$$h'(u_H) = \lambda_{IC}\left[1 - \frac{p_0}{p_1}\right] + \lambda_{IR}, \tag{4.25}$$

which, in conjunction with the complementary slackness conditions, (4.22), give the optimal solution.
(ii) The IR constraint binds.
(iii) The principal rewards the agent more for outcomes that are relatively more likely under the desired action, a_1.

Proof: (i) The first order conditions follow by setting $r = 0$ in (4.20), (4.21). This gives the two equations (4.24), (4.25). Since we have a convex minimization problem subject to linear inequality constraints, (4.24), (4.25), in conjunction with (4.22), give the solution to the optimal contract.

(ii) Suppose that the IR constraint does not bind at the optimal contract (u_L^*, u_H^*, a_1). Then consider a new contract $(u_L^* - \epsilon, u_H^* - \epsilon, a_1)$, where $\epsilon > 0$ is a small number. The IC and IR constraints continue to hold (because $r = 0$) and the expected payment to the agent falls, increasing the expected profits of the principal. Hence, the original contract (u_L^*, u_H^*, a_1) at which the IR constraint does not bind is not optimal.

(iii) Suppose $\lambda_{IC} = 0$, so from (4.24), (4.25), $h'(u_L) = h'(u_H) = \lambda_{IR}$. In this case, a flat wage $w_L = w_H$ is optimal. When there are no problems of incentives, then it is optimal to fully insure the risk averse agent. But this creates a problem of incentives in implementing a high effort level. To see this, a flat wage gives $u_L = u_H = \widehat{u}$. Then, using (4.16) we have $\overline{u}(a_1) = \widehat{u} - c_1$ and $\overline{u}(a_0) = \widehat{u} - c_0$. From the binding IR constraint we have $\widehat{u} = c_1$. The IC constraint then implies the contradiction $0 \geq \Delta c$. Thus, a flat wage is not optimal.

Since the Lagrangian multipliers are positive in the presence of inequality constraints, the other possibility is $\lambda_{IC} > 0$, so the IC constraint must bind (from (4.22)). Notice that in each of (4.24), (4.25), since $h'' > 0$, an increase in the RHS increases the corresponding wage levels, w_L, w_H. From the MLRP, stated above, we know that $\frac{p_1}{p_0} > \frac{1-p_1}{1-p_0}$, hence, $w_L < w_H$. Thus, the principal rewards the agent for observing an outcome that is more likely under the desired action, a_1. ∎

Let us now see how the results are modified in the presence of reciprocity ($r > 0$).

Proposition 4.6 *Let $r > 0$. Then the following hold.*

(i) If an agent with the reciprocity parameter $r = r_1$ is induced to choose action a_1 by the contract (u_L, u_H, a_1), then any agent with a reciprocity parameter $r = r_2 > r_1$ also chooses the action a_1.
(ii) The minimum expected cost of the principal, $V(r, \Delta\bar{\pi})$, defined in (4.23), is non-increasing in r and $\Delta\bar{\pi}$.
(iii) When the rent of the agent is high enough, a flat wage schedule can implement the action a_1. As the reciprocity parameter $r \to \infty$, the action a_1 can be implemented by a flat wage schedule with infinitesimal rents.

Proof: (i) Differentiating the LHS of the IC constraint with respect to r, we get $\bar{u}(a_1)(\bar{\pi}(a_1) - \bar{\pi}(a_0)) > 0$. Similarly, differentiating the LHS of the IR constraint with respect to r we get $\bar{u}(a_1)\bar{\pi}(a_1) > 0$. Thus, an increase in r relaxes both constraints. Hence, if the optimal contract can be implemented at r_1 it can be implemented at $r_2 > r_1$.

(ii) From part (i), an increase in r relaxes the IC constraint, and the IR constraint continues to hold. If IR does not bind then, by reducing wages, w_L, w_H, the expected profits of the principal will strictly increase as r increases. If IR binds, then the wage levels cannot be reduced, so expected profits are unchanged (but no lower). An increase in $\Delta\bar{\pi}$ relaxes the IC and IR constraints, hence, using a similar argument, the expected profits of the principal are also increasing in $\Delta\bar{\pi}$.

(iii) Suppose that there is a flat wage profile, so $w_L = w_H$ but the contract leaves positive rents for the agent. Constant state-contingent wages imply that $u_L = u_H = \tilde{u} > 0$. The outside option of the agent is zero, thus, the IR constraint is

$$(\tilde{u} - c_1)(1 + r\bar{\pi}(a_1)) > 0.$$

Evaluating the IC constraint at the stated contract, we get

$$r(\tilde{u} - c_1)\Delta\bar{\pi} > \Delta c.$$

Thus, for high enough $\tilde{u}$, the IC constraint is satisfied. Clearly, the larger the reciprocity parameter r, the smaller is the level of rents, $\tilde{u}$, required to satisfy the IC constraint. ∎

Comparing Propositions 4.5, 4.6 we see the following. In the absence of reciprocity, there is a conflict between insurance and incentives, so a flat wage is good for insurance but bad for incentives. However, in the presence of reciprocity, both insurance and incentives point in the same direction, hence, this may give rise to an optimal contract with flat wages. Indeed, the prediction of high-powered incentives in the absence of reciprocity (Proposition 4.5) is often violated in practice. See, e.g., the quote, due to Lemieux et al. (2009) in the chapter introduction.

Lemma 4.1 *In the presence of reciprocity, the IC constraint binds for all $r > 0$.*

Proof: First suppose that both constraints, IC and IR, are slack when evaluated at the contract (u_L, u_H, a_1). Then the principal's profits can be increased by the contract $(u_L - \epsilon, u_H - \epsilon, a_1)$, hence, this case cannot arise. The other possibility is that IC is slack but IR binds. Since IR binds, the agent gets no rents, hence, reciprocity of the agent become irrelevant. In effect, the behavior of the agent in this case is like a non-reciprocal agent ($r = 0$). If the IC is slack, so $\lambda_{IC} = 0$, then from (4.20), (4.21) we have $h'(u_L) = h'(u_H)$, so $w_L = w_H$, i.e., a flat wage schedule. But we know in this case that the self-regarding agent does not put in any effort, thus IC should be violated, contradicting the initial supposition that it does hold. Thus, the IC should bind when $r > 0$. ∎

Lemma 4.1 shows that IC will always bind, so we have two additional possibilities. (i) IR binds. (ii) IR is slack. The next proposition indicates when each of these cases is likely to arise.

Proposition 4.7 *There exists some finite reciprocity parameter r^* such that (i) for all $r \leq r^*$, IR binds, and (ii) for all $r > r^*$, the IR constraint is slack and the optimal contract provides strictly positive rents to the agent.*

We leave the proof of Proposition 4.7 as an exercise for the reader. In case (ii) of Proposition 4.7, since IR is slack we have $\lambda_{IR} = 0$. Substituting $\lambda_{IR} = 0$ in (4.20), (4.21) and using the fact that $h'(u_L) = \frac{1}{u'(w_L)}$ (see footnote 10 above on the properties of an inverse function) we have that the optimal contract specifies

$$\frac{u'(w_H)}{u'(w_L)} = \frac{1 - \frac{1-p_0}{1-p_1} + r\Delta\bar{\pi}}{1 - \frac{p_0}{p_1} + r\Delta\bar{\pi}}. \tag{4.26}$$

Thus, the ratio of marginal utilities depends not just on the likelihood ratios but also on the extent of reciprocal feelings of the agent. We leave it to the reader to explore the effects of the degree of informativeness of signals on the optimal contract. Englmaier and Leider (2012) show that when signals are more informative about the effort choice of the agent, then the principal relies more on incentives (as compared to reciprocity) in order to induce the desired effort level. One testable prediction of this model, therefore, is to compare the incidence of incentive contracts in firms with different levels of noise in the production technology. These sorts of models are also potentially useful to study the optimality of different organizational forms.[11]

4.3 Incomplete contracts under other-regarding preferences

Most real-life contracts are incomplete. In particular, in principal–agent relations, the effort level of agents is difficult to specify in full detail. When agents have self-regarding preferences, high-powered incentive contracts are predicted to induce high levels of effort. However, real-life incentives are typically not high-powered, and apart from top management, fixed wage payments or mildly increasing wage schemes are quite common.

In this section, we consider a simple model of moral hazard in a principal–agent relation but with (1) a rich menu of contracts, (2) the presences of other-regarding preferences, and (3) uncertainty about preferences (self-regarding or other-regarding). We show that in the presence of other-regarding preferences, a range of contracts, such as *bonus contracts* and *trust contracts* become potentially profitable for a principal; indeed, even more profitable than purely *incentive contracts*. Under purely self-regarding preferences, the bonus and the trust contracts are shown to be dominated by incentive contracts. The converse can be true under other-regarding preferences.

The treatment in this section is based on Fehr et al. (2007). We give a detailed treatment for two reasons. First, understanding the basic theoretical framework is important in the economics of incentives. Second, the predictions of this model have been empirically tested; we consider the empirical results in Section 4.3.3, below.

---

[11] Englemair and Leider (2012) make progress in this direction by identifying three different organizational forms in which there are two managers of a firm. They consider various heirarchical relations between them.

Consider a single, risk-neutral, principal who contracts a single, risk-neutral, agent to work for him. The reservation utilities of both parties are normalized at zero. The agent can expend effort $e \in [\underline{e}, \overline{e}]$ at some private cost $c(e)$ such that $c(\underline{e}) = 0$, $c' > 0$ and $c'' > 0$. The utility of the agent is given by

$$u = w - c(e) - C_A, \qquad (4.27)$$

where C_A are other possible costs associated with a contract that are incurred by the agent, such as fines for non-fulfillment of contractual obligations; these are specified in more detail below. w is the wage received by the agent from the principal.

The output of the principal is given by $\theta v(e)$, where $\theta > 0$ is a constant productivity parameter, and $v(\underline{e}) = 0$, $v'(e) > 0$, $v''(e) < 0$. We also assume that

$$c'(\underline{e}) < \theta v'(\underline{e}), \qquad (4.28)$$

i.e., the marginal benefit of the lowest effort level to the principal, exceeds the marginal cost.

Suppose the principal desires to induce the effort level e_c. If the effort is observable and verifiable, then e_c can be enforced through a legal contract. However, when the effort level is non-verifiable, even if it is observable, then e_c is non-binding and cannot be legally enforced. Effort is observed by both parties. However, the principal cannot provide hard evidence of the effort level to a third party unless he invests in a verification technology that costs $k > 0$ but produces hard evidence of the actual effort level with some probability $p \in (0, 1)$. Based on this evidence, the principal can impose a fine $f > 0$ on the agent. The maximum possible fine is $\overline{f}$. We assume that the maximum expected fine, $p\overline{f}$, exceeds the cost savings to the agent from shirking, i.e.,

$$c(e_c) - c(\underline{e}) \le p\overline{f}, \forall e_c. \qquad (4.29)$$

The profits of the principal are given by

$$\pi = \theta v(e) - w - C_P, \qquad (4.30)$$

where C_P captures other possible costs (positive or negative) associated with the contract that are incurred by the principal, such as investment in a verification technology, or receipt of fines from the agent.

The sequence of moves in the multi-stage game is as follows. In Stage 1, the principal makes a *take it or leave it* offer to the agent after choosing (a) the type of contract to offer, and (b) whether to invest in the verification technology. In Stage 2, the agent decides (a) to accept or reject the contract, and (b) the effort level to expend. In Stage 3, if the initial investment in the verification technology has been made, then hard evidence of the agent's effort level is obtained with probability $p > 0$ and the terms of the initial contract are enforced.

Consider the following three types of contracts.

1. *Incentive contracts*: This is the typical form of contracts in classical contract theory. Assume that the principal invests in the monitoring technology, so hard evidence of the agent's effort level can be produced with probability $p > 0$ and the agent expends an effort level e. The contract specifies a triple (w, e_c, f), where e_c is the contracted effort level and f is the

fine to be paid if verifiable evidence of shirking (i.e., $e < e_c$) is discovered. The ex-post utilities of the agent and the principal, u, π, are given respectively by:

$$u = \begin{cases} w - c(e_c) & \text{if } e = e_c \\ w - c(e) & \text{if } e < e_c \text{ (with probability } 1 - p) \\ w - c(e) - f & \text{if } e < e_c \text{ (with probability } p) \end{cases} \quad (4.31)$$

$$\pi = \begin{cases} \theta v(e_c) - w - k & \text{if } e = e_c \\ \theta v(e) - w - k & \text{if } e < e_c \text{ (with probability } 1 - p) \\ \theta v(e) - w - k + f & \text{if } e < e_c \text{ (with probability } p) \end{cases} \quad (4.32)$$

2. *Trust contract*: The trust contract specifies a pair (w, e_c) and there is no investment in the monitoring technology. Thus, shirking by the agent is never discovered and no fines are levied either. The contractual effort, e_c, is, therefore, legally non-binding. The wage payment $w \geq c(e)$ to the agent is not conditioned on the actual effort level of the agent. The contractual wage payment can be enforced by a court if necessary, so the agent is guaranteed to receive it, irrespective of the actual effort level, e. The respective utilities of the agent and the principal in a trust contract are:

$$u = w - c(e). \quad (4.33)$$

$$\pi = \theta v(e) - w. \quad (4.34)$$

Since e_c is unenforceable, the trust contract is more incomplete than the incentive contract.

3. *Bonus contract*: This contract is similar to a trust contract except for the presence of a non-enforceable bonus payment, $b \geq 0$, from the principal to the agent in Stage 3, conditional on having observed the Stage 2 outcome. Hence, the contract can be represented by a triple (w, e_c, b). As in the case of the trust contract, e_c is not legally enforceable. The respective, ex-post, utilities of the agent and the principal are:

$$u = \begin{cases} w - c(e) & \text{when no bonus is paid} \\ w - c(e) + b & \text{when bonus is paid} \end{cases} \quad (4.35)$$

$$\pi = \begin{cases} \theta v(e) - w & \text{when no bonus is paid} \\ \theta v(e) - w - b & \text{when bonus is paid} \end{cases} \quad (4.36)$$

The bonus contract is the most incomplete of the three contracts because b and e_c are both unenforceable.

We now make an important assumption that concerns the nature of reciprocity. We assume that this assumption holds in the subsequent analysis in this section. For the empirical evidence behind this assumption, see Section 4.6.

A1. When faced with an incentive contract, all types of principals and agents (other-regarding and self-regarding) behave in a self-regarding manner. *This is the sense in which the model captures concerns for reciprocity.* Incentive contracts are perceived as unkind behavior by the principal and induce agents to behave in a self-regarding manner. Trust and bonus contracts are perceived by the agent as kind behavior by the principal and induce other-regarding preferences (unless the agent is inherently self-regarding). Furthermore, in a bonus contract, if the principal is expected to be reciprocal, then the agent may put in high effort in the hope of receiving an, ex-post, bonus payment.

4.3.1 Optimal contracts under self-regarding preferences

If agents have self-regarding preferences, then reciprocity-based contracts, such as trust and bonus contracts, invite one-sided opportunism (trust contracts) or two-sided opportunism (bonus contracts). Self-regarding agents exert zero effort level because they are neither influenced by other-regarding preferences, nor by reciprocity. This contrasts with the observed evidence, say, in the gift exchange game.

Incentive contracts can, however, be very effective in eliciting the contracted effort, provided that the monitoring technology is effective (high p) and the maximum available fine, $\bar{f}$, is high enough. Proposition 4.8, below, formalizes these ideas and also characterizes the first best contract when both contractual parties have self-regarding preferences. The proofs in this section should be standard for most undergraduate students in economics, so they are all relegated as exercises.

Proposition 4.8 *Suppose that the principal and the agent have self-regarding preferences.*

(i) *Consider the first best contract that maximizes the total surplus* $u + \pi = \theta v(e) - c(e)$. *The socially optimal effort level, e^*, is given by*

$$\theta v'(e^*) = c'(e^*), \tag{4.37}$$

and $u + \pi > 0$.

(ii) *In the trust and the bonus contracts, the solution is summarized by*

$$e = \underline{e}, \, w = b = 0, \, u = 0, \, \pi = 0, \, u + \pi = 0. \tag{4.38}$$

(iii) *Suppose that the principal invests in the monitoring technology. If $p\bar{f} \geq c(e^*) - c(\underline{e})$, then the solution under the incentive contract is summarized by*

$$e = e^* > \underline{e}; u = 0; \pi = \theta v(e^*) - c(e^*) - k \geq 0; u + \pi \geq 0. \tag{4.39}$$

If the deterrence technology is potent enough ($p\bar{f} \geq c(e^*) - c(\underline{e})$), the equilibrium effort under the incentive contract is identical to the first best contract. However, the aggregate payoff is lower, on account of the cost of the verification technology, $k > 0$. Hence, this is the second best outcome. The trust and the bonus contracts elicit the lowest effort level $\underline{e}$; since $v(\underline{e}) = 0$, the firm's profits are zero in both cases.

The testable prediction of the model with self-regarding preferences, therefore, is that the principal will choose the incentive contract over the trust and the bonus contracts, when all three contractual forms are available; the evidence, described in Section 4.3.3, rejects this prediction.

4.3.2 Optimal contracts in the presence of other-regarding preferences

Now suppose that the principal and the agent have other-regarding preferences that take the Fehr–Schmidt (1997) form (abbreviated as FS preferences). Given assumption A1, individuals with FS preferences exhibit other-regarding preferences in the case of bonus and trust contracts but behave like self-regarding agents in the case of incentive contracts.

If all this is commonly known, then, in the trust contract, the principal could rationally hope that higher wages will be reciprocated by higher effort (as in the gift exchange game). Analogously, in a bonus contract, the agent rationally hopes the principal will reciprocate a high effort with a bonus payment. These factors are conducive for the agent to put in a high effort. Reciprocity arises here on account of inequity aversion and not beliefs, which is the case when we apply the machinery of psychological game theory (see Volume 4).

For pedagogical simplicity, we make the following assumptions.

$$v(e) = e; \ c(e) = \frac{1}{2}e^2; \ e \in [0,1]. \tag{4.40}$$

$$\theta = 1. \tag{4.41}$$

Equation (4.40) restricts the marginal benefit of effort to be linear, the effort cost function to be quadratic, and the effort choice to be made from the unit interval. Given these assumptions, the marginal product of effort, $\theta v'(e) = 1$, is strictly greater than the marginal cost of effort, $c'(e) = e$, for all $e \in [0,1)$ and equal at $e = 1$. Thus, from (4.37), a social planner would always want to elicit $e^* = 1$.

Under these specific functional forms, the utility of a self-regarding agent and a self-regarding principal is given, respectively, by

$$u = w - \frac{1}{2}e^2 - C_A \text{ and } \pi = e - w - C_P. \tag{4.42}$$

If the monetary payoffs of the agent and the principal are given by u and π as in (4.42) (which is a special case of (4.27), (4.30)), then their respective FS preferences, U and Π are given by:

$$U(u,\pi) = u - \alpha_A \max\{\pi - u, 0\} - \beta_A \max\{u - \pi, 0\} \tag{4.43}$$

$$\Pi(u,\pi) = \pi - \alpha_P \max\{u - \pi, 0\} - \beta_P \max\{\pi - u, 0\}, \tag{4.44}$$

where $\beta_i \in [0,1], \beta_i \leq \alpha_i, i = A, P$.

Let $0 < \lambda \leq 1$ denote the probability that the agent has self-regarding preferences, i.e., $\alpha_i = \beta_i = 0$. With probability $1 - \lambda$, the agent has other-regarding preferences. At the time of designing the incentive scheme of the agent in Stage 1, there is uncertainty: The principal does not know the agent's type, but knows the distribution of types. The principal cannot condition wage payments on the type of the agent; perhaps because the type information is non verifiable.

In line with the experimental evidence, we make the following assumption that applies to the subsequent analysis in this section.

A2. The preference parameters obey the restrictions, $\alpha_i \geq \beta_i > 0.5$.[12]

Due to uncertainty about the type of the agent, the profit of the principal, π, is a random variable. Theory does not provide sufficient guidance on how to extend (4.44) in the presence of risk. We make the simplest pedagogical assumption that the principal maximizes his expected payoffs $E\Pi$,

$$E\Pi = \lambda \Pi(u, \pi \mid \text{self-regarding agent}) + (1 - \lambda) \Pi(u, \pi \mid \text{other-regarding agent}), \tag{4.45}$$

where the first and the second terms on the RHS in (4.45) condition the profits of the principal on the type of the agent, self-regarding or other-regarding.

Suppose that the agent is other-regarding. It can then be shown that other-regarding agents are: (i) willing to transfer money to the other party to reduce disadvantageous inequality, and

---

[12] The assumption $\alpha_i > 0.5$ has better support than the assumption $\beta_i > 0.5$; see Table 2.1, above. However, the assumption $\beta_i > 0.5$ affords pedagogical simplicity.

(ii) engage in costly punishments, provided that punishments are not too costly and the envy parameter α is high enough. This is formalized in Lemma 4.2.

Lemma 4.2 *Suppose that $\alpha_A \geq \beta_A > 0.5$ (assumption A2) and the agent is other-regarding. Consider the Stage 2 problem of the agent to choose an effort level.*

(1) *If $u > \pi$, the agent is willing to reduce inequality by transferring resources to the principal.*
(2) *Suppose that the agent can, at a cost $\gamma < 1$, reduce the payoff of the principal by a unit. If $u < \pi$, the agent is willing to engage in costly punishment in order to reduce inequality if $\gamma \leq \frac{\alpha_A}{1+\alpha_A} < 1$.*

Proof: Let x_A and x_P be, respectively, the monetary payoffs of the agent and the principal. There are two cases to consider.

(a) $x_A > x_P$. In this case, the utility of the agent is given by $U(x_A, x_P) = x_A - \beta_A(x_A - x_P)$. Suppose now that the agent were to transfer a small amount $\varepsilon > 0$ of his own income to the principal, then his utility is

$$U(x_A, x_P) = x_A - \beta_A(x_A - x_P) + \varepsilon(2\beta_A - 1).$$

Since $\beta_i > 0.5$ it follows that the agent is better off by such a transfer of income. Hence, it follows that when inequality is to their advantage, other-regarding agents are willing to spend resources to benefit the disadvantaged partner.

(b) $x_A < x_P$. In this case, the utility of the agent is $U(x_A, x_P) = x_A - \alpha_A(x_P - x_A)$. Suppose that the agent can, at a cost $\gamma < 1$, reduce the payoff of the principal by a unit (it never makes sense to do so if $\gamma \geq 1$). The payoff of the agent in this case is

$$U(x_A, x_P) = (x_A - \gamma) - \alpha_A[(x_P - 1) - (x_A - \gamma)].$$
$$\Leftrightarrow U(x_A, x_P) = x_A - \alpha_A(x_P - x_A) + \alpha_A(1 - \gamma) - \gamma. \tag{4.46}$$

Thus, the agent will prefer to punish the principal to reduce inequality if $\alpha_A(1 - \gamma) - \gamma \geq 0$ or equivalently if

$$\gamma \leq \frac{\alpha_A}{1+\alpha_A} < 1. \tag{4.47}$$

This completes the proof. ∎

TRUST CONTRACTS

From Proposition 4.8, under a trust contract, the self-regarding agent puts in the effort level $e = 0$ (this result also holds in the special case of (4.40)). We now consider the effort choice of an other-regarding agent in Stage 2.

Lemma 4.3 *(a) Consider an other-regarding agent who accepts a trust contract. Then, in any "incentive compatible" trust contract, the agent will choose an effort level such that the payoffs of the principal and the agent are equated.*

The locus of (w, e) points that satisfy the incentive compatible contract are given by the condition

$$g(w,e) = e^2 + 2e - 4w = 0. \tag{4.48}$$

The effort reaction function of the other-regarding agent under an incentive compatible trust contract is given by[13]

$$e^T(w) = \sqrt{4w+1} - 1 \geq 0. \tag{4.49}$$

(b) A self-regarding agent chooses $e = 0$, irrespective of the wage paid.

From (4.49), the effort level of the other-regarding agent is increasing in the wage paid, as in gift exchange experiments and models of efficiency wage. This arises on account of the other-regarding preferences of the agent (see Lemma 4.2).

Lemma 4.4 *In equilibrium, in a trust contract, the individual rationality constraints of the self-regarding and the other-regarding agents are respectively given by $w \geq 0$ and $w - \frac{1}{2}e^2 \geq 0$, where e is some incentive compatible effort level.*

Proof of Lemma 4.4: We know from Lemma 4.3 that in a trust contract, an other-regarding agent chooses effort $e^T(w) \geq 0$ and the effort choice of the agent equates the payoff with the principal. Using (4.43), since the outside option of the agent is zero, the principal must offer a wage such that $w - \frac{1}{2}e^2 \geq 0$. From Lemma 4.3 the self-regarding agent puts in a zero effort level, hence, he accepts the contract if $w \geq 0$. ∎

We now state the next result that is simple to verify.

Lemma 4.5 *For a fixed $0 < e \leq 1$, the wage, w, that satisfies (4.48), the incentive compatibility condition of an other-regarding agent, is higher than the wage that satisfies the individual rationality constraint at equality for any strictly positive effort level, i.e., $w = \frac{1}{2}e^2$. When $e = 0$, the wage level that satisfies these two constraints is identical at $w = 0$. Hence, the satisfaction of the incentive compatibility constraint, for any strictly positive effort level by an other-regarding agent, will leave some rents to the agent.*

The result in Lemma 4.5 is analogous to the result in Proposition 4.7. Inequity averse agents repay the principal in terms of higher effort if the principal leaves them with rents.

We have considered, above, the Stage 2 problem for the case of an other-regarding and a self-regarding agent. We now consider the Stage 1 problem of the principal, separately, for the cases of other-regarding and self-regarding principals.

I. Trust contract offered by an other-regarding principal

Suppose that the principal has other-regarding preferences given in (4.44). Consider the Stage 1 problem of the principal.

With probability λ, the principal encounters a self-regarding agent who puts in zero effort level (see Lemma 4.3) and no output is produced. By definition, in a trust contract, the principal must honor the promise to pay a wage of w even if no output is produced. Thus, the principal faces disadvantageous inequity. Using (4.44), the principal's payoff in this case is $\Pi = -w(2\alpha_P + 1) < 0$.

With probability $1 - \lambda$, the principal encounters an other-regarding agent. Lemma 4.3 describes the outcome and (4.49) gives the effort level. The effort choice of the agent equalizes

---

[13] We are being a bit informal here because we also require that $e \in [0,1]$, thus, $e^T(w) = \min\{\sqrt{4w+1} - 1, 1\}$. We shall assume that $\min\{\sqrt{4w+1} - 1, 1\} = \sqrt{4w+1}$ to abstract from technical issues of boundary points. We trust that the reader can supply the necessary, but simple, formalism if required.

the payoffs of both parties, so there are no equity considerations in equilibrium. Given (4.40), (4.41), the principal's payoff is given by $\Pi = e^T(w) - w$, which is identical to the material payoff π.

Combining the two possibilities, and using (4.45), the expected payoff of the other-regarding principal is given by

$$E\Pi = -\lambda w(2\alpha_P + 1) + (1 - \lambda)(e^T(w) - w), \quad (4.50)$$

where $e^T(w)$ is defined in (4.49). The problem of the other-regarding principal is to maximize (4.50) subject to the individual rationality constraint of the other-regarding agent, $w \geq \frac{1}{2}(e^T)^2$; the effort reaction function e^T is already incentive compatible. Since e^T is increasing in w, it is not necessarily optimal to choose w, so that the individual rationality constraint of the other-regarding agent binds. We show this in the next proposition; w_F^T is the wage offered by the other-regarding (or fair) principal in a trust contract.

Proposition 4.9

(i) If $\lambda \geq \frac{1}{2(1+\alpha_P)}$, then in the only possible equilibrium, $(w_F^T, e_c) = (0,0)$, and the individual rationality constraint of both types of agents binds. The payoffs of both types of agents and the payoff of the principal are zero.

(ii) If $\lambda < \frac{1}{2(1+\alpha_P)} < \frac{1}{2}$, then there is an interior solution to the wage rate given by $w_F^T = \frac{(1-\lambda)^2}{(1+2\lambda\alpha_P)^2} - \frac{1}{4}$. The effort level of the other-regarding agent is given by $e_F^T = \frac{2(\lambda-1)}{(2\lambda\alpha_P+1)} - 1$. w_F^T is decreasing in α_P and λ, and both types of agents derive strictly positive rents. The expected profit of the other-regarding principal in a trust contract is

$$\Pi_F^T = -\lambda w_F^T(2\alpha_P + 1) + (1 - \lambda)(e_F^T - w_F^T). \quad (4.51)$$

(iii) It is never the case that the other-regarding principal elicits the maximum feasible effort level, $e = 1$, from the agent.

From Proposition 4.9(ii), if the probability of the self-regarding agent, λ, is low enough, then it is worthwhile for the principal to offer high enough rents. In response to these rents, the other-regarding agent responds with a high level of effort, on account of his inequity aversion. The self-regarding agent also benefits from the rents being offered but he puts in a zero effort level. This does create disadvantageous inequity for the other-regarding principal. But if the disadvantageous inequity parameter, α_P, of the principal is low, the costs are low relative to higher effort obtained from the other-regarding agent. Otherwise, the case in Proposition 4.9(i) obtains.

Finally, the surplus maximizing, or the most efficient effort choice of the agent is $e = 1$. The model predicts that we should not observe this choice. In other models, where agents care for efficiency, say, in Charness and Rabin (2002), agents may well choose $e = 1$. However, the empirical evidence shows that in gift exchange games, agents typically do not make the surplus maximizing choice (see Section 1.3, above).

II. Trust contract offered by a self-regarding principal

We can recover the case of the self-regarding principal from that of the other-regarding principal by setting $\alpha_P = 0$ in Proposition 4.9.

The comparison between the regimes of an other-regarding and a self-regarding principal under trust contracts is summarized below. The simple proof is omitted.

Remark 4.2 *The wage rate offered by an other-regarding principal is always lower relative to that of a self-regarding principal. The other-regarding agent reciprocates a higher wage by a higher effort, hence: (i) The effort level of the other-regarding agent is higher when the principal is self-regarding. (ii) Expected output is larger in the regime of a self-regarding principal as compared to the regime of an other-regarding principal.*

When $\lambda > \frac{1}{2}$, no principal (other-regarding or self-regarding) offers a positive wage, hence, the trust contract breaks down. The reason is that the self-regarding principal does not suffer from inequity aversion (which is costly for an other-regarding principal) when he meets a self-regarding agent. Thus, a self-regarding principal faces a lower marginal cost from a marginal increase in λ. If $\lambda \in \left(\frac{1}{2(1+\alpha p)}, \frac{1}{2}\right)$, then the self-regarding principal offers a trust contract but the trust contract breaks down if the principal is other-regarding. If $\lambda < \frac{1}{2(1+\alpha p)}$, then both types of principals, self-regarding and other-regarding, offer a trust contract. The effort level of the self-regarding agent is zero, regardless of the type of the principal.

Why does a self-regarding principal offer a higher wage than an other-regarding principal under a trust contract? The intuition is that the other-regarding principal, unlike a self-regarding principal, dislikes disadvantageous inequity. When the other-regarding principal encounters a self-regarding agent, he suffers disadvantageous inequity, which is increasing in the wage offered. Since the wage contract is offered prior to the type of the agent being revealed, the other-regarding principal offers a relatively lower wage.

INCENTIVE CONTRACTS

Recall our assumption that in the presence of an incentive contract, all parties to the contract behave as if they had self-regarding preferences (assumption A1). Consider now the incentive contract described above in which a self-regarding principal meets a self-regarding agent (with probability 1).

If the self-regarding agent were to shirk, relative to the contractual effort level, e_c, then it would pay to put in the minimum effort level, $e = 0$. This is because the probability of detection and fines is independent of the level of effort. Thus, the incentive compatibility condition of the self-regarding agent is

$$(1-p)w + p(w-f) \leq w - \frac{1}{2}(e_c)^2. \tag{4.52}$$

Rewriting (4.52),

$$e_c \leq \sqrt{2pf}, \tag{4.53}$$

gives the set of effort levels of the agent that are incentive compatible.

The self-regarding principal chooses a contract (w, e_c) to maximize expected profits

$$E\pi = (1-p)(e-w-k) + p(e-w-k+df) = e-w-k+pdf, \tag{4.54}$$

where d is a binary variable such that $d = 0$ if $e = e_c$ and $d = 1$ if $e \neq e_c$. There are two constraints, the incentive compatibility constraint in (4.53) and the individual rationality constraint $w - \frac{1}{2}e^2 \geq 0$. The satisfaction of these constraints at the contracted effort, e_c, ensures that $d = 0$. The objective function $E\pi$ is decreasing in w, and the incentive compatibility constraint is independent of w, hence, the individual rationality constraint always binds, i.e., $w = \frac{1}{2}e^2$. Denote the maximum value of the expected profit of the principal in an incentive contract by $E\Pi^I$. In light of the discussion, above, the results in the next proposition should not be surprising.

Proposition 4.10 *In an incentive contract, the optimal contracted effort level is given by*

$$e_I = \min\left\{1, \sqrt{2pf}\right\}. \tag{4.55}$$

There are two main cases.

(i) *If $\sqrt{2pf} \geq 1 \Leftrightarrow pf \geq 1/2$, then $e_I = 1$. The individual rationality constraint of the agent binds, so $w = 1/2$ and the expected profit of the firm is given by $E\Pi^I = \frac{1}{2} - k$.*
(ii) *If $\sqrt{2pf} < 1 \Leftrightarrow pf < 1/2$, then $e_I = \sqrt{2pf}$. The individual rationality constraint of the agent binds, so $w = pf$ and the expected profit of the firm is given by $E\Pi^I = \sqrt{2pf} - pf - k$.*

BONUS CONTRACT OFFERED BY AN OTHER-REGARDING PRINCIPAL

The bonus contract is described above. Analogous to the results in Lemma 4.2, 4.3, an other-regarding principal chooses a bonus, b, in Stage 3, in order to equate the monetary payoffs of the two parties, so,

$$e - w - b = w + b - \frac{1}{2}e^2.$$

Solving out for b we get

$$b = b(e, w) = \frac{1}{2}e - w + \frac{1}{4}e^2. \tag{4.56}$$

The bonus payment is increasing in the effort level of the agent, which captures the reciprocity of the principal. The bonus also depends negatively, and one to one, on the wage level because these are substitute instruments in ensuring equality of payoffs between the principal and the agent. The remaining analysis is similar to the case of trust contracts except that both parties know that in Stage 3, the bonus payment is given by (4.56).

The preferences of a self-regarding agent are given by $u = w + b(e, w) - \frac{1}{2}e^2$, which, using (4.56), is strictly concave in e. From the first order condition, we find that in a bonus contract, the optimal effort choice of a self-regarding agent is $e_S^b = 1$. Hence, even a self-regarding agent puts in the maximum possible effort level if he knows that the principal is other-regarding, who will, optimally, choose to honor his commitment to pay a bonus.

Now consider an other-regarding agent. From Lemma 4.2, 4.3 the optimal effort choice of the other-regarding agent will equate his monetary payoff with the principal, i.e.,

$$w + b(e, w) - \frac{1}{2}e^2 = e - w - b(e, w). \tag{4.57}$$

It turns out that (4.57) is satisfied for any value of e (because the choice of $b(e, w)$ ensures that payoffs are equated ex-post). Hence, the payoff of the other-regarding agent is identical to that of a self-regarding agent and is given by $U = w + b(e, w) - \frac{1}{2}e^2$. Substituting $b(e, w)$ from (4.56). we get $U = \frac{1}{2}e - \frac{1}{4}e^2$. Clearly this payoff is also maximized at $e_F^b = 1$.

Given that the Stage 3 bonus plays the same role as a wage, and is offset one for one with the wage, we can focus on the case where the Stage 1 wage offer of the principal is zero. Since the other-regarding and the self-regarding agents both put in the maximal effort level, the other-regarding principal's expected payoff in a bonus contract is $E\Pi = e - b(e,w)$, which is independent of λ. On substitution of $e = 1$, $w = 0$ and (4.56), the expected profit in a bonus contract is given by

$$E\Pi_F^B = \frac{1}{4}. \tag{4.58}$$

We summarize these results below.

Proposition 4.11 *In a bonus contract, when the principal is other-regarding, the self-regarding and the other-regarding agents exert identical effort levels equal to 1, i.e., $e_S^b = e_F^b = 1$. The expected profit of the principal is $E\Pi_F^B = \frac{1}{4}$.*

COMPARISON OF PROFITS UNDER THE THREE CONTRACTS

Does the other-regarding principal prefer an incentive contract or a bonus contract? The answer depends on the parameters and there are many possibilities. Classical contract theory under self-regarding preferences predicts that the incentive contracts should always dominate. We consider only one example here, in which bonus contracts dominate all others. Using Proposition 4.10, and (4.58), when $\sqrt{2pf} \geq 1$,

$$E\Pi^I \gtreqless E\Pi_F^B \text{ as } \frac{1}{4} \gtreqless k,$$

and when $\sqrt{2pf} < 1$

$$E\Pi^I \gtreqless E\Pi_F^B \text{ as } \sqrt{2pf} - pf \gtreqless \frac{1}{4} + k. \tag{4.59}$$

Thus, the incentive contract dominates the bonus contract when (1) the deterrence parameters p, f are high enough, so that hard evidence of shirking is discovered with high enough probability and then punished with severe enough consequences, and (2) the cost of the monitoring technology, k is low enough. When $\lambda > \frac{1}{2}$ the trust contract is not offered by either an other-regarding or a self-regarding principal (see Remark 4.2). In this case if $k > \max\{\frac{1}{4}, \sqrt{2pf} - pf - \frac{1}{4}\}$, then the bonus contract dominates all other contracts.

These results are only illustrative of the departures one gets from the standard model when individuals have other-regarding preferences. A classical game theorist might argue that the existence of non-competitive rents embodied in wage levels above the market level can equally well be explained using infinitely repeated games between purely self-regarding firms and workers. However, such arguments are not persuasive on empirical grounds. (1) The evidence strongly confirms the existence of economic agents who exhibit other-regarding preferences; much of Volume 2 of the book attempts to establish the relevant evidence base. (2) The model with other-regarding preferences generates these results without the machinery of repeated games and reputation formation. One can then design appropriate experiments to test the relative merit of these two alternative explanations, a task that we turn to in the next section.

4.3.3 Evidence on contract choice under contractual incompleteness

Fehr et al. (2007) examine, experimentally, the choice between incentive, trust, and bonus contracts. They ran several sessions with ten periods in each session and 20–24 individuals in each session. Agents are randomly matched with a different principal in each period. When principals are given a choice between trust and incentive contracts (the TI treatment), there is a strong trend towards the incentive contracts over successive rounds of the experiment. In the final three periods, more than 80% of all contracts offered were incentive contracts. Trust contracts were tried in one of the rounds by at least 70% of the principals but were not preferred. Effort was significantly higher in the incentive contracts relative to the trust contracts.

Profits were negative, on average, in the incentive contracts because the majority of the incentive contracts, 58.5%, violated the no-shirking constraint in (4.53). Most principals used the maximum fine and asked for an effort level that was too ambitious. However, the demanded effort fell over time and the share of incentive compatible contracts increased with time. The incentive-compatible incentive contracts are more profitable than the trust contracts but the non-incentive compatible ones are less profitable than trust contracts. The trust contracts in Fehr et al. (2007) do not perform as well as those in Fehr et al. (1993). A potential reason is that effort–wage relation is far steeper in the latter and the set of effort choices is discrete.

When principals are given a choice between bonus and incentive contracts (the BI treatment), then the overwhelming majority of principals chooses the bonus contract. The results, averaged across all sessions, are shown in Figure 4.1. From period 6 onward, the bonus contract is chosen in approximately 90% of the cases and approaches 96% in the final period. In the BI treatment, in the bonus contract, the average effort level is relatively higher and the gap between the demanded and actual effort is the lowest.

On average, the principal's profit in the bonus contracts is about four times higher. Roughly 40% of the compensation of agents is paid out as a bonus by the principal. The principals are not

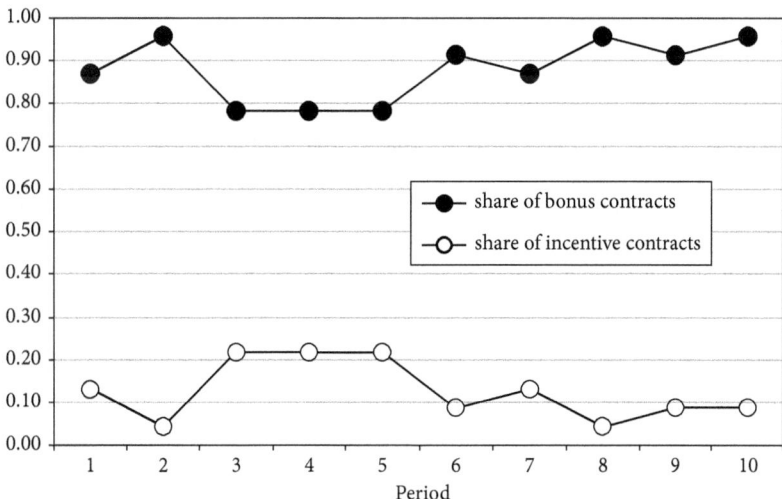

Figure 4.1 Share of bonus contracts and incentive contracts over successive rounds.
Source: Fehr et al. (2007) with permisssion of The Econometric Society.

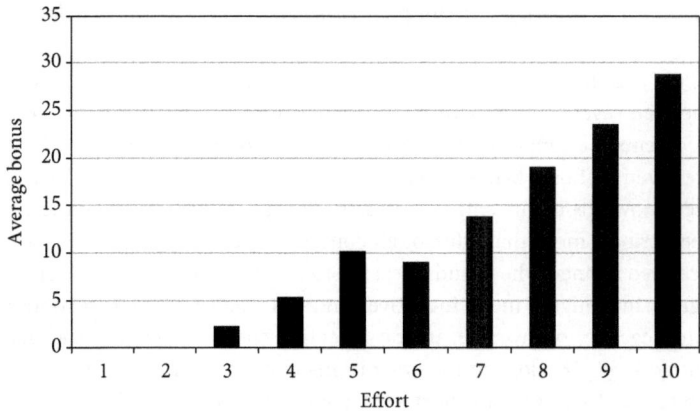

Figure 4.2 Relation between the actual bonus paid by the principal and effort level of the agent.
Source: Fehr et al. (2007) with permission of The Econometric Society.

fully committed to their announced bonuses. Rather, the actual bonus paid out depends heavily on the effort level of the agent, as shown in Figure 4.2. In conclusion, across all three contractual forms, the principals strongly prefer the bonus contract to the other contracts.

Fehr and Schmidt (2007) address one shortcoming of the Fehr et al. (2007) paper. They allow principals to combine a voluntary bonus (the carrot) with an incentive contract that allows for fines (the stick). It was hoped that this more general contract would probably perform the best. However, they found that two-thirds of the principals still preferred the pure bonus contract to the more general contract and the combined contract did not elicit greater effort.

A lower bonus is offered in the combined contract as compared to a bonus contract alone. Since agents might not know the type of the principal, they may take the choice of a combined contract by the principal as a signal that the principal is self-regarding and, so, less likely to offer a bonus. In anticipation, agents put in a low level of effort, which leads to lower profits in the combined contract relative to the bonus contract. The belief that principals who are less fair are also the ones more likely to choose the more general contract and less likely to pay a bonus is confirmed in the experimental findings.[14] This evidence further underpins assumption A2 in the theoretical model made above.

The evidence in Fehr et al. (2007) indicates that implicit contracts were chosen in 88% of the cases even when an explicit contract was available. Implicit contracts also elicited higher effort and were more profitable. The key to the success of the implicit contracts was the mutual

---

[14] In an insightful paper, Bénabou and Tirole (2003) consider the conflict between *intrinsic* and *extrinsic* motivation as a result of asymmetric information in a principal–agent framework. They find conditions under which incentives will or will not be an effective instrument. For instance, roughly paraphrased, one of their results is that incentives may crowd out intrinsic motivation when the principal is better informed and the agent has low ability in performing a task. Under these conditions, giving the agent a high-powered incentive may lead the agent to infer that his ability is actually low, which may be demotivating. These results also have a bearing on the difference in experimental practice in economics and psychology. Experimental economists emphasize the role of incentives, or extrinsic motivation, while experimental psychologists emphasize the role of intrinsic motivation and downplay the use of incentives in experiments. Most of the experimental results that we report are conducted under full information, so they are not suitable to test or apply the results of Bénabou and Tirole (2003).

reciprocity of the principal and the agent. For instance, reciprocal principals were expected to honor their promise to pay a bonus, hence, eliciting greater effort. Explicit contracts might on the other hand be perceived to be hostile, so they elicit lower effort.

Suppose that there are two parties to a contract and at least one party must make relation-specific investment in the relationship. An influential view in the property rights approach predicts that the institution of *joint ownership* will hamper short-term *relation-specific investment* because each party will fear that, ex-post, its investment will be held up by the other party (Hart, 1995). One proposed solution is to vest *residual control rights* in the hands of the party that makes the investment in the physical asset (Grossman and Hart, 1986).

A simplified version of the Grossman and Hart (1986) framework is considered in the two-player experiments conducted by Fehr et al. (2008). In the first stage, one or both players are asked to choose the form of their relationship, e.g., *single* or *joint* ownership (see below). In the second stage, the two players, A and B, make respective investments, $a, b \in \{1, 2, \ldots, 10\}$, that lead to a joint surplus $v(a, b)$. The cost of the investment equals the level of the investment. Investments are made sequentially: B invests first, followed by A who observes B's investment decision before choosing his own investment. Two possible regimes are considered.

1. Under *A-ownership*, A hires B on a fixed wage contract that pays a wage w. Net of the respective investments, the payoffs of A and B are respectively given by $v(a, b) - a - w$ and $w - b$.
2. Under *joint ownership*, each player gets one half of the total surplus, net of their respective investment costs. So the respective payoffs of A and B are: $\frac{1}{2}v(a, b) - a$ and $\frac{1}{2}v(a, b) - b$.

The game has been set up in such a way (by an appropriate choice of $v(a, b)$) that the first best levels of investments are $a = b = 10$. The predictions of the standard incomplete contracts model for self-regarding preferences are as follows. Under A-ownership, B has no incentive to invest, so b takes its lowest value, $b = 1$. Under joint ownership, each individual has to share half the marginal return with the other party. Given the setup of the problem, this induces the lowest possible investment for each player $a = b = 1$.[15]

The predictions of the model with self-regarding preferences are rejected by the experimental evidence. Player A chooses joint ownership in more than 80% of the cases. The respective investment levels chosen by the players, on average, under joint ownership, are $a = 6.5$ and $b = 8.9$. Furthermore, A earns more, on average, if he chooses joint ownership, relative to A-ownership. The explanation is that joint ownership is more conducive to reciprocal behavior. Player B expects A to behave reciprocally. This would be true even if player B is self-regarding but knew that player A has other-regarding preferences. Such expectations (which are fulfilled in equilibrium) induce player B to invest.

To summarize: the experimental evidence shows that incentive contracts are often outperformed by bonus contracts; incentive contracts can be viewed as hostile; and the institution of joint ownership can tap into the reciprocity of economic agents rather than holding-up investment through opportunistic channels.

Suppose that n ex-ante identical agents work in a team for a principal and everyone has self-regarding preferences. Each of the n agents undertakes a sub-project, whose success is guaranteed

---

[15] Essentially, A's choice of $a = a(b)$ is given from $0.5 v_a(a(b), b) = 1$. Substituting in the first stage, the optimal choice of b is found from $0.5 \left[v_a(a(b), b) \frac{da}{db} + v_b(a(b), b) \right] = 1$. For the functional forms chosen in the experiments, it turns out that $a = b = 1$.

by working hard; under shirking, the sub-project succeeds with probability $0 \leq p_i < 1$. Effort on the sub-project or its outcome cannot be contracted on. Each sub-project is part of a grand project whose success can be verified by all parties, hence, the wage vector of the n agents, $(w_1, w_2, \ldots, w_n)$, is conditioned solely on its outcome. Let $0 \leq \widehat{n} \leq n$ agents work hard on their sub-projects. Then the probability that the grand project succeeds is $p(\widehat{n})$ where p is an increasing and convex function. The aim of the principal is to minimize aggregate wage payments such that all the agents find it incentive compatible to work hard.

Under these conditions, Winter (2004) showed that it is optimal to pay unequal wages for equal work. Thus, wage inequality (or discrimination) among agents is efficient. The intuition is along the following lines. Since effort has the nature of a public good, agents would wish to free-ride on the effort levels of others. Each agent, if rational, can foresee this. Hence, he may withhold costly effort because if others do not work hard, the project is unlikely to succeed, which, in turn, does not justify his effort. If some agents are paid high enough discriminatory wages, so as to raise their stakes in the success of the grand project, the remaining agents feel sufficiently reassured to also work hard. Thus, discrimination in wages allows agents to coordinate their beliefs on the success of the grand project. Conditional on these beliefs, they indeed work hard, which fulfills the original beliefs.

Cabrales et al. (2010) and Goerg et al. (2010) report experimental support for this framework. The experiments show that efficiency is lower under equal pay for equal work, relative to pay discrimination. However, the experimental results of Abeler et al. (2010) that we have examined in Chapter 2 show that equal pay for unequal effort levels reduces effort levels in subsequent rounds and reduces output.

In actual practice, the implementation of a discriminatory wage scheme may run into difficulties with various employment legislations.[16] A more fundamental concern with this approach is that other-regarding preferences have been widely documented, not only in experimental games (Volume 2 of the book is a testament to this claim) but also in a range of principal–agent situations. Insofar as principals can rely on the other-regarding preferences of even a fraction of the agents, or on their reciprocity, the optimal contracts are likely to be markedly different. Indeed, the empirical contracts in Cabrales et al. (2010) and Goerg et al. (2010) concentrate on a narrow range of contracts that rule out reciprocity-based contracts such as bonus and trust contracts, which are found to be efficacious, as the evidence in this section suggests.

There might be substantial heterogeneity with respect to worker characteristics such as their risk aversion and other-regarding preferences. Will workers of different productivity levels and different personal characteristics self-select or sort themselves into fixed wage contracts and incentive contracts (such as piece-rate wages, tournaments, or revenue sharing)? It is quite difficult in field studies to observe the sorting decision. Hence, it is not clear if the observed positive effects of incentives on effort are the result of pure-incentive effects or the result of sorting of more productive workers into incentive contracts. By contrast, experiments allow a clean separation of these different motives.

Dohmen and Falk (2011) address these questions within a novel experimental design. They find that more productive workers self-select themselves into incentive schemes relative to fixed wage schemes. Output and effort are higher under the incentive contracts but these effects

---

[16] However, it is possible that firms may find other means of engaging in such practices. For instance, non-pecuniary discrimination or seniority based pay, etc. However, non-pecuniary discrimination and seniority-based pay have other well-known rationales also.

are driven largely by the sorting effects of workers. Furthermore, more risk averse subjects, and women, are more likely to self-select themselves into the fixed wage contract. Somewhat surprisingly, other-regarding preferences play only a marginal role in the self-selection decision.

Dohmen and Falk (2011) assume that it is not possible for firms to know the relevant traits of potential employees, hence the use of contractual forms as a screening device. Englmaier et al. (2014) give the complementary argument that several proxies about the characteristics of workers are available to firms. These include the CV of the workers (firms might shortlist, say, four candidates from an application pool of 100), ability, personality tests, and interviews.[17]

In a novel set of experiments, Englmaier et al. (2014) first elicit the productivity and reciprocity parameters of individuals. Productivity is elicited by giving subjects a real effort task that requires matching words to a four-digit code in a list. Reciprocity is elicited by the degree of *trustworthiness* in a trust game. Firms may be given no information (treatment N), only information about trust (treatment T), only information about productivity (P), or information about productivity and trust (treatment PT). Once the relevant information (which includes no information in treatment N) is given to the firm, the firm and the worker play a standard gift exchange game. One can then compare the wage, effort level, and profit level of the firm in each treatment.

The results are as follows. There is a substantial wage premium for productivity and trust. More productive and more trustworthy subjects receive significantly higher wages. However, the wage premium for productivity is twice as large as the premium for trust. In regression analysis, with the effort level of the worker as the dependent variable, once the wage is included as an explanatory variable, then productivity and trust add no further explanatory power. The reason is that wages are endogenous, and they correctly incorporate the effects of productivity and trustworthiness. Firms make the highest profits when the workers have both desirable features, productivity and trust. More trustworthy workers also induce a smaller variation in the profits and output levels of the firm.

4.4 Reciprocity and long-term contracts

The explanation of the structure of long-term relations, say, between firms and their suppliers, is of fundamental importance in industrial organization. Consider infinitely repeated games in which considerations of future costs and benefits of current actions give rise to *instrumental reciprocity*. In addition, suppose that individuals also exhibit *intrinsic reciprocity*. What is the interaction between these two different types of reciprocity? For instance, are these two types of reciprocity complementary or substitutes? These issues are addressed by Brown et al. (2004), which we now consider.

A repeated experiment was performed with 15 trading periods and 238 subjects who were assigned to play either the role of a firm or a worker. To model the importance of issues of reputation formation, each firm and worker were assigned an *ID* number. Each firm could only hire one worker in any period. Any period consisted of two subperiods. In the first subperiod,

---

[17] For instance, in the hiring process for academics in universities, the ability and personality characteristics are sought to be discovered through references, CV, one-to-one meetings with staff, job talk in the department, and interviews with committees.

a firm could offer a contract (w_b, e_n, ID), i.e., the contract specifies a *binding* wage level, w_b, a *non-binding* effort level, e_n, and the firm's identification number, *ID*. Firms can make either a *public offer* (open to all workers) or a *private offer* (open only to a worker with a particular *ID* number). In each period, and in each treatment, there were ten workers and seven firms, so there was always an excess supply of workers.

The experiments considered the following three treatments.

1. In the complete contracts condition, or *treatment C*, there is third party enforcement, i.e., the experimenter makes sure that the contracted effort level is always honored. Thus, the contracted effort level, e_n, equals actual effort level, e_a.
2. In the incomplete contracts condition, or *treatment ICF*, there is no third party enforcement of the contract, so it is possible that $e_n \neq e_a$.

In each of these two treatments, there is the possibility that the firm hires the same worker for more than one period, which constitutes a *long-term relation*. Hence, long-term relations, if they are observed, are purely endogenous.

3. To better understand the effectiveness of long-term relations, a control treatment, *treatment ICR*, is introduced. This is identical to treatment ICF, except that long-term relations are ruled out. In the actual experiments, this was achieved by jumbling the ID numbers of players at the end of each period, so that firms could not guarantee hiring the same worker through private offers even if they wanted to.

In the event of a successful contract between a firm and a worker, the payoff of the self-regarding firm, π, and the self-regarding worker, u, are respectively

$$\pi_s = 10e - w; \; u_s = w - c(e). \tag{4.60}$$

The cost function of effort, $c(e)$, is increasing and convex; it is shown in Table 4.1.

If a firm or a worker is unable to enter into a contract with the other party, then their respective payoffs are $\pi_s = 0$, $u_s = 5$, where the worker's outside option, e.g., unemployment benefits, is given by 5. Thus, the total social surplus in the worker–firm relationship (net of the worker's outside option) is given by

$$S = \pi_s + u_s - 5 = 10e - c(e) - 5. \tag{4.61}$$

4.4.1 The outcome with self-regarding preferences

We consider self-regarding preferences first, followed by other-regarding preferences in the next section.

Table 4.1 The cost of effort function.

e	1	2	3	4	5	6	7	8	9	10
$c(e)$	0	1	2	4	6	8	10	12	15	18

Source: Brown et al. (2004).

Lemma 4.6 *The socially efficient level of effort in any period is given by $e = 10$.*

Proof: In any period, marginal benefit of a unit of effort is 10, while the highest marginal cost is 3 (see Table 4.1). Further, the payoffs are independent across periods. Hence, in any period, it is optimal to choose the highest effort level, $e^* = 10$. ∎

Lemma 4.7 *In the ICF and ICR treatments, in any pairwise interaction, and in every period, the worker chooses the lowest effort level $e_I = 1$ and the firm pays a wage $w_I = 5$. The total social surplus $S_I = 5$ is reaped entirely by firms.*

Proof: Effort is not enforceable by a third party in the ICF and ICR treatments, workers receive a binding wage, w_b, and there is full information in each of the finite number of periods. Consider the last period. Self-regarding workers choose the least possible effort, i.e., $e_I = 1$. Anticipating this, firms choose a wage rate to ensure that the workers get no more than their outside option, so $w_I = c(1) + 5 = 5$. Substituting $w_I = 5$, $e_I = 1$ in (4.61) and using Table 4.1 we get that $S_I = 5$. However, since workers simply get their outside option, the entire surplus is reaped by firms. Now consider the penultimate period. In this period, the matching of firms and workers may be different but the solution is identical to that in the last period. Continuing backwards in this manner, we obtain an identical solution in each period. ∎

Lemma 4.8 *In the complete contracts treatment, treatment C, in every period, the optimal effort level is $e_c = 10$, wage is $w_c = 23$ and the surplus is $S_c = 77$.*

Proof: A third party, the experimenter, ensures that the contracted effort level in treatment C is binding. Consider the last period. As in the proof of Lemma 4.6, it is optimal to induce the highest effort level. The wage must now ensure that the worker's individual rationality constraint is satisfied, so $w_c = c(10) + 5 = 23$. Substituting $e_c = 10$ in (4.61) and using Table 4.1 we get that $S_c = 77$. By backward induction, the same outcome occurs every period.

Lemma 4.9 *Under self-regarding preferences, firms are indifferent between making private and public offers in the three treatments, C, ICF, ICR.*

Proof: Since there are no issues of reputation building, there is no additional gain from hiring a worker more than once. In any period, any worker is as good as another. Hence, private offers are just as good as public offers. ∎

4.4.2 The outcome with other-regarding preferences

Suppose that at least some workers have other-regarding preferences of the Fehr–Schmidt form (FS). Recall that there are 15 trading periods. We make the following assumptions.

A1. In any period, each individual compares his/her payoffs only with their trading partner. Thus, if i, j are trading partners, with respective material payoffs x_i and x_j, the FS utility of player i is:

$$U_i = x_i - \alpha_i \max\{x_j - x_i, 0\} - \beta_i \max\{x_i - x_j, 0\}. \quad (4.62)$$

A2. $\alpha_i = \beta_i = 0.5 + \epsilon$ where ϵ is some small but strictly positive number.
A3. By giving up a dollar, each player can punish the trading partner by an amount $\delta > 1 + \frac{1}{0.5+\epsilon}$.

A4. 60% of all players are other-regarding, while 40% are purely self-regarding (this is roughly consistent with some of the empirical evidence reviewed above).

A5. Other than in treatment ICR, in any period, firms can choose to fire the existing worker or hire the worker for the next period.

A6. There is no discounting of future payoffs.

Lemma 4.10 *Under assumptions A1–A6, if players have other-regarding preferences, they prefer to equalize payoffs with their trading partners.*

Proof: Suppose first that $x_j > x_i$. Using (4.62), the payoff of player i is $U_i = x_i - \alpha_i(x_j - x_i)$. Suppose that player i now gives up n units to punish the trading partner in order to equate payoffs, i.e., $x_j - n\delta = x_i - n$. Thus, $n = \frac{x_j - x_i}{\delta - 1}$. The post-punishment payoff of player i is $U_i = x_i - n = x_i - \frac{x_j - x_i}{\delta - 1}$. Given the original supposition that $x_j > x_i$, an equalization of payoffs improves player i's utility if $x_i - \frac{x_j - x_i}{\delta - 1} > x_i - \alpha_i(x_j - x_i)$ or $\alpha_i > \frac{1}{\delta - 1}$. Substituting $\alpha_i = 0.5 + \epsilon$ we get the condition $\delta > 1 + \frac{1}{0.5 + \epsilon}$, which is true by assumption A3 above.

Now suppose that $x_j < x_i$. Using (4.62), the payoff of player i is $U_i = x_i - \beta_i(x_i - x_j)$. In order to equalize payoffs, suppose that player i makes a transfer of $(x_i - x_j)/2$ to player j. The post-transfer payoff of player i is $U_i = x_i - \frac{x_i - x_j}{2}$. It is worth making the equalizing transfer if $x_i - \frac{x_i - x_j}{2} \geq x_i - \beta_i(x_i - x_j)$, which holds because $\beta_i > \frac{1}{2}$. Thus, both players find it optimal to equalize payoffs. ■

THE SOLUTION UNDER ASYMMETRIC INFORMATION

The remaining theoretical discussion is entirely organized around Proposition 4.12 below, which collects all the relevant results in this section. Workers have asymmetric information about the type of the firm, which can either be self-regarding or other-regarding. Prior to hiring a worker, firms also do not know if the worker is self-regarding, although, from assumption A4, they know that 60% are other-regarding and 40% are self-regarding. Thus, there is two-sided asymmetric information. Let us first offer the insights that underpin Proposition 4.12.

The finite period setup is realistic (e.g., because workers eventually retire). It also allows the workers' types to separate in the last period because self-regarding workers will always shirk in the last period. Since other-regarding workers respond to higher wages with higher effort (as in gift exchange games), the firm may find it profitable to offer rents to the workers. While self-regarding workers do not *intrinsically reciprocate*, however, the attractiveness of rents also induces them to *instrumentally reciprocate*. Hence, self-regarding workers would like to build a reputation for reciprocity and enjoy rents—they milk this reputation for as long as it is possible in the finite horizon game. This behavior suits other-regarding firms because profits are increasing in the effort levels of workers. Thus, *reputation effects interact in an important manner with reciprocity effects*.

The possibility that a fraction of the workers are other-regarding (assumption A4) means that even in the last period of the game, the firm can offer rents to the workers and, rationally, hope that other-regarding workers will respond with greater effort. Consider a self-regarding worker in the penultimate period of the game. If the worker shirks, then he will be fired, hence, he will be unable to avail himself of the last period rents. The contract offered in the penultimate period must ensure that the current gain to shirking of the self-regarding worker is smaller as compared to the expected future loss of rents, as in models of efficiency wages (Shapiro and Stiglitz, 1984).

Such repeated contracts that satisfy incentive compatibility in each period, provide the necessary inducement for self-regarding workers to put in greater effort. This, in turn, facilitates the endogenous formation of long-term contracts and we can expect the ICF treatment to foster greater effort and rents relative to the ICR treatment, which does not allow long-term relations. One may, thus, also expect a higher share of private offers relative to public offers in the ICF treatment.

Why does the firm not offer very low rents in the penultimate period? The reason is that it will then be perceived as being self-regarding itself and workers with other-regarding preferences would react negatively to lower wages offered by reducing their effort. As is typically the case with repeated games, there are a large number of equilibria. Finally, in treatment C, because the contracts are always enforced with the help of a third party, there is no need to give any incentives or rents. And there is no need to form long-term relations either. So one would expect a preponderance of public offers in treatment C.

We now use these insights to formalize the relevant results in Proposition 4.12.

Proposition 4.12 *Consider two-sided asymmetric information in which the type of the firm and the worker (self-regarding or other-regarding) is private information. The game is played over 15 periods and the outside option of any worker is 5. Assumptions A1–A6 hold. In the perfect Bayesian equilibrium of the model:*

I. *The strategy of the other-regarding and the self-regarding workers is as follows:*
   (a) *Other-regarding workers choose their effort levels to equalize payoffs with their trading partners every period and are willing to work if their individual rationality constraint is satisfied.*
   (b) *Faced with a contractual, but non-binding, effort level, e_n, self-regarding workers choose to shirk (i.e., choose $e < e_n$) in any period if the cost of effort, $c(e_n)$, is more than the expected loss from being fired.*

II. *The strategy of the other-regarding and self-regarding firms is as follows:*
   (a) *Firms renew the contract of a worker in period t if in period $t-1$ the worker put in $e = e_n$. Otherwise the worker is fired and earns his outside option in all future periods. Public offers are made by the firm in the first period and in any period following the decision of workers to shirk ($e < e_n$).*
   (b) *Both types of firms (self- and other-regarding) offer a pooling contract for the first 14 periods but offer separating contracts in the 15th period. In periods 1–13, the contract offered is $(w_b, e_n) = (59, 10)$. In period 14, the contract offered is $(w_b, e_n) = (40, 7)$. If $e = e_n$, then the payoffs of the firm and the worker are equalized in the first 14 periods. In period 15, the self-regarding firm offers the contract $(w_b, e_n) = (34, 6)$ but it is not unique. The other-regarding firm offers the contract $(w_b, e_n) = (5, 1)$.*

III. *The out of equilibrium beliefs are as follows:*
   (a) *All workers believe that the firm will terminate employment in period $t+1$ if it does not pay a fair wage (that equalizes payoffs) in period t.*
   (b) *Higher average effort levels can be sustained in the ICF treatment relative to the ICR treatment. Long-term relations arise endogenously in the ICF treatment and there are greater private offers in the ICF treatment relative to the ICR treatment.*

Proof: Consider self-regarding firms first. From Lemma 4.10 we know that an other-regarding worker will always equalize payoffs, i.e.,

$$10e - w = w - c(e). \tag{4.63}$$

Denote the solution to this equation by $e(w)$; this is the effort reaction function of the agent. The structure of the problem is discrete, but for pedagogical convenience we consider the continuous case, so let $c'(e)$ denote the marginal cost of effort. Using (4.63),

$$\frac{de(w)}{dw} = \frac{2}{10 + c'(e)} > 0, \tag{4.64}$$

hence, other-regarding workers will always reciprocate a higher wage offer with higher effort, as in gift exchange games.

We solve the game using backward induction.

(1) Consider first, the last period, period 15: Given the stated strategies in the proposition, a pooling equilibrium is played in the first 14 periods, hence, the type of the firm, other-regarding or self-regarding, is not revealed to the workers. Using (4.60) and assumption A4, the expected payoff of a self-regarding firm is given by

$$E\pi_s = 0.6[10e(w) - w] + 0.4[10 - w]. \tag{4.65}$$

The other-regarding worker reciprocates higher wage with higher effort (4.64). But the self-regarding worker chooses to shirk and put in the minimum effort level, $e = 1$, because it is the last period. Differentiating (4.65) with respect to w and using (4.64) we get

$$\frac{\partial E\pi_s}{\partial w} = \frac{12}{10 + c'(e)} - 1. \tag{4.66}$$

Since the cost of effort function is weakly convex throughout, for an interior solution, solving (4.66) gives $c'(e) = 2$. From Table 4.1, $c'(e) = 2$ for all effort levels in the set $\{3, 4, \ldots, 8\}$, hence, we have multiple equilibria. Let us choose the particular solution $e = 6$. To induce the other-regarding worker to undertake an effort level $e = 6$, the wage must be such that the payoffs of the worker and the firm are equalized (see Lemma 4.10). Substitute $e = 6$, $c(6) = 8$ in (4.63) to get $w = 34$. Hence, the (non-unique) contract offered by the self-regarding firm in period 15 is $(w_b, e_n) = (34, 6)$.

Since a pooling equilibrium is played in the first 14 periods, the type is unknown at the start of period 15. The expected payoff of the self-regarding firm $E\pi_s$ is given in (4.65). The payoff of the worker is $u = w - c(e)$. Using (4.62), the utility of an other-regarding firm is given by

$$\pi_f(k) = \pi_s - \alpha_f \max\{u_k - \pi_s, 0\} - \beta_f \max\{\pi_s - u_k, 0\},$$

where $k = f, s$ is the type of the worker—other-regarding or self-regarding—and π_s denotes the material payoff of the self-regarding firm, given in (4.60). Using assumption A4, the expected profit of the other-regarding firm from the contract (w_b, e_n) is given by

$$E\pi_f(w_b, e_n) = 0.6\pi_f(f) + 0.4\pi_f(s). \tag{4.67}$$

What is the optimal contract offered by the other-regarding firm in the last period? One can show that the other-regarding firm will prefer the contract $(w_b, e_n) = (5, 1)$ to any other contract that induces an effort level from the other-regarding worker belonging to the set $\{3,4,\ldots,8\}$. Recall that this is the set of effort levels that the self-regarding firm finds it optimal to induce from the other-regarding worker. The self-regarding worker, of course, only puts in the minimum effort level $e = 1$ in period 15 because there is no future to worry about. We show that it is non-optimal for the other-regarding firm to elicit the effort level $e = 3$ (a similar check can be made against the other effort levels, i.e., $4, 5, \ldots, 8$).

Suppose first that the other-regarding firm offers the contract $(w_b, e_n) = (5, 1)$. It is simple to check that the other-regarding worker also chooses the same effort as a self-regarding worker, i.e., $e = 1$, because it equalizes the payoffs with the firm (see Lemma 4.10) and ensures that the individual rationality constraint is met (recall that the outside option of the worker is 5). Since both types of workers choose $e = 1$, using (4.67), we get that, corresponding to the contract $(w_b, e_n) = (5, 1)$, the expected profit of the other-regarding principal is

$$E\pi_f(5, 1) = 5. \tag{4.68}$$

Let us now compute the payoff of the other-regarding firm from the contract $(w_b, e_n) = (w_b, 3)$, where the non-contractible effort level is $e_n = 3$. The actual effort level supplied by the self-regarding worker $e_a = 1$ because it is the last period. What level of wage, w_b, does the firm need to offer, so that the other-regarding worker chooses $e = 3$? Since the other-regarding agent equalizes material payoffs with the principal, substitute $e = 3$, $c(3) = 2$ in (4.63) to get $w_b = 16$. Substitute $w_b = 16$, $e = 3$ in (4.65) to get:

$$E\pi_s = 0.6[10 \times 3 - 16] + 0.4[10 - 16] = 6. \tag{4.69}$$

The respective payoffs of the self-regarding and other-regarding workers are $16 - c(1) = 16$ and $16 - c(3) = 14$. It is simple to calculate that $\pi_f(f) = 14$ and $\pi_f(s) = -6 - 22\alpha_f$. Thus, we get the payoff of the other-regarding firm as

$$E\pi_f(16, 3) = 0.6 \times 14 + 0.4(-6 - 22\alpha_f). \tag{4.70}$$

Comparing (4.68), (4.70), $E\pi_f(5, 1) > E\pi_f(16, 3) \Leftrightarrow 5 > 6 - 8.8\alpha_f \Leftrightarrow 8.8\alpha_f > 1$, which holds because $\alpha_f > 0.5$ (assumption A2). Hence, the contract $(5, 1)$ dominates the contract $(16, 3)$ for the other-regarding firm. A similar exercise shows that it is not optimal for the other-regarding firm to induce any effort level other than $e = 1$.

We conclude that in period 15, the self-regarding firm offers $(w_b, e_n) = (34, 6)$, while the other-regarding firm offers $(w_b, e_n) = (5, 1)$. Thus, the two types of firms offer a separating contract in period 15.

(2) Now consider period 14: Workers do not know the type of the firm. But given the strategies, they are aware of the contracts that will be offered in period 15 by both types of firms. From assumption A4, they know the respective proportions of the types of the firms. Hence, the expected future payoff of other-regarding workers, $E\pi_f$, from not shirking in period 14, so ensuring that they get hired by the same firm in period 15 is

$$E\pi_f = 0.6(5 - c(1)) + 0.4(34 - c(6)) = 13.4. \tag{4.71}$$

A self-regarding worker, on the other hand, will put in $e = 1$ in period 15, hence, his expected future payoff, $E\pi_s$, from not-shirking in period 14 is

$$E\pi_s = 0.6(5 - c(1)) + 0.4(34 - c(1)) = 16.6.$$

If the worker shirks in period 14, then given the strategies in the proposition, he is fired and earns his outside option of 5. So the expected future net gain from not-shirking in period 14 for the other-regarding and self-regarding workers is respectively $13.4 - 5 = 8.4$ and $16.6 - 5 = 11.6$. Since the worker receives a binding wage, the current gain to a self-regarding worker from shirking in period 14 is $c(e_n) - c(1) = c(e_n)$ (from Table 4.1, $c(1) = 0$) where e_n is the non-binding effort level in period 14. Hence, the self-regarding worker shirks if the current gain from shirking is greater than the expected future loss from shirking, i.e.,

$$c(e_n) > 11.6. \tag{4.72}$$

From Table 4.1, the set of effort levels which satisfy this inequality is $\{8, 9, 10\}$. Hence, in period 14, any effort level $e \leq 7$ will induce no-shirking from the self-regarding worker. A higher effort level leads to greater output and an other-regarding worker equalizes payoffs. Hence, inducing a higher effort level from the set of incentive-compatible effort levels for the self-regarding worker allows the principal to enjoy a higher payoff. Thus, it is optimal for the firm to induce $e_n = 7$ in period 14.

Using (4.63) and Table 4.1, the firm has to then pay a payoff equalizing wage $w_b = \frac{10 \times 7 + c(7)}{2} = 40$. Why is it not optimal to pay $w > 40$? If $w > 40$, then other-regarding workers will reciprocate with extra effort; however, self-regarding workers will not reciprocate because their no-shirking constraint will be violated. But does the extra effort from other-regarding workers make it worthwhile to offer $w > 40$? The answer is in the negative. The firm makes no additional profits from self-regarding workers. The extra profit made on account of the other-regarding workers is $\frac{d}{dw}(10e(w) - w)$, which when evaluated at $e = 7$ gives $\frac{20}{12} - 1 = 0.67$. However the extra wage cost on account of the self-regarding workers is 1. Hence, the net change in expected profit is $-1 + 0.67 = -0.33 < 0$. It is also not optimal to pay $w < 40$. Given out of equilibrium beliefs (see Proposition 4.12 III), $w < 40$ is construed as an unfair wage, hence, the expectation is that workers will not be rehired by the firm for period 15. But this induces full shirking from workers in period 14. Hence, $w_b = 40$ is the optimal wage for period 14.

In equilibrium, the firm must also make a private offer to the worker at the end of period 14. If it did not do this, then there is a (large) possibility that the current worker will not be rehired. This dilutes the incentives of the worker to work in period 14.

(3) Let us now focus on period 13: Workers know (from the firm's stated strategy) that for period 14, the pooling contract offered is $(w_b, e_n) = (40, 7)$, while for period 15, with probability 0.6, the firm is other-regarding and offers the contract $(w_b, e_n) = (5, 1)$, while with probability 0.4 the firm is self-regarding and offers the contract $(w_b, e_n) = (34, 6)$. The expected future rent (in periods 14 and 15) to a self-regarding worker who does not engage in shirking in period 13 is

$$[40 - c(7) - 5] + [0.6(5 - c(1)) + 0.4(34 - c(6)) - 5] = 33.4. \tag{4.73}$$

The two square brackets capture expected rents in periods 14 and 15 respectively. Analogous to (4.72), the self-regarding worker will shirk in period 13 if

$$c(e_n) > 33.4.$$

Hence, from Table 4.1, the set of effort levels that will not induce shirking is the entire set, i.e., $\{1, 2, \ldots, 10\}$. Since additional effort is valuable for the firm, in order to induce an other-regarding worker to supply $e = 10$, the firm must offer a payoff equalizing wage $w_b = \frac{10 \times 10 + c(10)}{2} = 59.0$. It is, therefore, optimal to offer the contract $(w_b, e_n) = (59, 10)$ in period 13. Using backward induction it is optimal to offer this contract also in the first 12 periods.

Since only one-shot interactions take place in the ICR treatment, the maximum effort level $e = 10$ cannot be sustained in this condition. Finally, accepting a wage equal to the outside option in period 15 is rational for an other-regarding worker because there is an oversupply of workers. If some of them are perceived to be self-regarding workers who will accept the outside option, then an other-regarding worker cannot punish the firm by rejecting a low offer. ∎

4.4.3 Experimental results

The experimental results are in line with the predictions of the theoretical model (Proposition 4.12). These results are as follows:

1. The relative share of private offers is substantially greater in the ICF treatment relative to the ICR and the C treatments. Furthermore, most of the private offers (63–79% after period 5) are made to workers already working for the firm. Hence, voluntary long-term relations are maintained through private offers when there is an opportunity to do so.
2. As predicted, about 90% of the trades in treatment C took place in interactions that lasted for one or two periods only. This contrasts with the ICF condition where only a third of the trades took place in one-shot encounters. About 50% of the trades in the ICF condition took place in relationships that lasted four or more consecutive periods and about 40% in relationships that lasted eight or more consecutive periods. The separation rate between workers and firms declined significantly after period 3, suggesting the possibility of a search phase for a good match in the initial periods. A comparison of the length of the relationship under the two treatments is shown in Figure 4.3, which plots the cumulative frequency of the length of relations. The cumulative distribution function under treatment ICF first order stochastically dominates the distribution function under treatment C.

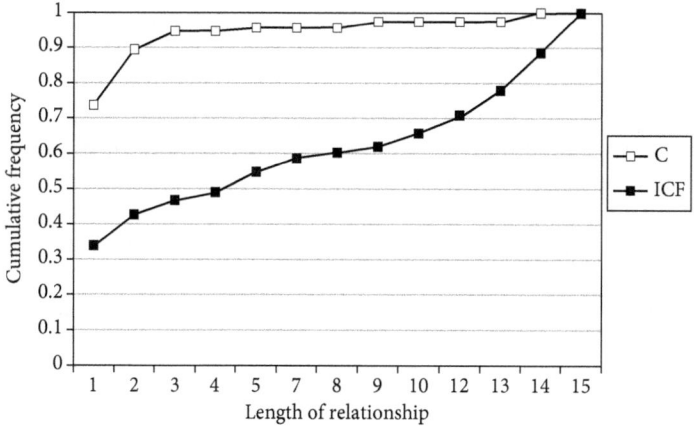

Figure 4.3 A comparision of the length of the worker–firm relationship under the two treatments.
Source: Brown et al. (2004) with permission of the Econometric Society.

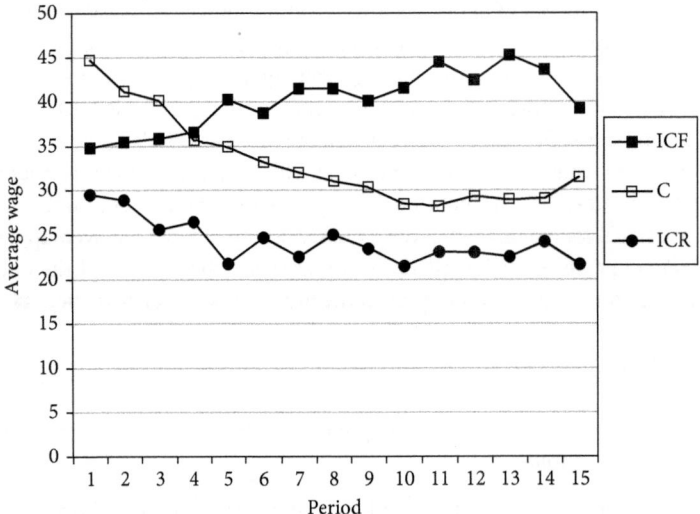

Figure 4.4 Average temporal wage in each treatment.
Source: Brown et al. (2004) with permission of the Econometric Soceity.

3. Under the ICF treatment, firms pay a rent to workers in order to induce them to put in the contracted effort level. Since rents enhance effort, due to the gift exchange mechanism, they can be interpreted as a form of *efficiency wages*. On the other hand, in treatment C, there is no need to pay efficiency wages because workers put in the contracted effort due to third party intervention. In the ICR treatment, on the other hand, there is no future to worry about, hence, efficiency wages are pointless. Thus, a clear prediction of the model is that wages and effort would be highest in the ICF treatment. These predictions are verified in Figures 4.4, 4.5. From Figure 4.4, it can be seen that the average wage is always highest in the ICF treatment except for the first few periods when the wage in the C treatment is higher. Further, the wage gap between the ICF and the ICR treatments increases over time and the gap in wages between the ICF and the other treatments is statistically significant. From Figure 4.5, there is an increase in effort over time in the ICF treatment. Effort drops off towards the end, as predicted in theory. Not surprisingly, effort is highest in treatment C, because it can be costlessly implemented through a third party and additional effort, net of the wage costs, is valuable. Furthermore, as predicted by the theory, the experimental results show that there is contingent contract renewal, i.e., a worker is more likely to have his contract renewed if he undertakes higher effort. For a worker providing the maximum effort level, the probability that the contract will be renewed in the following period is close to 1.
4. In choosing between alternative contractual forms, the incomplete contracts literature often takes the view that the contractual form which maximizes the total surplus in the relationship will be the institutional solution; for instance, the formation of firms in preference to the conduct of transactions at arms-length relationships (Hart, 1995). The experimental results indicate that the joint surplus in a relationship is higher, the longer it lasts. Since the ICF treatment is the one most conducive to long-term relations, it is not surprising that, on average, it has a higher joint surplus relative to the ICR treatment.

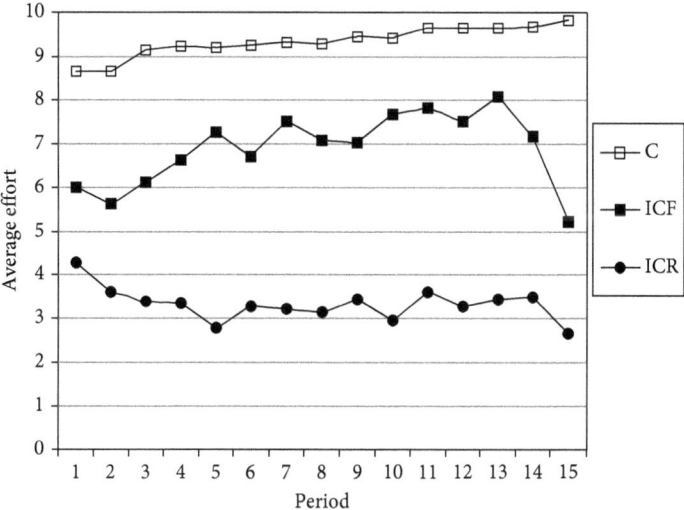

Figure 4.5 Average temporal effort in each treatment.
Source: Brown et al. (2004) with permission of the Econometric Soceity.

The highest surplus is in treatment C because the contract can be costlessly enforced. Insofar as contracts cannot be costlessly enforced in the real world, and treatment C is an idealized benchmark case, the predicted institutional solution is the ICF treatment. Figure 4.6 shows the association between profitability and the length of the relationship in the three treatments.

In Figure 4.6, the ICR and the C treatments are represented at the two extremes with the ICF treatment in the middle. Two important features of these results are the following. First,

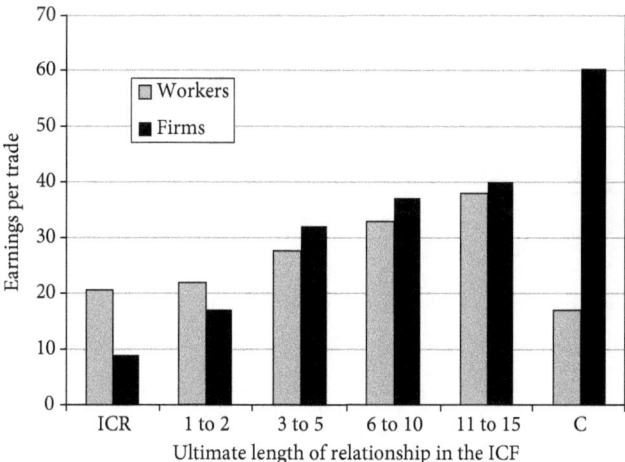

Figure 4.6 Average earnings per trade of the workers and firms in each treatment.
Source: Brown et al. (2004) with permission of The Econometric Society.

the surplus is shared less equally in the C and the ICR treatments relative to the ICF treatment. Second, the total surplus in the ICF treatment is increasing in the length of the relationship.

The experimental results suggest that initial conditions are the crucial determinant of a relationship developing into a long-term one. Of the initial relationships between workers and firms, 75% do not survive. However, 80% of the relations that survive for at least two periods go on to survive for the full duration of the experiment. Of the relationships that survive, an important factor seems to be the magnitude of the wage. If the initial wage is high, then initial effort is also high and the relation is more likely to survive. There is a gradual increase in wage and effort in relationships that survive longer than six periods. One can conjecture that this gradual increase in wage and effort creates greater mutual trust and makes the relationship more enduring.

In Brown et al. (2004) considered above, there is an excess supply of labor. In contrast, Brown et al. (2012) implement an experimental setup with an excess demand for labor. Denote the contracts C and ICF in Brown et al. (2004) by C-S and ICF-S to reflect the excess supply condition. Likewise denote the corresponding contracts under excess demand by C-D and ICF-D; contracts ICR-D and ICR-S are defined analogously. The point of the exercise is to see if the extent of unemployment has a bearing on the formation of relational contracts. Figure 4.7 compares the mean effort levels under the following two comparisons, ICF-D and ICF-S; ICR-D and ICR-S.

The evidence shows that firms are equally likely to offer contract renewal for non-shirking workers under conditions ICF-S and ICF-D. However, in the excess demand condition, workers turn down the contract renewals more often, so they switch firms more often. Hence, there is a lower formation of relational contracts. But the proportion of trades taking place in condition ICF-D is still larger than those taking place under C-D. In this sense, bilateral long-term contracts continue to play an important role even under excess demand. The effort levels under excess supply and excess demand for labor are similar.

What other factors are conducive for improving payoffs in finite period relationships? Van Dijk et al. (2002) produce experimental evidence to show that the continuation of relations produces

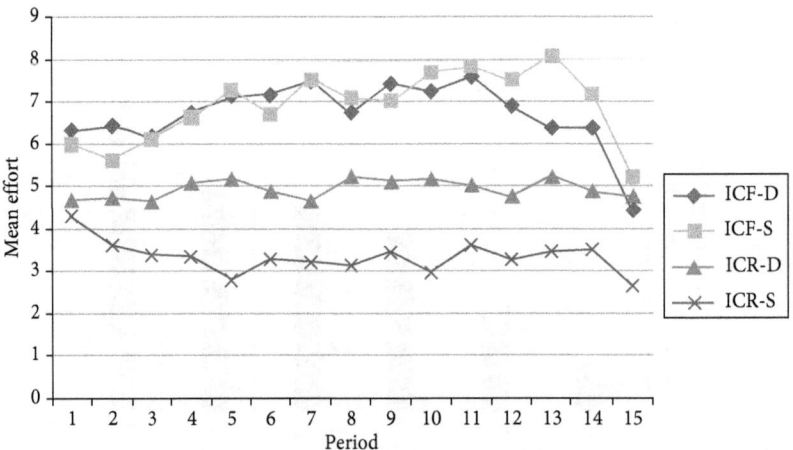

Figure 4.7 Comparison of mean effort levels under various treatments.

Source: "Competition and relational contracts: the role of unemployment as a disciplinary device," Brown, M., Falk, A., and Fehr, E., Journal of the European Economic Association, 10(4): 887–907. © 2012 by the European Economic Association.

social ties between the parties to a relationship. This strengthens their willingness to cooperate in the relationship, hence, providing an additional mechanism, other than instrumental reciprocity, that can sustain cooperative behavior. Gächter and Falk (2002) find that subjects in experiments cooperate more if they know there is a possibility that they will be paired with the same partners in the future.[18] Engelmann and Fischbacher (2009) confirm similar findings by giving a fraction of the subjects an opportunity to develop a reputation. They find that altruistic rewarding and the desire to build a reputation are important considerations for their subjects in experiments.

One argument that has been made in countering the results of cooperative behavior in one-shot games is that subjects in experiments are unable to distinguish between one-shot and repeated interactions. Hence, cooperation is some form of *maladaptation* that results from cognitive failure; for instance, Roth and Erev (1995) and Binmore et al. (1995). We have already considered these arguments, above, in the context of the ultimatum game. We have seen that individuals understand the strategic differences between one-shot and repeated interactions.

4.4.4 The nature of the firm and other-regarding preferences

When should transactions be carried out within a firm and when should they be carried out in arms-length relationships? This question has had a distinguished history in economics, particularly since Coase (1937). Simon (1951) posed this question as the choice between *employment contracts* within the firm and *sales contracts* offered by one entity to another. The advantage of an employment contract is that it offers greater flexibility in decisions to the employer. Within legal bounds, it allows the employer to control more closely the type of task that an employee will undertake. The cost of an employment contract is that employees may be treated more opportunistically by the employer (within legal bounds); this may reduce the intrinsic motivation of employees and make them reluctant to accept such a contract unless rents are high. The sales contract, by contrast, offers less flexibility to the employer but prevents opportunistic treatment of the employee, making the latter more likely to accept the contract at a lower rent.

Bartling et al. (2013) formalize similar trade-offs between two parties, a principal and an agent. The two parties sign one of two contracts, a sales contract or an employment contract, prior to the realization of one of two equiprobable states of the world—state 1 and state 2. There are three possible tasks, 1–3, that the principal can assign to the agent. Table 4.2 shows the relevant, state-contingent and task-contingent, economic information. This includes the revenues of the principal, the cost of the agent, the total surplus to be shared between the two parties, the principal's profit, and the agent's income. Task 3 always gives the highest revenues in each state but agents incur very high costs in undertaking it, hence, it is never efficient in any state. In state 1, task 1 is most efficient (total surplus is 160) and in state 2, task 2 is most efficient (total surplus is 160). The outside option of the principal and the agent is respectively 0 and 30.

A *sales contract* takes the form (w_b, task), where w_b is a binding wage and task specifies one of the three tasks. Thus, before any uncertainty about the state of the world is realized, the agent, in a sales contract, already knows which contractual task has been specified. An important cost of such a contract is that the ex-ante choice of the task may not be ex-post optimal. An *employment contract*, takes the form (w_b, principal chooses task ex-post). Thus, the principal has *residual*

---

[18] Dal Bó (2002) finds similar results for the prisoner's dilemma game. Cooperation increases when the probability of future interaction with the same partner increases from 0.5 to 0.75.

Table 4.2 The relevant economic information in each state of the world.

		Task 1	Task 2	Task 3
State 1	Revenue	160	80	190
	Cost	0	40	130
	Surplus	160	40	60
	Principal's profit	160-wage	80-wage	190-wage
	Agent's income	wage	wage-40	wage-130
State 2	Revenue	30	200	230
	Cost	0	40	130
	Surplus	30	160	100
	Principal's profit	30-wage	200-wage	230-wage
	Agent's income	wage	wage-40	wage-130

Source: Bartling et al. (2013).

control rights on the choice of one of the three tasks after observing the state of the world. Such a contract gives greater flexibility to the principal on task choice, but leaves open the possibility that the principal might choose the more exploitative task 3 and *abuse his legal power*. Thus, this is a problem of *employer moral hazard*. Once the state of the world is realized, the contracts are executed.

The game is played between eight principals and eight agents, over 15 periods. All players are assigned ID numbers at the start of the game. In the first stage, the principal makes a *private offer* that is addressed to a particular agent by specifying the ID number. This is followed by a *public offer* to other agents. In the second stage, agents observe these offers. If an agent receives more than two private offers he can accept only one. Once agents have accepted the private offers, if any, the unmatched agents are randomly matched with the public offers of the principal. At the end of this process, at least one agent is matched with one principal.

There are two main treatments. In treatment RANDOM, the ID numbers are randomly reassigned at the beginning of each period. Thus, when a principal makes contract offers or agents examine the contract offers, they cannot identify the past behavior of the other party. By contrast, in the treatment FIXED, the ID numbers stay fixed over the 15 periods, hence, principals can specify the ID number of the agent they would like to be matched with. In this case, the agent can use his past experience with the principal to make a more informed acceptance decision. In the treatment RANDOM, there is no point for the principal to build a reputation for not abusing authority (say, by not choosing task 3). However, building a reputation is critical in treatment FIXED. A third treatment, UNFAIR, is identical to RANDOM except that with an 80% chance, task 3 is exogenously chosen.

> **Proposition 4.13** *Suppose that the principal and the agent are self-regarding. The optimal contract for the principal is to offer a sales contract of the form (w_b, task 2). The employment contract is never optimal.*

Proof: Consider first, an employment contract. Suppose that we are in the last period, period 15, in any of the treatments RANDOM, FIXED, or UNFAIR. In an employment contract, since w_b is binding, the self-regarding principal will demand that the agent undertake task 3 because it is revenue maximizing. The cost of the agent is 130 and his outside option is 30. Hence, rational agents will accept an employment contract only if $w_b \geq 160$. These arguments also hold for the particular sales contract, (w_b, task 3). Since both states of the world are equiprobable, so the expected profit of the principal from an employment contract and from the sales contract (w_b, task 3) is $0.5(190 - 160) + 0.5(230 - 160) = 50$.

By contrast, the principal's expected profit from the sales contract (i) (w_b, task 1) is $0.5(160) + 0.5(30) - 30 = 65$, and (ii) ($w_b$, task 2) is $0.5(80 - 40) + 0.5(200 - 40) - 30 = 70$. Hence, the sales contract (w_b, task 2) is optimal in period 15. We can now solve the game with backward induction. The sales contract (w_b, task 2) is optimal in every period. In particular, note that in the treatment FIXED, both players know that the principal will act opportunistically in an employment contract in period 15, hence, there is no point for the principal to develop a reputation for non-abusive behavior in period 14. Using backward induction, the same applies, successively, in rounds 13, 12,...,1.

Thus, the sales contract (w_b, task 2) that gives the principal an expected profit of 70, dominates an employment contract that offers an expected profit of 50. ∎

Suppose now that we allow for a proportion, $\lambda \in (0, 1)$, of self-regarding principals and the remaining proportion $1 - \lambda$ of other-regarding principals who have the Fehr–Schmidt preferences. However, the preferences of each player is private information. This turns the game into a signaling game and one needs to find the perfect Bayesian equilibria of the game, as in Proposition 4.12 above. The presence of other-regarding principals potentially alters the solution because they do not try to exploit their residual control rights in an employment contract by choosing task 3. Unlike Proposition 4.12 that fully characterizes a perfect Bayesian equilibrium, here we offer an informal conjecture that illustrates the potential equilibria in the model.

Conjecture 4.1 *Suppose that there is asymmetric information about the type of the principal; with probability $\lambda \in (0, 1)$, the principal is self-regarding, and with probability $1 - \lambda$, the principal is other-regarding.*

(a) *In each treatment, and in each period, in one possible perfect Bayesian equilibrium, all principals offer the sales contract (w_b, task 2).*
(b) *Consider the treatment RANDOM. If a self-regarding agent is sufficiently optimistic that the principal is other-regarding $\left(\lambda \leq \frac{w-50}{110}\right)$, then he may accept the employment contract. Self-regarding principals always abuse their residual control rights by asking for task 3.*
(c) *There can be no employment contracts in the treatment UNFAIR.*
(d) *In the treatment FIXED, we "may" observe employment contracts and long-term contracts between the principal and the agent in which, ex-post, the principal requires the efficient tasks (task 1 in state 1 and task 2 in state 2).*

Basis for Conjecture 4.1: (a) Bayes' rule does not impose restrictions on out of equilibrium beliefs in such games. So let us impose the extreme beliefs that if the agent observes an employment contract, he assigns the posterior belief that the principal is self-regarding with probability 1. But this means that the agent is sure that the principal will abuse his authority by choosing task 3 in an employment contract. From Proposition 4.13 we know that the sales contract (w_b, task 2) is optimal in every period.

(b) Suppose that both types of principals offer an employment contract in period 15 and a pooling wage w. Agents believe that the self-regarding principal will choose to abuse his authority by choosing the revenue maximizing task 3, while the other-regarding principal will find it optimal to elicit an efficient task (task 1 or task 2). From Table 4.2, the cost of effort for tasks

1 and 2 is identical in states 1 and 2, and task 1 is efficient in state 1 and task 2 in state 2. Thus, a self-regarding agent should accept the employment contract if

$$\lambda\,[w-130]+(1-\lambda)\,[0.5(w)+0.5(w-40)]\geq 30 \Leftrightarrow \lambda \leq \frac{w-50}{110}. \quad (4.74)$$

Thus, given w, the self-regarding agent should accept the employment contract only if he believes that the probability of encountering a self-regarding principal is low. If the agent is other-regarding, then we have to proceed as in Proposition 4.13 by allowing extra rents for the inequity-averse agent. In the treatment RANDOM, there is no benefit for a self-regarding principal to try to build a reputation for not abusing residual control rights. Thus, such a principal will always choose to abuse authority. However, for a low enough λ there may be equilibria with employment contracts in each period.

(c) In treatment UNFAIR, task 3 is exogenously imposed with probability 0.8. Thus, even in the best case scenario in which task 1 is chosen in state 1 and task 2 in state 2, the surplus (net of the agent's outside option of 30) in the relation is

$$0.8\,[0.5\,(190+230)-130]+0.2\,[0.5(160)+0.5(200-40)]-30=66.$$

From Proposition 4.13, we know that this is dominated by a net surplus of 70 from a sales contract (w_b, task 2), hence, employment contracts should never be offered in treatment UNFAIR.

(d) Consider treatment FIXED. The formal proof can be given along the lines of Proposition 4.12. However, note that even self-regarding principals will attempt to pool with other-regarding principals in order to build a reputation for non-exploitative choice of efficient tasks (task 1 in state 1 and task 2 in state 2). The benefit of doing so is that the agent will not update his priors about the type of the principal and accept the principal's private employment offer in the next period. However, if the principal abuses the agent's trust in any period, then the agent rejects the private offer of the principal in the next period and, possibly, updates his posteriors that the type of the principal is self-regarding (this depends on the exact specification of the out of equilibrium beliefs). In the spirit of Kreps and Wilson (1982) and Milgrom and Roberts (1982) (see also Proposition 4.12) principals will try to build a reputation and milk it for a while, then revert back to their preferred contracts in the end. For instance, self-regarding principals will choose task 3 in period 15, irrespective of the treatment and this is foreseen by agents. ∎

The empirical results are as follows. In treatment RANDOM, the prediction is that authority will always be abused if players have self-regarding preferences (Conjecture 4.1). Yet, we observe that power is abused only in 51% of the cases (task 3 is chosen) but in the remaining cases one of the efficient tasks, 1 or 2, is chosen. Thus, the purely self-regarding preferences case is rejected.

Figure 4.8 shows the payoffs of the principal and the agent in the sales and employment contracts in treatment RANDOM (left panel) and treatment FIXED (right panel). In each case, on average, the principal earns a higher payoff in the employment contract, relative to the sales contract. In treatment RANDOM, on average, agents receive a higher payoff in sales contracts as compared to employment contracts. This finding is reversed in treatment FIXED and, in an employment contract, agents earn, on average, significantly higher than their outside option of 30 (i.e., they receive positive rents); by contrast agents barely earn their outside option, on average, in an employment contract in treatment RANDOM. In both treatments, principals who abuse

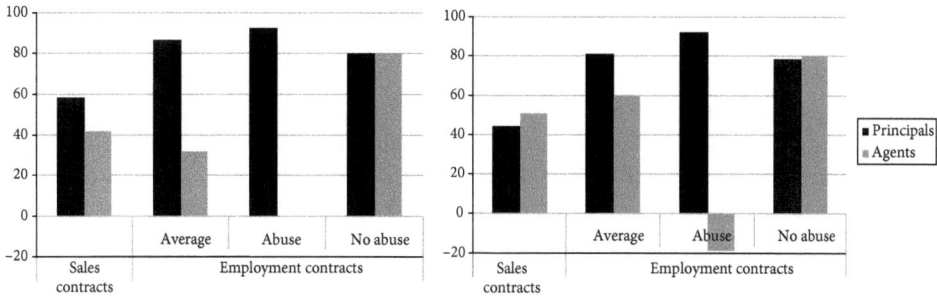

Figure 4.8 Payoffs of the principal and agent in treatment RANDOM (left panel) and treatment FIXED (right panel).

Source: "Use and abuse of authority: a behavioral foundation of the employment relation," Bartling, B., Fehr, E., and Schmidt, K.M., Journal of the European Economic Association, 11(4): 711–41. © 2013 Journal of the European Economic Association.

their residual control rights in employment contracts earn higher payoffs than those who do not, yet both types of principals earn more relative to a sales contract. Further insights into these results are provided in Figure 4.9.

From the left panel in Figure 4.9, in all treatments, the employment contract is predominantly offered in the beginning. However, over time, agents observe that the self-regarding principals abuse trust by choosing task 3. This, in particular, is the case in treatment RANDOM. Hence, agents who have had an abusive experience, begin in successive rounds to reject the employment contract in favor of the sales contract. In a sales contract, principals typically ask for one of the efficient tasks, task 2. Yet, one still observes that in treatment RANDOM, the share of the employment contract stabilizes at about 40%. What accounts for this high percentage, relative to the predictions of the self-regarding model?

A crucial role is played by the presence of principals with other-regarding preferences. We can see this by comparing the share of employment contracts in the following two treatments: RANDOM and UNFAIR. In the latter, an employment contract is never optimal (Conjecture 4.1(c)). The differences between the two treatments (left panel of Figure 4.9) are statistically significant and employment contracts are almost eliminated in the last few periods in treatment

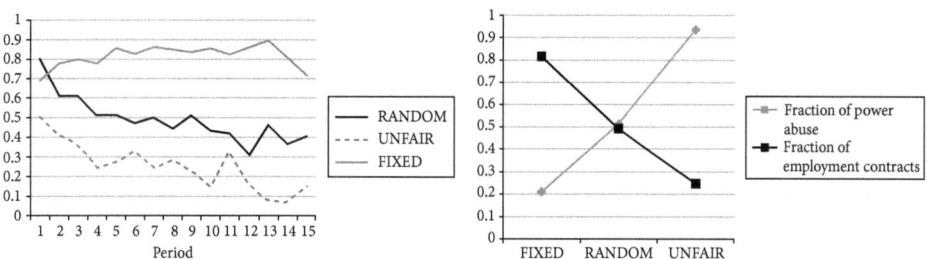

Figure 4.9 Share of employment contracts in different treatments (left panel). Frequency of power abuse and share of employment contracts in each treatment (right panel).

Source: "Use and abuse of authority: a behavioral foundation of the employment relation," Bartling, B., Fehr, E., and Schmidt, K.M., Journal of the European Economic Association, 11(4): 711–41. © 2013 Journal of the European Economic Association.

UNFAIR. Thus, it is likely to be the case that in treatment RANDOM, agents expect the presence of a significant fraction of principals with other-regarding preferences.

In contrast to these two treatments, the proportion of employment contracts in treatment FIXED begins from a high level and hovers around the 80–90% mark (there is also an endgame effect). The main reason for the prevalence of the employment contract in treatment FIXED is that principals do not abuse their residual control rights as much, in comparison to the other contracts. This is confirmed from the right panel of Figure 4.9, which shows a statistically significant negative correlation between the share of employment contracts and the abuse of power. This is the reason why in the right panel of Figure 4.8 (treatment FIXED), on average, the principal and the agent are better off relative to a sales contract. This is despite the fact that the agent has a negative payoff when he faces a principal who abuses his residual control rights.

The main reason that principals abuse their residual control rights relatively less in treatment FIXED is that agents terminate employment relations with abusive principals in the succeeding period. The cost to the principal of this event is that it might lead the principal to be identified as a self-regarding principal (this depends on the precise specification of out of equilibrium beliefs in a formal model). That this will lead to lower subsequent profits for the principal is also confirmed by the data.

Long-term relations do not emerge in a sales contract under the treatment FIXED but do emerge under an employment contract. The reason is that no reputation building is possible under a sales contract as there are no residual control rights that a principal can exploit.

The *efficiency* (actual surplus relative to maximum potential surplus) of employment contracts is significantly greater than sales contracts. This might be an important clue why *vertical integration* takes place in actual practice. The *transaction costs* identified in the traditional industrial organization literature typically originate from contract rigidity and the hold-up problem (Gibbons, 2010). However, the nature of the transaction costs identified in this paper is significantly distinct from the earlier ones. There are three main transaction costs: (i) Some potentially profitable contract offers are rejected by the agents (see also Bartling et al., 2012). (ii) Sales contracts are rigid and do not allow ex-post alteration of tasks. (iii) Some principals do abuse their residual control rights in an employment contract. Indeed, in the treatment FIXED, these transaction costs are lower in an employment contract relative to a sales contract and, hence, efficiency is higher.

Furthermore, these experiments provide exogenous variation in the principal's ability to build a reputation (FIXED versus RANDOM treatments) that alter the costs of integration such as the abuse of power by the principal but not the costs of non-integration (rigidity of task choice under sales contracts). By contrast, existing field evidence provides mainly correlational evidence only (Bartling et al., 2013, p. 715). This should also serve to caution those who might unconditionally espouse the superiority of field evidence relative to lab experiments.

4.5 Extrinsic and intrinsic motivation: theoretical framework

Consider the opening remarks from Ellingsen and Johannesson (2008):

Douglas McGregor's (1960) celebrated management book *The Human Side of Enterprise* argues that managers who subscribe to the conventional economic view that employees dislike work—McGregor labels it Theory X—may create workers who are "resistant, antagonistic, uncooperative". That is, managerial control and material incentives may trigger the very behaviors that they are designed to avert. Conversely, managers who subscribe to the more optimistic view that employees see their work as a source of self-realization and social esteem—Theory Y—may create workers who voluntarily seek to fulfill the organization's goals.

A major part of the agenda for the theoretical literature, that we consider in this section, is to provide some foundations for Theory Y.

In this section, we consider formal theoretical models that simultaneously examine the effect of incentives on extrinsic and intrinsic motivation. This is an active and productive area of research.[19]

4.5.1 Self-signaling and social signaling

In this section, we consider the models due to Bénabou and Tirole (2003, 2006). Consider first, a simplified version of the more general model in Bénabou and Tirole (2003). In this model, incentives signal the amount of trust that a principal has in an agent.

Consider a principal and an agent, both risk-neutral, who are engaged in some project. There is asymmetric information about the cost, $c \in [\underline{c}, \overline{c}]$, of the project that the agent will bear if the project is undertaken. The principal knows the actual value of c but the agent only knows the density, f, and the probability distribution of costs, F. For any wage, w, received by the agent and any cost, c, the agent's utility is $w - c$. The agent chooses the effort level, e, to either shirk, $e = 0$, or work hard, $e = 1$. If the project is unsuccessful, then both parties get a payoff of 0. If the agent works hard, then the project is successful with probability $\theta \in (0, 1]$ and the respective payoffs of the principal and the agent are $W > 0$ and $V > 0$; with probability $1 - \theta$, the project is unsuccessful. If the agent shirks, then the project is always unsuccessful. The outside option of the agent is normalized to 0.

The agent does not know the value of c, but he receives a private signal of the cost, c, given by $\sigma \in [0, 1]$ with conditional density $g(\sigma \mid c)$ and conditional distribution $G(\sigma \mid c)$. A higher value of the private signal, σ, is *good news* in the sense that it signals a lower value of the cost. This is formally incorporated by using the *monotone likelihood ratio property* (MLRP). For any two values of $\sigma : \sigma_L < \sigma_H$, and cost $c : c_L < c_H$, the MLRP property states that

$$\frac{g(\sigma_H \mid c_H)}{g(\sigma_L \mid c_H)} < \frac{g(\sigma_H \mid c_L)}{g(\sigma_L \mid c_L)}, \text{ or } \frac{g(\sigma_H \mid c_H)}{g(\sigma_H \mid c_L)} < \frac{g(\sigma_L \mid c_H)}{g(\sigma_L \mid c_L)}. \tag{4.75}$$

Using Bayes' rule,

$$\Pr(c_L \mid \sigma_H) = \frac{1}{1 + \frac{g(\sigma_H \mid c_H)}{g(\sigma_H \mid c_L)} \frac{f(c_H)}{f(c_L)}} \text{ and } \Pr(c_L \mid \sigma_L) = \frac{1}{1 + \frac{g(\sigma_L \mid c_H)}{g(\sigma_L \mid c_L)} \frac{f(c_H)}{f(c_L)}},$$

thus,

$$\frac{\Pr(c_L \mid \sigma_H)}{\Pr(c_L \mid \sigma_L)} = \frac{1 + \frac{g(\sigma_L \mid c_H)}{g(\sigma_L \mid c_L)} \frac{f(c_H)}{f(c_L)}}{1 + \frac{g(\sigma_H \mid c_H)}{g(\sigma_H \mid c_L)} \frac{f(c_H)}{f(c_L)}}. \tag{4.76}$$

---

[19] See, for instance, Hwang and Bowles (2011), Ellingsen and Johannesson (2008), Bénabou and Tirole (2003, 2006), and Besley and Ghatak (2005).

Using (4.75), (4.76) we get that $\Pr(c_L \mid \sigma_H) > \Pr(c_L \mid \sigma_L)$, which is the precise sense in which a higher value of σ is good news.

Lemma 4.11 *The MLRP in (4.75) implies that*
$$\frac{[1 - G(\sigma_H \mid c_L)]}{[1 - G(\sigma_L \mid c_L)]} \geq \frac{[1 - G(\sigma_H \mid c_H)]}{[1 - G(\sigma_L \mid c_H)]}.$$

The proof of Lemma 4.11 is left as an exercise for the reader.

The principal does not observe the effort level of the agent. If the project is successful, the principal contractually offers a performance based monetary bonus, b, to the agent. This is equivalent to an expected wage offer of $w = \theta b$, contingent on the agent working hard ($e = 1$). The bonus could alternatively be interpreted as the monetary value of working conditions, praise, and friendliness. Thus, in the event that the agent works hard and the project is successful, the respective gross payoffs of the principal and the agent are $W - b$ and $V + b$.

The agent may be willing to work hard if the cost of the project is not too high. The principal benefits if the agent works hard, otherwise each gets a payoff of only 0. Hence, the principal may wish to manipulate incentives in order to signal to the agent that the project has low cost and hope that this will boost the *self-confidence* of the agent and his interest in the task. The agent is aware of the principal's incentives to do so. Thus, he uses, jointly, his private signal, σ, and the bonus payment, b, to make an inference of the cost, c.

The full information benchmark is simple to find. The incentive compatibility condition and the individual rationality conditions are identical in this model. If the agent shirks, then the agent gets zero, which is also the outside option. The risk-neutral agent works hard if the expected payoff exceeds the outside option of zero, i.e., $\theta(V + b) - c \geq 0$. The principal only needs to ensure that this condition binds. Thus, a higher bonus makes it more likely that the agent will work hard.

Now consider the solution under asymmetric information. We derive a perfect Bayesian Nash equilibrium of the model. Under asymmetric information, the agent attempts to infer the cost of the project by observing, jointly, σ and b. Denote by $E[c \mid \sigma, b]$, the expected level of the cost, conditional on σ, b. Since a higher private signal, σ, is good news about costs, thus, for a fixed b, $E[c \mid \sigma, b]$ is strictly decreasing in σ.

The payoff of the agent from shirking ($e = 0$) is zero. Hence, the risk-neutral agent works hard ($e = 1$) if the expected payoff from working hard is positive; this is the incentive compatibility condition,

$$\theta(V + b) - E[c \mid \sigma, b] \geq 0. \tag{4.77}$$

Figure 4.10 gives a diagrammatic representation of the condition in (4.77) for two different levels of bonuses, $b_1 < b_2$. The curve $E[c \mid \sigma, b]$ is decreasing in σ. The shape is purely for illustrative purposes and the upward shift with respect to the bonus ($b_1 < b_2$) is proved in Proposition 4.14. It is obvious from Figure 4.10 and (4.77) that for any bonus, b, there is a cutoff point $\sigma^*(b)$ such that $E[c \mid \sigma^*(b), b] = \theta(V + b)$, and

$$\begin{cases} \sigma \geq \sigma^*(b) & \Rightarrow e = 1 \\ \sigma < \sigma^*(b) & \Rightarrow e = 0 \end{cases}. \tag{4.78}$$

The probability that $\sigma \geq \sigma^*(b)$ is given by $1 - G(\sigma^*(b))$. Given the best response function of the agent in (4.78), a principal who knows the actual cost to be c, chooses the bonus level, b, to maximize his expected profit

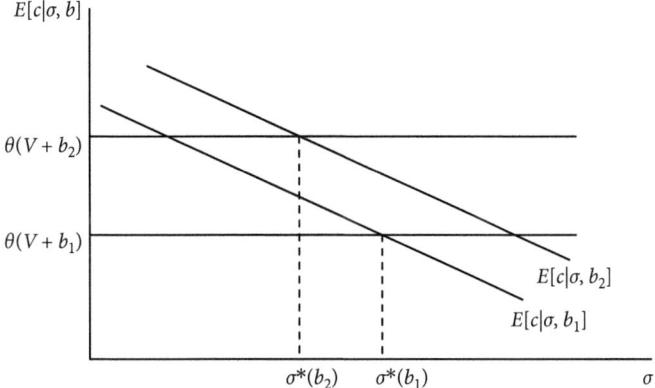

Figure 4.10 Diagrammatic representation of the condition in (4.77).

$$E\pi = \left[1 - G(\sigma^*(b) \mid c)\right]\theta(W - b), \tag{4.79}$$

where the expectation is taken over the distribution of σ. One may think of each possible level of cost, $c \in [\underline{c}, \overline{c}]$, as the type of the principal. Thus, an optimal strategy for the principal is a choice of b for each $c \in [\underline{c}, \overline{c}]$. Denote the set of optimal values of b by B^*. The results are summarized in the following proposition and we sketch a heuristic proof.

Proposition 4.14

(i) If $b_1, b_2 \in B^*$ and $b_1 < b_2$, then the cutoff private signal beyond which the agent decides to work hard is relatively lower under b_2, i.e., $\sigma^*(b_2) < \sigma^*(b_1)$.

(ii) A higher level of bonus is bad news for the agent. Let b_H and b_L be the optimal levels of bonus when the cost is respectively c_H and c_L, $c_H > c_L$. Then $b_H > b_L$.

(iii) Higher bonus payments reduce the perceived attractiveness of the task for the agent. For all pairs of signals (σ, σ'), and optimal bonus payments $b_1 < b_2$, $b_1, b_2 \in B^*$, we have $E[c \mid \sigma, b_1] < E[c \mid \sigma', b_2]$.

Proof: (i) Suppose that the statement in (a) is false. Then for some $b_1 < b_2$ in B^* we have $\sigma^*(b_2) > \sigma^*(b_1)$. But then, instead of offering b_2, the principal could offer a lower bonus b_1. This increases the expected profits of the principal, given in (4.79), in two ways. By reducing σ^* it increases the first term $[1 - G(\sigma^*(b) \mid c)]$. The second term, $\theta(W - b)$, increases directly when the bonus level falls. This contradicts the original supposition that b_2 is an optimal level of bonus. Thus, we cannot have $\sigma^*(b_2) > \sigma^*(b_1)$.

(ii) Suppose that the bonus b_i, $i = H, L$ is optimal when cost is c_i. Let $\sigma_2 = \sigma^*(b_H)$ and $\sigma_1 = \sigma^*(b_L)$ be the cutoff points for the private signals. Then, we get from (4.79) that

$$[1 - G(\sigma_2 \mid c_H)]\theta(W - b_H) > [1 - G(\sigma_1 \mid c_H)]\theta(W - b_L), \tag{4.80}$$

$$[1 - G(\sigma_1 \mid c_L)]\theta(W - b_L) > [1 - G(\sigma_2 \mid c_L)]\theta(W - b_H). \tag{4.81}$$

When the actual cost of the principal is c_H the bonus b_H is optimal ((4.80)) and when the actual cost is c_L the bonus b_L is optimal ((4.81)). From (4.80), (4.81) we get

$$\frac{[1 - G(\sigma_1 \mid c_L)]}{[1 - G(\sigma_2 \mid c_L)]} > \frac{(W - b_H)}{(W - b_L)} > \frac{[1 - G(\sigma_1 \mid c_H)]}{[1 - G(\sigma_2 \mid c_H)]}.$$

Since $c_L < c_H$, Lemma 4.11 implies that $\sigma_1 = \sigma^*(b_L) > \sigma_2 = \sigma^*(b_H)$. Since σ^* is a decreasing function it follows that $b_L \leq b_H$. Thus, a high bonus, b_H, conveys bad news for the agent that costs are high, c_H.

(*iii*) There cannot be a separating equilibrium. Suppose to the contrary that there is a separating equilibrium. Then each type of the principal, $c \in [\underline{c}, \overline{c}]$, announces a distinct level of bonus. Since the principal's action is fully revealing of his type in a separating equilibrium, hence, there is no need for the agent to use an imperfect private signal, σ. Suppose that we support such an equilibrium by imposing particularly pessimistic out of equilibrium beliefs that if the bonus payment in a separating equilibrium, b_i for some type $c_i \in [\underline{c}, \overline{c}]$ changes to any $b_j \neq b_i$, then the principal is of the worst, or highest cost, type, $\overline{c}$.

But if the agent is going to ignore his private signal, σ, then the principal of type $\overline{c}$, should choose the lowest bonus payment possible and improve his profits. This breaks the separating equilibrium. Thus, the proof of part (b) implies that pooling occurs over intervals. For $b_1 < b_2$, if the principal pays bonus b_1 for costs $c \in [\tilde{c}_0, \tilde{c}_1]$ and bonus b_2 for costs $c \in [\tilde{c}_2, \tilde{c}_3]$, then $\tilde{c}_1 < \tilde{c}_2$. Thus, all cost levels for which a higher bonus is offered are also higher, hence, the expected costs under the higher bonus are also higher, so for all pairs of signals (σ, σ'), $E[c \mid \sigma, b_1] < E[c \mid \sigma', b_2]$. Therefore, higher rewards are given for less attractive tasks (forbidden fruits) and they reduce intrinsic motivation. ∎

Bénabou and Tirole (2003) consider intrinsic and extrinsic motivation, and Bénabou and Tirole (2006) add to the mix a reputational motivation. For instance, while the Bénabou and Tirole (2003) model deals with situations where one party to a formal or informal contract has private information (child-rearing, education, monitoring of employees), a different framework is needed when one makes prosocial decisions such as blood donations, charitable giving, in-kind donations, choosing a fuel-efficient car, and voting. Such a framework is provided in Bénabou and Tirole (2006) that we now turn to.

Suppose that an agent can choose some prosocial action a from a set of real-valued numbers, A, at some cost $C(a)$. The action a confers some *intrinsic utility*, u_I, on the agent, per unit of the action, a (e.g., the agent may feel good about the act of donating blood). A principal chooses a monetary reward, $y \geq 0$, per unit of the action, a, for the agent. The *extrinsic utility* derived by the agent from the monetary reward per unit is u_E. For instance, the government (principal) may decide to tax exempt or subsidize the charitable contributions of citizens. Thus, the *private benefit* to the agent from the action, a is

$$P(a, y) = a(u_I + u_E y) - C(a). \tag{4.82}$$

The agent has private information on his *type* or *identity*, which is summarized by $(u_I, u_E) \in R^2$. The other players know that the pair (u_I, u_E) is drawn from the density $f(u_I, u_E)$. Others attempt to learn or infer (u_I, u_E) from the action taken by the agent, a, and the monetary reward given by the principal, y. The reward, y, creates additional difficulties in inferring intrinsic and extrinsic motivations from actions. For instance, society may wish to infer the degree of altruism of a contributor to charity, however, this calculation is made difficult if the tax regime allows charitable contributions to be tax exempt.

Social signaling is incorporated into the model by a concern for reputational payoffs. Denote by $E[u_I \mid a, y]$, $E[u_E \mid a, y]$, respectively, the posterior expectation of others about the agent's intrinsic utility and extrinsic utility. Then the *reputational payoff* is given by

$$R(a,y) = E[u_I \mid a,y] - E[u_E \mid a,y]. \tag{4.83}$$

An increase in $E[u_I \mid a,y]$ improves the reputation payoff of the agent by increasing the social perception of his intrinsic motivation. This term corresponds to the notion of *warm glow* from giving in the literature on charitable donations. On the other hand, an increase in $E[u_E \mid a,y]$ reduces the reputation payoff of the agent because it increases the social perception of his extrinsic motivation, or greed. In a more general model, the terms $E[u_I \mid a,y]$, $E[u_E \mid a,y]$ in (4.83) could be differentially weighted, as in Bénabou and Tirole (2006). Furthermore, there could be individual heterogeneity in these terms which make the problem of inferring motivations from actions even more difficult. We abstract from these considerations here.

The aggregate utility of the agent, U, indexed by the type $(u_I, u_E) \in R^2$, is given by $P(a,y) + R(a,y)$, thus,

$$U = a(u_I + u_E y) - C(a) + v\left(E[u_I \mid a,y] - E[u_E \mid a,y]\right). \tag{4.84}$$

In (4.84), the parameter $v > 0$ represents the *social visibility* of the action a (e.g., the number of people who observe the action) and it captures the extent of *reputational concerns* of the agent. The agent chooses action a to maximize U, defined in (4.84). Assuming that the problem is well-behaved, the first order condition that is sufficient to determine the optimal action is

$$(u_I + u_E y) + v R_a(a,y) = C'(a), \text{ where } R_a(a,y) = \left(\frac{\partial E[u_I \mid a,y]}{\partial a} - \frac{\partial E[u_E \mid a,y]}{\partial a}\right). \tag{4.85}$$

The LHS of (4.85) gives the marginal benefit of increasing a and the RHS, the marginal cost. The marginal benefit has three sources: *intrinsic*, *extrinsic*, and *reputational*. Suppose that we fix a particular value of $a > 0$. Then, from (4.85), the set of people who contribute (called the "high contributors") satisfy the inequality $(u_I + u_E y) + v R_a \geq C'(a)$, which can alternatively be written as

$$u_E \geq \frac{1}{y}\left(C'(a) - v R_a(a,y)\right) - \frac{1}{y}u_I. \tag{4.86}$$

When the inequality in (4.86) binds, the agent chooses a and when it does not bind, the agent chooses an action greater than a. Three different loci of combinations of (u_I, u_E) on which (4.86) binds are shown in Figure 4.11, as I, II, and III; these loci are created by varying the size of rewards, y. In u_I, u_E space, the region above any such locus gives the set of points (u_I, u_E) for which an action greater than a is chosen.

When there are zero rewards ($y = 0$), (4.86) reduces to $u_I^*(a,0) = C'(a) - v R_a(a,0)$. This is shown in Figure 4.11 by the vertical line, labeled I. Since there are no extrinsic rewards in this case, the actions of agents do not reveal anything about their extrinsic motivation. All the individuals whose identity or type (u_I, u_E) lies on or to the right of curve I contribute at least an amount a, under zero rewards, while those to the left contribute strictly less than a.

Now suppose that there is a jump in rewards to a strictly positive level ($y > 0$). The slope of the (u_I, u_E) locus is now given by $-\frac{1}{y}$. Two loci are shown in Figure 4.11, corresponding to $y > 0$; these are labeled as II and III. The curve labeled II shows the immediate effect, prior to the

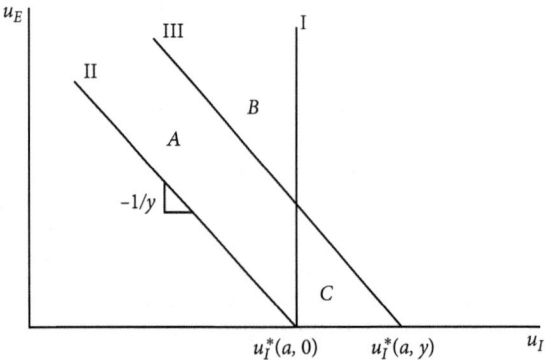

Figure 4.11 Loci of combinations of (u_I, u_E) on which (4.86) binds.
Source: Bénabou and Tirole (2006) with permission from the American Economic Association.

adjustments in the reputational concerns arising through the term R_a. Thus, there is no change in the abscissa (see (4.86)) which stays fixed at $u_I^*(a, 0)$. The curve labeled III shows the final effect once the reputational concerns have played out. In the case shown in the figure, reputational concerns shift the abscissa to the right. The abscissa is now given by $u_I^*(a, y) = C'(a) - \nu R_a(a, y)$. We now explain these effects in greater detail.

The immediate effect captured by curve II shows the extra set of individuals who now find it worthwhile to contribute at least a, in response to the presence of extrinsic incentives ($y > 0$ rather than $y = 0$). These people (new contributors) are represented by the area $A + B$. This is the classical positive effect of incentives. The reputational effect that is incorporated in curve III is more subtle. The relative intrinsic utility of the "new contributors" must be lower than that of the "high contributors" because the former did not find it worthwhile to contribute in the absence of extrinsic rewards. This reduces the overall average level of intrinsic utility of the set of contributors and the overall reputation of the set of contributors for prosocial behavior. However, the set of non-contributors has now also shrunk because the "new contributors" who have relatively high intrinsic utility among this group have transited to the set of contributors. Hence, the reputation from contributing an amount $a - \Delta a$ also goes down. Thus, the reputational effect for a marginal contributor is ambiguous, hence, the abscissa in (4.86) can go up or down. Curve III is drawn on the supposition that the reputation effect is negative ($R_a(a, y) < R_a(a, 0)$), so the abscissa goes up.

Comparing curves I and III, we are in a position to assess the final effect of incentives. Incentives stimulate contributions from a set of greedy individuals (high u_E relative to u_I). This is shown by the area B in Figure 4.11. However, there is an extra set of marginal contributors shown by the area C. The intrinsic utility u_I of these individuals is higher relative to their extrinsic utility u_E, so (based on (4.86)) they no longer find it optimal to take action a after the introduction of extrinsic incentives. This potentially explains several findings such as the work of Titmuss (1972) in the context of crowding-out effect of incentives for blood donations. Comparing curves I and III, the overall effect on total contributions will depend on the relative size of the areas, B and C as well as the shape of the probability density of individuals, $f(u_I, u_E)$, over these areas.

4.5.2 Intentions, altruism, and esteem

In this section, we consider theoretical models of principal–agent relations in which type-based reciprocity plays a key role (Ellingsen and Johannesson, 2008). These are models of two-sided asymmetric information in which both players can be self-regarding or altruistic. Players hold other players in greater esteem if they are perceived to be altruistic. Furthermore, players value being esteemed more by other players who are perceived to be altruistic. This can explain why a principal who chooses a kind action in the presence of an unkind action is regarded in greater esteem, because the principal signals clearly to the agent that he is kind. Agents then reciprocate, trusting actions by a kind principal, because the esteem received from a kind principal is valued more highly. Kindness may mean choosing a trusting action when a non-trusting action is available, or choosing a less controlling action when a more controlling action is available. We characterize an intuitive equilibrium of this two-sided signaling game and apply it to explain the experimental findings of McCabe et al. (2003) and Falk and Kosfeld (2006). We also consider the basic intuition behind some of the other related theoretical literature.

Consider two players $i \in N = \{Principal, Agent\}$. The pure strategy set of player $i \in N$ is denoted by S_i and the mixed strategy set by Σ_i. Consider the class of two-stage games where the principal first chooses a publicly observable strategy from the set Σ_P. The agent then sequentially chooses a strategy from the set Σ_A. There is two-sided asymmetric information about the altruism of the players. Each player belongs to one of two possible, privately known, types $\theta \in \Theta = \{\theta_L, \theta_H\}, 0 \leq \theta_L < \theta_H < 1$. The prior belief of player $i \in N$ that the opponent is of type θ_H is p_i^0.

Suppose player i of type θ_i chooses his action $s_i \in S_i$. Let h_i be the history of game, and let the belief of the player that his opponent is of type θ_H be $\mu_i(h_i, \theta_i)$. Let H_i be the set of all possible histories of the game when player i makes his move. Denote by $\overline{h}$, the terminal history of the game; it is summarized by the strategies followed by the two players for the whole game, σ_P, σ_A (defined below). Thus, we may write $\mu_i\left(\overline{h}, \theta_i\right) = \mu_i(\sigma_P, \sigma_A, \theta_i)$. We assume that players use Bayes' rule to update their beliefs.

The utility of a risk-neutral player $i \in N$ is given by

$$u_i = y_i + \theta_i y_j + \eta_i, \qquad (4.87)$$

where y_i is the monetary payoff of player $i \in N$ and y_j is the monetary payoff of the opponent, player $j \neq i$. The size of θ_i measures the degree of *altruism* that the player feels for the opponents; since we have restricted $\theta_j > 0, j = L, H$ we are ruling out spite or envy. The term η_i measures player i's feelings of being *esteemed* by player j. It is measured as follows. Let θ_{ij} be the esteem with which player i views player j. Conditional on the type of player i, θ_i, this is defined as the expected value of the altruism of player j at the terminal node.

$$\theta_{ij} = E\left[\theta_j \mid \theta_i, \overline{h}\right] = \mu_i\left(\overline{h}, \theta_i\right)\theta_H + \left[1 - \mu_i\left(\overline{h}, \theta_i\right)\right]\theta_L. \qquad (4.88)$$

Players hold their opponents in greater esteem if they think they are more altruistic. Thus, there is respect for character virtues.

Let $\chi_j = \chi\left(\theta_j\right)$ be the salience of the esteem that an opponent of type θ_j has for player i. Now define η_i as

$$\eta_i = \mu_i\left(\overline{h},\theta_i\right)\chi_H \text{ (Expected esteem of a type } \theta_H \text{ opponent for player } i) \qquad (4.89)$$
$$+ \left[1 - \mu_i\left(\overline{h},\theta_i\right)\right]\chi_L \text{ (Expected esteem of a type } \theta_L \text{ opponent for player } i)$$

or,

$$\eta_i = \mu_i\left(\overline{h},\theta_i\right)\chi_H\left[\left[\mu_j\left(\overline{h},\theta_H\right)\theta_H + \left[1 - \mu_j\left(\overline{h},\theta_H\right)\right]\theta_L\right]\right]$$
$$+ \left[1 - \mu_i\left(\overline{h},\theta_i\right)\right]\chi_L\left[\left[\mu_j\left(\overline{h},\theta_L\right)\theta_H + \left[1 - \mu_j\left(\overline{h},\theta_L\right)\right]\theta_L\right]\right]. \qquad (4.90)$$

We are now in a position to evaluate the utility function in (4.87). First, although (4.87) only incorporates altruism (through the second term), the authors claim that richer other-regarding preferences, such as those in Fehr and Schmidt (1999), do not alter their results. Second, the feeling of being esteemed by a player is greater if more virtuous opponents hold them in higher regard. Consider, for instance, the first term on the RHS of (4.89). The expected esteem of a more altruistic player j is weighted by the term $\mu_i\left(\overline{h},\theta_i\right)\chi_H$. Clearly this term is higher if the belief of player i about the altruism of player j, $\mu_i\left(\overline{h},\theta_i\right)$, is higher. Thus, the model is similar in spirit to models of type-based reciprocity, such as that by Levine (1998). Third, an alternative way of dealing with beliefs about esteem and beliefs about beliefs about esteem, require the machinery of psychological game theory. This is discussed in Volume 4 of the book.

A strategy for any player $i \in N$ is given by $\sigma_i : \Theta \times [0,1] \times H_i \to \Sigma_i$. It specifies a mixed strategy of a player for each possible type of a player, for any beliefs about the opponent, and for any history of the game. Let $\boldsymbol{\sigma}_P^* = \left(\sigma_P^*(\theta_H), \sigma_P^*(\theta_L)\right)$ and $\boldsymbol{\sigma}_A^* = \left(\sigma_A^*(\theta_H), \sigma_A^*(\theta_L)\right)$ denote the equilibrium type-contingent strategies of the principal and the agent. Let $\boldsymbol{\mu}_P^* = \left(\mu_P^*(\theta_H), \mu_P^*(\theta_L)\right)$ and $\boldsymbol{\mu}_A^* = \left(\mu_A^*(\theta_H), \mu_A^*(\theta_L)\right)$ be the respective equilibrium type-contingent beliefs.

Definition 4.2 *(Intuitive equilibrium): An equilibrium of the two-stage two-player game is a pair of type-contingent strategies $\left(\boldsymbol{\sigma}_P^*, \boldsymbol{\sigma}_A^*\right)$ and a pair of type-contingent beliefs $\left(\boldsymbol{\mu}_P^*, \boldsymbol{\mu}_A^*\right)$ such that the following hold.*

(1) Given the beliefs of any player $i \in N$, $\boldsymbol{\mu}_i^*$, the strategy $\boldsymbol{\sigma}_i^*$ maximizes the utility of player $i = A, P$.

(2) The beliefs $\boldsymbol{\mu}_i^*$ of player $i \in N$ satisfy Bayes' rule whenever possible.

(3) Off the equilibrium path, beliefs must satisfy the Cho–Kreps intuitive criterion.

Consider the trust game of McCabe et al. (2003) shown in Figure 4.12. In the voluntary trust game (VTG) in Panel A, player 1 (Principal) has two choices: Trust (T) or No Trust (NT). In the involuntary trust game (ITG) in Panel B, player 1 has only one choice, T. Player 2 (Agent) has identical choices in both cases: Reward (R) and Not Reward (N). In classical game theory, the choice of player 2 should be identical in both cases. However, McCabe et al. (2003) find that the frequency of the choice of R for player 2 is significantly higher in the VTG as compared to the ITG. Thus, the principal's choice of trust conveys a better signal of his sociality when the NT option is available.

Let us now explain these experimental results using the theoretical framework developed in this section. Assume that each player has two possible types $\theta \in \Theta = \{\theta_L, \theta_H\}$ such that θ_H is the relatively more altruistic type. The solution is set out in Proposition 4.15. The intuition behind the results is as follows. First, in the VTG, altruistic principals (high θ_H) are more likely to play T because they place a higher value on the payoffs of the agent that arise from playing T rather

4.5 Extrinsic and intrinsic motivation: theoretical framework | 235

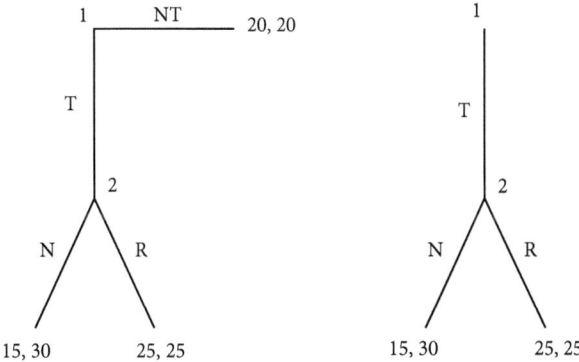

Figure 4.12 A trust game that differentiates between voluntary and involuntary trust.
Source: Ellingsen and Johannesson (2008) with permission from the American Economic Association.

than NT. Second, in a separating equilibrium where the more altruistic principal plays T but the self-regarding principal plays NT, the action of the principal fully reveals the type. More altruistic agents feel greater esteem from playing the action R, when they know that they are dealing with altruistic principals (type-based reciprocity). Hence, there is likely to be a separating equilibrium in which the more altruistic agent plays R and the self-regarding agent plays N in the VTG game.

> **Proposition 4.15** *(Ellingsen and Johannesson, 2008): Consider the trust games shown in Figure 4.12. For an open set of parameters, there exists a unique intuitive equilibrium (Definition 4.2) such that:*
>
> (i) *An altruistic principal (type θ_H) plays T and a self-regarding principal (type θ_L) plays NT.*
> (ii) *Both types of agents play N in the ITG. Altruistic agents (type θ_H) play R in the VTG.*

Proof: We only prove the existence part. For the proof of uniqueness, see Ellingsen and Johannesson (2008).

Consider first the ITG. Both types of player 2s must choose N in this game as part of the stated equilibrium in the proposition. A sufficient condition is that the altruistic player 2 who benefits most by gaining self-esteem prefers to play N over R. Player 1 never gets a chance to update his beliefs because he moves first. Hence, the relevant beliefs for him are captured by his initial belief that player 2 is of type θ_H (denoted by p_1^0). Similarly, since player 1 has no choice but to play T, player 2 does not update his beliefs either, hence, the belief of player 2 that player 1 is of type θ_H is given by p_2^0.

Using (4.87), (4.88), and (4.90), the utility of player 2 of type θ_H from playing N under the worst possible evaluation from player 1 (i.e., $\mu_1\left(\overline{h},\theta_H\right) = p_1^0 = 0$) is

$$u_2(N,\theta_H,p_1^0 = 0) = 30 + 15\theta_H + \theta_L \left(p_2^0 \chi_H + \left(1 - p_2^0\right) \chi_L\right).$$

Similarly, the utility of a type θ_H player 2 from playing R under the best possible evaluation from player 1 (i.e., $\mu_1\left(\overline{h},\theta_H\right) = p_1^0 = 1$) is

$$u_2(R,\theta_H,p_1^0 = 1) = 25 + 25\theta_H + \theta_H \left(p_2^0 \chi_H + \left(1 - p_2^0\right) \chi_L\right).$$

Under these conditions,

$$u_2(N,\theta_H,p_1^0=0) > u_2(R,\theta_H,p_1^0=1) \Leftrightarrow p_2^0 \chi_H + (1-p_2^0)\chi_L < \frac{5-10\theta_H}{\theta_H-\theta_L}. \qquad (4.91)$$

Now consider the VTG. As part of the separating equilibrium, player 1 of type θ_H always plays T in this case, while player 1 of type θ_L always plays NT. The prior beliefs of player 2 are updated in a manner that is consistent with Bayes' rule. Thus, on observing T, player 2 sets $\mu_2\left(\overline{h},\theta_H\right)=1$, and on observing NT he sets $\mu_2\left(\overline{h},\theta_H\right)=0$. So, conditional on being given the move $\left(\mu_2\left(\overline{h},\theta_H\right)=1\right)$, we first need to show that the altruistic player 2 will prefer to play R.

$$u_2(R,\theta_H,\mu_2=1) = 25 + 25\theta_H + \chi_H\theta_H.$$

In computing the last term, note that consistent with the strategies of player 2, player 1 sets $\mu_1\left(\overline{h},\theta_H\right)=1$ in (4.90). Similarly, the payoff of the altruistic player 2 from playing N is

$$u_2(N,\theta_H,\mu_2=1) = 30 + 15\theta_H + \chi_H\theta_L. \qquad (4.92)$$

If player 2 plays N, then, given the strategies, he is revealed to be a type θ_L player, hence, the beliefs of player 1 about him, at the terminal node are $\mu_1\left(\overline{h},\theta_H\right)=0$. Using this fact in (4.90) gives the last term on the RHS of (4.92), $\chi_H\theta_L$. Thus, the required condition for an altruistic agent to play R in the VTG game is

$$u_2(R,\theta_H,\mu_2=1) > u_2(N,\theta_H,\mu_2=1) \Leftrightarrow \chi_H > \frac{5-10\theta_H}{\theta_H-\theta_L}. \qquad (4.93)$$

Now consider a self-regarding agent (type θ_L) in the VTG. Proceeding analogously to the derivations above, such a player prefers to play N over R (as required in the equilibrium strategy profile) if

$$u_2(R,\theta_L,\mu_2=1) < u_2(N,\theta_L,\mu_2=1) \Leftrightarrow 25 + 25\theta_L + \chi_H\theta_H < 30 + 15\theta_L + \chi_H\theta_L,$$

or, if

$$\chi_H < \frac{5-10\theta_L}{\theta_H-\theta_L}. \qquad (4.94)$$

Now consider the incentive compatibility conditions of player 1 in the VTG. Player 1 believes that with probability p_1^0 he faces a type θ_H player 2 who will play R, and with probability $1-p_1^0$, a type θ_L player 2 who will play N. Hence, using (4.87), (4.88), and (4.90), the utility of a type θ_H player 1 from playing T is

$$u_1(T,\theta_H,p_1^0) = p_1^0\left[25 + 25\theta_H + \chi_H\theta_H\right] + (1-p_1^0)\left[15 + 30\theta_H + \chi_L\theta_H\right].$$

Since we are constructing a separating equilibrium, in the first term on the RHS, each of the players assigns probability one that the other is altruistic. Hence, we get the term $\chi_H\theta_H$. In the second term on the RHS, player 1 assigns probability zero that player 2 is type θ_H

$\left(\mu_1\left(\overline{h},\theta_H\right)=0\right)$, while player 2 assigns probability 1 that player 1 is type θ_H $\left(\mu_2\left(\overline{h},\theta_L\right)=1\right)$; substituting these facts in (4.90) gives the term $\chi_L\theta_H$. Similarly, we can define

$$u_1(NT,\theta_H,p_1^0) = p_1^0\left[20 + 20\theta_H + \chi_H\theta_L\right] + \left(1 - p_1^0\right)\left[20 + 20\theta_H + \chi_L\theta_L\right].$$

Thus,

$$u_1(T,\theta_H,p_1^0) > u_1(NT,\theta_H,p_1^0) \Leftrightarrow p_1^0 > \frac{5 - 10\theta_H - \chi_L(\theta_H - \theta_L)}{10 - 5\theta_H + (\theta_H - \theta_L)(\chi_H - \chi_L)}. \tag{4.95}$$

By now, the method of proof should be transparent to the reader. Proceeding analogously, a self-regarding player 1 (type θ_L) prefers to play NT (as stated in the equilibrium profile in the proposition) if

$$u_1(T,\theta_L,p_1^0) < u_1(NT,\theta_L,p_1^0) \Leftrightarrow p_1^0 < \frac{5 - 10\theta_L - \chi_L(\theta_H - \theta_L)}{10 - 5\theta_L + (\theta_H - \theta_L)(\chi_H - \chi_L)}. \tag{4.96}$$

We require that the inequalities in (4.93), (4.94), (4.95), and (4.96) hold simultaneously. One set of parameter values for which this is true is $p_1^0 = \frac{2}{5}$, $\chi_L = \theta_L = 0$, $\theta_H = \frac{1}{3}$ and $\chi_H = 6$. Since this statement is robust to small changes in the parameter values, it holds for an open set of parameter values around the stated values. ∎

We now consider the effects of *control-aversion* on the part of agents in a principal–agent relation. By choosing incentives that reveal a controlling nature, the agent's effort level may be reduced even when neoclassical theory predicts no such effect.

Consider the Falk and Kosfeld (2006) study in which a principal (player 1) can choose either to control or not control an agent (player 2). The agent is given an endowment of 120 money units and he can transfer any amount $[0,120]$ back to the principal. For every unit of transfer made by the agent, the experimenter ensures that the principal receives 2 units, hence, the amount received by the principal lies in the interval $[0,240]$.

Prior to the agent's decision, the principal has two options. (i) Either specify that the agent transfer a minimum amount $\overline{x} = 10$ (so that the principal receives at least $2\overline{x} = 20$). (ii) Or do not specify a minimum transfer. When a minimum transfer $\overline{x}$ is specified, the agent transfers an average amount of 17.5, while in the absence of such minimum transfers it is 23. About 70% of the principals choose to trust the agent by not specifying a minimum transfer. Further, if a minimum amount is exogenously specified, say, by the experimenter, then there is no difference in the amounts transferred. Hence, control-aversion seems to be the most likely explanation of these findings.

Consider now an explanation of these experimental results based on the Ellingsen and Johannesson (2008) framework. The strategy of the agent is $s_A \in [0,120]$ if the principal chooses to trust (T), and $s_A \in [10,120]$ if the principal choose to control (C). The strategy of the principal is a binary choice, $s_P \in \{T,C\}$. Thus, the utility functions of the principal and the agent are, respectively

$$u_P(s_P,\theta_i) = 2s_A + \theta_i(120 - s_A) + \eta_P, \tag{4.97}$$

$$u_A(s_A,\theta_i) = (120 - s_A) + \theta_i s_A + \eta_A. \tag{4.98}$$

As before, we assume that each player belongs to one of two possible, privately known, types $0 \leq \theta_L < \theta_H < 1$. The next proposition describes a separating equilibrium in this game that illustrates the negative effects of control-aversion. We leave the proof as an exercise.

Proposition 4.16 *(Ellingsen and Johannesson, 2008): There exists an open set of parameters such that there are intuitive equilibrium outcomes of the Falk and Kosfeld (2006) game with the following features:*

(i) *An altruistic principal (type θ_H) plays T, while a self-regarding principal (type θ_L) plays C.*

(ii) *A self-regarding agent (type θ_L) transfers the lowest amount possible, i.e., 0, when the principal plays T, and 10 when the principal plays C. An altruistic agent (type θ_H) transfers an amount $y \in (10, 120)$. However, the altruistic agent always transfers a greater amount if the principal plays T rather than C.*

Admittedly the results in Propositions 4.15, 4.16 hold for a simple class of games. However, they powerfully illustrate a view of incentives that runs contrary to existing models in neoclassical contract theory, in which incentives are typically, universally, good. These results qualify the existing models in important ways. If a principal mistrusts an agent, when he has an unused alternative that clearly signals trust, then agents may respond with lower effort levels. Furthermore, agents do not like being controlled—controlling them when there is an unused alternative that clearly signals mistrust also reduces effort.

Bénabou and Tirole (2006) also show (see Section 4.5.1), in a model where individuals have private information about multidimensional characteristics, that incentives may undermine effort. As in the blood donation example given above, incentives create an adverse selection problem by attracting individuals who are purely materialistic. Hence, it becomes difficult to signal one's esteem in the presence of such incentives. However, the Ellingsen and Johannesson (2008) model makes the additional prediction that when principals have a choice between two kinds of incentives—one signaling trust and the other signaling mistrust then the former elicits greater effort from the agent.

These results are related to those in Sliwka (2007). Here, in addition to the usual two kinds of *steadfast agents*, self-regarding and other-regarding, there is a third type, the *conformists*. The human virtues of conformists are more malleable and less steadfast. They behave like other-regarding agents if they think that there is a sufficiently large number of other-regarding agents. In other words, they are influenced by social norms. Thus, such an agent feels remorse from harming someone if he believes that there are sufficiently many other types of agents who would feel remorse.

The principal can choose either to trust or control the agent. The overall distribution of types of agents is unknown to the agents but the principal has superior information (perhaps he is more experienced). By choosing to trust, when control is available, the principal signals to the agents that the proportion of other-regarding agents is high. This is the signal that the conformists need in order to work hard. Such a transmission mechanism can also be invoked if the principal has a choice between say, a fixed wage scheme and an incentive scheme; the former may be used to signal to the conformists that the frequency of other-regarding agents is high.

Herold (2010) considers a principal–agent relation in which there are two types of agents. A *trustworthy agent* who shares the principal's concern to produce a high output level and a *self-regarding agent* who cares purely for the wage received and the cost of effort. The types of the agents are privately known to them. The principal receives a private signal of the type of the agent. Based on this signal, the principal has two possible types. The trusting principal has a high signal of the trustworthiness of the agent. The distrusting principal has a low signal of the trustworthiness of the agent. Conditional on the signal, each type offers either a trust contract that is independent of the realization of output (flat wage contract) or an incentive contract in which the wage is conditional on the output level. The principal can signal his type by a choice of the contract—trust or incentive contract.

The effort level of the trusting agent is positively influenced by his belief that the principal is trusting. Furthermore, the principal knows that the trusting agent shares his mission, and requires a lower cost in terms of incentives to produce the same output level. This effect is enhanced if the production function is such that the output depends on the joint efforts of the agent and the principal, and these effort levels are complementary. Hence, a trusting principal gains by separating from a mistrusting principal. In a separating equilibrium, the trusting principal chooses a trust contract and the distrusting principal chooses an incentive contract. An incentive contract, in this framework, is bad news for the trustworthy agent and leads to lower effort levels and output levels.

4.6 Extrinsic and intrinsic motivation: empirical evidence

Motivated by the theoretical models in Section 4.5, we now consider the empirical evidence on intrinsic and extrinsic motivation.

4.6.1 Incentives may signal a hostile intent

In principal–agent interaction, an agent might perceive the following two contractual situations in entirely different ways. In the first, a hostile incentive, say, a fine, is available to a principal and is used. In the second, the hostile incentive is available, but not used by the principal; see, for instance, Section 4.5.2. Empirical tests of these issues are considered by Fehr and Gächter (2001). They modify the basic gift exchange game in Fehr et al. (1997), in the following three potential ways. First, when agents exert inadequate effort (i.e., the actual effort e_a is lower than the non-enforceable, but desired, effort, e_n), they are caught with a probability $p = 0.3$ (in the standard gift exchange game, $p = 1$). Second, in the event that an agent is caught, a fine $f \in [0, f_{\max}]$ may be levied. Third, the contract may specify a *non-binding* bonus, $b_n \in [0, b_{\max}]$, in addition to the binding wage, w, and the non-binding effort, e_n; thus, this contract is even more incomplete relative to Fehr et al. (1997).

In order to differentiate the effects of various incentives, the following three conditions are considered. (1) *No incentives*, which is similar to the basic gift exchange game. (2) *Negatively framed incentives*, when a fine is possible. (3) *Positively framed incentives*, when a bonus is possible.

The main experimental results are summarized in Figure 4.13. The vertical axis measures the actual effort level, e_a, while the horizontal axis measures rents offered to the worker in different treatments. For a fixed level of rents, the effort levels are highest when no incentives are given. Instead of appealing to the instrumental reciprocity of agents (the incentive treatments) principals can do better by relying on the intrinsic reciprocity of agents (the no-incentive treatment).

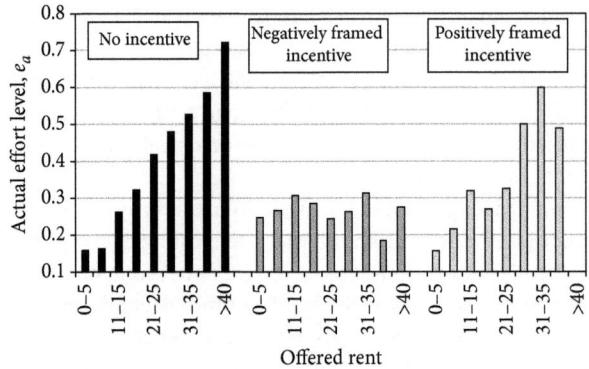

Figure 4.13 Effort and rents in three cases.

Source: Reprinted from European Economic Review, 46: 687–724. Fehr, E. and Falk, A., "Psychological foundations of incentives." © 2012, with permission from Elsevier.

One possible explanation of the results is to invoke the role of intentions, as in Section 4.5.2, or to explain the results using psychological game theory (see Volume 4 of the book). The no-incentive treatments indicate a trusting principal, thus, agents reciprocate the trust. The incentive treatments on the other hand indicate a lack of trust. In particular, fines might be interpreted as hostile intent. Accordingly, agents may respond with negative reciprocity by putting in a lower level of effort. Furthermore, it seems that the framing of incentives is quite important. Effort levels are higher in the positive frame (bonuses) relative to the negative frame (fines). These issues cannot be explained by using self-regarding preferences.

We quote here from Fehr and Gächter (2001): "it may be the case that explicit performance incentives reduce the willingness to voluntarily cooperate." This possibility may arise because explicit performance incentives may create an atmosphere of threat and distrust. Bewley (1999) reports that "many managers stress that explicit punishment should be rarely used as a way to obtain cooperation... In particular, explicit incentives may destroy trust—and reciprocity-based incentives, hence, may lead to welfare loss."[20]

Fehr and Rockenbach (2003) extend the trust game in the following way. Consider a static game played between an investor and a responder. Each of the players is endowed with 10 MUs (monetary units) and each MU is equivalent to half a German mark. The investor can decide to send (or invest) i MUs, that belong to the set $\{0, 1, 2, \ldots, 10\}$ to a responder, via the experimenter. The experimenter triples the amount and passes it on to the responder. The responder then returns r MUs back to the investor. The respective payoffs of the investor and the responder at the end of the game are $10 - i + r$ and $10 + 3i - r$. The investor can also announce some desired transfer, r^*, back from the responder.

The investor can decide to impose a fine on the responder if $r < r^*$. The fine reduces the responder's payoff but does not increase the investor's payoff. Hence, we have three possible cases. In the first, no fine is available. In the second, it is available and is used; this possibly signals unkind intentions to the responder. In the third, it is available and is not used, which signals kind intentions to the responder. Fehr and Rockenbach (2003) find that the total surplus between the

---

[20] There is a large psychological literature which suggests that incentives might crowd out intrinsic motivation. Within the Fehr–Schmidt model, intrinsic motivation may be interpreted as reciprocity-driven effort.

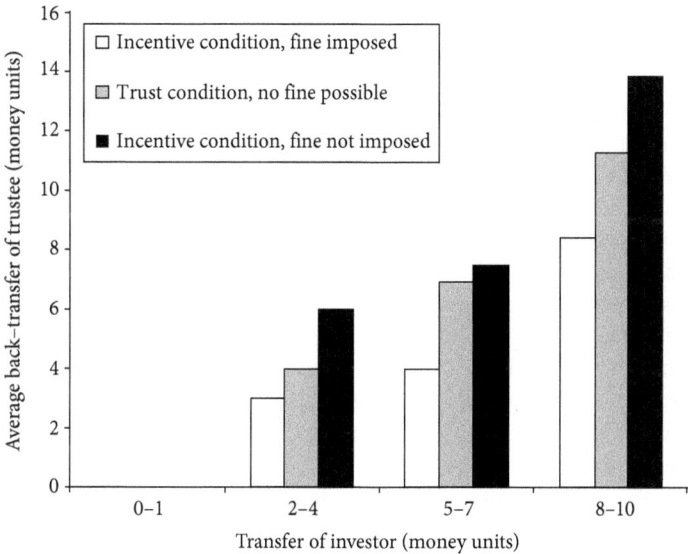

Figure 4.14 Effect of intentions in the trust game.
Source: Reprinted by permission from Macmillan Publishers Ltd.: Nature, Fehr, E. and Rockenbach, B., "Detrimental effects of sanctions on human altruism," 422: 134–40. © 2003.

investor and the responder and the average payoff of the investor are highest in the third case; see Figure 4.14. Hence, the responder's perception of the principal's intentions (hostile or kind) determines the outcome; kinder intentions produce better outcomes.[21]

In experiments conducted by Dickinson and Villeval (2008), a principal chooses different probabilities of monitoring the agent's effort; these probabilities are observed by the agent. When the effort of the agent directly increases the principal's payoff, then an increase in the monitoring intensity is found to reduce the agent's effort. Similar findings about the potentially negative effect of incentives on effort are reported in other papers that we describe in greater detail elsewhere in this chapter (Fehr et al., 2007; Fehr and Schmidt, 2007).

4.6.2 Control aversion and choking under high incentives

Incentives may signal a desire on the part of principals to "control" agents. Agents may be *aversive to control*. This idea goes back to a literature in psychology (Deci and Ryan, 1985; Deci et al., 1999). In this view, incentives conflict directly with the desire of agents for *autonomy* and *independence*. Consider the following example from Ryan and Deci (2000): "Students who are overly controlled not only lose initiative but also learn less well, especially when learning is complex or requires conceptual, creative processing... Similarly, studies show children of parents who are more autonomy supportive to be more mastery oriented—more likely to spontaneously explore and extend themselves—than children of parents who are more controlling."

---

[21] There is some evidence that the amounts given in the trust game might be influenced by demographic variables such as age, marital status, health status, etc.; see, for instance, Fehr and Schmidt (2006). The elderly and the more healthy tend to give back more in the role of a responder.

In Falk and Kosfeld (2006), an agent can choose some action $x \in [0,\bar{x}]$ for a principal. Increasing x is costly to the agent but beneficial to the principal. There are two treatments. In the first, the agent's choice is unrestricted—call this a *trust contract*. In the second treatment, the principal sets a binding lower limit, $\underline{x} > 0$, to the agent's action. Thus, the agent now must choose x from the interval $[\underline{x},\bar{x}]$—call such a contract an *incentive contract*. If the agent had purely self-regarding preferences, then in the trust contract he would choose $x = 0$ and in the incentive contract he would choose $x = \underline{x}$. It turns out that for low levels of $\underline{x}$, the principal's profits under the trust contract are greater than the profits under the incentive contract. Only when $\underline{x}$ is high enough does the incentive contract do as well as the trust contract.

Falk and Kosfeld (2006, p. 1611) summarize their main result as follows: "Explicit incentives backfire and performance is lower if the principal controls, compared to if he trusts." Their main transmission mechanism (pp. 1611–12) is that "agents do not like to be restricted and perceive control as a negative signal of distrust." Consistent with this hypothesis, principals who try to control the behavior of agents, relative to those who do not, are found to hold more pessimistic beliefs about the performance of the agent.

In order to test this mechanism further, they implement a control treatment in which the experimenter (but not the principal) directly enforces x from the interval $(\underline{x},\bar{x}]$, where $\underline{x}$ is identical to that chosen in the incentive contract. The control treatment does not signal a lack of trust or the desire to control on part of the principal, because the choice is made by the experimenter. Consistent with the authors' suggested transmission mechanism, the principal's profits are higher in the control treatment relative to the profits in the incentive contract.

In a second control treatment, the authors embed their game in a gift exchange game in which the principal chooses the pair $(w,\underline{x})$ where w is a fixed wage. The results are shown in Figure 4.15. As expected, the agent chooses a higher x when w is higher; this is the gift exchange channel. Furthermore, for most wage levels (30 or above in Figure 4.15), the choice of x is lower in the contract $(w,\underline{x}), \underline{x} > 0$ (labeled "principal controls" in Figure 4.15) relative to the contract $(w,0)$ (labeled "principal does not control" in Figure 4.15), which is consistent with the control aversion hypothesis.

The relation between incentives and effort in economics relies on two sequential channels. In the first, performance-based pay increases the worker's motivation. In the second

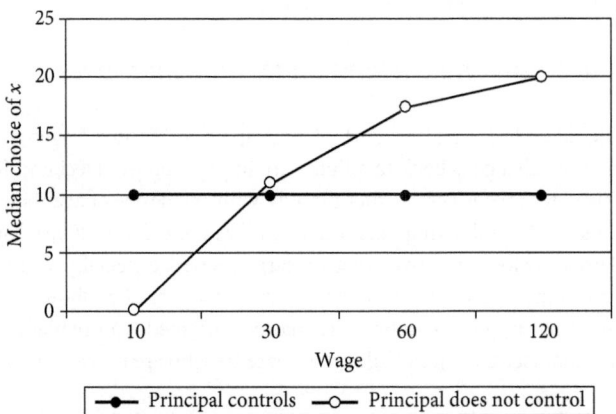

Figure 4.15 Median choice of action by the agent when the principal does, and does not, control.
Source: Falk and Kosfeld (2006) with permission from the American Economic Association.

channel, improved motivation results in greater effort. Ariely et al. (2009a) test for the second channel. They rely on several factors, which indicate that an increase in incentives may have a detrimental effect on effort (p. 2): "These include increased arousal, shifting mental processes from 'automatic' to 'controlled', narrowing of attention, and preoccupation with the reward itself." The Yerkes–Dodson law in psychology, based on experiments on rats, posits an optimum level of arousal for each task, with effort falling as the level of arousal differs from the optimal in both directions. The results of Neiss (1988) for human motor performance are consistent with this law. Thus, it is possible that high incentives over-arouse the subject, focus attention away from the task to the reward, or highlight negative emotions, such as feelings of regret, in case the reward is missed.

Choking refers to emotional responses that make high incentives counterproductive for the sorts of reasons described above (Loewenstein, 2000). The meaning of the term is well understood in common usage. Consider, for instance, the following typically self-effacing quote from Simon Hattenstone in the *Guardian* dated June 22, 2012, prior to the London Olympics:

> Britain is no stranger to the choke. Reading the newspapers, or overhearing pub conversations, you might well imagine it's a national pastime. The England football team? Ach, we'll crack up when it comes to penalties. Murray at Wimbledon? Wait till it comes to the crunch. The Olympics? More tears from Paula Radcliffe. Of course, this is an unfair generalization. All those cited have performed at the highest level, and Britain has produced any number of champions. Yet it's undoubtedly true that in a summer in which so many will be playing for the highest stakes, many of the great sporting hopes, from whatever country, will buckle under the pressure.

Ariely et al. (2009a) give six tasks to subjects in an experiment that test memory, motor skills, and creativity. Subjects were randomly assigned to the tasks. There are three treatments, differentiated by the level of incentives: Incentives are very small, medium, or very large. The six tasks are simple games. A game called "Packing quarters" measures creativity; this involved fitting nine metal pieces into a wooden frame in a fixed amount of time. Two games, "Simon" and "Recall last three digits" test for memory; these involve recalling a sequence of numbers. Motor skills are tested using three games: "Labyrinth," "Dart Ball," and "Roll-Up." The results are shown in Figure 4.16.

The measure of performance that is used in these six tasks is share of earnings relative to maximum possible earnings. Figure 4.16 shows the average performance in each of the games (Panel(a) pools across all games). It is obvious that relatively high monetary incentives can have perverse effects on performance, but there was no noticeable difference between the low and the medium incentive conditions.

These results used a between-subjects treatment in rural India. A potential criticism of these results is that the subjects might not have played these kinds of games before. Hence, in a second set of experiments, a within-subjects treatment is implemented for MIT students, using games that the subjects would be familiar with. Subjects perform two possible tasks—adding a fixed set of numbers within a certain amount of time that measures cognitive skills, and repeatedly pushing a small sequence of keys to proxy for a physical task. The results are shown in Figure 4.17. The results of the cognitive task are similar to the earlier between-subjects treatment and high incentives are detrimental to effort. However, the results of the physical task are the opposite; high incentives are effective in this case.

Bartling et al. (2012) propose a new framework to test for the trade-off between control aversion caused by limited discretion on the one hand, and the misuse of discretion by workers

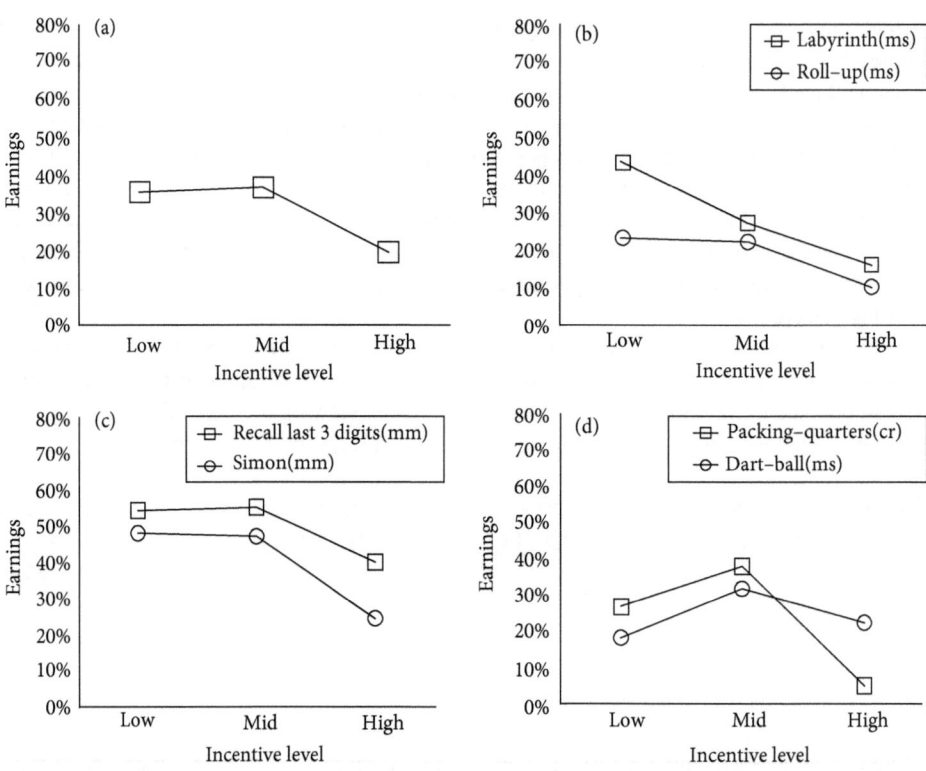

Figure 4.16 Mean earnings as a percentage of maximum earnings in different games.

Source: Ariely, D., Gneezy, U., Loewenstein, G., and Mazar, N. "Large stakes and big mistakes," Review of Economic Studies (2009) 76(2): 451–69, by permission of Oxford University Press.

on the other. Suppose that an employer hires an employee by offering a contract (w_b, e_n), where w_b is the binding wage level and e_n is the non-binding effort level (or *requested effort* that cannot be contractually enforced). The payoffs of the employer and the employee are, respectively, $\pi = be_a - w_b$ and $u = w_b - e_a$, where e_a is the actual effort level, and $b > 0$ is the marginal productivity of effort.

The employer can offer one of two possible contracts. In the *full discretion contract* (contract-F), the employee chooses $e_a \in \{1, 2, \ldots, 10\}$ and the productivity parameter $b = 5$. By contrast, in the *limited discretion contract* (contract-L) the employee chooses $e_a \in \{3, 4, \ldots, 10\}$ and $b = 4$. These numbers illustrate the trade-off between *efficiency* and *control*; contract-F is more efficient because b is higher, but the employee may shirk. The reason b is lower under contract-L is that the employee's flexibility is reduced; for instance, control may be associated with inflexible hours that do not suit the employee. The payoff functions and the technology is known to all players and the outside option of the employee is zero.

The employers and employees are matched randomly over 15 periods. There are two treatments. In the *base treatment*, the employer does not receive any information about the past effort levels of the agent. In the *screening treatment*, the employer is told about the effort choice of the

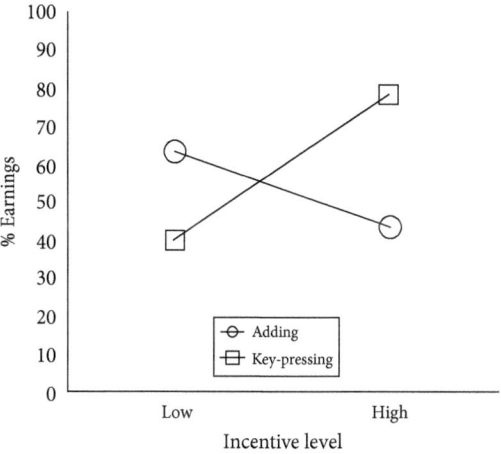

Figure 4.17 Mean earnings as a percentage of maximum earnings in different games.
Source: Ariely, D., Gneezy, U., Loewenstein, G., and Mazar, N. "Large stakes and big mistakes," Review of Economic Studies (2009) 76(2): 451–69, by permission of Oxford University Press.

employee, e_a, in the last three rounds but not the type of contracts (contract-F or contract-L) that were offered or the requested effort level, e_n.[22]

Consider the solution under self-regarding preferences. In the last round, the employee puts in the minimum effort possible under each of the two contracts ($e = 1$ under contract-F and $e = 3$ under contract-L). The employer offers a wage to ensure that the individual rationality constraint of the employee binds, so $w - e = 0$. It is straightforward to check that the profit of the employer under contracts F and L is, respectively, 4 and 9. Thus, the employer optimally chooses contract-L. By backward induction, this is the solution in each round and it is identical under the base treatment and the screening treatment.

The solution under other-regarding preferences of the employer and the employee is along the lines discussed in Section 4.4; see for instance, Proposition 4.12. In this case, employers (self-regarding or other-regarding) will attempt to tap into the reciprocity of other-regarding agents. Self-regarding employees will tend to mimic the actions of the other-regarding employees in order to get rents. The results depend on the proportion of self-regarding and other-regarding employees, and the magnitudes of the inequity parameters of other-regarding players (as in Proposition 4.12).

While we do not prove these results here, under reasonable restrictions, one gets the following results.[23] In the base treatment, employers choose contract-L, i.e., they choose to control. In the screening treatment, however, employers offer contracts conditional on the previous levels of efforts of the employees (screening). When the previous effort levels are high, the employers offer contract-F and a high wage level in order to tap into the employees' reciprocity. For low previous effort levels, they offer the contract-L. The opportunity to build a reputation also induces

---

[22] For instance, employers may have access to reference letters of potential employees that may not provide all possible information.
[23] Readers can consult Section A1 of the online appendix in Bartling et al. (2012) for the details.

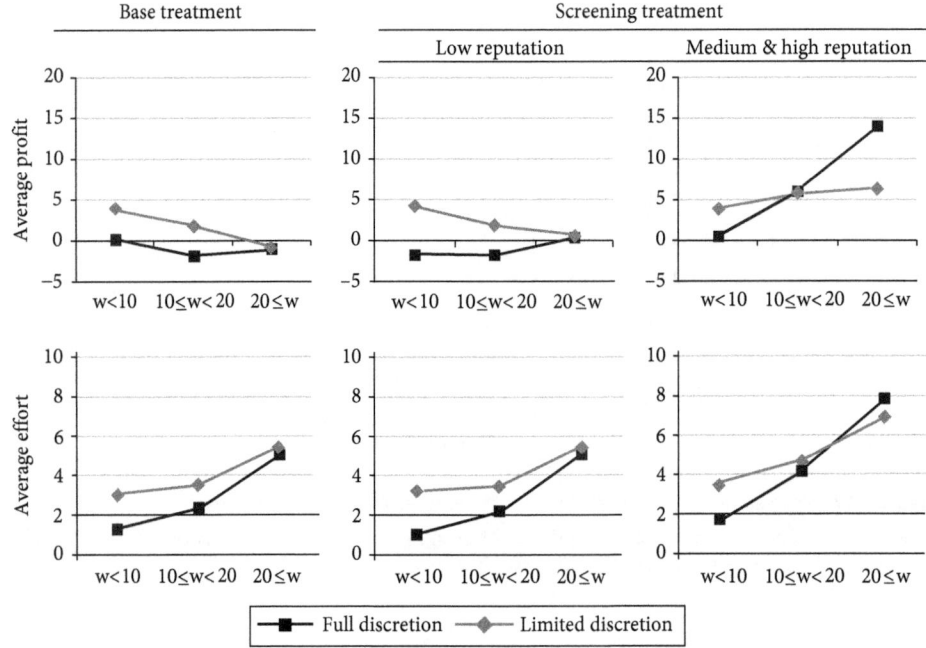

Figure 4.18 Average profits and average effort levels conditonal on the employees' reputations.
Source: Bartling et al. (2012) with permission from the American Economic Association.

employees to put in higher effort levels. Such an incentive is even higher if employers compete for workers, putting more upward pressure on wages.

In principle, one could have highly variable contracts. For instance, contract-F or contract-L, any positive wage level, and any, feasible, requested effort level. However, predominantly, two types of jobs are offered by the employers that we may call, respectively, as the *trust strategy* and the *control strategy*. The trust strategy has the following four features: (contract-F, high w_b, high e_n, high employee surplus). By contrast, the control strategy has the following four features: (contract-L, low w_b, low e_n, low employee surplus).[24] The trust strategy is based on tapping into the other-regarding employees' reciprocity, while the control strategy is designed to minimize shirking by self-regarding employees.

Which of the two strategies, trust and control is more profitable? The answer, as shown in the upper row of Figure 4.18, depends on the reputation of the employees. Let us group employees into three groups by their average past effort levels, $\bar{e}$, over three rounds: *Low reputation* if $\bar{e} < 3.5$, *medium reputation* if $3.5 \leq \bar{e} < 6.5$, and *high reputation* if $6.5 \leq \bar{e}$.

In the base treatment, contract-L is significantly more profitable than contract-F for employers, conditional on workers of all three types of reputations. In the base treatment, employers who offer contract-F, make losses for all levels of wages. The outcome is identical in the screening treatment when workers are of low reputation. However, the opposite is true for workers of medium and high reputation. In this case, under a screening contract, contract-F is relatively

---

[24] The employee surplus is defined as $\min\left\{1, \frac{w_b - e_n}{be_n - e_n}\right\}$.

more profitable. The main reason for these results can be seen in the second row of Figure 4.18. The slope of the effort–wage response is too flat in the base treatment to justify the cost of a higher wage payment. By contrast, in the screening treatment, the effort–wage response is sufficiently steep to justify higher wage payments. Indeed, in an attempt to build a reputation, even self-regarding employees may mimic other-regarding employees and respond with a high effort choice. Regression results confirm the insights from Figure 4.18.

Recall the results of Falk and Kosfeld (2006) and Ariely et al. (2009a), above. These papers show that greater control reduces effort. This finding is not replicated in the second row of Figure 4.18. In fact, other than the high reputation employees in the screening treatment, one gets the opposite result, namely, that average effort is higher in contract-L. However, the high reputation employees also receive higher wages in a screening contract. Hence, these results neither support nor reject the *hidden costs of control.*

It turns out that most employers in the two treatments converge towards the optimal contract over time. In other words, when the reputation of the employees is medium or high, employers choose to control in the base treatment and trust in the screening treatment. The results are shown in Figure 4.19. However, not all employers optimize. There is greater optimization in the base treatment. For instance, in the screening treatment, 45% of the employers fail to optimize when faced with employees of medium to high reputations.

A similar trend is found with respect to the employees. A significant percentage of self-regarding employees do not attempt to mimic the other-regarding employees by responding to high wages with high effort levels. Hence, they forgo an opportunity to improve their payoffs. This leads to *segmented labor markets*. Some employees work hard, are offered good jobs (the trust strategy of the employers) and have higher payoffs relative to others who shirk and get offered bad

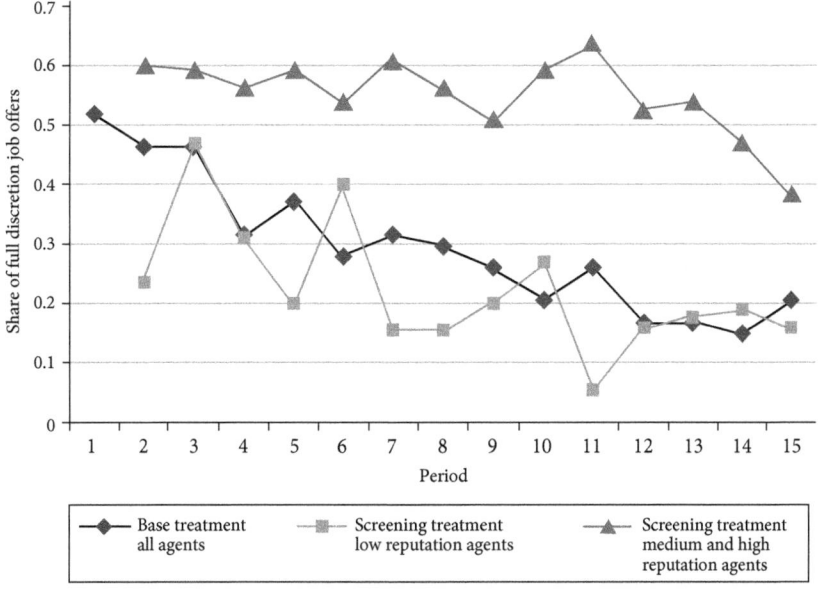

Figure 4.19 Share of contract-F in each treatment.
Source: Bartling et al. (2012) with permission from the American Economic Association.

jobs (the control strategy). Despite the presence of a positive fraction of these non-optimizing employees, the opportunity to screen workers increases the profits of the employers. The reason is that there is a sufficiently large fraction of employees who take the opportunity of screening to build reputations for hard work and they are rewarded by good jobs. These features of the results are strengthened even further when competition is introduced in a separate treatment.

4.6.3 Moral disengagement

Implicit incentives such as bonuses may engage the *moral frame*, while *explicit incentives* may sometimes turn off the moral frame. Bowles and Polanía-Reys (2012, p. 373) write: "market-like incentives trigger what psychologists term 'moral disengagement' (Bandura, 1991), a process that occurs because 'people can switch their ethicality on and off' (Shu et al. 2011)." In a similar vein, Schotter et al. (1996, p. 38) write: "While we are not claiming that people change their nature when they function in markets, it may be that the competition inherent in markets and the need to survive offers justifications for actions that, in isolation, would be unjustifiable... The morality of economic agents embedded in a market context may therefore be quite different from their morality in isolation."

Hoffman et al. (2008) consider two treatments. In the first treatment, subjects are randomly assigned to the roles of proposers and responders in a standard ultimatum and dictator game. In the second treatment, subjects have to earn the right to be proposers. This is achieved by ranking the subjects, based on the number of correct answers to a general knowledge quiz. The top half of the ranked students is then assigned the role of a proposer and the bottom half is assigned the role of a responder. Further, proposers are told that they are "sellers" and responders are told that they are "buyers."

In this "exchange version" of the ultimatum game, subjects play the game shown in Figure 4.20. Note that this game is identical to a standard ultimatum game, although it is framed differently, hence, standard frame-invariant economic theory predicts that the results should be identical in the two games. However, in the exchange version of the ultimatum game, sellers (or proposers) make lower offers relative to the standard ultimatum game and this difference is statistically significant. Buyers (or responders) are also less likely to reject offers in the exchange version of the game. Similar results carry over to the dictator game when a standard dictator game is compared with its exchange version: dictators make significantly lower offers. One plausible interpretation of these results is that the "moral frame" of the ultimatum and the dictator games is altered when these are framed as exchange games.

		Seller chooses PRICE											
		$0	$1	$2	$3	$4	$5	$6	$7	$8	$9	$10	
Buyer chooses to	BUY	$0	$1	$2	$3	$4	$5	$6	$7	$8	$9	$10	Seller profit
		$10	$9	$8	$7	$6	$5	$4	$3	$2	$1	$0	Buyer profit
	NOT BUY	$0	$0	$0	$0	$0	$0	$0	$0	$0	$0	$0	Seller profit
		$0	$0	$0	$0	$0	$0	$0	$0	$0	$0	$0	Buyer profit

Figure 4.20 Buyer/seller profits as a function of buyer/seller choices.
Source: Reprinted from Hoffman, E., McCabe, K., and Smith, V., "Preferences and property rights in ultimatum and dictator games," in Charles R. Plott and Vernon L. Smith (eds.), Handbook of Experimental Economics Results, Volume 1. © 2008, with permission from Elsevier.

In Schotter et al. (1996), subjects in the experiment play two rounds of an ultimatum game and subjects are split into three groups. The first group forms the set of proposers in round 1. The second and third groups are, respectively, the responders in rounds 1 and 2. The proposers in round 1 play a tournament in the sense that they are ranked by the amounts that they could keep for themselves successfully (i.e., in cases where their offer was accepted). The top half of the proposers in round 1, who win the tournament, then go on to play the ultimatum game in round 2. Thus, as in Hoffman et al. (2008), proposers have to earn the right to play in round 2. The competitive tournament environment produces lower offers by proposers in round 2, i.e., the presence of incentives induces more self-regarding outcomes.

Cardenas et al. (2000) conduct experiments in three rural areas in Colombia among communities that live on the edge of forests. As part of their lives, these communities harvest a common resource, wood, from the forest. Subjects in the experiments engage in a common pool resource game. As is typical in these problems, the efficient solution involves a degree of resource conservation, while in the Nash solution there is an over-exploitation of resources on account of free-riding.

The authors consider two groups of subjects. All subjects first play nine rounds of the common pool resource game. As expected, there is over-exploitation of the common resource. In the subsequent nine rounds, one group of subjects can communicate (Com), while the other cannot (Reg). Further, group Reg is subjected to government incentives to prevent over-exploitation in the form of a quota. Communication in group Com is designed to mimic the real-world alternative to regulation in such problems, namely, local cooperative efforts.[25] It was found that group Reg, who faced government incentives made choices close to the Nash equilibrium, while group Com made much more efficient choices.

Henrich et al. (2010) consider results for three games, the dictator game (DG), the ultimatum game, and the third party punishment game (TPG). The TPG is a three-player game in which the first two players play a dictator game, while the third player can punish the proposer in the dictator game for low offers, by levying a fine at a personal cost. The subjects in the experiments are drawn from 15 diverse societies that include Amazonian tribes, African hunter-gatherers, and US students. Fines were not uncommon. Across all societies, the average offer in DG is 37%, while in the TPG it is 32%. In four out of the six societies where the offers in DG and the TPG are significantly different in a statistical sense, the offers are significantly lower in the TPG. Thus, the incentives embodied in the fines actually reduce offers. This crowding-out effect of incentives disappeared if one restricted attention to offers made by dictators who subscribed to one of the world's religions such as Islam or Christianity (as compared to other local or traditional religions).

Gneezy and Rustichini (2000a) explore the implications of introducing a fine in private day care centers in Haifa. They choose ten day care centers that are observed over 20 weeks. In the first four weeks, the number of parents who came late to pick up their children was observed for all ten centers. In six out of the ten centers, a fine of 10 Israeli Shekels for picking up children late was announced in week five. The remaining four centers were the control group that continued to operate without a fine. The six centers where the fine was levied between periods 5 and 16, had the fine removed in the beginning of week 17. Parents were observed again for the remaining four weeks to see if incentives have long-lasting effects.

---

[25] See, for instance, Ledyard (1995) in the context of public goods.

The results are shown in Figure 4.21. There was an immediate jump in the number of parents arriving late after the introduction of the fine. The *reciprocity relation* between the parents and day care center staff seems to have altered with the introduction of the fine to an *exchange relation* (a form of switching-off of ethicality). Those parents who had a high opportunity cost of their time, seemed to be willing to pay the fine to pick up their children late (although this was not formally tested). There is no reason to believe that the opportunity cost altered after the imposition of the fine. It was also found that from weeks 17–20, when the fine was removed, the parents in day care centers where the fine had been levied, continued to come late and their late arrival stabilized at the end of the period. Thus, incentives may have a long-lasting effect on reciprocity relations. Similar results are found by Holmås et al. (2010) who find that disincentives in the form of fines for prolonging hospital stay in Norway prolonged hospital stay.

One possible explanation for the negative effect of incentives is that incentives may be too low. On the other hand, higher incentives may have a positive effect. This line of reasoning is pursued in Gneezy and Rustichini (2000b).[26] In the first experiment, the IQ experiment, university subjects with an average age of 23 are asked GMAT style questions. Four treatments, with 40 students each, are implemented that differ in the degree of incentives offered; the respective rewards for a correct answer in these treatments are 0, 0.1, 1, and 3 New Israeli Shekels (NIS). In a second experiment, the donation experiment, students were grouped in twos and had to collect money for a good cause. There were three treatments here. In treatment 1a, students were given no monetary incentives but were told that the results of their efforts would be made public and that society wishes for them to collect as much money as possible. In treatment 1b, students were promised an incentive of 1% of the amount they collected and in treatment 1c, an incentive of 10% of the money collected.

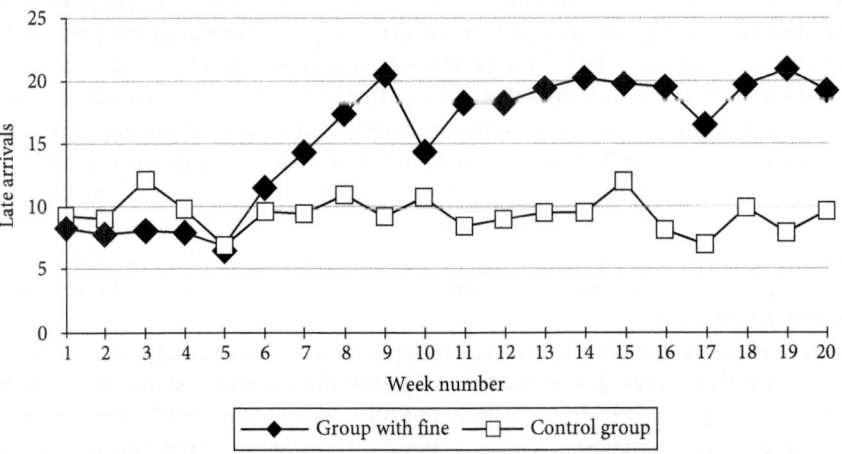

Figure 4.21 Average number of parents who arrive late.
Source: Gneezy, U. and Rustichini, A., (2000a), "A fine is a price," Journal of Legal Studies, 29: 1–17, © 2000. The University of Chicago Press, with permission of the University of Chicago Press.

---

[26] See also Heyman and Ariely (2004) who find that giving no incentives is better than giving small incentives; the latter reduce motivation and effort.

The results are as follows. In the IQ experiment, the number of correct answers in the four treatments is respectively 28.4, 23.075, 34.7, 34.1. The number of correct answers with low incentives (monetary incentives 0, 0.1) is significantly lower as compared to high incentives (monetary incentives 1, 3). There is a significant marginal reduction in the number of correct answers when one moves from zero incentives (intrinsic motivation) to very low incentives (0.1). There is no statistical difference in the number of correct answers when incentives are already high (1, 3).

In the donations experiment, the average collections in the three treatments, 1a, 1b, and 1c, respectively, are NIS 238.67, 153.67, 219.33. There is a statistically significant reduction in collections when one goes from treatment 1a (intrinsic motivation) to treatment 1b (1% monetary payments). There is a statistically significant increase in collections as one moves from low incentives in treatment 1b to higher incentives in treatment 1c (10% monetary payments). However, even with high incentives, the collections are not higher than those that arise from purely intrinsic motivation.

Frey and Oberholzer-Gee (1997) showed that Swiss residents were more likely to agree to nuclear waste disposal in their communities out of a sense of civic duty as compared to a situation where they were offered monetary compensation. The monetary compensation may also potentially indicate to the residents that the potential risks of the plant are high.

In an unusual and interesting experiment, Falk and Szech (2013) explore if markets erode morality when subjects could choose between earning money and saving the life of a mouse. In the individual (or non-market) treatment, subjects had to choose between receiving 10 euros, or saving the life of a young, healthy mouse, who could live for two more years. One may presume that in most cultures, the unjustified and intentional taking of a life must be considered immoral. In the bilateral treatment, a seller and a buyer bargain over the division of 20 euros. Should bargaining conclude successfully, then the life of the mouse is lost, but the two players get to share 20 euros. The multilateral treatment is similar to the bilateral treatment except that there are several buyers and sellers who simultaneously bid in a double auction format.

The authors conjecture three possible channels through which morality may be eroded in markets. First, in the bilateral and the multilateral treatments, responsibility for killing the mouse is more diffused relative to the individual treatment. Hence, guilt may be shared, and shared even more widely in the multilateral treatment, relative to the bilateral treatment. Second, the observation that others are willing to engage in trade (at the moral cost of the mouse's life) may loosen one's own morality in favor of the self-interest motive. Third, markets may draw attention to a non-moral frame by focusing the attention of individuals on negotiations, bargaining, and competition.

In the individual treatment, 45.9% of the subjects are willing to accept 10 euros, rather than save the mouse's life. In the bilateral and the multilateral treatments, 72.2% and 75.9%, respectively, of the subjects are willing to enter into a bargaining agreement that potentially gives them 10 euros, rather than save the mouse's life. These percentages are significantly higher relative to the individual treatment. Further, in the individual treatment, 72.2% and 75.9% of the subjects are willing to have the mouse killed, but only in return for much higher sums of money, respectively, 47.50 and 50 euros. Hence, morality would appear to diminish in markets. It would be of interest to examine the precise channels through which these effects operate.[27]

---

[27] Falk and Szech (2014) already make headway in this direction by considering alternative treatments that differ in the extent to which any one subject is pivotal in the decision to kill the mouse.

Ellman and Pezanis-Christou (2010) use insights from social psychology to explore the effect on the ethicality of decisions by varying the organizational form within firms and the levels of communication among players. In their three-player variant of the dictator game, a third player is passive. The first two players, who are members of the firm, decide whether to take an action that improves the profits of the firm, but harms the third player. In the *vertical organizational form*, the two-player firm has one boss who makes the decision and the other player is a subordinate. The subordinate cannot take a decision but can quit, which shuts down the firm. In the *horizontal organizational form*, both players in the firm take a decision by consensus.

When responsibility for the decision is diffused, such as in the horizontal organizational form, then each of the players feels a lower level of responsibility for an unethical decision. Indeed, the authors find that with unrestricted communication between the two players in the firm, vertical organizational forms exhibit more ethical behavior. The authors also recover an important role for communication. Communication may enhance ethicality for several reasons. For instance, communication may aid in transmitting norms of ethicality. Subordinates in horizontal structures may also feel a greater sense of social responsibility when they are able to transmit their views to superiors. Communication may also create an *observer effect*, whereby when one is observed by others one exhibits greater sociality (recall the evidence from dictator games in Section 1.2).

4.6.4 Morality may be difficult to signal in the presence of incentives

Consider the work of Bénabou and Tirole (2006) in Section 4.5.1 that addresses issues of altruism and social participation in several diverse contexts such as charitable contributions, voting, and blood donation. Positive actions by an individual, such as higher charitable contributions, may improve one's own self-image (self-signaling) and could also be a medium through which one engages in social signaling to others such as family, friends, relatives, and colleagues. Individuals may be privately informed of their degree of altruism and they may derive utility from positive signals of their altruism to themselves and to others. Incentives may, however, dilute the reputational value of the signal by making it noisier. Hence, incentives may be counterproductive in eliciting greater effort.

In a pioneering study, Titmuss (1971) found that individuals are more likely to donate blood on a voluntary basis as compared to the case where they are compensated to donate blood; this became known as the *crowding-out effect of incentives*. Mellström and Johannesson (2008) use Swedish subjects to test the crowding-out effect, taking account of gender differences among subjects. Three treatments are considered. In the first, there are no incentives for giving blood and in the second there is a fixed monetary incentive of SEK 50 (the equivalent of US$7) for donating blood. The results are shown in Figure 4.22.

Across all subjects in experiments, as we move from treatment 1 to treatment 2, the percentage of subjects who decide to donate blood falls from 43% to 33% but this difference is not statistically significant. However, there are noticeable gender differences. There is no crowding-out for men, but for women there is a statistically significant crowding-out effect and blood donations fall from 52% to 30%. A third treatment offers the kind of incentives that the *Economic Journal* gives to its referees. Subjects can choose to receive SEK 50 for their blood donations or have SEK 50 contributed, on their behalf, to a Swedish charity. In this case, when individuals choose the option to contribute to charity, there is no crowding-out. This result is consistent with the Bénabou and Tirole (2006) explanation because contributions to charity may allow one to use contributions to signal one's type.

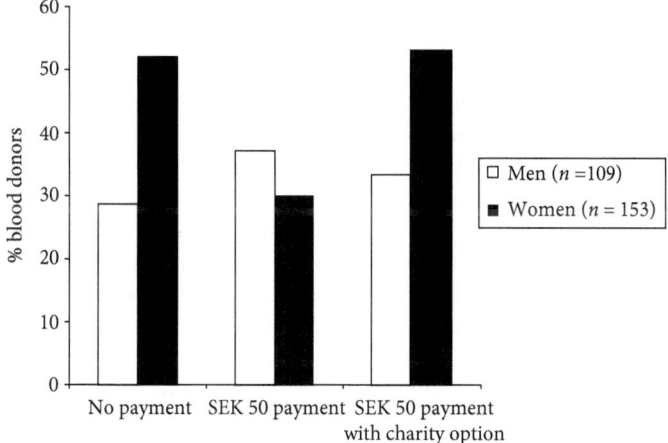

Figure 4.22 Percentage of blood donors under varying levels of incentives.
Source: "Crowding out in blood donation: was Titmuss right?" Mellström, C. and Johanneson, M., Journal of the European Economic Association, 6: 845–63. © 2008 European Economic Association.

Lacetera et al. (2012) consider a very large sample of 500,000 blood donations to the American Red Cross (ARC) in Ohio between 2006 and 2008. The ARC collects blood in so called *blood drives*; each blood drive is a single event that solicits blood donations and there are an average of 36 donors per blood drive. They find a positive effect of non-monetary incentives (blankets, T-shirts, mugs, coupons) on blood donations. Higher incentives induce greater blood donations on two accounts: An increase in the turnout and an increase in the number of units donated. A significant part of this increase in donations, about 45%, is caused by substitution from other spatially and temporally separated blood drives. Thus, one should exercise caution in estimating the overall effect of incentives on blood donations.

Reich et al. (2006) find no effect of incentives, in the form of T-shirts, on blood donation. Goette and Stutzer (2008) find a positive effect of incentives that take the form of a free lottery ticket worth USD 5, although the bulk of the effect came from occasional donors, while committed donors exhibited no effect. In their review, Goette et al. (2010) opine that non-monetary incentives are more likely to induce greater blood donations, which is consistent with the signaling hypothesis. Furthermore, while survey evidence suggests that health-related incentives (e.g., free cholesterol test for donors) are most effective, randomized trials show that they are not. In general, the evidence does not allow one to make conclusive policy implications. As Goette et al. (2010) say: "Overall, the results provide no support for the predictions from theories of motivational crowding. They provide moderate support for the view that incentives help to tip the balance in favor of more blood donations. However, several studies also found no effects, and this type of heterogeneity remains to be explained."

Angrist and Lavy (2009) consider incentives given to high school grade 12 students in Israel (Bagrut certification) to improve grades. Successful students go on to university, while the unsuccessful ones have an uncertain future. Hence, the economic gains for the students from doing well in these examinations would seem to be very high. However, anti-dropout measures for children taking these exams and measures to improve their grades have not been very successful. Given the widespread trend towards offering financial incentives to high school students for better grade performance, the authors wonder if financial incentives could work.

They find that incentives are effective in the case of girls but not boys. Furthermore, incentives work only for those girls whose predicted grades are higher relative to the average. These marginal students would seem to have the most to gain from putting in extra effort or adjust their test-taking strategy. Five years after the intervention, these girls were also more likely to enroll in higher education, suggesting that incentives may have longer-term effects.

Charitable donations may be publicly revealed or not. Under private information, donations are anonymous and carry no signal about the goodness or the altruism of the donor. Public information can take several forms, such as publicly revealing the list of donors, or giving donors special privileges, or simply giving tokens such as wristbands that publicly identify the donors. Ariely et al. (2009b) conjecture that in the private information case, incentives for donations (e.g., tax exempt donations) may enhance donations. However, in the public information case, if donations are made to signal one's image to others (or to oneself), then incentives reduce the value of such signals. In this case, incentives may be counterproductive.

This conjecture is verified in their empirical results. Figure 4.23 shows donations to either a good cause (as determined by an individual) or to the Red Cross, which was determined to be a good cause by a majority of the subjects. Hence, the latter is particularly revealing for the signaling value of one's donations in the public information case. The vertical axis is the number of presses; subjects were asked to press buttons and the experimenter made donations to the chosen charity that were directly proportional to the number of presses. In each case, incentives reduce prosocial behavior in the public information case but increased such behavior in the private information case.

Carpenter and Myers (2010) consider the decision to volunteer as a firefighter and the decision to respond to a call. They find that subjects who are more altruistic, as identified by their performance in a dictator game, are more likely to be volunteer firefighters and also put in more training hours. However, altruism is not necessarily associated with the decision to respond to calls. The decision to respond to calls is more strongly correlated with incentives that boost one's public image such as a vanity license plate. For decision makers who are motivated by such reputational concerns, extrinsic motivation in the form of monetary incentives is ineffective.

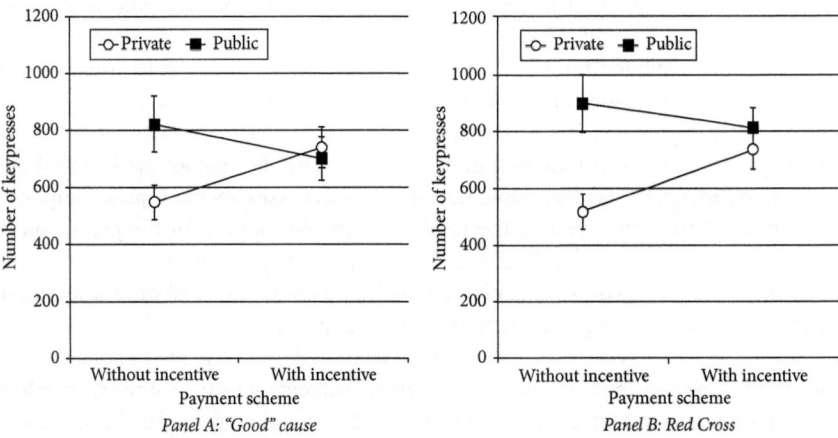

Figure 4.23 The effect of incentives on prosocial behavior in different treatments. Vertical bars are standard errors of means.

Source: Ariely et al. (2009b) with permission from the European Economic Association.

Gneezy et al. (2012) conduct three field experiments to examine the effect of incentives on the degree of self-regarding behavior in markets. These experiments are similar in nature to the Prucker and Sausgruber (2013) experiments that we considered in Chapter 3. In the first experiment, an amusement park sells photos taken during a ride to potential customers. Potential customers can *pay the price that they want* (PWYW pricing) including a price of zero. Under purely self-regarding preferences, they should not pay at all. However, 8.39% of the customers choose to buy under PWYW pricing. In a second treatment (PWYW + charity), customers are told that half of the sales proceeds will go towards charitable contributions. In this case 4.49% buy their photos but they pay a price $5.33 relative to a price of $0.92 in under PWYW pricing. Indeed, the PWYW and PWYW + charity pricing scheme are profitable to the amusement park. The data supports the hypothesis that people buy less under PWYW + charity because they avoid the possibility that they will pay too little and harm their self-image.[28]

In another field experiment, customers in a restaurant in Vienna could directly, and publicly, pay the owner or, under PWYW pricing, pay privately in an envelope. Under self-regarding preferences, customers should not pay under PWYW pricing, at least in a static game. The direct payment to the restaurant owner rules out any prosocial signaling. However, under PWYW pricing, one may self-signal prosocial behavior, or other desirable human virtues, by paying-up. Indeed, under PWYW pricing, customers paid more relative to direct public payments to the owner. A major conclusion of this study is that the desire to maintain a favorable self-image induces departures from self-regarding outcomes in markets.

4.6.5 *Economic environment, learning, and incentives*

We have reviewed the empirical evidence in Henrich et al. (2001) in Chapter 1, which showed that participation in a market environment is correlated with sociality among individuals from diverse cultures. Perhaps individuals learn to alter their preferences in such environments because doing so is advantageous to them. Furthermore, the effects of incentives can be long lasting; some examples of this are as follows. The association between educational incentives and long-term enrollment in higher education (Angrist and Lavy, 2009); the link between fines and lateness in the arrival of parents in after care centers in Israel (Gneezy and Rustichini, 2000a). We now consider some additional, related results.

Bohnet et al. (2001) consider the effects of the legal environment on contracts. They consider a two-player game in which a principal decides whether to enter or not into a contract with an agent; this is a measure of the *trust* of the principal. The principal does not know if the agent will perform; the probability that the agent performs is a measure of his *trustworthiness*. If the agent does not perform, then he is penalized with some probability that depends on the strength of the law enforcement institutions. The agent may experience psychological costs (such as guilt, or aversion to lying) from not performing or he may be completely self-regarding. In classical enforcement theory, formulated under purely self-regarding preferences, there is a monotonic relation between the strength of law enforcement and the trustworthiness of the agent. However, in the presence of human virtues, and malleable preferences, this monotonic relation may not hold.

Clearly, when the enforcement institutions are weak, the principal will only offer a contract if his belief about the trustworthiness of the agent is high. A low belief in the trustworthiness of the agent protects the principal from being exploited under these circumstances. A high

---

[28] For a similar experiment and results, see also Gneezy et al. (2010).

degree of belief in trustworthiness may ensure that, over time, more trustworthy agents are hired (the authors formalize this in terms of an evolutionary argument). Hence, in an environment with weak enforcement, trustworthiness may be crowded-in. With medium enforcement, the probability of law enforcement is high enough so that it is worthwhile for the principal to enter into a contract, based on expected utility calculations. In this case, the self-regarding agents will maximize their payoffs by not performing and the honest agents will maximize their payoff by performing. Thus, with medium enforcement, trustworthiness may be crowded-out. When the enforcement institutions are strong, then non-performance is always detected and all types of agents perform. The predictions on the relation between the strength of the legal institutions and the degree of trustworthiness are verified in the experiments conducted by the authors.

In a field study, Meier (2007) examines the effect of temporary incentives and the long-term effect on behavior once the incentives are removed. His subject pool is Swiss students who can contribute to one of two possible social funds. It is announced in a treatment group that the contributions of those who contribute to both funds will be matched to varying degrees (in one sub-treatment, the match is 25% and in another it is 50%). It is found that incentives in the form of matching contributions increase donations to the social funds. However, once the incentive is removed, (1) the average contributions in the treatment group are significantly lower than the control group in which no incentives were given, and (2) most of the subjects in the treatment group who had originally contributed to one of the two social funds, stop contributing altogether to any fund.

Reeson and Tisdell (2008) run three treatments of a public goods game without punishments, over 12 rounds. Rounds 1–4 comprise the initial stage, rounds 5–8 the middle stage, and rounds 9–12 the final stage. The control treatment is the standard public goods game experiment run over 12 rounds. In the *moral suasion treatment*, a standard text is read out to the subjects, which says that everyone will be better off if they contributed to the public good. This text was read out at the beginning of each stage, i.e., in rounds 1, 5, and 9. Finally the *regulation treatment* is identical to the moral suasion treatment except that in the middle stage, i.e., rounds 5–8, in addition to moral suasion, the experimenter announces a minimum required contribution of 100 cents to the public good. The results are shown in Figure 4.24 that shows the average contributions to the public good in cents in the three treatments.

The Nash equilibrium that is consistent with free-riding is constructed in such a way that it is 600 cents. Contributions are significantly higher in the moral suasion treatment relative to the control treatment in the initial stage. Consistent with the dominant finding in public goods games, the level of contributions declines over successive rounds in the initial stage. Reading out the moral suasion text at the beginning of round 5 boosts contributions in the middle stage to a level similar to that of the initial stage (the authors call this the "groundhog day" effect). In the middle stage, contributions are highest in the regulation treatment and these are significantly higher than the control treatment. However, once the regulations are removed in round 9, contributions in the regulation treatment drop below the level of the moral suasion treatment and are significantly lower relative to the initial stage. Thus, not only does moral suasion play an important role, it dominates incentives, in the form of regulation, in the long run.

Burks et al. (2009) consider the effect of economic incentives on Swiss and American bicycle couriers. When distinguished by their compensation, bicycle messengers belong to two main groups. (1) The first group receives performance based pay or commission payment in which couriers typically receive 40–45% of the revenues they generate. (2) The second group is made up of two subgroups that do not receive performance-based pay. They either receive a fixed hourly wage or they are members of cooperatives that simply share the total revenues.

4.6 Extrinsic and intrinsic motivation: empirical evidence | 257

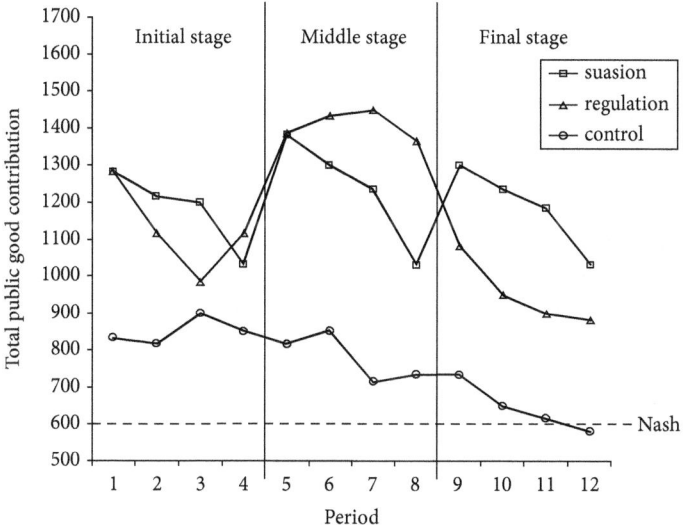

Figure 4.24 Total public goods contributions over successive rounds when the incentives are varied.
Source: Reprinted from Journal of Economic Behavior and Organization 68(1), Andrew F. Reeson and John G. T. Sdell, "Institutions, motivations and public goods: an experiments test of motivational crowding," 273–81. ©2008, with permission from Elsevier.

Members of both groups are asked to play a sequential prisoner's dilemma game, which really is a standard prisoner's dilemma game except that the first player makes a choice that is observed by the second player who then sequentially makes his choice. In this game, respondents are asked to choose their strategy (cooperate or defect) in the role of the first player and the second player.[29] They are also asked what percentage of the other players are likely to cooperate. Players are randomly assigned to be the first player or the second player; once the roles are chosen each player is randomly paired with another player. The stated responses of both players in their respective roles are then implemented.

The outcomes are used to classify respondents into one of three groups. *Egotists* always defect, *altruists* always cooperate, and *conditional cooperators* are second players who cooperate when the first player plays cooperate and defect when the first player plays defect.[30] The same game is also played with students. The results are as follows.

On average, player 1s who played the strategy "cooperate," estimated that 67% of players 2 will also cooperate. This was an underestimate—the actual figure was 86%. Thus, players may have other-regarding preferences. Respondents who are exposed to performance-based pay, choose significantly lower levels of the strategy "cooperate" relative to those who are not exposed to performance-based pay. They also expect others to cooperate less. The experimental classification of respondents into egotists, altruists, and conditional cooperators is a good predictor of the

---

[29] The *strategy method* is used to enhance the number of observations. In this method, the second player is asked what choice they would make for each possible observed choice of the first player (cooperate or defect).
[30] There is a fourth category of players, who the authors term as "Wingnuts" who do not appear to have understood the game. Since these are only 3% of the total, they are excluded from the sample.

answers to survey questions that further probe their behavior at work and off work. There are significantly more egotists in the student population relative to the population of bicycle couriers.

4.6.6 Crowding-in effect of incentives

It is possible that, in certain cases, there might be a synergy between incentives and other-regarding preferences. For instance, punishments by one's peers may trigger feelings of guilt and shame, thus pushing individuals towards a more prosocial outcome. It can often, however, be difficult to isolate the channels that are involved. For instance, punishment in public goods games may contribute to achieving an outcome close to the first best; see Section 1.4.3 above. However, it is also found that non-monetary punishments such as social ostracization can enhance contributions in public goods games (Masclet et al., 2003). Do non-contributors contribute more in the presence of punishment simply because they anticipate being punished and so they contribute, or because the punishment activates feeling of guilt, shame, lower self-evaluation, or even stigma if punishments are publicly implemented?

Herrmann et al. (2008), which was considered in Section 1.4.6, show that in public goods games with punishments, cooperation is higher when there is already a strong social norm of cooperation. In the presence of such norms, punishments trigger feelings of shame rather than resentment against the punishers. When such social norms are absent, then there is a crowding-out effect of punishment. In the absence of social norms of contributing, non-contributors who have been punished in the past turn on the contributors in subsequent rounds by engaging in antisocial punishments.[31]

Xiao and Houser (2011) ask if the negative effect of incentives arise because the punishments are privately implemented. They consider a public goods game in which the punishments are publicly announced. Yet the anonymity of the target of the punishment is maintained in order to rule out any effects arising from "naming and shaming" of the non-cooperators. They announce a probability with which any round of the public goods game is monitored. In the monitored round, the individual whose contribution is the lowest is punished in proportion to the difference between the average contribution and the lowest contribution. They conjecture that the transmission channel through which incentives work is that public punishments help establish the norm of "contribute at least as much as the average of one's group members." Contributions are found to be much higher in the treatment with public punishment relative to the baseline case of private punishment.

Carpenter et al. (2009) reconsider the public goods game with punishments. In the strangers treatment, subjects are randomly assigned to a new group at the beginning of each round. They find that being punished seems to trigger feelings of shame and guilt among non-contributors, who then contribute more. The efficacy of punishments depends on there being a high enough proportion of players who exhibit indirect reciprocity and a group size that is not too large.

Cappelen et al. (2015) consider if giving behavior in dictator games is motivated by intrinsic motivation or extrinsic motivation. In different treatments, the authors vary the morality associated with giving, for instance, by varying entitlements and needs; differences in giving

---

[31] Evidence for antisocial punishments is also found in Hopfensitz and Reuben (2009) using a social dilemma game such as the sequential prisoners' dilemma and the trust game. They find that punishment is effective only when it induces feelings of shame and guilt among the punished.

between these treatments reflect changes in intrinsic morality in different moral frames. Extrinsic motivation is altered by varying the information given to the receiver about the dictator's giving behavior. Such motivation is caused by factors such as shame and guilt that, however, are better captured using psychological game theory that we develop in Volume 4. The two main experimental findings are as follows. First, intrinsic motivation, which reflects human virtues, is fundamentally important. Second, intrinsic motivation crowds-in extrinsic motivation; in the absence of intrinsic motivation, extrinsic motivation is irrelevant.

Tyran and Field (2006) consider two kinds of sanctions on non-contributors in a public goods game. Sanctions imposed by the experimenter and sanctions imposed by a referendum among group members. Although both kinds of sanctions raised the cost of free-riding, sanctions imposed by the experimenter were not effective, while those imposed by a referendum were effective. One possible explanation is that the referendum conveys a signal of the moral disapproval by one's peers, so it is more effective in triggering feelings of guilt and shame.[32]

Fryer (2011) conducted experiments in four school districts in the US in which an amount of USD 6.3 million was distributed as incentive payments in 261 schools. In Dallas and Columbia, incentives were given for "inputs" such as attendance, good behavior, and reading a book, followed by a quiz to test the understanding of students. In New York City and Chicago, incentive payments were made for "outputs" such as exam grades. If students understand the production function that links inputs to outputs and if behavioral factors such as self-control are absent, then incentives based on outputs may be superior. The reason is that incentives based on inputs may distort the use of inputs, while output-based incentives allow users to optimally combine inputs. The results of the study are not easy to interpret. However, no link is found between intrinsic motivation and incentives. An important finding of the experiments is that incentives for output are ineffective, while incentives for inputs are effective, in a statistical sense, for some measures of performance in some of the districts. This suggests that we need to reconsider the underlying model of incentives in neoclassical economics.

Levitt et al. (2012) consider the effect of short-term educational incentives that are not confounded by issues of time discounting. They find that the effects of financial incentives, framed as gains, are mixed. However, there are stronger effects of financial incentives framed as losses.[33] Among younger students, non-financial incentives such as awards and trophies are as effective as financial incentives. There are also significant treatment effects such as age-specific effects (older children respond more to financial incentives) and gender effects (boys are more responsive to short-term incentives).[34] When incentives are delayed in the experiments (e.g. students are paid a month later), then the beneficial effects of incentives are substantially curtailed. In actual practice the rewards to education, such as jobs, salaries, and perks (which are the corresponding incentives in the real world) follow with substantial delay, suggesting that there could be underinvestment in education.

---

[32] For a theoretical model of the formation of a sanctioning institution (e.g., a court, or an arbitration board) that enables punishment of non-cooperators in a public goods game, see Kosfeld et al. (2009). Institutional punishments may also evoke feelings of guilt and shame.

[33] The framing effect of incentives jives well with the importance of framing considered elsewhere in the book. For instance, in the context of social preferences, Liberman et al. (2004) find that the manner in which a prisoner's dilemma game is framed (a cooperative or competitive game) significantly affects the prosocial behavior of participants.

[34] The gender specific effects of incentives were also found in some of the studies considered above that examine educational incentives, e.g., Fryer (2011) and Angrist and Lavy (2009).

260 | CHAPTER 4 *Incentives and Other-Regarding Preferences*

A regular exercise regime coupled with a healthy diet, taken in moderation, has well-known benefits. These include higher self-esteem, better body image, a lower likelihood of being depressed, and a lower risk factor for several health problems such as cardiovascular disease. Hence, it may be argued that there are already high incentives in place to induce a regular exercise regime, yet such a regime is not universally observed. Charness and Gneezy (2009) ask if financial incentives can aid in developing a habit to exercise.

In Study 1, they first give a handout that describes the benefit of exercise. Then they distribute the subjects into three groups. In the first group, the control group, no financial incentives are given. In the second group, the *one-time group*, $25 are given for exercising once a week. The third group, the *eight-times group*, starts off with a payment of $25 for exercising once a week, followed by a payment of $100 for exercising eight more times in the next four weeks. In study 2, subjects were given $75 to show up, have biometric readings taken, and receive a handout that described the benefits from exercise. At this time, subjects were divided into three groups and invited to come back two more times with the promise of a payment of $50 each time as well as the recording of biometric readings. In the first group, the control group, there was no requirement to exercise. In group 2, the one-time group, participants were asked to attend the gym once in the intervening period, while in group 3, the eight-times group, participants were asked to attend the gym eight times in the intervening period.

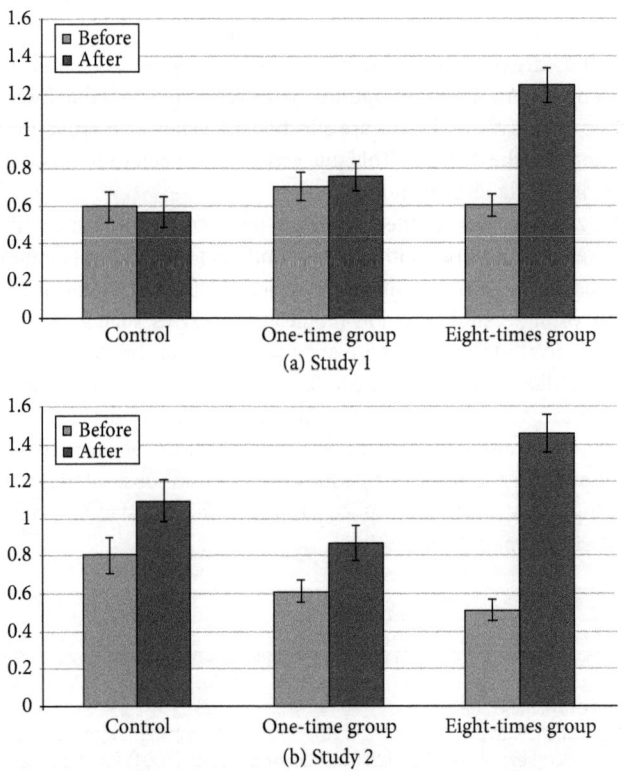

Figure 4.25 Number of weekly visits to the gym. Error bars reflect one standard error.
Source: Charness and Gneezy (2009) with permission of The Econometric Society.

The results are shown in Figure 4.25. The vertical axis shows visits to the gym per week. The period "before" records gym visits in the eight weeks before the intervention and the period "after" records gym visits in the seven weeks after the intervention. There is no statistical difference between the control group and the one-time group. However, the eight-times group, the high incentive group, reveals significantly higher gym attendance in the "after" period. There is also a significant improvement in the biometric measures for this group. The positive effect of incentives in this group is driven largely by people who did not attend the gym regularly in the "before" period.

CHAPTER 5
A Guide to Further Reading

I include below some of the key papers that were published after I submitted my book draft to OUP in September 2015. This is not merely an addendum to Volume 2. It contains critical new advances in the literature. As such, it is an essential requirement for developing a more complete understanding of the subject. In particular, there is an extended discussion of social norms that was missing in Dhami (2016). I have tried to organize the readings below roughly in the same order as the material presented in this volume.

5.1 More evidence from gift exchange experiments

In Section 1.3, in our exposition of the gift exchange game, we considered duration effects in the gift exchange game. Rajshri et al. (2016) examine duration effects for tea plantation workers in India, who were given a 30% increase in wages following the introduction of minimum wage legislation. The neoclassical model with self-regarding preferences predicts that workers should not put in any extra effort. By contrast, the evidence showed that there was a short-term increase in the productivity of workers of 20–40 percent after controlling for rainfall and the effects arising from greater supervision of workers following a wage increase. However, in the longer term, the effects of the increase in wage began to reverse. Two months after the wage increase, productivity started to decline, and four months after the wage increase, output returned to the same level that it was prior to the wage increase. This suggests the need to conduct more research on duration effects.

Malmendier and Schmidt (2017) consider situations such as the following. A pharmaceutical company gives a small gift to a doctor to influence the doctor's prescription of medicine to a third party, the patient. Should doctors be influenced by this small gift, particularly when they know that the intentions of the pharmaceutical company might not be benign? Empirical evidence suggests that while doctors deny any influence of such small gifts on their decisions, they also believe that most other doctors are influenced by the small gift. In their experiments, the authors find that small gifts are reciprocated despite there being no informational or incentive confounds. The authors' preferred explanation for their findings is sociological. They believe that humans are programmed to respond positively to gifts; gifts simply create a pre-programmed obligation to reciprocate.

5.2 Social preferences and political choices

In Section 2.5, we introduced theoretical models that incorporate other-regarding preferences into models of political economy. Fisman et al. (2017) provide evidence for the external validity of lab evidence from the domain of political behavior. In the US, in recent decades, the Democrats have been the party of greater redistribution and higher taxes, relative to the Republicans. Do Democrat voters vote for Democrats because they share this preference for greater fairness and redistribution or is it other aspects of the Democratic party platform that they are attracted to? A similar question could be asked of Republican voters in terms of a preference for lower degree of fairness and redistribution. Using a dictator game with a variable price of giving to the receiver, the authors show that subjects who have a greater degree of fairness, as measured in the lab, are more likely to vote for Democrats and those who have a greater degree of concern for efficiency are more likely to vote for Republicans.

Similar results for the external validity of lab evidence are presented by Kerschbamer and Muller (2017) for German data. Based on how subjects decide to allocate money between two players, they classify subjects into various categories. The most common category is inequity-averse subjects. The main finding is that social preferences found in the lab are a good predictor of political choices. Thus, subjects who are found to be self-regarding in the lab are more likely to support right-wing parties. More inequity averse subjects in the lab are more likely to support left-wing parties and also favor relatively greater redistribution.

5.3 Other-regarding preferences and children

Cappelen et al. (2018) examine the effects of different methods of early childhood education on social preferences. Children 3–4 years old were randomly allocated to one of three possible treatments. (1) A full-time preschool treatment, which is a full day preschool for nine months. (2) A parent academy, also a nine-month program, in which parents teach the child at home but are given 90 minute sessions every two weeks and also suggested homework. (3) A control treatment which is neither (1) nor (2). The same children are then followed up when they are 6–8 years old and are asked to do a series of simple incentivized experiments to elicit their social preferences; the experiments may involve sharing a sum of money with another child or acting as a spectator to influence the allocation between two other children. The main finding is that children exhibit the greatest prosociality in the preschool treatment. However, children participating in the parenting program care relatively more for efficiency. The authors identify social learning as the main mechanism through which these effects occur—egalitarian preferences from teachers in preschool and efficiency from parents.

Deckers et al. (2017) study the evolution of social preferences by using data from 435 German children, aged 7–9. Families are classified as low and high by socio-economic status (low SES and high SES). Low SES families have low income, low parental education, and are headed by single parents; high SES families are defined in a complementary manner. The children and their mothers participated in two incentivized experiments, held 16 months apart. In the experiments, they filled in a questionnaire on parenting style and income; tested for their IQ; and played experimental games that elicited patience, risk taking, and altruism. The main result is that SES is a strong predictor of preferences and of IQ. Children coming from low SES families exhibited greater impatience, lower IQ, less altruism, and were more risk taking as compared to those coming from high SES families. It is interesting that these differences in preferences and in IQ, which are likely to be correlated with economic success over their lifetimes, arise at such an early age. The authors locate the main reason for these differences in parental investment of effort and time (relatively low investment in low SES families). Clearly, one policy implication for narrowing down the gap between the two sets of children is to subsidize parental investment such as fostering parent–child interaction and home visiting programs.

5.4 Other-regarding preferences around the globe

We have examined differences in preferences between countries in several places in this book. For instance, there is substantial cultural variation in the outcomes from ultimatum game across the world (Section 1.2), and the incidence of antisocial punishment is relatively higher in societies that lack a rule of law and the norm of civic cooperation (Section 1.4.6). In an ambitious research program, Falk et al. (2018) study global variation in economic preferences by using the Global Preference Survey (GPS). Using an experimentally validated survey, based on the method described in Falk et al. (2016), they study risk preferences, time preferences, and social preferences of 80,000 individuals across 76 countries.[1] Some of the findings that are relevant for other-regarding preferences are as follows.

1. There is heterogeneity of preferences across the continents. Other-regarding preferences are strong in Asia but much weaker in sub-Saharan Africa. Surprisingly, the within-country variation in these preferences is even greater relative to the between-countries variation in preferences.
2. Several kinds of preferences are highly correlated; an example is the preferences for positive reciprocity, trust, and altruism.
3. The absolute latitude of a country and the presence of large domesticable animals are positively correlated with trust and negative reciprocity.
4. Other-regarding preferences as measured in the lab have ecological validity across countries. For instance, they are positively correlated with prosocial actions such as charitable donations, gifts of time, and helping friends/strangers. The average level of negative reciprocity in a country is positively and highly correlated with the frequency of armed conflicts.
5. The preferences for positive/negative reciprocity and altruism are positively correlated with cognitive ability.
6. Altruism is independent of age but positive reciprocity plots as a hump-shaped curve with respect to age.

5.5 Types of other-regarding preferences

We have argued in this volume that a mixture of self-regarding and other-regarding people, even if the latter are in a minority, may have a significant effect on outcomes. We have applied these ideas to explain the pattern of contributions to public goods (Section 1.4.4); to behavioral

---

[1] The data are publicly available at: https://www.briq-institute.org/global-preferences/home.

political economy; and to the nature of optimal contracts (Chapter 4). However, this left open the critical question of the precise empirical mix of other-regarding and self-regarding preferences that we observe in society. In an important advance, Bruhin et al. (2018) use a structural model to endogenously estimate the mixture of other-regarding preferences in the population. The structural model allows for inequity averse preferences and for reciprocity in two-player experimental games such as dictator games and trust games. Denote the two players by $i = A, B$. Let their respective material payoffs be given by m_A and m_B, and their respective psychological payoffs by U_A and U_B. The utility of player A is given by

$$U_A = (1 - \alpha s - \beta r)m_A + (\alpha s + \beta r)m_B. \tag{5.1}$$

The utility of player B, U_B, is defined in an analogous manner. In (5.1), s, r are binary variables. If $m_A < m_B$ then $s = 1$ and $r = 0$. If $m_A \geq m_B$, then $s = 0$ and $r = 1$. Values of (α, β) can be used to differentiate between the following types of preferences.

(a) If $\alpha = \beta = 0$, then $U_A = m_A$. Such players are purely self-regarding.
(b) Rewriting (5.1), player A has the preferences

$$U_A = \begin{cases} (1-\alpha)m_A + \alpha m_B & \text{if} \quad m_A < m_B \\ (1-\beta)m_A + \beta m_B & \text{if} \quad m_A \geq m_B \end{cases}. \tag{5.2}$$

If $\alpha < 0$ and $m_A < m_B$, then from the first row of (5.2) player A places a negative value on the material utility of player B. In this case, player A is said to be *behindness averse*.
(c) If $\beta > 0$ and $m_A \geq m_B$, then player A is *aheadness averse* because player A places a positive weight on the material payoff of player B.

Combining (b), (c), if $\alpha < 0 < \beta$ then player A is both behindness averse and aheadness averse. Such a type is termed as *difference averse*. By examining the behavior of subjects in, say, the dictator game with varying costs of making transfers to the receiver, one can estimate their α, β parameters and classify them into various types.

The authors are also interested in classifying subjects by their reciprocity preferences. This requires a modification of (5.1), which is given next:

$$U_A = (1 - \alpha s - \beta r - \gamma q - \delta v)m_A + (\alpha s + \beta r + \gamma q + \delta v)m_B. \tag{5.3}$$

In (5.3), if player B has behaved kindly towards player A, then $q = 1$, otherwise $q = 0$ (positive reciprocity). To capture negative reciprocity, if B has behaved unkindly towards player A, then $v = 1$, otherwise $v = 0$. If A has a preference for rewarding kind behavior with kind behavior, then $\gamma > 0$ and if A has a preference for punishing unkind behavior, then $\delta < 0$. One may use reciprocity games, for instance, players might be asked to play the role of trustors in a trust game, and then the reciprocity parameters γ, δ may be elicited.

The four parameters $(\alpha, \beta, \gamma, \delta)$ are estimated using a random utility model for discrete choices. This model gives the probability that subjects take a particular action in a game. A finite mixture model is then used to classify subjects into $k = 1, 2, \ldots, K$ different types such that the parameters of type k are given by $(\alpha_k, \beta_k, \gamma_k, \delta_k)$. The estimated parameters of each subject $(\alpha, \beta, \gamma, \delta)$ are then used to classify them into one of the K types. This is a different procedure from the one used in many other papers on mixture models that do not allow for an endogenous distribution of types. The problem with allowing only an exogenous distribution of types is that if a type is not initially allowed for, it cannot be found in the data. The results are as follows:

1. Roughly 40% of the subjects are *strong altruists*. They put a weight on the payoff of others, irrespective of whether their material payoff is higher or smaller. In order to increase the payoff of the other player by $1, they are willing to sacrifice 86 cents when ahead and 19 cents when behind. They display moderate positive reciprocity and weak negative reciprocity.
2. The most common type, comprising 50% of the subjects, is the *moderate altruists* who put a lower but still positive weight on the payoffs of others, as compared to the strong altruists. In order to increase the payoff of the other player by $1, they are willing to sacrifice 15 cents when ahead and 7 cents when behind. So this type is willing to engage in low-cost altruism but not high-cost altruism; the scope of low-cost altruism is not necessarily limited.
3. About 10 percent of the subjects are behindness averse. They are willing to pay 78 cents to reduce the income of others by $1 when behind, but not willing to pay to increase the incomes of others when they are ahead.
4. For the specific context and the types of the games used (dictator and trust games), no self-regarding types are found even though the mixture model would have picked out this type if it existed.
5. The endogenous type classification derived above, predicts quite well in "out of sample" data (when subjects play another set of games, e.g., trust games, that can detect prosocial actions). Thus, the underlying preferences are stable and meaningful in making predictions.

Relative to the OECD countries, income inequality is significantly higher in the US. Yet, in the US, the rates of redistribution and the size of the welfare state are relatively lower. Several competing hypotheses have been proposed. One possibility is that Americans prefer less fairness relative to the OECD countries. However, there are other explanations. (1) Empirical evidence suggests that Americans believe that the source of income inequality lies in the differences in productivity and skill rather than luck. By contrast, Europeans appear to believe that this source lies in luck rather than differences in productivity/skills. (2) Americans might carry out lower redistribution because they believe that redistribution is relatively costly (e.g., inefficient governments). Due to these differences in beliefs, one cannot identify the greater observed inequality and lower redistribution in the US with a lower preference for fairness. So how can we identify the relative fairness concerns of Americans relative to Europeans?

Almås et al. (2018) address these issues with the following experimental design. 1,000 spectators were recruited from the US and Norway, each. The spectators observed a division of a sum of money between two players (one of whom had been assigned $6 and the other $0) and then spectators may redistribute the $6 in any proportion between the two players, i.e., $(6, 0)$, $(5, 1), \ldots (0, 6)$. Each spectator was randomly assigned to one of three treatments, luck, merit, or efficiency, depending on the source of income inequality and the cost of redistribution. Only in the efficiency treatment is there a cost of redistribution. In the luck treatment, the original distribution arises purely from a lottery. In the merit treatment, the player who gets $6 solves a productivity task relatively better than the other player. The only difference between the luck and the efficiency treatments is that there is a cost of redistribution in the latter (one unit of payoff is lost for every unit redistributed).

The authors propose three types of social preferences. *Egalitarians* are those who divide the $6 equally in the merit treatment. The share of *meritocrats* is the difference in shares of spectators who allocate more to the productive worker in the merit treatment and those who allocate more to the lucky worker in the luck treatment. *Libertarians* are those who allocate everything to the lucky worker in the luck treatment.

The results are as follows:

1. Spectator choices are quite heterogeneous in both countries. Across both countries and across all treatments, 52.8% spectators completely equalize incomes between both players. However, 23.6% of the spectators do not redistribute at all. There are country-specific differences: 42.3% Americans divide equally, while 63.3% Norwegians divide equally.
2. In the luck treatment, the modal action is complete equalization of incomes (53.5% among Americans and 78.4% among Norwegians). However, the behavior in both countries changes in the merit treatment: In this case, complete equalization is carried out by 15.3% of Americans and 35.6% Norwegians. This suggests that Americans are more tolerant of income inequality arising from differences in productivity and skills.
3. For each treatment, Norwegian spectators chose a significantly more equal distribution of income as compared to American spectators, suggesting that there are differences in fairness preferences between the two countries. In both countries, inequality is accepted more in the merit treatment as compared to the luck treatment.
4. There is little difference in the inequality that is tolerated across the two treatments: luck and efficiency. Thus, the costs of redistribution do not alter peoples preferences towards inequality in any of the two countries.
5. There are significant gender differences. Men tolerate more inequality than women. Supporters of the conservative parties (i.e., those who would vote Republicans in the US elections) are willing to tolerate relatively greater inequality. American spectators who are more educated implement relatively greater inequality when compared to less educated American spectators. No such effect of education on inequality preferences is found for Norwegian spectators.
6. Meritocrats are the most prevalent in both countries (37.5% in America and 42.5% in Norway). However, there are significant differences in the presence of the other two types. Libertarians are 13.8% in Norway and more than double at 29.4% in America. However egalitarians are twice more prevalent in Norway relative to the US (35.6% versus 15.3%).

5.6 Recent evidence on human virtues

This section provides a short account of some of the recent work on human virtues (Chapter 3). A more detailed survey can be found in Dhami (2017).

5.6.1 *Lab studies on lying behavior*

We know from Volume 1 that loss aversion is one of the most salient human characteristics. Are individuals more likely to lie when they perceive that they are in the domain of losses? Grolleau et al. (2016) give subjects a matrix solving task in a 2 × 2 design (gain vs loss frame and monitored vs unmonitored reporting). In the gain frame, subjects are given a payment for the number of correct solutions. In the loss frame, subjects are initially given the maximum possible payment that would accrue from correctly solving all the matrices. Then, based on their actual/reported performance in the matrix task, a fraction of the initial payment is clawed back from them for the unsolved matrices.

Under monitored reporting, no cheating is possible, and it is found that there is no significant difference in performance between the gain and the loss frames. Thus, the frames do not produce any innate differences in the motivation to solve extra matrices. However, under unmonitored reporting, when cheating to the full extent is possible, there is significantly greater cheating in the loss frame: Relative to the unmonitored frame, solved matrices increases by 43% in the gains frame and by 296% in the loss frame.

Evidence of differences in morality in gain and loss frames is also provided by Schindler and Pfattheicher (2017). They use a variant of the Fischbacher–Föllmi-Heusi method and ask subjects to privately roll a die 75 times and report the number of occurrences of 4. Since the probability of a 4 in each throw is 1/6 and the throws are independent, the statistical prediction under truthtelling is $75(1/6) = 12.5$. In the gain frame, subjects are told that they will gain 10 cents for each reported 4. In the loss frame, subjects are initially endowed with 7.5 euros and told that they will lose 10 cents for every report of a number that is not 4. This is identical to the opportunity cost of not reporting a 4 in the gain frame. On average, subjects in the loss frame reported significantly higher 4s as compared to the prediction under truthtelling ($p = 0.031$), which indicates significant dishonesty in the loss frame. In contrast, in the gain frame, no statistically significant dishonesty was found.

In the matrix task in Mazar et al. (2008), where subjects in a lab experiment self-report the number of correctly solved matrices, an increase in incentives to lie reduces the extent of lying. The authors interpret these results to imply that there is a convex cost of lying, so that when lying for higher amounts, the marginal cost of lying to an individual increases. In contrast, in their die-throwing experiments, Fischbacher and Föllmi-Heusi (2013) find that even when incentives are tripled, the extent of lying does not change. These findings are supported in the meta-analysis of Abeler et al. (2016). How can these apparently conflicting results be reconciled?

Kajackaite and Gneezy (2017) argue that subjects who lie in the die-throwing experiments may assign some residual probability of being found out. They propose a new game, the *mind game*, in which subjects first think of a number, then they roll a six-sided die. If they self-report to the experimenter that the number on the die is identical to the number they originally thought of, then they receive a prize that was varied in different treatments to reflect changing incentives for lying. They find that there is greater lying in the mind game relative to the die throwing experiments for all levels of incentives. While men lie significantly more than women in the die-throwing experiments, no gender differences in lying were found in the mind game.

Do the size of the stakes influence the extent of cheating? Using a meta-analysis of 90 studies that use the Fischbacher and Föllmi-Heusi framework, Abeler et al. (2016) found that, on average, subjects forgo three-quarters of the potential gain from lying. This result is robust to increasing the payoff levels 500-fold relative to a baseline level, to take account of higher stakes.

5.6.2 Artifactual and field studies of lying

Balafoutas et al. (2017) conducted a real effort experiment with professional German internal auditors who were given a set of 30 calculations and told that 10 were incorrect. Subjects had to identify the incorrect calculations in three minutes, without using a calculator; they received 1 point for a correct identification and a deduction of 0.5 points for each incorrect identification. A 3×2 design (3 treatments and 2 different methods of evaluation) is used. Under *individual incentives*, subjects received a piece rate of 2 euros for each point. Under *competitive incentives*, groups of two individuals were formed; the individual in each group who gives more correct answers gets

4 euros for each point, while the partner gets nothing. Under *team incentives*, each player gets 1 euro for a correct answer given by any of the two players in the team. Under *objective evaluation*, players report on the other players' performance, but such reports are payoff-irrelevant; the actual payoffs are determined by the experimenter's directly evaluation of the number of correct answers. Under *peer evaluation*, the payoff of a player is determined by the report of the partner, which can be honest or dishonest. The results are as follows:

1. There is no misreporting in the absence of monetary incentives. Under *individual incentives* and *peer evaluation*, the actual performance (6.07 points) and the report on the performance of peers (5.96 points) is statistically indistinguishable.
2. Under *objective evaluation* and *team incentives*, players under-report the performance of the team member, despite their report being payoff-irrelevant. One potential explanation is that this enhances the *self-image* and *status perception* of individuals.
3. Under *peer evaluation* and *competitive incentives*, players under-report the number of correct answers of the partner. On average, reported points are 22% lower than actual points. The opposite, i.e., over-reporting, occurs under *team incentives* in which player reports inflate the number of correct points by 16%.
4. The share of truthful reports ranges from 70% (under peer reporting and team incentives) to 86% (under peer reporting and individual incentives). Thus, dishonest behavior is driven by a minority of the subjects, while most subjects are honest. Yet, the behavior of the small minority does lead to differences in the averages across treatments (as in points 2 and 3 above). The share of dishonest subjects is higher under competitive incentives and team incentives relative to individual incentives.

Dai et al. (2017) examine the correlation between fare evasion by passengers using public transport in Lyon and their self-reported outcomes in the die-throwing task introduced by Fischbacher and Föllmi-Heusi. Subjects were recruited from those who had just arrived at a tram/bus stop, and volunteered to participate in the experiment. The following three measures of dishonesty in the field were used. (1) At the end of the experiment, subjects were given the opportunity to exchange their ticket for a superior option, a day pass. Inability to produce a ticket may identify fare-dodgers. (2) Self-reports of subjects on the number of times they evaded fare for every ten trips in the past; cheaters (or *self-fraudsters*) evade the fare at least once, while *non-fraudsters* never evade. (3) Passengers who were known to have just paid a fine for dodging the fare.

These three groups of people were then asked to participate in a die-throwing experiment. Subjects privately threw a three-colored but six-sided die, such that each of the three colors, red, blue, and yellow, came up with 1/3 probability in a random throw of the die. Subjects then self-reported the outcome. The rewards were as follows: blue (0 euros), yellow (3 euros), and red (5 euros). Clearly amoral subjects with self-regarding preferences, as under neoclassical economics, should only report the color red.

There was widespread cheating behavior in the field. When asked to produce a valid ticket to exchange for a day pass, 41.8% could not produce one. On the basis of self-reports, 54.92% travelled without a ticket once every ten trips. For each of the different categories of subjects, based on their field behavior, we can now compare their self-reports in the lab die-throwing task. Under complete truthtelling, the die throwing task predicts a uniform probability of 1/3 for each of the three colors, blue, yellow, and red. Thus, we are interested in examining the correlation in behaviors in the field and in the lab. The field data can be used to generate several categories. For instance, the category non-ticket/self-fraudster refers to those subjects who could not produce a ticket in exchange for the day pass, and who confessed to evading the fare at least once in the last ten trips; by contrast, in the non-ticket/self-non-fraudster category, subjects do not evade fares. The remaining two categories, ticket/self-fraudster and non-ticket/self-fraudster, can be defined in an analogous manner.

The results are as follows.

1. For all the four categories of subjects, the outcome with the highest payoff (red) is overreported, and the worst outcome (blue) is under-reported. Thus, in each category, the observed distribution of self-reports is statistically different from the predicted uniform distribution.
2. Fare evaders in the field are also more dishonest in self-reporting the outcome of the die throw in the lab. Comparing the data for ticket holders and non-ticket holders, a p-test shows that non-ticket holders lie significantly more. Self-reported fraudsters under-report the worst outcome (blue) significantly more than self-reported non-fraudsters, but these two categories of subject exhibit no difference in reporting the best outcome (red).
3. Those who self-report never traveling without a ticket in the last ten trips are significantly more honest in the lab, relative to those who self-report traveling without a ticket at least thrice in the last ten trips.
4. Subjects who have just been caught evading fares behave honestly in the lab experiment. The distribution of their self-reports is statistically indistinguishable from ticket holders. One possibility is that there might be some sort of *conscience-accounting* at play (Gneezy et al., 2014). The *conscience-accounting hypothesis* postulates that guilt may depreciate over time, so an individual is more likely to engage in good deeds (e.g., contributions to charity) immediately after a moral transgression, relative to a delayed opportunity to do good deeds.
5. Since the die task might be unfamiliar to the subjects, when it is replaced by a contextualized lab public transport game that allows for fare evasion, then self-reported fraudsters in the field also behave more dishonestly than the rest.

Overall, these results suggest that lab behavior has a high degree of external validity.

Do taxpayers respond to moral suasion? Hallsworth et al. (2017) randomized five different messages across 100,000 taxpayers who had declared their incomes, but had not yet paid their taxes, so this study is not about tax evasion but rather about the timeliness of tax payments. A control group received a standard letter without moral suasion. In the letters where moral suasion was involved, three of the five messages highlighted *descriptive norms* and *injunctive norms*. The former tell subjects about what others *actually do* (e.g., "most other taxpayers pay with minimal delay") while injunctive norms tell subjects about what others think *should be done* (e.g., "most people believe that taxpayers should not delay payments beyond a month"). The remaining two messages were public service messages (e.g., "taxes fund public services"). Relative to the control treatment, the five messages resulted in an increase in the likelihood of an earlier repayment of taxes. The most successful of these messages produced a treatment effect of 5.1% over the control treatment. It is also found that descriptive norms are relatively more effective in persuading taxpayers to pay early.

5.6.3 Markets and morality

Section 4.6.3 considered some issues on markets and morality. We explore these issues further in this section.

Many economic activities are associated with negative externalities in which actions by one party cause harm or disutility to another party. In this case, the parties may be made to internalize the social costs of their actions through a range of policy choices, such as corrective Pigouvian taxes. However, if economic agents have a preference for social responsibility, could they internalize negative externalities without recourse to public policy? Anecdotal evidence suggests several examples. Many corporations increasingly stress the idea of corporate social responsibility that requires them to take account of the larger social interest, even at a cost in terms of private profits. Consumers may sometimes be willing to pay for more expensive, but socially responsible, products that do not involve child labor or cruelty to animals, or those that are made with greener, more expensive, technologies.

Bartling et al. (2015) design experiments to consider these issues in two different datasets from Swiss and Chinese subjects. In the baseline condition, there are six firms, five consumers, and five third parties. Firms can produce either a costless product that causes negative externalities worth 60 units to the third parties; or a costly externality-free product that costs 10 units. Each firm can sell one unit to one consumer, and makes an independent choice of price and the type of the product. Both types of products give each customer an identical value of 50 units, and once the firms have made their choices consumers enter the market sequentially. The game is played over 24 rounds. Reputational effects are minimized or eliminated by maintaining anonymity of the ID numbers of players and randomly rematching subjects in each round.

Suppose that consumers and firms are self-regarding and have no social responsibility. In this case, consumers will wish to buy the cheapest product and firms will wish to maximize monetary profits. Thus, we should only observe the externality-causing product in the market, leading to a negative social surplus $(50 - 60 = 10)$ for each product sold. However, if social responsibility is strong enough, the model predicts that we may observe the exchange of the costly externality-free product.

The results are as follows.

1. Over successive rounds, in the baseline condition, the externality-free products quickly stabilize at 45% of the total. Since such products are costlier, they are sold at a relatively higher price, but the price difference between the externality–free and the externality-causing product is lower than the extra production costs of the externality-free product. Thus, in equilibrium, both sellers and buyers share in the costs of being socially responsible in competitive markets.
2. As greater competition between the sellers is introduced, the price drops further, but social responsibility does not diminish. However, when the cost of production of the externality-free product is raised sufficiently (from 20% of the surplus to 80% of the surplus), the degree of observed social responsibility falls. The estimated preferences of players are best described by a combination of material utility and utility for socially responsible products.
3. When the same experiment is repeated in China, the share of the externality-free product stabilizes at a lower level of 16%, suggesting lower norms of socially responsible behavior.
4. Do markets reduce ethicality? To check this, the Swiss and the Chinese subjects are asked to play another "non-market allocation game" with similar payoffs as those that arise in the market game described above. In this game, the outcomes arising in the Chinese and the Swiss subject pools are similar, which suggests that they possess a similar preference for prosociality. Furthermore, the frequency of choices in the non-market setting that mitigate the negative effects on third parties (the analogue of negative externalities in the market setting) is relatively higher. Hence, markets do appear to reduce ethicality, which is consistent with the findings of Falk and Szech (2013) that were reported in Section 4.6.3.

Bartling and Özdemir (2017) show that existing norms influence the degree to which markets reduce or enhance ethicality. Hence, without studying the interaction effects between the two, we might get misleading results. They consider the possibility that firms may engage in an unethical business opportunity on the grounds that if they did not, someone else will (the "replacement excuse"). Whether the replacement excuse is exercised by subjects in the experiment depends on the norm for such excuses. If there are no such norms, then the replacement excuse is more likely to be exercised. However, if there exists a norms that such an excuse is immoral, then this excuse is not used.

We showed in Section 1.2 that the variations in the outcomes of the ultimatum game across societies suggest that human sociality was enhanced by the degree of market integration in the community and the degree of cooperation in production. Thus, *markets enhance sociality, even if they might diminish ethicality*. By not making this important distinction, researchers risk drawing erroneous conclusions. Ethicality does appear to be influenced by norms for ethicality, but this also begs the interesting question of why there are norms for some types of ethical behavior, but not others.

5.6.4 Public and private personas

It is useful to separate the domains of individual actions into a *private sphere* and a *public sphere*. In the private sphere, individuals make private everyday decisions such as the following: Which consumer durables to buy? How to allocate a portfolio among alternative assets? How much to save? When to retire? On the other hand, the public sphere is defined as (Gintis, 2017, p. 47): "...the locus of activities that create, maintain, transform, interpret, enforce, and execute the rules of the game that define society itself." Examples include actions such as voting in elections, participating in civil rights movements, and signing a petition for a social cause. Actions in the public sphere are *non-consequentialistic* in the sense that they do not lead to a private material gain, nor individual actions, by themselves, alter social outcomes. For instance, in signing a public petition, one person's signature is unlikely to have an effect on the final outcome. The main insight of Gintis (2017, Chapter 3) is that individuals appear to behave "as if" they have different preferences in the private and public spheres.

In the private sphere, individuals have *private personas* that make choices in a self-regarding or in an other-regarding manner. However, in the public sphere, individuals have *public personas* that give rise to direct utility from participating in actions in the public sphere. For instance, individuals might derive direct utility from voting in elections or from participating in social movements. However, such a preference is not absolute. Individuals could weigh the extra utility from these actions against the extra cost, which is possibly subjective. If the cost of participating in social actions is too high, then an individual may not engage in such actions.

It follows that rational choice theory which tries to explain social actions, such as voting, is based on the incorrect assumption that individuals take purely consequentialistic actions by engaging their private personas. Gintis suggests that the appropriate equilibrium notion in the public sphere is a form of *social rationality*, as encapsulated in a Kantian equilibrium. In a symmetric n-player game, a Kantian equilibrium strategy is such that every player prefers it to all other strategies if "everyone who shares their preferences were to act according to the same rule" (Gintis, 2017, p. 51).

5.6.5 A microfoundation for gender differences in lying

Houser et al. (2016) give one possible explanation for gender differences in lying behavior. Parents (88% mothers) were asked to privately toss two coins; each coin had a green side and a blue side. If the parent self-reports that both coins had come up green, then a reward is given, otherwise there is no reward. The accuracy of the self-report could not be verified by the experimenter, so individual lying was unobservable. However, aggregate lying could be discovered by comparing the self-reports with the objective probability of 25% of winning the reward under truthtelling. The authors chose a 2 × 2 design: (1) The reward was for either the parent ($10), or the child (a toy), and (2) the decision to lie was either made privately, or in front of the child, whose gender was recorded by the experimenter. The results were as follows:

1. Parents lied less in the presence of their child. In the presence of the child, the claimed win rate dropped down to 33% from 46% in the absence of the child; the difference is significant at 10% ($p = 0.09$).
2. When the reward is for the parent, the claimed win rate was 36%. But when the reward is for the child, the claimed win rate was 43%; the difference is not significant ($p > 0.10$).
3. The greatest claim rate, 58%, occurs when parents report privately, but the reward is for the child. This is statistically higher than the average claim rate of 33%, averaged across all treatments.
4. The claimed win rate in the presence of a daughter is 28%, close to the predicted rate of 25% under complete honesty. This is significantly lower than the claimed average win rate of 42% in the presence of sons ($p < 0.01$). This suggests that a potential explanation for lower dishonesty among women may lie in the manner in which they are socialized when young, relative to men. The authors tie this to a result in Hays and Carver (2014), which shows that children who are exposed to dishonest behavior when young, are more likely to be dishonest when adults. However, this still begs the interesting question of why people chose to behave differently with daughters, relative to sons, on moral issues.

Do people lie relatively more in groups? What group features may induce more or less honesty? A-priori, the arguments could go either way. (1) Groups might be able to use a more sophisticated analysis relative to individuals and ensure a better understanding of the underlying game (Kocher et al., 2006; Sutter, 2009). (2) Individuals might be able to disguise their lying in groups. (3) Individuals might lie more in groups on account of social preferences (Gino et al., 2013; Wiltermuth, 2011). (4) Concerns for one's social image might reduce lying in groups (Bénabou, 2013; Bénabou and Tirole, 2006). (5) Group interaction may reveal social norms about honesty or dishonesty, which could either increase or reduce honesty, depending on what one observes and learns.

Kocher et al. (2017) test some of these alternative explanations. In their novel use of the Fischbacher and Föllmi-Heusi method, individual cheating behavior can be identified by the experimenter. In the *individual treatment*, subjects observe the throw of a die on a computer screen and self-report the observed number; payoffs equal the number reported, except for the number 6, which results in a zero payoff. The experimenter also observes the outcome of the die on the computer screen, allowing an identification of individual lying. This may, however, also create greater uncertainty on the part of subjects that their lying could be observed by others.

Once subjects have participated in the individual treatment, they participate in either of two group cheating tasks. In the group tasks, subjects observe the throw of a die on the computer, but then have the opportunity to chat and exchange free-form messages before they submit their self-reports. In the treatment GroupPC, if all subjects report an identical number, then their individual payoffs equal the number (except for a payoff of zero for the number 6), otherwise if they do not report a common number, then all get a zero payoff. This treatment activates group concerns and social preferences. By contrast, in the treatment GroupNoPC, the payoff of each player depends only on the self-report, so social concerns are absent.

Comparing the results across the three treatments, the main results are as follows.

1. There is significantly more lying in both group treatments, 89.7% in GroupPC and 86.3% in GroupNoPC, as compared to the individual treatment that precedes it (61.5%). There is no statistical difference in lying between the two group treatments, suggesting that social preferences are not important in this context. The choices made in the individual treatment (honest or dishonest) have no bearing on the choices made in the group treatments.
2. There is a high degree of coordination among group members in both group treatments. Coordination is in everyone's best interests in GroupPC, and all subjects are found to coordinate. However, there is also surprisingly high coordination in GroupNoPC, where coordination has no payoff relevance; here 33 out of 39 groups coordinate after the group chat.
3. What causes increased lying in groups? First, group chat increases the beliefs of players about the dishonesty of others, relative to the individual treatment. Second, communication during the group chat plays a key role in the decision to lie. Research assistants are used to categorize free-form chat arguments into those that reflect honesty and dishonesty; when the research assistants cannot agree, their median value is taken. Arguments for dishonesty are made far more frequently (in 51% of the groups) as compared to arguments for honesty (in only 24% of the groups). The number of arguments for dishonesty are indistinguishable among the two groups. Thus, payoff commonality (as in GroupPC) does not appear to be a factor in dishonest behavior in groups. Finally, arguments for honesty significantly reduce lying in groups.

In conjunction, the results are driven by a shift in the perception of individuals in groups about the honesty norms in the rest of the population.

5.7 Norms and social preferences

There has been a growing interest in the empirical study of social norms in economics; for a wide ranging and thoughtful survey, see Fehr and Schurtenberger (2018a). The reason for the relatively brief treatment of social norms in Dhami (2016) was that despite some progress, there is much confusion and disagreement in this literature. Some of the most basic questions, such as the following four, remain unaddressed in a satisfactory manner.

1. What is the appropriate definition of a norm?
2. Can observed behavior be accounted for by social preferences or by norms?
3. Do social preferences influence conformity with norms?
4. Do norms influence social preferences?

Several factors have contributed to limited progress in answering these four basic questions. The main contributory factor is the different, inconsistent, and imprecise usages of the term "norm." The following two illustrative quotes highlight some of this frustration. Gächter et al. (2013, p. 544) write: "Explaining phenomena by appealing to the influence of social norms can be problematic because of the difficulties of precisely identifying and measuring norms. In particular, often what may or may not constitute a norm is based on intuition or casual empiricism." Similarly Schram and Charness (2015) write: "It has become fairly common practice to refer to 'social norms' or 'internalized social norms' when discussing experimental (or field) data that appear unexplainable by existing economic theories of behavior. Essentially, much of this literature has used 'social norms' as a black box meant to capture some of the influence of the social environment on individuals' decisions." Clearly, this is a highly unsatisfactory state of affairs.

In an important study on norms, Bicchieri (2006) has argued that two kinds of expectations are critical in the formation of norms—*empirical expectations* (EE) and *normative expectations* (NE). EE are the expectations of individuals about the actions of others in some given situation. In many cases of interest, these expectations are likely to have been generated by direct observation of what others have done in the past. In a more general framework, EE may be generated by *social projection* or *evidential reasoning*, i.e., individuals may undertake a mental exercise in which they ask themselves: What are other like-minded people likely to do in the given situation (Cialdini et al. 1990; al-Nowaihi and Dhami, 2015)?

In contrast to EE, the NE of a player, say player A, is player A's beliefs about the actions that others expect player A *should* or *ought* to take. NE are distinct from the following two kinds of expectations. (1) *Personal normative expectations*, which are personal expectations of player A about the actions that player A ought to take. Such expectations underpin many *moral norms* (Elster, 1989). (2) *Second order empirical beliefs* (SOB) as in psychological game theory (see details in Volume 4), which are the expectations of player A about the first order expectations of others.

> **Example 5.1** *As an illustration of the difference between NE and SOB, consider a prisoners' dilemma game between two players, A and B, who simultaneously choose to either cooperate, C, or defect, D. If both players play C they get 20 each and if both play D they get 10 each. If one plays C and the other plays D, they get, respectively, 0 and 30.*
> *Player A may have the NE that player B expects that player A ought to cooperate. However, the SOB of player A could be that player B thinks that player A will, in fact, defect. In this case, there is clearly a conflict between NE and SOB. Such a situation is likely to arise, when norms (either of cooperation or defection) have not yet been established. Indeed, norms, once they are established, are likely to act as a mechanism that coordinates NE, EE, and SOB.*

EE are necessary, yet they are not sufficient for norm compliance. Suppose that in a social dilemma situation, one's EE are that others will cooperate. Then, *ceteris paribus*, it might also be in one's self-regarding interests to actually withdraw cooperation. For instance, in a public goods game, if players with self-regarding preferences believe that most others will cooperate, then they may maximize their payoffs by free-riding.

For this reason, NE are a critical component in sustaining norms (Bicchieri, 2006; Sugden, 1998, 2004) and EE alone might not be enough. If NE lead players to believe that "others expect that they ought to" take a particular action, then not taking the required action may generate feelings of *guilt* or *shame*. Indeed, such emotions are the *internal psychological mechanisms* that may successfully support social norms, even in the absence of social sanctions (Elster, 1989, 1999, 2011). In the context of public goods games, and taking account of the *false-consensus effect*, Dhami et al. (2018) show that guilt-aversion is a powerful determinant of public goods contributions at the individual and aggregate levels.

As a guide to a common problem among many empirical studies, consider some social scenario where players may choose from a set of actions S. Another set of players N is asked to rate the "social appropriateness" of actions in the set S. If the social appropriateness ratings of the set of players in N is not conveyed to player A, then there is no guarantee that player A's internal psychological mechanisms propagated through guilt-aversion and shame will be fully activated. Yet, several existing papers implicitly make the contrary assumption by not conveying the appropriateness ratings to player A. It is not clear how to interpret the results in this case.

When EE and NE are in conflict, there is some evidence that EE are more important (Bicchieri and Xiao, 2009). While EE and NE may jointly suffice to support social norms for many people, this is not always the case. In addition to EE and NE, norm compliance often requires the existence of *sanctions* or *punishments* that are imposed on those who break the norm. There is a sizeable experimental and non-experimental literature that supports this view.[2] Sometimes, a distinction is drawn between *descriptive norms* (actions of players are based on EE alone) and *injunctive norms* (actions of players are based on NE alone). However, most norms are likely to be a result of both EE and NE, as well as sanctions.

The discussion above suggests the following working definition of a norm. We distinguish between a *strong norm* and a *weak norm* based on whether sanctions are present or not.

> **Definition 5.1** *(Weak norm): A weak norm is characterized by the following:*
> *(a) Actions of individuals are jointly determined by their observation of empirical expectations and normative expectations.*
> *(b) The empirical and normative expectations of players are correct (Bicchieri, 2006, p. 52).*

Sanctions are not a part of the definition of a weak norm. Next, we define a strong norm that includes such sanctions.

> **Definition 5.2** *(Strong norm): A weak norm becomes a strong norm if, in addition, sanctions are present, so that actions of individuals are jointly determined by their observation of empirical expectations, normative expectations, and sanctions, and these expectations are correct.*

Not everyone will follow a norm, even if such a norm exists; some people may break the norm.

Definitions 5.1, 5.2 suggest an *equilibrium interpretation of norms*; see, e.g., Definition 5.1(b). When norms are not yet established, there is no guarantee that the EE and NE of players turn out to be correct; i.e., out of equilibrium, the beliefs of players need not be correct. But once established, the beliefs of players are assumed to be correct.

> **Example 5.2** *In a prisoner's dilemma game (see Example 5.1), suppose that a cooperative norm has not yet developed. Then, we may have the entirely reasonable situation described in Example 5.1, and there may be a conflict between NE and SOB. However, once a norm of cooperation has developed in this game, then we expect the following. Players observe that most others cooperate (EE); they also believe that others think that they ought to cooperate (NE); and, the EE and NE are correct. In addition, if this is a strong norm, then players who defect may expect to be sanctioned. A norm of defection may be constructed in an analogous manner. Which of the two norms develops, a cooperative norm or a norm of defection, is an interesting empirical question.*

---

[2] See, for instance, Fehr and Gächter (2000), Fehr et al. (2002), Fehr and Fischbacher (2004), Elster (2011), Dhami (2016), and Gintis (2017).

A norm is to be distinguished from a *convention*. A convention is a set of behaviors such that it is in the material best interests of an individual to follow the convention if others follow it too (Sugden, 1989).[3] Unlike strong norms, no sanctions are required to sustain conventions (e.g., driving on the left or the right side of a road).[4]

Elster (1989, 1999, 2011) distinguishes between *moral norms* and *social norms*. Moral norms are rules of behavior followed by an individual that do not depend on being observed by others, nor do they invite sanctions from others. Such norms are maintained by *internal psychological mechanisms* such as *guilt*. Social norms, on the other hand, require one's actions to be observed and typically sanctioned by others for norm violation. Such norms are sustained by emotions such as *shame*, triggered by contempt demonstrated by a third party, the observer, who observes the violation of the norm. A measure of the contempt of the third party may be garnered by the amount of costly punishment that the third party is willing to undertake. Social norms are likely to involve a shared understanding of situation-specific actions. This is probably also true for most moral norms but is not a necessary condition.

Three features of Definitions 5.1, 5.2 need further discussion.

(1) For some individuals, EE and NE are sufficient to follow norms (weak norms), while for others, in addition, sanctions are needed (strong norms); see Bicchieri (2006). For instance, contributions in public goods games are high when sanctions are allowed, otherwise not (Fehr and Gächter, 2000). For many kinds of norms, such as the norm against incest and cannibalism, sanctions are observed in most societies (Elster, 1989). Thus, the relevant definition of a norm here is the strong norm. In contrast, for moral norms such as being punctual for appointments, or waiting in a queue, no formal sanctions are needed (Elster, 1989). Furthermore, conventions also do not require formal sanctions, but do require EE and NE. Thus, a "weak norm" may suffice in such cases.

(2) We emphasize the "direct observations" of EE, NE and sanctions for successful norms. Since norms are often shared understandings of situation-specific actions, one would expect that for successful norms, EE, NE, and the associated sanctions, would be well known and understood. Thus, experiments that implement norms need to ensure that these are directly and clearly observable to players who then take the relevant actions. Direct observation also ensures that the second condition in Definition 5.1 is more likely to be satisfied.

In particular, having defined a norm, one needs to demonstrate a (possibly context-dependent) *mapping* or *decision rule* from EE, NE, and sanctions, to individual actions. A major and fatal drawback of most existing papers on norms is that such a decision rule is not provided. Hence, the future literature not only needs to build on the insights of the existing literature, it needs a more formal and less arbitrary approach to defining norms.

Ostrom (2000), in a much-cited passage writes (pp. 143–4): "social norms are shared understandings about actions that are obligatory, permitted, or forbidden." Definitions 5.1, 5.2 are more general than the simple and intuitive idea that norms provide a "shared understanding" of an action.

---

[3] This appears closely related to the idea of a Kantian equilibrium (Gintis, 2017, p. 51).

[4] The British constitution is a good example of unwritten conventions. For instance, consider the following conventions that appear to require only EE and NE (Elster, 2011, p. 210): "The monarch cannot refuse to sign a bill that has been passed by both Houses of Parliament. Assent has not been withheld since 1708. Parliament should meet at least once a year. The House of Lords does not originate any money bills ... The House of Lords does not vote against the principle of a bill that has been announced in the manifesto of the governing party. The Prime Minister must be a member of the House of Commons. The Cabinet cannot instruct the Attorney General."

Remark 5.1 *Suppose that the preconditions for the existence of a norm in Definitions 5.1, 5.2 are not met. Then, one may still argue that the behavior of subjects in experiments is determined by norms that they have learnt outside the lab (Binmore, 2010). However, this criticism can be addressed in the following manner. First, one can study the contrast between different treatments within an experimental session that have EE, NE and sanctions, and treatments that do not have such features. Such a contrast is likely to pick out the effect of a norm. Second, it is often not clear what outside-the-lab norm should apply to an unfamiliar experimental game and further it is even less likely that there is an immediate shared understanding of a norm imported from outside the lab that will apply to a lab experiment.*

Several literatures have tried to explain norms (and conventions) as a means of choosing among multiple equilibria. In Volume 6, we demonstrate how stochastic social dynamics can be used justify a punctuated equilibria in which the underlying game tips into the basin of attraction of various Nash equilibria (Young, 1998). Gintis (2009) shows that norms may act as a social choreographer to bring about mutual consistency of beliefs, which is an unjustified construct in classical game theory (see Volume 4 for a discussion).

Other than Fehr and Schurtenberger (2018b) that we review below, none of the experimental papers examine the mapping from EE, NE, and sanctions to the actual actions taken by players. Hence, while what they say might ultimately have something to add to our understanding of norms, they do not work from an acceptable definition of norms. Nor do these contributions directly answer the four questions that we posed at the beginning of this section.

The Krupka and Weber (2013) approach to norms has been fairly influential. Krupka–Weber focus only on injunctive norms (what others ought to do) as distinct from *descriptive norms* (what others actually do). There are no sanctions/punishments. They consider a dictator game with two treatments. In the "give treatment" dictators split $10 with a passive receiver. In the "take treatment", the dictator and the receiver are given $5 each and the dictator can take any amount $\{1,\ldots,5\}$ from the passive receiver. Clearly the "social appropriateness" of different allocations, in the eyes of a third party, in each treatment is different. For instance, to achieve an allocation of (8,2), implies that in the give treatment, the dictator gives $2 to the receiver, while in the take treatment, the dictator takes $3 from the receiver.

The authors then propose a utility function that augments material utility with the social appropriateness of actions. Actions are then chosen probabilistically using a conditional logit model. The main finding is that the social appropriateness of actions *as judged by a third party* explains more prosocial choices by the dictator. The authors reach the strong conclusion that norms are important, social preferences are not. However, one may equally argue that social preferences are richer than just inequity averse preferences. For instance, such preferences may themselves be conditioned by moral norms (Elster, 1989). Thus, the dictator might feel *guilty* (internal psychological mechanism) taking $3 from the passive receiver in the take treatment to reach the allocation (8,2). This eminently plausible explanation, based on psychological game theory, is not considered in that paper.

The fact that the majority of subjects consider an action as socially appropriate does not necessarily constitute a norm. For instance, in corrupt countries, where the norm is to take bribes, surveys show that corruption is not considered socially appropriate; there is also no norm to take public transport even in many crowded cities, even though people believe that it is more socially appropriate as compared to using private transport (Elster, 1989; Bicchieri, 2006).

Gächter et al. (2013) use a gift exchange game to run a horse race between the social preferences model of Fehr and Schmidt (1999), and a model of social norms, using the Krupka–Weber framework. There is one firm and two employees, who choose their effort levels sequentially; Employee 1 chooses publicly observable effort first, followed by Employee 2. Suppose that Employee 1 chooses a high effort level and suppose that Employee 2 has inequity averse social preferences with respect to the firm and to Employee 1. Then, Employee 2 responds to high wages with high effort, and to high effort of Employee 1 with high effort, in order to avoid disadvantageous inequity with respect to, respectively, the firm and to Employee 1. A second, alternative, explanation is in terms of norms. A high effort level by Employee 1 may draw Employee 2's attention towards a norm of reciprocity, hence, Employee 2 also puts in a higher effort level. No social preferences are invoked in the second explanation.

In an improvement over the basic Krupka–Weber design, in the first stage, Gächter et al. (2013) gauge the social appropriateness of various effort choices from the point of view of Employee 2, who makes the relevant decisions, rather than a third party. They then augment the material utility of Employee 2 to include (1) inequity aversion with respect to the firm and to Employee 1, and (2) respect for the social appropriateness of various effort levels (as judged by Employee 2). In other respects they are faithful to the Krupka–Weber design. The main finding is the opposite of Krupka and Weber (2013); they find that once material payoffs and social preferences are accounted for, norms (albeit in the form of social appropriateness) add no explanatory value. This is a valuable result but it also takes a limited view of norms by proposing a mapping or decision rule only between personal normative expectations and actions, leaving out NE and sanctions.

Krupka and Weber (2009) introduce another definition of a norm by asking people what they believe are the NE others have of them. It might well be that individuals are uncertain of the relevant NE and if they are directly informed about the NE that others actually have of them, their actions may be different. In any case, the framework falls short of a more complete definition of a norm.

Schram and Charness (2015) consider a 2×2 design in which a third party can provide advice to a dictator about the social appropriateness of actions and the dictator's actions/payoffs can either be (1) publicly observed (leading to potential shame), or (2) only privately observed (leading to no shame). The design allows them to separate moral norms from social norms in terms of the underlying emotions involved (guilt-aversion for moral norms and shame for social norms). The main effect on the dictator's actions arises from a combination of advice and public information. This paper is an improvement over most of the papers directly using the Krupka–Weber framework because the advice of the third party about the normative expectations is directly conveyed to the dictator; hence, actual NE are used to try to isolate a norm. However, EE and sanctions play no role in influencing actions.

Kimbrough and Vostroknutov (2016) first use a *rule-following game* (RF) based on a monetary incentive to break traffic rules. They find that those who have a greater proclivity to follow rules in the RF game also exhibit more prosocial behavior in several experimental games such as the public goods game, the trust game, and the ultimatum/dictator games. The authors conclude that social preferences are unimportant and norms (to follow traffic rules in this case) alone suffice to explain behavior in the experimental games on other-regarding preferences. This conclusion is inappropriate. The results show, at best, that there is a correlation between the propensity to follow rules and prosocial behavior in experiments. We already know this to be the case from cross-country evidence (Hermann et al., 2008). Similarly, Gächter and Thöni (2005) show that more prosocial groups (based on the first-round contributions in a public goods game) make higher contributions over successive rounds of a public goods game, even without punishment.

The cumulative density functions of choices in the RF game in various treatments (e.g., RF game followed by the public goods game; public goods game followed by the RF game) in Figure E1 in the appendix of Kimbrough–Vostroknutov look very different to the naked eye. No tests of the statistical differences between these distributions are reported. However, if these differences between the cumulative density functions are confirmed, then the authors' framework, based on stable norms but unstable social preferences, would appear to be suspect. Furthermore, there is no demonstration of any mapping from EE, NE, and sanction to actions. Often what appear to be social preferences are termed as norms. Consider this example: "... a norm of conditional cooperation accounts for our observations in the PG." Arguably, conditional cooperation might well be a preference rather than a norm. Indeed, conditional reciprocity appears so hardwired in humans that even when we remove EE, NE, and sanctions (the sufficient conditions for a norm) conditional reciprocity is likely to persist; Volume 2 has already provided rich evidence for this view.

Most of the existing literature on norms uses the *direct elicitation of beliefs* method in computing EE and NE. In this method, players are asked their beliefs about the actions and beliefs of others. For instance, Xiao and Bicchieri (2010) elicited subjects' first order and second order EE by posing questions such as "how much do you think other participants in your role will transfer to their counterpart?" and "what does your counterpart think you will do?" NE were elicited by asking questions such as "how much do you think your counterpart believes you should transfer to her?"

It is now well known that studies using direct belief elicitation are subject to the *false consensus effect*, also sometimes known as *social projection* or *evidential reasoning* (al-Nowaihi and Dhami, 2015). These findings in the literature on psychological game theory do not appear to have penetrated the literature on norms. For instance, Ellingsen et al. (2010) showed that when people are directly asked to state their beliefs, say their second order beliefs, then they simply impute their own first order beliefs to the other player and imagine these to be the other player's second order beliefs. The problem of false consensus is widespread and even experts behave in this manner; this includes judges and finance professionals; see Volume 5 for the evidence. Even more concerning for the norms literature is the finding that with such direct belief elicitation, there is no guilt-aversion and the variation in subject responses could be explained by the false consensus effect alone (Ellingsen et al., 2010). As noted above, guilt-aversion is a key internal psychological mechanism that supports norms.

Finally, we consider the paper by Fehr and Schurtenberger (2018b), which offers a more satisfactory approach to the formation of norms in a repeated public goods game. They elicit normative requests from players (how much "should" others contribute to the public good). Each player is then told the average normative request; this serves as the NE. Players can also observe the contributions of others in the past; this serves as the EE. Without a punishment option, cooperation in the public goods game decays over successive rounds, despite the normative requests. However, in the presence of the punishment option, a norm of cooperation successfully develops. In terms of the terminology that we have used in this section, a weak norm is not effective in this case, but a strong norm is effective.

5.8 Exercises for Volume 2

1. Prove Lemma 2.4.
2. (Fehr and Schmidt, 1999) Consider the ultimatum game with responder competition when all agents are other-regarding. Suppose that there are n players. Player 1 is the

proposer and the remaining players are the responders, whose Fehr–Schmidt preference parameters are commonly given by (α, β). The proposer offers a share $s \in [0,1]$ that is observed by all responders who simultaneously choose to accept or reject. If more than one responder accepts, then one among this set is chosen randomly as the winner. The winning responder gets s, the proposer gets $1 - s$, and all other responders get 0. Suppose that $\beta < \frac{n-1}{n}$. Show that there exists a subgame perfect equilibrium in which all responders accept any $s \geq 0$ and the proposer offers $s = 0$. Show also that the highest offer that can be sustained as a subgame perfect equilibrium is given by $s^* = \frac{\alpha}{(1-\beta)(n-1)+2\alpha+\beta} < \frac{1}{2}$.

3. (Fehr and Schmidt, 1999) Prove Proposition 2.3.
4. (Fehr and Schmidt, 1999) Consider the public goods game in Section 1.4. Suppose that all contributors have Fehr–Schmidt preferences. Show that:
    (a) If $r + \beta_i < 1$ for player i, then it is a dominant strategy for that player to choose $g_i = 0$.
    (b) Let k denote the number of players with $r + \beta_i < 1$, $k \in [1, n]$. If $\frac{k}{n-1} > \frac{r}{2}$, then there is a unique equilibrium with $g_i = 0$ for all i.
    (c) If $\frac{k}{n-1} < \frac{r+\beta_j^{-1}}{\alpha_j+\beta_j}$ for all players $j = 1, 2, \ldots, n$ and $r + \beta_j > 1$, then there exist other equilibria with positive contribution levels. In these equilibria, all players with $r + \beta_i < 1$ choose $g_i = 0$, while all other players contribute $g_j = [0, y]$. Further, $\frac{r+\beta_j^{-1}}{\alpha_j+\beta_j} < \frac{r}{2}$.
5. (Fehr and Schmidt, 1999) Prove Proposition 2.4.
6. In a public goods game experiment that is repeated over several rounds, contributions stabilize at a very low level. Does this provide support for self-regarding preferences?
7. Consider the three-player experiments by Güth and van Damme (1998), which combine an ultimatum and a dictator game. There is a single proposer (player 1) and two responders, an active responder (player 2), and a passive responder (player 3). The proposer makes an offer of the form (x_1, x_2, x_3) such that the proposer's share is x_1, the active responder's share is x_2, and the passive responder's share is x_3. Player 2 can (as in ultimatum games) either accept or reject the offer. Player 3 does not have any actions. The main empirical finding is that the proposer allocates very low amounts to player 3 and the rejection decision of player 2 does not seem to be significantly influenced by the amount offered to player 3. What are the implications of these results for maximin preferences (as in Charness and Rabin, 2002) and for models of inequity aversion such as the Fehr–Schmidt model and the Bolton–Ockenfels model?
8. (al-Nowaihi and Dhami, 2015) Consider the prisoner's dilemma game.

	C	D
C	2,2	0,x
D	x,0	1,1

Each player has two choices: cooperate (C) or defect (D). The payoff matrix shows material payoffs of the two players and $x > 2$. In terms of the material payoffs, (C,C) is not a Nash equilibrium. Now suppose that players are inequity averse and have Fehr–Schmidt preferences.
    (a) Suppose that $x = 3$. What is the lower bound on β that achieves the cooperative outcome (C,C)?

(b) Now suppose that $x = 10$. How does your answer to (a) change? Is the lower bound on β consistent with the experimental evidence? What can you conclude about the ability of Fehr–Schmidt preferences to explain the empirical results that in the static prisoner's dilemma games we observe the outcome (C, C) about 50% of the time?

(c) "It has been suggested that players achieve a higher degree of cooperation in prisoner's dilemma games when the game is framed as a community game (cooperative frame) rather than as a Wall Street game (competitive frame). It has also been shown that preplay communication improves cooperation in the prisoner's dilemma game." Can models of inequity aversion explain these results? What additional features might you need to explain this finding?

9. There is a positive level of giving in dictator games. Which of the three main types of theories—inequity aversion, intention-based reciprocity, or type-based reciprocity—can explain this finding?

10. Equal splits (50–50) are often observed in the ultimatum game. Can these equal splits be rationalized in terms of the Bolton–Ockenfels (2000), ERC model? What restrictions are needed on the parameters α, β in the Fehr and Schmidt (1999) model to account for the empirical finding of equal splits? Can the model of Rotemberg (2008) (see Section 2.8.2) account for the equal splits, and if so, what is the difference in the transmission channel relative to the Fehr–Schmidt model?

11. Charness (2004) conducts two treatments in a gift exchange game. In the random choice condition, the firm's wage choice is randomly determined. In the human choice condition, a human proposer makes the choice. What is the prediction of intention-based theories? What is the prediction of type-based reciprocity theories about the relative correlation between wage and effort in the two different treatments? The empirical finding in these experiments was that there is a significant positive correlation between wages and effort in the random choice condition. This correlation was only slightly lower in the human choice condition. What are the implications of these experiments for the three main types of theories—inequity aversion, intention-based reciprocity, or type-based reciprocity?

12. (a) Eckel and Gintis (2010, p. 111) make the following comment: "Binmore and Shaked's defense of the neoclassical analysis on the grounds that 'all possible divisions of the money in the ultimatum game are Nash equilibrium outcomes' is transparently faulty." Do you agree with the comment?
(b) Evaluate the following quotes from Eckel and Gintis (2010):
(b1) (p. 111) "Binmore and Shaked also argue that other-regarding behavior disappears or is greatly attenuated when the stakes are high. It is not clear why this is a criticism."
(b2) On p. 114, Eckel and Gintis quote Binmore and Shaked, thus: "Behavioral economists sometimes claim that neoclassical economists hold that people are self-regarding... But no such [selfishness] axiom appears in neoclassical economics textbooks... When utility functions of various kinds are fitted to data obtained in laboratory experiments, neoclassical economics is therefore in no danger of being refuted." Evaluate this claim in the context of a general equilibrium neoclassical model.

13. (Dhami and al-Nowaihi, 2013) Prove Proposition 2.8.

14. (Dhami and al-Nowaihi, 2013) Prove Propositions 2.9, 2.10.

15. (Dhami and al-Nowaihi, 2010a) Prove Proposition 2.11.

16. (Dhami and al-Nowaihi, 2010a) Prove Lemmas 2.6 and 2.7.

17. (Dhami and al-Nowaihi, 2010a) Consider the model in Section 2.5. (a) Prove Proposition 2.12.

(b) Show that if utility is quasilinear

$$\widetilde{u}(c, 1 - l) = c - \frac{1}{2}l^2,$$

then a majority prefers the tax rate that is optimal for the median-skill voter. In particular, show that assumption A1 holds and assumption A2 in Proposition 2.12 is not needed in this case.

18. (Dhami and al-Nowaihi, 2010a) Prove Proposition 2.13.
19. (Dhami and al-Nowaihi, 2010a) Prove Proposition 2.14.
20. (Bartling et al., 2013) Consider the model of vertical integration in Section 4.4.4. How does this model offer at least a partial justification for the role of trade unions and labor market legislation?
21. (Itoh, 2004) Prove Propositions 4.3 and 4.4.
22. (Englmaier and Leider, 2012) Prove Proposition 4.7.
23. (Fehr et al., 2007) Prove Lemma 4.3. [Hint: Use the same method that you used in Lemma 4.2].
24. (Fehr et al., 2007) Prove Proposition 4.9. [Hint: Set up the Kuhn–Tucker conditions for the other-regarding principal's optimization problem and consider the various combinations of the complementary slackness conditions.]
25. (Fehr et al., 2007) Prove Proposition 4.8. [Hint: For each of the contracts, solve, using backward induction, the two-stage game in which the principal first chooses the contractual parameters followed by the agent's choice of effort].
26. Prove Lemma 4.11. [Hint: Rewrite the MLRP in (4.75) as $g(\sigma_H \mid c_H)g(\sigma_L \mid c_L) < g(\sigma_L \mid c_H)g(\sigma_H \mid c_L)$. Then integrate both sides twice, first over σ_L from σ_L to 1 and then over σ_H from σ_H to 1.
27. (Bénabou and Tirole, 2003) (a) Show that the conclusions of Proposition 4.14 are unaltered if the outside option of the agent is $\overline{U} > 0$.

    (b) Consider the setting of the Bénabou–Tirole (2003) model in Section 4.5.1. Suppose now that costs are public information but that the principal has private information about the agent's ability to perform the task, θ, that is drawn from the distribution $F(\theta)$. The principal observes θ perfectly. The agent observes an imperfect signal of θ given by $\sigma \in [0, 1]$ that has conditional distribution function $G(\sigma \mid \theta)$ and conditional density $g(\sigma \mid \theta)$ that satisfies the monotone likelihood ratio property (see (4.75)). In all other respects we have the model given in Section 4.5. The principal does not observe the agent's effort e but pays a performance contingent reward, b, in the event that the project is successful. Show that all the results in Proposition 4.14 continue to hold with appropriate changes in notation and terminology.
28. Can you explain the following empirical findings using standard models of neoclassical economics in a plausible manner using reasonable assumptions? If not, what assumptions might you need on human sociality or non-standard human motivations to explain them.

    (a) (Restivo and van de Rijt, 2012) Contributors to Wikipedia were randomly chosen to be given Barnstar rewards, a form of status-reward that was publicly displayed. Over the next three months, the individuals who were given the reward were 60% more productive as compared to a control group that was not given the reward.

    (b) (Kosfeld and Neckermann, 2011) In a single data entry task, subjects in a gift exchange experiment were told that the top two performers will receive a congratulatory card and a personal thank-you note from the managing director. This simple intervention increased performance by 12%, which is identical to the hypothetical effect of an increase in wage of 35–72%, based on output elasticity measured in previous gift exchange games.

(c) (Ashraf et al., 2014) In a field experiment in Zambia, barbers were recruited by the public health organization to sell condoms. Four treatments varied in their reward structure. In a control treatment, there were no rewards; in two treatments, the margins offered were 10% and 90% of sales; in the star treatment there was a non-pecuniary reward in the form of a star stamped on a publicly displayed chart. The star treatment was supposed to capture the esteem associated with a sense of public duty. After a year it was found that barbers in the star treatment had sold twice as many condoms as in any other treatment.

29. Use the material in this chapter to explain the interaction between other-regarding preferences and incentives in the following description of events from Bowles and Polanía-Reys (2012, p. 369). "On December 1, 2001, the Boston Fire Department terminated its policy of unlimited paid sick days, replacing it with a fifteen-day sick day limit; pay would be docked for firemen exceeding the limit. The firemen responded to the new incentives: those calling in sick on Christmas and New Year's Day increased tenfold over the previous year. The Fire Commissioner retaliated by canceling their holiday bonus checks (Belkin 2002). The firemen were unimpressed: the year following they claimed 13,431 sick days; up from 6,432 the previous year (Greenberger 2003). Many of the firemen, apparently angered by the new system, abused it or abandoned their previous ethic of serving the public even when injured or not feeling well."

30. (Ariely et al. 2009b) Consider the following example. "An individual is considering buying a new hybrid car. This car is more expensive than an equivalent car operating with a standard gasoline engine, but the hybrid car helps in preserving the environment. Driving a car which is clearly a hybrid automobile would probably add to one's positive image, especially for those who live in a community that values environmentally friendly technologies. Suppose now that the government gives a large tax benefit to those who decide to purchase a hybrid car (and everybody knows about this). The tax incentive, of course, reduces the price of hybrid cars and therefore should make the hybrid car more attractive for the individual." Will the tax incentive be necessarily successful in boosting sales of the hybrid car among all groups of individuals?

31. (Ellingsen and Johannesson, 2008) Prove Proposition 4.16.

REFERENCES FOR VOLUME 2

Abbink, K., Brandts, J., Herrmann, B., and Orzen, H. (2010). Intergroup conflict and intra-group punishment in an experimental contest game. *American Economic Review* 100(1): 420–47.

Abbink, K., Irlenbusch, B., and Renner, E. (2000). The moonlighting game. An experimental study on reciprocity and retribution. *Journal of Economic Behavior and Organization* 42(2): 265–77.

Abeler, J., Altmann, S., Kube, S., and Wibral, M. (2010). Gift exchange and workers' fairness concerns: when equality is unfair. *Journal of the European Economic Association* 8(6): 1299–324.

Abeler, J., Becker, A., and Falk, A. (2014). Truth-telling: a representative assessment. *Journal of Public Economics* 113: 96–104.

Abeler, J., Nosenzo, D., and Raymond, C. (2016). Preferences for truth-telling. CEDEX Discussion Paper No. 2016-13.

Ackert, L. F., Martinez-Vazquez, J., and Rider, M. (2007). Social preferences and tax policy design: some experimental evidence. *Economic Inquiry* 45(3): 487–501.

Akerlof, G. A. (1982). Labor contracts as partial gift exchange. *Quarterly Journal of Economics* 97(4): 543–69.

Akerlof, G. A. and Kranton, R. E. (2000). Economics and identity. *Quarterly Journal of Economics* 115(3): 715–53.

Akerlof, G. A. and Kranton, R. E. (2005). Identity and the economics of organizations. *Journal of Economic Perspectives* 19(1): 9–32.

Akerlof, G. A. and Kranton, R. E. (2008). Identity, supervision, and work groups. *American Economic Review* 98(2): 212–17.

Akerlof, G. A. and Yellen, J. L. (1990). The fair wage-effort hypothesis and unemployment. *Quarterly Journal of Economics* 105(2): 255–83.

Alexander, R. D. (1987). *The Biology of Moral Systems*. New York: Aldine De Gruyter.

Almås, I. Cappelen, A., and Tungodden, B. (2018). Cutthroat capitalism versus cuddly socialism: are Americans more meritocratic and efficiency-seeking than Scandinavians? Mimeo, Norwegeian School of Economics.

al-Nowaihi, A. and Dhami, S. (2015). Evidential equilibira: heuristics and biases in static games of complete information. *Games* 6(4): 637–77.

Andersen, S., Ertaç, S., Gneezy, U., Hoffman, M., and List, J. A. (2011). Stakes matter in ultimatum games. *American Economic Review* 101(7): 3427–39.

Andreoni, J. (1988). Why free ride?: strategies and learning in public goods experiments. *Journal of Public Economics* 37(3): 291–304.

Andreoni, J. and Bernheim, B. D. (2009). Social image and the 50–50 norm: a theoretical and experimental analysis of audience effects. *Econometrica* 77(5): 1607–36.

Andreoni, J. and Miller, J. H. (1993). Rational cooperation in the finitely repeated prisoner's dilemma: experimental evidence. *Economic Journal* 103(418): 570–85.

Andreoni, J. and Miller, J. H. (2002). Giving according to GARP: an experimental test of the consistency of preferences for altruism. *Econometrica* 70(2): 737–53.

Andreoni, J. and Petrie, R. (2008). Beauty, gender and stereotypes: evidence from laboratory experiments. *Journal of Economics Psychology* 29: 73–93.

Andreoni, J. and Vesterlund, L. (2001). Which is the fair sex? Gender differences in altruism. *Quarterly Journal of Economics* 116(1): 293–312.

Angrist, J. and Lavy, V. (2009). The effects of high stakes high school achievement rewards: evidence from a randomized trial. *American Economic Review* 99(4): 1384–414.

Ariely, D., Bracha, A., and Meier, S. (2009b). Doing good or going well? Image motivation and monetary incentives in behaving prosocially. *American Economic Review* 99(1): 544–55.

Ariely, D., Gneezy, U., Loewenstein, G., and Mazar, N. (2009a). Large stakes and big mistakes. *Review of Economic Studies* 76(2): 451–69.

Ashraf, N., Bandiera, O., and Jack, B. K. (2014). No margin, no mission? A field experiment on incentives for public services delivery. *Journal of Public Economics* 120: 1–17.

Axelrod, R. (1984). *The Evolution of Cooperation.* New York: Basic Books.

Axelrod, R. and Hamilton, W. D. (1981). The evolution of cooperation. *Science* 211(4489): 1390–6.

Babcock, L. and Loewenstein, G. (1997). Explaining bargaining impasse: the role of self-serving biases. *Journal of Economic Perspectives* 11(1): 109–26.

Balafoutas, L., Czermak, S., Eulerich, M., and Fornwagner, H. (2017). Incentives for dishonesty: an experimental study with internal auditors. Working Papers in Economics and Statistics, University of Innsbruck No. 2017–06.

Bandiera, O., Barankay, I., and Rasul, I. (2005). Social preferences and the response to incentives: evidence from personnel data. *Quarterly Journal of Economics* 120(3): 917–62.

Bandura, A. (1991). Social congnitive theory of moral thought and action. In W. M. Kurtines, J. Gewirtz, and J. L. Lamb (eds.), *Handbook of Moral Behavior and Development: Volume I, Theory.* Hillsdale, MI: Lawrence Erlbaum and Associates, pp. 45–103.

Baran, N. M., Sapienza, P., and Zingales, L. (2010). Can we infer social preferences from the lab? Evidence from the trust game. NBER. Working Paper 15654.

Barmettler, F., Fehr, E., and Zehnder, C. (2012). Big experimenter is watching you! Anonymity and prosocial behavior in the laboratory. *Games and Economic Behavior* 75(1): 17–34.

Bartling, B. (2011). Relative performance or team evaluation? Optimal contracts for other-regarding agents. *Journal of Economic Behavior and Organization* 79(3): 183–93.

Bartling, B., Fehr, E., and Schmidt, K. M. (2012). Screening, competition, and job design: economic origins of good jobs. *American Economic Review* 102(2): 834–64.

Bartling, B., Fehr, E., and Schmidt, K. M. (2013). Use and abuse of authority: a behavioral foundation of the employment relation. *Journal of the European Economic Association* 11(4): 711–42.

Bartling, B. and Fischbacher, U. (2012). Shifting the blame: on delegation and responsibility. *Review of Economic Studies* 79(1): 67–87.

Bartling, B., and Özdemir, Y. (2017). The Limits to Moral Erosion in Markets: Social Norms and the replacement excuse. CESifo Working papers Volume 17, No. 93.

Bartling, B. and von Siemens, F. A. (2010). The intensity of incentives in firms and markets: moral hazard with envious agents. *Labour Economics* 17(3): 598–607.

Bartling, B., Weber, R., and Yao, L. (2015). Do markets erode social responsibility? *Quarterly Journal of Economics* 130(1): 219–66.

Bateson, M., Nettle, D., and Roberts, G. (2006). Cues of being watched enhance cooperation in a real-world setting. *Biology Letters* 2: 412–14.

Battigalli, P. and Dufwenberg, M. (2007). Guilt in games. *American Economic Review* Papers and Proceedings 97(2): 170–6.

Battigalli, P. and Dufwenberg, M. (2009). Dynamic psychological games. *Journal of Economic Theory* 144(1): 1–35.

Belkin, D. (2002). Boston firefighters sick—or tired of working 15-day allowance seen fueling call-ins. *Boston Globe* Jan. 18 B1.

Bellemare, C., Kröger, S., and Van Soest, A. (2008). Measuring inequity aversion in a heterogeneous population using experimental decisions and subjective probabilities. *Econometrica* 76(4): 815–39.

Bellemare, C. and Shearer, B. S. (2007). Gift exchange within a firm: evidence from a field experiment. IZA, Discussion Paper 2696.

Bénabou, R. (2013). Groupthink: collective delusions in organizations and markets. *Review of Economic Studies* 80(2): 429–62.

Bénabou, R. and Tirole, J. (2003). Intrinsic and extrinsic motivation. *Review of Economic Studies* 70(3): 489–20.

Bénabou, R. and Tirole, J. (2006). Incentives and prosocial behaviour. *American Economic Review* 96(5): 1652–78.

Bénabou, R. and Tirole, J. (2011). Identity, morals, and taboos: beliefs as assets. *Quarterly Journal of Economics* 126(2): 805–55.

Benjamin, D. J., Choi, J. J., and Strickland, A. J. (2010). Social identity and preferences. *American Economic Review* 100(4): 1913–28.

Benz, M. and Meier, S. (2008). Do people behave in experiments as in the field?—evidence from donations. *Experimental Economics* 11(3): 268–81.

Berg, J., Dickhaut, J., and McCabe, K. (1995). Trust, reciprocity, and social history. *Games and Economic Behavior* 10(1): 122–42.

Bernhard, H., Fehr, E., and Fischbacher, U. (2006). Group affiliation and altruistic norm enforcement. *American Economic Review* 96(2): 217–21.

Besley, T. and Ghatak, M. (2005). Competition and incentives with motivated agents. *American Economic Review* 95(3): 616–36.

Bewley, T. (1999). *Why Wages Don't Fall During a Recession*. Cambridge, MA: Harvard University Press.

Bewley, T. (2005). Fairness, reciprocity and wage rigidity. In H. Gintis, S. Bowles, R. Boyd, and E. Fehr (eds.), *Moral Sentiments and Material Interests* Cambridge, MA: MIT Press, pp. 303–38.

Bicchieri, C. (2006). *The Grammar of Society: The Nature and Dynamics of Social Norms*. New York: Cambridge University Press.

Bicchieri, C. and Xiao, E. (2009). Do the right thing but only if others do it. *Journal of Behavioral Decision Making* 22: 191–208.

Billig, M. and Tajfel, H. (1973). Social categorization and similarity in intergroup behaviour. *European Journal of Social Psychology* 3(1): 27–52.

Binmore, K. (ed.) (1998). *Just Playing: Game Theory and the Social Contract, Volume 2*. Cambridge, MA: MIT Press.

Binmore, K. G. (2010). Social norms or social preferences? *Mind and Society* 9:139–58.

Binmore, K. G., Samuelson, L., and Gale, J. (1995). Learning to be imperfect: the ultimate game. *Games and Economic Behavior* 8(1): 56–90.

Blanco, M., Engelmann, D., and Normann, H. T. (2011). A within-subject analysis of other-regarding preferences. *Games and Economic Behavior* 72(2): 321–38.

Blount, S. (1995). When social outcomes aren't fair: the effect of causal attributions on preferences. *Organizational Behavior and Human Decision Process* 63(2): 131–44.

Bochet, O., Page, T., and Putterman, L. (2006). Communication and punishment in voluntary contribution experiments. *Journal of Economic Behavior and Organization* 60(1): 11–26.

Bohnet, I., Frey, B. S., and Huck, S. (2001). More order with less law: on contractual enforcement, trust, and crowding. *American Political Science Review* 95(1): 131–44.

Bohnet, I., Harmgart, H., Huck, S., and Tyran, J.-R. (2005). Learning trust. *Journal of the European Economic Association* 3(2–3): 322–9.

Bohnet, I. and Kübler, D. (2005). Compensating the cooperators: is sorting in the prisoner's dilemma possible? *Journal of Economic Behavior and Organization* 56(1): 61–76.

Bolle, F. and Kritikos, A. (1998). Self-centered inequality aversion versus reciprocity and altruism. Mimeo, Europa-Universität Viadrina.

Bolton, G. E. (1991). A comparative model of bargaining: theory and evidence. *American Economic Review* 81(5): 1096–136.

Bolton, G. E., Brandts, J., Katok, E., Ockenfels, A., and Zwick, R. (2008). Testing theories of other-regarding behavior: a sequence of four laboratory studies. In C. R. Plott and V. L. Smith (eds.), *Handbook of Experimental Economics Results* Amsterdam: North Holland, pp. 488–99.

Bolton, G. E., Brandts, J., and Ockenfels, A. (1998). Measuring motivations for the reciprocal responses observed in a simple dilemma game. *Experimental Economics* 1(3): 207–19.

Bolton, G. E., Brandts, J., and Ockenfels, A. (2005). Fair procedures: evidence from games involving lotteries. *Economics Journal* 115(506): 1054–76.

Bolton, G. E., Greiner, B., and Ockenfels, A. (2013). Engineering trust: reciprocity in the production of reputation information. *Management Science* 59(2): 265–85.

Bolton, G. E., Katok, E., and Ockenfels, A. (2004). How effective are electronic reputation mechanisms? *Management Science* 50(11): 1587–602.

Bolton, G. E. and Ockenfels, A. (1998). Strategy and equity: an ERC-analysis of the Guth-van Damme Game. *Journal of Mathematical Psychology* 42(2): 215–26.

Bolton, G. E. and Ockenfels, A. (2000). ERC: a theory of equity, reciprocity, and competition. *American Economic Review* 90(1): 166–93.

Bolton, G. E. and Ockenfels, A. (2005). A stress test of fairness measures in models of social utility. *Economic Theory* 25(4): 957–82.

Bolton, G. E. and Ockenfels, A. (2006). Measuring efficiency and equity motives: a comment on "inequality aversion, efficiency, and maximin preferences in simple distribution experiments". *American Economic Review* 96(5): 1906–11.

Bolton, G. E. and Ockenfels, A. (2014). Does laboratory trading mirror behavior in real world markets? Fair bargaining and competitive bidding on eBay. *Journal of Economic Behavior and Organization* 97: 143–54.

Bolton, G. E. and Zwick, R. (1995). Anonymity versus punishment in ultimatum bargaining. *Games and Economic Behavior* 10(1): 95–121.

Bolton, G. E., Zwick, R., and Katok, E. (1998). Dictator game giving: rules of fairness versus acts of kindness. *International Journal of Game Theory* 27(2): 269–99.

Bowles, S. and Gintis, H. (2003). Origins of human cooperation. In P. Hammerstein (ed.), *Genetic and Cultural Evolution of Cooperation*. Cambridge, MA: MIT Press, pp. 429–43.

Bowles, S. and Gintis, H. (2013). *A Cooperative Species: Human Reciprocity and Its Evolution*. Princeton, NJ: Princeton University Press.

Bowles, S., Gintis, H., and Osborne, M. (2001). The determinants of earnings: a behavioral approach. *Journal of Economic Literature* 39(4): 1137–76.

Bowles, S. and Polania-Reyes, S. (2012). Economic incentives and social preferences: substitutes or complements? *Journal of Economic Literature* 50(2): 368–425.

Brandts, J. and Charness, G. (2004). Do labour market conditions affect gift exchange? Some experimental evidence. *Economic Journal* 114(497): 684–708.

Brandts, J., Saijo, T., and Schram, A. (2004). How universal is behavior? A four country comparison of spite and cooperation in voluntary contribution mechanisms. *Public Choice* 119: 381–424.

Brandts, J. and Schram, A. (2001). Cooperation and noise in public goods experiments: applying the contributions function approach. *Journal of Public Economics* 79(2): 399–427.

Brown, M., Falk, A., and Fehr, E. (2004). Relational contracts and the nature of market interactions. *Econometrica* 72(3): 747–80.

Brown, M., Falk, A., and Fehr, E. (2012). Competition and relational contracts: the role of unemployment as a disciplinary device. *Journal of the European Economic Association* 10(4): 887–907.

Bruhin, A., Fehr, E., and Schunk, D. (2018). The many faces of human sociality: uncovering the distribution and stability of social preferences. *Journal of the European Economic Association*, forthcoming.

Burks, S., Carpenter, J., and Goette, L. (2009). Performance pay and worker cooperation: evidence from an artefactual field experiment. *Journal of Economic Behavior and Organization* 70(3): 458–69.

Burnham, T., McCabe, K., and Smith, V. L. (2000). Friend-or-foe intentionality priming in an extensive form trust game. *Journal of Economic Behavior and Organization* 43(1): 57–73.

Cabrales, A., Miniaci, R., Piovesan, M., and Ponti, G. (2010). Social preferences and strategic uncertainty: an experiment on markets and contracts. *American Economic Review* 100(5): 2261–78.

Cadsby, C. B. and Maynes, E. (1998). Gender and free riding in a threshold public goods game: experimental evidence. *Journal of Economic Behavior and Organization* 34(4): 603–20.

Camerer, C. F. (2003). *Behavioral Game Theory: Experiments in Strategic Interaction*. Princeton, NJ: Princeton University Press.

Camerer, C. F. (2015). The promise and success of lab-field generalizability in experimental economics: a critical reply to Levitt and List. In G. R. Fréchette and A. Schotter (eds.), *Handbook of Experimental Economic Methodology*. Oxford: Oxford University Press, pp. 249–95.

Camerer, C. F. and Thaler, R. H. (1995). Anomalies: ultimatums, dictators, and manners. *Journal of Economic Perspectives* 9(2): 209–19.

Camerer, C. F. and Weigelt, K. (1988). Experimental tests of a sequential equilibrium reputation model. *Econometrica* 56(1): 1–36.

Cameron, L. A. (1999). Raising the stakes in the ultimatum game: experimental evidence from Indonesia. *Economic Inquiry* 37(1): 47–59.

Cappelen, A. W., Sørensen, E. Ø., and Tungodden, B. (2013). When do we lie? *Journal of Economic Behavior and Organization* 93: 258–65.

Cappelen, A. W., Halvorsen, T., Sorensen, E., and Tungodden, B. (2015). Face-saving or fair-minded: what motivates moral behavior? Mimeo, Norwegian School of Economics.

Cappelen, A., List, J., Samek, A., Tungodden, B. (2018) The effect of early childhood education on social preferences. Mimeo, Norwegian School of Economics.

Cardenas, J. C., Stranlund, J. K., and Willis, C. E. (2000). Local environmental control and institutional crowding-out. *World Development* 28(10): 1719–33.

Carpenter, J. P. (2007). Punishing free-riders: how group size affects mutual monitoring and the provision of public goods. *Games and Economic Behavior* 60(1): 31–51.

Carpenter, J. P., Bowles, S., Gintis, H., and Hwang, S. H. (2009). Strong reciprocity and team production: theory and evidence. *Journal of Economic Behavior and Organization* 71(2): 221–32.

Carpenter, J., Corrolly, C., and Myers, C. (2008). Altruistic behavior in a representative dictator experiment. *Experimental Economics* 11: 282–98.

Carpenter, J. and Myers, C. (2010). Why volunteer? Evidence on the role of altruism, image, and incentives. *Journal of Public Economics* 94 (11–12): 911–20.

Carpenter, J. P. and Seki, E. (2011). Do social preferences increase productivity? Field experimental evidence from fishermen in Toyama Bay. *Economic Inquiry* 49(2): 612–30.

Carpenter, J. P., Verhoogen, E., and Burks, S. (2005). The effect of stakes in distribution experiments. *Economics Letters* 86(3): 393–8.

Charness, G. (2000). Responsibility and effort in an experimental labor market. *Journal of Economic Behavior and Organization* 42(3): 375–84.

Charness, G. (2004). Attribution and reciprocity in an experimental labor market. *Journal of Labor Economics* 22(3): 665–88.

Charness, G., Cobo-Reyes, R., and Jiménez, M. (2008). An investment game with third-party intervention. *Journal of Economic Behavior and Organization* 68(1): 18–28.

Charness, G., Du, N., and Yang, C. L. (2011). Trust and trustworthiness reputations in an investment game. *Games and Economic Behavior* 72(2): 361–75.

Charness, G. and Dufwenberg, M. (2006). Promises and partnership. *Econometrica* 74(6): 1579–601.

Charness, G., Frechette, G. R., and Kagel, J. H. (2004). How robust is laboratory gift exchange? *Experimental Economics* 7(2): 189–205.

Charness, G. and Gneezy, U. (2009). Incentives to exercise. *Econometrica* 77(3): 909–31.

Charness, G. and Rabin, M. (2002). Understanding social preferences with simple tests. *Quarterly Journal of Economics* 117(3): 817–69.

Charness, G., Rigotti, L., and Rustichini, A. (2007). Individual behavior and group membership. *American Economic Review* 97(4): 1340–52.

Chaudhuri, A., Graziano, S., and Maitra, P. (2006). Social learning and norms in a public goods experiment with intergenerational advice. *Review of Economic Studies* 73(2): 357–80.

Chaudhuri, A. and Paichayontvijit, T. (2006). Conditional cooperation and voluntary contributions to a public good. *Economics Bulletin* 3(8): 1–14.

Chen, R. and Chen, Y. (2011). The potential of social identity for equilibrium selection. *American Economic Review* 101(6): 2562–89.

Chen, Y. and Li, S. X. (2009). Group identity and social preferences. *American Economic Review* 99(1): 431–57.

Cherry, T. L., Frykblom, P., and Shogren, J. F. (2002). Hardnose the dictator. *American Economic Review* 92(4): 1218–21.

Childs, J. (2012). Gender differences in lying. *Economics Letters* 114(2): 147–9.

Cialdini, R., Kallgren, C., and Reno, R. (1990). A focus theory of normative conduct: a theoretical refinement and reevaluation of the role of norms in human behavior. *Advances in Experimental Social Psychology* 24: 201–34.

Cinyabuguma, M., Page, T., and Putterman, L. (2005). Cooperation under the threat of expulsion in a public goods experiment. *Journal of Public Economics* 89(8): 1421–35.

Cleave, B. L., Nikiforakis, N., and Slonim, R. (2012). Is there selection bias in laboratory experiments? The case of social and risk preferences. *Experimental Economics* 16(3): 372–82.

Coase, R. (1937). The nature of the firm. *Economica* 4(16): 386–405.

Cohn, A., Fehr, E., and Goette, L. (2012). Fair wages and effort: evidence from a field experiment. Mimeo, Department of Economics, University of Zurich.

Cohn, A., Fehr, E., Herrmann, B., Schneider, F. (2011). Social comparison in the workplace: evidence from a field experiment. IZA, Discussion Paper 5550.

Cohn, A., Maréchal, M. A., and Noll, T. (2013). Bad boys: how criminal identity affects rule violation. Mimeo, Department of Economics, University of Zurich.

Conrads, J., Irlenbusch, B., Rilke, R. M., and Walkowitz, G. (2013). Lying and team incentives. *Journal of Economic Psychology* 34: 1–7.

Cox, J. C. (2000). Trust and reciprocity: implications of game triads and social contexts. University of Arizona. Working Paper 00–11.

Cox, J. C. (2004). How to identify trust and reciprocity. *Games and Economic Behavior* 46(2): 260–81.

Cox, J. C., Friedman, D., and Gjerstad, S. (2007). A tractable model of reciprocity and fairness. *Games and Economic Behavior* 59(1): 17–45.

Crawford, V. (1997). Theory and experiment in the analysis of strategic interaction. In D. Kreps and K. Wallis (eds.), *Advances in Economics and Econometrics: Theory and Applications, Seventh World Congress, Volume I*. Cambridge: Cambridge University Press, pp. 206–42.

Croson, R. and Gneezy, U. (2009). Gender differences in preferences. *Journal of Economic Literature* 47(2): 448–74.

Dai, Z., Galeotti, F., and Villeval, M.C. (2018). Cheating in the lab predicts fraud in the field. An experiment in public transportations. *Management Science* 64(3): 1081–100.

Dal Bó, P. (2002). Cooperation under the shadow of the future: experimental evidence from infinitely repeated games. Brown University, Department of Economics. Working Paper 2002-21.

Dal Bó, P., Foster, A., and Putterman, L. (2010). Institutions and behavior: experimental evidence on the effects of democracy. *American Economic Review* 100(5): 2205–29.

Dana, J., Cain, D. M., and Dawes, R. M. (2006). What you don't know won't hurt me: costly (but quiet) exit in a dictator game. *Organizational Behavior and Human Decision Processes* 100(2): 193–201.

Dana, J., Weber, R. A., and Kuang, J. X. (2007). Exploiting moral wriggle room: experiments demonstrating an illusory preference for fairness. *Economic Theory* 33: 67–80.

Davis, D. D. and Holt, C. A. (1993). *Experimental Economics*. Princeton, NJ: Princeton University Press.

Dawes, C. T., Fowler, J. H., Johnson, T., McElreath, R., and Smirnov, O. (2007). Egalitarian motives in humans. *Nature* 446: 794–6.

Dawes, R. M. (1980). Social dilemmas. *Annual Review of Psychology* 31: 169–93.

Dawes, R. M. and Thaler, R. H. (1988). Anomalies: cooperation. *Journal of Economic Perspectives* 2(3): 187–97.

Dawkins, R. (1989). *The Selfish Gene*. 2nd edition. Oxford: Oxford University Press.

de Quervain, D. J.-F., Fischbacher, U., Treyer, V., et al. (2004). The neural basis of altruistic punishment. *Science* 305(5688): 1254–8.

Deci, E. L. (1975). *Intrinsic Motivation*. New York: Plenum Press.

Deci, E. L., Koestner, R., and Ryan, R. M. (1999). A meta-analytic review of experiments examining the effects of extrinsic rewards on intrinsic motivation. *Psychological Bulletin* 125(6): 627–68.

Deci, E. L. and Ryan, R. M. (1985). *Intrinsic Motivation and Self-Determination in Human Behavior*. Berlin: Springer.

Deckers, T., Falk, A., Kosse, F., Pinger, P., and Schildberg-Hörisch, H. (2017). Socio-economic status and inequalities in children's IQ and economic preferences. IZA Discussion Paper No. 11158.

DellaVigna, S. (2009). Psychology and economics: evidence from the field. *Journal of Economics Literature* 47(2): 315–72.

Dhami, S. (2016). *The Foundations of Behavioral Economic Analysis*. Oxford: Oxford University Press.

Dhami, S. (2017). Human ethics and virtues: rethinking the homo-economicus model. CESifo Working Paper Series No. 6836.

Dhami, S. and al-Nowaihi, A. (2010a). Existence of a Condorcet winner when voters have other-regarding preferences. *Journal of Public Economic Theory* 12(5): 897–22.

Dhami, S. and al-Nowaihi, A. (2010b). Redistributive policy with heterogeneous social preferences of voters. *European Economic Review* 54(6): 743–59.

Dhami, S. and al-Nowaihi, A. (2013). Stochastic dominance for Fehr-Schmidt preferences. University of Leicester, Discussion Papers in Economics. Working Paper 13/09.

Dhami, S., Wei, M. and al-Nowaihi, A. (2018). Public goods games and psychological utility: theory and evidence. Forthcoming in the special issue on Psychological Game Theory in *Journal of Economic Behavior and Organization*.

Dickenson, D. and M.-C. Villeval (2008). Does monitoring decrease work effort? The complementarity between agency and crowding-out theories. *Games and Economic Behavior* 63(1): 56–76.

Dohmen, T. and Falk, A. (2011). Performance pay and multidimensional sorting: productivity, preferences, and gender. *American Economic Review* 101(2): 556–90.

Dohmen, T., Falk, A., Huffman, D., and Sunde, U. (2009). Homo reciprocans: survey evidence on behavioural outcomes. *Economic Journal* 119(536): 592–612.

Dreber, A. and Johannesson, M. (2008). Gender differences in deception. *Economics Letters* 99(1): 197–9.

Duesenberry, J. S. (1949). *Income, Saving, and the Theory of Consumer Behavior*. Cambridge, MA: Harvard University Press.

Dufwenberg, M., Heidhues, P., Kirchsteiger, G., et al. (2011). Other-regarding preferences in general equilibrium. *Review of Economic Studies* 78(2): 613–39.

Dufwenberg, M. and Kirchsteiger, G. (2004). A theory of sequential reciprocity. *Games and Economic Behavior* 47(2): 268–98.

Eckel, C. C. and Gintis, H. (2010). Blaming the messenger: notes on the current state of experimental economics. *Journal of Economic Behavior and Organization* 73(1): 109–19.

Eckel, C. C. and Grossman, P. J. (1996). Altruism in anonymous dictator games. *Games and Economic Behavior* 16(2): 181–91.

Eckel, C. C. and Petrie, R. (2011). Face value. *American Economic Review* 101(4): 1497–513.

Egas, M. and Riedl, A. (2008). The economics of altruistic punishment and the maintenance of cooperation. *Proceedings of the Royal Society B: Biological Sciences* 275(1637): 871–8.

Ellingsen, T. and Johannesson, M. (2004). Promises, threats and fairness. *Economic Journal* 114(495): 397–420.

Ellingsen, T. and Johannesson, M. (2008). Pride and prejudice: the human side of incentive theory. *American Economic Review* 98(3): 990–1008.

Ellingsen, T., Johannesson, M., Tjøtta, S., and Torsvik, G. (2010). Testing guilt aversion. *Games and Economic Behavior* 68: 95–107.

Ellman, M. and Pezanis-Christou, P. (2010). Organizational structure, communication and group ethics. *American Economic Review* 100(5): 2478–91.

Elster, J. (2011). Norms. In Peter Bearman and Peter Hedström (eds.), *The Oxford Handbook of Analytical Sociology*. Oxford: Oxford University Press.

Elster, J. (1999). *Alchemies of the Mind: Rationality and the Emotions*. Cambridge: Cambridge University Press.

Elster, J. (1989). Social norms and economic theory. *Journal of Economic Perspectives* 3(4), 99–117.

Engelmann, D. and Fischbacher, U. (2009). Indirect reciprocity and strategic reputation building in an experimental helping game. *Games and Economic Behavior* 67(2): 399–407.

Engelmann, D. and Strobel, M. (2004). Inequality aversion, efficiency, and maximin preferences in simple distribution experiments. *American Economic Review* 94(4): 857–969.

Engelmann, D. and Strobel, M. (2006). Inequality aversion, efficiency, and maximin preferences in simple distribution experiments: reply. *American Economic Review* 96(5): 1918–23.

Englmaier, F. and Leider, S. (2012). Contractual and organizational structure with reciprocal agents. *American Economic Journal: Microeconomics* 4(2): 146–83.

Englmaier, F., Strasser, S., and Winter, J. (2014). Worker characteristics and wage differentials: evidence from a gift-exchange experiment. *Journal of Economic Behavior and Organization* 97: 185–203.

Englmaier, F. and Wambach, A. (2010). Optimal incentive contracts under inequity aversion. *Games and Economic Behavior* 69(2): 312–28.

Erat, S. and Gneezy, U. (2012). White lies. *Management Science* 58(4): 723–33.

Falk, A. (2007). Gift exchange in the field. *Econometrica* 75(5): 1501–11.

Falk, A., Becker, A., Dohmen, T., Huffman, D., and Sunde, U. (2016). The preference survey module: a validated instrument for measuring risk, time, and social preferences. IZA Discussion Paper No. 9674.

Falk, A., Becker, A., Dohmen, T. J., Enke, B., Huffman, D., and Sunde, U. (2018). Global evidence on economic preferences. Forthcoming in *Quarterly Journal of Economics*.

Falk, A., Fehr, E., and Fischbacher, U. (2003). On the nature of fair behavior. *Economic Inquiry* 41(1): 20-6.

Falk, A., Fehr, E., and Fischbacher, U. (2005). Driving forces behind informal sanctions. *Econometrica* 73(6): 2017-30.

Falk, A., Fehr, E., and Fischbacher, U. (2008). Testing theories of fairness and reciprocity—intentions matter. *Games and Economic Behavior* 62(1): 287-303.

Falk, A., Fehr, E., and Zehnder, C. (2006). Fairness perceptions and reservation wages—the behavioral effects of minimum wage laws. *Quarterly Journal of Economics* 121(4): 1347-81.

Falk, A. and Fischbacher, U. (2006). A theory of reciprocity. *Games and Economic Behavior* 54(2): 293-315.

Falk, A. and Kosfeld, M. (2006). The hidden costs of control. *American Economic Review* 96(5): 1611-30.

Falk, A., Meier, S., and Zehnder, C. (2013). Do lab experiments misrepresent social preferences? The case of self-selected student samples. *Journal of the European Economic Association* 11(4): 839-52.

Falk, A., and Szech, N. (2013). Morals and markets. *Science* 340(6133): 707-11.

Falk, A. and Szech, N. (2014). Organization, diffused pivotality and immoral outcomes. Mimeo, University of Bonn.

Fehr, E. (2009). On the economics and biology of trust. *Journal of the European Economic Association* 7(2-3): 235-66.

Fehr, E. and Falk, A. (1999). Wage rigidity in a competitive incomplete contract market. *Journal of Political Economy* 107(1): 106-34.

Fehr, E. and Falk, A. (2002). Joseph Schumpeter lecture: psychological foundations of incentives. *European Economic Review* 46(4-5): 687-24.

Fehr, E. and Fischbacher, U. (2002). Why social preferences matter—the impact of non-self-regarding motives on competition, cooperation and incentives. *Economic Journal* 112(478): C1-C33.

Fehr, E. and Fischbacher, U. (2003). The nature of human altruism. *Nature* 425: 785-91.

Fehr, E. and Fischbacher, U. (2004). Third-party punishment and social norms. *Evolution and Human Behavior* 25(2): 63-87.

Fehr, E. and Fischbacher, U. (2005). Human altruism: proximate patterns and evolutionary origins. *Analyse & Kritik* 27(1): 6-47.

Fehr, E., Fischbacher, U., and Gächter, S. (2002). Strong reciprocity, human cooperation, and the enforcement of social norms. *Human Nature* 13(1): 1-25.

Fehr, E., Fischbacher, U., and Tougareva, E. (2002). Do high stakes and competition remove reciprocal fairness? Evidence from Russia. University of Zurich, Institute for Empirical Research in Economics, Working Paper 120.

Fehr, E. and Gächter, S. (1999). Cooperation and punishment in public goods experiments. University of Zurich, Institute for Empirical Research in Economics, Working Paper 10.

Fehr, E. and Gächter, S. (2000). Cooperation and punishment in public goods experiments. *American Economic Review* 90(4): 980-94.

Fehr, E. and Gächter, S. (2001). Do incentive contracts crowd out voluntary cooperation? University of Zurich, Institute for Empirical Research in Economics, Working Paper 34.

Fehr, E. and Gächter, S. (2002). Altruistic punishment in humans. *Nature* 415: 137-40.

Fehr, E., Gächter, S., and Kirchsteiger, G. (1997). Reciprocity as a contract enforcement device: experimental evidence. *Econometrica* 65(4): 833-60.

Fehr, E., Goette, L., and Zehnder, C. (2009). A behavioral account of the labor market: the role of fairness concerns. *Annual Reviews: Economics* 1: 355-84.

Fehr, E., Kirchsteiger, G., and Riedl, A. (1993). Does fairness prevent market clearing? An experimental investigation. *Quarterly Journal of Economics* 108(2): 437-59.

Fehr, E., Kirchsteiger, G., and Riedl, A. (1998). Gift exchange and reciprocity in competitive experimental markets. *European Economic Review* 42(1): 1-34.

Fehr, E., Klein, A., and Schmidt, K. M. (2007). Fairness and contract design. *Econometrica* 75(1): 121-54.

Fehr, E., Kremhelmer, S., and Schmidt, K. M. (2008). Fairness and the optimal allocation of ownership rights. *Economic Journal* 118(531): 1262-84.

Fehr, E. and Leibbrandt, A. (2011). A field study on cooperativeness and impatience in the Tragedy of the Commons. *Journal of Public Economics* 95(9–10): 1144–55.

Fehr, E. and List, J. A. (2004). The hidden costs and returns of incentives: trust and trustworthiness among CEOs. *Journal of the European Economic Association* 2(5): 743–71.

Fehr, E., Naef, M., and Schmidt, K. M. (2006). Inequality aversion, efficiency, and maximin preferences in simple distribution experiments: comment. *American Economic Review* 96(5): 1912–17.

Fehr, E. and Rockenbach, B. (2003). Detrimental effects of sanctions on human altruism. *Nature* 422: 137–40.

Fehr, E. and Schmidt K. M. (1999). A theory of fairness, competition and cooperation. *Quarterly Journal of Economics* 114(3): 817–68.

Fehr, E. and Schmidt, K. M. (2006). The economics of fairness, reciprocity and altruism: experimental evidence and new theories. In S.-C. Kolm and J. M. Ythier (eds.), *Handbook of the Economics of Giving, Altruism and Reciprocity, Volume 1*. Amsterdam: Elsevier, pp. 615–94.

Fehr, E. and Schmidt, K. M. (2007). Adding a stick to the carrot? The interaction of bonuses and fines. *American Economic Review* 97(2): 177–81.

Fehr, E. and Schneider, F. (2010). Eyes are on us, but nobody cares: are eye cues relevant for strong reciprocity? *Proceedings of the Royal Society B: Biological Sciences* 277: 1315–23.

Fehr, E. and Schurtenberger, I. (2018a). Normative foundations of human cooperation. *Nature Human Behavior* 2: 458–68.

Fehr, E. and Schurtenberger, I. (2018b) The dynamics of norm formation and norm decay. Working Paper Department of Economics, University of Zurich.

Fehr, E., Tougareva, E., and Fischbacher, U. (2014). Do high stakes and competition undermine fair behaviour? Evidence from Russia. *Journal of Economic Behavior and Organization*, 108: 354–63.

Fischbacher, U. and Föllmi-Heusi, F. (2013). Lies in disguise: an experimental study on cheating. *Journal of the European Economic Association* 11(3): 525–47.

Fischbacher, U., Fong, C. M., and Fehr, E. (2009). Fairness, errors and the power of competition. *Journal of Economic Behavior and Organization* 72(1): 527–45.

Fischbacher, U. and Gächter, S. (2010). Social preferences, beliefs, and the dynamics of free riding in public good experiments. *American Economic Review* 100(1): 541–56.

Fischbacher, U., Gächter, S., and Fehr, E. (2001). Are people conditionally cooperative? Evidence from a public goods experiment. *Economics Letters* 71(3): 397–404.

Fisman, R., Jakiela, P., and Kariv, S. (2017). Distributional preferences and political behavior. *Journal of Public Economics* 155: 1–10.

Fisman, R., Kariv, S., and Markovits, D. (2007). Individual preferences for giving. *American Economic Review* 97(5): 1858–76.

Forsythe, R., Horowitz, J. L., Savin, N. E., and Sefton, M. (1994). Fairness in simple bargaining games. *Games and Economic Behavior* 6(3): 347–69.

Fréchette, G. R. (2015). Laboratory experiments: professionals versus students. In G. R. Fréchette and A. Schotter (eds.), *Handbook of Experimental Economic Methodology*. Oxford: Oxford University Press, pp. 360–90.

Fréchette, G. R., Kagel, J. H., and Lehrer, S. F. (2003). Bargaining in legislatures: an experimental investigation of open versus closed amendment rules. *American Political Science Review* 97(2): 221–32.

Frey, B. S. and Oberholzer-Gee, F. (1997). The cost of price incentives: an empirical analysis of motivation crowding-out. *American Economic Review* 87(4): 746–55.

Fryer, R. G. (2011). Financial incentives and student achievement: evidence from randomized trials. *Quarterly Journal of Economics* 126(4): 1755–98.

Gächter, S. and Falk, A. (2002). Reputation and reciprocity: consequences for the labour relation. *Scandinavian Journal of Economics* 104(1): 1–26.

Gächter, S. and Herrmann, B. (2009). Reciprocity, culture, and human cooperation: previous insights and a new cross-cultural experiment. *Philosophical Transactions of the Royal Society B* 364(1518): 791–806.

Gächter, S., Nosenzo, D., and Sefton, M. (2012). The impact of social comparisons on reciprocity. *Scandinavian Journal of Economics* 114(4): 1346–67.

Gächter, S., Nosenzo, D., and Sefton, M. (2013). Peer effects in pro-social behavior: social norms or social preferences? *Journal of the European Economic Association* 11(3): 548–73.

Gächter, S., Renner, E., and Sefton, M. (2008). The long run benefits of punishment. *Science* 322(5907): 1510.

Gächter, S. and Thöni, C. (2005). Social learning and voluntary cooperation among like-minded people. *Journal of the European Economic Association* 3(2–3): 303–14.

Geanakoplos, J., Pearce, D., and Stacchetti, E. (1989). Psychological games and sequential rationality. *Games and Economic Behavior* 1(1): 60–79.

Ghiselin, M. T. (1974). *The Economy of Nature and the Evolution of Sex*. Berkeley, CA: University of California Press.

Gibbons, R. (2010). Transaction cost economics: past, present, and future? *Scandinavian Journal of Economics* 112(2): 263–88.

Gibson, R., Tanner, C., and Wagner, A. F. (2013). Preferences for truthfulness: heterogeneity among and within individuals. *American Economic Review* 103(1): 532–48.

Gino, F., Ayal, S., and Ariely, D. (2013). self-serving altruism? The lure of unethical actions that benefit others. *Journal of Economic Behavior and Organization* 93: 285–292.

Gintis, H. (2000). Strong reciprocity and human sociality. *Journal of Theoretical Biology* 206(2): 169–79.

Gintis, H. (2009). *The Bounds of Reason: Game Theory and the Unification of the Behavioral Sciences*. Princeton, NJ: Princeton University Press.

Gintis, H. (2017). *Individuality and Entanglement: The Moral and Material Bases of Social Life*. Princeton, NJ: Princeton University Press.

Gintis, H., Bowles, S., Boyd, R., and Fehr, E. (2003). Explaining altruistic behavior in humans. *Evolution and Human Behavior* 24(3): 153–72.

Gintis, H. and Fehr, E. (2012). The social structure of cooperation and punishment. *Behavioral and Brain Sciences* 35(1): 28–9.

Gintis, H., Smith, E. A., and Bowles, S. (2001). Costly signaling and cooperation. *Journal of Theoretical Biology* 213(1): 103–19.

Gneezy, A., Gneezy, U., Nelson, L. D., and Brown, A. (2010). Shared social responsibility: a field experiment in pay-what-you-want pricing and charitable giving. *Science* 329(5989): 325–7.

Gneezy, A., Gneezy, U., Riener, G., and Nelson, L. D. (2012). Pay-what-you-want, identity, and self-signaling in markets. *Proceedings of the National Academy of Sciences of the United States of America* 109(19): 7236–40.

Gneezy, U. (2005). Deception: the role of consequences. *American Economic Review* 95(1): 384–94.

Gneezy, U., Imas, A., Madarász, K. (2014). Conscience accounting: emotion dynamics and social behavior. *Management Science* 60(11): 2645–2658.

Gneezy, U. and List, J. A. (2006). Putting behavioral economics to work: testing for gift exchange in labor markets using field experiments. *Econometrica* 74(5): 1365–84.

Gneezy, U., Rockenbach, B., and Serra-Garcia, M. (2013). Measuring lying aversion. *Journal of Economic Behavior and Organization* 93: 293–300.

Gneezy, U. and Rustichini, A. (2000a). A fine is a price. *Journal of Legal Studies* 29(1): 1–17.

Gneezy, U. and Rustichini, A. (2000b). Pay enough or don't pay at all. *Quarterly Journal of Economics* 115(3): 791–810.

Goerg, S. J., Kube, S., and Zultan, R. (2010). Treating equals unequally: incentives in teams, workers' motivation and production technology. *Journal of Labor Economics* 28(4): 747–72.

Goette, L. F., Huffman, D., and Meier, S. (2012). The impact of social ties on group interactions: evidence from minimal groups and randomly assigned real groups. *American Economic Journal: Microeconomics* 4(1): 101–15.

Goette, L. F. and Stutzer, A. (2008). Blood donations and incentives: evidence from a field experiment. IZA, Discussion Paper 3580.

Goette, L. F., Stutzer, A., and Frey, B. M. (2010). Prosocial motivation and blood donations: a survey of the empirical literature. *Transfusion Medicine and Hemotherapy* 37(3): 149–54.

Greenberger, S. S. (2003). Sick day abuses focus of fire talks. *Boston Globe* Sept. 17 B7.

Grolleau, G., Kocher, M. G. and Sutan, A. (2016). Cheating and loss aversion: do people lie more to avoid a loss? *Management Science* 62(12): 3428–38.

Grossman, S. J. and Hart, O. D. (1983). An analysis of the principal–agent problem. *Econometrica* 51(1): 7–45.

Grossman, S. J. and Hart, O. D. (1986). The costs and benefits of ownership: a theory of vertical and lateral integration. *Journal of Political Economy* 94(4): 691–719.

Guala, F., Mittone, L., and Ploner, M. (2013). Group membership, team preferences, and expectations. *Journal of Economic Behavior and Organization* 86: 183–90.

Gunnthorsdottir, A., Houser, D., and McCabe, K. (2007). Disposition, history and contributions in public goods experiments. *Journal of Economic Behavior and Organization* 62(2): 304–15.

Gürerk, Ö., Irlenbusch, B., and Rockenbach, B. (2006). The competitive advantage of sanctioning institutions. *Science* 312(5770): 108–11.

Güth, W., Schmittberger, R., and Schwarze, B. (1982). An experimental analysis of ultimatum bargaining. *Journal of Economic Behavior and Organization* 3(4): 367–88.

Güth, W. and Tietz, R. (1990). Ultimatum bargaining behavior: a survey and comparison of experimental results. *Journal of Economic Psychology* 11(3): 417–49.

Güth, W. and van Damme, E. (1998). Information, strategic behavior and fairness in ultimatum bargaining: an experimental study. *Journal of Mathematical Psychology* 42(2–3): 227–47.

Gylfason, H. F., Arnardottir, A. A., and Kristinsson, K. (2013). More on gender differences in lying. *Economics Letters* 119(1): 94–6.

Halali, E., Bereby-Meyer, Y., and Ockenfels, A. (2013). Is it all about the self? The effect of self-control depletion on ultimatum game proposers. *Frontiers in Human Neuroscience* 7: 240.

Haley, K. J. and Fessler, D. M. T. (2005). Nobody's watching? Subtle cues affect generosity in an anonymous economic game. *Evolution and Human Behavior* 26(3): 245–56.

Hallsworth, M., List, J. A., Metcalfe, R. D., and Vlaev, I. (2017). The behavioralist as tax collector: using natural field experiments to enhance tax compliance. *Journal of Public Economics* 148, 14–31.

Hamermesh, D. and Biddle, J. (1994). Beauty and the labor market. *American Economic Review* 84(5): 1174–94.

Hamilton, W. D. (1964). The genetical evolution of social behavior. *Journal of Theoretical Biology* 7(1): 1–52.

Hannan, R. L., Kagel, J. H., and Moser, D. V. (2002). Partial gift exchange in experimental labor markets: impact of subject population differences, productivity differences and effort request on behavior. *Journal of Labor Economics* 20(4): 923–51.

Hargreaves Heap, S. P., Tan, J. H. W., and Zizzo, D. J. (2013). Trust, inequality and the market. *Theory and Decision* 74(3): 311–33.

Hargreaves Heap, S. P. and Varoufakis, Y. (2002). Some experimental evidence on the evolution of discrimination, cooperation and the perception of fairness. *Economic Journal* 112(481): 679–703.

Hargreaves Heap, S. P., Verschoor, A., and Zizzo, D. J. (2012). A test of the experimental method in the spirit of Popper. *Journal of Economic Methodology* 19(1): 63–76.

Hargreaves Heap, S. P. and Zizzo, D. J. (2009). The value of groups. *American Economic Review* 99(1): 295–323.

Harrison, G. W. and McCabe, K. A. (1996). Expectations and fairness in a simple bargaining experiment. *International Journal of Game Theory* 25(3): 303–27.

Hart, O. (1995). *Firms, Contracts, and Financial Structure.* Oxford: Oxford University Press.

Hays, C., and Carver, L. J. (2014). Follow the liar: the effects of adult lies on children's honesty. *Developmental Science* 17(6): 977–83.

Henrich, J., Boyd, R., Bowles, S., et al. (2001). Cooperation, reciprocity and punishment in fifteen small-scale societies. *American Economic Review* 91: 73–8.

Henrich, J., Ensminger, J., McElreath, R., et al. (2010). Markets, religion, community size, and the evolution of fairness and punishment. *Science* 327(5972): 1480–4.

Herold, F. (2010). Contractual incompleteness as a signal of trust. *Games and Economic Behavior* 68(1): 180–91.

Herrmann, B. and Thöni, C. (2009). Measuring conditional cooperation: a replication study in Russia. *Experimental Economics* 12(1): 87–92.

Herrmann, B., Thöni, C., and Gächter, S. (2008). Antisocial punishment across societies. *Science* 319(5868): 1362–7.

Heyman, J. and Ariely, D. (2004). Effort for payment: a tale of two markets. *Psychological Science* 15(11): 787–93.

Hoffman, E., McCabe, K. A., Shachat, K., and Smith, V. L. (1994). Preferences, property rights, and anonymity in bargaining games. *Games and Economic Behavior* 7(3): 346–80.

Hoffman, E., McCabe, K. A., and Smith, V. L. (1996). On expectations and the monetary stakes in ultimatum games. *International Journal of Game Theory* 25(3): 289–301.

Hoffman, E., McCabe, K., and Smith, V. L. (2008). Preferences and property rights in ultimatum and dictator games. In: C. R. Plott and V. L. Smith (eds.), *Handbook of Experimental Economics Results, Volume 1*. Amsterdam: North-Holland, pp. 417–22.

Hoffman, E. and Spitzer, M. L. (1982). The Coase theorem: some experimental tests. *Journal of Law and Economics* 25(1): 73–98.

Holmås, T. H., Kjerstad, E., Lurås, H., and Straume, O. R. (2010). Does monetary punishment crowd out pro-social motivation? A natural experiment on hospital length of stay. *Journal of Economic Behavior and Organization* 75(2): 261–7.

Holmstrom, B. and Milgrom, P. (1991). Multitask principal–agent analyses: linear contracts, asset ownership and job design. *Journal of Law, Economics and Organization* 7: 24–52.

Hopfensitz, A. and Reuben, E. (2009). The importance of emotions for the effectiveness of social punishment. *Economic Journal* 119(540): 1534–59.

Hopkins, E. (2008). Inequality, happiness and relative concerns: what actually is their relationship? *Journal of Economic Inequality* 6(4): 351–72.

Houser, D., List, J. A., Piovesan, M., Samek, A., and Winter, J. (2016). Dishonesty: from parents to children. *European Economic Review* 82: 242–254.

Huck, S., Lünser, G. K., and Tyran, J.-R. (2012). Competition fosters trust. *Games and Economic Behavior* 76(1): 195–209.

Huck, S., Müller, W., and Normann, H.-T. (2001). Stackelberg beats Cournot—on collusion and efficiency in experimental markets. *Economic Journal* 111(474): 749–65.

Hurkens, S. and Kartik, N. (2009). Would I lie to you? On social preferences and lying aversion. *Experimental Economics* 12(2): 180–92.

Hwang, S.-H. and Bowles, S. (2011). A note on optimal incentives with state-dependent preferences. Sogang University, Research Institute for Market Economy, Working Paper 1118.

Iriberri, N. and Rey-Biel, P. (2013). Elicited beliefs and social information in modified dicatator games: what do dictators believe other dictators do? *Quantitative Economics* 4: 515–47.

Isaac, R. M., McCue, K., and Plott, C. R. (1985). Public goods provision in an experimental environment. *Journal of Public Economics* 26(1): 51–74.

Itoh, H. (2004). Moral hazard and other-regarding preferences. *Japanese Economic Review* 55(1): 18–45.

Iturbe-Ormaetxe, I., Ponti, G., Tomás, J., and Ubeda, L. (2011). Framing effects in public goods: prospect theory and experimental evidence. *Games and Economic Behavior* 72(2): 439–47.

Jex, S. M. and Britt, T. W. (2008). *Organizational Psychology: A Scientist-Practitioner Approach*. 2nd edition. New Jersey: John Wiley & Sons.

Johnson, N. D. and Mislin, A. A. (2011). Trust games: a meta-analysis. *Journal of Economic Psychology* 32(5): 865–89.

Kagel, J. H., Kim, C., and Moser, D. (1996). Fairness in ultimatum games with asymmetric information and asymmetric payoffs. *Games and Economic Behavior* 13(1): 100–10.

Kahneman, D., Knetsch, J. L., and Thaler R. H. (1986). Fairness as a constraint on profit seeking: entitlements in the market. *American Economic Review* 76(4): 728–41.

Kajackaite, A. and Gneezy, U. (2017). Incentives and cheating. *Games and Economic Behavior* 102: 433–444.

Karlan, D. (2005). Using experimental economics to measure social capital and predict financial decisions. *American Economic Review* 95(5): 1688–99.

Kartik, N. (2009). Strategic communication with lying costs. *Review of Economic Studies* 76(4): 1359–95.

Kartik, N., Ottaviani, M., and Squintani, F. (2007). Credulity, lies, and costly talk. *Journal of Economic Theory* 134(1): 93–116.

Kerschbamer, R. and Muller, D. (2017). Social preferences and political attitudes: an online experiment on a large heterogeneous sample.

University of Innsbruck Working Papers in Economics and Statistics No. 2017-16.

Keser, C. and Van Winden, F. (2000). Conditional cooperation and voluntary contributions to public goods. *Scandinavian Journal of Economics* 102(1): 23-39.

Kimbrough, E. O. and Vostroknutov, A. (2016). Norms make preferences social. *Journal of the European Economic Association* 14(3): 608-38.

Knoch, D., Pascual-Leone, A., Meyer, K., Treyer, V., and Fehr, E. (2006). Diminishing reciprocal fairness by disrupting the right prefrontal cortex. *Science* 314(5800): 829-32.

Kocher, M. G., Cherry, T., Kroll, S., Netzer, R. J., et al. (2008). Conditional cooperation on three continents. *Economics Letters* 101(3): 175-8.

Kocher, M. G. and Schudy, S. (2017). I lie? We lie! Why? Experimental evidence on a dishonesty shift in groups. *Management Science*. 64(9): 3971-4470.

Kocher, M., Strauß, S., and Sutter, M. (2006). Individual or team decision making-causes and consequences of self-selection. *Games and Economic Behavior* 56(2): 259-70.

Koford, K. and Penno, M. (1992). Accounting, principal-agent theory, and self-interested behavior. In N. E. Bowie and R. E. Freeman (eds.), *Ethics and Agency Theory: An Introduction*. New York: Oxford University Press, pp. 127-42.

Kosfeld, M. and Neckermann, S. (2011). Getting more work for nothing? Symbolic awards and worker performance. *American Economic Journal: Microeconomics* 3(3): 86-99.

Kosfeld, M., Okada, A., and Riedl, A. (2009). Institution formation in public goods games. *American Economic Review* 99(4): 1335-55.

Kreps, D. and Wilson, R. (1982). Reputation and imperfect information. *Journal of Economic Theory* 27: 280-312.

Krueger, A. B. and Mas, A. (2004). Strikes, scabs, and tread separations: labor strife and the production of defective Bridgestone/Firestone tires. *Journal of Political Economy* 112(2): 253-89.

Krupka, E. and Weber, R. (2009). The focusing and informational effects of norms on pro-social behavior. *Journal of Economic Psychology* 30(3): 307-20.

Krupka, E. and Weber, R. (2013). Identifying norms using coordination games: why does dictator game sharing vary? *Journal of the European Economic Association* 11(3): 495-524.

Kube, S., Maréchal, M. A., and Puppe, C. (2006). Putting reciprocity to work positive versus negative responses in the field. University of St. Gallen, Economics, Discussion Paper 2006-27.

Kube, S., Maréchal, M. A., and Puppe, C. (2012). The currency of reciprocity: gift exchange in the workplace. *American Economic Review* 102(4): 1644-62.

Kube, S., Maréchal, M. A., and Puppe, C. (2013). Do wage cuts damage work morale? Evidence from a natural field experiment. *Journal of the European Economic Association* 11(4): 853-70.

Kurzban, R. and Houser, D. (2004). Experiments investigating cooperative types in human groups: a complement to evolutionary theory and simulations. *Proceedings of the National Academy of Sciences of the United States of America* 102(5): 1803-7.

Lacetera, N., Macis, M., and Slonim, R. (2012). Will there be blood? Incentives and displacement effects in pro-social behaviour. *American Economic Journal: Economic Policy* 4(1): 186-223.

Lambert, P. J. (2001). *The Distribution and Redistribution of Income*. 3rd edition. Manchester: Manchester University Press.

Ledyard, J. O. (1995). Public goods: a survey of experimental research. In J. H. Kagel and A. E. Roth (eds.), *Handbook of Experimental Economics*. Princeton, NJ: Princeton University Press, pp. 111-94.

Lee, D. and Rupp, N. G. (2007). Retracting a gift: how does employee effort respond to wage reductions? *Journal of Labor Economics* 25(4): 725-61.

Leibbrandt, A. (2012). Are social preferences related to market performance? *Experimental Economics* 15(4): 589-603.

Lemieux, T., MacLeod, W. B., and Parent, D. (2009). Performance pay and wage inequality. *Quarterly Journal of Economics* 124(1): 1-49.

Levine, D. K. (1998). Modeling altruism and spitefulness in experiment. *Review of Economic Dynamics* 1(3): 593-622.

Levitt, S. D. and List, J. A. (2007). What do laboratory experiments measuring social preferences reveal about the real world? *Journal of Economic Perspectives* 21(2): 153-74.

Levitt, S. D. and List, J. A. (2008). Homo economicus evolves. *Science* 319: 909–10.

Levitt, S. D., List, J. A., Neckermann, S., and Sadoff, S. (2012). The behavioralist goes to school: leveraging behavioral economics to improve educational performance. NBER, Working Paper 18165.

Liberman, V., Samuels, S. M., and Ross, L. (2004). The name of the game: predictive power of reputations versus situational labels in determining prisoner's dilemma game moves. *Personality and Social Psychology Bulletin* 30(9): 1175–85.

List, J. A. (2004). Young, selfish, and male: field evidence on social preferences. *Economic Journal* 114(492): 121–49.

List, J. A. (2006). The behavioralist meets the market: measuring social preferences and reputation effects in actual transactions. *Journal of Political Economy* 114: 1–37.

List, J. A. (2007). On the interpretation of giving in dictator games. *Journal of Political Economy* 115(3): 482–93.

List, J. A. and Cherry, T. L. (2000). Learning to accept in ultimatum games: evidence from an experimental design that generates low offers. *Experimental Economics* 3(1): 11–29.

List, J. A. and Cherry, T. L. (2008). Examining the role of fairness in high stakes allocation decisions. *Journal of Economic Behavior and Organization* 65(1): 1–8.

Loewenstein, G. F. (2000). Emotions in economic theory and economic behavior. *American Economic Review* 90(2): 426–32.

Loewenstein, G. F., Bazerman, M., and Thompson, L. (1989). Social utility and decision making in interpersonal contexts. *Journal of Personality and Social Psychology* 57(3): 426–41.

Lotz, S., Schlösser, T., Cain, D. M., and Fetchenhauer, D. (2013). The (in)stability of social preferences: using justice sensitivity to predict when altruism collapses. *Journal of Economic Behavior and Organization* 93: 141–8.

Malmendier, U., and Schmidt, K. (2017). You owe me. *American Economic Review* 107(2): 493–526.

Mas, A. (2006). Pay, reference points, and police performance. *Quarterly Journal of Economics* 121(3): 783–821.

Mas, A. (2008). Labor unrest and the quality of production: evidence from the construction equipment resale market. *Review of Economic Studies* 75(1): 229–58.

Masclet, D., Noussair, C., Villeval, M.-C., and Tucker, S. (2003). Monetary and non-monetary punishment in the voluntary contributions mechanism. *American Economic Review* 93(1): 366–80.

Mas-Colell, A., Whinston, M. D., and Green, J. R. (1995). *Microeconomic Theory*. New York: Oxford University Press.

Matsusaka, J. G. (2005). Direct democracy works. *Journal of Economic Perspectives* 19(2): 185–206.

Maximiano, S., Sloof, R., and Sonnemans, J. (2007). Gift exchange in a multi-worker firm. *Economic Journal* 117(522): 1025–50.

Mazar, N., Amir, O., and Ariely, D. (2008). The dishonesty of honest people: a theory of self-concept maintenance. *Journal of Marketing Research* 45(6): 633–44.

McCabe, K. A., Rassenti, S. J., and Smith, V. L. (1998). Reciprocity, trust, and payoff privacy in extensive form bargaining. *Games and Economic Behavior* 24(1–2): 10–24.

McCabe, K. A., Rigdon, M. L., and Smith, V. L. (2003). Positive reciprocity and intentions in trust games. *Journal of Economic Behavior and Organization* 52(2): 267–75.

McDermott, R. (2009). Psychological approaches to identity: definitions, measurement and experimentation. In R. Abdelal, Y. M. Herrera, A. I. Johnson, and R. McDermott (eds.), *Measuring Identity: A Guide for Social Science Research* Cambridge: Cambridge University Press, pp. 345–68.

McGregor, D. (1960). *The Human Side of Enterprise*. New York: McGraw-Hill.

Meier, S. (2007). Do subsidies increase charitable giving in the long run? Matching donations in a field experiment. *Journal of the European Economic Association* 5(6): 1203–22.

Mellström, C. and Johannesson, M. (2008). Crowding out in blood donation: was Titmuss right? *Journal of the European Economic Association* 6(4): 845–63.

Milgrom, P. and Roberts, J. (1982). Predation, reputation, and entry deterrence. *Journal of Economic Theory* 27: 280–312.

Mobius, M. and Rosenblat, T. (2006). Why beauty matters. *American Economic Review* 90(1): 222–35.

Muller, L., Sefton, M., Steinberg, R., and Vesterlund, L. (2008). Strategic behavior and learning in repeated voluntary contribution experiments. *Journal of Economic Behavior and Organization* 67(3–4): 782–93.

Neilson, W. S. (2006). Axiomatic reference-dependence in behavior toward others and toward risk. *Economic Theory* 28(3): 681–92.

Neiss, R. (1988). Reconceptualizing arousal: psychological states in motor performance. *Psychological Bulletin* 103(3): 345–66.

Nikiforakis, N. and Normann, H.-T. (2008). A comparative statics analysis of punishment in public good experiments. *Experimental Economics* 11(4): 358–69.

Ockenfels, A. and Werner, P. (2012). Hiding behind a small cake in a newspaper dictator game. *Journal of Economic Behavior and Organization* 82(1): 82–5.

Ockenfels, A. and Werner, P. (2014). Beliefs and ingroup favoritism. *Journal of Economic Behavior and Organization* 108(C): 453–62.

Offerman, T. (2002). Hurting hurts more than helping helps. *European Economic Review* 46(8): 1423–37.

Okada, A. and Riedl, A. (2005). Inefficiency and social exclusion in a coalition formation game: experimental evidence. *Games and Economic Behavior* 50(2): 278–311.

Ostrom, E. (2000). Collective action and the evolution of social norms. *Journal of Economic Perspectives* 14: 137–58.

Ostrom, E., Walker, J., and Gardner, R. (1992). Covenants with and without a sword: self-governance is possible. *American Political Science Review* 86(2): 404–17.

Owens, M. F. and Kagel, J. H. (2010). Minimum wage restrictions and employee effort in incomplete labor markets: an experimental investigation. *Journal of Economic Behavior and Organization* 73(3): 317–26.

Page, T., Putterman, L., and Unel, B. (2005). Voluntary association in public goods experiments: reciprocity, mimicry, and efficiency. *Economic Journal* 115(506): 1032–53.

Parrett, M. (2006). An analysis of the determinants of tipping behavior: a laboratory experiment and evidence from restaurant tipping. *Southern Economic Journal* 73(2): 489–514.

Persson, T. and Tabellini, G. E. (2000). *Political Economics: Explaining Economic Policy*. Cambridge, MA: MIT Press.

Pruckner, G. J. and Sausgruber, R. (2013). Honesty on the streets: a field study on newspaper purchasing. *Journal of the European Economic Association* 11(3): 661–79.

Rabin, M. (1993). Incorporating fairness into game theory and economics. *American Economic Review* 83(5): 1281–302.

Rajshri, J., Ray, D. and de Véricourt, F. (2016). Anatomy of a Contract Change. *American Economic Review* 106 (2): 316–58.

Reeson, A. F. and Tisdell, J. G. (2008). Institutions, motivations and public goods: an experimental test of motivational crowding. *Journal of Economic Behavior and Organization* 68(1): 273–81.

Rege, M. and Telle, K. (2004). The impact of social approval and framing on cooperation in public good situations. *Journal of Public Economics* 88(7–8): 1625–44.

Reich, P., Roberts, P., Laabs, N., et al. (2006). A randomized trial of blood donor recruitment strategies. *Transfusion* 46(7): 1090–6.

Restivo, M. and van de Rijt, A. (2012). Experimental study of informal rewards in peer production. *PLoS ONE* 7(3): e34358.

Rey-Biel, P. (2008). Inequity aversion and team incentives. *Scandinavian Journal of Economics* 110(2): 297–320.

Riedl, A. and Vyrastekova, J. (2002). Social preference in three-player ultimatum game experiments. Tilburg University, Center for Economic Research, Discussion Paper 2002-5.

Rotemberg, J. J. (2008). Minimally acceptable altruism and the ultimatum game. *Journal of Economic Behavior and Organization* 66(3–4): 457–76.

Roth, A. E. and Erev, I. (1995). Learning in extensive-form games: experimental data and simple dynamic models in the intermediate term. *Games and Economic Behavior* 8(1): 164–212.

Roth, A. E., Prasnikar, V., Okuno-Fujiwara, M., and Zamir, S. (1991). Bargaining and market behavior in Jerusalem, Ijubljana, Pittsburgh, and Tokyo: an experimental study. *American Economic Review* 81(5): 1068–95.

Rothschild, M. and Stiglitz, J. E. (1970). Increasing risk: I. A definition. *Journal of Economic Theory* 2(3): 225–43.

Rothschild, M. and Stiglitz, J. E. (1971). Increasing risk: II. Its Economic Consequences. *Journal of Economic Theory* 3(1): 66–84.

Rustagi, D., Engel, S., and Kosfeld, M. (2010). Conditional cooperation and costly monitoring explain success in forest commons management. *Science* 330(6006): 961–5.

Ryan, R. M. and Deci, E. L. (2000). Intrinsic and extrinsic motivations: classic definitions and new directions. *Contemporary Educational Psychology* 25(1): 54–67.

Sánchez-Pagés, S. and Vorsatz, M. (2007). An experimental study of truth-telling in a sender–receiver game. *Games and Economic Behavior* 61(1): 86–112.

Schmitt, M., Baumert, A., Gollwitzer, M., and Maes, J. (2010). The justice sensitivity inventory: factorial validity, location in the personality facet space, demographic pattern, and normative data. *Social Justice Research* 23(2–3): 211–38.

Schmitt, M., Neumann, R., and Montada, L. (1995). Dispositional sensitivity to befallen injustice. *Social Justice Research* 8(4): 385–407.

Schotter, A., Weiss, A., and Zapater, I. (1996). Fairness and survival in ultimatum and dictatorship games. *Journal of Economic Behavior and Organization* 31(1): 37–56.

Sefton, M., Shupp, R., and Walker, J. M. (2007). The effect of rewards and sanctions in provision of public goods. *Economic Inquiry* 45(4): 671–90.

Segal, U. and Sobel, J. (2007). Tit for tat: foundations of preferences for reciprocity in strategic settings. *Journal of Economic Theory* 136(1): 197–216.

Seinen, I. and Schram, A. (2001). Social status and group norms: indirect reciprocity in a helping experiment. University of Amsterdam, Department of Economics and Econometrics, Working Paper.

Selten, R. and Ockenfels, A. (1998). An experimental solidarity game. *Journal of Economic Behavior and Organization* 34(4): 517–39.

Serra-Garcia, M., van Damme, E., and Potters, J. (2013). Lying about what you know or about what you do? *Journal of the European Economic Association* 11(5): 1204–29.

Schindler, S. and Pfattheicher, S. (2017). The frame of the game: loss-framing increases dishonest behavior. *Journal of Experimental Social Psychology* 69: 172–7.

Schram, A. and Charness, G. (2015). Inducing social norms in laboratory allocation choices. *Management Science* 61(7): 1531–46.

Shapiro, C. and Stiglitz, J. (1984). Equilibrium unemployment as a worker discipline device. *American Economic Review* 74(3): 433–44.

Shih, M., Pittinsky, T. L., and Ambady, N. (1999). Stereotype susceptibility: identity salience and shifts in quantitative performance. *Psychological Science* 10(1): 80–3.

Shu, L. L., Gino, F., and Bazerman, M. H. (2011). Dishonest deed, clear conscience: cheating leads to moral disengagement and motivated forgetting. *Personality and Social Psychology Bulletin* 37(3): 330–49.

Simon, H. A. (1951). A formal theory of the employment relationship. *Econometrica* 19(3): 293–305.

Sliwka, D. (2007). Trust as a signal of a social norm and the hidden costs of incentive schemes. *American Economic Review* 97(3): 999–1012.

Slonim, R. and Roth, A. E. (1998). Learning in high stakes ultimatum games: an experiment in the Slovak Republic. *Econometrica* 66(3): 569–96.

Sloof, R. and Sonnemans, J. (2011). The interaction between explicit and relational incentives: an experiment. *Games and Economic Behavior* 73(2): 573–94.

Smith, V. L. (1962). An experimental study of competitive market behavior. *Journal of Political Economy* 70(2): 111–37.

Sobel, J. (2005). Independent preferences and reciprocity. *Journal of Economic Literature* 43(2): 392–436.

Soetevent, A. R. (2005). Anonymity in giving in a natural context—a field experiment in 30 churches. *Journal of Public Economics* 89(11–12): 2301–23.

Sonnemans, J., Schram, A., and Offerman, T. (1999). Strategic behavior in public good games: when partners drift apart. *Economics Letters* 62(1): 35–41.

Sugden, R. (1989). Spontaneous order. *Journal of Economic Perspectives* 3: 85–97.

Sugden, R. (1998). Normative expectations: the simultaneous evolution of institutions and norms. In A. Ben-Ner and L. Putterman (eds.), *Economics, Value, and Organization*. Cambridge: Cambridge University Press, pp. 73–100.

Sugden, R. (2004). *The Economics of Rights, Cooperation and Welfare*. 2nd edition. London: Macmillan.

Sutter, M. (2009). Deception through telling the truth?! Experimental evidence from individuals and teams. *Economic Journal* 119: 47–60.

Stoop, J., Noussair, C., and van Soest, D. (2012). From the lab to the field: public good provision with fishermen. *Journal of Political Economy* 120(6): 1027–56.

Tajfel, H., Billig, M. G., Bundy, R. P., and Flament, C. (1971). Social categorization and inter-group behavior. *European Journal of Social Psychology* 1(2): 149–78.

Tajfel, H. and Turner, J. (1979). An integrative theory of intergroup conflict. In W. G. Austin and S. Worchel (eds.), *The Social Psychology of Intergroup Relations*. Monterey, CA: Brooks Cole, pp. 33–47.

Tajfel, H. and Turner, J. (1986). The social identity theory of intergroup behavior. In W. G. Austin and S. Worchel (eds.), *The Psychology of Intergroup Relations*. Chicago: Nelson-Hall, pp. 7–24.

Thaler, R. H. (1988). Anomalies: the ultimate game. *Journal of Economic Perspectives* 2(4): 195–206.

Titmuss, R. M. (1971). *The Gift Relationship: From Human Blood to Social Policy*. New York: Pantheon Books.

Trivers, R. L. (1971). The evolution of reciprocal altruism. *Quarterly Review of Biology* 46(1): 35–57.

Turner, J. C., Hogg, M. A., Oakes, P. J., Reicher, S. D., and Wetherell, M. S. (1987). *Rediscovering the Social Group: A Self-Categorization Theory*. Oxford and New York: Wiley & Sons.

Tyran, J.-R. and Feld, L. P. (2006). Achieving compliance when legal sanctions are non-deterrent. *Scandinavian Journal of Economics* 108(1): 135–56.

Tyran, J.-R. and Sausgruber, R. (2006). A little fairness may induce a lot of redistribution in a democracy. *European Economic Review* 50(2): 469–85.

Vanberg, C. (2008). Why do people keep their promises? An experimental test of two explanations. *Econometrica* 76(6): 1476–80.

van der Weele, J. J., Kulisa, J., Kosfeld, M., and Friebel, G. (2014). Resisting moral wiggle room: how robust is reciprocal behavior? *American Economic Journal: Microeconomics* 6(3): 256–64.

van Dijk, F., Sonnemans, J., and van Winden, F. (2002). Social ties in a public good experiment. *Journal of Public Economics* 85(2): 275–99.

Veblen, T. (1899). *The Theory of the Leisure Class. An Economic Study of Institutions*. New York: Random House.

Volk, S., Thöni, C., and Ruigrok, W. (2012). Temporal stability and psychological foundations of cooperation preferences. *Journal of Economic Behavior and Organization* 81(2): 664–76.

Vrij, A. (2000). *Detecting Lies and Deceit: The Psychology of Lying and the Implications for Professional Practice*. New York: John Wiley & Sons.

Vrij, A. (2008). *Detecting lies and deceit: pitfalls and opportunities*. Wiley Series in the Psychology of Crime, Policing and Law. Chichester: John Wiley & Sons.

Williams, G. C. (1966). *Adaptation and Natural Selection: A Critique of Some Current Evolutionary Thought*. Princeton, NJ: Princeton University Press.

Wilson, E. O. (2012). *The Social Conquest of Earth*. New York: Liveright Publishing Corporation.

Wiltermuth, S. S. (2011). Cheating more when the spoils are split. *Organizational Behavior and Human Decision Processes* 115: 157–68.

Winter, E. (2004). Incentives and discrimination. *American Economic Review* 94(3): 764–73.

Xiao, E. and Bicchieri, C. (2010). When equality trumps reciprocity. *Journal of Economic Psychology* 31: 456–70.

Xiao, E. and Houser, D. (2011). Punish in public. *Journal of Public Economics* 95(7–8): 1006–17.

Yamagishi, T. (1986). The provision of a sanctioning system as a public good. *Journal of Personality and Social Psychology* 51(1): 110–16.

Yamagishi, T. and Kiyonari, T. (2000). The group as the container of generalized reciprocity. *Social Psychology Quarterly* 63(2): 116–32.

Young, P. H. (1998). *Individual Strategy and Social Structure: An Evolutionary Theory of Institutions*. Princeton, NJ: Princeton University Press.

Zizzo, D. J. (2010). Experimenter demand effects in economic experiments. *Experimental Economics* 13(1): 75–98.

AUTHOR INDEX

Note: Tables are indicated by an italic *t* following the page number.

Abbink, K. 45, 56, 78, 79, 81, 134
Abeler, J. 20, 44, 59, 158, 208, 268
Ackert, L. F. 114, 115, 116
Akerlof, G. A. 35, 43, 55, 154, 165, 173
Alexander 93
Allais, M. 9, 16
Almås, I. 266
al-Nowaihi, A. 7, 14, 31, 98, 101, 110, 113, 114, 115, 116, 118, 119, 120, 121, 122, 127, 275, 280, 281, 282, 283
Altmann, S. 59
Andersen, S. 18, 42, 48
Anderson, J. 20
Andreoni, J. 43, 49, 52, 54, 66, 70, 74, 97, 130, 132
Angrist, J. 182, 253, 255, 259
Ariely, D. 23, 181, 243, 244, 245, 247, 250, 254, 284
Arkes, H. R. 23
Ashraf, N. 9, 284
Axelrod, R. 4

Babcock, L. 3
Balafoutas, L. 268
Bandiera, O. 85, 180
Bandura, A. 248
Baran, N. M. 47, 84, 91
Bardsley, N. 9, 12, 15, 16, 19, 23, 24, 25
Barmettler, F. 19, 46, 85, 86
Bartling, B. 137, 271, 272, 283
Bateson, M. 50
Battigalli, P. 43, 52
Becker, G. M. 10, 24
Belkin, D. 284
Bellemare, C. 44, 60, 61, 84, 101*t*
Bénabou, R. 3, 23, 43, 51, 176, 180, 181, 206, 227, 230, 231, 232, 238, 252, 273, 283
Benjamin, D. J. 28, 153, 166, 167, 176
Bentham, J. 9
Benz, M. 47, 92
Berg, J. 44, 56, 64
Bernhard, H. 171
Bernheim, B. D. 52
Besley, T. 227
Bewley, T. 2, 44, 61, 62, 240
Bicchieri, C. 275, 276, 277, 278, 280
Biddle, J. 66
Billig, M. 153, 166
Binmore, K. G. 43, 49, 221, 278, 282
Blanco, M. 101
Blaug, M. 11, 12
Blount, S. 99, 131, 137, 139

Bochet, O. 45, 67, 68, 74
Bohm, P. 25
Bohnet, I. 182, 255
Bolle, F. 130
Bolton, G. E. 1, 18, 23, 66, 68, 85, 97, 98, 99, 100, 108, 109, 114, 115, 116, 131, 133, 135, 136*t*, 137, 138, 139, 140, 141, 142, 145, 281, 282
Bowles, S. 5, 83, 90, 227, 248, 284
Braga, J. 25
Brandts, J. 61, 72, 139, 140
Britt, T. W. 174
Brown, M. 4, 179, 209, 210, 217, 218, 219, 220
Brown, R. 16
Bruhin, A. 2, 265
Bruni, L. 9
Burks, S. 84, 182, 256
Burnham, T. 68

Cabrales, A. 208
Cadsby, C. B. 167
Camerer, C. F. 9, 10, 18, 19, 20–1, 22, 23, 27–8, 47, 50, 64, 92
Cameron, L. A. 20, 48
Cappelen, A. W. 160, 258, 263
Cardenas, J. C. 181, 249
Carpenter, J. P. 20, 46, 47, 48, 73, 84, 86, 109, 182, 254, 258
Carver, L. J. 273
Chamberlin, E. H. 16
Charness, G. 44, 57, 58, 61, 65, 94, 99, 109, 110, 130, 131, 137, 139, 143, 144, 145, 147, 148, 153, 164, 168, 169, 182, 201, 260, 275, 279, 281, 282
Chaudhuri, A. 45, 73, 74
Chen, R. 172
Chen, Y. 168, 171, 172
Cherry, T. L. 19, 48, 49
Childs, J. 160
Cialdini, R. 275
Cinyabuguma, M. 45, 73
Cleave, B. L. 20, 46, 84
Coase, R. 221
Cohn, A. 44, 47, 58, 86, 87, 169
Colander, D. 32
Conrads, J. 160
Cox, J. C. 62, 99, 130, 137, 148
Crawford, V. 3
Croson, R. 66, 160

Dai, Z. 269
Dal Bó, P. 73, 221

Dana, J. 18, 43, 50, 51
Daruvala 101t
Davidson, D. 16
Davis, D. D. 22, 58, 102
Dawes, R. M. 70, 74, 132
Dawkins, R. 83
Deci, E. L. 181, 241
Deckers, T. 263
Dekel, E. 12, 33
DellaVigna, S. 180
De Marchi, N. 12
de Quervain, D. J.-F. 49, 72
Dhami, S. 7, 31, 98, 101, 110, 113, 114, 115, 116, 118, 119, 120, 121, 122, 127, 262, 267, 274, 275, 276, 280, 281, 282, 283
Dickenson, D. 241
Dohmen, T. 44, 62, 63, 208, 209
Dreber, A. 160
Duesenberry, J. S. 4
Dufwenberg, M. 43, 52, 96, 98, 125, 126, 127, 128, 129, 135, 136t, 136, 153, 164

Eckel, C. C. 44, 66, 100, 101, 282
Edgeworth, F. 9
Edwards, W. 16
Egas, M. 73
Einstein, A. 12
Ellingsen, T. 3, 101t, 146, 153, 160, 226–7, 233, 235, 237, 238, 280, 284
Ellman, M. 252
Ellsberg, D. 9
Elster, J. 275, 276, 277, 278
Engel, S. 91
Engelmann, D. 47, 49, 94, 99, 131, 145, 221
Englmaier, F. 178, 189, 190, 194, 209, 283
Erat, S. 152, 154, 160
Erev, I. 49, 221

Falk, A. 2, 18, 20, 21, 46, 49, 56, 57, 61, 63, 82, 84, 88, 99, 130, 133, 134, 135, 136t, 136, 137, 138, 145, 180, 181, 208, 209, 220, 221, 233, 237, 238, 240, 242, 247, 251, 264, 271
Farmer, J. D. 32
Fehr, E. 1, 2, 3, 9, 20, 42, 43, 44, 45, 47, 48, 49, 50, 55, 56, 57, 58, 61, 64, 66, 71, 72, 75, 76, 80, 84, 85, 86, 88, 89, 94, 95, 97, 99, 100, 101, 101t, 117, 130, 131, 132, 133, 134, 135, 136t, 136, 138, 142, 145, 148, 150, 151, 178, 179, 180, 181, 194, 197, 205, 206, 207, 220, 225, 234, 239, 240, 241, 274, 276, 277, 278, 280, 281, 282, 283
Feld, L. P. 109, 182, 259
Fessler, D. M. T. 18, 43, 50, 85
Feynman, R. 29
Fischbacher, U. 2, 42, 43, 45, 47, 49, 71, 74, 75, 76, 94, 95, 99, 104, 130, 134, 135, 136t, 136, 137, 145, 152, 156, 157, 158, 159, 221, 268, 269, 273, 276
Fisman, R. 54, 101, 263
Foley, D. 32
Föllmi-Heusi, F. 152, 156, 157, 158, 159, 268, 269, 273
Forsythe, R. 43, 50, 54
Fouraker, L. E. 16
Fréchette, G. R. 20, 46, 146

Frey, B. S. 251
Friedman, D. 148
Friedman, M. 13–14, 16
Fryer, R. G. 182, 259

Gächter, S. 2, 42, 44, 45, 46, 49, 57, 58, 71, 72, 73, 75, 80, 81, 82, 83, 132, 134, 180, 181, 221, 239, 240, 275, 276, 277, 278–9
Geanakoplos, J. 43
Ghatak, M. 227
Ghiselin, M. T. 83
Gibbons, R. 226
Gibson, R. 152, 156
Gilboa, I. 12–13, 19, 29
Gino, F. 273
Gintis, H. 1, 3, 5, 8, 10, 12, 14, 28, 31, 33, 47, 72, 82, 83, 86, 100, 101, 272, 276, 277, 278, 282
Gjerstad, S. 148
Glimcher, P. W. 9, 32
Gneezy, U. 23, 24, 44, 57, 59, 60, 66, 138, 152, 154, 155, 156, 158, 159, 160, 181, 182, 244, 245, 249, 250, 255, 260, 268, 270
Godfrey-Smith, P. 14
Goeree 101t
Goerg, S. J. 208
Goette, L. F. 153, 170, 171, 172, 182, 253
Greenberger, S. S. 284
Grether, D. M. 27
Grolleau, G. 267
Grossman, P. J. 66
Grossman, S. J. 191, 207
Guala, F. 16, 172
Gunnthorsdottir, A. 73
Gürerk, Ö. 76, 77
Güth, W. 42, 47, 105, 281
Gylfason, H. F. 160

Halali, E. 53
Haley, K. J. 18, 43, 50, 85
Hallsworth, M. 270
Hamermesh, D. 66
Hamilton, W. D. 4, 83
Hands, D. W. 11, 12
Hannan, R. L. 57, 84
Hargreaves Heap, S. P. 67, 91, 93, 154, 172
Harrison, G. W. 49
Hart, O. 191, 207, 218
Hattenstone, S. 243
Hausman, D. 11
Hays, C. 273
Heckman, J. J. 18, 21
Henrich, J. 43, 48, 49, 162, 249, 255
Herbst, D. 22
Herold, F. 238
Herrmann, B. 45, 46, 72, 80, 81, 82, 83, 109, 182, 258, 279
Hertwig, R. 22, 23
Heyman, J. 250
Higgs, P. 15
Hoffman, E. 18, 48, 49, 85, 181, 248, 249
Hogarth, R. M. 18, 20, 22, 23
Holmås, T. H. 250

Holmstrom, B. 180
Holt, C. A. 22, 58, 101t, 102
Hopfensitz, A. 258
Hopkins, E. 112–13
Houser, D. 72, 258, 273
Huck, S. 67, 68, 148
Huffman, D. 63
Hume, D. 9
Hurkens, S. 156
Hwang, S.-H. 227

Iriberri, N. 54, 130
Irlenbusch, B. 77
Isaac, R. M. 70
Itoh, H. 177, 182, 184, 186, 189, 283
Iturbe-Ormaetxe, I. 74

Jevons, S. 9
Jex, S. M. 174
Johannessen, M. 3, 101t, 146, 153, 160, 181, 226–7, 233, 235, 237, 238, 252, 253, 284
Johnson, M. D. 44, 65
Judd, K. L. 32

Kagel, J. H. 61, 133
Kahneman, D. 2, 9, 16, 25–6, 31
Kajackaite, A. 268
Karlan, D. 47, 90
Kartik, N. 156, 160
Katok, E. 140
Kerschbamer, R. 263
Keser, C. 75
Kessler, J. B. 22
Kim, E. H. 26
Kimbrough, E. O. 279, 280
Kirchsteiger, G. 96, 135, 136t, 136
Kiyonari, T. 171
Knetsch, J. 25
Knoch, D. 49
Kocher, M. G. 72, 273
Koford, K. 156
Kosfeld, M. 91, 181, 233, 237, 238, 242, 247, 259, 283
Kranton, R. E. 35, 154, 165, 173
Kreps, D. 224
Kritikos, A. 130
Kröger, S. 101t
Krueger, A. B. 57
Krupka, E. 278, 279
Kube, S. 44, 57, 59, 61, 62
Kübler, D. 68
Kuhn, T. S. 11, 12
Kupers, R. 32
Kurzban, R. 72

Lacetera, N. 182, 253
Lakatos, I. 11–12
Lambdin, C. G. 18
Lambert, P. J. 115
Lavy, V. 182, 253, 255, 259
Ledyard, J. O. 70, 74, 147, 249
Lee, D. 57
Leibbrandt, A. 47, 88, 89

Leider, S. 178, 189, 190, 194, 283
Lemieux, T. 177, 193
Levine, D. K. 99, 144, 146, 148, 234
Levitt, S. D. 17, 20, 46, 50, 84, 85, 92, 182, 259
Li, S. X. 168, 171
Liberman, V. 259
Lichtenstein, S. 27
Lipman, B. L. 12
Lipsey, R. G. 14–15
List, J. A. 17, 20, 21, 44, 46, 48, 49, 50, 57, 59, 60, 84, 85, 92, 138
Loewenstein, G. F. 3, 8, 9, 243, 244, 245
Lotz, S. 52
Lünser, G. K. 67

McCabe, C. 248
McCabe, K. A. 49, 56, 233, 234
McDermott, R. 166
McGregor, D. 226
Malmendier, U. 262
Maréchal, M. A. 62
Markowitz, H. 9
Mas, A. 22, 57
Masclet, D. 45, 73, 258
Mas-Colell, A. 111
Matsusaka, J. G. 115
Maximiano, S. 58
Maynes, E. 167
Mazar, N. 158, 244, 245, 268
Meier, S. 47, 92, 256
Mellström, C. 181, 252, 253
Milgrom, P. 180, 224
Miller, J. H. 43, 49, 54, 97, 130, 132
Mislin, A. 44, 65
Mitchell, J. 32
Mobius, M. 66
Muller, D. 263
Muller, L. 55
Myers, C. 254

Neckermann, S. 283
Neilson, W. S. 99, 150, 151
Neiss, R. 243
Nikiforakis, N. 72
Nordhaus, W. 15
Normann, H.-T. 72
Nosenzo, D. 20

Oberholzer-Gee, F. 251
Ockenfels, A. 1, 50, 51, 98, 99, 100, 108, 109, 114, 115, 116, 131, 133, 135, 136t, 139, 140, 141, 142, 145, 165, 281, 282
Offerman, T. 133, 137
Okada, A. 146
Ortmann, A. 22, 23, 24
Ostrom, E. 75, 277
Owens, M. F. 61
Özdemir, Y. 272

Page, T. 45, 68, 73
Paichayontvijit, T. 45, 73
Parrett, M. 49

Penno, M. 156
Persson, T. 115, 116
Petrie, R. 44, 66
Pezanis-Christou, P. 252
Pfattheicher, S. 268
Phelps, E. 9
Plott, C. 16, 27
Polanía-Reys, S. 248, 284
Pollak, R. A. 9
Popper, K. 10–11
Pruckner, G. J. 152, 158, 255
Puppe, C. 62

Rabin, M. 99, 100, 109, 110, 130, 131, 143, 144, 145, 147, 148, 168, 201, 281
Rajshri, J. 262
Read, D. 24
Reeson, A. F. 182, 256, 257
Rege, M. 52
Reich, P. 182, 253
Restivo, M. 283
Reuben, E. 258
Rey-Biel, P. 54, 130, 189
Riedl, A. 73, 146
Roberts, J. 224
Rockenbach, B. 57, 77, 159, 181, 240, 241
Rosenblat, T. 66
Rotemberg, J. J. 147, 282
Roth, A. E. 1, 16, 20, 22, 42, 47, 48, 49, 103, 221
Rothschild, M. 98, 110
Rubinstein, A. 13
Rupp, N. G. 57
Rustagi, D. 47, 90, 91
Rustichini, A. 23, 24, 181, 249, 250, 255
Ryan, R. M. 181, 241
Rydval, O. 24

Samuelson, P. A. 9, 15
Sausgruber, R. 114, 115, 116, 152, 158, 255
Schindler, S. 268
Schmidt, K. M. 2, 50, 71, 75, 97, 99, 100, 101, 101t, 117, 130, 132, 133, 135, 136t, 142, 145, 148, 150, 151, 164, 179, 180, 197, 206, 225, 234, 241, 262, 278, 280, 281, 282
Schmitt, M. 52
Schneider, F. 50, 85
Schotter, A. 14, 181, 249
Schram, A. 47, 72, 93, 94, 275, 279
Schubik, M. 16
Schurtenberger, I. 274, 278, 280
Sefton, M. 45, 72
Segal, U. 99, 149
Seinen, I. 47, 93, 94
Seki, E. 20, 46, 47, 86
Selten, R. 9, 16, 50
Serra-Garcia, A. 159, 160
Shaffer, V. A. 18
Shaked, A. 282
Shapiro, C. 212
Shearer, B. S. 44, 60, 61
Shih, M. 167
Shu, L. L. 248

Siegel, S. 16
Simon, H. A. 9, 16, 221
Siniscalchi, M. 33
Sliwka, D. 238
Slonim, R. 20, 42, 48
Sloof, R. 180
Slovic, P. 27
Smith, A. 9
Smith, V. L. 16, 19, 22, 58, 248
Sobel, J. 99, 130, 149
Soetevent, A. R. 52
Sonnemans, J. 75, 180
Spitzer, J. L. 49
Starmer, C. 25
Stiglitz, J. E. 98, 110, 212
Stoop, J. 92
Strobel, M. 99, 131, 145
Stutzer, A. 182, 253
Sugden, R. 9, 275, 277
Sunde, U. 63
Suppes, P. 16
Sutter, M. 273
Szech, N. 251, 271

Tabellini, G. E. 115, 116
Tajfel, H. 153, 165, 166
Telle, K. 52
Tesfatsion, L. 32
Thaler, R. H. 8, 9, 12, 20, 25, 27, 31, 47, 70
Thöni, C. 45, 72, 73, 82, 83, 279
Tietz, R. 47
Tirole, J. 3, 23, 43, 51, 176, 180, 181, 206, 227, 230, 231, 232, 238, 252, 273, 283
Tisdell, J. G. T. 182, 256, 257
Titmuss, R. M. 3, 181, 232, 252
Trivers, R. L. 4, 83
Tullock, G. 78
Turner, J. C. 153, 165, 166
Tversky, A. 9, 16, 25–6, 31
Tyran, J.-R. 67, 109, 114, 115, 116, 182, 259

Vanberg, C. 153, 164
van Damme, E. 281
van de Rijt, A. 283
van der Weele, J. J. 51
van Dijk, F. 179, 220
Van Soest, A. 101t
Van Winden, F. 75
Varoufakis, Y. 93
Veblen, T. 4
Vesterlund, L. 22, 130
Villeval, M.-C. 241
Volk, S. 54
von Siemens, F. A. 189
Vostroknutov, A. 279, 280
Vrij, A. 154
Vyrastekova, J. 146

Walker, J. M. 22
Wambach, A. 189
Weber, R. 278, 279

Weigelt, K. 64
Werner, P. 51, 165
Wibral, M. 59
Williams, G. C. 83
Wilson, E. O. 4
Wilson, R. 224
Wiltermuth, S. S. 273
Wimsatt, C. W. 14
Winter, E. 208

Xiao, E. 258, 276, 280

Yamagishi, T. 75, 171
Yellen, J. L. 55
Young, P. H. 278

Zehnder, C. 86
Zizzo, D. J. 17, 84, 154, 172
Zwick, R. 85, 140

SUBJECT INDEX

Note: Tables and Figures are indicated by an italic *t* and *f*, respectively, following the page number.

age factors
   altruism 264
   educational incentives 259
   lying 160
   reciprocity 264
agent-based computational economics (ACE) 32
agreeableness, public goods games 55
Allais paradox 24
all causes model 21
altruism 4, 5, 96–8
   axiomatic foundations 149
   cultural factors 264
   dictator game 50, 51, 52, 54
   evolution 83
   fairness and stochastic dominance 112–13
   Fehr–Schmidt model 116
   genuine 43, 52
   incentives 230, 233–9, 252, 254
   interdependent preferences models 146–7
   public goods games 75
   reciprocal 4
   reluctant 43, 51, 52
   social identity 168, 171
   trust game 66
   types of other-regarding preferences 266
   white lies 155, 160
animals, cooperation 5
antecedents of behavioral economics 9–10
antisocial punishments 46
   crowding-in effect of incentives 258
   equity, reciprocity, and competition model 109
   public goods games 80–3
artificial social identity 165
as-if-classical consumers 126, 127
attribution hypothesis, intention-based reciprocity 138, 139, 141, 142
audience effect 52, 85
automatic choices 52–3
autonomy 241

bargaining impasse 3
battle of the sexes (BOS) game, and social identity 169–70, 169*f*
Becker–DeGroot–Marshak mechanism (BDM) 24–5
betrayal aversion 66
blame the theory argument 20
blood donations incentives 252–3, 253*f*
bonus contracts 178–9, 194, 196
   evidence on contract choice under contractual incompleteness 205–6, 205*f*, 206*f*, 207, 208

   other-regarding preferences 197, 203–4
   self-regarding preferences 197

case-based decision theory 13
charitable donations, and incentives 254, 254*f*
Charness–Rabin hybrid model 143–6
cheap talk 155, 160
children, other-regarding preferences 263–4
choking under high incentives 243–8
civic cooperation, norms of 45, 46, 80, 82
communication and morality 252
competition
   Fehr–Schmidt model 101–5
   preferences 54
   trust game 67–8
competitive equilibrium (CE), gift exchange game 58
complexity theory 32
conditional cooperation 4, 5
   public goods games 55, 72–3, 75
      external validity of lab evidence 88, 90
Condorcet winner 116–20, 121–2
conformists 238
conscience accounting hypothesis 270
contracts
   bonus vs. incentive 3
   employment 179–80, 221–6
   explicit 206–7
   implicit 206–7
   independent 188
   legal environment 255–6
   long-term 179, 209–26
   relative performance 188, 189
   team 188–9
   see also bonus contracts; incentive contracts; incomplete contracts; optimal contracts; trust contracts
control aversion 237–8, 241–8
conventions 277, 278
cooperation 4–5
   conditional *see* conditional cooperation
   Fehr–Schmidt model 105–8
   in production 48
   ultimatum game 48
Cox–Friedman–Gjerstad model 148
critical cost-efficiency index (CCEI) 54
crowding-in effect of incentives 258–61
crowding-out effect of incentives 252, 258
cultural factors
   gift exchange game 58
   other-regarding preferences 264
   public goods games 81, 82

decision theory, hard core of 12
deliberative choices 52–3
democracy, direct 115–25
descriptive methodology 11
descriptive norms 276, 278
dictator game (DG) 42, 43, 50–3
    altruism 96–7
    Charness–Rabin hybrid model 144, 146
    crowding-in effect of incentives 258–9
    envy 97
    equity, reciprocity, and competition model 109
    human virtues 160
    incentives 248, 249, 252, 258–9
    intention-based reciprocity 137–8
    interdependent preferences models 147
    internal validity 18–19
    norms and social preferences 278, 279
    rationality of other-regarding preferences 53–5
    social identity 165
    social preferences models, evidence on 130–1, 132, 263
    student subject pool 85, 86f
    third party punishments 94, 95f
    types of other-regarding preferences 265, 266
    and ultimatum game, comparison between 50
distribution hypothesis, intention-based reciprocity 138, 140, 142
Duhem–Quine thesis (DQT) 11
duration effects, gift exchange game 59–60, 60f, 61f, 262

economic environment 182, 255–8
economy, defined 126
educational incentives
    crowding-in effect 259
    extrinsic and intrinsic motivation 253–4, 255, 259
efficiency
    and control, trade-off between 244–7
    preferences 131, 263
empirical expectations 275–8, 280
empirically progressive research programs 11
employment contracts 179–80, 221–6
endowment effect, public goods games 74
entitlement norm, ultimatum game 49
envy 4, 97
    incentives 199
    political economy 116, 120
    social identity 168
epistemic foundations of equilibrium concepts 33
equity, reciprocity, and competition (ERC) model 98, 108–10
    evidence on 132
esteem incentives 233–9
ethnicity factors
    social identity 167
    trust game 66
evidential reasoning 275, 280
evolution, and public goods games 83
exercise incentives 260–1, 260f
expected utility theory (EU)

Becker–DeGroot–Marshak mechanism 24–5
    incentive compatibility 24, 25
    random lottery incentive mechanism 24
    second price auction 25
    see also independence axiom of expected utility theory
experimental economics 10, 15–28
    and behavioral economics, relation between 8
experimental scrutiny 46, 84, 85
experimenter demand effect 17, 18, 46, 84
    other-regarding preferences 84
explicit contracts 206–7
external validity
    of experiments 17, 20–2
    of other-regarding preferences 84, 86–93
extrinsic motivation
    asymmetric information in principal–agent framework 206
    empirical evidence 181, 239–61
    in experiments 22–4, 25
    theoretical framework 180–1, 226–39

fairness
    axiomatic foundations 149
    Fehr–Schmidt model 99, 101–8
        political economy 116
    general equilibrium and welfare 125–9
    intention-based reciprocity 137
    interdependent preferences models 147
    of lies 156
    motivations 25
    norm
        dictator game 52, 53
        third party punishment game 94
        ultimatum game 49
    preferences, acquired nature of 53
    reference points 137–43
    social preferences models, evidence on 263
    stochastic dominance 98, 110–15
    types of other-regarding preferences 266–7
false consensus effect 280
feasibility and Pareto optimality 128
feedback market 66–7
Fehr–Schmidt model 97–8, 99, 100–8
    and equity, reciprocity, and competition model, comparison between 109
    evidence on 132
    political economy 116–17
Fehr–Schmidt preferences
    fairness and stochastic dominance 110–14, 115
    fairness, general equilibrium, and welfare 127
    general form 110–11
    incentives
        incomplete contracts 197, 198
        moral hazard 183
        reciprocity and long-term contracts 211, 223
    promises and threats model 162, 163
Fehr–Schmidt utility 117, 118, 120
firefighter volunteers, incentives 254
firm, nature of the 221–6
first order Fehr–Schmidt dominance 114, 115

first order stochastic dominance
  defined 111
  and fairness 110, 114
  incentives 217
framing effects
  dictator game 50
  gift exchange game 58
  incentives 259
  survey data 26
free-riding 2
  incentives
    crowding-in effect 259
    extrinsic and intrinsic motivation 249, 256, 259
    incomplete contracts 208
  norms and social preferences 275
  public goods games 55, 75, 76, 77
    empirical evidence 70, 71, 73
    external validity of lab evidence 89, 90
    Fehr–Schmidt model 106
    unproductive expenditures 80
    with punishments 71
    without punishments 69

gender factors
  crowding-out effect of incentives 252
  educational incentives 259
  incentives 252, 254, 259
  income inequality 267
  lying 160, 268, 273
  social identity 167
  trust game 66
general equilibrium, fairness and welfare 98–9, 125–9
general form of Fehr–Schmidt preferences 110–11
generalized axiom of revealed preference (GARP)
  altruism 97
  defined 54
  dictator game 43, 53, 54
generalized Lorenz dominance 110, 115
genuine altruism 43, 52
gift exchange game 42, 43–4, 55–64, 262
  envy 97
  equity, reciprocity, and competition model 109
  experiments and internal validity 17–18
  external validity of lab evidence 86, 87f
  incentives 239–40, 242
  intention-based reciprocity 139
  norms and social preferences 278–9
  social preferences models, evidence on 132
  student subject pool 84
  and trust game, relation between 64–8
group factors, lying behavior 273–4
guilt
  aversion 164
  norms and social preferences 275–80

happiness economics
  altruism 113
  survey data 27
hard core of a research program 11–12
hawk-dove game 93
helping game 93
history of behavioral economics 9–10

honesty, evidence on 154, 156, 157–9
hostile intent 181, 239–41
house money effect 26
human sociality *see* sociality, human
human virtues *see* virtues, human
hybrid models of other-regarding preferences 96, 99, 143–51

identity
  social *see* social identity
  soldier vs. civilian 3
  within firms 3
identity economics 173–6
impatience 167
implicit contracts 206–7
incentive contracts 178–9, 194, 195–6
  evidence on contract choice under contractual incompleteness 205, 205f, 206, 207
  extrinsic and intrinsic motivation 239, 242
  other-regarding preferences 197, 202–3, 204
  self-regarding preferences 197
incentives 177–82
  extrinsic and intrinsic motivation
    empirical evidence 239–61
    theoretical framework 226–39
  identity economics 173–6
  incomplete contracts 194–209
  for lying/truth-telling 154, 155–6, 159, 160
  moral hazard 182–94
  reciprocity and long-term contracts 209–26
  role in economics 22–5
income inequality 266–7
incomplete contracts 178–9, 210, 218
independence 241
independence axiom of expected utility theory 24, 33
independent contracts 188
indirect reciprocity 5, 47, 93–5
  equity, reciprocity, and competition model 109
inequity aversion 4
  axiomatic foundations 149, 150, 151
  Charness–Rabin hybrid model 143, 145, 146
  dictator game 50, 51, 54
  equity, reciprocity, and competition model 132
  Fehr–Schmidt model 100–1, 101t, 105, 106, 132
  gift exchange game 62
  intention-based reciprocity 133, 137–43
  moral hazard 177–8, 182–9
  norms and social preferences 278, 279
  promises and threats model 163, 164
  social preferences models, evidence on 130, 131, 132, 263
injunctive norms 276, 278
instrumental position 13, 14
instrumental reciprocity 4, 209, 212
intention-based reciprocity, models of 96, 132
  evidence on 132–43
intentions
  axiomatic foundations 150
  Charness–Rabin hybrid model 143, 144, 145
  extrinsic and intrinsic motivation 233–9
interdependent preferences, models of 96, 146–8
internal validity of experiments 17–19

intrinsic motivation
  asymmetric information in principal–agent framework 206
  empirical evidence 181, 239–61
  employment contracts 221
  in experiments 22–4, 25
  gift exchange game 62
  theoretical framework 180–1, 226–39
intrinsic reciprocity 4
  gift exchange game 55, 56, 57
  long-term contracts 209, 212
  public goods games 75

justice sensitivity (JS) 52

lab evidence, representativeness 46–7, 84–93
labor supply, properties of 119
law, rule of 45, 46, 80, 82
learning
  incentives 255–8
  models 49
Leontief preferences 54
long-term contracts 179, 209–26
loss aversion
  lying behavior 267
  prospect theory 74
  survey data 26
lotteries 24, 33
lying
  artifactual and field studies of 268–70
  evidence on 154–60
  gender factors 160, 268, 273
  group factors 273–4
  lab studies 267–8
  neoclassical economics 152, 154, 157

markets
  integration 48
  and morality 270–2
maximin preferences
  Charness–Rabin hybrid model 145–6
  social preferences models, evidence on 131
methodology in economics 10–16
minimal groups, social identity 166, 168, 170–1, 172f
minimum effort games 172
minimum wage 61, 262
model building 13–14
modified public goods (MPG) game 87–8
monotone likelihood ratio property (MLRP), and incentives 190, 192, 227
moonlighting game 134–7
moral disengagement 181, 248–52
moral hazard
  employer 222
  incentives 177–8, 182
    inequity aversion 182–9
    reciprocity 189–94
  trust game 67
moral norms 275, 277
morality

and markets 270–2
signaling 182, 252–5
multitask agency models 177

neoclassical economics 7
  and behavioral economics, relation between 8
  experiments 19–20
  frame-invariance assumption 26
  incentives 237, 238, 259
  other-regarding preferences 1, 4
  promises and threats 153, 160
  selfish black liars 152, 154, 157
neuroeconomics 29
  ultimatum game 49
normative expectations 275–80
norms
  descriptive 276, 278
  equilibrium interpretation 276
  injunctive 276, 278
  moral 275, 277
  social *see* social norms
  and social preferences 274–80
  strong 276, 277, 280
  weak 276, 277, 280

optimal contracts
  incomplete contracts 197–204
  moral hazard 184–6, 187, 188, 189, 191, 192, 194
  reciprocity and long-term contracts 214–15
other-regarding preferences 1–6
  children 263–4
  global variation 264
  human sociality 42–95, 262
  human virtues 153, 154–60
  incentives 177–261
  models 96–151, 263
  social identity 153–4, 165–72
  types of 264–7
  see also social preferences

paradigm shifts 11
Pareto optimality and feasibility 128
Pareto white lies 155, 160
pay what you want (PWYW) pricing 255
personal normative expectations 275
personas, public and private 272
policy view of experiments 20
political economy, behavioral 98, 115–25, 263
preference reversals 27
prescriptive methodology 11
pride 113
primates, cooperation 5
priming, and social identity 165–6
  evidence on 166, 167, 168, 169, 172
prisoner's dilemma (PD) game
  antisocial punishments 82–3
  democracy 73
  future interaction with same partner 221
  incentives
    crowding-in effect 258, 259
    extrinsic and intrinsic motivation 257, 258, 259

prisoner's dilemma (PD) game (*cont.*)
   norms and social preferences 275, 276
   reciprocity 4
   social identity 169–70, 169f, 171–2
private personas 272
productivity incentives 209
promises and threats, model of 153, 160–5
prosocial behavior 3
   children 263
   cultural factors 264
   equity, reciprocity, and competition model 109
   evolution 83
   incentives 254, 255
   markets and morality 271
   norms and social preferences 279
   public goods games 72
      evolution and reciprocity 83
      external validity of lab evidence 89–90, 91, 92–3
      punishments 81
   social identity 170
   student subject pool 84–5
prosocial punishments 46
prospect theory (PT)
   public goods games 74
   survey data 25–6
public goods (PG) games 42, 44–6, 68
   contributions 54–5
   empirical evidence 70–4
   evolution and reciprocity 83
   external validity of lab evidence 87–90
   Fehr–Schmidt model 105
   heterogeneous preferences and the pattern of contributions 74–7
   inequity aversion 132
   modified public goods game 87–8
   norms and social preferences 275, 277, 279, 280
   threshold 74
   unproductive expenditures 77–80
   with punishments 69–70
      altruism 97
      antisocial punishments 80–3
      Charness–Rabin hybrid model 143, 144
      crowding-in effect of incentives 258
      empirical evidence 70–4
      equity, reciprocity, and competition model 109
      Fehr–Schmidt model 106–8
      heterogeneous preferences and the pattern of contributions 75–7
      intention-based reciprocity 134–5
      unproductive expenditures on public goods 77–9, 80
   without punishments 68–9
      empirical evidence 70–1, 72, 74
      equity, reciprocity, and competition model 109
      external validity of lab evidence 87–8
      Fehr–Schmidt model 106
      heterogeneous preferences and the pattern of contributions 74
      incentives 256, 257f
      unproductive expenditures on public goods 79–80

public personas 272
punishments
   antisocial *see* antisocial punishments
   human sociality 5
   incentives 199, 258
   norms and social preferences 276, 277, 278, 280
   prosocial 46
   social identity 170, 171, 172f, 172
   see also public goods (PG) games, with punishments; third party punishment (TPG) game

random lottery incentive mechanism (RLI) 24, 33
reciprocal altruism 4
reciprocal fairness equilibrium (RFE) 145
reciprocity 4, 5
   axiomatic foundations 149–50
   Charness–Rabin hybrid model 145
   Cox–Friedman–Gjerstad model 148
   cultural factors 264
   external validity of lab evidence 92, 93
   gift exchange game 60, 61f, 62, 63f, 63–4, 262
   incentives
      extrinsic and intrinsic motivation 233, 234, 235, 239, 240, 246, 250
      incomplete contracts 196, 197, 207, 208, 209
   instrumental 4, 209, 212
   intention-based 96, 132
      evidence on 132–43
   long-term contracts 179, 209–26
   models 99, 132–43
   moral hazard 178, 189–94
   norms and social preferences 279
   public goods games 75, 76, 83
   social identity 168
   strong 5
   student subject pool 84
   and tenure, relation between 60, 61f
   types of other-regarding preferences 265, 266
   see also indirect reciprocity; intrinsic reciprocity
reference dependence 61–2, 62f
reference points
   fairness 137–43
   gift exchange game 60, 61
relative performance contracts 188, 189
reluctant altruism 43, 51, 52
rent dissipation 79, 80, 81f
reputation
   incentives 230–2, 245–7, 246f, 248, 254
   indirect reciprocity 93, 94
   other-regarding preferences 90
   reciprocity and long-term contracts 209, 211, 212, 221, 222, 224, 226
   ultimatum game 49
revealed preferences
   dictator game 53
   generalized axiom *see* generalized axiom of revealed preference
revenge 81
rewards, and human sociality 5

risk aversion 208–9
Roberts–Romer–Meltzer–Richards (RRMR) model 116
rule-based reasoning 13
rule following (RF) games 279–80
rule of law 45, 46, 80, 82

sales contracts 179–80, 221–6
scientific view of experiments 20–1
second order empirical beliefs 275, 276, 280
second order Fehr–Schmidt dominance 114–15
second order stochastic dominance
   defined 111
   and fairness 110, 114, 115
second price auctions 25
selfish black lies
   evidence on 155, 157, 158, 159, 160
   neoclassical economics 152, 154, 157
self-referent separability axiom 150–1
self-regarding preferences 1–4
   children 53
   dictator game 50, 54
   evolution 83
   fairness and stochastic dominance 110, 111
   fairness, general equilibrium, and welfare 127–8
   Fehr–Schmidt model 103, 104–5
   gift exchange game 55, 56, 58
   incentives 177
      extrinsic and intrinsic motivation 236, 237, 238, 240, 245, 247, 255
      incomplete contracts 207
      moral hazard 183–4, 187, 188, 189, 191, 193
      optimal contracts 197, 198, 199, 200, 201–2, 203, 204
      reciprocity and long-term contracts 210–11, 212–17, 222–6
   intention-based reciprocity 135, 136–7
   markets and morality 271
   norms and social preferences 275
   political economy 115, 116, 117, 118, 119, 120, 121–4
   promises and threats 160, 161, 162, 164
   public goods games 75, 76
      empirical evidence 70–1
      unproductive expenditures 78
      with punishments 69, 71
      without punishments 69, 70–1
   trust game 64–5
   ultimatum game 47, 49
self-signaling 227–32, 252
sender–receiver games 158–9, 160
separability
   axiom 150–1
   preferences 126
shame 275, 276, 277, 279
signaling
   incentives
      extrinsic and intrinsic motivation 252, 253
      self-signaling 227–32, 252
   social 227–32, 252
social comparisons 58–9
social dilemma game 139–40, 139f, 140f

social identity 153–4, 165–6
   artificial 165
   and economic incentives 173–6
   and other-regarding preferences, evidence on 166–72
sociality, human
   evidence on 42–95
   other-regarding preferences 5
   see also prosocial behavior
social monotonicity 129
social norms 277
   dictator game 52
   ultimatum game 49
social preferences
   models 96, 129–32, 263–4
      axiomatic foundations 149
      Charness–Rabin hybrid model 143–4
      equity, reciprocity, and competition model 108–10
      fairness and stochastic dominance 110–15
      fairness, general equilibrium, and welfare 125–9
      Fehr–Schmidt model 100–8
      political economy 115–25, 263
   and norms 274–80
   see also other-regarding preferences
social projection 275, 280
social psychology 165
social rationality 272
social signaling 227–32, 252
social status 93, 94
social ties 221
social welfare maximization 54
societal redistribution 115
solidarity game 50
spite 4
stake effects 20
   gift exchange game 58
   lying behavior 268
   ultimatum game 48
Stackelberg game 148
stochastic dominance
   and fairness 98, 110–15
   see also first order stochastic dominance; second order stochastic dominance
strong norms 276, 277, 280
strong reciprocity 5
Stroop task 53
student subject pool 84–6
subject pools in experiments 19–20
survey data 25–7

team contracts 188–9
theoretically progressive research programs 11
third party punishment (TPG) game
   equity, reciprocity, and competition model 109–10
   incentives 249
   indirect reciprocity 94, 95f, 95
threats and promises, model of 153, 160–5
trust 64–8, 65f
   cultural factors 264

trust (cont.)
   incentives
      extrinsic and intrinsic motivation 227, 238–41, 246
      incomplete contracts 209
   legal environment for contracts 255
trust contracts 178–9, 194, 196
   evidence on contract choice under contractual incompleteness 205, 208
   extrinsic and intrinsic motivation 242
   other-regarding preferences 197, 199–202
   self-regarding preferences 197
trust game 44, 64–8
   altruism 97
   Charness–Rabin hybrid model 144
   envy 97
   external validity of lab evidence 90–2
   incentives
      crowding-in effect 258
      extrinsic and intrinsic motivation 234, 235f, 235, 240–1, 241f
   indirect reciprocity 94–5
   intention-based reciprocity 137
   norms and social preferences 279
   social identity 170–1, 171f, 172
   student subject pool 84, 85, 86f
   types of other-regarding preferences 265, 266
trustworthiness 64–8, 65f
   legal environment for contracts 255–6
truthfulness, evidence on 154, 156, 157–9

ultimatum game 42–3, 47–9
   Charness–Rabin hybrid model 143, 145–6
   Cox–Friedman–Gjerstad model 148
   deliberative vs. automatic choices 52–3
   and dictator game, comparison between 50
   envy 97
   equity, reciprocity, and competition model 109
   Fehr–Schmidt model 101, 102–3, 104
   incentives
      extrinsic and intrinsic motivation 248–9
      moral hazard 185
   intention-based reciprocity 133–4, 134f, 138, 139, 140–3, 141f, 142f
   interdependent preferences models 147, 148
   internal validity 18, 19
   norms and social preferences 279
   promises and threats model 162
   student subject pool 85, 86f
   willpower, depletion of 53

Vickery auctions 25
virtues, human 152–3, 267–74
   evidence on 154–60
   promises and threats model 160–5

Walrasian competitive equilibrium 98–9, 127, 128, 129
weak norms 276, 277, 280
welfare
   fairness and general equilibrium 98–9, 125–9
   social identity 172
well-being externalities 128
white lies
   altruistic 155, 160
   evidence on 154–5
   Pareto 155, 160
willpower 53

Yerkes–Dodson law 243